Computers and
Application
Software

SECOND EDITION

Computers and Application Software

ROBERT A. SZYMANSKI
DONALD P. SZYMANSKI
NORMA A. MORRIS
DONNA M. PULSCHEN

Macmillan Publishing Company
New York

Collier Macmillan Canada, Inc.
Toronto

Maxwell Macmillan International Publishing Group
New York   Oxford   Singapore   Sydney

Cover art copyright 1989 J. P. Thirion—LIENS/CNRS (Paris)

Executive Editor: Vernon R. Anthony
Developmental Editor: Peggy H. Jacobs
Production Editor: Sharon Rudd
Art Coordinator: Lorraine Woost
Photo Editor: Gail Meese
Text Designer: Cynthia Brunk
Cover Designer: Brian Deep
Production Buyer: Pamela D. Bennett

This book was set in Meridien and Univers.

Macmillan Publishing Company
866 Third Avenue, New York, New York 10022

Collier Macmillan Canada, Inc.

Library of Congress Cataloging-in-Publication Data
Computers and application software / Robert A.
    Szymanski . . . [et al.].—2nd ed.
        p. cm.
    Includes index.
    ISBN 0-675-21269-3
    1. Computers. 2. Application software.
    I. Szymanski, Robert A.
QA76.5.C61388   1991
005.3—dc20   90-23019
                                                  CIP

Printing: 1 2 3 4 5 6 7 8 9
Year: 1 2 3 4

Photographs without specific credits following their captions are by Macmillan Publishing/Cobalt Productions.

Part opening quotations: Part One (p. 1). Asimov, Isaac. "Asimov Ponders PCs." *PC World.* (September 1985): 190. Part Two (p. 217), Case, John. *Digital Future: The Personal Computer Explosion—Why It's Happening and What It Means.* (New York: William Morrow & Co., 1985): 177.

All screen representations of software are used with permission of their respective copyright owners: Multimate®, MultiMate Advantage™, MultiMate Advantage II, and dBASE III PLUS are copyright © Ashton-Tate Corporation, 1987. MultiMate Advantage and MultiMate Advantage II are trademarks, and MultiMate is a registered trademark of Ashton-Tate Corporation, Torrance, California; SideKick by Borland International, Inc., Scotts Valley, California; PC-TALK III by The Headlands Press, Tiburon, California; The Twin Spreadsheet by Mosaic Software, Inc., Cambridge, Massachusetts; Lotus 1-2-3® is a registered trademark of the Lotus Development Corporation. Lotus 1-2-3 is © Lotus Development Corporation, 1986; Open Access II by Software Products International, Inc., San Diego, California; PFS:First Choice by Software Publishers Corporation, Mt. View, California; WordPerfect by WordPerfect Corporation, Orem, Utah; Commodore Educational by Commodore Computer Systems Division, West Chester, Pennsylvania; MultiPlan by Microsoft Corporation, Redmond, Washington; and Apple Desktop Publishing by Apple Computer, Inc., Coopertino, California. Apple, Macintosh, and LaserWriter are trademarks of Apple Computer, Inc.

Part opening artwork courtesy of: Lasergraphics, Inc., pp. xxiv−1, 160−161.

Chapter opening artwork courtesy of: Alias Research Corporation, pp. 218, 343 (bottom), 375 (bottom); Autodesk, Inc., pp. 2 (top), 28 (bottom), 176, 177; Luz Bueno, Berkeley, California, pp. 3 (bottom), 72, 73 (bottom), 249 (bottom); Sheriann Ki-Sun Burnham, p. 313 (bottom); fractal landscape generated by computer from the decimal expansion of pi, Gregory and David Chudnovsky, Columbia University Department of Mathematics, p. 343 (top); Tracy Colby, p. 313 (top); D. Cox/S. Meyers/D. Sandin/E. Sandor, Electronic Visualization Laboratory, University of Illinois at Chicago, p. 139 (bottom); Phil Cunningham, Purdue University CADLAB, p. 3 (top); David S. Ebert,

To Laura for her love and friendship, and for making it all worthwhile, and to my loving parents

R. A. S.

For the truly meaningful part of my life, my wife Sue and children Paul, Stacy, and Michael

D. P. S.

To Edward, Erin, Jason, and Rachel who lovingly encouraged and supported me throughout this project

N. A. M.

For the Chip in my main memory and my dear Mother "bored"

D. M. P.

PREFACE

On the premises that information is essential to survival and that computers are essential to the best use of information, this book explains how computers and information systems work, where they work, and how they affect the physical, political, and ethical environment of society. This work reflects our commitment to students and their need to prepare for the demands of the information age. Whether a student wishes simply to understand the use of computers and the role they play in today's world, to work with computers to manage information in his or her own life, or to design information systems, this text offers a comprehensive, up-to-date look at computers and their considerable impact.

Note to the Student

Computers *will* be an important part of your future, whether in your personal life or at your workplace. Some experts think that if you do not know how to use a computer, you eventually will be just as handicapped in performing your job as the person today who cannot read.

To be computer literate, you must know not only who uses computers, but also how and where they can be used, the tasks they perform, how they affect our society and economy, and how to use them to benefit your own life and career. If you are taking this course to familiarize yourself with the world of computers, you will find *Computers and Application Software* an interesting and informative guide on your journey to computing literacy. If you intend to become a computer professional, this book will give you the broad-based background you need to pursue more advanced coursework.

Long after you have completed this course, this book will remain a handy reference. When you select and purchase your own personal computer system, you can use the consumer information, checklists, and tips in Appendix E, "Buying and Caring for a Microcomputer System," on page

431. The five chapters on popular application software will provide additional information when you are ready to evaluate and select your own software. The glossary at the end of the book contains standard definitions of common computer-related terms that you may encounter.

Computers in Preparation of This Text

The existence of this textbook confirms the relevance and importance of the new technologies of the information age. From the contract negotiation stage, when the publisher ran computer budgeting and production analysis, to the drafting, revising, and typesetting of the manuscript, the computer was a team member.

The image on the cover was created using state-of-the-art computer graphics equipment, and computer-generated graphics appear on all pages that begin each part and chapter. Computers even enhanced the color in many photographs.

The manuscript was prepared using microcomputers and word processing software. It was then sent on floppy diskettes to the editor for copyediting. After these changes were made, the manuscript was transmitted electronically through telephone lines to a compositor's larger computers and typesetting equipment located in another state. There, exact margins were set and text lines were justified. Then, the text was retransmitted electronically to the publisher for further corrections. Finally composition of the pages was executed on computer, and pages were printed out for editorial review. Final film was sent to the printer, and computer-controlled presses produced the finished book. Finally, computers were key players in the sale and distribution of the book.

While computers played an important role in the preparation of this text, so did a talented group of publishing professionals. Computers and people working together made this book possible.

Key Features of the Text

To present thorough coverage of concepts, hardware, software, computer systems, information systems, and related topics that educators have indicated are important, we have included these key features:

- ☐ **Readability** at the appropriate level, and a conversational writing style to hold the student's interest.
- ☐ **Sound and effective pedagogy** designed to facilitate student understanding and interest in the subject matter.
- ☐ **Current examples** of computer applications that relate concepts to actual situations.
- ☐ **Comprehensive coverage** which, beyond the usual core coverage, includes discussions of contemporary issues such as:

    - ☐ Artificial intelligence, neural networks, and artificial reality
    - ☐ Expert systems
    - ☐ Work monitoring
    - ☐ Robotics

- ☐ Legal issues, computer-related legislation, and ethics
- ☐ Trends in new chip technologies, optoelectronics, parallel processing, and communication
- ☐ Object-oriented programming languages, object-oriented databases, and computer-assisted systems engineering (CASE)
- ☐ Popular types of application software
- ☐ Increasing use of communication technology
- ☐ Increasing use of networks, commercial information services, and database services by professionals, organizations, businesses, and home users
- ☐ Increasing home use of computers and helpful microcomputer and software buyers' tips
- ☐ Career information about computer professions and about non-computer professions that use computers
- ☐ Structured programming concepts
- ☐ The BASIC programming language

- ☐ **Written for everyone**—not only introductory level students who may be interested in continuing their study of computers and information systems as a career, but also for those who plan to enter noncomputer fields.

Pedagogy

The following pedagogical devices were chosen with both students and instructor in mind:

- ☐ **Chapter objectives** alert students and instructor to the major points or concepts to be gleaned from the chapter.
- ☐ **Chapter outlines** preview chapter topics and organization so students can see the relationships among the topics covered.
- ☐ **Profiles** acquaint students with people who have made major contributions to the information age.
- ☐ **Highlight boxes** focus on current computer uses and issues.
- ☐ **Sidebars,** placed in the margin near relevant text, reiterate key points and serve as memory joggers.
- ☐ **Summaries** review major concepts in the chapter.
- ☐ **Vocabulary Self-Tests** spotlight words that are important to understanding the material. These words are boldfaced in the text and listed alphabetically at the end of the chapter with text page numbers for reference and review. They are also listed in the glossary.
- ☐ **Review questions** check the student's understanding of the main topics in the chapter. They appear at the end of each chapter as a self-test comprised of about 30 questions.
- ☐ **Glossary,** a handy reference at the end of the book, defines all of the key terms.
- ☐ **Index** presents a detailed guide to text topics. A boldfaced page number indicates the page on which a key term is defined.

Finally, full-color functional illustrations and over 150 photographs clarify concepts, depict applications, and show equipment.

Comprehensive Coverage

The text includes chapters on hardware, software, information systems, communication, and application software. Also discussed are basic concepts and the ways in which these concepts are integrated into work situations, personal business, school activities, and leisure-time activities.

Because microcomputers are the easiest to use, and because most people will encounter them (rather than larger systems) in their daily lives, we have included significant microcomputer coverage throughout the text.

Organization

The text is divided into two parts. Part One (Chapters 1 through 6) provides an overview of computers and computing, describes computer systems, and explains information systems. Part Two (Chapters 7 through 12) presents an introduction to application software and describes five popular types of application software. The seven appendixes, written in chapter format, follow the twelve basic chapters.

Chapter 1, "Computers in Your World," introduces computers, gives examples of where they are used, and briefly explains how they work, what they can and cannot do, and the importance of becoming computing literate.

Chapter 2, "Computer Essentials," overviews the internal design and operation of the central processing unit. It explains data representation. It explains input and output concepts and describes devices for both large and small computer systems. Finally, it describes various secondary storage media and ways to organize and access data on media.

Chapter 3, "Computer Systems," describes computer systems, gives criteria for classifying large computers, and describes the popularity of microcomputers.

Chapter 4, "Computer Software," describes systems and application software, emphasizing operating systems and their importance. It also looks at different levels of computer programming languages; introduces the latest programming techniques, including object-oriented programming; and lists criteria for choosing a programming language.

Chapter 5, "Communication and Networks," explains how data are transferred from one computer to another and describes applications of data communications. It also explains local-area networks, wide-area networks, topologies, and distributed data processing.

Chapter 6, "Information Systems," defines information systems and describes transaction processing systems, management information systems, decision support systems, and executive support systems. It also describes steps in a system development life cycle. Finally, it describes the use of files and databases. It includes coverage of file management systems, database management systems, database models, and concerns for developing a database.

Chapter 7, "Introduction to Application Software for Microcomputers," introduces the five major application software programs and distinguishes among the various types of integrated packages. It also describes several features common to most application software.

Chapter 8, "Word Processors," describes the uses and features of a typical word processor. It also describes desktop publishing.

Chapter 9, "Data Managers," describes the uses and features of a typical data manager. It also describes hypertext and multimedia software.

Chapter 10, "Spreadsheets," describes the uses and features of a typical electronic spreadsheet.

Chapter 11, "Graphics for Microcomputers," describes the types of, applications for, and features of typical graphics software.

Chapter 12, "Microcomputer Communications," describes the uses and features of typical communications software.

Appendix A, "History of Computers," provides a summary of events, significant people, and their contributions throughout the history of computers and computing.

Appendix B, "Issues and Trends," discusses major social concerns including privacy of personal data, computer crimes, electronic work monitoring, health and safety, and computer ethics. A section on legal issues and legislation discusses responsibility and liability for computer errors and incorrect information. It also presents software reliability, copyright infringement, and a table of some computer-related federal legislation. It presents some technological trends—chip technologies, neural networks, artificial reality, parallel processing, and optoelectronics. It also discusses some societal trends, the emergence of a "global village," and progress and competition at the international level.

Appendix C, "Careers in an Information Age," describes major computer-related professions and discusses how computers affect other jobs and professions.

Appendix D, "Knowledge-Based (Expert) Systems," describes the evolution, components, and operation of expert systems.

Appendix E, "Buying and Caring for a Microcomputer System," offers suggestions for selecting and purchasing hardware and software for a microcomputer system. It also offers microcomputer owners many helpful tips on maintaining and protecting their systems and data.

Appendix F, "Structured Programming Concepts," covers structured programming concepts including top-down design, the qualities of a good program, and the importance of documentation.

Appendix G, "The BASIC Programming Language," introduces BASIC.

The Instructional Package

☐ **Instructor's Resource Manual** contains chapter-by-chapter lecture outlines, answers to all questions in the text, suggestions for using alternative instructional material, and a list of sources for additional reading. For instructors who prefer to use an integrated software package, the manual includes an explanation of how

Microsoft Works can be used with the text; 100 questions on Works are included in the computerized test bank. An ASCII disk copy of the manual is included to allow instructors to modify material and add their own teaching notes. In addition, an electronic disk copy of transparencies is included, along with a display show for ease of use in the classroom.

- ☐ **Computerized Test Bank** includes more than 2,500 true/false, short answer, multiple choice, and fill-in questions. Questions are coded with the chapter number and organized by objective. This versatile test bank program allows the instructor to generate tests, edit existing questions, and add new questions.

- ☐ **Printed Test Bank** is a hard-copy version of all questions in the computerized test bank.

- ☐ **Transparency Package** consists of overhead transparencies that illustrate concepts presented in the text.

- ☐ **Electronic Transparency Package** utilizes a graphics program and allows instructors to present transparencies in the classroom using their PC.

- ☐ **Data Diskettes** (packaged with the Instructor's Manual) are files that save keyboarding time for instructors and eliminate the possibility of introducing incorrect data during rekeying.

- ☐ Videotapes can be purchased by adopters of *Computers and Application Software, Second Edition,* directly from American Micro Media at a discounted rate:

  "Electronic Words" — Word Processing and Microcomputers

  "Keeping Track" — Data Management and Microcomputers

  "Computer Calc" — Electronic Spreadsheets and Microcomputers

  "Computer Talk" — Microcomputer Communications

  "Computer Images" — Computer Graphics

Reviewers

We wish to thank the following people who reviewed the manuscript and provided thoughtful and helpful suggestions for this second edition of *Computers and Application Software:* Joyce Able, Dupage College; Virginia Anderson, University of North Dakota; Robert Barrett, Indiana University; Beth DeFoor, Eastern New Mexico University; Kevin Duggan, Midlands Tech.; John Eatman, University of North Carolina; Richard Ernst, Sullivan Junior College; Barbara Felty, Harrisburg Community College; David Harris, College of the Redwoods; Edward Henning, Marywood College; John Kautz, American University—Washington, D.C.; Chris Luna, Truckee Meadows Community College; Ken Martin, University of North Florida; Judy Ogden, Johnson County Community College; John Pharr, Cedar Valley College; John Rezac, Johnson County Community College; Megan Jennings Tucker, Community College—Vermont; and James Westfall, University of Evansville.

Acknowledgments

Once again, we have had the pleasure of working with a very professional and friendly group of individuals throughout this endeavor. So many people were involved in the development, production, and creative aspects of this project that the list of names would go on and on. All of the professionals we worked with at Macmillan provided support, enthusiasm, and helpful suggestions. Special acknowledgment, however, goes to our executive editor and friend, Vernon Anthony, for once again bringing his unparalleled talents and steadfast dedication to this project. The developmental editorial support of Peggy Jacobs is unrivaled. Everyone in Macmillan's production, art, and design department is to be commended for their creativity, dedication, and hard work. In particular, we thank Sharon Rudd, production editor; Lorry Woost, art coordinator; Cindy Brunk, text designer; and Brian Deep, cover designer. Additionally, we are grateful to the organizatons and businesses that provided photographs and technical material for use in this book. We also appreciate the work of Seth Hock, who developed the instructor's manual and test bank for this book. Last but not least, thank you to Teresa George for many jobs well done.

Robert A. Szymanski

Donald P. Szymanski

Norma A. Morris

Donna M. Pulschen

BRIEF CONTENTS

CONTENTS

Computers and Application Software

PART ONE

Information Age: An Overview of Computing and Computers

In my opinion, the future will see computers and humans, each representing totally different forms of intelligence, working in cooperation rather than in competition and accomplishing more together than either could possibly achieve alone.

Isaac Asimov, science fiction writer

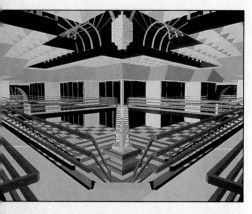

OBJECTIVES

☐ Describe the importance of understanding and being able to use computing technology.

☐ Describe what a computer is and give examples of how computers are used.

☐ Identify four basic ways in which computers are used.

☐ Recognize the three tasks that computers perform.

☐ Identify the flow of data.

☐ Distinguish between what computers can and cannot do.

☐ Identify the components of a computer system.

☐ Grasp the scope of where computers are used.

CHAPTER ONE

Computers in
Your World

PROFILE
Raymond Kurzweil

Raymond Kurzweil is impatient—and hopeful—so when he gets an idea for a computer application, his first thought seems to be, "How quickly can we get it on the market?"

It is no wonder, then, that the native New Yorker didn't bother with a lot of formal schooling before plunging into the infant computer world of the late 1950s and early 1960s. In fact, he was only 12 years old when he developed a software package so useful and well-constructed that IBM agreed to distribute it.

As the child of a music professor who was a refugee from Nazi Germany, Kurzweil spent his early years in a working-class neighborhood in New York City. His two passions as a youngster were the piano and computer technology, and Kurzweil found ways to enjoy both enthusiasms.

In 1964, when he was 16, Kurzweil won seven national awards, including first prize at the International Science Fair in Electronics and Communications, for his pioneering work in artificial intelligence. By the age of 18, he had sold a software package for $100,000 to a New York publishing company. Clearly, the bright young man had a bright future.

Blind singer and composer Stevie Wonder first encountered Kurzweil after the young computer whiz began marketing a machine that could scan books and then read them aloud by translating the signals into a synthesized voice. Wonder bought one of the first reading machines.

Then, in talking to Kurzweil about the exotic work being performed by computers, Wonder complained that the music synthesizers available, while useful in their own right, could not simulate the richly varied sounds of traditional acoustic instruments. Out of this conversation grew the idea for the Kurzweil Model 250 keyboard. Although some professional musicians say the Model 250 lacks the depth and range of a grand piano, others are enthusiastic, praising both its "natural" sound and its portability. Prince, Herbie Hancock, the Pat Metheny Group, Lynn Stanford of the American Ballet Theatre, and other top musicians also have used the Kurzweil 250. These days, Kurzweil's name and inventions are as well-known to performers as they are to the U.S. Patent Office.

Another Kurzweil enthusiasm is the VoiceWriter, a system that "hears" the spoken word and instantly prints it onto paper. A great deal of the inventor's success is attributable to his zeal for self-promotion. He is remarkably agile in both the laboratory and the boardroom. Kurzweil founded and presently directs several companies, and he personally raised the money to get them started. In 1982, at the age of 34, Kurzweil was inducted into the Computer Industry Hall of Fame, and in 1988, he received Boston's Inventor of the Year award.

A lthough the courses you choose in school may not demand technical knowledge of computers and programming, you will eventually be a computer user, either directly or indirectly. Many jobs and careers depend on some familiarity with computers and the ability to use them. This may be your formal introduction to computers, but you probably already use them—perhaps without realizing it. Did you ever make a withdrawal from your bank account using an automated teller machine (Figure 1–1)? Did you ever play a video game (Figure 1–2)? Did you ever get a printout of your class registration? Well then, you have been a computer user.

This text takes you on a journey through the world of computers and shows how computing affects your personal and professional life. It stresses the importance of being able to put computers to work for yourself.

THE NEED FOR COMPUTING LITERACY

It is likely that you will become a computer user, knowingly or unknowingly, when you begin your career. From accounting to zoology, computers have touched nearly every profession. In business, computers play vital roles from the factory floor to the boardroom. Unless you intend to be a hermit, computers will affect you.

What is computing literacy, and why would you want or need it? **Computing literacy** is learning how to use computers to benefit your life or work. This encompasses a general knowledge of computers, including who uses them, what functions they perform, how they are (or can be)

FIGURE 1–1
This automated teller machine is conveniently located in the lobby of an office building. (Courtesy of Diebold, Inc.)

FIGURE 1–2
Students enjoy playing video games, which are informal introductions to computing. (Photo by Larry Hamill/Macmillan)

used by yourself and others, and how they are affecting society. This text provides valuable knowledge to help you move into a workplace environment that uses computers. Some experts think that the person who does not know how to use computers eventually will be as handicapped in performing his or her job as the person who cannot read.

WHAT COMPUTERS ARE

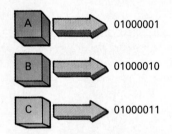

A **computer** is simply a problem-solving tool for people to use; it is a machine that accepts data, stores data, performs certain operations on that data, and presents the results of those operations. A computer is generally thought of as belonging to one of two categories—analog or digital—depending on the logic it uses.

Analog computers recognize data as continuous measurements of a physical property. The output of analog computers is usually in the form of readings on dials or graphs. Voltage, pressure, speed, and temperature are some physical properties measured in this way. For example, a furnace thermostat may be considered an analog computer.

Digital computers are high-speed, programmable, electronic devices that perform mathematical calculations, compare values, and store the results. They recognize data by counting discrete signals representing either a high-voltage electrical state (on) or low-voltage electrical state (off). Numbers and special symbols are reduced to representation by 1s (on) and 0s (off). Figure 1–3 shows how the capital letters A, B, and C are reduced to representation by a number system of 1s and 0s.

The focus of this text is on digital computers because they are the most widely used and are the category of computers you are most apt to work with.

FIGURE 1–3
A computer can recognize only characters that are coded as a series of 1s and 0s. Here, the letters A, B, and C are shown with this numeric representation.

A → 01000001
B → 01000010
C → 01000011

HOW WE USE COMPUTERS

Many of today's computers are easy to use because programs (called software) are geared to specific applications such as word processing, spreadsheets, data management, communication, and graphics. These special programs allow you to use a computer with very little experience. You can create term papers with the same word-processing package that lawyers use to draft legal briefs. You can track your finances with the same spreadsheet software that corporate finance managers use to track a major company's accounts. You can organize and maintain addresses, birthdays, and other vital statistics for family and friends with a data management program similar to ones that business managers use to handle the many details of their operations.

The same art and graphics programs that let you design greeting cards are implemented by architects to create blueprints for shopping centers and skyscrapers. Hobbyists use programs similar to those that sophisticated corporations and government agencies use for worldwide data communication.

Classes of Computers

- Analog—measures physical properties
- Digital—counts discrete signals

WHAT COMPUTERS CAN DO

Computers are used in four basic ways: (1) data processing, (2) control, (3) design and development, and (4) data communication.

Data Processing

Converting **data** (raw facts) into **information** (data in organized, usable form) is called data processing. Data processing includes statistics, mathematical calculations (such as for payrolls), filing tasks, and even word processing—all of which are traditional business data-processing applications. (Although the trend is to call data processing "information processing," it is the data that are processed *into* information.)

Control

Computers control many mechanical devices and processes. They direct robots in factories and monitor traffic lights at intersections throughout many cities. At the heart of many of these computer-controllers are sensors that activate a device or system of devices. For example, sensors are embedded in the streets of some cities to control traffic flow by adjusting traffic-light timing during peak hours at busy intersections. Computers are used in controllers that direct factory operations, monitor assembly lines, and operate machinery for many manufacturers.

Design and Development

Engineers can design a product and test it by computer before their company begins manufacture. For example, using computers, engineers can design new airplane wings and test them by simulation to see how they will function under specific conditions.

A TEACHER IN OVER HIS HEAD!

Jason, Jr., played hide and seek among the waterlogged ruins of the *Titanic,* and his sibling, also called Jason, is going to be a teacher. Jason is a 7-foot-long robot who is a whiz at underwater exploration. "Seeing" with a powerful video camera and "feeling" with his maneuverable arms, Jason can dive to depths that could injure or kill a human diver.

Jason's video eye is linked to a two-way satellite that carries back the images it sees to hundreds of thousands of school children throughout the United States and Canada. Jason conducted his first lesson in early 1989 from the bottom of the Mediterranean Sea—a long way from his base at the Woods Hole Oceanographic Institute on Cape Cod.

The million-dollar instructor came close to missing the first day of school when the cable attached to his carrier ship snapped and Jason dropped 2,100 feet to the ocean floor. After some delicate rescue moves, Jason was snatched from the deep—recess was over!

Surgeons and design engineers collaborate using computers to design and produce artificial joints and limbs (Figure 1–4). Not only do the prostheses fit better but most are developed in one-third the time and at one-third the cost of hand-drafted designs. Raw data are fed into a computer in the form of computerized tomography scans (CTs), X-rays, and

Computerized robot, Jason, Jr., leaves its "garage" aboard the manned submersible *Alvin* and sets out for a day's work photographing the remains of the luxury liner *Titanic,* over 13,000 feet below the surface of the North Atlantic. (Courtesy of Woods Hole Oceanographic Institution)

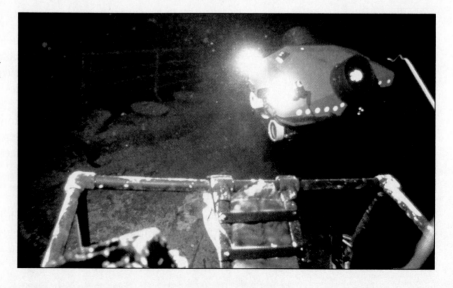

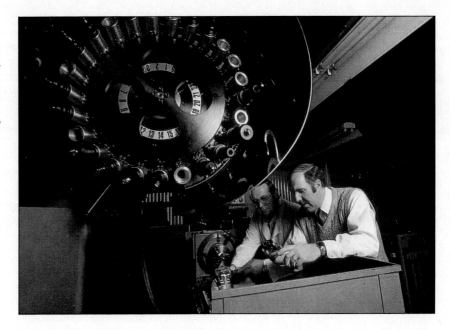

other variables such as a patient's age, body size, and the amount of activity that the new part must sustain. The computer then analyzes these data to help create a design that will best fit the patient.

Data Communication

Data communication is the process of electronically sending data from one point to another. Linking one computer to another makes it possible to share and update data at different locations. Computer users who subscribe to services such as the Dow Jones News Retrieval Service or CompuServe are able to combine their computers, software, and telephone lines to access huge banks of data on various topics.

FUNCTIONS OF A COMPUTER

Although computers have many applications in each of their four basic uses, they actually can perform only three basic tasks:

1. Perform arithmetic functions on numeric data (adding, subtracting, multiplying, and dividing).
2. Test relationships between data items by comparing values.
3. Store and retrieve data.

These skills are really no more than people can do, but computers can accomplish the tasks faster, more accurately, and more reliably.

A computer can solve complex mathematical problems in a fraction of a second; it can work with the highest accuracy imaginable; and it can store great volumes of data. The disparity of performance between a computer and a person is readily evident when each is asked to multiply two 32-digit numbers.

Computer Functions

- Arithmetic
- Comparisons
- Storage and retrieval

HOW COMPUTERS OPERATE

Before a computer can begin any solution, the data must be presented. Data must flow through a system in these general steps: (1) input, (2) processing, and (3) output. Data and information also can be stored during this flow.

Input involves collecting, verifying, and encoding data into a machine-readable form for the computer. Before processing can occur, the data must be entered into the system by means of an input device, such as a keyboard.

In **processing,** a computer creates useful information from data through such operations as classifying, sorting, calculating, summarizing, and storing. The data can be processed immediately or can be stored on a storage device for future processing. **Storage** includes **main memory** (internal storage within a computer) as well as **secondary storage** (storage external to the computer; typically used for long-term retention of instructions or data.)

Data processing requires careful planning and appropriate instructions. Accurate data must be input for the information delivered to be useful—garbage in, garbage out (GIGO) means that output is only as accurate as the input. By the same token, a program must be accurate for subsequent processes to be performed correctly.

Output includes retrieving data, converting them into human-readable form, and displaying the information to the user (for example, on a display screen or printer).

Figure 1–5 illustrates the basic flow of data through a computer system.

Note: Even if data are entered and processed correctly, the output can still be misinterpreted, misused, or ignored by the user. Once the computer does its job, it is important that the user has both the knowledge and the ethics to use that information appropriately.

Flow of Data

- Input
- Processing (including storage)
- Output

WHAT COMPUTERS CANNOT DO

It may seem that the solution to any problem is a computer. However, computers are merely tools. Computers cannot (a) operate without humans, (b) identify a problem to be solved, (c) decide the output needed to solve a problem, (d) identify and collect the data needed to produce output, (e) design the software necessary to transform data into a desired output, or (f) interpret and use information to solve a problem. These tasks must be completed by humans. If the tasks are conceived, designed, and executed appropriately, then a computer becomes a valuable tool to accomplish them faster, more accurately, and more reliably.

In some cases, it may seem that a computer is doing its work without the benefit of human involvement—for example, when a computer automatically generates software instructions or initiates a process. However, the software that automatically generates other instructions was conceived and designed by humans, and the decision criteria that lead to a particular process initiated by a computer were defined and programmed by humans.

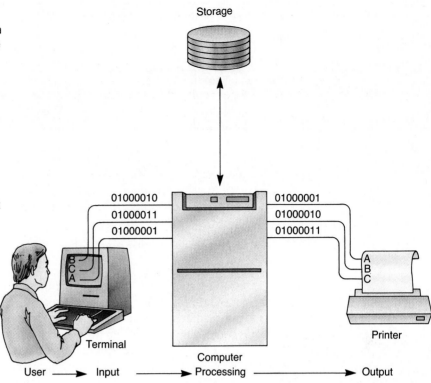

FIGURE 1–5
The basic flow of data through a computer system involves three steps: (1) input, (2) processing, and (3) output. A user enters data at an input device, and the computer converts the data to machine-readable form. In this example, the computer's instructions specify that the data should be alphabetized. After the computer completes that procedure, the output, in human-readable form, prints out on the output device. Data can be stored during this flow.

COMPUTER SYSTEMS

What components make up a computer system? The components include hardware, software, and users:

1. **Hardware,** or equipment, includes:
   a. The computer, where the processing occurs.
   b. **Storage devices,** including peripheral devices used for data storage, such as floppy disks and hard disks.
   c. **Input devices,** including peripheral devices through which data are entered into the computer, such as the keyboard and the mouse.
   d. **Output devices,** including peripheral devices that translate machine-readable code into a form that humans can use, such as printers and monitors.
2. **Software,** a set of instructions that tells the computer what to do.
3. A **user,** who is required to activate the system, and an **end user,** a noncomputer professional who accesses the computer, such as a manager, doctor, clerical worker, or student who lacks computer expertise.

Examples of computer use in this text identify situations where you may be either a user or an end user.

The size and configuration of a system depend on the processing requirements, functions necessary, and budget constraints. Computers are

Computer Components

- Hardware
  - Computer
  - Storage devices
  - Input devices
  - Output devices
- Software
- User

grouped into four main categories: supercomputers, mainframes, mini-computers, and microcomputers.

Supercomputers

Supercomputers are the fastest, most powerful, and most expensive computers. They are used where vast quantities of data must be manipulated, primarily by government agencies, scientific laboratories, and large corporations.

As early as 1984 supercomputers were used to generate innovative special effects for the movie *The Star Fighter*. Supercomputers are widely used in aerodynamic design and simulation, processing geologic data, processing data on genetic coding, and collecting and processing weather data.

Mainframe Computers

Mainframe computers are less powerful, not quite as fast, and somewhat less expensive than supercomputers. Mainframes got their name because they were first built by incorporating modules on a chassis, or "main frame." They are often used as the "traditional" computer for a company where many users at separate work stations share the same computer.

Federal and local government agencies, banks, hospitals, and commercial and industrial users need a mainframe's capabilities.

Minicomputers

Minicomputers are smaller than mainframe computers, providing somewhat less memory and processing capability, and are less expensive. They can serve several users simultaneously.

They usually are used by small and medium-sized businesses, scientific laboratories, research groups, some colleges, engineering firms, and even industrial and manufacturing plants.

Microcomputers

Computers that contain a lesser amount of memory and processing capability at a lower cost than minicomputers are called **microcomputers**. Microcomputers are used in homes for hobbies, entertainment, or personal business. They are used in schools for research, education, and practice drills. Businesses of all sizes and corporate executives use microcomputers for general business, managing finances, and improving productivity.

Chapter 3 examines these four major types of computer systems in detail.

WHERE COMPUTERS ARE USED

Even when you don't see them, computers are working behind the scenes—at home, at school, and where you shop, work, or transact business. Some computers are responsible for your leisure enjoyment and en-

tertainment; others are found in government operations and most professions.

Business and Industry

Computers are used in business for many information-processing tasks. Information processing includes word processing, filing, and assembling numbers and facts associated with general office functions such as accounting, payroll processing, personnel record keeping, and compliance with federal regulations.

Science, Medicine, and Technology

With their capability for accumulating and storing data, computers have been important to advances in health care. The ability to simulate hazardous conditions without involving risk to humans has been important to advances in space flight and earthbound vehicle-safety testing. The computer's ability to compare and make inferences has been important in many fields of study.

Health Care. If all this talk about computers has your head in a spin and you go to the emergency room of a major hospital for relief, you will find that information about your admission will be entered into a computer. Indeed, your entire hospital stay will be recorded—all prescribed medications, visits from doctors, and other hospital services (Figure 1-6). In fact, your itemized bill most likely will be ready when you are released.

Some of today's medical students are learning anatomy and physiology lessons using *The Electric Cadaver*. This "electronic book" uses a microcomputer such as a Macintosh II to display text and images—even depictions of muscles and tendons at work—and to study the body's internal organs and skeletal structure.

Dentists are using small computer systems to diagnose and treat jaw misalignments. A magnetic square containing three sensors is placed between the front teeth and lips and the sensors are attached to a computer. They follow the movement of the magnet, tracing a line on the screen as the patient's mouth opens. If the jaw moves improperly, the line bends, and corrective action is indicated. On the other hand, if the line is straight, the patient just needs to keep flossing. A computer can be programmed to send a reminder for a checkup in six months.

Simulation. Because supercomputers have huge memories, fast processing speeds, and capability for processing vast amounts of data, they are used widely in simulation tests. Simulation of automobile crashes or airplane emergency landings involves a variety of factors that must be evaluated to locate weaknesses in new designs without risking human life (Figure 1-7). NASA astronauts train by studying computer simulations of problems they could encounter during launch, in space, or upon return to Earth. In addition, supercomputers help design aircraft models and simu-

FIGURE 1–7
(a) A General Motors technician adjusts a robotic testing device that simulates a body's reaction during crash testing. (b) The body model simulates the mass and other characteristics of an actual human body to test a proposed seat belt design. Computer simulation aids engineers in identifying the most effective seat belt design to eliminate shoulder belt slack on impact. (a, courtesy of General Motors Technical Center; b, courtesy of Daimler-Benz and Evans & Sutherland)

(a)

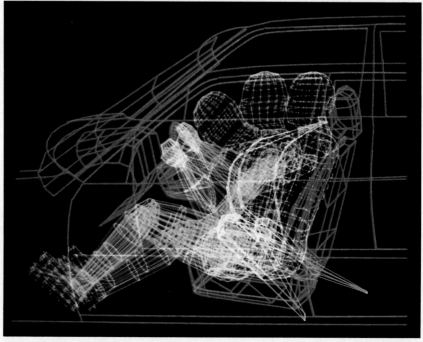

(b)

late the effects that winds and other environmental forces might have on those designs.

Making Inferences. At Stanford University, civil engineers use a computer program called SEISMIC to evaluate the effects of an earthquake on structures in the Palo Alto, California area. Buildings are assessed on their age, proximity to the San Andreas fault, soil type, size, shape, and construction material. Even though SEISMIC contains enough information about earthquakes to be labeled an expert, an engineer must interpret and evaluate the information provided and then draw conclusions.

Education

Nearly all public schools in the United States have computers, which are located in science laboratories, classrooms, and registration offices. Many educators find computers to be valuable aids for instruction and tutoring. Computers are tireless and nonjudgmental when drilling students on mathematical facts or offering specialized lessons on particular subjects. Because many science laboratory experiments can be simulated by computer, young students become interested and excited by the interactions and the feelings of accomplishment that they gain from right answers and vivid color graphics (Figure 1–8).

The Smithsonian Institution, Apple, and Lucasfilm (creator of the *Indiana Jones* movie series) have collaborated on interactive instructional media. In *Life Story,* they combine videodisc technology and film production to bring art, text, graphics, and sound effects to the screen.

Colleges and Universities. Students on many campuses use telephones to access computerized programs for registration or dropping and adding classes. Computer lab facilities are available to most students. Some colleges and universities *require* computer ownership for their incoming students. Educators are observing that today's students view the computer as another work tool, comparing it to the calculator in past decades. Graduates often attribute success in their chosen professions to computer skills learned and used in college.

Libraries. Many libraries, including those at Stanford, Harvard, and Yale, offer on-line searching capabilities. At Stanford, Socrates is an electronic card catalog system of eight million books—including all books purchased by the library since 1970. Computers with on-line databases in the libraries allow easy and quick research. Gone are the tiresome hand searching of card catalogs, physical finding of the particular volume and page, and then reading of an article only to find that the citation isn't exactly what you expected.

Government

The federal government is the largest user of computers and one of the largest funders of computer research. By one estimate, the federal govern-

(a)

(b)

FIGURE 1-8

(a) This youth uses a math drill that requires him to determine if the addition and subtraction problems presented on the screen are correct or incorrect. (b) This student learns to tell time with an easy-to-operate program called Timekeeper. By touching the screen or typing in the time on the keyboard, the student can move the clock hands to match digital time or time displayed in words. (c) Elementary schools use computers as tools to teach a variety of subjects. (Courtesy of International Business Machines Corp.)

(c)

ment holds over four billion personal files on U.S. citizens. The U.S. Patent and Trademark Office receives over 20,000 documents every day and the Securities and Exchange Commission receives more than six million pages of documents and reports a year.

The IRS processes over 100 million tax returns a year, making it the federal government's largest computer user. The returns are first handled at a regional office, where clerks key the data into a computer through terminals. Then, the returns are processed by a computer that checks for arithmetic accuracy. The returns are further checked by a computer that compares them to information that was supplied by banks and employers. Some IRS auditors even take small laptop computers on location when making tax audits.

Politics. Computers have been used to tally national election votes since 1952, when the UNIVAC I first attracted worldwide attention. In the na-

IS THAT A BUG ON THE MENU? Computers have changed the language a great deal already, and the changes continue. To begin with, words, such as *byte, microchip, bubble memory, bar code, floppy disk, microprocessor,* and *artificial intelligence,* were coined as names for devices and processes that didn't exist (or which had limited uses) until computers came into their own. Then, some commonly used terms began to have specific computer-related meanings: *boot, address, BASIC, bit, bug, bus, disk, dump, execute, file, flag, input, interpreter, list, load, loop, menu, monitor, mouse, network, output, plotter, program, PROM, prompt, RAM, swapping, terminal,* and *track.* While some of these words will no doubt become obsolete, our computer-based society will assure a long, active life for others.

In 1987, the Merriam-Webster Company published a supplement to its 1961 Third International Dictionary. The list of new terms contained 12,000 words, many originating from the computer field. A supplement to the Oxford English Dictionary (the final volume of the dictionary's update) also contains some new American computer terminology, including *update* and *user friendly.* Perhaps it is poetic justice that the machine that brought so many new words into the language is now the main tool for helping dictionary makers keep track of the changing language.

tional presidential election that year, it correctly predicted Dwight Eisenhower's victory over Adlai Stevenson after only five percent of the vote had been counted. Because of the different time zones across the United States, there is much controversy about predictions of election outcomes while the polls on the West Coast are still open.

Political parties maintain databases of voter registration and past election results. Potential candidates use computers to analyze opinion polls and to draw lists of names of volunteers or contributors. After candidates have been elected to the legislature, they use other computer database services. The House Information System contains data on federal grants, pending legislation, and U.S. Supreme Court decisions. The LEGIS system provides information on the status of all bills currently pending. A computerized tally board displays the results of members' votes.

Defense. Military organizations such as NORAD (North American Air Defense Command) use computers to detect missiles that might be headed toward the United States. Computers are part of the early warning systems in satellites and AWACS (Airborne Warning and Control System) aircraft, and they compile data from surveillance and intelligence operations. Computers are also used inside weapons such as the Cruise missile to guide them to their targets.

States. Most states use computers for financial accounting. In many states, computers in the Division of Motor Vehicles process driver's license applications, check titles, and print registration forms. Michigan provides a terminal in the offices of all state senators and representatives. Alaska, where travel is often difficult, has networked various information offices to link sites across the state with audio conferencing capabilities.

Local Government. Two especially important computer uses in local governments are in fire and police protection. One of the first cities to computerize its fire response systems was San Francisco. SAFER (Systems for Assigning of Fire Equipment and Resources) was implemented to assign equipment efficiently for approximately 30,000 calls a year.

In Detroit, a $20 million computer system called DETERS (Detroit Emergency Response System) was implemented in 1989. This system, in which police, fire, and emergency vehicles are equipped with computers, allows the emergency 911 system to handle more calls and dispatch the appropriate aid in much less time than previously. Officers can immediately check automobile registration and driver's licenses and verify that a driver has no outstanding arrest warrants. Some police departments use computerized robots as part of an educational and safety training program (Figure 1–9).

FIGURE 1–9
With the help of a robot, a police officer in Orlando, Florida, gives students instructions on safety topics. (Courtesy of Orlando Police Department)

Traffic Control. State and local governments use computers for city planning and traffic control. For example, some cities have enlisted computer expertise to eliminate the dreaded gridlock. A real-life traffic jam is defined as gridlock when traffic is at a total standstill in an area of eight or more blocks for 15 minutes. Beyond being an annoyance, gridlock is a threat to public safety because emergency vehicles cannot get through.

To alleviate gridlock, traffic engineers designed a system that includes loops of wire embedded in the asphalt at many intersections across a city. As cars drive over the wires, a central computer counts electrical pulses, translates them into a number of cars, converts the numbers to a rate of flow, and tells the traffic lights when to change. The computer also saves the information for predictions of potential gridlock areas or gridlock days. If necessary, the chief of operations can send additional traffic patrols to problem areas.

Legal System

By using computers to search through huge data banks such as LEXIS or Shepard's Citations, lawyers shorten the time required to conduct legal precedent and case research. They use an electronic retrieval system to look through millions of individual cases; find whether similar or parallel cases were approved, denied, criticized, or overruled; and decide whether to use them in their arguments for the current case (Figure 1–10). Lawyers then formulate strategies based on past case decisions.

Attorneys also use computers to track their appointments, case dockets, time journals, and clients' bills. Word processors help many legal secretaries prepare legal documents and briefs in time for filings with the courts.

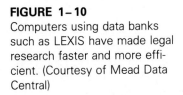
FIGURE 1–10
Computers using data banks such as LEXIS have made legal research faster and more efficient. (Courtesy of Mead Data Central)

Court reporters find that Kurzweil's VoiceWriter (see the profile at the beginning of this chapter) may become as much of an asset as the transcription machine. With the VoiceWriter, records are dictated directly into a voice-activated typewriter instead of first being spoken into one machine and later transcribed by a typist.

Recreation and Entertainment

Our recreation and leisure-time pursuits, entertainment, and even our homes have been affected by computerization.

Recreation. A health and fitness obsession continues in the United States. Users stay in shape with computer-controlled monitoring devices that combine a personal computer, a road bicycle, and an exerciser in a personally programmed course of exercise. The course can be created to give the effect of hills and to let you select speed, wind, and slope conditions. A screen simulation offers a panorama of the particular course you select.

Sports. In most sports, computers are used to compile statistics, sell tickets, create training programs and diets for athletes, and suggest strategies based on the past performance of competitors. The graphic art displays flashed on scoreboards also are generated by computers.

If you're a sports fan watching in an armchair, do computers affect you? Well, television networks use computers in the control room to bring you play-by-play action. With the help of a computer, a technician calls up replays of the action and inserts the commercial breaks on schedule. It is possible that the sport shoes you're wearing were designed using computers that checked stress points and then created a style and shape to offer maximum support for the foot. Brooks, Nike, and other athletic shoe manufacturers use computers to design and produce footwear.

FIGURE 1–11
Computers are used in restaurants to record purchases and keep track of inventory.

Entertainment. Almost everyone has played video games like Nintendo. Also, you are probably familiar with the order entry system found at fast-food restaurants, where a clerk enters your order by indicating choices on a special cash register. This device actually enters data directly into a computer that, in turn, lists your order, calculates the cost, and prints a receipt.

Computers are found in the fancier restaurants, too (Figure 1–11). For example, the Las Casuelas Terraza in Palm Springs, California, has a seating capacity of 200. In 1983, Internal Revenue Service regulations required that the owner keep records of each employee's tips. That seemed an appropriate time to computerize everything, including the cash register system.

Having a Macintosh computer and PageMaker software in the restaurant office means that menus can be printed quickly and easily to reflect any price changes brought about by droughts, inflation, or desire for higher profits. Service is greatly improved with a 50-page handbook that was prepared for all servers. The success of special promotions can be seen quickly, and predictions of future volume of business and amount of revenue can be made. The owner credits the use of computers for the restaurant's growth, including sales of over $4 million.

Music. Electronic pianos contain digital computers. The Kurzweil Ensemble Grande creates the sounds of a piano and 32 other instruments, plays preset rhythms, and stores and replays 4,000 notes. The Kurzweil 250 synthesizer is another computer used in music.

A musical instrument digital interface (MIDI) links musical instruments to a personal computer, thereby enabling the computer to control a wide variety of instrument sounds (Figure 1–12). Often, the background music in movies, television shows, and commercials is electronically generated. In addition, when you buy concert tickets, the ticket agency is

FIGURE 1–12
(a) Musician and entertainer Steve Loren of Columbus, Ohio, uses eight pieces of computerized equipment, a microcomputer, a keyboard, and (b) a MIDI device, such as The Box, to produce synthesized music.

(a)

(b)

probably part of a computerized network that registers the number of seats sold.

Movies. Computer-generated art lets designers create sets, special effects, and even imaginary characters in movies, videos, and commercials. Creatures, spaceships, and entire galaxies are created and manipulated by computers and then photographed by computer-driven cameras. Computer-controlled lighting systems used on sound stages or in theaters can produce a dramatic range of atmospheres. Not all special effects are computer creations, though. The mine walls seen in *Indiana Jones and the Temple of Doom* were created by the not-so-high-tech scrunching and painting of aluminum foil.

Games. A computer can be programmed to play the banker in the ever-popular game of Monopoly. Of course, computer checkers and chess are the old faithfuls of computer games. Computer Scrabble is a relatively sedate and safe offering, but in the computerized game Photon, a player dodges through a futuristic environment (Figure 1–13).

FIGURE 1–13
In the computerized game Photon, the player dodges through a futuristic environment of passageways, mazes, and catwalks. The object of the game is to reach the enemy team's goal, somewhere beyond the fog and past the enemy's lasers, without being terminated. Points are automatically racked up on the central computer. (Courtesy of Photon Entertainment, Inc.)

Travel and Tourism. Want to get away from it all? Computers will help prepare your ticket, confirm your hotel room and rental car reservations (Figure 1–14), monitor the route of your train, or guide your plane to a safe landing. Tulsa, Oklahoma, is the hub for the American Airlines reservation system SABRE, the world's largest network of nonmilitary computers. The system processes data at 1,400 messages per second. With over 700,000 miles of wire and circuits connecting five large computers, SABRE confirms your reservation while you wait.

Computers also control animations—voices, lights, music, and speed of the action—of attractions found at many theme parks around the country.

Home. In more and more home offices, people use computers to continue their daytime work, organize their personal information needs, or conduct business for themselves. Microwave ovens, sewing machines, and coffee makers now are among the standard computerized appliances in most kitchens. Many of our home entertainment equipment such as TVs, VCRs, and stereos also are computer-controlled.

Home automation systems with prices from $1,500 to $15,000 are available to create so-called "smart homes" that maximize computer use.

FIGURE 1–14
With help from a computer, a travel agent can quickly identify availability and the price that suits a client's needs when booking airline flights, hotel rooms, and car rentals.

FIGURE 1–15
This demonstration "smart" house, a prototype by American Electric Power and Columbus Southern Power, has many computerized features. At the heart of the system is a microcomputer, software, and special wiring with an integrated cable. The computer system controls security, energy use and cost, and an array of "smart" appliances—from the stereo, to the washer and dryer, to the heating and air-conditioning units. Strategically placed sensors monitor energy distribution throughout the building. (Photo by Larry Hamill/Macmillan)

Lighting, heating, cooling, and security systems are among the computer-controlled functions found in many smart homes (Figure 1–15). Sensors warn owners of fire or vandalism. Lawns are sprinkled automatically, hot tub temperatures are regulated, and motion sensors even turn lights and heat on or off when a person enters or leaves a room.

If you still are among the skeptical who believe that they are not affected by computers, you should know that the manuscript for this textbook was written, revised, and edited on microcomputers using word-processing software. Many of the color photos were computer enhanced to give the final pictures their best clarity and color. Not only that, but the art designs that open each chapter were created with computer-graphics software. Every word in this book was electronically typeset on a computer system. The UPC (Universal Product Code) bar symbol on the back cover was placed there for scanning into computer inventory and cash-register systems!

Without doubt, computers are a part of your world. Developing the knowledge and skills to put them to work for you is essential to a well-rounded education in the information age in which you live.

ABOUT THIS BOOK

This first chapter is just an introduction to the computers in your world. In subsequent chapters, you will learn more about the operation of computers and their specific parts, find out what devices are used with computers, and discover how those devices are related. You will see how computers can be used to help solve problems. We devote one chapter to computer systems, where you will study the differences among systems and the types of jobs that each performs. You will learn how computers communicate with each other and how data communication expands what computers can do for you or your business. You'll also see the varied ways in which people use computers and understand why computer users have wisely acquired a powerful working partner.

We introduce several microcomputer application software packages, such as word processor, data manager, spreadsheet, graphics, and communication. These programs give you the powerful advantage of performing tasks that are commonly aided by computers.

Appendix A addresses the history of computers and computing since the early 1950s. Appendix B presents the latest computer trends and some concerns people have about the effects of computers on our society. Because innovations are occurring rapidly, it is impossible to predict the future with any degree of accuracy. However, this appendix ventures some observations and a general forecast.

Many careers and jobs now require some familiarity with computers. Some of these positions are described in Appendix C. If you are interested in a career or job that is directly involved with information technology or computer technology, many possibilities exist—entering data, defining the ways in which data are processed, managing a computer system, and using information generated from computers to make the best business decisions. Other possibilities include designing computer systems, marketing and selling them, and maintaining them.

Appendix D describes knowledge-based "expert systems" and gives examples showing how and where these expert systems are being applied.

Appendix E discusses buying and caring for your own microcomputer system. You will find many helpful hints and things to be aware of before buying. We also look at taking care of your investment.

Appendix F explains the purpose of structured programming, including the qualities of a good program and the importance of documentation.

Appendix G introduces the BASIC programming language.

SUMMARY

Computing literacy is a general knowledge about computers, who uses them, what functions they perform, how they are used, where they are used, how they affect society, and how to use them yourself. A computer is a machine that can help solve problems by accepting data, performing certain operations, and presenting the results of those operations. Analog computers recognize data as measurements of a physical property; digital computers are high-speed programmable electronic devices that perform mathematical calculations, compare values, and store results.

Computers are used in four basic ways: (1) data processing, (2) control, (3) design and development, and (4) data communication. Data processing is converting raw data into usable information. Controllers use sensors to activate devices. Computers design, develop, and test products. Computers communicate data from point to point electronically.

Although computers can perform only three basic tasks—(1) arithmetic functions, (2) comparisons, and (3) storage/retrieval—they can do these tasks faster, more accurately, and more reliably than people.

Data must flow through a computer in this sequence: input, processing, and output. Input involves collecting, verifying, and encoding data so that the machine can read them. In processing, a computer classifies, sorts, calculates, summarizes, and stores the results. Storage means the computer saves the data, either internally or externally. Output involves retrieving and collecting data so a person can read the results.

Computers *cannot* identify a problem, decide how to solve it, identify and collect the data to solve it, design the software to solve it, or interpret information that is obtained.

A computer system includes hardware, software, and a user. Computers are categorized as supercomputers, mainframe computers, minicomputers, and microcomputers. Computers are found in diverse areas—business and industry, science and technology, medicine, education, government, law, recreation, entertainment, and the home.

Vocabulary Self-Test

Can you define the following?

analog computer (p. 6)

computer (p. 6)

computing literacy (p. 5)

data (p. 7)

data communication (p. 8)

digital computer (p. 6)

end user (p. 11)

hardware (p. 11)

information (p. 7)

input (p. 10)

input device (p. 11)

mainframe computer (p. 12)

main memory (p. 10)

microcomputer (p. 12)

minicomputer (p. 12)

output (p. 10)

output device (p. 11)

processing (p. 10)

secondary storage (p. 10)

software (p. 11)

storage (p. 10)

storage device (p. 11)

supercomputer (p. 12)

user (p. 11)

Review Questions

Multiple Choice

1. The _____ computer is the type that recognizes data as measurements of a physical property.
   a. analog   c. mainframe
   b. digital   d. dataprocessing

2. Which is an example of using a computer as a controller?
   a. Calculating payroll
   b. Creating artificial limbs
   c. Sending data
   d. Directing robots

3. _____ is the process of electronically sending data from one point to another.
   a. Word processing
   b. Data management
   c. Data retrieval
   d. Data communication

4. Computers are capable of all but one of the following functions. Which answer does not belong?
   a. Adding, subtracting, multiplying, and dividing
   b. Testing relationships by comparing values
   c. Solving problems by thinking
   d. Storing and retrieving data

5. The process of collecting, verifying, and encoding data into a machine-readable form for the computer is called _____.
   a. input   c. processing
   b. output   d. store and retrieve

6. _____ occurs when the computer creates useful information from data.
   a. Input   c. Processing
   b. Output   d. Storage

7. External storage that is typically used for long-term storage of instructions or data is known as _____.
   a. primary storage
   b. main memory
   c. output
   d. secondary storage

8. If inaccurate data are input, the output is useless; this phenomenon is sometimes called _____ .
   a. computing illiteracy
   b. data processing
   c. garbage in, garbage out (GIGO)
   d. miscommunication

9. The mouse is an example of a(n) _____ device.
   a. user   c. output
   b. input   d. supercomputer

10. A(n) _____ device could be a monitor or a printer.
    a. input   c. keyboard
    b. output   d. software

Fill-in

1. The computer that recognizes data by counting on and off states of electricity is a(n) _Digital_ computer.
2. Converting data into information is known as _Processing_
3. _Data Processing_ is the process of electronically sending data from one point to another.
4. People can perform the same functions as computers, but computers can perform their functions _more accurately, more reliably_, and _faster_ than people.
5. _output_ is the method of retrieving data, converting it into human-readable form, and displaying the information.
6. Storage includes _Main men_ (the internal storage unit of the computer) and _Secondary_ (external storage).
7. _Floppy disk_ and _hard disk_ are the two types of computer storage devices.
8. The keyboard and the mouse are _input_ devices.
9. Printers and monitors are also called _output_ devices.
10. _Software_ is the set of instructions that tells the computer what to do.

Short Answer

1. List several kinds of software programs that make today's computers easy to use. _wp Lotus Paint brush_
2. Computers are used in basically four ways. Name them. _see page 25_
3. What are the three functions of a computer? _Arithmetic comparisons Storage Retrieval_
4. Explain what is involved during each step in the flow of data through a computer. _Input Processing held storage and output_
5. List the components of a computer system. In your opinion, which is the most important? _Hardware, storage input, output, software and user_
6. Give examples of how the medical profession uses computers.
7. How are computers used in the field of education?
8. Give examples of how computers are applied in the legal system.
9. Explain how computers might affect your vacation.
10. Describe three scenarios in which you imagine computers affecting your education, career, or home.

COMPUTERS IN YOUR WORLD   □   27

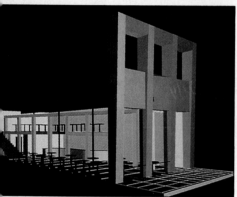

OUTLINE

OBJECTIVES

- ☐ Understand the function of each part of the central processing unit (CPU).

- ☐ Distinguish among bits, bytes, words, and encoding systems.

- ☐ Distinguish between the two ways data are prepared for input.

- ☐ Explain the two modes of updating files.

- ☐ Know the two ways of ensuring accuracy as data are entered.

- ☐ Define input and briefly describe various input devices.

- ☐ Define output and briefly describe various output devices.

- ☐ Describe the transfer of data using serial and parallel interfaces.

- ☐ Understand the purpose of secondary storage.

- ☐ Name and describe several different forms of secondary storage.

- ☐ Describe the basic hierarchy of data organization.

- ☐ Contrast three methods of storing and accessing a file.

CHAPTER TWO

Computer Essentials

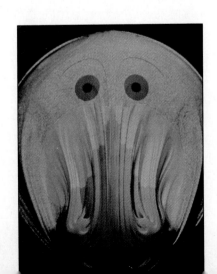

□ □

PROFILE
M. E. (Ted) Hoff

It's hard to imagine the world today if it weren't for people with vision like Ted Hoff. Even he probably didn't realize what would become of the work he started on that fateful day in 1969.

After working at Stanford University as a research assistant, Ted Hoff joined Intel Corporation in 1969. At Intel, Hoff led a team that helped a Japanese firm, Busicom, design a custom circuit for its calculator. The Busicom design called for 12 integrated circuit chips, each with 3,000–5,000 transistors. The chips that made up the processor were matched to the specific tasks of the calculator. After reviewing the design, however, Hoff decided it was too complex and would be too expensive to produce. Consequently, he used a totally different approach. He decided to design the calculator around a general-purpose processor, relying more on software than on electronics. Although more memory space was needed to store the software, this approach enabled Hoff to put the entire processor on a single integrated-circuit chip, called a microprocessor.

What a chip it was! The Intel 4004 could handle four bits of information at a time, and its computational powers came close to those of the ENIAC, one of the early electronic digital computers that required an entire room to house it. This single microprocessor performed as well as some of the early (1960s) IBM machines that cost around $30,000 and had processing units the size of a large desk. Hoff's microprocessor was about one-sixth by one-eighth inch and cost about $200. The reductions in size and cost made it possible to design small, relatively inexpensive computers. This discovery heralded the beginning of the microcomputer revolution. Thanks to Ted Hoff's creativeness, microprocessors are everywhere—in our computers, homes, cars, factories, and yes, still in our calculators.

The purpose of the computer is to help turn data into useful information. In this chapter you will learn about the central processing unit of the computer, the place where the processing of data occurs. You will also look at methods and devices for getting data into the computer, as well as methods and devices that output the results of data processing. Finally, we will examine methods of organizing and storing data, including the storage media.

THE CENTRAL PROCESSING UNIT

The **central processing unit (CPU)** is an integrated circuit or circuits comprised of (1) the arithmetic and logic unit (ALU), (2) the control unit, and (3) the main memory unit. Some sources define the CPU as only the arithmetic and logic unit and the control unit. However, because the ALU, the control unit, and main memory are closely related and function as a whole, the CPU is functionally defined here as containing all three elements (Figure 2–1). Large computer systems may have multiple CPUs, whereas microcomputers generally have only one.

An **integrated circuit,** also called a **microchip** or just **chip,** is used for logic and memory circuitry. For example, an IC can be designed to function as part of the ALU or as a memory chip.

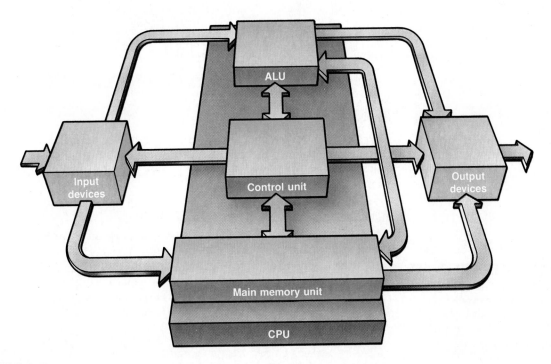

FIGURE 2–1
The central processing unit (CPU) includes the arithmetic and logic unit (ALU), control unit, and main memory unit. The relationship between a CPU and input and output devices also is shown. Arrows show movement of data or instructions among these elements.

Until the developmental work by Ted Hoff (see profile at beginning of chapter), the parts of the central processing unit were on separate chips. Hoff combined them on a single chip called a **microprocessor** (Figure 2–2), which is the CPU of a microcomputer. To be called a microprocessor, a chip must contain at least the arithmetic and logic unit and the control unit, but it may also contain main memory. Microprocessors made possible the rapid development of microcomputers. You may hear someone refer to a computer as, for example, a "386 machine." What the person is referring to is the microprocessor, in this case the Intel 80386. Many times, you will hear a computer described by its processor rather than its brand name. In a microcomputer, the microprocessor and other support chips are mounted on the main circuit board, often called the motherboard or system board (Figure 2–3).

The Arithmetic and Logic Unit

The **arithmetic and logic unit (ALU)** is the part of a CPU in which all arithmetic and logical functions are performed:

Main Components of a CPU

- Arithmetic and logic unit (ALU)
- Control unit
- Main memory unit

FIGURE 2-3
The motherboard, or main circuit board, of a computer.

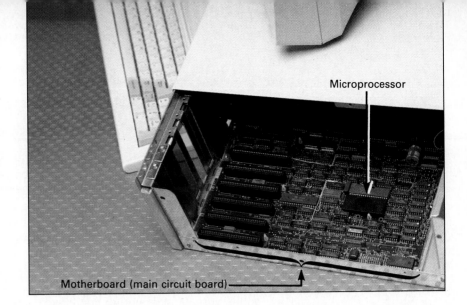

Microprocessor

Motherboard (main circuit board)

□ The arithmetic functions include basic addition, subtraction, multiplication, and division as well as advanced mathematical functions such as logarithms, trigonometry, and specialized operations.
□ The **logic functions,** where numbers or conditions are compared
to each other, include greater than ($>$), less than ($<$), equal to ($=$),
not equal to ($\neq$), greater than or equal to ($\geqq$), and less than or
equal to ($\leqq$).

The Control Unit

The **control unit** interprets any instructions it receives from memory and
directs the sequence of events necessary to execute each instruction. It also
establishes the timing of these events. It is basically the "traffic cop" of the
system. For example, data can flow both into and from the CPU, but the
control unit keeps this from happening simultaneously in order to prevent
garbled information.

The Main Memory Unit

The **main memory unit** is the internal memory of a computer. It provides temporary storage of computer program instructions and data during
program execution. Part of the main memory may contain permanently
stored instructions that tell the computer what to do when it is turned on.
Examples are checking that everything is working properly and checking
what peripheral devices—disk drives, printers, monitors—are attached.
Because the main memory is located inside a computer and is linked
directly to the other components of the CPU, access to instructions and
data is very fast.

The process of entering data into the main memory is called **writing**.
When data are placed in—"written to"—the main memory, they replace
what was originally there. This procedure is equivalent to deleting a word
with a pencil eraser and writing a new word in its place. The process of

CHIPS TO LIVE BY It's not too hard to see how computers benefit us in our jobs. We can even imagine how computers might be used in all sorts of machines ranging from robots to microwave ovens. They even help save lives. "Sure," you say, "there are plenty of applications, such as pacemakers, magnetic resonance imaging, and numerous monitoring functions, but how about on a smaller, more unusual scale?"

A company in Fremont, California, called Aprex markets a medication event monitoring system (MEMS). MEMS is a medicine bottle with a tiny computer contained in the cap. Every time the bottle is opened, the date and time are recorded by the computer chip. The doctor can insert the cap into a special machine to discover when the patient took the pills. Regular medication is important with many ailments. One test at Yale University found that epilepsy patients suffered more seizures when they did not use the medicine correctly.

Often, a full-sized computer cannot go where a computer could be used to help save a life, but integrated circuits have made thumbnail-sized computers possible. Scuba divers depend on the functions that underwater decompression computers (the size of a wristwatch) can perform. A battery-operated computer keeps track of information, such as dive depth and duration of dive. Then, the computer displays the appropriate rate of ascent numerically so that the diver avoids getting the bends when surfacing.

retrieving data from the main memory is called **reading.** The reading process does not change the data in any way.

Semiconductor integrated circuits can be designed to function as memory chips. Most memory today is comprised of semiconductor technology. The two commonest forms of semiconductor memory are random-access memory and read-only memory:

☐ **Random-access memory (RAM)** is the part of main memory where data and program instructions are held while being manipulated or executed. This type of memory allows you to enter data into memory (write) and then to retrieve it from main memory (read). Most of main memory consists of RAM. RAM is *volatile,* which means that the contents of memory are lost when the power to a RAM chip is interrupted.

☐ **Read-only memory (ROM)** can only be read, as the name implies. Data cannot be written into read-only memory. ROM may contain information on how to start the computer and even in-

Semiconductor Main Memory

- Random-access memory (RAM)
  - ☐ Read–write
  - ☐ Volatile
- Read-only memory (ROM)
  - ☐ Read only
  - ☐ Nonvolatile

structions for the entire operating system. The actual contents of ROM are usually set by the computer manufacturer, and they are unchangeable and permanent. Because the contents cannot be altered and they are not lost when the electric current is turned off, ROM is *nonvolatile*.

The amount of main memory is important in determining the capabilities of a computer. More main memory available means that more instructions and data can be loaded into the computer. Many applications require a specific amount of memory. If your computer doesn't have that amount, the application software may not work or may run slowly and inefficiently because you must keep swapping diskettes. Most computers have provisions either for adding individual RAM chips to the main circuit board or for adding RAM cards. A RAM card is a group of integrated circuits already assembled on a printed circuit board (Figure 2–4). It can

This scuba diver uses a wristwatch-size decompression computer, which tracks dive depth and duration and displays the safest rate of ascent. (David Hiser/Photographers Aspen. Inset: Macmillan Publishing/Cobalt Productions)

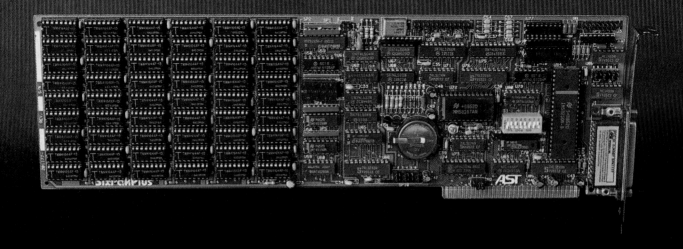

FIGURE 2–4
A RAM card for extending memory. Some RAM cards, such as this AST Six
Pac Plus, offer additional functions such as a parallel printer port and a battery-
operated system clock. RAM cards often are called multifunction boards.

be plugged into the main circuit board of a computer to increase the
amount of RAM.

DATA REPRESENTATION

In Chapter 1, you learned that digital computers identify only signals in the
form of digital pulses that represent either a high-voltage state (on) or a
low-voltage state (off). The on and off conditions are commonly labeled
with the numbers 1 and 0, respectively. (This convention has become
commonplace in labeling ON/OFF switches on computers and copiers: 1
for ON, 0 for OFF.)

The number system using only 1s and 0s is called the **binary system**. Various combinations of 1s and 0s represent all of the numbers,
letters, and symbols that can be entered into a computer. Although you see
numbers, letters, and symbols assembled to form English words and
phrases, the computer sees things totally differently. For example, the uppercase letter D is represented by the binary sequence 11000100.

Because the language of the computer, "machine language," is based
on the binary system, data entered into a computer must be interpreted
into binary code before they can be used by the computer. Fortunately,
programs take care of this conversion.

Bits and Bytes

The smallest piece of data that can be recognized and used by a computer
is the bit, a binary digit. A **bit** is a single binary value, either a 1 or a 0. A
grouping of eight bits is a **byte**. (Occasionally, the term "nibble" is used,
meaning half of a byte, or four bits.) The byte is the basic unit for mea-

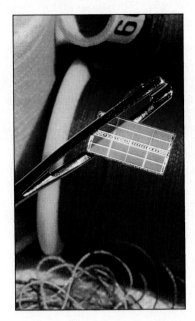

Chip sizes are shrinking. This IBM chip contains one megabit of memory, but it is so small it can fit through the eye of a needle. (Courtesy of International Business Machines Corp.)

Data Representation

- Bit
- Byte
- Word
- Encoding systems
  - ASCII
  - EBCDIC

suring memory size. However, because today's memories are so big, it is more common to hear the term *kilobyte* (K or KB) or *megabyte* (MB). To give you an idea of how many English words are in a kilobyte, the text material in this chapter is approximately 60,000 bytes, or 60 kilobytes (60K).

There is some confusion over the prefixes *kilo-* and *mega-*. In strict scientific notation, *kilo-* means 1,000 and *mega-* means 1,000,000. However, in the language of computers, *kilo-* actually is 1,024 and *mega-* is 1,048,576. The disparity occurs because computers are binary machines, that is, machines based on "powers of 2." If 2 is raised to the 10th power (2^{10}), the decimal number is 1,024. Because this is very near 1,000 (10^3), the prefix *kilo-* was adopted for computer use. The same reasoning lies behind the prefixes *mega-*, and *giga-* (one billion). Before long, memory capacities in the *tera*bytes (one trillion bytes) may be common in the largest computer systems.

Computer Words

A computer **word** is the number of adjacent bits that can be stored and manipulated as a unit. Just as English vocabulary words are of varying lengths, so are computer words. Many microcomputers have the ability to manipulate a 32-bit word, whereas some models have word lengths of 8 and 16 bits. In general, the longer a computer word that a computer can use, the faster the computer can process the data.

Encoding Systems

Computers must be capable of interpreting more than just numbers. Letters of the alphabet, as well as symbols such as @, #, and *, are used in programming. In fact, any character that can be entered from the keyboard must be converted into 1s and 0s before a computer can use it. Letters, numbers, and symbols are collectively called *alphanumeric characters*. In addition to alphanumeric characters, coding systems represent various control functions, such as carriage return, escape, and backspace.

Encoding systems permit alphanumeric characters to be coded in terms of bits using 1 and 0. Because of marketing reasons and competition, more than one encoding system was developed. The two most widely used are EBCDIC (Extended Binary Coded Decimal Interchange Code, pronounced "EB-si-dik") developed by IBM, and ASCII (American Standard Code for Information Interchange, pronounced "ASK-ee"), developed by several computer manufacturers. Table 2−1 lists some alphanumeric characters, their ASCII codes, and their EBCDIC codes. Table 2−2 shows a comparison of decimal, binary, octal, and hexadecimal numbers.

ASCII and EBCDIC codes allow a computer to distinguish among a number, letter, or symbol. When a computer sees the ASCII bit pattern 1100 1011, it interprets this pattern as a capital letter *K*. A system using EBCDIC, however, sees the capital letter *K* as 1101 0010.

TABLE 2–1
ASCII and EBCDIC alphanumeric chart.

Character	8-Bit ASCII	8-Bit EBCDIC	Character	8-Bit ASCII	8-Bit EBCDIC
0	1011 0000	1111 0000	K	1100 1011	1101 0010
1	1011 0001	1111 0001	L	1100 1100	1101 0011
2	1011 0010	1111 0010	M	1100 1101	1101 0100
3	1011 0011	1111 0011	N	1100 1110	1101 0101
4	1011 0100	1111 0100	O	1100 1111	1101 0110
5	1011 0101	1111 0101	P	1101 0000	1101 0111
6	1011 0110	1111 0110	Q	1101 0001	1101 1000
7	1011 0111	1111 0111	R	1101 0010	1101 1001
8	1011 1000	1111 1000	S	1101 0011	1110 0010
9	1011 1001	1111 1001	T	1101 0100	1110 0011
A	1100 0001	1100 0001	U	1101 0101	1110 0100
B	1100 0010	1100 0010	V	1101 0110	1110 0101
C	1100 0011	1100 0011	W	1101 0111	1110 0110
D	1100 0100	1100 0100	X	1101 1000	1110 0111
E	1100 0101	1100 0101	Y	1101 1001	1110 1000
F	1100 0110	1100 0110	Z	1101 1010	1110 1001
G	1100 0111	1100 0111	+	1010 1011	0100 1110
H	1100 1000	1100 1000	$	1010 0100	0101 1011
I	1100 1001	1100 1001	.	1010 1110	0100 1011
J	1100 1010	1101 0001	<	1011 1000	0100 1100

INPUT AND OUTPUT

The CPU can turn raw data into usable information quickly and efficiently. But how do you, the user, get data into the computer for processing? How are the results of that processing communicated back to you? We now introduce some important data entry concepts, define input and output, and look at some common I/O (input/output) devices.

Data Entry Concepts

Input is the *process* of entering and translating incoming data into machine-readable form so that they can be processed by a computer: "The data have been *input* into the computer." The term input also often refers to the data itself: "The *input* is of good quality for processing."

A major problem in generating information is *data entry,* the entering of data into a computer in a timely manner, at a reasonable cost, and with minimal error. Here we discuss the two basic ways in which data are prepared for input.

Data Preparation Methods. Two basic ways in which data are entered for input are transcriptive data entry and source-data entry:

☐ In **transcriptive data entry,** the data are entered on documents at the source, or place of origin (for example, handwritten or typed sales invoices). The data must then be transcribed to another medium that can be read and interpreted by a computer.

TABLE 2–2

Decimal, binary, octal, and hexadecimal number chart.

Decimal	Binary	Octal	Hexadecimal	Decimal	Binary	Octal	Hexadecimal
0	0	0	00	50	110010	62	32
1	1	1	01	51	110011	63	33
2	10	2	02	52	110100	64	34
3	11	3	03	53	110101	65	35
4	100	4	04	54	110110	66	36
5	101	5	05	55	110111	67	37
6	110	6	06	56	111000	70	38
7	111	7	07	57	111001	71	39
8	1000	10	08	58	111010	72	3A
9	1001	11	09	59	111011	73	3B
10	1010	12	0A	60	111100	74	3C
11	1011	13	0B	61	111101	75	3D
12	1100	14	0C	62	111110	76	3E
13	1101	15	0D	63	111111	77	3F
14	1110	16	0E	64	1000000	100	40
15	1111	17	0F	65	1000001	101	41
16	10000	20	10	66	1000010	102	42
17	10001	21	11	67	1000011	103	43
18	10010	22	12	68	1000100	104	44
19	10011	23	13	69	1000101	105	45
20	10100	24	14	70	1000110	106	46
21	10101	25	15	71	1000111	107	47
22	10110	26	16	72	1001000	110	48
23	10111	27	17	73	1001001	111	49
24	11000	30	18	74	1001010	112	4A
25	11001	31	19	75	1001011	113	4B
26	11010	32	1A	76	1001100	114	4C
27	11011	33	1B	77	1001101	115	4D
28	11100	34	1C	78	1001110	116	4E
29	11101	35	1D	79	1001111	117	4F
30	11110	36	1E	80	1010000	120	50
31	11111	37	1F	81	1010001	121	51
32	100000	40	20	82	1010010	122	52
33	100001	41	21	83	1010011	123	53
34	100010	42	22	84	1010100	124	54
35	100011	43	23	85	1010101	125	55
36	100100	44	24	86	1010110	126	56
37	100101	45	25	87	1010111	127	57
38	100110	46	26	88	1011000	130	58
39	100111	47	27	89	1011001	131	59
40	101000	50	28	90	1011010	132	5A
41	101001	51	29	91	1011011	133	5B
42	101010	52	2A	92	1011100	134	5C
43	101011	53	2B	93	1011101	135	5D
44	101100	54	2C	94	1011110	136	5E
45	101101	55	2D	95	1011111	137	5F
46	101110	56	2E	96	1100000	140	60
47	101111	57	2F	97	1100001	141	61
48	110000	60	30	98	1100010	142	62
49	110001	61	31	99	1100011	143	63

□ In **source-data entry,** the data are prepared at the source in a machine-readable form that can be used directly by a computer without a separate, intermediate data-transcription step. Such data are called source data.

The greatest advantage of the source data-entry method is that it reduces the number of errors made during input because it eliminates the transcription process (where errors often occur). Various studies show that, of all errors detected in data, approximately 85 percent are due to transcription errors and only 15 percent actually occur in the source data.

Anyone supplying data to a computer system is performing data entry. The device used to enter the data can be either on-line or off-line. **On-line** refers to devices that are directly connected to a CPU. **Off-line** refers to devices that are not directly connected.

File Updating Modes. Updating is the processing of data to keep files current. Two updating modes are used, batch processing and real-time processing:

□ **Batch processing** is the collecting of data into a file over time and later processing it as a batch. During batch processing, a computer program reads the file and processes new data without any interaction with users, clerks, or others. Advantages of batch processing are that (1) the computer does not have to interact with users, (2) the programming function is rather simple, (3) computer processing time is held to a minimum, and (4) such processing is cheaper than real-time processing because less hardware and software are needed to handle batch files. An example is the updating of magazine subscription files in a batch at night when computer demand is low.

□ **Real-time processing** involves entering the data on-line and adding, deleting, or modifying records instantly. Processing data in real-time requires the user terminal to be on-line. Data entered into a system in a real-time environment are processed immediately, an ideal arrangement for airlines and banks. Such processing permits customers to reserve seats on flights, cancel them if plans change, or change the dates if necessary. Bank customers can have their funds available immediately or can instantly determine their balances. The advantages of real-time processing are speed and continual updating of files.

Input Accuracy. Given the vast amount of data entered into computers and the humanness of data-entry personnel, errors are bound to occur. Two of the various methods used to help eliminate errors are verification and validation:

□ **Verification,** performed by the operator or user, is corroborating the data entered by checking them against a known source. For example, in a transcriptive data entry environment, the operator

Input Concepts

- Data Preparation Methods
  □ Transcriptive and source data entry
- File Updating Modes
  □ Batch processing and real-time processing
- Ensuring Input Accuracy
  □ Verification and validation

can match the computer input data against the original paper documents that provided the data.

□ **Validation,** performed by the computer, involves programming the computer to accept only a certain range of data. Validation is checking for data that deviate from this range. For example, if the input calls for a number corresponding to a day of the year, the computer can be programmed to accept only the numbers 1 to 365. If a number greater than 365, or a negative number, or an alphabetic character is entered instead, the computer presents an error message and will not proceed until data in the proper range are entered. (In leap years, the range would be changed to 1–366.)

Input Devices

Before discussing input devices, let's define some terms:

□ **Hardware** is all of the physical components of a computer system.
□ A **peripheral device** is any hardware item attached to the main unit of a computer (the main unit houses the CPU).
□ An **input device** is a peripheral device through which data are entered and transformed into machine-readable form.
□ The **cursor** is a special character or symbol, usually controlled by the input device, that indicates a user's position on the screen or focuses attention to a specific area to allow communication and interaction between the user and the program.

This section introduces you to a variety of input devices.

Keyboard. One of today's most familiar input devices is the **keyboard**. The traditional QWERTY typewriter keyboard comprises the basic portion. (It is called QWERTY because the first six letters on the top row form this fanciful name.) A typical computer keyboard contains all of the letters, numbers, and symbols of a regular typewriter plus a variety of other keys. The other keys may include (a) a numeric keypad that looks and functions much like a calculator, (b) function keys which can be preprogrammed by the software or reprogrammed by the user to perform various functions, and (c) special keys, such as those used to control cursor movement on a computer screen (Figure 2–5).

Other Electromechanical Input Devices. Other devices include:

□ Mouse (Figure 2–6)
□ Joystick (Figure 2–7)
□ Trackball (Figure 2–8)
□ Touch screen (Figure 2–9)
□ Light pen (Figure 2–10)
□ Digitizer (Figure 2–11)
□ Scanner (Figure 2–12)

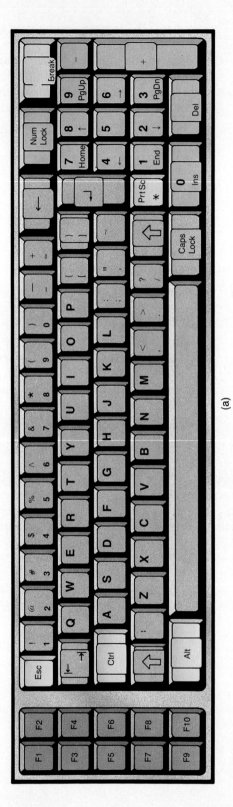

FIGURE 2–5

(a) Standard IBM PC keyboard.

= QWERTY keyboard containing alphabetic, numeric, and special character keys

= Numeric keypad and cursor movement keys

= Function keys

= Other special keys

(b)

FIGURE 2–5 (continued)
(b) Enhanced IBM PC keyboard.

FIGURE 2–6 (right)
Mouse moves the cursor on screen. Pressing a mouse button marks your place or selects from a menu.

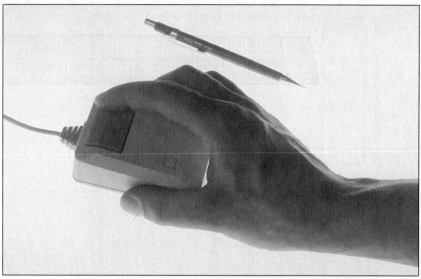

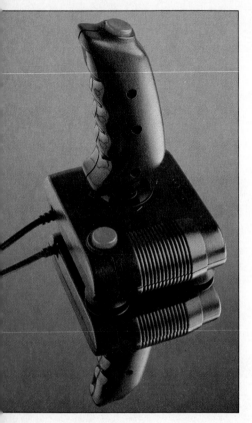

FIGURE 2–8
Trackball moves the cursor on screen. (Macmillan Publishing/Cobalt Productions)

FIGURE 2–7
Joystick moves the cursor on screen.

(a)   (b)

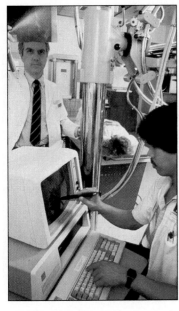

FIGURE 2–10
X-ray technician uses a light pen to enter data into a computer. (Courtesy of Travenol Laboratories, Inc.)

FIGURE 2–11
Using a digitizer to transfer images to a computer screen. (Macmillan Publishing/Cobalt Productions)

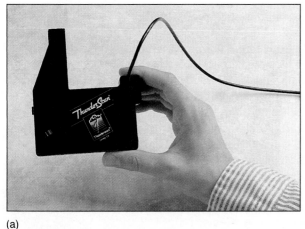

(a)   (b)

FIGURE 2–12
(a) This small hand-held scanner is attached to a computer. (b) This scanner reads the image on the paper and sends it to the computer. (Both courtesy of Thunderware)

FIGURE 2–9 (opposite)
(a) Touch screen registers input when a finger or other object interrupts infrared or ultrasonic waves. (Courtesy of Hewlett-Packard Co.) (b) Touch-screen lottery machine. (Macmillan Publishing/Cobalt Productions)

FIGURE 2–13

With a voice-recognition data-entry system, an operator's hands are free to write while the operator speaks commands to the computer. (Courtesy of Texas Instruments)

Input Devices

- Keyboards
- Joysticks and track-balls
- Touch screens
- Light pens
- Digitizers
- Voice recognition (voice input)
- Source-data input devices

Voice Recognition Devices. Voice recognition, or voice input, is one of the most complex input techniques used to interact with computers. Computer experts have made headway in creating machines that can "listen" to a person speak and then translate the speech into a form that the computer can process. One example is translating speech into print. A user inputs data by speaking into a microphone (Figure 2–13).

Source-Data Input. Conventional input methods require that data be written or typed as an intermediate step between the source and the computer (transcriptive data entry). However, when data are entered with a device *directly* into a computer system at their source, these data are *source data*. Methods of source-data input include magnetic and optical.

Magnetic methods include magnetic-ink character recognition (MICR) and magnetic strips (Figures 2–14 and 2–15).

Optical recognition occurs when a device scans a printed surface and translates the image seen by the scanner into a machine-readable format. The three types are optical-mark recognition (Figure 2–16), optical-bar recognition (Figure 2–17), and optical-character recognition (Figure 2–18).

Output Concepts

Output is the *process* of translating data that are in machine-readable form into a form understandable to humans or readable by other machines. The term output also often refers to the *information that is the result of processing*. An **output device** is a peripheral device that enables a computer to communicate information to humans or other machines. Output devices receive data from a computer and transform them into a usable form.

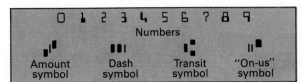

(a) Magnetic-ink character set

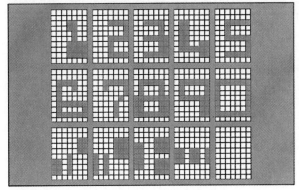

(b) Matrix patterns for magnetic-ink characters

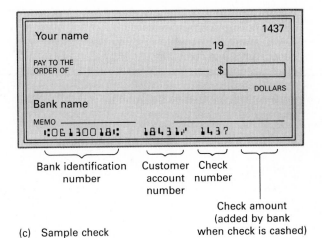

(c) Sample check

FIGURE 2–14
Magnetic-ink character recognition (MICR) is the interpretation by a computer
of a line of characters written in a special magnetic ink. Banks use magnetic-ink
characters on checks to ensure fast and efficient processing.

FIGURE 2–15
Magnetic strips are thin bands of magnetically encoded data found on the
backs of many credit cards and automated teller cards. Stored data can be
highly sensitive or personal because they are invisible. The magnetic strip on
this automated teller card records the card number and customer password.
(Courtesy of The Huntington National Bank)

FIGURE 2–16

Simple optical-mark recognition (OMR) scans and translates pencil marks into computer-readable form, as on this multiple-choice test form. (NCS General Purpose Answer Sheet courtesy of National Computer Systems, Inc. © 1977)

GENERAL PURPOSE - NCS - ANSWER SHEET
FOR USE WITH ALL NCS SENTRY OPTICAL MARK READING SYSTEMS
SEE IMPORTANT MARKING INSTRUCTIONS ON SIDE 2

	A B C D E		A B C D E		A B C D E		A B C D E		A B C D E
1	① ② ③ ④ ⑤	11	① ② ③ ④ ⑤	21	① ② ③ ④ ⑤	31	① ② ③ ④ ⑤	41	① ② ③ ④ ⑤
2	① ② ③ ④ ⑤	12	① ② ③ ④ ⑤	22	① ② ③ ④ ⑤	32	① ② ③ ④ ⑤	42	① ② ③ ④ ⑤
3	① ② ③ ④ ⑤	13	① ② ③ ④ ⑤	23	① ② ③ ④ ⑤	33	① ② ③ ④ ⑤	43	① ② ③ ④ ⑤
4	① ② ③ ④ ⑤	14	① ② ③ ④ ⑤	24	① ② ③ ④ ⑤	34	① ② ③ ④ ⑤	44	① ② ③ ④ ⑤
5	① ② ③ ④ ⑤	15	① ② ③ ④ ⑤	25	① ② ③ ④ ⑤	35	① ② ③ ④ ⑤	45	① ② ③ ④ ⑤
6	① ② ③ ④ ⑤	16	① ② ③ ④ ⑤	26	① ② ③ ④ ⑤	36	① ② ③ ④ ⑤	46	① ② ③ ④ ⑤
7	① ② ③ ④ ⑤	17	① ② ③ ④ ⑤	27	① ② ③ ④ ⑤	37	① ② ③ ④ ⑤	47	① ② ③ ④ ⑤
8	① ② ③ ④ ⑤	18	① ② ③ ④ ⑤	28	① ② ③ ④ ⑤	38	① ② ③ ④ ⑤	48	① ② ③ ④ ⑤
9	① ② ③ ④ ⑤	19	① ② ③ ④ ⑤	29	① ② ③ ④ ⑤	39	① ② ③ ④ ⑤	49	① ② ③ ④ ⑤
10	① ② ③ ④ ⑤	20	① ② ③ ④ ⑤	30	① ② ③ ④ ⑤	40	① ② ③ ④ ⑤	50	① ② ③ ④ ⑤

Product category — 0 code

Manufacturer's identification

Product/part code

(a)

(b)

FIGURE 2–17

More sophisticated optical-bar recognition (OBR) scans and interprets line patterns. (a) Universal Product Code (UPC) used on consumer products. (b) Using a bar-code scanner to enter inventory data into a computer. (Courtesy of Intermec Corp.)

Output Concepts

- Human-readable output
  - □ Hard copy
  - □ Soft copy
- Secondary storage

Output is divided into two general categories: (1) output that is read and used by people and (2) data that are sent to secondary-storage devices for later use, either as input for further computer processing or for use by another machine.

In today's information society, people require clear, legible output—a major consideration when purchasing output devices. Output that is readable to users is categorized as either hard copy or soft copy:

□ **Hard copy** is output, such as paper, that can be read immediately or stored and read later. It is a relatively stable and permanent form of output.

□ **Soft copy,** such as screen-displayed output, is a transient form of output. It is lost when the computer is turned off. However, if the data used to create that soft copy have been saved on disk or tape, the soft copy can be reproduced on the screen repeatedly.

Output Devices

Graphics and text material can be produced with a wide selection of printers and plotters. A **printer** is an output device that prints output, usually text, on paper; however, some printers can produce graphics. A **plotter** is an output device that draws graphic images on paper. Before looking at the major categories of printers and plotters, let's consider print quality, an important feature of any hard-copy device.

Print Quality. The print quality available from hard-copy output devices varies considerably. You may have heard the terms *typeset quality, near-typeset quality, letter quality, near-letter quality, standard quality,* and *compressed print* (Figure 2–19).

Typeset-quality print is that provided by commercial typesetters and is the type you see in most magazines or books like this one. Letters and characters are fully formed, using solid lines. Near-typeset-quality print is similar; characters are fully formed, but with tightly packed dots.

Letter-quality print, equivalent to good typewriter print, also is made using fully formed (solid-line) characters, but the printing is not as sharp as typeset quality. Near-letter-quality print generates high-quality documents with characters composed of dots or short lines; this is achieved on some printers when the print head makes multiple passes over each letter, filling in the spaces between the dots or lines.

Standard-quality print, sometimes called draft-quality print, is produced when characters composed of dots or lines are formed by a single pass of the print head. With compressed print, which is sometimes used for listing or printing the code in computer programs, characters are printed very close together (compressed) to conserve space. The characters are formed with a minimum number of dots or lines and are smaller than the standard-quality characters.

The quality of type that a printer produces is determined mainly by its printing mechanism. A printer uses one of two basic types of printing mechanisms: impact and nonimpact.

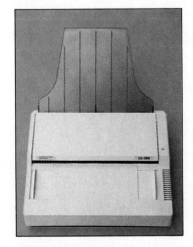

FIGURE 2–18

Most sophisticated optical-character recognition (OCR) system recognizes special alphabetic and numeric characters. State-of-the-art scanners read graphics and text.

This is an example of typeset-quality print.

This is an example of near-typeset quality print.

This is an example of letter-quality print.

This is an example of near-letter quality print.

This is an example of standard-quality print.

This is an example of draft-quality (compressed) print.

FIGURE 2–19
A comparison of the different qualities of print.

Impact Printers. An **impact printer** produces characters when a hammer or pin strikes an ink ribbon, which in turn presses against a sheet of paper and leaves an impression of the character on the paper. These are character-at-a-time printers, meaning that they print one character at a time. This is also how an ordinary typewriter works. The two impact printers most often used with microcomputers are the dot-matrix printer and the daisy-wheel printer.

The dot-matrix printer uses a print head containing from 9 to 24 pins (the more pins, the higher the quality). These pins produce patterns of dots to form the individual characters. Dot-matrix printers are capable of producing both draft-quality and letter-quality print.

A daisy-wheel printer produces letter-quality type like that on modern typewriters. The characters are on a wheel that resembles a daisy (Figure 2–20). At the end of each "petal" is a fully formed character. When a hammer strikes a petal against the ribbon, the character image prints on the paper. Daisy-wheel printers produce solid-line print rather than dots.

In businesses that use mainframes or other large computer systems and print enormous amounts of material, character-at-a-time printers are too slow. A **line printer,** or line-at-a-time printer, uses a special mechanism that prints a whole line at once. It can typically print 1,200–6,000 lines per minute. Drum, chain, and band printers are line-at-a-time printers.

FIGURE 2-20
A daisy wheel.

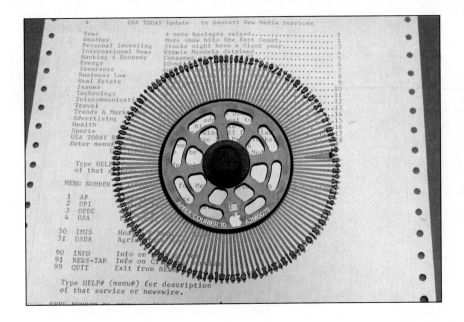

Nonimpact Printers. A **nonimpact printer** does not use a striking device to produce characters on paper. Rather, it uses one of several newer technologies. Because nonimpact printers do not hammer against paper, they are much quieter. Major technologies used are ink-jet, thermal-transfer, dye-diffusion, laser, and electrostatic:

☐ An *ink-jet printer* forms characters on paper by spraying ink from tiny nozzles through an electrical field that arranges the electrically charged ink droplets into characters. The ink is absorbed into the paper and dries instantly.

☐ The *thermal-transfer printer* transfers and bonds ink onto paper by heating pins that press against a special ink ribbon. Thermal wax printers produce color images by melting colored wax onto paper. These printers produce near-letter-quality.

☐ A *dye-diffusion printer* produces images by heating a ribbon to vaporize the dye and diffuse it onto paper. Although expensive, this process can print millions of different color shades. These printers create near-photographic-quality images.

☐ A *laser printer* does the job when near-typeset quality is required. A laser printer produces images on paper by directing a laser beam at a mirror which reflects the beam onto a drum. The laser beam leaves a negative charge on the drum, to which positively charged black toner powder sticks. As paper rolls by the drum, the toner is transferred to the paper. A hot roller then bonds the toner to the paper.

☐ The *electrostatic printer* is a fast, high-resolution printer used where complex images are needed, as in mapping, integrated circuit design, and satellite imaging.

Plotters. The growth of computer-aided design and drafting technology has created a demand for devices that can produce high-quality graphics in multiple colors on hard copy. Some plotters reproduce drawings using a pen attached to a movable arm. The pen is directed across the surface of a stationary piece of paper. Many plotters, however, combine a movable pen arm with a mechanism that rolls the paper back and forth to make the drawing. This two-way movement allows the plotter to draw any configuration (Figure 2–21).

Computer Output Microform. Hard-copy photographic images recorded on microfilm or microfiche are called computer output microform (COM). In some cases, a computer can output directly to a COM machine. In other cases, data are first recorded on magnetic tape, and the tape is used as input to a COM machine. Microfilm and microfiche readers are used to read the data.

Monitors. The most popular soft-copy output device is the monitor (Figure 2–22). A **monitor** is a televisionlike device that displays data or information. Like other output devices, monitors come in many styles and price ranges.

Monitor quality is measured in **resolution,** the number of picture elements that the display screen of a monitor contains. A picture element,

(a)

(b)

FIGURE 2–21

(a) Desktop plotters are used in offices to generate graphics that enhance business presentations. (b) Large plotters allow images such as this circuit diagram to be drawn to a size that users can view in detail. (Both courtesy of Houston Instrument)

FIGURE 2–22
Several monitors used to view output. Note the difference between the color
display of the monitor on the left and the monochrome (single color) display of
the monitor on the bottom right. (Courtesy of TRW, Inc.)

or **pixel,** is the smallest increment of a display screen that can be controlled. The more pixels, the clearer and sharper the image. A 640×480
pixel screen contains 640 horizontal pixels and 480 vertical pixels.

The screen in a monitor is a cathode-ray tube (CRT). To produce an
image on the CRT, an electron beam moves across a phosphor-coated
screen. Intensifying the strength of the beam, the phosphor coating glows
in certain places, forming the characters. Instructions from the computer
intensify the beam on certain pixels, making the phosphor glow to form
the characters. The most common CRT can display 24 lines of 80 characters
each. Other sizes are available, including ones used in desktop publishing
that display two full 8½×11-inch pages at full size.

A monochrome (single-color) monitor is used where output consists
mainly of text and numbers, although with the appropriate circuitry, some
monochrome monitors can display graphics. A monochrome monitor usually displays either green, amber, or white characters on a black screen. A
typical text resolution in monochrome monitors is 640×350 pixels, and
graphics resolution is 720×348 pixels.

A color monitor is often preferred for output containing graphics. Just
as in a standard TV set, three colors of phosphor dots (red, green, and blue)
form a pixel on color monitors. These colors blend to make other colors by
varying the intensity of the electron beam focused on the phosphor dots.

A cathode-ray tube is too cumbersome to use in today's small, portable computers. However, a flat-panel display does not use a CRT and can
be manufactured small enough to fit a battery-powered portable computer.

Soft-copy Output Devices

- Monitors
  - Cathode-ray tube (CRT)
  - Gas plasma flat panel
  - LCD flat panel
- Voice output

Some desktop microcomputers also use flat-panel displays. A common type of flat-panel display is the liquid-crystal display (LCD), which produces images by aligning molecular crystals. When voltage is applied, the crystals line up to block light from passing through them. The absence of light is seen as characters on the screen.

Another type of flat-panel display is the gas-plasma display, which contains an ionized gas (plasma) between two glass plates. One glass plate contains a set of horizontal wires, and the other has a set of vertical wires. The intersection of each horizontal and vertical wire identifies a pixel. A pixel is turned on when current is sent through the appropriate vertical and horizontal wires. The plasma at the pixel emits light as the current is applied. Characters are formed by lighting the appropriate pixels. Figure 2–23 compares gas-plasma and LCD screens. Besides size, another advantage of flat-panel screens is that they do not flicker. CRTs flicker due to the electron beams moving across the screen, and the flicker can cause eye strain and fatigue during prolonged use.

Voice Output. Another type of output is voice output, the technology in which a computer "talks." Voice output systems are used where a display screen is not appropriate, for example in automobile warning systems, systems for the blind and visually impaired, and in toys and games. Speech coding, one type of voice output, is the storage of many actual human

(a)

(b)

FIGURE 2–23

Comparison of (a) gas-plasma display screen and (b) LCD display screen.

sounds which the voice output system draws upon to build the words needed to communicate. Another approach is voice synthesis, the process of electronically mimicking the human voice.

SECONDARY STORAGE

Often, main memory is not large enough to hold all the instructions and data you require. Also, recall that main memory is volatile: when the power is turned off, data and instructions in main memory are lost. They require reentry for each new use. Because of these limitations, a supplemental form of storage is necessary. This supplemental form is called secondary storage.

Which secondary storage medium is best? First, consider what you want secondary storage to do. Do you need quick access to data, or do you plan to store it for a long time? By learning the advantages and disadvantages of various types of secondary storage, you can make an informed choice.

Secondary storage is nonvolatile memory that is external to the main memory of a computer. A secondary-storage medium is usually used to store large amounts of data or for permanent or long-term storage of data or programs. Secondary storage media are also used for storing backups—copies of data and programs. An input/output (I/O) hardware device allows you to store and access data and instructions on secondary storage media.

Secondary-storage media used with all sizes of computers are (1) magnetic tapes, (2) magnetic disks, and (3) optical technology. These media can hold much more data than main memory, and they are nonvolatile. However, access to the data is relatively slower than access from main memory.

Magnetic Tape

Typically, **magnetic tape** is a one-half or one-quarter inch ribbon of mylar (a plastic material), coated with a thin layer of iron oxide material. The **tape drive** is an input/output device that reads and writes data on tape. In the drive, the tape passes by a read/write head, which reads, writes, and erases data on the tape. When the head writes data to a tape, the tiny, haphazardly arranged iron oxide particles are aligned through magnetization, storing data as magnetized areas. To read the tape, the drive again passes the tape by the head, which interprets the magnetized areas as pieces of data.

Magnetic tape stores records (groups of related data). It stores records sequentially (one after another). To find the data you're looking for, a computer must read every record preceding the one you need. Because tapes can store large quantities of data inexpensively, they are often used as backup storage media. Magnetic tapes are erasable, reusable, and durable.

Although mainly found with large computers, magnetic tapes can be used with all sizes. They come in three formats: reel-to-reel (Figure 2–24),

---

Forms of Magnetic Tape

- Reel-to-reel
- Cassette
- Cartridge

(a)

(b)

FIGURE 2–24
(a) Magnetic reel-to-reel tape with raw iron oxide. (Courtesy of BASF Corporation Information Systems) (b) Magnetic reel-to-reel tape mounted on tape drives. (Courtesy of U.S. Department of the Navy)

cassette (Figure 2–25), and cartridge (Figure 2–26). Each form stores data magnetically, but each holds different amounts of data and accesses them at different rates.

Magnetic Disk

A **magnetic disk** is a mylar or metallic platter on which electronic data can be stored. Although disks resemble phonograph records, they do not

FIGURE 2–25
Cassette tapes for data storage are similar to audio cassettes. (Macmillan Publishing/Cobalt Productions)

FIGURE 2-26
This tape cartridge is approximately one-half the size of a
videocassette and holds about
20,000 pages of information.
(Courtesy of BASF Corporation
Information Systems)

have the characteristic spiraling groove; however, data are accessed in much the same way as an individual song is selected on a record. Data files on a magnetic disk can be read either sequentially (like tape) or directly. The main advantages of a magnetic disk over magnetic tape include (1) ability to access the data stored on it directly, (2) ability to hold more data in a smaller space, and (3) ability to attain faster data access speeds.

Magnetic disks are manufactured in both floppy diskette and hard disk styles. New technology, such as thin film coatings for disks and composite read/write heads, are allowing more and more data to be packed onto magnetic disks.

Floppy Diskette. A **floppy diskette,** also called simply a diskette or disk, is a small, flexible mylar disk coated with iron oxide (similar to magnetic tape) on which data are stored. It is available in three sizes—the 3½-inch microfloppy, as well as the 5¼-inch size and 8-inch size (Figure 2-27).

The 8-inch and 5¼-inch disks are covered by stiff, protective jackets with various holes and cutouts—Figure 2-28(a). The disk drive engages the hub ring to rotate the disk. An elongated read/write window allows the read/write head of the drive to write data to or read data from the disk. Beside the hub ring is an index hole with which the computer determines the position of the disk when locating data. The write-protect notch, when covered with tape, protects data on the disk from being erased or written over.

A 3½-inch disk has a hard plastic cover and protective metal piece that covers the read/write window when the disk is not in use—Figure 2-28(b). This additional protection makes the disk less prone to damage from handling, dust, or other contaminants. The 3½-inch diskette is growing in popularity, as evidenced by IBM's Personal System/2 computers— all are equipped with 3½-inch drives. The Apple Macintosh series also uses 3½-inch diskettes. However, each of these systems can be equipped to use a 5¼-inch drive.

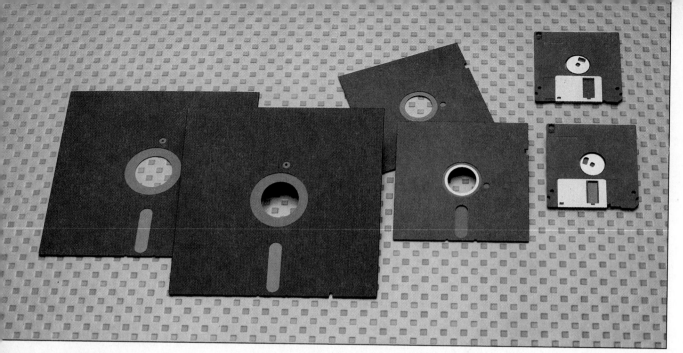

FIGURE 2–27
Floppy diskettes are available in three different sizes: 8-, 5¼-, and 3½-inch.

You must prepare a disk for use before you can store data or programs on it. This preparation is called *formatting*. Formatting records invisible magnetic tracks and sectors on the diskette. All disks, regardless of size, are divided into concentric circles called tracks, where data are stored (Figure 2–29). A disk is also divided into pie-shaped wedges called sectors, which further specify data-storage locations. The number of tracks and sectors is usually determined by the operating system of the computer during the formatting operation. The operating system labels each sector of each track with an address. Then, when the computer is seeking data, it can go directly to a specific sector and track, rather than start at the beginning as with magnetic tape.

Hard Disks. A **hard disk** is hard and inflexible, made from materials such as aluminum instead of mylar. The input/output device used to transfer data to and from a hard disk is called a **hard-disk drive**. The read/write head of a hard-disk drive floats above the surface of the disk at a height of about 50 millionths of an inch (0.00005 inches). In comparison, a human hair is about a hundred times thicker (Figure 2–30).

Because of the high rotation speed of the hard disk (approximately 3,600 revolutions per minute), if the read/write head runs into any particles of dirt, dust, or even smoke, a "head crash" results. When this occurs, a foreign particle is pushed into the disk, and the head actually bounces and comes into physical contact with the disk. Severe damage can result to the head or the disk, destroying the data stored there.

A hard disk has several advantages over a floppy diskette. Its rigid construction allows it to be rotated 10 times as fast as a floppy disk, which turns at only 360 rpm. Thus, data can be transferred much faster to or from

---

Forms of Magnetic Disk

- Floppy diskette
  - □ 8-inch
  - □ 5¼-inch
  - □ 3½-inch
- Hard disk
  - □ Fixed disk
  - □ Removable cartridge
  - □ Disk pack

FIGURE 2–28
(a) A 5¼-inch floppy disk.
(b) A 3½-inch diskette.

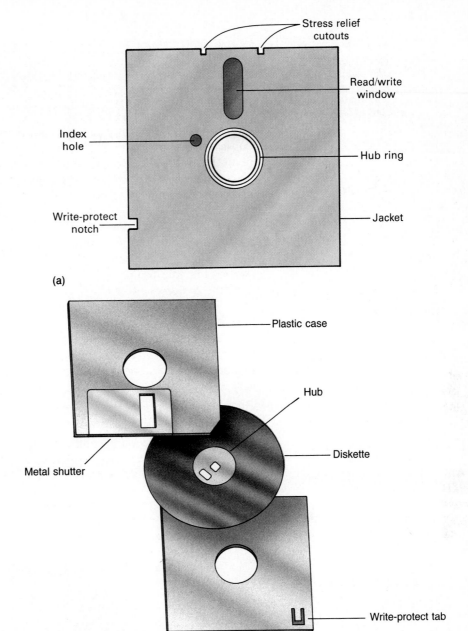

Stress relief cutouts

Read/write window

Index hole

Hub ring

Write-protect notch

Jacket

(a)

Plastic case

Hub

Metal shutter

Diskette

Write-protect tab

A protective liner covers both sides of the diskette.

(b)

a hard disk because it takes less time to find the storage location. Also, because of its hard construction, this disk allows data to be stored more densely—more data can be packed into a smaller area, giving the hard disk far more storage capacity than a floppy disk of the same size.

Hard-disk drives are available for all sizes of computers, from home microcomputers to business-oriented system computers. Hard disks are

HAND-IN OPERATION   You curl your fingers as if you're holding a ball, and then you "throw" it. At the same time on your computer screen, a detached hand duplicates every motion of your own hand, right down to the pitching of a three-dimensional object that arcs and bounces like a ball. Usually, you would use a keyboard or a mouse to input information to your personal computer, but what you've just witnessed is input by DataGlove.

The DataGlove, developed by VPL Research in California, is a spandex glove with optical sensors placed at the 10 major points of the human hand. A fiber optic cable carries the signals generated by hand movements into the computer and onto the screen. Greenleaf Medical Systems employs VPL's glove in a system for use by doctors who specialize in hands, to measure how much the different joints of the hand can bend. A patient would wear the glove while moving his or her hand and the glove would feed the data into the computer. Applications of the new technology are still being studied, but the glove has already been adapted by some video game manufacturers, like Mattel's Nintendo, to replace the "old-fashioned" joystick.

even available for laptop computers with storage capabilities of many megabytes. Hard disks may be permanently installed in a drive (Figure 2–31) or may be in the form of a removable cartridge (Figure 2–32) or disk pack (Figure 2–33) that can also be removed from the drive.

FIGURE 2–29
A diskette divided into tracks and sectors.

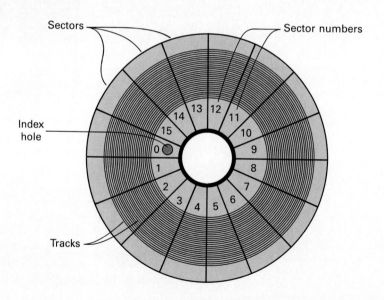

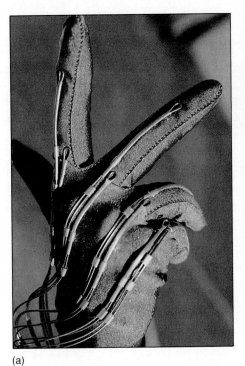
(a)

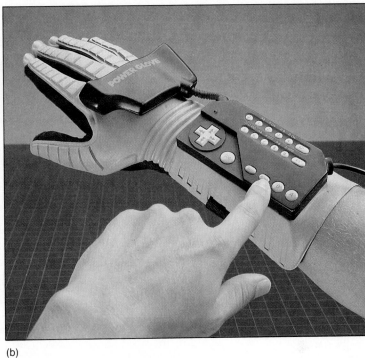
(b)

(a) Original data glove showing fiber optic sensors (Courtesy of VPL Research, Inc.) (b) Data glove with programmable keyboard as used with Nintendo game. (Courtesy of Mattel Toys)

FIGURE 2–30
Notice the size of the disk contaminants compared with the distance between the read/write head and the hard disk.

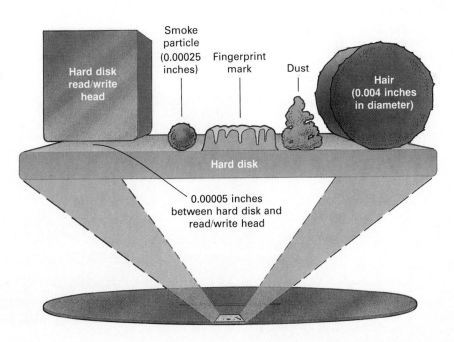

Hard disk read/write head

Smoke particle (0.00025 inches)

Fingerprint mark

Dust

Hair (0.004 inches in diameter)

Hard disk

0.00005 inches between hard disk and read/write head

FIGURE 2–31

A fixed disk is protected in a sealed case. Fixed-disk systems contain one or more hard disks. They can be used in all types of computers. Microcomputers for homes use 5¼-inch or 3½-inch fixed-disk drives, with storage typically from 10 to 150 megabytes. Fixed disks in large computers provide storage in the gigabyte range (billions of bytes). Here the case has been removed to show the hard disk and a read/write head. (Courtesy of Seagate)

Optical Technology

Optical technology uses lasers—highly concentrated beams of light. The word *laser* is an acronym for *l*ight *a*mplification through *s*timulated *e*mission of *r*adiation. Laser beams are used to write to the optical storage medium and read data from it. As costs decrease, optical storage may overtake magnetic media as the preferred method for storing data and instructions because optical storage has much greater storage capacity and reliability. It is also removable. Optical storage is commonly seen in disk format, but it also is available as optical cards and tape.

Optical laser disks, metal disks ranging from 4.72 inches to 14 inches, were originally developed as compact disks for video and audio applications. Whether an optical disk is used for computer data, video, or audio, the storage is in binary form. The data are read by a laser beam. The laser

FIGURE 2–32

A storage system using removable cartridges has the same speed and capacity as a system with a fixed disk. The Bernoulli Box is a device from which cartridges can be removed and stored in a secure location.

FIGURE 2–33

A disk pack is another removable device in which several hard disks (a common number is 11) are packed into a single plastic case. Disk-pack drives are designed for systems that require large storage capacities. Disk packs can be interchanged, giving a computer a virtually unlimited amount of secondary storage. Here, an operator installs a disk pack for mainframe computer storage. (Courtesy of BASF Corporation Information Systems)

beam is either reflected back to a sensor or scattered due to microscopic pits in the disk. The presence or absence of pits represents a binary 1 or 0.

To illustrate the enormous storage capacity of optical media, *Academic American Encyclopedia,* a nine-million-word (21-volume) reference, is stored on a single compact disk less than five inches in diameter, with room to spare (Figure 2–34). Grolier Electronic Publishers sells it to consumers for about $200.

A credit card-size optical card, or laser card, has an optical laser-encoded strip that can store approximately four megabytes of data. Such

FIGURE 2–34

The *Academic American Encyclopedia* on a single CD-ROM. (Courtesy of Grolier Electronic Publishing, Inc.)

cards have many potential uses, most notably as credit records or medical histories.

Optical tape is similar to magnetic tape in that it is read sequentially, but on optical tape, data are stored by optical-laser techniques. A 14-inch reel of optical tape is capable of storing one terabyte of data, equivalent to thousands of ordinary magnetic tapes or about a half billion pages.

CONNECTIONS

A computer requires special hardware to connect the CPU and any peripheral device, such as a printer. The connection is called an **interface**. Data are transferred with either a serial interface or a parallel interface (Figure 2–35).

When a **serial interface** is used, data are transferred between the CPU and a peripheral device one bit at a time. The most common serial interface in microcomputers is called the RS–232C. It is usually available as a plug-in card, but sometimes is built into a computer's circuitry by the manufacturer.

In a **parallel interface,** data are transferred between the CPU and a peripheral device one byte (eight bits) at a time. Parallel interfaces are faster and more expensive than serial interfaces. The term *parallel* is used because data are sent over conductors running next to each other. The Centronics standard and the IEEE–488 standard are parallel interfaces used in many microcomputers. Like the serial interface, these are either built in by the manufacturer or available as plug-in cards.

DATA ORGANIZATION

Organization of ideas or tangible objects is the key to productivity. For example, finding the right wrench is easy if your wrenches are laid out in order from smallest to largest, rather than scattered in a box. The same logic applies to data stored on tape or disk. In this section we'll explore ways in which files are organized and accessed.

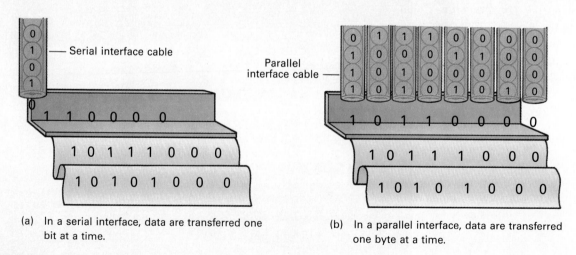

(a) In a serial interface, data are transferred one bit at a time.

(b) In a parallel interface, data are transferred one byte at a time.

FIGURE 2–35
Serial versus parallel data transfer.

Data Hierarchy

The basic hierarchy of data organization, going from most general to most specific, is database, file, record, and field:

Data Hierarchy

Data base bank
- Database
- File
- Record
- Field
  - Byte
  - Bit

☐ A **database** is a collection of files, cross-referenced and designed to minimize repetition of data. For example, a bursar might maintain a database of all student grades.

☐ A **file** is a collection of records (similar groups of data) that fit under one name or heading. An instructor's gradebook is an example; all data therein deal with students and their grades. A file may be further separated into records.

☐ A **record** is a collection of fields containing data that relate to an entity. For example, that entity may be a student, employee, or product. In a file of class grades, information about an individual student, such as name and test scores, might be contained in a record. Information in the record pertains to that student only, but all of that information is related to the file topic—class grades.

☐ In a record, space must be allocated for data. Each individual classification of data stored in the record is called a **field**. Each record may contain one or more fields. Once again, in the instructor example, there are many fields: one for the student's name, one for each test grade, one for each homework grade, and one for each computer lab report grade (Figure 2–36).

☐ To round out the hierarchy, each character in a field is represented internally to the computer as a byte. Each byte is composed of

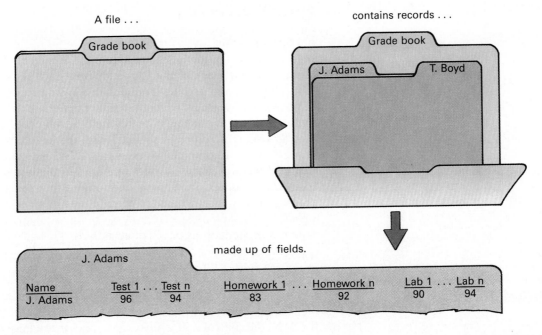

FIGURE 2–36
Organization of data by file, record, and field.

eight bits. A bit is the smallest unit of data the computer can recognize.

File-access Methods

■ Sequential
■ Direct
■ Indexed sequential

File Storage And Access Methods

There are three primary methods of placing files in, and retrieving them from, secondary storage: (1) sequential-access file processing, (2) direct-access file processing, and (3) indexed sequential-access file processing:

☐ **Sequential-access file processing** stores the records of a file in sequential order. Records appear one after another *in the order in which they were entered into the computer* and subsequently stored on the medium. Access to any one record requires access to all preceding records. Magnetic tape is a sequential storage medium by nature—to access a particular record, you first must read all preceding records. You could use the sequential-access method to record individual student grades each week because you must access and update all of the records of the students anyway.

☐ **Direct-access file processing,** also called random-access file processing, stores the records of a file in random order. A direct-access file has a key, called a key field or access key, that lets the computer locate, retrieve, and update any record in the file without reading each preceding record. A **key field** is a field that uniquely identifies each record. Examples of key fields are account numbers, employee identification numbers, and social security numbers.

☐ **Indexed sequential-access file processing** allows both sequential and direct access to records in a file. An indexed sequential file can be set up in many ways. Basically, records are stored sequentially when the indexed sequential file is created. The computer keeps an index of the key fields from each record. It automatically sorts and updates the index to allow both sequential and direct access. To access a record, the computer searches the index by key field. When it finds the key field, it can access the record directly using an address associated with the key field. To search sequentially, the computer accesses the record associated with the first key field in the sorted index and follows the rest of the index in sequential order. The sorted index allows the computer to find records in sequence no matter where they are physically located on a disk. (This type of file access does not work with tape because tape is a sequential-access medium only.)

SUMMARY

A central processing unit (CPU) is comprised of an arithmetic and logic unit (ALU), a control unit, and the main memory unit. Modern technology has put the ALU, the control unit, and in some cases the memory unit onto one integrated circuit (microchip or chip), called a microprocessor. The

ALU handles mathematical and comparison operations. The control unit regulates the timing and sequence of all processing within a computer. The main memory unit is the computer's internal storage where programs and data are stored.

The most used technology for the main memory is semiconductor memory. Semiconductor memory comes in two basic types: RAM and ROM. Program instructions or data can be stored internally in random-access memory (RAM) or read-only memory (ROM). RAM is used primarily for temporary storage and is volatile, meaning that it can only function while receiving power. ROM is used for permanent storage and is nonvolatile, meaning that it does not rely on a continuous source of power.

Within a computer, data are represented as binary system numbers comprised of 1s and 0s. The smallest piece of data that a computer understands is a bit. A grouping of eight bits is a byte. A kilobyte is 1,024 bytes. A computer word is the number of adjacent bits that can be stored and manipulated as a unit; word length varies from computer to computer. ASCII and EBCDIC are two of the encoding schemes used to represent all alphanumeric characters and control codes in binary code.

Before a CPU processes data and makes the results available, there must be a way for people to move data into and from the computer. Transcriptive data entry and source-data entry are two ways in which data are input. The data can be entered either on-line or off-line, depending on the application. Files are updated using either batch processing or real-time processing. Any data being input should be checked for accuracy, either by human verification or computer validation.

The process of entering data (data entry) and translating the data into machine-readable form is called input. The data to be entered are often called input, too. The numerous input methods and devices include the keyboard, mouse, light pen, voice recognition, magnetic-ink character recognition, optical-mark recognition, optical-bar recognition, and optical-character recognition.

The process of translating machine-readable data into a form that can be understood by humans or a form that can be read by other machines is called output. The information that is the result of processing is also referred to as output. Output readable by people can be categorized as either hard copy or soft copy. Hard-copy output devices include printers, plotters, and computer-output microform devices. Printers are categorized as either impact or nonimpact printers, based on how the mechanism prints the characters. Soft-copy output devices include monitors and voice-output systems.

Peripheral devices are connected to a CPU by a connection called an interface. An interface provides a standard means of communication between the computer and its peripheral devices. Two basic types of interfaces are used: (1) a serial interface transfers data one bit at a time, and (2) a parallel interface transfers data one byte, or eight bits of data, at a time.

Main memory sometimes is inadequate for data storage needs because it is limited in size and is volatile. To supplement main memory, secondary storage—nonvolatile memory external to the computer—is used. Three types of secondary-storage media are magnetic tape, magnetic disk, and optical technology.

Data are organized in a hierarchy that includes database, file, record, and field designators. A database is a group of related files stored together in a logical fashion. A file is a collection of similar groups of data that fit under one category. A record contains data related to one particular item in that category, such as a person's name. A field is the name given to each classification of data in a record.

The three primary storage and access methods are sequential access, direct access, and indexed sequential access. Sequential-access file processing accesses and stores records in a file one after another. Direct-access file processing allows a user to retrieve a record without reading each one in front of it. In indexed sequential-access file processing, an index of key fields allows records to be sequentially or directly accessed.

Vocabulary Self-Test

Can you define the following?

arithmetic and logic unit (ALU) (p. 32)

batch processing (p. 40)

binary system (p. 36)

bit (p. 36)

byte (p. 36)

central processing unit (CPU) (p. 31)

chip (p. 31)

control unit (p. 33)

cursor (p. 41)

database (p. 65)

direct-access file processing (p. 66)

encoding system (p. 37)

field (p. 65)

file (p. 65)

floppy diskette (p. 57)

hard copy (p. 49)

hard disk (p. 58)

hard disk drive (p. 58)

hardware (p. 41)

impact printer (p. 50)

indexed sequential-access file processing (p. 66)

input (p. 38)

input device (p. 41)

integrated circuit (IC) (p. 31)

interface (p. 64)

keyboard (p. 41)

key field (p. 66)

line printer (p. 50)

logic function (p. 33)

magnetic disk (p. 56)

magnetic tape (p. 55)

main memory unit (p. 33)

microchip (p. 31)

microprocessor (p. 32)

monitor (p. 52)

nonimpact printer (p. 51)

off-line (p. 40)

on-line (p. 40)

optical technology (p. 62)

output (p. 46)

output device (p. 46)

parallel interface (p. 64)

peripheral device (p. 41)

pixel (p. 53)

plotter (p. 49)

printer (p. 49)

random-access memory (RAM)
(p. 34)

reading (p. 34)

read-only memory (ROM) (p. 34)

real-time processing (p. 40)

record (p. 65)

resolution (p. 52)

secondary storage (p. 55)

sequential-access file processing
(p. 66)

serial interface (p. 64)

soft copy (p. 49)

source-data entry (p. 40)

tape drive (p. 55)

transcriptive data entry (p. 38)

validation (p. 41)

verification (p. 40)

word (p. 37)

writing (p. 33)

Review Questions

Multiple Choice

1. A microprocessor contains both the _____.
   a. ALU and main memory
   b. control unit and RAM
   c. RAM and ROM
   d. ALU and control unit

2. Which of the following is a logic function?
   a. addition
   b. greater than
   c. division
   d. logarithmic

3. Main memory refers to _____.
   a. permanent ROM storage only
   b. internal storage for programs or data
   c. disk storage of data
   d. external permanent storage only

4. The number of adjacent bits that can be stored and manipulated as a unit is called a _____.
   a. byte
   b. nibble
   c. word
   d. MIP

5. Data preparation requiring that data be transcribed to an intermediate medium that, in turn, can be read by the computer is _____.
   a. real-time data entry
   b. peripheral data entry
   c. source data entry
   d. transcriptive data entry

6. Source-data entry is the concept of _____.
   a. collecting data as it is output and storing it for future processing
   b. collecting data at their source and sending them directly to the computer
   c. collecting data in batches and storing them in files
   d. bypassing the input process

7. The special symbol or character that indicates a user's position on the screen is the _____.

a. mouse
b. digitizer
c. cursor
d. monitor

8. A _____ interface is used to connect a peripheral device such as a printer to the CPU and can transfer data one bit at a time.
a. synthetic interface
b. parallel interface
c. serial interface
d. byte interface

9. Preparing a disk for use is called _____.
a. sectioning
b. tracking
c. readying
d. formatting

10. Which of the following is the correct hierarchy of data?
a. File, database, record, field
b. Database, file, field, record
c. Database, file, record, field
d. Field, file, database, record

Fill-in

1. The processing unit responsible for mathematical computations is the _ALU_.

2. The process of entering data into memory is called _____.

3. The _Binary_ number system is used to represent the electrical conditions of ON or OFF in computers.

4. A kilobyte is equal to _1024_ bytes and a byte is equal to eight _Bits_.

5. When an input device is on-line, it is directly connected to the _CPU_.

6. A hardware item that is attached to the main unit of a computer is a(n) _Monitor_.

7. Screen output is considered _Soft_ (hard or soft) copy.

8. A(n) _Pixel_ is the smallest increment of a display screen that can be controlled individually.

9. _Secondary_ is the nonvolatile memory external to a computer.

10. Through a(n) _____, a computer determines the relative position of a disk for locating data.

Short Answer

1. What three major units comprise the CPU, and what is CPU an acronym for?

2. Give four examples of a logic function.

3. What does the term *volatile* mean as it pertains to computer memory?

4. Contrast batch processing and real-time processing.

5. Describe the accuracy-checking methods of validation and verification.

6. How do resolution and pixels relate to monitors?

7. Describe secondary storage and explain why it is needed.

8. What are the advantages of magnetic tape over magnetic disks?

9. What is the main difference between a serial interface and a parallel interface?

10. Contrast the three basic methods of file storage and retrieval.

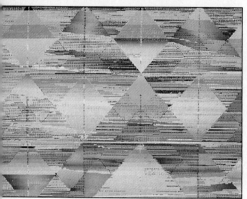

OUTLINE

OBJECTIVES

☐ Recognize the four major classifications of computers.

☐ Know why microcomputers are popular.

☐ Identify the basic components of a typical microcomputer system.

☐ Describe a microprocessor and briefly explain how microprocessors are used in devices other than computers.

☐ Distinguish among the various sizes of microcomputers and their uses.

☐ Understand the importance of compatibility.

CHAPTER THREE

Computer Systems

PROFILE

Seymour Cray

In an age emphasizing small personal computers, there is one man who continues to do quite the opposite. Seymour Cray marches to a different drummer, working to create the fastest, most powerful computers in the world. Cray first worked at Control Data Corporation (CDC), where he helped invent supercomputers. In 1972 he left CDC and, using half a million dollars of his own plus over $2 million from venture capitalists, he formed his own company, Cray Research, in Minneapolis. Cray's primary objective was to build large computers.

By 1976, Cray Research delivered the first in a series of Cray supercomputers. The Cray–1 computed at the rate of roughly 150 million floating-point operations per second. Its nearly $7 million price tag made it affordable to organizations needing massive computing power, primarily government agencies and large corporations.

In 1989 Cray Research split into two separate corporations. Seymour Cray now heads Cray Computer Corporation, based in Colorado Springs. He expects to devote more time to his Cray–3 supercomputer, increasing its power through use of new circuitry based on the compound, gallium arsenide. Computer-industry watchers speculate whether the original firm, Cray Research, will survive without the genius of Seymour Cray.

Cray has designed his offices for extreme quiet. "I just can't think when it's noisy," he once said. In fact, to be alone, he often works in the late afternoons and evenings. A curious paradox is that Cray usually prefers to work using paper, pencil, and occasionally a desktop computer, not his own supercomputer.

Adding credibility to claims of his eccentricity, when stumped by a problem, Cray thinks while digging an eight-foot-high by four-foot-wide tunnel under his home in the Wisconsin woods. An hour of digging completes four more inches in the tunnel. Cray suggests that, while he is busy excavating his tunnel, elves come in from the woods and solve his problems. Then when he returns to his office, he can resume his computer design.

No one has designed more supercomputers than Seymour Cray, and without his contributions, the United States would not have technological supremacy in this area. Competitors in the field of supercomputers know that Cray's are the ones to beat.

Cray continues doing what he does best—thinking, digging, and working on his next supercomputer.

All computers do basically the same thing and have the same basic components. However, there is great variation in their size and power. This chapter describes computers of all sizes, how they work, and their uses.

Computers traditionally have been grouped according to power, speed, and price. Large, powerful computer systems are divided into three categories: supercomputers, mainframe computers, and minicomputers. Small computer systems include a wide variety of microcomputers, including desktop, portable, and laptop models. Size distinctions now overlap because rapid advances in technology have given smaller machines many of the characteristics and capabilities of larger machines. Large computers are becoming smaller, and small computers are becoming more powerful. In this rapidly evolving technology, the categories we use here soon may be obsolete, but we will use these labels for ease of identification.

CRITERIA FOR CLASSIFYING COMPUTERS

Computers are grouped into four major size classifications: (1) supercomputers, (2) mainframes, (3) minicomputers, and (4) microcomputers. They are placed into these groups based on criteria which include architecture, processing speed, amount of main memory, capacity of external storage devices, speed of output devices, number of users, and cost. These factors are described below.

The architecture of a computer is the design of the internal circuitry. It includes the quantity and type of components that perform the actual computing tasks.

Processing speed is the number of instructions that a computer can process per second. Speed is usually measured in *millions of instructions per second* (MIPS). Generally, the larger the classification, the faster a computer can process data.

The amount of main memory includes the internal storage that a computer can access and use. Larger computers have more main memory than smaller computers. Generally, too, the larger the classification of computer, the larger the number of secondary storage devices that it is capable of supporting.

The speed of the output device of a computer is how fast it can print or otherwise produce output. Usually, the larger the computer, the faster the output devices. Output from small computers is usually measured in characters per second (cps), whereas output from larger computers is usually measured in lines per minute.

Typically, small computers can be accessed only by a single user at one time. Large computers can easily support hundreds of users.

Price of a computer usually reflects the power of the system. The larger the classification, the higher the price tends to be. Price also depends on the options purchased. Thus, a complete computer system classified in a lower category may actually cost more than one in a higher category. Small computers generally range from hundreds to thousands of dollars, and the largest computers cost millions of dollars.

Classifications of Computers

- Supercomputers
- Mainframe computers
- Minicomputers
- Microcomputers

SUPERCOMPUTERS

Supercomputers (Figure 3–1) are the most powerful and most expensive, as well as the fastest. Supercomputers are used where vast quantities of data must be manipulated, primarily by government agencies, scientific laboratories, and large corporations. Because of the sophistication of supercomputers and their adaptability and importance for use in weapon designs, the U.S. government is very cautious about the sale of supercomputers to certain countries.

The supercomputers developed by Seymour Cray (see Profile at beginning of chapter) contain up to 60 miles of wiring in their internal circuitry for the main memory alone. Because tremendous heat is generated by that circuitry, special cooling devices and separate computer rooms are required. Main memory is measured in billions of bytes. Supercomputers routinely execute *billions of instructions per second* (bips). Highly trained data-processing professionals are required to operate supercomputers. Thousands of users can access a supercomputer simultaneously. Prices range from several million dollars up to $27 million. Companies that manufacture supercomputers include Cray Research, Fujitsu, Hitachi, and NEC, and Cray is the largest of all producers.

Scientific applications include aerodynamic design and simulation, processing of geological data, processing of data in genetic decoding, and collecting and processing weather data. Oil companies process millions of pieces of data to determine the most productive oil exploration sites. As early as 1984, supercomputers were used to generate innovative special effects for the movie *The Star Fighter*.

In the aerospace field, aerodynamics and structural design are studied with supercomputers. Several aerospace programs will benefit from the capabilities of supercomputers because they require some experiments that are impossible to physically create. For example, a proposed space station

(a)

(b)

FIGURE 3–1
(a) The Cray YMP supercomputer. (b) Terminals and other hardware needed to support the Cray YMP. (Photo by Jo Hall/Macmillan)

would collapse under its own weight if built in the gravity of Earth, so it must be designed by computer for assembly in space. Another program is a transatmospheric space plane that must take off from a runway on Earth and accelerate directly into orbit at speeds over 8,800 mph. Many of its test conditions cannot be duplicated, even in a wind tunnel. Testing in space could be accomplished, but the expense would be prohibitive. The simulations and modeling for these designs and tests include processing billions of pieces of data and solving numerous complex mathematical calculations—a perfect application for supercomputers.

MAINFRAME COMPUTERS

Mainframe computers are less powerful, not quite so fast, and somewhat less expensive than supercomputers (Figure 3–2). Mainframe computers were so named because they were first built by incorporating modules on a chassis, or "main frame." They are often used in companies where many users at separate workstations must share the same computer.

Mainframes are generally found in "computer rooms" where environmental factors such as temperature, humidity, and dust are closely monitored. The circuitry for a mainframe is not nearly so complex as the circuitry for a supercomputer. Main memory is measured in millions of bytes, and secondary storage depends on the devices chosen. Mainframes process data at the rate of many millions of instructions per second. More than 1,000 remote stations can be accommodated by a typical mainframe computer; however, users do require specific training.

Mainframes can be rented from a manufacturer, leased through leasing companies, or purchased for amounts ranging from several hundred thousand dollars to as much as several million. Manufacturers include IBM, National Cash Register Company, Digital Equipment Corporation (DEC), UNISYS (formerly Burroughs and Sperry), and Amdahl. IBM, the

FIGURE 3–2
The Amdahl 5890–300E mainframe computer is shown on the manufacturing test floor. Mainframes are most often used for business processing in medium-sized to large corporations. (Courtesy of Amdahl Corp.)

largest supplier, has produced mainframes for 30 years and accounts for the majority of mainframes sold in North America. The IBM 3090 mainframe contains circuitry that stores 1 million bits of information on a chip and takes only 80 billionths of a second to retrieve it.

Mainframe capabilities are needed by federal and local government agencies, banks, hospitals, and commercial and industrial users. Mainframes typically coordinate and manage vast amounts of data in giant data banks. Korea's Stock Exchange in Seoul uses two mainframes to process nearly 25 million shares of stock orders from 400 branch offices of 25 security companies. The Metro Toronto Police in Canada store hundreds of thousands of fingerprints in a mainframe computer. They also monitor and service all ''911'' emergency telephone calls requesting police, fire, and ambulance assistance. Arresting officers, managing officers, and dispatchers can access the computer data bank at the same time.

MINICOMPUTERS

Minicomputers are smaller than mainframe computers. They contain somewhat less memory and processing capability and are less expensive. Small and medium-sized businesses use them, and they can serve several users simultaneously (Figure 3–3). Main memory can consist of several million bytes of data. It is possible to expand memory by using secondary

FIGURE 3–3
Minicomputers generally have less power than mainframes. They are used in many small and medium-sized organizations. (Courtesy of Hewlett-Packard Co.)

storage devices. Processing speeds are several millions of instructions per second. As many as a hundred users, with minimal training, can access a minicomputer. Minicomputer prices range from tens of thousands to several hundred thousand dollars.

Minicomputers were first introduced in the mid-1960s by Digital Equipment Company (DEC). They were small-scale mainframe computers, having less power and speed, popular because of their low price, approximately $20,000. Many companies manufacture minicomputers, including Hewlett-Packard, Data General, Texas Instruments, Honeywell, UNISYS, Wang, IBM, and Prime. However, the innovator of minicomputers, DEC, remains the leader.

Scientific laboratories, research groups, some colleges, engineering firms, and even industrial and manufacturing plants also use minicomputers. At the University of Miami's Rosenstiel School of Marine and Atmospheric Science, minicomputers condense more than two billion bytes of information daily. Research there includes image processing, in which complex data are compiled from satellite observations of the Earth's oceans to create color images depicting winds, surface temperatures, and even chlorophyll content. The reasonable price of minicomputers makes them available to smaller organizations, such as the American Association of University Women. A minicomputer in its Washington, DC headquarters keeps 175,000 members in 2,000 communities in touch with issues important to women, their communities, and the nation.

MICROCOMPUTERS

Computers that contain less memory and processing capability at a cheaper price than minicomputers are called **microcomputers** (Figure 3–4). Microcomputer processing speeds are at the lowest range—approximately one million instructions per second. Main memory in microcomputers is also considerably smaller than in larger systems. Users can read the documentation and manuals and learn how to operate microcomputers without specialized training. Unlike a larger computer, a single microcomputer is generally used by only one person at a time. However, with appropriate software, some of the more powerful microcomputers can be used by several users at once.

To share data and computing power, microcomputers can be connected to a large system in **micro-to-mainframe links**. These links, or connections, enable microcomputer users to share data and computing power with a larger system. For example, dealers for the French automaker, Peugeot, place orders for specific interiors and specific parts on personal computers that are networked into a mainframe system in Paris.

Networks and data communication play an important role in business computing. Businesses and industries have expanded across the country and around the world, and the physical distance and fast pace require rapid transmission and reception of information. Data communication technology helps keep pace and meet the demands of this fast-moving economy. In Chapter 5 we will examine data communication.

Distinctions in computing power are becoming blurred because of technological innovations that process data more quickly and store greater

Classification Criteria

- Architecture
- Processing speed
- Main memory
- Secondary storage
- Speed of output
- Number of users
- Price

FIGURE 3–4
Microcomputers are used not only in offices but at home for a wide variety of tasks.

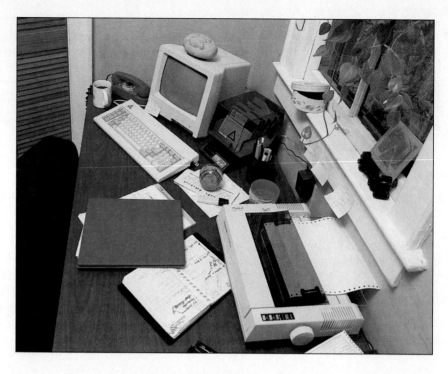

FIGURE 3–5
Because technological advances have increased computing power and decreased prices, categorical distinctions among computer systems are becoming increasingly blurred.

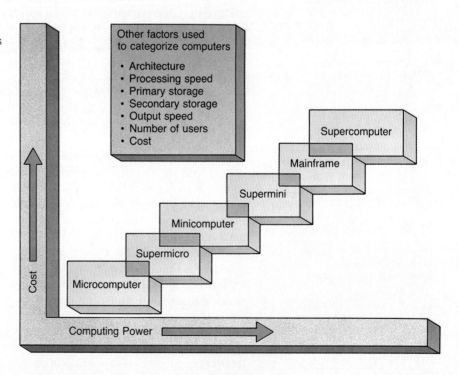

Other factors used to categorize computers

- Architecture
- Processing speed
- Primary storage
- Secondary storage
- Output speed
- Number of users
- Cost

Cost

Supercomputer

Mainframe

Supermini

Minicomputer

Supermicro

Microcomputer

Computing Power

amounts of data in smaller areas (Figure 3–5). Therefore, many of the small new machines have characteristics and capabilities of the large older ones of only a few years ago. Two new classifications—superminicomputers and supermicrocomputers—have emerged as a result of recent advances. Superminicomputers bridge the gap between standard mainframes and minicomputers. Supermicrocomputers bridge the gap between minicomputers and microcomputers. However, large systems are still needed to handle the needs of many users.

The rest of this chapter focuses on microcomputers, the type you are most likely to come in contact with and use.

A MICROCOMPUTER SYSTEM

A microcomputer is the smallest, least expensive of the computers, but don't let the prefix *micro* or the word *small* fool you. *Micro* refers mainly to the physical size of a computer and its circuitry rather than its capabilities. Originally, microcomputers had limited capabilities compared to large mainframes, but now microcomputers are more powerful than the early mainframes.

All computers have the same basic elements—input devices, a central processing unit (CPU), main memory, output devices, software, and usually some secondary storage. The key differences between microcomputers and large computers today are that microcomputers have smaller memory, less power, and permit fewer peripherals. They accommodate fewer users, and are physically smaller.

Microcomputers range in price from a few hundred dollars for the simplest ones to tens of thousands of dollars. Microcomputers also have been called **personal computers,** or PCs for short. When Steven Jobs and Stephen Wozniak were designing their first Apple, they had in mind a computer to put on your desk, ready for individual use (see Profile, Chapter 11). Today, however, some microcomputers can be used by several users, each with a terminal connected to a central microcomputer.

Components of a Microcomputer System

A microcomputer and its peripheral devices and software are called a **microcomputer system.** Depending on its purpose, a microcomputer system can be configured with a variety of input and output devices. Figure 3–6 shows a configuration for a typical microcomputer system. The major components are:

- ☐ System unit (the basic computer, containing the microprocessor and main memory).
- ☐ Keyboard for input.
- ☐ Disk drive(s) for secondary storage of data and programs.
- ☐ Monitor (display screen) for soft-copy output.
- ☐ Printer for hard-copy output.
- ☐ Software (including the operating system and application software).

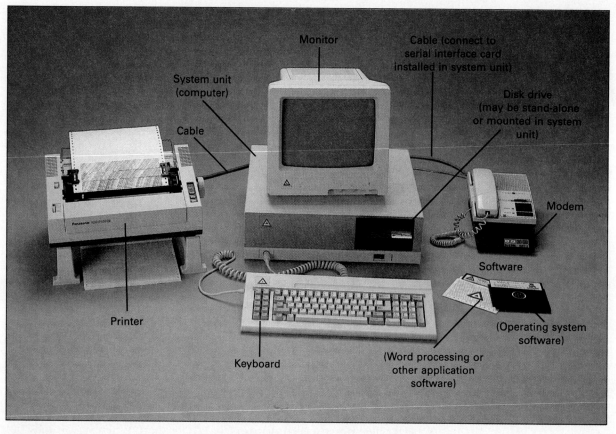

FIGURE 3–6
A typical microcomputer system.

☐ Modem connected to the telephone line for telecommunication.
☐ Serial interface card to permit modem connection.
☐ Serial or parallel interface card to permit a serial or parallel printer and other peripheral device connections.
☐ Cables to connect all of the hardware components.

Earlier chapters described most of these components in more detail; Chapter 5 describes modems.

A Multiuser Microcomputer System

Some organizations and businesses use **multiuser microcomputer systems**. In this type of system, a number of terminals, typically two to thirty, are attached to one powerful microcomputer, a hard-disk drive, and a printer. These terminals are usually located in the same office or building. They also can have individual disk drives. A microcomputer used in this way needs a great deal of main memory to handle all the input from each terminal.

The advantage of a multiuser system is that several people can share the same computer, peripheral equipment, and data. This configuration is similar to a minicomputer or mainframe system with multiple terminals. A disadvantage is limited computer resources: the more terminals that are added, the less memory, disk space, and CPU time are available to each user. And, if the computer breaks down, all users are affected.

WHY MICROCOMPUTERS ARE POPULAR

Since the first Apple II personal computer hit the market in 1977, people have been excited about the possible uses of microcomputers. Why have microcomputers gained such acceptance?

First, it is because they clearly have proved to be *tools that increase productivity*. After a network of microcomputers was installed at Gulfstream Aerospace Corporation of Savannah, Georgia, productivity increased 25 percent in its Vehicle Design and Flight Sciences departments. Engineers there used microcomputers and specialized software to test aircraft design and thereby reduce time-consuming and expensive tests with wind tunnels. Overall, Gulfstream was able to speed its production schedule.

In a typical business office, a typist's productivity can be significantly increased by using a computer and word processing software. A bookkeeper's tasks are speeded up with an electronic spreadsheet.

The second reason for their acceptance is that microcomputers have proved to be *effective problem-solving tools*. Computing power is no longer just a corporate tool or a tool in the hands of computer professionals. By using microcomputers, individuals and small businesses can accomplish tasks that would ordinarily take too much time or too much effort to even attempt manually.

A third reason is that microcomputers are *useful to a variety of people for a variety of tasks* (Figure 3–7). They can be used to play games, teach math to children, create new musical sounds, predict stock market trends, or serve as handy references.

A fourth reason is that *microcomputers are inexpensive*. Students, families, and home businesses can afford small systems (Figure 3–8).

Finally, there is *an abundance of easy-to-use software*. People don't need to know how a computer operates to use one. Much of the ready-to-use software displays instructions on the computer screen to guide users through the task at hand.

Input and output devices also have been simplified. Some computers accept commands when you touch the screen. Others, with the appropriate hardware and software, respond to voice commands.

Now the power of computers is available to almost anyone. People can own microcomputers or have access to them in schools, public libraries, or even neighborhood photocopy shops. In the same way that most people drive automobiles without giving much thought to their complex machinery, people use computers without thinking of their complexity.

Why Microcomputers Are Popular

- Increased productivity
- Problem-solving abilities
- Usefulness to variety of people for variety of tasks
- Inexpensiveness
- Availability of easy-to-use software

FIGURE 3–7
A musical instrument digital interface (MIDI) links computers to musical instruments to control and create sounds. (Courtesy of Apple Computer, Inc.)

FIGURE 3–8
Computers are used in homes for entertainment, education, and business tasks. This boy is learning to use a microcomputer to type reports for class. (Photo by Larry Hamill/Macmillan)

HIGHLIGHT 3-1

HISTORICAL HACKERS

In many circles these days, hacker is a synonym for technological terrorist. The bad name came from movies that pictured these zealous computer fans as masters of espionage and from news stories that told of the aberrant genius who broke through computer-erected barriers to make free long-distance telephone calls or change data in some high-security database. Not long ago, though, the hacker was still a romantic figure in an industry that had precious little romance to offer. The computer hackers of this first generation are, in fact, the pioneers in microcomputer development and application. They designed the early video games, created the understandable and useful software for everyday use, and dreamed of a society in which computers are as vital and commonplace as running water.

A few years ago, some of the best hackers in the business got together to see what they had in common and what they could offer each other and the public. This historically important Hackers Conference took place in Marin County, California, on a winter weekend in 1984. The Hackers Conference of 1984 did not lay out political plans for its representatives or issue manifestoes about the rightful place of computers in the world, but it did bring together some of the best and brightest minds in the country: Steve Wozniak (Apple computer designer and cofounder), Bob Frankston (VisiCalc developer), and Lee Felsenstein (leader of the Home Brew Computer Club, a pioneering computer brainstorming organization).

Except for being unanimous in their belief in the benefits and usefulness of computers, the 150 hackers agreed on virtually nothing else. Some thought that all software should be free and available to everyone; others argued that the software their brains had created was as much their own property as their souls. However, the important part of this historic meeting was not what the representatives agreed upon. Rather, for the first time, the leading minds of the computer revolution met to talk, plan, inspire, and challenge each other. They finally saw themselves as members of a community—not as isolated thinkers. Subsequent meetings of these creative minds (and those who follow their lead) are destined to liberate the potential that computers hold for us all.

MICROPROCESSORS

Entry into a new generation of computer technology occurred with the introduction of the microprocessor. Changes happened so fast that some describe the period since 1975 as a "microcomputer revolution."

The heart of a microcomputer is the **microprocessor,** which is the master controller of the whole system. Sometimes called a "computer on a chip," the microprocessor is a remarkably miniaturized electronic circuit. It is a logic chip on which parts of a CPU are placed (the arithmetic and logic unit plus the control unit). Some microprocessor designs even include the arithmetic and logic unit, control unit, *and* main memory on a single chip.

Often, a microcomputer is identified by the name of the microprocessor that controls it. Four manufacturers of microprocessors dominate the microcomputer industry: (1) Motorola, (2) Intel, (3) Zilog, and (4) MOS technology. The companies introduce new microprocessors in their lines as technology advances (Table 3–1).

Popular and powerful microprocessors include Intel's 32-bit microprocessor (the Intel 80386), other 32-bit chips (such as Motorola's 68030), and Intel's 80486 (i486). Also popular, but less powerful than the 32-bit chip, are 16-bit chips including Intel's 80286 and Motorola's 68020. The popularity of 8-bit chips such as the Zilog Z–80, Intel 8088, and MOS technology 6502 series has dwindled for most applications because the

TABLE 3–1

Microcomputers and their microprocessors

Microcomputer	Microprocessor
Apple Macintosh	Motorola 68000
Apple Macintosh II	Motorola 68020
Apple Macintosh SE/30	Motorola 68030
Apple II	MOS Technology 6502
Apple IIc	MOS Technology 65C02
Atari 520ST	Motorola 68000
AT&T UNIX PC	Motorola 68010
AT&T 6300	Intel 8086
Commodore Amiga	Motorola 68000
Compaq Deskpro 286	Intel 80286
Compaq Deskpro 386	Intel 80386
Compaq Portable Computer	Intel 8088
DataWorld's Data 386-16	Intel 80386
Dell System 310	Intel 80386
IBM PC AT	Intel 80286
IBM PC XT	Intel 8088
IBM PS/2 Model 80	Intel 80386
Kaypro II	Zilog Z-80A
Leading Edge Model D	Intel 8088
NeXt	Motorola 68030
Tandy 1000	Intel 8088
Tandy 3000	Intel 80286
Radio Shack TRS-80 Model 4	Zilog Z-80A
Radio Shack TRS-80 Model 16	Intel 8086

8-bit chip does not have the power to efficiently run most of today's applications. However, the MOS technology 6502 has retained some popularity in the educational market because a great deal of software exists for the Apple II series of computers which are used by many elementary and secondary schools.

The first microprocessor was not intended for use in a computer at all. Instead, it was intended for use in a Japanese line of calculators. The same type of microprocessor is also found in a large array of modern automatic devices and appliances. **Embedded microprocessors** control certain functions of such devices, making them "smart." The chips are preprogrammed by manufacturers so that users usually do no more than turn on the devices or press buttons to choose features or functions.

In microwave ovens, an embedded microprocessor controls cooking time and temperature. All you do is set the cooking time and select the temperature. The microprocessor does the rest. In some automatic cameras, a microprocessor senses the light level at several points on the viewing screen, averages the light, and computes and sets the correct lens opening and shutter speed.

Some automobile engines use one or more microprocessor chips to monitor and control certain engine functions. The microprocessor receives information from strategically located sensors about speed, temperature, and pressure. It also controls the air and fuel mixture, spark timing, and emissions control to get the best engine economy and efficiency.

In offices, modern typewriters and photocopiers contain microprocessors. The control panel on a modern copier reflects its many microprocessor-controlled functions, such as reduction or enlargement sizes, paper selection, automatic exposure (which controls the degree of contrast on the copy), and the copy counter. Most copiers even have self-diagnostics to explain problems in the equipment when they occur.

In gasoline pumps, microprocessors measure the amount of gasoline pumped and calculate the price. Most pumps are programmed to stop when a certain dollar amount or number of gallons is reached.

Many modern games and toys use microprocessors. For example, the popular computer game Nintendo has an embedded microprocessor, as do toy robots that walk, pick up and carry items, and respond to commands.

SUPERMICROCOMPUTERS

Some high-performance desktop computers are called **supermicrocomputers**. They are used mainly in businesses to support a multiuser system, where a number of terminals are connected to the same microcomputer. They also are used as local area network servers (discussed in Chapter 5) and for complex applications, such as computer-aided design. Supermicrocomputers usually contain 32-bit, high-speed microprocessors and include extensive memory. Here, too, main memory can be expanded by adding memory cards.

Supermicrocomputers challenge the speed and power of minicomputers. In fact, they are competing with minicomputers in the marketplace because of their comparatively low price, their ability to handle multiple

PC PERSUASION In its mania to reach all of the people all the time, American advertising is now making its way into computer software. In at least one case, the consumer actually had to pay for the ad. In 1989 Ford Motor Company sold ads on home computer disks for $5. Of course, there was an appealing bonus: the consumer could pop the disk in, bring up the data and images on the computer screen, and then "test drive" any of 29 Ford vehicles. An added feature enabled the user to select a model, add and subtract options, and calculate cost, right down to the monthly payments.

Advertisers like using disks to promote their wares because upscale and well-educated consumers often work daily with personal computers. American International Group, for instance, has used advertising disks to promote its financial services to company treasurers.

Besides targeting a very narrow but very affluent audience, computer advertising may be a way of bringing down the price of creating new software packages. However, because not everyone wants to look at advertising every time they pop a disk into their machines, some advertisers are looking into methods that would allow the ads to fade out after the software has been used a certain number of times.

New car buyers who feel a need to kick the tires before buying will obviously not get a "kick" out of this kind of sales device.

users, and their ability to store large amounts of data. Large-capacity, hard-disk drives are the usual storage devices used with supermicrocomputers. Examples of such systems are the Prime EXL MBX, IBM Personal System/2 Model 80, AT&T UNIX PC, Hewlett-Packard Vectra, and DEC Microvax I and II.

DESKTOP MICROCOMPUTERS

Desktop microcomputers are the most common microcomputers used; they fit nicely on the top of a desk at home or in an office. Averaging about 30 to 50 pounds, they are too heavy and cumbersome to carry easily, but they are certainly more portable than are mainframes (Figure 3–9).

At the core of a desktop computer is a circuit board called the **motherboard**. Mounted on it are the microprocessor, memory chips, and chips that handle input, output, and storage. This circuit board is placed inside the system unit at the factory. However, there are usually slots for adding other circuit boards, such as a board that adds graphics capabilities or one that expands memory capacity.

FIGURE 3–9
The NeXT computer uses an
erasable optical disk for storage.
(Courtesy of NeXT Computers)

In contrast to the early one kilobyte of memory, today's microcomputers contain memory ranging from 256 kilobytes to several megabytes. For example, Apple's Macintosh II has four megabytes of internal memory, and the IBM Personal System/2 Model 40 has two megabytes.

Some companies incorporate 32-bit microprocessors in their desktop computers (Figure 3–10). Some of the most powerful use the high-speed Intel 80386 chip. Introduced in late 1986 in the Compaq Deskpro 386 computer, this and other 32-bit chips (such as the Motorola 68030) created a great leap in microcomputer capabilities. Recently, faster 32-bit chips such as the Intel 80486 have been introduced, but the lower-priced 80386 chips remain the most popular. With the appropriate operating system, these chips provide multiprocessing capabilities, give more speed, and accommodate more powerful programs than 8-bit or 16-bit chips. Complex tasks once possible only with large computers, such as speech recognition

FIGURE 3–10
The Compaq Deskpro 386 was
the first of a new generation of
personal computers in 1986 to
use the Intel 80386 microprocessor. (Courtesy of Compaq
Computer Corp.)

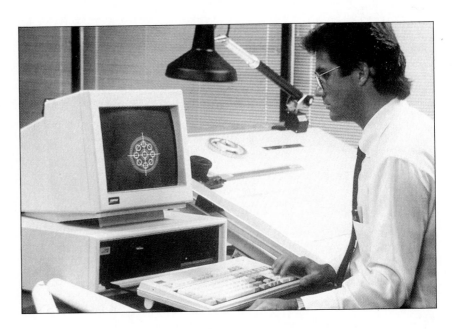

and humanlike decision-making functions, are becoming possible with microcomputers as more software takes advantage of 32-bit chip power.

On the rear panel of a desktop computer and almost all microcomputers, openings called **ports** allow attachment of peripheral devices such as printers or modems (Figure 3–11).

Manufacturers of popular desktop computers whose names you might recognize were listed in Table 3–1. Dozens of name brands of desktop computers are available to consumers for home and business use (see Figure 3–12).

FIGURE 3–11

Ports allow peripheral devices to be connected to a microcomputer. (Photo by Jo Hall/Macmillan)

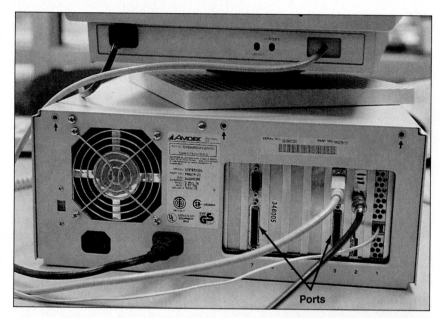

FIGURE 3–12

The Apple Macintosh II microcomputer (Photo by Jo Hall/Macmillan)

PORTABLE MICROCOMPUTERS

People on the go—writers on assignment, traveling salespeople who transmit typed orders by telephone communication, or students using computers on campus—need a computer small and lightweight enough to carry easily—a **portable computer**. For thousands of executives, salespeople, and field service managers, the "portable office" is a necessity and a reality. (Figure 3–13).

Until just a few years ago, portable computers were actually "transportable" computers—microcomputers lightweight enough to move (20–30 pounds and suitcase-sized) but still needing external power supplies. True portables, small enough to carry easily and briefcase-sized or smaller, use either replaceable or rechargeable batteries. Some also permit using either standard AC power or DC power (batteries). Typical portables average 10 to 30 pounds.

Although features and cost vary from computer to computer, some portables have the same range of features and microprocessor power as desktop computers. Display screens are generally smaller to save space, but most can show 25 lines of text. Most are equipped with a 3½-inch disk drive and a hard disk as well as expansion slots for peripheral devices.

Prices of portables range from approximately $1,000 to $5,000. The category of portables can be further subdivided into laptop computers and hand-held/pocket computers, described next.

Sizes of Microcomputers

- Supermicrocomputers
- Desktop microcomputers
- Portable microcomputers
  □ Laptop
  □ Hand-held/pocket

FIGURE 3–13
A portable microcomputer being used at a construction site. (Photo by Cobalt Productions/ Macmillan)

FIGURE 3–14
Laptop computers are convenient for salespeople who have to make client contacts either in person or by telephone. This salesman is able to give his client current prices, which are stored in the computer, and to key in the client's order as it is placed.

Laptop Computers

Laptop computers, sometimes called briefcase computers, actually can be used on your lap. They are very portable (Figure 3–14). Some models weigh about 4 pounds; others weigh up to 18. Like desktop microcomputers, laptop computers have full typewriter keyboards. Some laptops equal the memory capacity of some desktop models, ranging from 256 kilobytes to several megabytes. Most are IBM compatible. Display screens are either color or monochrome, and they typically display several lines on a flat screen using either a liquid crystal display (LCD) or gas plasma display.

Most laptops have built-in modems or serial interfaces so users can send data to a larger computer or receive data from it. Some have built-in software packages (such as word processors) and built-in tape or disk drives. In the office, a laptop can be connected to larger peripherals—regular-sized printers or larger monitors, for example.

The manageable size of laptop computers enables businesspeople to work while traveling. One can work on a laptop in an airport while awaiting a flight, and when the flight is announced, slip the computer into its case. On the plane, the case can be stored under the seat. Some airlines even permit use of laptops during flights, although certain types of laptops can cause radio interference. Laptops now are common sights on commuter trains. And if you travel by car, you can secure a handy car seat for your computer to the passenger seat to facilitate working while traveling (not while driving, of course!). With laptops, journalists can file stories from the field. IRS auditors are using laptops to perform audits right in taxpayers' offices or homes.

College students now find laptops almost as necessary as textbooks (see Figure 3–15). Half of the students at Harvard Business School now take their exams on laptops rather than in the traditional blue books. Even the space shuttle carries a couple of laptop computers that are powerful enough to help land the shuttle should the main on-board computer fail!

Apple, NEC, Tandy, Grid, Toshiba, and others manufacture laptop computers.

Hand-held Computers

More power in less space—that's the direction in which personal computer designers continue to move. The result is pocket-size or **hand-held computers**. These have been around since 1981, when Radio Shack introduced one about the size of a small book. It weighed only seven ounces.

Despite their small size, light weight (sometimes only a few ounces), and limited LCD displays of one or a few lines, hand-held computers have full keyboards and sometimes include built-in printers (Figure 3–16). They sell for $200 to $1,000.

Surprisingly powerful, Sharp's tiny Wizard computer, for example, stores as much information as did the original IBM microcomputer. It has a full keyboard and an eight-line screen. The 6½×3¾-inch device, which

FIGURE 3–15
This student uses a portable computer in the library to make research notes. Back at her room, she will organize the notes, prepare a rough draft, revise the text, and then print a final copy for her class assignment.

FIGURE 3–16
A pocket computer being used to design new pricing strategies for service-station dealers. (Courtesy of Chevron Corp.)

TABLE 3-2

Comparison of microcomputers

	Super-microcomputer	Desktop	Typical Portable	Laptop	Hand-held
Price range	$7,000–$20,000	$300–$6,000	$1,000–$5,000	$500–$3,000	$200–$1,000
Size	Desktop	Desktop	Suitcase	Briefcase	Book or pocket
Weight	30–70 lbs.	30–50 lbs.	10–30 lbs.	4–18 lbs.	Several ounces
Display screen	25 lines	25 lines	25 lines	8–25 lines	1–8 lines
Processor	16-, 32-bit	8-, 16-, 32-bit	8-, 16-, 32-bit	8-, 16-, 32-bit	8-, 16-bit
Power source	External	External	Battery/external	Battery/external	Battery/external

can be used to calculate as well as to make notes, holds up to 700 telephone numbers and lets you mark dates and appointments on a 200-year calendar.

The hand-held size is particularly appropriate for people who work on location, such as engineers or repair and maintenance personnel. Marquette Electronics, Inc., a manufacturer of high-tech computerized electrocardiogram equipment, supplies its service technicians with hand-held computers to compile and transmit reports on service calls. Instead of hand-writing and mailing work orders to headquarters each day, the technicians file the reports by computer. Reports include the technician's identification number, expenses incurred, customer's account number, part numbers, and quantities used on a service call. IBM is another example; its thousands of repairpeople are equipped with hand-held computers to send messages to and from the home office through a nationwide network of radio towers.

How small can computers be made and still have readable screens and usable keyboards? The displays on hand-held and pocket-size computers are already small and the keyboards are difficult to use. Researchers think computer shrinkage will continue, possibly by dispensing with keyboards altogether and making portable computers that can read handwriting or recognize voices as input. Table 3-2 compares several sizes of microcomputers.

THE ISSUE OF COMPATIBILITY

A major problem affecting both the microcomputer industry and users has been a lack of compatibility of equipment and software among manufacturers. **Compatibility** is the ability of hardware and software from one computer to work with another computer. The whole problem of compatibility reflects the rapid growth and extreme competitiveness of the computer marketplace. For example, why are IBM computers and Apple computers incompatible? The different internal circuit designs of each make them incompatible.

Disk size also varies from computer to computer. For example, the Apple Macintosh uses a 3½-inch diskette enclosed in hard plastic, but other Apple microcomputers use a 5¼-inch floppy diskette. The IBM PS/2 series uses 3½-inch diskettes, but many IBM compatibles use 5¼-inch floppy diskettes. However, even using the same size of floppy diskette does not guarantee compatibility. A program designed to work with a particular microprocessor and a particular operating system will run under those conditions only. Even disk drives, printers, and software are designed to operate with specific computers.

For consumers, this means that linking one computer to another to exchange data, or sharing equipment or data in a network, requires that the hardware and software of the two computers be compatible. However, for reasons of features and price, Consumers want to mix and match products from various manufacturers. They don't want to be forced to the same vendor for every purchase.

Because the IBM was, for a time, the most popular microcomputer, other manufacturers introduced their versions, called *IBM compatibles*— machines that run IBM software and work with other IBM peripheral equipment. The term "IBM compatible" is a bit misleading because these machines are compatible with the IBM family in varying degrees. Compatibles generally use the same microprocessors and the same operating systems.

However, IBM software and hardware are not always compatible with clones, and vice versa. Some software runs on the same operating system and accesses only DOS-level routines. Other software accesses codes contained in the built-in portions of the operating system that reside in ROM. (This is the ROM–Basic Input Output System, or ROM–BIOS.) Such software is not interchangeable because of copyrighted differences between ROMs from manufacturer to manufacturer. To maintain its competitive advantage, IBM decided not to make its ROM–BIOS available to other manufacturers. However, software developers such as Phoenix Software Associates, Limited, designed a ROM–BIOS that is nearly 100 percent compatible and licensed it to manufacturers of IBM compatibles. Still, some peripherals and other hardware that claim to be compatible actually need modification before they will work.

One way that computer manufacturers are helping consumers handle the compatibility problem is by inserting a second microprocessor on a plug-in board. This lets a computer switch between the two microprocessors and permits running software (including operating systems) designed for either system. A second way is the development of networks that allow incompatible computers to share data and resources.

A third way of addressing the compatibility problem is creation of industry standards. Various organizations and manufacturers are making recommendations for standardization of hardware and software. Standard interfaces and data formats for input and output devices, as well as standards for programming languages, would help alleviate compatibility problems.

SUMMARY

Computers are classified by architecture, processing speed, main memory, external storage capability, speed of output devices, number of users, and cost. Large computers are categorized as supercomputers, mainframe computers, and minicomputers. Small computers are called microcomputers.

Development of the microprocessor ushered in a new generation of computer technology, making invention of the microcomputer possible. A microcomputer, sometimes called a personal computer (PC), is the smallest, least-expensive computer. Its capabilities, however, are nearing those of large computers. Micro-to-mainframe links allow microcomputers to share data with larger systems.

A basic microcomputer system comprises several items: the system unit, a keyboard, disk drive(s), a monitor, a printer, software, a modem, connecting cables, and serial and parallel interfaces. A multiuser microcomputer system is one in which several terminals are connected to a single powerful microcomputer.

Microcomputers have become popular because their use increases productivity, they are useful problem-solving tools, they appeal to a variety of people for a variety of tasks, they are inexpensive, and the availability of software makes them easy to use.

The introduction of the Apple II computer spurred the microcomputer industry and moved microcomputers into homes, schools, and businesses. The industry received an even greater boost when IBM presented its microcomputer.

Today, there are many imitations (clones) of the IBM. An owner of an IBM-compatible machine can use equipment and software originally intended for the IBM.

A microprocessor, sometimes called a "computer on a chip," is a logic chip on which parts of a central processing unit are placed. Microprocessors are used not only in computers but also in electronic devices and appliances that are not computers themselves. You can find embedded microprocessors in automobile engines, photocopiers, electronic typewriters, and many other appliances.

Desktop computers are the most common microcomputers. They weigh about 30 to 50 pounds and are small enough to fit on a desk. Some businesses use very powerful desktop-sized supermicrocomputers, which have almost as many capabilities as minicomputers and are used as multiuser systems.

Portable computers, small microcomputers that are lightweight enough to be carried from place to place, come in various sizes. Portables have components similar to but sometimes smaller than those of desktop computers. However, many portables are as powerful as desktops and can be connected to large peripheral devices, such as standard monitors or printers.

Compatibility of equipment and software from one computer to another has always been a problem. Different internal circuit designs make computers incompatible. New hardware developments, the creation of networks that allow incompatible computers to share data and resources, and the creation of hardware and software standards are helping to relieve the problem.

Vocabulary Self-Test

Can you define the following?

compatibility (p. 94)
desktop microcomputer (p. 88)
embedded microprocessor (p. 87)
hand-held computer (p. 92)
laptop computer (p. 92)
mainframe computer (p. 77)
microcomputer (p. 79)
microcomputer system (p. 81)
microprocessor (p. 85)
micro-to-mainframe link (p. 79)

minicomputer (p. 78)
motherboard (p. 88)
multiuser microcomputer system (p. 82)
personal computer (p. 81)
portable computer (p. 91)
ports (p. 90)
supercomputer (p. 76)
supermicrocomputer (p. 87)

Review Questions

Multiple Choice

1. The largest, most expensive, and most powerful computer is the
   _____ .
   a. microcomputer
   b. minicomputer
   c. mainframe computer
   d. supercomputer

2. Microcomputers run under the control of a(n) _____.
   a. disk drive
   b. interface
   c. transistor
   d. microprocessor

3. The microprocessor is a logic chip that contains _____.
   a. parts of the CPU
   b. a modem
   c. secondary storage
   d. the motherboard

4. Because so many technological changes have occurred in computers, the
   period since 1975 is sometimes known as the _____.
   a. microcomputer age
   b. computer revolution
   c. microcomputer revolution
   d. microprocessor age

5. Which of the following can be found embedded in some household
   appliances?
   a. disk drives
   b. microtablets
   c. microcomputers
   d. microprocessors

6. The most common size of microcomputer is the _____.
   a. minicomputer
   b. desktop microcomputer

    c. supermicrocomputer

    d. hand-held computer

7. At the core of the desktop computer is the main circuit board called the
    _____ .

    a. microcircuit

    b. motherboard

    c. port

    d. interface

8. _____ are the openings on a microcomputer that allow peripheral devices to be connected.

    a. modems

    b. transistors

    c. interfaces

    d. ports

9. Most portable computers use microprocessors as powerful as those found in _____ .

    a. desktop computers

    b. transistor computers

    c. supercomputers

    d. mainframe computers

10. _____ is the capability of hardware and software from one computer to work with another computer.

    a. Linkage

    b. Compatibility

    c. Word processing

    d. Supercomputing

Fill-in

1. Many functional distinctions among the different sizes of computers have _____ over time because advances in technology have given smaller machines many of the characteristics and capabilities of larger machines.

2. _____ is the main difference between a typical microcomputer system and a multiuser microcomputer system.

3. A microcomputer runs under the control of the _____ , the heart of a microcomputer.

4. A microprocessor is sometimes called a(n) _____ on a(n) _____ .

5. Microprocessors were originally developed for use in a line of _____ .

6. A(n) _____ is a very powerful desktop microcomputer.

7. A(n) _____ -bit chip is used in the most powerful desktop computers.

8. Any computer that is small and lightweight enough to be easily carried or moved around is a(n) _____ computer.

9. A(n) _____ computer is even smaller than a laptop computer.

10. Two computers are incompatible if their _____ is different.

Short Answer

1. Computer systems are grouped into which four classifications? List three criteria used in classifying computer systems.

2. Why are microcomputers sometimes called personal computers?

3. List the basic components of a typical microcomputer system.

4. Explain why microcomputers have become so popular in the United States.

5. Give examples describing how supercomputers, mainframes, minicomputers, and microcomputers have affected your life.

6. Describe a microprocessor. Name three devices with embedded microprocessors.

7. Explain how the categorical distinctions among computer systems have become blurred.

8. What is a motherboard and where is it found?

9. Describe a laptop computer. What are some typical uses?

10. With regard to size and cost, how does a microcomputer compare with other computers?

OBJECTIVES

☐ Understand the difference between system software and application software.

☐ Understand the functions and capabilities of an operating system, and know the major parts of an operating system.

☐ Identify the major operating systems used on microcomputers.

☐ Know the difference between the two broad categories of application software—generalized and specialized.

☐ Identify the categories of programming languages and know the applications for which they are used.

☐ Know the names of common programming languages and the purposes for which they are used.

CHAPTER FOUR

Computer Software

PROFILE

William H. Gates

At the age when boys are trying to find ways to impress girls, 13-year-old Bill Gates was losing his heart to computers. An extraordinarily bright student in mathematics, Gates became fascinated with computer programming. In the late 1960s, while he was in high school, Gates and some friends volunteered to work evenings for no salary at Computer Center Corporation in Seattle. Their job was to find bugs in the elaborate programs provided to the Center by Digital Equipment Corporation for its DEC computer. While several teenagers took part in this operation, the clear leaders were Gates and his friend, Paul Allen, who was 2 years older.

Computer Center didn't turn over its computer to the youngsters simply as an act of community good will. According to its contract with DEC, as long as it was able to uncover bugs in DEC's programs, the company did not have to pay for the use of the DEC computer. Of the original team, only Gates and Allen stayed long enough to get paying jobs with Computer Center.

By the time that Gates was 15, he and Allen had formed Traf-O-Data, a company that sold computer analyses of traffic patterns. The effort grossed them around $20,000 a year.

Then, in 1974, they developed Microsoft BASIC, the first high-level language for microcomputers. Later, in 1975, the language became part of the MIS Altair, the first personal computer.

Subsequently, Gates and Allen founded a second company, Microsoft, to market Microsoft BASIC and create other software for microcomputers. Gates, a student at Harvard, had to leave to find the time to manage the daily operations of the new company. In 1981, IBM adopted Microsoft DOS and Microsoft BASIC for its personal computer line, a move that turned Microsoft into a thriving company.

Allen left Microsoft before it really started to bloom financially. Gates stayed on, however, serving as not only a developer of ideas, but also an effective salesman. Gates saw PC-DOS and MS-DOS, the company's biggest successes, become the operating systems that run millions of personal computers.

By the time Gates was 30 years old, Microsoft went public in search of investors. Gates's share of the stock was worth more than $300 million—enough to compensate for the work he did as an unpaid whiz kid.

Computer hardware cannot perform alone. To perform any task, that hardware must receive a series of instructions, called software, telling it what to do. This chapter introduces two types of software: system software and application software. They are your link to the hardware. System and application software are the keys that let you tap the power of computers and utilize it for problem solving, decision making, and increased productivity. Together, system and application software allow you to direct the hardware to perform various tasks. Knowing the functions and capabilities of system software and application software will help you select the right software to accomplish your tasks.

We will discuss the application software commonly used by many organizations and individuals. We also will look at programming languages—the software-development tools used to write both system and application software.

SYSTEM SOFTWARE

System software is the program (or programs) that directly control the computer hardware. System software does not accomplish specific applications, such as creating documents or analyzing data. System software includes *operating systems* (the most important), data-management software, computer-language-oriented software, and aids and utilities that assist users with various functions. Our look at system software focuses on operating systems, but the other types of system software will be briefly presented.

What Is an Operating System?

When computers were first invented, someone had to program every detail of hardware operation into a computer by setting switches or hard-wiring circuits. This long, tedious process had to be repeated for *each* program executed. The programmer required specific and detailed knowledge about the ways in which a particular computer operated, and the central processing unit (CPU) sat idle while the details were being programmed. Because hardware costs for the early computers were so high, users wanted to increase computer efficiency. To accomplish this goal, a type of system software called an operating system was created.

An **operating system** is a core set of programs that control and supervise computer hardware and provide services to other system software, application software, programmers, and users of a computer. The purposes of an operating system are (1) to remove from the user the task of managing hardware and give this job to the more-efficient computer, and (2) to provide an interface between the hardware and a user or between the hardware and an application program.

The portion of the operating system in use resides in main memory, so the computer receives and executes the details of an operation at computer speeds. This eliminated the long delays that existed when humans had to intervene by hard wiring and setting switches. Thus, an operating system dramatically increases the efficiency of a CPU, because it automates the details of programming and removes this burden from the programmer or computer user. There is not, however, one universal operating system for all computers.

Parts of an Operating System

The programs that make up an operating system are generally divided into two types: control programs and service programs.

Control programs manage computer hardware and resources. The main program in most operating systems is the supervisor program. A **supervisor program** is a control program that is known in some operating systems as the monitor, executive, or kernel. It is responsible for controlling all other operating-system programs as well as other system and application programs. The supervisor program controls the activities of all hardware components of a computer.

Service programs are external operating-system programs that provide a service to the user or programmer. They perform routine but essential functions such as preparing a disk for use and copying files from one location to another. Service programs are included in the purchase price of an operating system. However, they must be installed separately because they are not automatically loaded when the operating system is loaded.

Operating System Capabilities

An operating system might incorporate several basic processing capacities, including single-user processing, multiuser processing, single tasking, context switching, multitasking, multiprocessing, multithreading, interprocessing, time sharing, virtual storage, real-time processing, and virtual-machine processing. (Don't be intimidated by all of these technical names—we explain them all in the following pages.) A particular operating system may incorporate one or more of these capabilities.

Single-User Processing. An operating system with **single-user processing** allows only one user at a time to access a computer. Most operating systems used on microcomputers, such as DOS, are single-user operating systems.

Multiuser Processing. An operating system with **multiuser processing** allows two or more users to access a computer at the same time. The actual number of users depends on the hardware and the operating system design. Large computers have much greater computing capacity than can be used by one user, so they commonly use operating systems with multiuser capabilities. Some operating systems used on microcomputers, such as Unix, are also capable of multiuser support.

Single Tasking. An operating system with the capability of **single tasking** allows one program to execute at a time, and that program must finish executing completely before the next program can begin. This characteristic is typical of many microcomputer operating systems. For example, MS-DOS by Microsoft is a single-tasking operating system for IBM-

---

Operating System Parts

- Control programs
- Service programs

Operating System Capabilities

- Single-user processing
- Multiuser processing
- Single tasking
- Context switching
- Multitasking
- Multiprocessing
- Multithreading
- Interprocessing
- Time sharing
- Virtual storage
- Real time processing
- Virtual-machine (VM) processing

compatible microcomputers. The goal of this type of operating system is maximum ease of use and minimum professional support.

Context Switching. Slightly more sophisticated is the capability called **context switching** which allows several programs to reside in memory but only one to be active at a time. The active program is said to be in the *foreground*. The other programs in memory are not active and are said to be in the *background*. However, instead of having to quit a program, erase it from memory, and then load another, you can simply switch it to the background with a few keystrokes and bring another program into the foreground to receive attention from the CPU. You don't have to quit a program to place it in the background. You can simply suspend its operation until you switch it back to the foreground to receive attention from the CPU again.

Multitasking. An operating system with the capability of **multitasking,** also called multiprogramming, allows a single CPU to appear to execute more than one program at a time. The CPU switches its attention between two or more programs in main memory as it receives requests for processing from one program and then another. This switching happens so quickly that the programs appear to be executing simultaneously. Another term for this method is "executing concurrently." Multitasking can increase the overall performance of a CPU because the CPU can devote its time to processing instructions from one program while another goes through input/output operations. This capability can be found on a variety of operating systems for large computers and microcomputers.

Advances in microcomputer hardware and this operating system capability allow for what some call "true multitasking," wherein several programs run simultaneously (concurrently), but independently of each other. For example, software can electronically divide the Intel 80386 microprocessor to emulate or behave like up to four Intel 8086 microprocessors working simultaneously. These reside in random-access memory (RAM) and work independently of each other. Each can be dedicated to truly execute a single program simultaneously. In effect, what you have is a simple multiprocessing environment even though the computer contains only one physical CPU.

Multiprocessing. An operating system with the capability of **multiprocessing** (also called parallel processing) allows the simultaneous, or parallel, execution of programs by a computer that has two or more CPUs. Each CPU can be dedicated to one program, or each CPU can be dedicated to specific functions and then used by all programs. Many computers, such as mainframes and supercomputers, have more than one CPU and use multiprocessing operating systems.

Multithreading. An operating system with the capability of **multithreading** can support several simultaneous functions with the same application. For example, with only one copy of a database management system in memory, one database file can be sorted while data are simultaneously entered into another database file.

Interprocessing. An operating system with the capability of **interprocessing,** also called dynamic linking, allows any change made in one application to be automatically reflected in any related, linked application. For example, suppose that you incorporate a financial statement created in your spreadsheet program into a word-processing document and you have defined these two applications as linked applications. If you make a change in the financial statement, that change is automatically reflected in the word-processing document without your loading the document and making the change manually.

Time Sharing. An operating system with the capability of **time sharing** allows multiple users to access a single computer. This capability is typically found on large computer operating systems where many users need access at the same time. The attention of the CPU is shifted among the users on a timed basis that is controlled by the operating system. As long as the computer does not have more users than the operating system can handle, it appears that each user has uninterrupted access to the CPU. However, if the number of users exceeds the capability of the operating system, noticeable delays in processing result. TSO is a time-sharing operating system used on many mainframes.

Virtual Storage. An operating system with the capability of **virtual storage,** also called virtual memory, allows you to use a secondary-storage device as an extension of main memory. A problem experienced by some computer users is insufficient main memory to contain an entire program and its data. This is common on large computers where a number of users are vying for the available main memory. A virtual-storage operating system can resolve this problem because the entire program and data do not have to reside in main memory. Portions of a program and its data can be rapidly swapped between a secondary-storage device and main memory as needed, allowing the computer to function as if the entire program and its data were in main memory. With a virtual-storage operating system, users need not worry about how much main memory is available.

Real-time Processing. An operating system with **real-time processing** allows a computer to control or to monitor the task performance of other machines and people by responding to input data in a specified amount of time. To control processes, immediate response is usually necessary; to simply monitor processes, periodic response is generally adequate. Real-time operating systems generally have fewer functions than more general-purpose operating systems. Real-time systems offer only the services required to respond to a set of monitored events within certain set periods. Often, real-time operating systems are written specifically for an intended application. For example, in a large computer, a real-time system might be used for monitoring the position of a rocket. On a microcomputer, it might be used to monitor the vital signs of a heart transplant patient. With real-time operating systems, CPU efficiency is often sacrificed in favor of quicker response time.

Virtual-Machine (VM) Processing. An operating system with virtual-machine processing is very powerful. **Virtual-machine (VM) processing** creates the illusion that there is more than one physical machine when in fact there is only one. Such programming allows several users of a computer to operate as if each had the only terminal attached to the computer. Thus, users feel as if each is on a dedicated computer and has sole use of the CPU and input and output devices.

When a VM operating system is loaded, each user chooses the operating system that is compatible with his or her intended application. Another operating system appears as just another application program to the VM operating system. Thus, the VM operating system gives users flexibility and allows them to choose operating systems that best suit their needs. A virtual-machine operating system is typically used on supercomputers and mainframes.

Focus on Microcomputer Operating Systems

In your career, you probably will be working directly with microcomputers rather than large computers. You often will hear the term *disk operating system* when dealing with microcomputers. A **disk operating system (DOS)** is an operating system that allows and manages the use of disk drives for storing and accessing data and programs.

The User Interface. The operating system provides a set of programs that are used to direct the computer to perform the desired tasks. Each operating system also has a **user interface,** which is the portion of a program that users interact with—entering commands to direct the operating system and viewing the results of those commands. User interfaces can take two forms: text-based interfaces and graphics-based interfaces. **Text-based user interfaces** require a user to type in the desired commands at a command line. **Graphics-based user interfaces** operate in a graphics mode. A graphics-based user interface typically includes the following parts:

- ☐ Pointing device, typically a mouse.
- ☐ On-screen pull-down menus that can appear or disappear under the control of the pointing device.
- ☐ Windows that graphically display what the computer is doing.
- ☐ Icons, which are graphical images that represent certain items, such as files and directories.
- ☐ Other graphic devices that let you tell the computer what to do and how to do it—for example, dialog boxes and buttons (see Chapter 7).

Graphics-based user interfaces can dramatically improve the ease of use of an operating system and have helped in the design of user interfaces with greater human orientation. Human-oriented user interfaces are designed to respond to the needs of users rather than to the specifics of a computer.

An operating system's user interface equips application software developers with standardized names, functions, and icons. By using these elements, developers can create application programs that have consistent interfaces. Consistent interfaces mean that programs are easier to use and take less time to learn. For example, the command you give to print with one application will be the same for all other applications, if all are based on the user interface supplied by the operating system.

Operating Environments. An **operating environment** is software that can enhance the functions of an operating system and improve its user interface. Operating environments often use windows to increase the flexibility of a program. A **window** is a separate area or box on the screen that encloses independent applications. With windows, several applications can be displayed on the screen concurrently and data can be transferred among them.

The most common disk operating systems used on microcomputers include DOS (PC-DOS for use on IBM microcomputers and MS-DOS for use on IBM-compatible microcomputers), OS/2, the Apple Macintosh operating system, and various versions of the Unix operating system. We describe these on the following pages.

DOS. DOS originated as an operating system called 86–DOS. This operating system was designed in 1979 to take advantage of Intel's 16-bit 8086 microprocessor. Shortly after its development, Microsoft Corporation acquired the rights to it. Microsoft then struck a deal with IBM to help develop and use the operating system on the IBM PC, which was introduced in 1981. IBM called the operating system PC-DOS. Because of the success of the IBM PC, many other vendors began marketing compatible computers. Microsoft supplied the generic version of this operating system to the manufacturers of compatibles and called it MS-DOS (Microsoft–Disk Operating System).

DOS was designed as a single-user, single-tasking operating system. This design means that the computer can accommodate only one user and one application program at a time. DOS uses a text-based, command-line-oriented user interface. This means that in order to direct the operating system to perform a function, a user must type a command at the command line to enter it into the computer. Figure 4–1 shows a DOS command line and the command used to list the files from a disk. The newest version, DOS 4.0, is still command-line based, but it includes a menu-based option for selecting commands.

DOS can be used on computers built around the Intel 8088, 8086, 80286, 80386, and 80486 microprocessors. However, it cannot take full advantage of the 80286, 80386, and 80486 microprocessors, because it was developed strictly as an 8088/8086 operating system. The limitations of DOS include its inability to effectively use memory larger than 640 kilobytes, lack of support for multitasking, and a weak file-management system. In addition, DOS is not very easy to use. There are, however, three

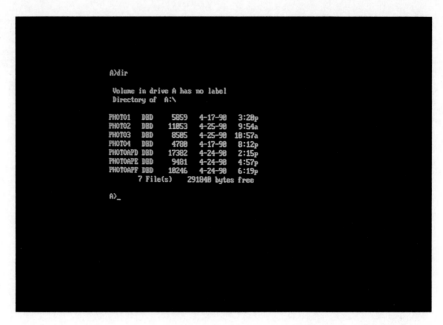

```
A>dir

Volume in drive A has no label
Directory of  A:\

PHOTO1   DBD     5859   4-17-90   3:20p
PHOTO2   DBD    11053   4-25-90   9:54a
PHOTO3   DBD     8505   4-25-90  10:57a
PHOTO4   DBD     4780   4-17-90   8:12p
PHOTOAPD DBD    17382   4-24-90   2:15p
PHOTOAPE DBD     9481   4-24-90   4:57p
PHOTOAPF DBD    10246   4-24-90   6:19p
        7 File(s)   291040 bytes free

A>_
```

ways of getting around the limitations of DOS. DOS extenders, DOS enhancers, and DOS replacements are available to increase the power of DOS and make it easier to use.

DOS extenders, such as Phar Lap's 386/DOS Extender or Qualitas's 386−to−the−Max, allow a computer to access more than 640 kilobytes of main memory without substantially changing the way in which DOS operates. This extension allows programs that require more than 640 kilobytes of main memory to run under DOS.

DOS enhancers are operating environments that utilize the DOS kernel but add functions and improve the ease of use. Support for large amounts of main memory and multitasking are common added functions. The operating environment may supply a user interface that is either text-based or graphics-based. DESQview, from Quarterdeck Office Systems, is a popular text-based operating environment for DOS. Microsoft Windows, Tandy's DeskMate, and Digital Research's GEM Desktop are popular graphics-based operating environments. Microsoft Windows is the most popular operating environment for DOS (Figure 4−2).

DOS replacements are operating systems that are compatible with DOS but take better advantage of the 80286, 80386 and 80486 chip capabilities. Examples include Digital Research's Concurrent DOS 386 and Software Link's PC−MOS/386. Among other things, these operating systems add multitasking and multiuser support.

Currently, DOS is the most popular operating system in use on microcomputers. Although not officially declared a standard, it has become what is known as a **de facto standard;** that is, DOS is recognized as the most popular and widely used operating system. Vendors generally recognize the popularity of DOS and most new software is developed to run on it. DOS is likely to stay around through the 1990s because a large amount

FIGURE 4–2

Microsoft's Windows is a graphics-based operating environment for DOS. (Photo by Jo Hall/Macmillan)

of application software is available for it and because 15 to 20 percent of the computers purchased by Fortune 500 companies are DOS-dependent 8086 and 8088 computers.

OS/2. OS/2 is an operating system developed by IBM and Microsoft, released in 1988 to take advantage of the 80286 and 80386 microprocessors. It is a single-user, multitasking operating system. OS/2 requires at least an 80286 microprocessor and needs much more memory than DOS.

The improvements of OS/2 over DOS include multitasking capability, support for larger main memory, and a more sophisticated file-management system. To take full advantage of many capabilities of OS/2 and the new microprocessors, DOS programs must be rewritten specifically for OS/2. However, DOS programs can be run as is in OS/2. Like DOS, OS/2 uses a command-line-oriented user interface, but a graphics-based user interface is available in an operating environment called the Presentation Manager (Figure 4–3). Presentation Manager was developed by IBM and Microsoft and closely resembles the Microsoft Windows operating environment for DOS.

Although growing in popularity, OS/2 has available less application software that specifically takes advantage of its capabilities than does DOS. However, the application base for OS/2 is growing. As this base grows and the operating system matures, OS/2 is expected to become the most popular operating system for IBM and compatible computers.

Macintosh Operating System. The Apple Macintosh operating system, which is called the System, made its debut with the introduction of the first Macintosh in 1984. Much of this operating system is rooted in the Xerox 8010 Star Information System developed at Xerox's Palo Alto Research

Microcomputer Operating Systems

- DOS
  □ Single user
  □ Single tasking
- OS/2
  □ Single user
  □ Multitasking
- Macintosh Operating System
  □ Single user
  □ Multitasking
- Unix
  □ Multiuser
  □ Multitasking

FIGURE 4–3
Presentation Manager is a
graphics-based operating environment for OS/2. (Courtesy of
Microsoft Corp.)

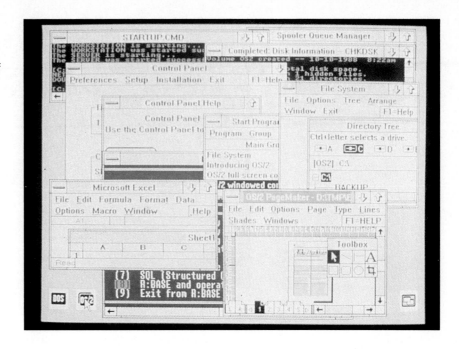

Center in the 1970s. Many of the well-known user-friendly features of the Macintosh were borrowed from the Xerox computer.

The Apple Macintosh operating system has little in common with DOS or OS/2 because it is designed for a different series of microprocessors, the Motorola 68000 family. Early versions for the 68000 microprocessor were single-user and single-tasking. Current versions for the Motorola 68030 include support for multitasking.

The operating environment for the Apple Macintosh operating system, called the Finder, is a standard part of the Macintosh computer and has a graphics-based user interface (Figure 4–4). This interface was designed with the idea that computers should adapt to users, rather than users adapting to computers. The Apple Macintosh initially found a niche in business for such graphics applications as desktop publishing, but it has been slowly establishing itself in more traditional business applications since the late 1980s.

Unix. The Unix operating system is a multiuser, multitasking operating system developed at AT&T's Bell Labs in the late 1960s. In the 1970s, Unix was distributed almost exclusively to colleges and universities through donations because, at the time, government regulation prohibited AT&T from entering the commercial-computer business. Unix was originally designed to run on minicomputers made by DEC. Subsequently, it was rewritten primarily in the C programming language, which allowed it to be easily moved to any size of computer that could run C, supercomputer to microcomputer. Unix was not made available for microcomputers until 1980.

FIGURE 4–4
Finder, the Apple Macintosh's
graphics-based operating environment, is a standard part of
the computer. (Photo by Jo Hall/
Macmillan)

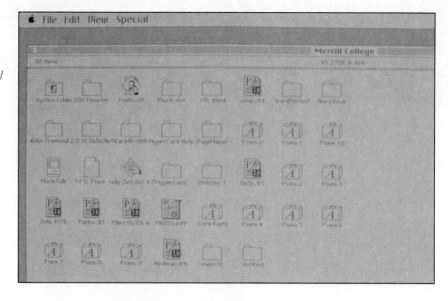

Unix supports multiple users, allowing each to run several concurrent tasks. It is well suited for use by software developers because it contains a large number of ready-made, built-in utilities that make application software development easier. However, novice users have found Unix difficult to work with because of its structure, including its large volume of commands. Further, several competing versions are available, and no version is fully compatible with the others. This lack of a standard version causes confusion.

AT&T Unix System V is the major version used by many large computers. Xenix, Microsoft's version of Unix for IBM and compatible 80286 and 80386 microcomputers, is based on System V. A/UX is a version of Unix for the Macintosh. Various operating environments try to make Unix easier to work with; two popular ones are the graphics-based OSF/Motif and SUN/OpenLook. The industry is trying to combine these and the many other Unix variants into one standard operating system.

Unix has been used on minicomputers by colleges and universities across the country since early 1970. It has been popular with scientists and engineers because of its capabilities, but it hasn't been used much in business because of the difficulties in learning and using it. In the past few years, IBM, Apple, Microsoft, AT&T, and others have shown increased interest in Unix as a microcomputer operating system. Development of a standard Unix operating system and operating environment for microcomputers may see Unix play a bigger part in business in the 1990s.

Other Types of System Software

Although operating systems are the most essential type of system software, there are other types:

☐ Data-management software includes database and file-management programs that manage data for an operating system. It also includes data-center management programs that control program execution, monitor system usage, track system resources and utilization, and bill users accordingly.

☐ System software associated with programming languages includes language translators such as assemblers, interpreters, and compilers. It also includes program generators (programs that automatically generate program code), debugging and testing programs, and various other programming utilities.

☐ Utilities and aids are programs that users can purchase as separate products to perform a wide range of functions. This software includes such products as data conversion programs that convert data from one format to another, data recovery programs which restore data that has been damaged or accidentally erased, librarians that are used to log and track the location of disk or tape program files, security and auditing programs, and merge and sort programs, to name a few.

APPLICATION SOFTWARE

The key to making a computer useful is to combine it with software for a particular application. An "application" is any job or task you want to accomplish through a computer. **Application software** includes programs that help perform a specific task. For example, application software enables you to write a letter or create a graph. It helps you work faster, more efficiently, and thus more productively than would manual performance. Application software creates a communication bridge whereby you can tell system software how to direct the hardware to perform desired functions. Figure 4–5 shows the relationships among system software, application software, hardware, and the user.

Application software comes in varying levels of sophistication and complexity. Demand for human-oriented interfaces (designed for the way humans work best rather than for how computers work best) has made software developers more sensitive to the needs of novices and nontechnical users. The term *user friendly* refers to software interfaces that are easy to learn and use. However, users vary in skill, sophistication, and need, and

FIGURE 4–5
The relationships among system software, application software, hardware, and a user.

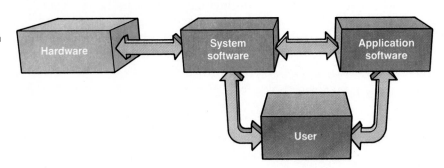

**THE WANG FREESTYLE
SYSTEM**

User interfaces that work the ways that humans do are beginning to show up on application software. Wang's Freestyle is a DOS application that automates handwritten notes, marked-up documents, telephone messages, and spoken discussions. The application uses a combination of hardware and software to accomplish its tasks.

Freestyle's user interface displays a desk top containing icons that represent typical office equipment, such as an "in" box, a trash can, a printer, a fax machine, a copy machine, pads of paper, folders, a file cabinet, a stapler, and a staple remover. Users can manipulate all of these icons by using a tablet and pen rather than a mouse as in other applications. You can set up the desk top by selecting icons from an icon catalog and placing them where you want. Freestyle uses a page as the basic system object. You create a page by performing a DOS screen capture, receiving a fax transmission, scanning an image with a scanner, or selecting a blank or lined page from on-screen pads.

When you select a page Freestyle enlarges that page to full size on the Annotator screen. This screen allows you to annotate the page. You use a keyboard to make typewritten additions to the page. A tablet and pen allow you to write comments or make sketches on the page. If you don't like what you just wrote, you simply turn the pen around and erase it.

There is also a telephonelike device and a tape recorder console to add voice annotation to a page. You can synchronize voice annotation and free-form writing with the pen. For example, if you sent a page to another user, that person might hear, "Ted, please verify this number," while a circle was drawn around the number in question. The recipient of the message could then make any necessary changes and voice annotate the document before sending it back.

You can store pages in folders, staple them together to form documents, print them, fax them, or send them as mail over a network. Performing these operations is as easy as dragging the page to the appropriate icon. For example, to print a page, you select the desired page icon with the pen and tablet and drag it to the printer icon. To copy a page, you simply drag it to the copier-machine icon. The easy manipulation of the icons and the ability to use free-form writing and voice annotation gives a glimpse of where user interfaces for application software are headed. Still, Freestyle has limited text-entry capabilities and is not a full-fledged word processor. Thus, the text of a page is better created through text entry or word processing than through Freestyle.

software that is easy for a novice may be so simple that it's not useful for a more experienced user.

Yet, some powerful and complex programs take human factors into consideration. Apple Macintosh applications are known for this. The Macintosh has made easier the learning of applications by supplying a consistent graphics-based user interface. Some other application software programs provide interfaces that can be changed to suit the needs of different users. Regardless of a user's technical level, application software probably is available to match those needs and abilities. Highlight 4–1 looks at an application program called Wang Freestyle that takes the user interface one step further than other programs.

Types of Application Software

Application software can be grouped into two broad categories: generalized and specialized. **Generalized application software** can be applied to a wide variety of tasks and is found on both large computers and microcomputers. It includes such applications as electronic spreadsheets, data managers, word processors, graphics, and communications—the five generalized application software programs most used by business and home users of microcomputers. For example, a generalized spreadsheet program can create one spreadsheet to calculate a payroll and another to perform cost analysis. Chapters 7 through 12 focus on generalized application software.

Specialized application software performs a specific task and cannot be changed or programmed to perform a different task. For example, a payroll application program is designed to be used exclusively for payroll functions. It cannot be programmed to do other tasks, such as cost analysis. Popular specialized application programs found on large computers and microcomputers include business-oriented programs, vertical-market programs, engineering and scientific programs, educational programs, and entertainment programs:

☐ Business-oriented application software includes accounting programs (payroll, accounts receivable, accounts payable, general ledger, budgeting, and financial planning, all of which are used in almost every kind of business), banking software, financial software, and investment software.

☐ Vertical-market application software handles the unique needs of specific markets (businesses), such as medicine and health services, legal services, the automotive industry, and property management. Highlight 4–2 examines an application software program being used in courtrooms.

☐ Engineering and scientific application software includes such programs as computer-aided design (CAD, which automates mechanical drawing), chemical engineering, scientific calculations, and structural analysis.

☐ Educational application software includes computer-assisted instruction (CAI), which guides an individual through a course of

COMPUTERS IN THE COURTROOM

Every day, it seems, someone has thought of a new application software program. One application software program is computer-aided transcription (CAT) for court stenographers. A common delay in court is due to the stenographer's having to search through notes for specific testimony. Usually, there are also substantial delays in obtaining typed transcripts of the stenographer's notes.

With CAT, a stenographer records the testimony on a 22-button stenotype machine. However, the stenotype machine is wired directly to a computer that transcribes the stenographic shorthand into English and sends the output almost immediately to monitors on the judge's bench and the lawyers' tables. The judge and attorneys can easily scroll through the transcript displayed on the monitors to review earlier testimony. Edited and typed transcripts are available in a matter of hours. CAT also reduces the waste of time and redundancy of having a stenographer dictate notes to a typist.

study; administration; library services; student services; typing tutors; and gradebook programs to assist instructors in the process of recording student scores.

☐ Entertainment application software is plentiful, including games, flight simulators, and music programs.

Sources of Application Software

Application software is created and acquired in three main ways: (1) prewritten by an outside source for public sale, (2) custom-developed in-house, and (3) custom-developed by an outside source. Generally, prewritten software is available for purchase through a vendor, a distributor such as a computer store, or the author. The use of prewritten application software has several advantages:

1. It can be quickly installed, so it is ready for immediate use.
2. It is usually less expensive than application software produced in-house.
3. It is available for almost any task required.
4. It has already been tested.
5. Some can be quickly customized or modified to meet a user's specialized requirements.

The primary disadvantage of prewritten application software is that it may not precisely fit the special needs of a user.

Instead of purchasing prewritten application software, programmers or skilled users sometimes write their own. In-house custom-developed application software is designed and coded by skilled personnel within a firm. The main advantage of in-house software is that it can be tailored to the user's exact specifications. An additional advantage is that the creator may, in turn, be able to market and sell the software to others. A major disadvantage is cost; skilled programmers are expensive, and determining precise specifications can be time-consuming and costly.

If personnel, expertise, time, or money are not available for in-house custom development, another option is to contract with a person or group that specializes in developing software. Many such firms employ skilled programmers to develop customized software for the specialized needs of clients.

Users must balance the need for customized software against the cost. Often, rather than spending the time or money in-house or out-of-house for development of customized software, businesses decide to compromise and select prewritten application software that comes close but doesn't precisely meet the need.

PROGRAMMING LANGUAGES—SOFTWARE DEVELOPMENT TOOLS

Those who choose to develop their own software are faced with deciding which programming language to use. The information here will help you become familiar with several common programming languages.

To take advantage of the capabilities of computer hardware, you need some means of communicating to the computer exactly what needs to be done. A computer must be instructed through each detail of an operation. For example, to print a document, you must give the computer detailed instructions on how to access the file, set up the printer, send data to the printer, and so on. A **programming language** is a set of written symbols that instruct computer hardware to perform specified operations. Use of these symbols is governed by a set of rules called **syntax,** the equivalent of grammatical rules in English and other languages.

BASIC INSTRUCTIONS OF A PROGRAMMING LANGUAGE

Several hundred programming languages are used for computers today. Although the specifics of each language vary, certain basic instructions are included in all of them:

Types of Programming Language Instructions

- Input/output
- Arithmetic
- Logic
- Control
- Data movement
- Specification

□ Input/output instructions transfer instructions and data between the CPU and input and output devices.

□ Arithmetic instructions perform mathematical operations, such as addition, subtraction, multiplication, and division.

□ Logic instructions determine comparisons, such as equal to, not equal to, less than, greater than, greater than or equal to, and less than or equal to. Logic instructions also test conditions. A condition involves testing the values or logical relationships of one or more data items. For example, in the statement "If $x > 10$, then $y = 1$, else $y = 2$," the condition being tested is $x > 10$. If x is greater than 10, then the value of y is set to 1. If x is not greater than 10, the value of y is set to 2.

□ Control instructions alter the order in which program instructions are to be executed.

□ Data movement instructions copy and move data within main memory.

□ Specification instructions specify various parameters, such as constants, the portions of memory to be used, and the file access method.

Even though every programming language is capable of these basic functions, the methods used to accomplish them vary widely.

CATEGORIES OF PROGRAMMING LANGUAGES

Of the hundreds of different programming languages available, all fit into one of five general categories: (1) machine languages, (2) assembly languages, (3) high-level languages, (4) fourth-generation languages, and (5) fifth-generation languages.

Machine Language

Machine language is a binary code made up of 1s and 0s. It is the only programming language that a computer can understand. There is not, however, a universal machine language. The arrangement of 1s and 0s to represent similar instructions, data, and memory locations differs among computers because of different hardware designs.

Machine language programs have the advantage of fast execution speeds and efficient use of main memory. However, writing machine language is a tedious, difficult, and time-consuming method of programming. As a **low-level language,** machine language requires that programmers have detailed knowledge of how computers work, because every detail of an operation must be specified. As you might imagine, it is easy to make an error but very difficult to find and remove ("debug") a machine-language program.

If machine language were the only means of programming a computer, there probably wouldn't be many programmers, and there certainly wouldn't be the vast number of application programs available for use. To make programming simpler, other easier-to-use programming languages have been developed. These languages, however, must ultimately be translated into machine language before a computer can understand and use them.

Assembly Language

The next higher level of programming language is **assembly language**. It is also classified as a low-level language because detailed knowledge of hardware specifics is still required. An assembly language uses mnemonics in place of 1s and 0s to represent the instructions (Figure 4–6). A **mnemonic** is an alphabetical abbreviation used as a memory aid. For example, instead of using a combination of 1s and 0s to represent an addition operation, a programmer might use the mnemonic *AD*.

Categories of Programming Languages

- Machine — _Low level_
- Assembly
- High-level
- Fourth-generation
- Fifth-generation (natural languages)

FIGURE 4–6

Assembler code (mnemonics)	Machine-language instructions

```
Assembler code (mnemonics)

sseg                   segment stack
                       db 256  dup (?)
sseg                   ends
dseg                   segment
data                   db "2 x 4 =  "

dseg          ends
cseg                   segment
assume     cs:cseg,ds:dseg,ss:sseg,es:nothing
start         proc far
                       push ds
                       mov ax,0
                       push ax
                       call main
start         endp

main                   proc near
                       cld
                       mov ax, dseg
                       mov ds, ax
                       mov ax, 0b000h
                       mov es, ax
                       mov dx, 0
                       mov bx, 0
                       lea si, data
                       mov di, 32848
                       mov al, 02h
                       mov bl, 04h
                       mul bl
                       or al, 30h
                       mov al, data+9
   msgsb:     mov cx,9
   lbl:                movsb
                       inc di
                       mov al, 135
                       mov [di], al
                       loop lbl
main                   endp
cseg                   ends
                       endstart
```

```
Machine-language instructions

0100
110010  100000  1111000  100000  110100  100000
111101  100000  100000
11110
10111000
1010000
11101000
11111100
10111000
10001110  11011000
10111000
10001110  11000000
10111010
10111011
10001101  110110
10111111
10110000  00000010
10110011  00000100
11110110  11100011
00001100  110000
10100000
10111001
10100100
1000111
10110000  10000111
10001000  00000101
11100010  1111000
```

FIGURE 4–6
This is a comparison of assembler codes (mnemonics) and machine-language instructions for a program that computes and prints out the result of 2 × 4.

Assembly languages use *symbolic addressing* capabilities that simplify the programming process so that a programmer need not know or remember the exact storage locations of instructions or data. Symbolic addressing is the expression of an address (location) in terms of symbols chosen by a programmer rather than an absolute numerical location. Instead of assigning and remembering a number that identifies the address of a piece of data, a programmer can assign data to a symbolic name, such as TOTAL. The assembly language then automatically assigns an address when it encounters that symbolic name and remembers all of the assigned addresses.

Before a computer can use an assembly language, it must translate it into a machine language. The computer makes this conversion with a **language-translator program,** a system program that converts programming language code into machine language. The language-translator program used to translate assembly language code into machine language is called an **assembler.**

Assembly languages provide easier and more efficient ways to program than machine languages, but they still maintain control over the internal functions of a computer at the most basic level. In addition, assembly languages produce programs that are efficient, use less storage, and execute much faster than programs using high-level languages. However, assembly languages are still machine oriented and require thorough knowledge of computer hardware. Compared with high-level languages, they are tedious and prone to errors.

High-Level Language

A **high-level language** is one with instructions that closely resemble human language and mathematical notation. High-level languages do not require that a programmer have detailed knowledge about the internal operations of a computer. Because they closely resemble human language, high-level languages are much easier to learn and use than machine or assembly languages. Typically, less time and effort are required for high-level programming because errors are easier to avoid and correct.

Many high-level languages are also designed to be machine-independent. Thus, they can be transported from computer to computer and executed with few changes. As a result, high-level languages are used more often than machine or assembly languages. The American National Standards Institute (ANSI) has developed standards to help make high-level languages more machine-independent.

Sometimes, portions of a program may require more speed or efficiency than can be achieved with the high-level programming language being used. Most high-level languages allow the use of assembly language programs to supply a boost in capabilities.

A high-level language must also be translated into a machine language before a computer can use it. Two different language-translator programs are used to translate high-level languages: compilers and interpreters.

A **compiler** translates a whole program, called the source code, into machine language all at one time before the program is executed. Once converted, the program is stored in machine-readable form, called the object code. The object code can be immediately executed anytime thereafter. The source code remains intact after the conversion and can be updated and changed as required and then recompiled into the object code.

An **interpreter** translates a program into machine language one line at a time, executing each line of the program after it is translated. With most interpreters, the machine-readable form is not stored in main memory or on a secondary storage medium. Therefore, the program must be interpreted each time it is executed.

Fourth-Generation Language

The different categories of languages are sometimes labeled by generations—from lowest to highest. Machine languages are considered the first generation; assembly languages, the second generation; and high-

---

Types of Language-Translator Programs

- Assemblers
- Compilers
- Interpreters

level languages, the third generation. A **fourth-generation language** is one of a variety of programming languages that require much less effort in creating programs than high-level languages. The objectives of a fourth-generation language include (1) increasing the speed of program development, (2) minimizing end-user effort to obtain information from a computer, (3) decreasing the skill level required of end users (so they can concentrate on an application rather than on the intricacies of coding and thus solve their own problems without the aid of a professional programmer), and (4) minimizing maintenance by reducing errors and making programs easy to change.

The sophistication of fourth-generation languages varies widely. They usually are used in conjunction with a database. Fourth-generation languages include database query languages, report generators, and application generators.

A **database query language** permits user formulation of inquiries that relate to records from one or more files. The appropriate records are then printed or displayed in a suitable format. Examples include IBM's SQL and Artificial Intelligence's INTELLECT.

A **report generator** allows data from a database to be extracted and formatted into reports. It also allows substantial arithmetic and logic operations to be performed on data before they are displayed or printed. NOMAD by NCSS and GIS by IBM are examples of report generators.

An **application generator** allows data entry and permits a user to specify how to update a database, what calculations or logic operations to perform, and what output to create. This language allows a user to build an entire application. Examples include FOCUS by Information Builders and MANTIS by Cincom Systems.

Fifth-Generation Language

Many individuals consider natural languages to be **fifth-generation languages**. **Natural languages** are similar to query languages, but they eliminate the need for a user or programmer to learn and use a specific vocabulary, grammar, or syntax. A natural language closely resembles normal human speech. For example, if a user enters the command "Get me sales figures for January 1992," a computer understanding natural language could interpret this and supply the desired information.

Because of the complexity involved in interpreting a command entered in a human-speech format, natural languages require very powerful hardware and sophisticated software. Although advances in hardware have produced computers powerful enough, a deficit exists in the development of programming languages and techniques.

PROCEDURAL VERSUS NONPROCEDURAL LANGUAGES

Programming languages are classified into two different types, procedural and nonprocedural:

☐ **Procedural languages** specify *how* something is accomplished. Common procedural languages include BASIC, Pascal, C, Ada, COBOL, and FORTRAN.

☐ **Nonprocedural languages** specify *what* is accomplished without going into the details of how. Database query languages and report generators are examples of nonprocedural languages.

The difference between procedural and nonprocedural languages can be illustrated with the analogy of giving directions to a taxi driver. Using a procedural language, the directions might go as follows: "Drive 600 yards forward. Turn right. Drive 350 yards forward. Turn left. Drive 500 yards forward. Stop." Using a nonprocedural language, you would simply tell the driver what you want: "Take me to the Fairview Hotel."

OBJECT-ORIENTED PROGRAMMING LANGUAGES

A traditional programming language treats the data and procedures in a program as separate entities. A programmer is responsible for applying active procedures (programming instructions) to passive data structures (such as files). However, an **object-oriented programming language (OOPL)** treats a program as a series of objects and messages. An **object** is a combination of data and procedures stored together as a reusable unit. **Messages** are procedures sent between objects.

OOPLs provide ways of designing and programming software that are more understandable to users. *Object-oriented* implies that things are looked at as people normally see them. For example, users perceive the world around them as a variety of objects—trees, houses, people, and so on. In everyday life, this means that people look at a tree and see a tree, not a collection of atoms. In programming, it means that applications are broken down in ways that seem normal to users. Traditional programming languages would deal with the atoms, OOPLs with the tree.

The combining of data and procedures into a reusable structure is called **encapsulation,** and it is one of the basic principles of an OOPL. One of the most powerful features of an OOPL is **inheritance**. This is the ability of the programming language itself to define a new object or class of objects that is just like an old object or class of objects with a few minor differences. This ability helps increase code sharing. Inheritance is the major feature distinguishing OOPLs from other programming languages.

The program code of an application written in an OOPL is much easier to comprehend by nonprogrammers and by programmers who were not involved with coding the original program than is the program code of an application written using traditional programming procedures and control structures. It is useful to develop generic objects that can easily be used in other applications. That is precisely one of the points of an OOPL. Object-orientation encourages:

☐ Code reuse, rather than reinvention, to speed the development and maintenance of large applications.
☐ Development of generic functions to allow easy assembly of applications from prefabricated parts.
☐ Development of programs that users can readily comprehend and share with others.

Smalltalk, Objective-C, and C++ are examples of object-oriented programming languages.

MAJOR HIGH-LEVEL LANGUAGES

Major high-level languages include FORTRAN, COBOL, BASIC, PL/1, Pascal, Modula-2, RPG, C, Ada, LISP, Prolog, and Logo. They are described on the following pages.

FORTRAN

FORTRAN (FORmula TRANslator) was introduced in 1957 and is the oldest high-level programming language. It was designed primarily for use by scientists, engineers, and mathematicians in solving mathematical problems. However, most early business applications were written in FORTRAN and later converted to COBOL, and it is not uncommon even today to find business application programs written in FORTRAN. FORTRAN is well suited to complex numerical calculations. However, because it lacks strength for some input/output and nonnumeric operations, FORTRAN is not widely used for manipulation of large data files. Figure 4–7 gives a brief example of a FORTRAN program.

COBOL

COBOL (COmmon Business-Oriented Language) is a widely used programming language for business data processing. It was developed in the late 1950s by the Conference on Data Systems Languages (CODASYL)

FIGURE 4–7
A FORTRAN program that computes the sum and average of ten numbers.

```
C    COMPUTE THE SUM AND AVERAGE OF 10 NUMBERS
C
          REAL NUM, SUM, AVG
          INTEGER TOTNUM, COUNTR
C
          SUM = 0.0
C    INITIALIZE LOOP CONTROL VARIABLE
          COUNTR = 0
          TOTNUM = 10
C
C    LOOP TO READ DATA AND ACCUMULATE SUM
    20 IF (COUNTR .GE. TOTNUM) GO TO 30
          READ, NUM
          SUM = SUM + NUM
C    UPDATE LOOP CONTROL VARIABLE
          COUNTR = COUNTR + 1
          GO TO 20
C    END OF LOOP - COMPUTE AVERAGE
    30 AVG = SUM / TOTNUM
C    PRINT RESULTS
          PRINT, SUM
          PRINT, AVG
          STOP
          END
```

committee, which consisted of manufacturers, users, and government agencies. It was specifically designed to manipulate the large data files typically encountered in business.

COBOL uses descriptive Englishlike statements, a feature which makes the logic of the program easy to understand and follow. It also makes COBOL programs self-documenting. A COBOL program is generally much longer than one for other high-level languages that accomplish the same task because COBOL is designed to make future program changes more efficient. The language is deliberately redundant to make program maintenance easier. This approach is important because an organization typically spends 85 percent of its business programming dollars on maintenance programming.

FIGURE 4–8
A COBOL program that computes the sum and average of ten numbers. (The program continues on the next page.)

```
IDENTIFICATION DIVISION.
PROGRAM-ID.        AVERAGES.
AUTHOR.            DEB KNUDSEN.
DATE-COMPILED.
ENVIRONMENT DIVISION.
CONFIGURATION SECTION.
    SOURCE-COMPUTER. HP-3000.
    OBJECT-COMPUTER. HP-3000.
INPUT-OUTPUT SECTION.
FILE-CONTROL.
    SELECT NUMBER-FILE ASSIGN TO "NUMFILE".
    SELECT REPORT-FILE ASSIGN TO "PRINT,UR,A,LP(CCTL)".
DATA DIVISION.
FILE SECTION.
FD  NUMBER-FILE
    LABEL RECORDS ARE STANDARD
    DATA RECORD IS NUMBER-REC.
01  NUMBER-REC                      PIC S9(7)V99.
FD  REPORT-FILE
    LABEL RECORDS ARE STANDARD
    DATA RECORD IS REPORT-REC.
01  REPORT-REC                      PIC X(100).

WORKING-STORAGE SECTION.
01  END-OF-NUMBER-FILE-FLAG         PIC X(3) VALUE SPACES.
    88  END-OF-NUMBER-FILE                   VALUE "YES".
01  SUM-OF-NUMBERS                  PIC S9(7)V99.
01  AVERAGE-OF-NUMBERS              PIC S9(7)V99.
01  NUMBER-OF-NUMBERS               PIC 9(5).

01  WS-REPORT-REC.
    05  FILLER                      PIC X(2)   VALUE SPACES.
    05  FILLER                      PIC X(17)  VALUE
                                    "Sum of Numbers = ".
    05  WS-SUM-OF-NUMBERS           PIC Z,ZZZ,ZZZ.99-.
    05  FILLER                      PIC X(3)   VALUE SPACES.
    05  FILLER                      PIC X(15)  VALUE
                                    "# of Numbers = ".
    05  WS-NUMBER-OF-NUMBERS        PIC ZZZZ9.
    05  FILLER                      PIC X(3)   VALUE SPACES.
    05  FILLER                      PIC X(21)  VALUE
                                    "Average of Numbers = ".
    05  WS-AVERAGE-OF-NUMBERS       PIC Z,ZZZ,ZZZ.99-.
    05  FILLER                      PIC X(8)   VALUE SPACES.
```

Although other programming languages perform the same operations more efficiently, COBOL is likely to be the predominant language in business for some time to come because businesses need programs that are easy to maintain and update. In addition, the expense in time and money to convert existing programs and retrain programmers is prohibitive to many organizations. Figure 4–8 is a brief example of a COBOL program.

PL/1

PL/1, Programming Language One, was created in the early 1960s. Intended to be all things to all people, it was designed to replace FORTRAN, ALGOL, and COBOL. Users of these languages found themselves needing

FIGURE 4–8
(continued)

```
PROCEDURE DIVISION.

100-MAIN-PROGRAM.
    OPEN INPUT  NUMBER-FILE
         OUTPUT REPORT-FILE.
    MOVE SPACES TO REPORT-REC.
    MOVE ZEROS TO SUM-OF-NUMBERS.
    MOVE ZEROS TO AVERAGE-OF-NUMBERS.
    MOVE ZEROS TO NUMBER-OF-NUMBERS.

    READ NUMBER-FILE
      AT END MOVE "YES" TO END-OF-NUMBER-FILE-FLAG.

    IF END-OF-NUMBER-FILE
      NEXT SENTENCE
    ELSE
      PERFORM 200-PROCESS-NUMBER-FILE
        UNTIL END-OF-NUMBER-FILE.

    PERFORM 300-COMPUTE-AVERAGE.

    PERFORM 400-PRINT-RESULTS.

    CLOSE NUMBER-FILE
          REPORT-FILE.

    STOP RUN.

200-PROCESS-NUMBER-FILE.
    ADD 1 TO NUMBER-OF-NUMBERS.
    ADD NUMBER-REC TO SUM-OF-NUMBERS.

    READ NUMBER-FILE
        AT END MOVE "YES" TO END-OF-NUMBER-FILE-FLAG.

300-COMPUTE-AVERAGE.
    DIVIDE SUM-OF-NUMBERS BY NUMBER-OF-NUMBERS
        GIVING AVERAGE-OF-NUMBERS.

400-PRINT-RESULTS.
    MOVE SUM-OF-NUMBERS TO WS-SUM-OF-NUMBERS.
    MOVE NUMBER-OF-NUMBERS TO WS-NUMBER-OF-NUMBERS.
    MOVE AVERAGE-OF-NUMBERS TO WS-AVERAGE-OF-NUMBERS.

WRITE REPORT-REC FROM WS-REPORT-REC.
```

more than any single one of the languages could provide. They wanted a general-purpose language that allowed powerful computations and sophisticated data structures.

Although the designers of PL/1 produced a good programming language, PL/1 failed to gain a large following. One reason may be that its initial version was finished too late; the COBOL revolution had already begun. In addition, the size of the PL/1 language posed a drawback for users who needed only a fraction of its capabilities. After failing to capture the business and scientific markets, PL/1 was promoted as a systems programming language. However, it is not competitive with modern languages like C, which are specifically designed for systems programming. PL/1 is largely used in the oil industry today. Figure 4–9 is an example of a simple PL/1 program.

BASIC

BASIC (Beginner's All-Purpose Symbolic Instruction Code) was developed at Dartmouth College in the mid-1960s to provide students with an easy-to-learn, interactive language on a time-sharing computer system. In an interactive language, each statement is translated into machine language and executed as soon as it is entered into the computer. If a statement contains an error, BASIC provides an error message immediately.

BASIC was developed as a shortened and simplified version of FORTRAN. It allowed novices to learn and begin programming in a few hours. Because it is easy to learn and use, BASIC has become the most popular language for microcomputers, and it is available for most microcomputers in use today.

Many extensions to BASIC have been developed to take advantage of specific hardware. Thus, there are many different nonstandardized versions of the language. The American National Standards Institute set standards for the most essential portion of BASIC, called Minimal BASIC, in 1978. However, because Minimal BASIC and its various extensions are not well suited to structured programming methods, structured versions of BASIC,

FIGURE 4–9

A PL/1 program that computes the sum and average of ten numbers.

```
START: PROCEDURE OPTIONS (MAIN);
  DECLARE (N, K) DECIMAL FIXED (2),
          VALUE (N) DECIMAL FIXED (5,2) CONTROLLED,
          SUM        DECIMAL FIXED (6,2) INITIAL (0.0),
          AVERAGE    DECIMAL FIXED (6,3);
  GET DATA (N); ALLOCATE VALUE;
      GET LIST (VALUE);
      DO K = 1 TO N; SUM = SUM + VALUE (K); END;
      AVERAGE = ROUND(SUM/N,3); PUT DATA(N, SUM, AVERAGE);
END START;

DATA:

N=10; 1.0 2.0 3.0 4.0 5.0 6.0 7.0 8.0 9.0 10.0
```

FIGURE 4–10

A BASIC program that computes the sum and average of ten numbers.

```
10   REM COMPUTE SUM AND AVERAGE OF 10 NUMBERS
20   LET SUM = 0
30   FOR I = 1 TO 10
40      INPUT N(I)
50      LET SUM = SUM + N(I)
60   NEXT I
70   LET AVG = SUM / 10
80   PRINT "SUM = ",SUM
90   PRINT "AVERAGE = ",AVG
999 END
```

such as True BASIC, have also emerged. Figure 4–10 shows a BASIC program in the Microsoft BASIC language.

Pascal and Modula-2

Niklaus Wirth of Zurich developed **Pascal** in the late 1960s and named it after Blaise Pascal, the French mathematician and philosopher who invented the first practical mechanical adding machine. The Pascal language is suited to both scientific and file-processing applications. It was originally designed to teach the concepts of structured programming and top-down design to students. Because of Pascal's structured nature, some schools have replaced BASIC with it in introductory programming classes. Like BASIC, Pascal is not standardized and has many versions. A short Pascal program is shown in Figure 4–11.

Because Pascal was originally designed as a teaching tool, it initially lacked some features of a good application-software development tool. To add these features and correct existing problems, Wirth redesigned his creation and called it **Modula-2**. Modula-2 improves the modularity, input and output capabilities, and file-handling capabilities of the language. Figure 4–12 is a short Modula-2 program. Pascal also remains in use and has been greatly enhanced since its initial development.

FIGURE 4–11

A PASCAL program that computes the sum and average of ten numbers.

```
PROGRAM average(input, output);
{ Compute the sum and average of ten numbers }
VAR num, sum, avg : real;
    i : integer;

BEGIN
    sum:=0.0;
    FOR i := 1 TO 10 DO
    BEGIN
        read(num);
        sum:=sum + num;
    END;
    avg:=sum/10;
    writeln('Sum =',sum);
    writeln('Average =',avg);
END.
```

FIGURE 4-12

A Modula-2 program that computes the sum and average of ten numbers.

```
MODULE averageNum;
FROM InOut IMPORT WriteLn, WriteString, ReadCard;
FROM RealLnOut IMPORT WriteReal;

VAR
    i:CARDINAL;
    sum, average:REAL;
    Nmbs:Array[1..10] OF CARDINAL;

BEGIN
    WriteLn;
    WriteString("Enter number: ");
    WriteLn;
    FOR i := 1 TO 10 BY 1 DO
      ReadCard(Nmbs[i]);  (* get numbers from keyboard *)
      WriteLn;
    END;
    sum := 0.0;
    FOR i := 1 TO 10 BY 1 DO (* sum numbers *)
      sum := sum + FLOAT(Nmbs[i]);
    END;
    average := sum / 10.0;  (* calculate average *)
    WriteLn;
    WriteString("Sum = ");
    WriteReal(sum,10);
    WriteLn;
    WriteString("Average = ");
    WriteReal(average,10);
END AverageNum.
```

RPG

RPG (Report Program Generator) was developed in the mid-1960s. Because most people at that time had no programming experience, RPG was designed to be especially easy to learn and use. A programmer uses coding sheets (Figure 4-13) to specify input, output, processing operations, and file specifications. Although RPG is easy to learn, it has limited capabilities. It can be used for producing reports and processing files on tape or disk, but it is not well suited to mathematical or scientific applications.

C

The **C** programming language, developed at Bell Laboratories in the early 1970s, incorporates many advantages of both low-level and high-level languages. Like assembly language, C gives programmers extensive control over computer hardware, but because C uses Englishlike statements, which are easy to read, it is often classified as a high-level language. C also incorporates sophisticated control and data structures, which make it a powerful but concise language.

C is well suited to development of system software, which was its original purpose. The Unix operating system was developed largely with C. However, C is also becoming a popular choice for developing application programs because of its power, structured nature, and portability. (In software, portability means that a program written for one computer can be

FIGURE 4–13
RPG coding sheets (Courtesy of International Business Machines Corp.)

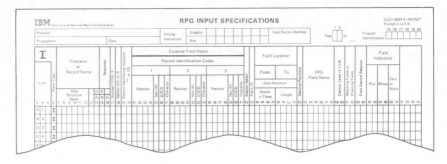

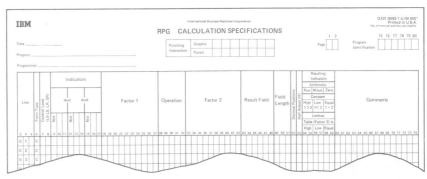

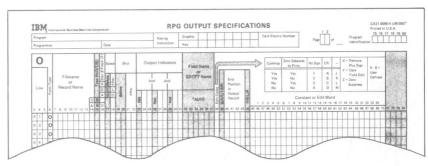

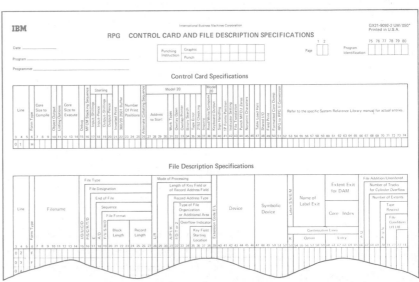

FIGURE 4–14

A C program that computes the sum and average of ten numbers.

```
#include <stdio.h>

main ()
    {
        int i, num;
        float sum;

        printf("Enter numbers \n");
        sum = 0;
        for (i = 0; i < 10; i++)
            {
                scanf("%d",&num);
                sum = sum + num;
            }
        printf("Sum = %3.1f\n",sum);
        printf("Average = %3.1f\n",sum / 10.0);
    }
```

Major High-Level Languages

- FORTRAN
- COBOL
- BASIC
- PL/1
- Pascal
- Modula-2
- RPG
- C
- Ada
- LISP
- Prolog
- Logo

used on another computer with little or no modification.) Many of today's popular applications—such as WordPerfect and Lotus 1-2-3, which were originally written in machine-specific assembly language—have been converted to C. Figure 4–14 shows a brief C program.

Ada

The **Ada** programming language was developed in the late 1970s with the support of the U.S. Department of Defense. It was named for Augusta Ada, Countess of Lovelace, who is considered by many to be the world's first programmer.

In developing Ada, the goal was to build a very powerful, complete, and efficient structured language for military applications, such as controlling weapon systems. To accomplish this, the language was designed with powerful control and data structures and with a set of commands that allowed it to control hardware devices directly. Currently, Ada is used primarily by the U.S. Department of Defense, but the powerful and efficient nature of the language suggests that it may see greater use in other applications in the future. Figure 4–15 is a brief Ada program.

Other High-Level Languages

LISP is a language used to process symbol sequences (lists) rather than numbers. It uses the same constructs to handle both instructions and data and allows each user to define new language elements. **Prolog** is another language used for symbol processing. Both LISP and Prolog are heavily used for artificial intelligence applications.

Logo is an interactive education-oriented language designed to teach inexperienced users logic and programming techniques. Logo uses a triangular object called a turtle that allows users to draw, animate, and color images very simply. It also includes list-processing capabilities.

FIGURE 4–15
An Ada program that computes
the sum and average of ten
numbers.

```
PROCEDURE average number IS
    USE simple io;
    num, sum, avg: REAL;

BEGIN
    sum := 0;
    FORiIN 1...10 LOOP
      GET(num);
      sum:=sum + num;
    END LOOP;
    avg:=sum / 10;
    PUT("Sum ="); PUT(sum);
    PUT("Average ="); PUT(avg);
END average number;
```

CHOOSING A PROGRAMMING LANGUAGE

With so many programming languages to choose from, several factors must be considered before selecting one for programmer use. First, what is the nature of the problem? Is the programming language designed for this type of problem? For example, COBOL is suited for business data processing, but it is not suited for robotics because it doesn't have the vocabulary or features to control such things as robot arm movements.

Second, what is the speed at which the program needs to execute? If the program will be used frequently and requires efficient execution, a programming language such as an assembly language or C may be necessary to reduce execution time.

Third, what is the expertise of the programming staff? Do the programmers already know the language under consideration? If not, can they learn it in the required time period, and is the additional cost for training justifiable?

Fourth, what is the portability of the language? Will the program have to run on more than one type of computer? Machine and assembly languages are machine-specific and require extensive changes or complete rewrites for new hardware. High-level languages are more portable, and they can usually be run on different computers with few or no changes.

Fifth, what is the amount of program maintenance expected? Will the program be subject to periodic updates and revisions? If so, a structured high-level language may be the best choice.

SUMMARY

System software is the program (or programs) that directly control the computer hardware, rather than performing a specific application (such as creating a document or analyzing data). The most important type of system software is the operating system, a core set of programs that controls and supervises a computer's hardware and provides services to other system software, application software, programmers, and users of a computer.

An operating system is composed of two types of programs: control programs and service programs. Control programs manage computer hardware and resources. Service programs are external operating-system programs that must be loaded separately to provide a service to the user or programmer of a computer.

Operating systems may incorporate a number of capabilities, including single-user processing, multiuser processing, single tasking, context switching, multitasking, multiprocessing, multithreading, interprocessing, time sharing, virtual storage, real-time processing, and virtual-machine processing.

A disk operating system (DOS) is an operating system that allows and manages the use of disk drives for storing and accessing data and programs. The user interface of an operating system is the portion of a program that users interact with; it can be text-based or graphics-based. An operating environment is software used to enhance the functions of an operating system and improve its user interface. Operating environments use windows to display several applications on the screen concurrently and to facilitate data transfer among them.

Popular microcomputer operating systems include MS-DOS, OS/2, the Apple Macintosh operating system, and Unix. Popular operating environments include Microsoft Windows, Tandy's DeskMate, and Digital Research's GEM Desktop for DOS; Presentation Manager for OS/2; and OSF/Motif and SUN/OpenLook for Unix. The operating environment for the Apple Macintosh operating system, called the Finder, comes as a standard part of the Macintosh computer.

Many tasks that people perform manually can be done faster and more efficiently with a computer. Application software includes programs that direct a computer to perform a specific task for the user. The two broad categories of application software are generalized and specialized.

Generalized application software can be applied to a wide variety of tasks and includes such programs as electronic spreadsheets, data managers, word processors, graphics, and communication.

Specialized application software performs a specific task and cannot be changed to perform a different task. Such software includes business-oriented, vertical market, engineering and scientific, educational, and entertainment programs.

Application software can be prewritten software, in-house custom-developed software, or outside custom-developed software.

A set of symbols, called a programming language, is used to construct the program that will instruct a computer to perform specific tasks. Each programming language has a set of rules, or syntax, for governing the use of the symbols. There are many programming languages, but each performs these basic functions: input/output, arithmetic, logic, control, data movement, and specifications. Programming languages are divided into five categories: (1) machine language, (2) assembly language, (3) high-level language, (4) fourth-generation language, and (5) fifth-generation language.

Procedural languages are those that specify *how* something is accomplished. Nonprocedural languages specify *what* is accomplished without going into the details of how. An object-oriented programming language (OOPL) treats a program as a series of objects and messages.

Common high-level languages include FORTRAN, COBOL, BASIC, Pascal, Modula-2, RPG, C, Ada, LISP, Prolog, and Logo. When choosing a programming language, one should consider the nature of the problem; the speed at which the program needs to execute; the expertise of the programming staff; the portability of the language; and the amount of program maintenance expected.

Vocabulary Self-Test

Can you define the following?

Ada (p. 130)

application generator (p. 121)

application software (p. 113)

assembler (p. 119)

assembly language (p. 118)

BASIC (p. 126)

C (p. 128)

COBOL (p. 123)

compiler (p. 120)

context switching (p. 105)

control program (p. 104)

database query language (p. 121)

de facto standard (p. 109)

disk operating system (DOS) (p. 107)

DOS enhancer (p. 109)

DOS extender (p. 109)

DOS replacement (p. 109)

encapsulation (p. 122)

fifth-generation language (p. 121)

FORTRAN (p. 123)

fourth-generation language (p. 121)

generalized application software (p. 115)

graphics-based user interface (p. 107)

high-level language (p. 120)

inheritance (p. 122)

interpreter (p. 120)

interprocessing (p. 106)

language-translator program (p. 119)

LISP (p. 130)

Logo (p. 130)

low-level language (p. 118)

machine language (p. 118)

message (p. 122)

mnemonic (p. 118)

Modula-2 (p. 127)

multiprocessing (p. 105)

multitasking (p. 105)

multithreading (p. 105)

multiuser processing (p. 104)

natural language (p. 121)

nonprocedural language (p. 122)

object (p. 122)

object-oriented programming languages (OOPL) (p. 122)

operating environment (p. 108)

operating system (p. 103)

Pascal (p. 127)

PL/1 (p. 125)

procedural language (p. 121)

programming language (p. 117)

Prolog (p. 130)

real-time processing (p. 106)

report generator (p. 121)

RPG (p. 128)

service program (p. 104)

single tasking (p. 104)

single-user processing (p. 104)

specialized application software (p. 115)

supervisor program (p. 104)

syntax (p. 117)

system software (p. 103)

text-based user interface (p. 107)

time sharing (p. 106)

user interface (p. 107)

virtual-machine (VM) processing (p. 107)

virtual storage (p. 106)

window (p. 108)

Review Questions

Multiple Choice

1. Programs that directly control and use computer hardware rather than accomplishing a specific application for a user are called _____.
   a. service programs
   b. programming languages
   c. system software
   d. application software

2. The core set of programs that controls and supervises the hardware of a computer and provides services to other system software, application software, programmers, and users of a computer system is called a(n) _____.
   a. operating system
   b. specialized application
   c. data manager
   d. programming language

3. The _____ operating system capability allows the use of a secondary storage device as an extension of main memory.
   a. virtual-machine
   b. time-sharing
   c. multiprocessing
   d. virtual storage

4. An operating system with _____ capabilities allows a computer to control or monitor the task performance of other machines and people by responding to input data within a specified amount of time.
   a. real-time
   b. multithreading
   c. multiprogramming
   d. interprocessing

5. The portion of a program with which the user interacts to enter commands and view results is called a(n) _____.
   a. operating environment
   b. control program
   c. user-interface
   d. window

6. _____ is a multiuser, multitasking operating system that can be run on microcomputers.
   a. OS/2
   b. Unix
   c. Macintosh System
   d. DOS

7. _____ software can be applied to a wide variety of tasks.
   a. Generalized application
   b. All application
   c. Specialized application
   d. System

8. A set of written symbols that instruct the computer hardware to perform specified operations is called a(n) _____ .
   a. interpreter
   b. operating system
   c. programming language
   d. interface

9. _____ is the only programming language that a computer can understand.
   a. BASIC
   b. Machine language
   c. Assembly language
   d. C

10. A programming language that specifies *how* something is accomplished rather than *what* is accomplished is called a(n) _____ .
    a. procedural language
    b. nonprocedural language
    c. object-oriented language
    d. high-level language

Fill-in

1. The _____ is a control program that is responsible for controlling all other operating system programs as well as other system and application programs.

2. Operating system programs that provide a service to the user or programmer of a computer are called _____ .

3. _____ is a capability of an operating system that allows a single CPU to execute what appears to be more than one program at a time.

4. The operating system that allows simultaneous execution of programs by a computer that has two or more CPUs is called _____ .

5. An operating system that has _____ capabilities can run several other operating systems at the same time.

6. A microcomputer operating system that allows and manages the use of disk drives is referred to as a(n) _____ .

7. A(n) _____ is a separate area on the screen that encloses independent applications.

8. A program that helps a user perform a specific task is called _____ .

9. A(n) _____ is a language-translator program that translates assembly language program into machine language.

10. A(n) _____ uses objects and messages to construct programs.

Short Answer

1. What impact will system software and application software have on your chosen profession?

2. What are the purposes of an operating system?

3. List and describe the twelve general capabilities of operating systems that were discussed in the chapter.

4. What effect do you think the design of a user interface has on a user?

5. Identify and briefly discuss the four microcomputer operating systems presented.

6. Identify the two broad categories of application software and give examples of each.

7. Identify and discuss the three main sources from which software is created or obtained.

8. Describe the basic instructions that are included in a programming language.

9. Describe an object-oriented programming language.

10. Discuss some factors that must be considered when choosing a programming language.

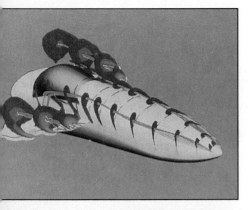

OUTLINE

OBJECTIVES

- ☐ Define data communication and telecommunication, and describe applications of each.

- ☐ Explain the differences between analog and digital data transmissions, and describe the processes of converting one to the other.

- ☐ Describe a communication channel, and discuss the three basic types.

- ☐ Describe two configurations of communication channels.

- ☐ Identify factors that determine the speed at which data are transmitted along a communication channel.

- ☐ Name and describe the three modes of data transfer.

- ☐ Describe and contrast a local-area network and a wide-area network.

- ☐ List and explain four network topologies.

- ☐ Define distributed data processing, and discuss some of its advantages and disadvantages.

- ☐ Explain the advantages of cellular communication networks to travelers.

- ☐ Identify several ways in which data communication is used.

CHAPTER FIVE

Communication and Networks

PROFILE
Andrew
Fluegelman

A lawyer by training, an editor by profession, and a San Francisco Giants fan by day and night, Andrew Fluegelman left several bright marks on the computer world before his death at age 41. Fluegelman made his first major contribution in the field of data communication when he wrote his own computer program to transfer files between his IBM PC and an acquaintance's North Star computer. The program worked so well that friends and colleagues suggested he publish it.

Because Fluegelman was familiar with the software publishing process, he had some reservations about putting his own program through it. Instead of following this traditional route, which he had little patience for, he tried a new way of getting the program out to users—a way that retained the excitement then being felt about the many promises of computers. The standard way of publishing a program involved the insertion of an element that prevented the software from being copied. However, all of the elements being used at that time for copy protection were easily broken, and Fluegelman did not have the technical skill to create a better form of protection.

After watching a local public television station carry on its fund-raising drive, Fluegelman developed the concept of user-supported software, which is similar to the television station's viewer support of programming.

Thus, he began encouraging people to copy his data communication program, called PC Talk, and to send him a voluntary contribution of $35 for each copy. He referred to this process as "free-ware." This concept helped promote the use of data communication among early PC users by supplying them with an inexpensive communication software package.

A graduate of Yale Law School, Fluegelman practiced law for five years before turning to book publishing. His new profession made it necessary for him to learn such skills as publishing, distribution, and advertising—all of which he used when he developed and marketed his own software. Fluegelman also became a gifted writer and editor near the end of his life. He co-authored the book *Writing in the Computer Age* and served as editor-in-chief of *PC World* and *Macworld*. Throughout his life, Fluegelman took great delight in baseball, particularly in the fortunes of the San Francisco Giants. He once told a friend that if he ever became disabled, wheeling him out to the ballpark would restore his happiness.

Earlier we introduced you to the different classifications of computers—supercomputers, mainframes, minicomputers, and microcomputers. These computers offer a wide range of computing power. If more computing power is needed, one way to get it is to buy a larger system. This route may be fine if the money and facilities are available, but many businesses and individuals simply can't afford to purchase a larger system.

Another concern arises for users who are geographically dispersed but who want to share data and other computer resources. They may need to send data to, or use data in, several different locations. One solution to this need is to keep separate data files at each location, but this can be costly and potentially disastrous: it is expensive to maintain redundant data files and difficult to ensure the continuing accuracy.

What, then, is an alternative solution to these problems of needing more power and data exchange and sharing? The alternative is the use of *data communication technology*. This chapter examines basic concepts of data communication and some ways in which you can use it to enable computer systems to share data, hardware, and software, including local-area networks, wide-area networks, and distributed data processing.

DATA COMMUNICATION

Data communication is the process of sending data electronically from one point to another. Linking one computer to another permits the power and resources of each to be tapped. It also makes possible the sharing and updating of data in different locations.

Computers that are physically close to each other, either in the same room or building, can communicate data through a direct-cable link. Computers located far apart use a special form of data communication—telecommunication. **Telecommunication,** or teleprocessing, is the use of communication facilities, such as the telephone system and microwave relays, to send data between computers.

The Effects of Data Communication

In today's business world, data communication technologies are as important as the computer technologies that support them. Many organizations, including banking and financial firms, could not exist as they do today without data communication. Businesses use data communication to communicate with a wide variety of individuals—other personnel within the same organization, banking and financial services personnel outside the organization, customers, suppliers, shareholders, government officials, consumer groups, advertisers, and more. Communication can take place locally, nationally, or internationally.

Users must send and receive data and information in timely fashion to identify and solve problems and make effective decisions. In this fast-paced electronic environment, even a slight delay can mean a missed opportunity.

However, getting data to a desired destination in a timely manner is not the only concern. Communication systems must transmit the data accurately and in a form that can be understood and used by the receiving system.

One day, you may be faced with deciding which data communication hardware and software options are right for the organization you own or are employed by. This crucial decision must consider numerous factors, including cost and performance. In addition, you will need to be aware of current or emerging data communication standards in the industry so that the hardware and software you select will be compatible with current and future needs. Even if you won't need to select or purchase communication hardware and software, it is essential to understand what data communication can do and how it works so that you can identify opportunities where it can help achieve your goals.

Data communication is also important for the home computer user. It allows access to services that supply information on countless topics. Through data communication, individuals can also link their home computers to office computers and share data, software, and hardware.

Analog and Digital Data Transmissions

The two forms of data transmission are analog and digital. **Analog data transmission** is the transmission of data in continuous-wave form—Figure 5–1(a). The telephone system is an example of a system designed for analog data transmission.

Digital data transmission is the transmission of data using distinct on-and-off electrical states—Figure 5–1(b). Remember that data in digital form are represented as a sequence of 1s and 0s, with each 1 representing the "on" state and each 0 representing the "off" state.

Because most computers work in digital form, and because digital data communication is faster and more efficient than analog communica-

Forms of Data Transmission

- Analog
- Digital

FIGURE 5–1
(a) Analog and (b) digital data transmissions.

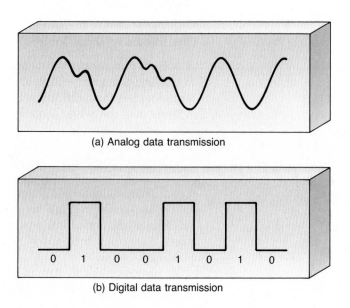

(a) Analog data transmission

```
0   1   0   0   1   0   1   0
```

(b) Digital data transmission

tion, it would seem that all data communication between computers would be in digital form. However, this is not the case. A completely digital system is possible, but the present telephone system (an analog system) is used for a great percentage of data communication because it is the most widely available communication system already in place. To avoid the expense of converting to a digital system or establishing a duplicate digital system over a large geographic area, a method was devised to transmit digital signals over telephone lines. This method is called modulation-demodulation.

Modulation, Demodulation, and Modems

Data in a computer are formatted as digital signals. Because telephone lines were designed to transmit the human voice, they format data as analog signals. Thus, for communication between computers to take place over a telephone line, the digital signal must be converted to an analog signal before it is transmitted. After its journey over the telephone lines, the analog signal must then be reconverted to a digital signal so that the receiving computer can use it. The process of converting a digital signal to an analog signal is called **modulation**—Figure 5–2(a). **Demodulation** is the process of reconverting the analog signal back to a digital signal—Figure 5–2(b). The device that accomplishes both of these processes is a **modem,** short for *mo*dulator–*dem*odulator.

FIGURE 5–2
(a) Modulation is the conversion of a digital signal to an analog signal. (b) Demodulation is the conversion of an analog signal to a digital signal.

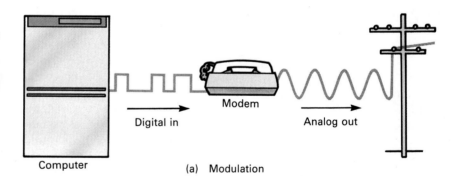

Computer   Digital in   Modem   Analog out

(a) Modulation

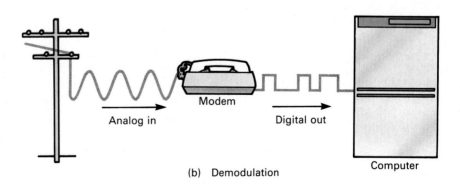

Analog in   Modem   Digital out   Computer

(b) Demodulation

FIGURE 5-3
External direct-connect modems connect to a computer via a serial interface cable and to the telephone line via a modular phone jack. (Photo by Larry Hamill/Macmillan)

Three Types of Modems

- Acoustic modem (acoustic coupler)
- External direct-connect
- Internal direct-connect

COMMUNICATION CHANNELS

The three basic types of modems used with microcomputers are (1) acoustic, (2) external direct-connect, and (3) internal direct-connect. An **acoustic modem,** or acoustic coupler as it is sometimes called, has two cups into which the handset of a telephone is placed. This type of modem sends data through the mouthpiece and receives data through the earpiece of the handset. Acoustic modems are not used very often today because their signals are much more susceptible to distortion than are those of other types of modems. Also, the carbon microphones used in a telephone handset limit the rate of data transmission.

An **external direct-connect modem** is external to a computer and connects directly to the telephone line with a modular phone jack (Figure 5-3). The direct connection greatly reduces the distortion of signals and permits faster data transfer rates. A popular external direct-connect modem is the Hayes Smartmodem.

Most external direct-connect modems have a variety of features not found on acoustic modems, including checks of the operating status using status lights and speakers, change of the speeds at which data are transmitted, automatic dialing and answering of the phone, response to commands from a communication program, and self-testing of their ability to correctly transmit data. Because the specialized circuitry in these modems allows them (rather than the computer) to perform these and other functions, they are often called "smart" or "intelligent" devices.

Both acoustic modems and external direct-connect modems require that a computer be equipped with a communication adapter or other serial port with a connector used as a serial interface. A serial interface provides a standard method for serial transmission of data. A modem cable to connect the modem to the serial port is also needed. On most microcomputers, the RS232C interface is used. It has 25 pins, called a male connector, to which one end of a modem cable is connected, and the modem has 25 receptacles, called a female connector, to which the other end of the modem cable is connected.

An **internal direct-connect modem** has all of its communication circuitry on a plug-in board that fits into one of the expansion slots (empty spaces) inside a computer. Not needed are a separate communication board or an RS232C serial interface board. Internal direct-connect modems also link directly to telephone lines with modular phone jacks. These modems have many of the same special features that external direct-connect modems have. In addition, they take up no desk space and are ideal for use in portable computers.

A **communication channel** is the medium, or pathway, through which data are transmitted between devices. Communication channels fall into three basic types: wire cable, microwave, and fiber optics.

Wire cable includes telegraph lines, telephone lines, and coaxial cables. It is the most common type of data communication channel in use today. Telegraph and telephone lines are often referred to as "twisted-pair" lines because they consist of a pair of wires, each wrapped in a protective coating and twisted around the other. Coaxial cable consists of a single wire surrounded by insulating material, which in turn is surrounded by a metal sheath that shields transmitted data from interference. The cable used to connect TV sets to cable systems is one form of coaxial cable.

Because the extensive wire-cable networks that already exist are easier and cheaper to use than establishing new systems, wire-cable channels are the most popular. They are also popular because the technology used to transmit data along wire cables is standardized, which reduces compatibility problems.

One disadvantage of wire cables is that data must be transmitted in analog form. Conversion of digital data not only requires special hardware but also slows transmission. Another disadvantage is that wire cables are subject to electrical interferences that make them less reliable than other communication channels. In addition, it is difficult to create the physical links needed where users are separated by large distances or by natural barriers, such as mountains or large bodies of water.

FIGURE 5-4

Data communication is accomplished with the help of computers, satellites, and satellite dishes located at Earth stations (see inset photo). The Space Shuttle is now being used along with rockets to deploy satellites in orbit. (Courtesy of Chromatics, Inc. Inset: Photo courtesy of American Satellite Co., part of Contel's Information Systems sector)

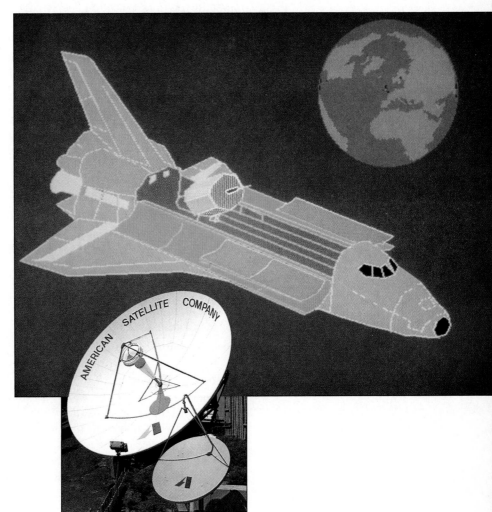

SATELLITE COMMUNICATIONS HELP AUTOMAKERS GAIN COMPETITIVE EDGE

Automakers are beginning to incorporate satellite communication technologies to help gain a competitive edge. Using this technology, automakers can provide their dealers with up-to-date customer records, information about the latest service offering, pricing changes, and other important data. Chrysler Corporation and Toyota Motor Corporation are using Very Small-Aperture Terminal (VSAT) dishes from Hughes Aircraft Company in a satellite network that links them to their dealers.

The automakers plan to use the data and video capabilities of the system to offer customers and dealers services not found in most of the auto industry. For example, currently a customer's records are available from the seller only. However, with a national database and the satellite communication system, an automaker can supply on-line information about a customer's car, including its complete maintenance history to any dealership. In addition, inventory information for both cars and parts can be transmitted. The video capabilities of the system allow an automaker to keep its dealers up to date through live broadcasts from top management, technical service information, and parts announcements.

The drive behind this system is to improve customer service. The automakers, especially those in the higher markets, see service as one way in which a manufacturer can differentiate itself from the competition.

Toyota's system links together the dealers for its Lexus LS400 luxury sedan and its main office in Torrance, California. The network includes a hub satellite station and a video broadcasting studio at company headquarters. Each dealer is equipped with a VSAT satellite dish. The hardware for the network and the satellite are provided by Hughes Network Systems in Germantown, Maryland. Each of the Lexus dealers (the network nodes) is equipped with an IBM Application System/400 computer to handle its computing needs. Lexus also hopes that the improved customer service will give them a strategic advantage over the competition.

Microwave is another type of analog communication channel. Microwave signals are transmitted through the atmosphere rather than through wire cables, in much the same ways as radio and television signals are transmitted. However, microwave signals must be transmitted in straight lines because they cannot bend around corners or follow the curvature of the earth. You've probably seen microwave transmitter stations, with their distinctive dish-, cone-, or trapezoid-shaped antennas. They must be located about every 30 miles to accommodate the curvature of the Earth. The transmitter stations are relays that redirect and boost the signals.

Satellites are also used to direct microwaves over large, geographically dispersed areas. A communication **satellite** is an electronic device placed in an orbit around Earth to receive, amplify, and then transmit signals. Microwave signals are sent from a transmitter station to an Earth station and then are beamed to an orbiting satellite (Figure 5–4). From there, they are beamed directly back to another Earth station if a direct line of sight is possible. If such direct transmission is not possible, the signal is transmitted to another satellite that does have a direct line of sight, and then back to an Earth station. Only three satellites are required to send a signal anywhere on Earth. Highlight 5–1 describes how automakers are taking advantage of satellite communication networks to improve the competitive edge of their dealers.

Compared with wire cable, microwave transmission by either earth-bound systems or satellite has a much lower error rate. Thus, it is more reliable. Also, because there are no physical connections between the sending and receiving systems, communication links can be made over large distances and rough terrains. One disadvantage, however, is the high cost of ground stations and satellites to support a microwave network.

Fiber optics is the third type of communication channel (Figure 5–5). Unlike wire cable and microwave, a fiber-optic channel transmits data in digital form. It uses light impulses that travel through clear, flexible tubing. The tubing is thinner than a human hair and hundreds of tubes can fit in the amount of space required for only one wire cable.

Fiber optics are very reliable communication channels. In addition, they can transmit data at very high speeds (several billions of bits per

FIGURE 5–5
Tiny fibers of transparent glass in fiber-optic cables transmit data at the speed of light. The beam of light sent through these fibers can be turned on or off at about 1 billion times per second. These cables are replacing traditional telephone lines and are used to connect computers in telecommunication systems. (Courtesy of United Telecommunications)

second) with few or no errors. Unlike wire cables, fiber-optic cables are not subject to electrical interference. They do, however, require "repeater stations" to read and boost signal strength because light pulses lose their strength over long distances. Technical developments continue to drive down the cost of installing, using, and manufacturing fiber optics, so they are becoming competitive with traditional cabling. Some long-distance telephone companies, such as U.S. Sprint, have already converted to a fiber-optic system, and others are in the process of conversion.

Channel Configurations

The two principal communication-channel configurations are point-to-point and multipoint (Figure 5-6). In a **point-to-point channel configuration,** a device (such as a terminal or computer) is connected directly to another device by a dedicated communication channel, giving those devices sole use of that channel. A point-to-point configuration can be inefficient and costly if a terminal is not active enough to keep the channel busy. Large computers that continuously communicate with each other often use point-to-point channel configurations.

An alternative configuration is **multipoint channel configuration,** in which three or more devices are connected to a single line. A multipoint configuration uses a communication channel more efficiently and reduces the amount of intercabling needed, thus lowering costs. However, this configuration requires a way of determining which device gets access to the single channel, and when. Two methods are used to determine which device gets access to a channel: polling and contention.

In **polling,** the computer checks each device, one at a time, to see whether it has a message to send. If the device has a message ready, transmission begins; if not, the computer polls the next device. After all of the devices have been individually polled, the process begins again. A disadvantage to polling is that the processor of a computer will be idle if no messages are to be sent by the devices being polled, and this wastes expensive processor time.

Contention, the second method, puts the devices in control: each device monitors the communication channel to see whether it is available. If it is, the device sends its message. If the communication channel is being used, the device waits a predetermined amount of time and tries again, repeating the process until the channel is available. One problem with this approach is that a single device can tie up the communication channel for long periods of time.

Channel Sharing

Two methods are used to regulate the flow of data from communication channels into a computer: multiplexing and concentration. Their purpose is to increase the efficiency of use of a communication channel.

Multiplexing is the process of combining the transmissions from several devices into a single data stream that can be sent over a single

FIGURE 5-6
Communication channel configurations: (a) point-to-point; (b) multipoint.

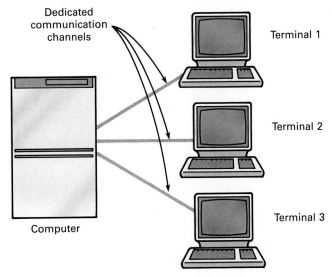

Dedicated communication channels

Terminal 1

Terminal 2

Terminal 3

Computer

(a) Point-to-point channel configuration

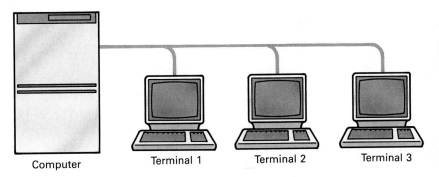

Computer

Terminal 1

Terminal 2

Terminal 3

(b) Multipoint channel configuration

high-speed communication channel. The unit that electronically accomplishes this is called a **multiplexer**. On the sending end, a multiplexer collects data from several devices and sends them over one channel; on the receiving end, a multiplexer separates the transmissions back into their original order for processing (Figure 5−7). The rationale behind this process is that most communication channels can transmit much more data at one time than a single device can send. Thus, a multiplexer allows a communication channel to be used more efficiently, thereby reducing the cost of using the channel.

Frequently it is necessary to connect more devices to a computer than a communication channel can handle at one time. **Concentration** is the process of connecting and serving these devices. A **concentrator,** itself often a minicomputer, is the hardware that provides concentration (Figure 5−8). When the number of devices transmitting exceeds the capacity of a communication channel, the data are stored in a buffer for later transmission. Many multiplexers also provide concentration.

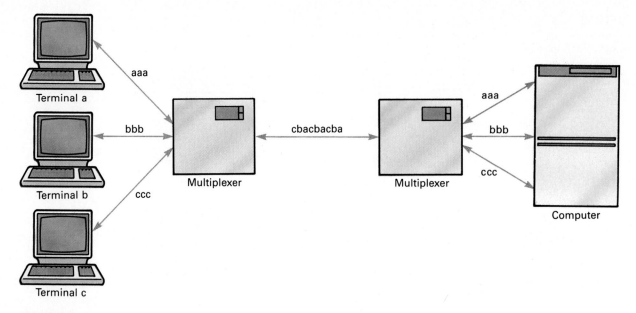

FIGURE 5–7
A multiplexer allows several terminals to share a communication channel.

Front-End Processors

A **front-end processor** is a special-purpose computer that handles all data-communication control functions (Figure 5–9). Thus, while the CPU in a front-end processor handles all of the communication tasks, the CPU of a main computer is free to work on other tasks. The two processors interact only to pass data between them. A typical front-end processor might control scores of communication channels of varying types and speeds coming from a number of diverse remote terminals.

A front-end processor can be programmed to perform a variety of functions, such as concentration, error control, code conversion, buffering, and channel sharing, which are activities related to data and message control. Front-end processors also can contain their own secondary storage devices to log (record) the communication activities for billing and audit trails.

Common Carriers

A company that is licensed and regulated by federal or state government to transmit the data owned by others at regulated rates is called a **common carrier**. There are thousands of licensed common carriers of data commu-

FIGURE 5–8 (opposite)
A concentrator allows connection and service to a greater number of devices than the communication channel is capable of serving at one time.

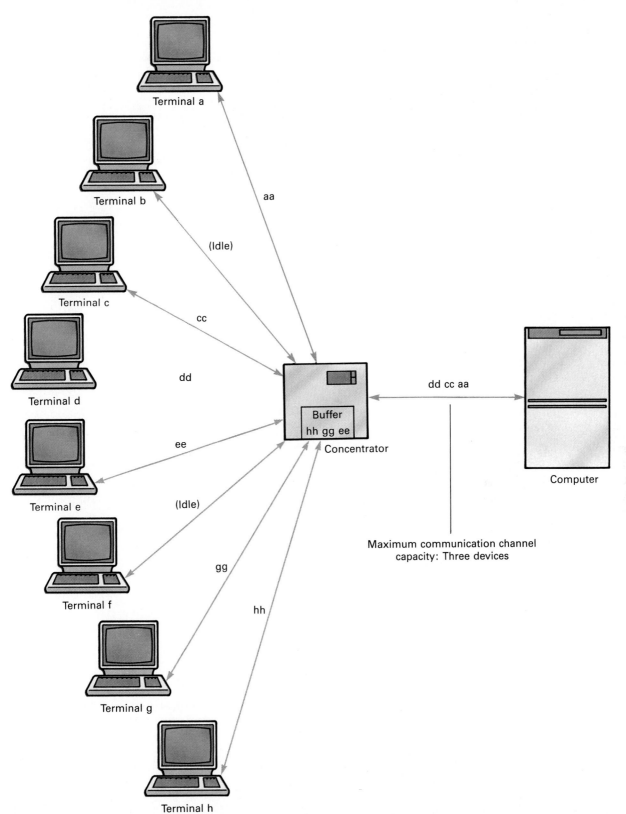

Terminal a

Terminal b

(Idle)

aa

Terminal c

cc

Terminal d

dd

Terminal e

ee

(Idle)

Terminal f

gg

Terminal g

hh

Terminal h

Buffer
hh gg ee

Concentrator

dd cc aa

Computer

Maximum communication channel
capacity: Three devices

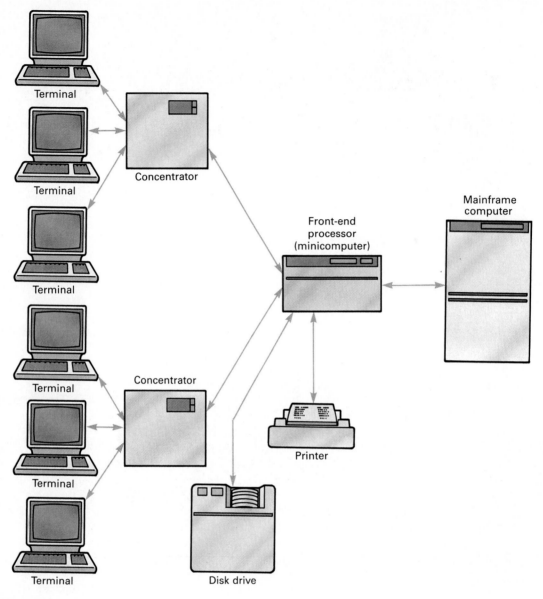

FIGURE 5–9
A front-end processor processes and routes all input and output operations.

nications. Three of the largest are American Telephone and Telegraph (AT&T), Western Union, and General Telephone & Electronics (GTE). All common carriers dealing with communication are regulated by the Federal Communications Commission (FCC) and various state agencies.

Specialized common carriers and value-added carriers are alternatives to the major common carriers. A *specialized common carrier* supplies limited data-communication services, usually restricted to selected areas.

A *value-added carrier* leases communication channels from common carriers and adds extra services over and above the those that the common carriers provide. Such services include electronic mail, voice messaging, information retrieval services, time sharing, and distributed data processing. Tymnet and Telenet are value-added carriers.

RATE OF DATA TRANSMISSION

As people become accustomed to the speeds at which computers can transfer data, they seem to want even faster transfer. Information that once took days to receive now seems slow if it has taken a few minutes by computer. The rate at which data are transferred is the **baud rate,** which is the number of times per second that the signal being transmitted changes (modulates or demodulates). Baud is often equated with bits per second (bps); however, this comparison is not entirely accurate because a signal does not always carry one bit.

Although higher speeds are possible, typical data transmission speeds are 300, 1200, 2400, 4800, and 9600 baud. Modems used with microcomputers typically use 300, 1200, or 2400 baud. Large computer systems used for business communication typically transmit data at speeds of 4800 baud or higher, using high-speed modems. Factors that determine the rate at which data can be transmitted include the bandwidth of the communication channel and the method of data transmission (asynchronous or synchronous), all discussed below.

Communication Channel Bandwidths

> **Communication Channel Bandwidths**
>
> - Narrow-band
> - Voice-band
> - Broad-band

The **bandwidth** of a communication channel, also called the "grade," determines the rate (speed) at which data can be transmitted over the channel. The term bandwidth is often shortened to *band*. There are three types of bands for communication channels: (1) narrow-band, (2) voice-band (also called voice-grade), and (3) broad-band.

The slowest of these is the **narrow-band channel,** which transmits data at rates between 40 bits per second (bps) and 100 bits per second. A telegraph line is a narrow-band channel. A **voice-band channel** transmits data at rates between 110 bits per second and 9600 bits per second. Telephone lines are voice-band channels.

The fastest of these channels is the **broad-band channel,** which can transmit data at rates up to several million bits per second. Advances in technology will soon allow data to be transmitted on some types of broad-band channels at speeds exceeding a billion bps. Microwaves, coaxial cables, and laser beams are broad-band channels.

Asynchronous and Synchronous Transmissions

> **Methods of Data Transmission**
>
> - Asynchronous
> - Synchronous

Asynchronous transmission of data is a method that sends one character at a time. The transfer of data is controlled by *start bits* and *stop bits*. Thus, each character is surrounded by bits that signal the beginning and ending of the character. These characters allow the receiving terminal to synchronize itself with the transmitting terminal on a character-by-character basis. Asynchronous transmission is often used in low-speed transmissions of data in conjunction with narrow-band and some slower-speed voice-band channels (less than 1200 baud) for which the transmitting device operates manually or intermittently.

Synchronous transmission of data sends blocks of characters in timed sequences. Rather than having start and stop bits around each character, each block of characters is marked with synchronization characters. The receiving device accepts data until it detects a special ending character or counts a predetermined number of characters, at which time the device knows the message has come to an end.

Synchronous transmission is much faster—and more expensive—than asynchronous transmission. It commonly uses the faster voice-band (greater than 1200 baud) and broad-band channels, and usually is used when data-transfer requirements exceed several thousand bits per second. Synchronous transmission is used in direct computer-to-computer communications of large computer systems because of its high data-transfer speeds. The equipment required for synchronous transmission of data is more sophisticated than that needed for asynchronous devices.

The special characters used by asynchronous and synchronous transmissions to alert a modem that data are being sent or that transmissions are complete are **message characters**. Before data transmission, however, a set of traffic rules and procedures called **protocol** must be established. The purpose of protocol is to perform such tasks as getting the attention of another device, identifying all of the devices involved in the communication, checking to see whether a message has been sent correctly, and initiating any necessary retransmission or error recovery. Protocol varies, depending on the devices being used, but the same protocol must be followed by all devices participating in a communication session. Prearranged signals defining the protocol are sent between computers in an exchange called **handshaking**.

MODES OF TRANSMISSION

The transfer of data over communication channels occurs in three modes: (1) simplex, (2) half-duplex, and (3) full-duplex. In the **simplex mode,** data can be transmitted in only one direction—Figure 5–10(a). A device using the simplex mode of transmission can either send or receive data, but it cannot do both. This mode might be used in a burglar alarm system with the source located in a building and the destination being the local police station. The simplex mode allows no means of feedback to ensure correct interpretation of the signal received. In the burglar alarm example, police officers have no way of knowing whether the alarm had been set off by a test, a malfunction, or a burglar.

The **half-duplex mode** allows a device to send and receive data, but not at the same time. In other words, the transmission of data can occur in only one direction at a time—Figure 5–10(b). An example of a half-duplex transmission is a Citizens Band (CB) radio. A user can talk or listen but cannot do both at the same time.

Modes of Data Transfer
■ Simplex
■ Half-duplex
■ Full-duplex

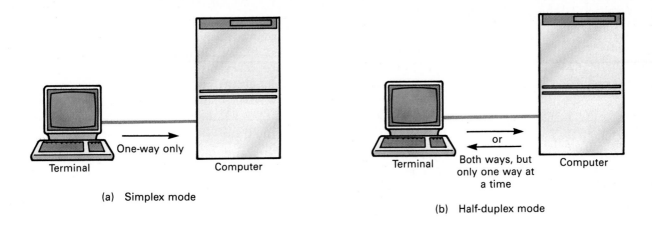

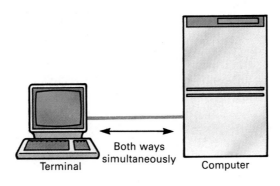

FIGURE 5–10
The transfer of data over a communication line can take place in one of three
modes: (a) simplex, (b) half-duplex, or (c) full-duplex.

The most sophisticated of the transmission modes is the **full-duplex
mode,** which allows a device to receive and send data simultaneously—
Figure 5–10(c). For example, a telephone system using a full-duplex mode
allows the users to talk and listen at the same time. Telephone systems use
either the half-duplex or full-duplex mode.

MICRO-TO-MICRO LINKS

Microcomputers are often connected for data communication in a **micro-
to-micro link** so that microcomputer users with incompatible data formats can share data. For example, users of an Apple Macintosh and an
IBM PS/2 cannot swap data disks because the data are saved on the disks
in different formats. However, data that are in a standard format, such as
ASCII, can be interchanged via modem and telephone lines. Transmission
of data is possible in either direction—Apple to IBM or IBM to Apple.
    If the two computers are near each other, another option is to directly
connect them (hard-wire) using a null modem cable. A **null modem**

cable uses a different pin configuration from that of a modem cable and eliminates the need for a modem by directly matching the data transmit pin from one computer to the data receive pin on the other computer. Hard wiring with a null modem cable allows incompatible computers to transfer data at speeds up to 9600 bits per second and eliminates the need for modems at each computer. However, this method provides no error detection capabilities.

MICRO-TO-MAINFRAME LINKS

Microcomputers can also be connected to large systems in a **micro-to-mainframe link** to share data and computing power. As the number of microcomputers used in business increases, this connection is being seen more and more. As with micro-to-micro communication, micro-to-mainframe communication can be accomplished either via modems and telephone lines or by hard wiring.

However, the connection of microcomputers and mainframes is not so simple, because the large systems use communication formats different from those of their microcomputer counterparts, and they handle data differently. To complicate the problem even further, the communication and data formats used by the various mainframes also differ. Hardware designed for the particular type of computer involved is usually needed to make the data compatible. Before a micro-to-mainframe link can be made, three factors must be considered: (1) the type of mainframe being linked, (2) the specific data format of the mainframe, and (3) the specific communication protocols (or handshaking signals) of the mainframe.

NETWORKS AND DISTRIBUTED DATA PROCESSING

One application of data communication technology is the development of computer networks. A **computer network** is created when data-communication channels link several computers and other devices, such as printers and secondary storage devices. Each computer in a network can have its own processing capabilities and can share hardware, data files, and programs. The two primary types of networks are wide-area networks and local-area networks.

Network Topology

Each computer or device in a network is called a **node**. The arrangement by which the nodes are connected is the **topology** of the network. A network can be arranged in one of four different topologies: (1) a star network, (2) a ring network, (3) a tree network, or (4) a bus network.

Star Network. A **star network** consists of several devices connected to one centralized computer (Figure 5–11). All communications go through this computer, allowing it to control the operations, workload, and resource allocation of the other computers in the network. For example, a bank with several branch offices would typically use a star network to control and coordinate its branches. The advantage is relative simplicity,

---

Network Topologies

- Star network
- Ring network
- Tree network
- Bus network

FIGURE 5–11
Star network.

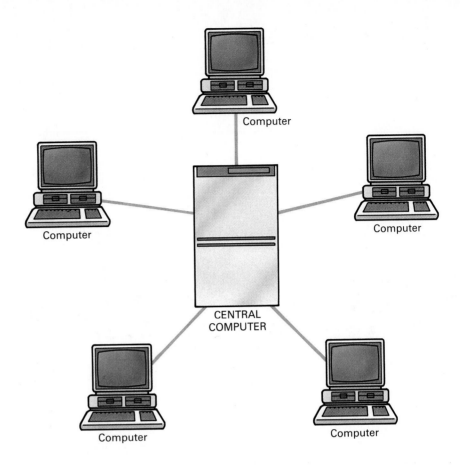

but the single-point vulnerability of the network may be a problem. If the central computer breaks down, none of the other computers can communicate with each other.

Ring Network. A **ring network** consists of several devices connected to each other in a closed loop by a single communication channel (Figure 5–12). No computer is central or predominant in this network. Data must travel around the ring to each station in turn until they arrive at the desired station. A unidirectional ring moves data in one direction only; a bidirectional ring moves data in both directions, but in only one direction at a time. When one node malfunctions in a bidirectional ring, a message can usually be sent in the opposite direction. This ability allows communication among all active nodes in the network.

Tree Network. A **tree network** links computers in a hierarchical fashion and requires data to flow through the branches (Figure 5–13). In this figure, to move from the computer at Node 1 to Node 7, data must go through Nodes 3, 5, and 6 before arriving at 7.

One advantage of a tree structure is that functional groupings can be created. For example, one branch could contain all of the general ledger terminals, another branch all of the accounts receivable terminals, and so

FIGURE 5–12
Ring network.

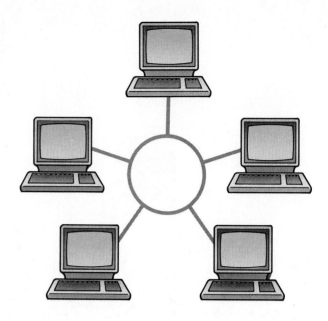

on. Another advantage is that the other branches in a tree network are not affected if one branch stops functioning. However, data movement through a tree network can be slow.

Bus Network. In a **bus network** each computer is connected to a single communication cable via an interface. Thus, every computer can communicate directly with every other computer or device in the network (Figure 5–14). Each node is given an address, and a user simply needs to know the address to access a particular node. Going through a hierarchy of nodes is not necessary here, as it is in a tree network. This topology is frequently used with local-area networks (described later).

Wide-Area Networks

A **wide-area network (WAN)** consists of two or more computers that are geographically dispersed but are linked by communication facilities provided by common carriers, such as the telephone system or microwave relays. This type of network is often used by large corporations and government agencies to transmit data. Satellites are often used to transmit the data across large distances that are divided by geographic barriers, such as oceans or mountains. For example, the National Science Foundation (NSF) in Washington, DC has linked six supercomputers together in a wide-area network that links their computers with schools and research centers around the nation.

Several methods are used to move data through a wide-area network, including circuit switching, message switching, and packet switching.

Circuit switching opens up a complete, predetermined transmission route from sender to receiver before a message is transmitted. An entire

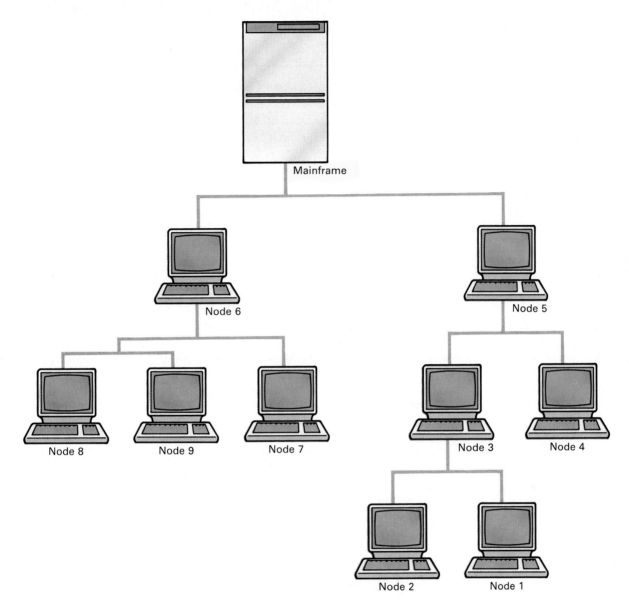

FIGURE 5–13
Tree network.

message is then transmitted at once. This method guarantees exclusive use of the transmission route and uninterrupted message transmission. However, if all of the possible transmission routes to a receiver are being used, the sender must wait for a link to become free.

Message switching also involves sending an entire message at one time over a predetermined transmission route, but in this case, the transmission route is not dedicated to just one message. It is possible that a message will encounter a portion of the transmission route that is not available. When this happens, the message is temporarily stored. When that part of the

FIGURE 5–14
Bus network.

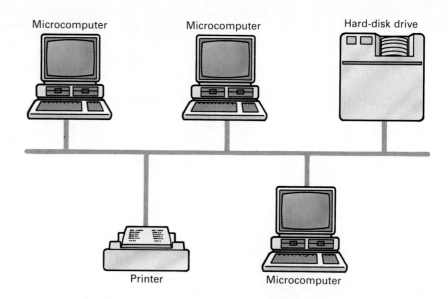

route becomes available, the message is retrieved from storage and transmission continues.

Packet switching is the most complex of the data-movement methods discussed in this section. Its advantage is increased utilization of a network, thus decreasing the cost of using the network. In packet switching, there is no temporary storage of messages in secondary storage devices. Instead, messages are divided into packets, or blocks, of standard size. A single message may be made up of one or more packets. Each packet is sent along a transmission route that is determined in one of two ways—either predetermined at the time of transmission or dynamically determined at transmission time and at each node, depending on the traffic and the availability of portions of transmission routes. Value-added common carriers use packet switching.

Local-Area Networks

A **local-area network (LAN)** consists of two or more computers directly linked within a relatively small, well-defined area, such as a room, building, or cluster of buildings. A LAN may include only microcomputers or any combination of microcomputers and large systems. Popular LANs available for microcomputer users include Ethernet (DEC, Xerox, and others), EtherLink (3Com), StarLAN (AT&T), and Token Ring (IBM). The difference between a LAN and a multiuser system is that a LAN is made up of stand-alone computers, whereas a multiuser system typically has one computer that is shared among two or more terminals.

LANs can be connected to WANs through the use of gateways. A **gateway** is an interface that converts the data codes, formats, addresses, and transmission rates of one network into a form usable by another network.

LAN Components. A LAN usually includes the following components:

- ☐ Two or more computers.
- ☐ Network server(s).
- ☐ Peripheral devices, such as printers and hard-disk drives.
- ☐ Special twisted-pair, coaxial, or fiber-optic cables to connect the computers and other devices. The length of the cable connecting a computer to a network varies, depending on the LAN. Most LANs allow cables of about 1,000 feet, but some allow cables of several miles to be used. The data transfer speeds range from several thousand bps to around 50 million bps.
- ☐ Plug-in adapter boards to handle data transmissions.
- ☐ Software to control the computers or other devices connected to the LAN.

The number of computers in a LAN varies widely, from smaller LANs that typically connect 2 to 25 computers to larger LANs that can connect as many as 10,000 computers.

LANs use a **network server,** a hardware device that provides file, print, or communication services to other network devices. A network server may include one or more of these functions:

- ☐ A *file server* to store and control access to program and data files. It not only eliminates the need for each node to store separate copies of program or data files but also facilitates file sharing.
- ☐ A *print server* to control printing operations. It temporarily stores files to be printed in queue while waiting for the printer. It both eliminates the need for each node to have a printer and allows computers sharing a printer to store files to be printed directly in the server instead of sitting idle while awaiting access to the printer.
- ☐ A *communications server* to handle communication functions for a LAN, avoiding the need for each node to be equipped with communication hardware and software.

In addition to hardware, a LAN needs software: a LAN operating system to control operation of the computers and other devices connected to the LAN. LAN operating systems vary in features. For example, some allow only one computer operating system on a LAN, whereas others allow more than one. Thus, some LANs require all computers to be of a certain type (such as MS-DOS compatible), whereas others allow a variety of types to be connected (such as MS-DOS, Unix, and Macintosh systems). Some allow single-user file access, whereas others permit simultaneous multiuser file access. A popular LAN operating system is Novell NetWare. Highlight 5–2 examines ways in which LANs are benefiting a medical center that specializes in cancer treatment.

Security and privacy of data are two concerns of LAN users. A LAN must get data to the proper destination, transmit the data correctly, and prevent unauthorized users from gaining access to the data. These tasks are

NETWORKS PROVIDE LIFELINE FOR MEDICAL CENTER

Local-area networks are playing an important role at The M.D. Anderson Cancer Center in Houston, Texas. The center is part of the University of Texas, and it is the busiest and largest medical facility of its kind, employing 6,500 people. Anderson has the highest cancer cure rate in the world.

The Anderson Center has one of the world's largest and most varied LANs, using the Ethernet technology. The networked computer system is the lifeblood of the center. The LAN system uses mostly the Novell Netware LAN operating system and Ethernet adapters. The system supports 3,000 computers, ranging from Apple Macintoshes to DEC Vaxes. The network is made up of a conglomeration of smaller networks of personal computers that are interconnected and tied into other types of computers.

The corporate information system of the center consists of three DEC Vaxes. Personal computer networks that stand alone or that are connected to the Vaxes are used to support the various administrative, business, and medical departments.

The Vax version of the LAN operating system allows a Vax to act as a file server for DOS applications. The center uses a wide variety of DOS applications, including basic productivity applications, such as word processors, database management systems, and spreadsheets. Users at Anderson are comfortable and confident working with the network because they can still use the DOS applications that they have already learned. This is an important factor in keeping productivity high at the bustling center.

The LAN operating system also allows personal computer users access to Vax data files. Storing the vast amounts of data the center generates on the Vaxes, the center makes that data easily available to other users who need it. Having the data stored on the Vaxes also takes the burden off departments that cannot manage a network themselves—they shift it to the Vax support personnel. Most departments take advantage of the shared data stored on the network.

accomplished through both the hardware and the LAN operating system software.

Benefits of LANs. There are several benefits to using LANs. They reduce cost by allowing users to share computer hardware (laser printers, color printers, hard-disk drives, modems), software, and data files. LANs facilitate communication between users via electronic mail—a method of using computers and communication technology to store and send messages.

For example, the facilities and engineering staff at the center maintain a library of drafting schematics of the complex. Using PC-based drafting software, an electrician can download a master drawing at a personal computer, then apply an overlay of the electrical system, and then save the modified drawing on the Vax so that others can review it.

The network has not only increased productivity but has also reduced operating expenses for individual departments on the system. For example, each department doesn't have to pay a network administrator or add administrative duties to the workload of its employees. The network also has the advantage of encouraging and fostering independence. Staff members can think more about what they need to do their jobs well and the systems department is better able to meet their requests. For example, at the request of two blind users, the center purchased customer keyboard/headphone combinations that let the users hear the characters they type. Benefits to using the network have been increased personal satisfaction and productivity and the ability to maintain the Anderson Center's high success rate in treating cancer. The network has proved to be one of its most vital elements.

Anderson also runs its own hotel that serves patients who don't require hospital stays but who need to be in close contact with the medical center, the families of patients, and resident doctors. The hotel is equipped with a local-area network that handles all management, from registration to staff scheduling.

In addition, the center maintains its own police department. Personal computers connected to a Vax are used to track dispatch records. Whenever a car is dispatched, all the information about that call and the officer's reports are entered into the departmental database. This database is used to supply a very detailed audit of the activities. The center is also planning a network that will aid university medical researchers.

LANs allow different brands of computers to communicate, such as Apple Macintoshes and IBMs. LANs give an organization control over a communication channel without having to deal with common carriers.

Drawbacks of LANs. With the benefits of LANs come several drawbacks. Users must be trained, which takes time and money, and users often resist change. LAN operation incurs certain costs. It requires upkeep and usually a LAN Administrator to oversee its operation. Although LANs make communication between users and the sharing of files easier, they also increase security and privacy concerns for data.

Distributed Data Processing

Distributed data processing (DDP) is dispersing computers, devices, software, and data into areas where they are used, and connecting them via communication channels. The computers are distributed by function and geographical boundaries, but work together as a cohesive system.

DDP contrasts with a centralized system, where all data-processing resources are in one location. Typically, a centralized system has one large general-purpose computer with many terminals attached to it. Although the centralized computer can perform many tasks, it may do few of them efficiently or cost-effectively. A DDP system allows the tailoring of many smaller, more specialized computers to perform particular tasks efficiently and cost-effectively.

Thus, three advantages of DDP are (1) cost-effectiveness, (2) user-controlled computing facilities with a shorter response time, and (3) shared resources. Hardware costs used to argue against DDP, but most computer system components have decreased in cost and improved in performance. However, the cost of communication channels has not decreased as much. Consequently, many organizations have discovered that distributing computers and data storage to local areas can actually save money by decreasing use of expensive communication channels. In addition, because a DDP network allows remote sites to share equipment and data, redundancy of both can be reduced with proper management and control of the DDP system.

DDP has also become popular because users gain more control over individual information system needs. Users need not consult a centralized computer staff which attempts to fulfill everyone's needs. A DDP system typically uses many minicomputers and microcomputers, which are simpler and require less maintenance than a larger centralized system. Users of the smaller systems access them directly and can use their full power. Nevertheless, for tasks such as managing extremely large, complicated databases, mainframes still play a vital role in many DDP systems.

Response times for many applications are faster in a DDP system. The concept of distributing management is referred to as decentralized management. When DDP system management is decentralized, the system is often called a "fully distributed system." Of course, there are varying degrees of both DDP and decentralized management. As with many things, it is not a simple case of one extreme or the other.

Another advantage of DDP is that users share equipment, software, and data with other computers in the DDP system to meet their total information needs.

On the other hand, DDP brings several disadvantages. First, problems can occur if the system is poorly managed. If an organization loses control over data-processing resources, management will have difficulty controlling costs and maintaining standards throughout the distributed areas of the organization.

DDP Advantages

- Cost efficiency
- User control of computer facilities
- Shared resources

DDP Disadvantages

- Loss of management control
- Redundancies of resources and data
- Compatibility problems
- Unskilled users
- Support difficulties

A second problem that can arise is redundancy of resources and data. Without proper management and control, each distributed site may try to develop an information system to meet all needs of the site, creating several systems that are the same or nearly so. This duplication can lead to higher hardware and software costs than would exist if the distributed sites shared resources. Uncontrolled data redundancy also can lead to differences in data among the distributed sites, causing discrepancies in reports, and this problem can be difficult and expensive to resolve.

Third, if distributed sites do not coordinate their selection of hardware and software, compatibility problems can arise. Different protocols at distributed sites may result in an inability of the hardware to communicate with hardware at other distributed sites.

A fourth problem can occur if a site is controlled by untrained and inexperienced users, resulting in poor selection of hardware and software, inferior programming, and little if any documentation. This can lead to a costly, complex system or even to one that is inappropriate for the job.

Finally, obtaining timely support at some distributed sites can be difficult because they are too far from the support staff of the vendor or organization. However, maintaining a separate support staff at each location may be too expensive for some organizations.

Thus DDP is not appropriate for all situations. To ensure that DDP meets the needs of an organization, both central management and dispersed users should be integrally involved in the design of the system. Its success or failure ultimately depends on management planning, commitment, and control, as well as user acceptance.

Cellular Networks

Cellular mobile phones now enable travelers to maintain high-quality communication with office or home while on the road. In a **cellular network,** transmitters are placed in a checkerboard pattern throughout the service area (Figure 5–15). The geographical area that each transmitter covers is a *cell*. Each cell has radio frequencies assigned to it that are not available to other cells in the network.

When a user places a call, the local cell (in which the call is made) detects it and assigns specific frequencies for the call. A computer system monitors the strength of the signal. As a caller travels out of the cell, the signal gets weaker. When the signal strength falls to a predetermined level, the computer interprets this to mean that the caller has left the cell and checks all surrounding cells to determine which one is now picking up the transmission. The call is then taken over by that cell, and the user's telephone is assigned new frequencies for transmitting and receiving. This handoff between cells is fully automatic and usually happens fast enough that it goes undetected by the user.

Business use of cellular telephones is growing rapidly. Executives who travel by car frequently can stay in touch with their offices and receive last-minute information on their ways to meetings. Supervisors and repair technicians working at remote sites can stay in touch with their offices. Portable computers can be connected to the home office through modems

---

Types of Networks

- Wide-area
- Local-area
- Distributed data processing
- Cellular

FIGURE 5–15
A cellular network.

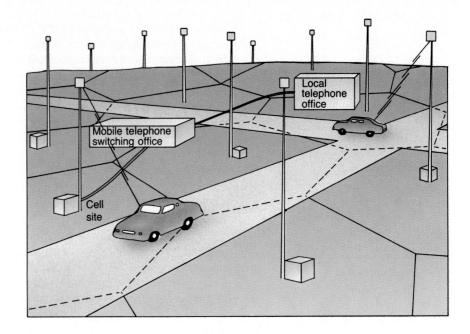

and cellular phones to exchange information conveniently. Terminals are also available to transmit facsimile (fax) images over a cellular network. Portable cellular computers transmit data directly over a cellular network without a modem or cellular phone.

Public transportation is beginning to make cellular phones available to patrons. Examples include commuter trains and ferry boats that cater to a business clientele.

Cellular networks are found in most major cities. Presently, not all networks are compatible; however, the trend is toward nationwide compatibility that will enable users to use their phones in any system nationwide.

COMMUNICATION CHALLENGES

Use of data communication is not without its challenges. Many computer systems are incompatible with each other and cannot easily establish communication linkages. In addition, data sent over communication channels are subject to various kinds of interference, which may alter or destroy some of the data. Besides ensuring data security, data privacy also must be protected. Passwords and access codes may be helpful. However, to prevent unauthorized access to highly sensitive data, they may have to be encrypted (scrambled) before transmission. Then, of course, they must be decoded (unscrambled) when received.

DATA COMMUNICATION AT WORK

Numerous businesses make extensive use of telecommunication systems. One of the earliest and biggest success stories was that of American Hospital Supply Corporation and its installation of order-entry terminals on hospital premises in 1974. Hospitals could then simply enter or check the status of an order at any time, without having to wait for a salesperson.

Today Federal Express uses a parcel tracking system known as Cosmos. This on-line system enables inquiries from remote locations about the status of a parcel. In addition, it locates delayed shipments and automatically sends invoices to customers. Federal Express delivery vans are even equipped with on-board terminals to improve customer service. With the use of telecommunication, drivers can call the Cosmos system directly and answer customers' questions as to the whereabouts of a parcel.

On-line reservations systems have also revolutionized the travel industry, from car rentals to hotels to airlines. All of these organizations, as well as travel agencies, send and receive information on reservations and flight schedules through data communication channels. Saber (American Airlines) and Apollo (United Airlines) are two of the largest reservation systems.

Many of the stories in newspapers and magazines are filed by journalists using portable computers and data-communication channels in remote locations. Many supermarket merchants and other retailers link their cash registers to a large computer at a distant location to track inventories.

Another application of data communication is **electronic data interchange (EDI),** a communication protocol which allows retailers and their suppliers to conduct business transactions electronically. Use of EDI reduces the paperwork, human involvement, and time associated with processing a single order. Turnaround time on orders has been reduced in some cases by as much as 50 percent.

Electronic funds transfer (EFT), the electronic movement of money among accounts, is another widely used data-communication application. A large portion of money in the business and financial communities changes hands through EFT. One popular form of EFT is the automated teller machine. In fact, Society for Worldwide Interbank Financial Telecommunications (SWIFT), the most sophisticated private interbank system in the world, averages 750,000 transactions daily for 1,300 member banks in 46 countries. After it is upgraded, the mainframe and communication network of the system will process 1 million messages daily.

Right now approximately 1,500 member banks in 46 states use the Cirrus banking network to process some 200 million transactions annually. The network provides such services as cash withdrawals and balance inquiries for checking, savings, and credit accounts and supports more than 6,500 automated teller machines.

Some companies have adopted a method of employment called **telecommuting**. This method permits some personnel to work at home and use their computers to communicate with an office computer.

Data communication has made the computer one of the most vital tools in our information-using society. It links two or more computers via communication channels and enables users to send and receive electronic data with little regard for time or distance.

Equipping a personal computer with communication hardware and software can open a whole new world of information resources. One of the easiest and least expensive ways to begin exploring communication capa-

TABLE 5–1

Hints on using a bulletin board system (BBS).

<table>
<tr><td colspan="1"></td></tr>
<tr><td>

☐ Keep pencil and paper near your computer to write down names of files, list commands and other instructions, and note names of people or messages that are of interest.

☐ Write down the password, if there is one, and keep it handy.

☐ Ask questions of the system operators (sysops) and BBS users. These are usually people who like to share their thoughts and experiences with others.

☐ If the BBS line is always busy, try early morning hours.

☐ If calling long distance, prepare messages before going on-line to save on phone charges.

☐ Most BBSs use the remote bulletin board system (RBBS) or Hostcomm bulletin board system program. If the BBS you use requires a long-distance call, try to find out what program that BBS uses. Then find a local bulletin board that uses the same program to familiarize yourself with the operating environment. This saves money because you do not spend time on a long-distance phone connection learning how that BBS operates.

☐ For public domain software, try local BBSs. If the software is not available locally, then try long-distance BBSs.

</td></tr>
</table>

bilities is by using a bulletin board system (Table 5–1). A **bulletin board system (BBS)** is the electronic equivalent of a conventional bulletin board. Many BBSs are established to let users exchange information about any topic; others are set up for people who own a specific brand or model of computer. The first electronic bulletin board system was created in 1978 by Ward Christensen and Randy Suess to help the members of the Chicago Area Computer Hobbyists Exchange trade information.

Electronic mail refers to a variety of methods used to electronically transmit mail and messages almost anywhere in the world. It is a system used by computers and communication channels to store and send messages. Many businesses use electronic-mail systems to reduce paperwork and the time it takes messages to reach their destinations.

Facsimile is a specialized type of electronic mail. **Facsimile (fax)** transmission allows a copy of an original document to be electronically sent and reproduced at another location. To send a copy, you insert the original document into the fax unit. The fax machine scans the document and then sends digital electronic signals representing its text, graphics, photographs, and even handwriting over telephone lines. (Many fax units are directly connected to a phone line; if not, you must place the phone receiver into a coupler.) Another fax machine at the receiving end receives the electronic signals and converts them into a facsimile of the original document, producing a hard-copy print (Figure 5–16). Fax machines must be compatible to communicate with each other, and fax standards are beginning to emerge.

Fax boards are new developments that allow a personal computer to function as a fax machine. Through the use of facsimile technology, doc-

FIGURE 5–16
A facsimile (fax) machine sends
a document electronically to a
branch office in another city.

uments that are urgently needed can now be sent between offices anywhere in the world in minutes. Facsimile is rapidly growing in popularity,
so much so that "junk fax mail" is considered a problem by many.

Even with the introduction of many new forms of electronic communication, the telephone remains the most-used device for communication between businesspeople. It is simple, efficient, easy for people to understand and use, and it can be combined with a computer to form a
voice-messaging system. **Voice-messaging systems** are computer-
supported systems that allow a message to be sent as human voice from
standard push-button telephones, without the need for the recipient to be
available to receive the message.

Messages can be sent and received from standard push-button telephones. When you prepare a message, the voice-messaging system stores
it. You then can review and edit it before sending to the recipient's voice
mailbox. When you instruct the computer to do so, it sends the message to
the mailbox for storage. When convenient, the recipient can dial his or her
mailbox and hear the message.

The latest and most promising technology is **electronic teleconferencing,** where computer systems are connected by the telephone system
and participants key in their conversations. Participants at a teleconference

can be anywhere in the world. Although teleconferencing won't replace business travel, it can replace nonessential trips.

Participants need not be at their computers at the same time to have a successful conference. A question might be asked of a participant and sent to that individual's mailbox. The recipient can access and read the message at a convenient time.

Teleconferencing systems are similar to BBSs, but they are much larger and require large computer systems to run them and store the data. Most BBSs operate on microcomputer systems.

A business that supplies information to subscribers on numerous topics of general interest is an **information service**. These services use powerful, large-computer systems that store millions of pieces of data. In some ways, information services are similar to BBSs; however, they are run on a much larger scale, supply much more information, and operate as businesses for profit.

In addition to information about general topics, **commercial database services** offer information on highly specialized topics. Such services are collections of large-scale databases that contain millions of articles, abstracts, and bibliographic citations from thousands of books, periodicals, reports, and theses. A subscriber is permitted to electronically search these collections for information.

A **gateway service** buys large quantities of connect time at wholesale rates from information or commercial database services and then resells the time to its own subscribers at retail rates. With a single call to a gateway service, a subscriber can connect to several different services.

Videotext is an interactive information service similar to other information services, but it uses color displays and graphics. The other services we have discussed thus far transmit and receive data as text and have no graphic capabilities. Videotext is designed to heighten consumer interest with color and graphics. (Users, of course, must have computer systems that can display the color and graphics.)

Data communication has made the computer one of the most vital tools in our information-hungry society. It links two or more computers via communication channels and enables users to send and receive electronic data with little regard for time or distance.

SUMMARY	Data communication is the process of sending data electronically from one point to another. Using communication facilities such as the telephone system and microwave relays to send data between computers is a type of data communication often referred to as telecommunication.

The transmission of data takes one of two forms: analog or digital. Analog data transmission is the passage of data in continuous-wave form. Digital data transmission is the passage of data in distinct on-and-off pulses.

Modulation is the process of converting a digital signal into an analog signal. Demodulation is the process of converting the analog signal back into a digital signal. A modem (*mo*dulator–*dem*odulator) is the device that converts the signals. |

A communication channel is a pathway along which data are transmitted between devices. The three basic types of communication channels are (1) wire cable, (2) microwave, and (3) fiber optic.

Multiplexing is the process of combining the transmissions of several computers or devices so they share the same communication channel. Concentration allows a communication channel to be connected to and serve more devices than the capacity of that channel normally allows. A front-end processor is a computer that handles all data-communication control functions, freeing the CPU of a main computer to work on other tasks.

Common carriers are companies licensed and regulated to transmit data owned by others. Specialized common carriers and value-added carriers are alternatives to the major common carriers for data communication.

The baud rate of a communication channel is the number of times per second that the transmitted signal changes (modulates or demodulates). The bandwidth, or band, of a communication channel determines the speed at which that channel can transmit data.

Asynchronous transmission transmits data one character at a time. Synchronous transmission transmits data as a block of characters in timed sequences. Protocol is the set of rules and procedures defining the technical details of data transfer between two devices. Data transfer can occur in three modes: (1) simplex, (2) half-duplex, and (3) full-duplex.

Data communication has allowed the linking of microcomputer to microcomputer and microcomputer to mainframe so that data and capabilities can be shared. A computer network is created when several computers and other devices, such as printers and secondary storage devices, are linked together by data-communication channels. Each computer or device in a network is called a node. The way in which these nodes are connected is the network's topology. Network topologies include a star network, ring network, tree (hierarchical) network, and bus network.

A wide-area network (WAN) consists of two or more computers that are geographically dispersed but linked by communication facilities provided by common carriers, such as the telephone system or microwave relays. A local-area network (LAN) consists of two or more computers directly linked within a small, well-defined area, such as a room, building, or cluster of buildings. LANs can be connected to WANs through the use of gateways, which convert the data codes, formats, addresses, and transmission rates of one network into a form usable by another network.

Distributed data processing (DDP) is dispersing the computers, devices, software, and data that are connected through communication channels into the areas where they are used. The computers are organized on a functional or geographical basis, and they work together as a cohesive system to support user requirements.

A cellular network permits mobile communication from cellular telephones. Computers can send and receive data over a cellular network through the use of modems and cellular phones. Cellular computers can transmit data directly over a cellular network without the use of modems or phones.

Data communication has allowed computers to share data in spite of the boundaries of time or distance. It has found many applications in our society, including reservation systems, electronic funds transfer, and tele-commuting.

Vocabulary Self-Test

Can you define the following?

acoustic modem (p. 144)

analog data transmission (p. 142)

asynchronous transmission (p. 153)

bandwidth (p. 153)

baud rate (p. 153)

broad-band channel (p. 153)

bulletin board system (BBS) (p. 168)

bus network (p. 158)

cellular network (p. 165)

commercial database service (p. 170)

common carrier (p. 150)

communication channel (p. 144)

computer network (p. 156)

concentration (p. 149)

concentrator (p. 149)

contention (p. 148)

data communication (p. 141)

demodulation (p. 143)

digital data transmission (p. 142)

distributed data processing (DDP) (p. 164)

electronic data interchange (EDI) (p. 167)

electronic mail (p. 168)

electronic teleconferencing (p. 169)

external direct-connect modem (p. 144)

facsimile (fax) (p. 168)

fiber optics (p. 147)

front-end processor (p. 150)

full-duplex mode (p. 155)

gateway (p. 160)

gateway service (p. 170)

half-duplex mode (p. 154)

handshaking (p. 154)

information service (p. 170)

internal direct-connect modem (p. 144)

local-area network (LAN) (p. 160)

message characters (p. 154)

micro-to-mainframe link (p. 156)

micro-to-micro link (p. 155)

microwave (p. 146)

modem (p. 143)

modulation (p. 143)

multiplexer (p. 149)

multiplexing (p. 148)

multipoint channel configuration (p. 148)

narrow-band channel (p. 153)

network server (p. 161)

node (p. 156)

null modem cable (p. 155)

point-to-point channel configuration (p. 148)

polling (p. 148)

protocol (p. 154)

ring network (p. 157)

satellite (p. 147)

simplex mode (p. 154)

star network (p. 156)

synchronous transmission (p. 154)

telecommunication (p. 141)

telecommuting (p. 167)

topology (p. 156)

tree network (p. 157)

videotext (p. 170)

voice-band channel (p. 153)

voice messaging system (p. 169)

wide-area network (WAN) (p. 158)

wire cable (p. 144)

Review Questions

Multiple Choice

1. _____ is the process of using communication facilities such as the telephone system and microwave relays to send data between computers; it is a form of data communication.
   a. Telecommunication
   b. Modulation
   c. Demodulation
   d. Multiplexing

2. A _____ communication channel transmits data in digital form through clear flexible tubing.
   a. wire-cable
   b. fiber-optics
   c. simplex
   d. microwave

3. _____ is a method of determining access to a communication channel when the computer checks with the device to determine if the device has a message to send.
   a. Contention
   b. Polling
   c. Multiplexing
   d. Concentration

4. Multiplexing and concentration are two _____.
   a. data transfer modes
   b. communication bandwidths
   c. channel configurations
   d. channel sharing methods

5. The _____ (or grade) of a communication channel determines the rate (speed) that data can be transmitted over the channel.
   a. bits per second
   b. baud rate
   c. bandwidth
   d. protocol

6. _____ transmission of data is a method whereby blocks of characters are transmitted in timed sequences.
   a. Asynchronous
   b. Half-duplex
   c. Full-duplex
   d. Synchronous

7. The set of rules and procedures for transmission of data are called _____.
   a. handshaking
   b. protocol
   c. message characters
   d. links

8. A _____ network is one in which each computer is connected to a single communication cable via an interface and every computer can communicate with every other computer.
   a. star
   b. ring
   c. tree
   d. bus

9. A _____ is two or more computers directly linked within a small, well-defined area, such as a room, building, or cluster of buildings.
   a. wide-area network
   b. local-area network
   c. cellular network
   d. network topology

10. Which one of the following is not a feature of distributed data processing?
   a. user-controlled computing facilities
   b. centralization
   c. cost efficiency
   d. shared resources

Fill-in

1. The process of sending data electronically from one point to another is called _____ .

2. A(n) _____ configuration connects one device to another device by a dedicated communication channel.

3. The process whereby each terminal monitors the communication channel to determine if it is available is called _____ .

4. _____ is the process of combining the transmissions from several devices into a single data stream that can be sent over a single high-speed communication channel.

5. The process of connecting and serving more devices to a computer than a communication channel can handle at one time is called _____ .

6. A(n) _____ is a special-purpose computer that handles all data-communication control functions.

7. A company that is licensed and regulated by federal or state government to transmit the data-communication property of others at regulated rates is called a(n) _____ .

8. In _____ transmission messages are transmitted one character at a time and in _____ transmission messages are transmitted as blocks of characters in timed sequences.

9. A set of traffic rules and procedures that govern how data are transmitted is called _____ .

10. A(n) _____ is created when data-communication channels link several computers and other devices, such as printers and secondary storage devices.

Short Answer

1. How does data communication differ from telecommunication?
2. Describe the difference between analog and digital data transmission.
3. When is a modem needed? Why are two needed?
4. Describe the purpose of a communication channel and discuss the three types presented in the chapter.
5. Describe how the processes of polling and contention operate.
6. What are the three bandwidths for communication channels? Discuss their differences.

7. List and describe the three modes in which the transfer of data can occur.

8. List three factors to consider for a microcomputer to communicate with a large system computer.

9. Name and describe the four different network topologies.

10. Define wide-area network, local-area network, and distributed data processing.

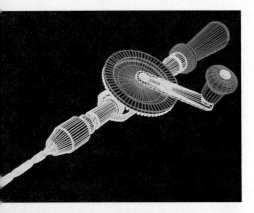

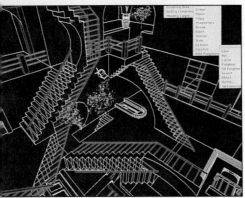

OBJECTIVES

☐ Define system, information system, and computer-based information.

☐ Describe the three basic functions of an information system.

☐ Describe the different levels of management and the types of information each needs.

☐ Describe how transaction processing systems, management information systems, decision support systems, and executive support systems are used by the different levels of management.

☐ List and describe the four phases of the system development life cycle (SDLC).

☐ Understand the role of prototyping and the importance of automation in the SDLC.

☐ Define file management system (FMS) and describe its advantages and disadvantages.

☐ Discuss the advantages and disadvantages of database processing.

☐ Describe the purpose and function of a database management system (DBMS).

☐ List and describe the four database models.

☐ Identify database design considerations.

CHAPTER SIX

Information Systems

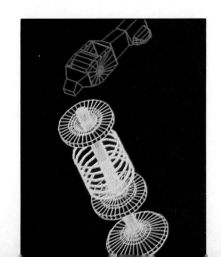

PROFILE
E. F. Codd

Experience is one of life's best teachers. Most of us can see how something can be accomplished by doing. Some, however, can see how something is done and devise a new and better way of doing it. So it was with Edgar F. Codd, the creator of the relational database structure. Codd received his master's degree in mathematics from Oxford University in England in 1949. Later, he incorporated the mathematical concepts he had learned at Oxford to develop his strategy for a database management system. This development did not happen overnight, for Codd had 20 years of computer experience before proposing his ideas on a relational database model.

Codd, who was born in England and served as a pilot for the Royal Air Force in World War II, went to work at IBM in 1949. His work there included helping design IBM's first stored-program computer, the IBM 701. Codd also lived briefly in Canada, where he managed the computer center for the Canadian Guided Missile Program. A short time later he returned and became a citizen of the United States.

Some 2 decades after starting at IBM, Codd found himself at a seminar on database management systems. Here Codd saw something amiss with the structure.

Finding data was a potentially complex process under this current structure. Codd reasoned that by using sound mathematical principles, called predicate logic, the database structure could be simplified into tables. In mathematical terms, these tables were called relations. From there, Codd's idea became known as a relational database structure.

New ideas are not always welcomed with open arms, however. Codd struggled for many years to persuade IBM to accept his concept. In fact, it was 1981 before IBM announced its first relational database product. Still, perseverance paid off for Codd, as the relational model became the standard for databases.

The battles were not over, though. Codd had to fight back from a serious fall that left him in a coma. He retired 2 years later from IBM, in 1985. Not one to rest on his laurels, Codd formed his own company with a friend. Codd and Date Consultants continued his work to improve the relational database model. His new battles come from the proponents of object-oriented databases, who say the relational system is outmoded.

No matter what your career path, you will likely be responsible for identifying and solving problems and for making decisions in your work. Some decisions may be inconsequential, and others may have monumental impact on you and your organization. To ensure that the decisions you make are in the best interest of your organization, you must understand how to recognize and acquire appropriate information to make those decisions. Thus, you must understand how to use computers and information systems to their best advantage.

Information is a key to a successful business. Organizations realize that next to people, information is their most valuable resource. Computers and information systems have been a primary force in enabling people to collect, process, and manage information that they need to solve problems and make decisions.

Because of the changing makeup of businesses, employees and managers alike must understand the importance of information in problem solving and decision making, the role of computers in information systems, and the effect of information systems on strategies and goals of organizations. Computers and information systems have become the foundation of most businesses and the primary tools for managers to use in problem identification and decision making. The ways in which organizations use computers will profoundly affect the growth, profitability, and productivity of the organizations.

In this chapter we define the terms *system* and *information system*, look at the functions of information systems and ways in which management uses them, and discuss several of the major types of information systems in use. We also will look at the system development life cycle (SDLC). Finally, we'll discuss two types of program used by information systems to manage data—file management systems and database management systems.

WHAT IS A SYSTEM?

A **system** is a set of components that interact with each other to form a whole and work together toward a common goal. The four major components of a system are (1) inputs, (2) processes, (3) outputs, and (4) feedback control. Figure 6–1 illustrates a simple system.

Input is anything that enters the system, such as energy, materials, or data. For example, raw material such as iron ore may be input into a

FIGURE 6–1
A simple system.

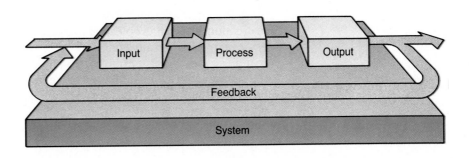

? not
always

production system, and data in the form of market share figures may be input into a marketing system. A system may have one or many inputs.

Output is anything leaving the system. Outputs are the goal of the system, the purpose for which the system exists. Products, services, or information may be the outputs of a system, and the outputs from one system can become the inputs for another system. For example, the output of one system (an organization that produces tires) might be automobile tires. These tires might then be used as an input in another system (an automobile production company) that assembles automobile parts.

A *process* transforms an input into an output.

Feedback reintroduces a portion of the output from a system as a special kind of input into the same system. Feedback is used as a control mechanism within a system to indicate the difference between the goals and actual performance of a system. The thermostat used in home heating-and-cooling systems provides feedback to control the temperature.

INFORMATION SYSTEMS DEFINED

An **information system** is a set of people, data, and procedures that work together to achieve the common goal of information management. Information management includes the tasks of (1) gathering data, (2) processing them into reliable, accurate, and usable information, and (3) distributing them in a timely fashion for use in decision making, problem solving, and control. People, data, and procedures are the minimum components of an information system.

The most valuable resource an organization has is its people. From the production line through top management, people make products, deliver services, solve problems, and make decisions. Good people are the backbone of an organization.

Data also play an important role in an information system; they are the basis for information. The data gathered must be complete and accurate. If not, the information generated from the data will not be valid or accurate, and errors in decision making may result.

A large portion of the resources of an organization are put into gathering and storing data about business transactions, competitors, the marketplace, and a host of other topics. An organization must determine what data are essential to generate the information needed, where to obtain the data, and whether the data gathered are correct. All of this must be done in a cost-effective manner.

The final component in an information system is procedures, the instructions that tell people how to operate and use an information system. For example, procedures tell how to format data for input into an information system, what steps to use to process specific data, and ways to use the output. Procedures also explain the steps to be taken if errors occur. Common sources of procedures include operations manuals (which provide instructions on how to operate the computer system) and user's manuals (which tell how to use the information system to get the information needed).

COMPUTER-BASED INFORMATION SYSTEMS

Even though an information system does not require a computer, when most people read or hear the term *information system* they think of computer-based information systems. A **computer-based information system** is a set of people, data, procedures, hardware, and software that work together to achieve the common goal of information management. We have already discussed people, data, and procedures. Hardware is any physical device or connection of a computer system, such as a computer, disk drive, printer, modem, or cable. Software is the set of instructions that tell the hardware how to operate. From here on, we'll use the term *information system* to mean a computer-based information system.

Computers are used to increase the efficiency and effectiveness of an information system (Figure 6–2). Computers allow the data to be processed and stored in less time than ever before. Because of the speed of computers in processing data and the capability of electronic communications to distribute information, users can take advantage of information that would otherwise have been impossible to gather, process, analyze, and distribute in timely fashion. Thus, decisions can be based on better or more complete information.

However, the use of computers does not automatically create a better information system. Computers simply are *tools* to reach this goal. The advantage of using computers in information systems is that they perform arithmetic functions, test relationships, and store and retrieve data faster, more accurately, and more reliably than people can. However, people still

FIGURE 6–2
At Ford Motor Company, computers enable engineers to easily collect, process, and manage test data on automobiles. The information can help the engineers detect and solve problems and improve designs. (Courtesy of Ford Motor Company)

determine what data to collect, how to process the data, and how to use the information generated.

Computers can also act as equalizers. They can enable smaller companies to compete effectively with larger ones. In many cases, large companies can no longer overpower smaller companies simply by using their size to make the cost of entering the market very high. Computers are also used to achieve a twofold strategic advantage:

- By differentiating the products and services of an organization from those of others in the field. (J. C. Penney used computers to create a credit card network; this created a new business that other companies pay to use and helped differentiate J. C. Penney from its competitors.)
- By applying automation to become the low-cost producer in an industry. (Northeast Utilities is using the latest computer and communication technologies to help keep down costs.)

FUNCTIONS OF AN INFORMATION SYSTEM

An information system has three basic functions: (1) to accept data (input), (2) to convert data to information (process), and (3) to produce and communicate information (output) in a timely fashion to users for decision making. Many banks and other financial institutions use information systems to help determine whether a customer applying for a loan is a good risk (Table 6–1). Data about the customer, lending policies, and interest rates are input into the information system, which then processes the data using previously defined procedures for determining credit worthiness, and generates information for the loan officer (the user) in the form of a recommendation to grant or deny the loan. The information is output in a form usable by the loan officer. It is important to note, however, that no matter what the output indicates, the user of an information system must make the actual decision.

Because of the ever-increasing importance of information to organizations, the efficiency and effectiveness of an information system's information management are becoming more and more critical to the success of the organization.

TABLE 6–1
Functions of an information system in determining customer credit.

Input	Process	Output
Data	*Data to Information*	*Information*
Customer specifics Lending policy Interest rate	Algorithms to convert data into desired information (e.g., customer credit worthiness, recommendation of whether to grant loan or not)	Transformed into a form usable by loan officer (e.g., screen display, paper copy)

MANAGERS AND INFORMATION NEEDS

In business, managers at all levels make decisions. Each level has its own need for specific types of information to handle problems. Before defining the different levels of management, we'll describe what managers are and what they do.

The Roles of Managers

A **manager** is a person responsible for using available resources—people, materials/equipment, land, information, money—to achieve the goals of an organization. Managers are the key decision makers and problem solvers within organizations. To perform most efficiently and effectively, managers must receive information they need when they need it.

Managers work toward goals through five major functions:

1. *Planning* is the future-oriented process of developing courses of action to meet short-term and long-term goals of an organization.
2. *Staffing* is assembling and training personnel to achieve the goals.
3. *Organizing* provides resources and a structure in which personnel are responsible and accountable for working toward the goals.
4. *Directing* supplies leadership in supervising personnel, via communication and motivation.
5. *Controlling* involves developing procedures to measure actual performance against goals and making adjustments to keep the organization moving toward its goals.

Functions of a Manager

- Planning
- Staffing
- Organizing
- Directing
- Controlling
- *Debugging*

Management Levels and Information Needs

Management is divided into three basic levels: (1) strategic (top-level) managers, (2) tactical (middle-level) managers, and (3) operational (low-level) managers (Figure 6–3). Although all three levels of management work toward organizational goals and are involved to varying degrees in all five of the management functions, each level requires different types of information.

Management Levels

- Strategic (top-level)
- Tactical (middle-level)
- Operational (low-level)

Strategic Managers. **Strategic (top-level) managers** make decisions involving long-range, or strategic, goals of organizations. Of the five major management functions, top-level managers spend most of their time planning and organizing. They need summarized information that covers past and present operations as well as future projections. Information drawn from internal sources gives them broad views of the internal situations of their companies. Information drawn from external sources permits them to evaluate industry trends, world economic trends, government regulations, and other outside activities that influence the business health of corporations. A strategic manager such as Lee Iacocca, chief executive officer of Chrysler, might be required to decide whether a new plant should be opened or a new sports car produced.

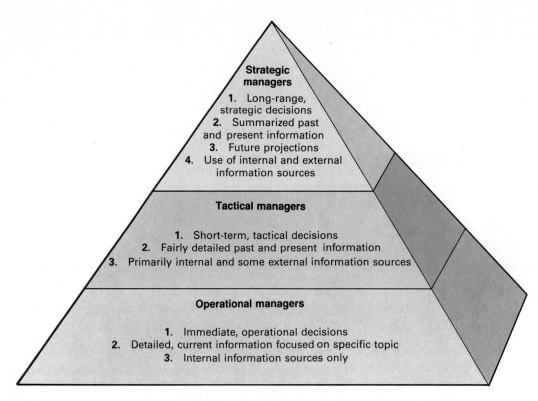

FIGURE 6–3
Levels of management, types of decision making, and information needs.

Tactical Managers. **Tactical (middle-level) managers** divide their time among all five functions of management. They are concerned with short-term, tactical decisions directed toward accomplishing the organizational goals established by the top-level managers. Middle-level managers work on budgets, schedules, and performance evaluations and need information that is fairly detailed to permit them to compare present and past results and make adjustments where necessary. Middle-level managers require mainly internal information but also use some external information. A tactical manager for Chrysler might decide how long to advertise a new car on television in a particular state. Many organizations are using computerization to reduce the number of tactical managers and cut costs.

Operational Managers. **Operational (low-level) managers** are directly involved with the day-to-day operations of business. They are responsible for seeing that the tactical decisions of middle-level managers are implemented by personnel at the operations level. The information of operational managers must be detailed, current, and focused. It comes from such sources as inventory lists, historical records, and procedures manuals. An operational manager at Chrysler might decide to use a newer and less-expensive method for cleaning paint-nozzle jets.

TYPES OF INFORMATION SYSTEMS

To accommodate the differences in information needs of the various management levels, several different types of information systems have evolved. We have been looking at the organization from the top down; now let's look at it from the bottom up. On the operational level are transaction processing systems (TPSs). At the tactical level, management information systems (MISs) provide support. Decision support systems (DSSs) can be found on both tactical and strategic levels. Executive support systems (ESSs), a variation of DSSs, operate on the strategic level.

Transaction Processing Systems

A **transaction** is a business activity or event. Transactions include buying a product such as clothes at a department store or a service such as cable television from the local cable company. The information system that records and helps manage these transactions is known as a **transaction processing system (TPS)**. Certain transaction processing systems are commonly seen in business organizations: accounts payable, order entry, accounts receivable, inventory control, payroll, and general ledger. These systems are grouped into one broad category—accounting information systems.

Management Information Systems

The purpose of a **management information system (MIS)** is to provide information to managers for use in problem detection and solution. An MIS is used in decision making for situations that recur and are highly structured. The manager knows the information requirements in advance. An MIS can use data from a transaction processing system as well as data collected and processed to assist in a particular decision. For example, an MIS could collect transactions from an order-entry system for all customers and then summarize them to show the total sales volume each month compared with that of the same month for the previous year.

Information from an MIS is available to managers either as reports or via on-line retrieval. Reports are hard-copy printouts containing masses of information, whereas on-line retrieval generates small amounts of information tailored to managers' inquiries.

Reports are the primary form of information presented to all levels of management in an organization. They often are classified according to their production schedule and contents. **Scheduled reports,** generated on a regular basis such as weekly or monthly, are useful primarily to operating managers and their staffs. They may be detailed or summarized, depending on purpose.

Demand reports are generated only on demand from an individual. In other words, such reports are not produced unless someone asks for them. Such reports are needed for special purposes; for example, a personnel manager might need to know which employees have shown unsatisfactory job performance for 2 consecutive years. Such a report is not

---

Types of Information Systems

- Transaction processing systems (TPSs)
- Management information systems (MISs)
- Decision support systems (DSSs)
- Executive support systems (ESSs)

produced on a regular basis but may be required at special times, such as before staff cuts.

Exception reports highlight out-of-control activities that need management action, allowing more efficient use of the manager's time by focusing on activities that have problems. Exception reports might target late activities for a project manager, delinquent customers for a credit manager, slow-moving items for an inventory manager, or absentee workers or machine down-time for a manufacturing manager.

A manager may have specific questions about something that does not warrant a full report, but still needs answers very quickly. The on-line retrieval feature of a management information system offers this capability: a manager asks a question by keying in a request, and the computer responds to the question immediately. On-line retrieval applications include inquiries by credit managers on the credit status of applicants or customers, airlines reservation managers on flight schedule information, and inventory managers on the status of items in inventory.

Regardless of format, an MIS presents information to a manager only in a predetermined form. It cannot provide any other views of the information or incorporate new information without being reprogrammed. To give managers greater flexibility in entering, retrieving, and analyzing the data they need, decision support systems are used.

Decision Support Systems

A **decision support system (DSS)** is an interactive, computer-based information system that helps solve structured, semistructured, or unstructured management problems. To explain some of this terminology, an **interactive system** allows a user to communicate with a computer through dialogue. *Unstructured problems* refer to those without any clear-cut solutions, such as problems that do not repeat or problems that cannot be predicted in advance. *Structured problems* have well-known solutions and are repetitive. *Semistructured problems* fall in between.

As its name indicates, a decision support system does not make decisions for users, but *supports* decision making. Managers must use their judgment, intuition, and experience to evaluate solutions proposed by a DSS.

Because a semistructured or unstructured problem does not have a clear-cut solution, a DSS can present several possible solutions for one problem. It allows a user to enter, retrieve, and analyze data in an ad hoc manner. The user does not have to rely on the systems department to change the program, create new relationships among existing data, enter new data, or analyze the data in a new way. As a result, information is available almost immediately. DSSs are used by middle-level and top-level managers, but primarily by middle management. They are often oriented toward models and data analysis. Managers often use both internal and external data to support their decisions.

Reports generated by a DSS are known as **predictive reports**. Such reports are useful in suggesting what might happen, given certain planning decisions.

There are numerous DSS applications in business organizations. Some of the most important and widely used applications are in financial planning, manufacturing, mergers and acquisitions, new product development, plant expansions, and sales forecasting. In financial planning, banks use DSSs for budgeting and for analyzing the impact of changes in money market rates, financial regulations, and interest rates. Manufacturing firms use DSSs to study the impact that different combinations of production processes, labor rates, and machine capacities have on production costs.

DSSs are used in new product development to analyze the impact that different marketing strategies and competitive actions have on the success of a new product. In plant expansions, application of DSSs involves analyzing the effect of different expansion alternatives on cost and production. Sales forecasting incorporates DSSs to evaluate profitability estimates of a company being considered for acquisition.

Executive Support Systems

Executive is usually synonymous with *strategic* or *top-level management*. An executive has the responsibility of setting long-range planning goals and a strategic course for an organization for the years ahead. Although different levels of management can benefit from decision support systems, DSSs are used predominantly by middle management for assistance in decision making. A DSS that caters specifically to the special information needs of executives—managerial planning, monitoring, and analysis—is called an **executive support system (ESS)**. Figure 6–4 illustrates the relationships of TPSs, MISs, DSSs, and ESSs for various levels of management.

An executive support system incorporates large volumes of data and information gathered from the external environment of an organization.

FIGURE 6–4
Relationships among TPSs, MISs, DSSs, ESSs, and the levels of management.

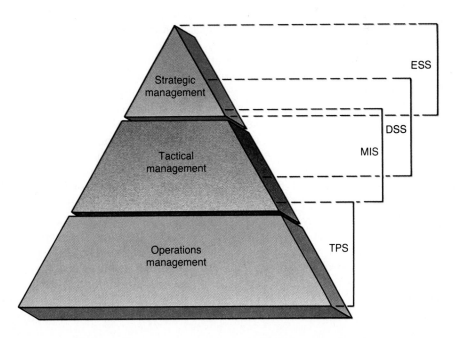

That information, used in conjunction with information generated by MISs within functional areas of the organization, accommodates the specialized information needs of executives. An ESS is vital in summarizing and controlling the volume of information that an executive must read. An executive can assign values to the various information sources from which data are drawn, so as to receive information from those sources deemed most important for decision making. Thus, ESSs can be tailored to meet the specific needs of each executive in an organization.

THE SYSTEM DEVELOPMENT LIFE CYCLE

The **system development life cycle (SDLC)** is the structured sequence of operations required to conceive, develop, and make operational a new information system. The term *cycle* stresses that a newly designed system will not last forever; ultimately, it will need replacement, and the development cycle will start again.

The system development life cycle can be broken into four major phases (illustrated in Figure 6–5):

1. System *analysis* includes problem definition, analysis of requirements, and project justification.
2. System *design* includes logical system design and physical system design.
3. System *implementation* includes testing, installation, and training.
4. System *maintenance* includes continually monitoring and adjusting the system until it is time for a total reevaluation.

Developing an information system throughout the system development life cycle involves continual, clear communication among users and "system personnel"—the people responsible for designing and implementing the information system.

Users are those who will use an information system once it has been installed. Users include computer operators and managers who require information from the system. System personnel include system analysts, system designers, and programmers. A **system analyst** works with users to determine their information-processing needs. A **system designer** designs a system to fulfill users' needs. A **programmer** uses a programming language to code instructions for a computer to solve a problem. In large organizations, these positions are usually separate; in smaller enterprises one person may do all or several of the tasks.

To help make the communication process easier and more efficient, a project management team is often established.

Project management is the structured coordination and monitoring of all activities involved in a one-time endeavor (project). Three basic functions are required for management of an information system project: (1) planning, (2) monitoring, and (3) resource control.

During planning, detailed task lists are developed to specify timing, sequencing, and responsibilities. During monitoring, all project tasks are periodically measured to determine progress, in both time and cost. During resource control, planned progress is compared with actual progress to

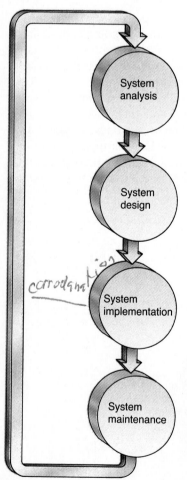

FIGURE 6–5
System development life cycle.

FIGURE 6-6
A project management team composed of system personnel and users must agree on the nature and scope of a problem. (Courtesy of Honeywell, Inc.)

System Development Life Cycle

- Analysis
- Design
- Implementation
- Maintenance

determine whether resource or schedule adjustments are needed. A project management team usually consists of a project manager and, depending upon project size, various numbers of users, system analysts, programmers, and other specialists (Figure 6-6).

The role of user involvement cannot be overemphasized. Users are the ultimate "consumers" of an information system and must accept the system if it is to be successful. The best way to ensure this acceptance is close communication between the team and the users throughout the development process.

Accurate and complete documentation throughout the entire cycle is important. **Documentation** is a written or graphic record of the steps carried out during the development of an information system. System personnel are responsible for accurately documenting each task they perform. Then, a system librarian compiles the documentation, maintains it, and makes it available to other personnel.

Keeping accurate and complete documentation is important. First, many people may be involved in development of an information system, and many tasks rely on work already completed by other members of a development team. Documentation allows system personnel and management to review what was previously done and understand why. A second reason is that many system development projects extend over a long period of time. During that time there will be personnel changes to the team. New personnel can review documentation to understand what is going on and thus be able to contribute even in the middle of a project.

SYSTEM ANALYSIS

System analysis, the first phase of system development, includes identifying a system problem or new opportunity, analyzing the current system in light of the problem or opportunity, and justifying development of a new system or modification of an old system to meet the needs of users. Many of you will eventually become part of management in an organization. Managers control the system analysis process and make the final decision on whether to proceed into the next phase of system design. To make sound decisions, managers must understand what should take place during system analysis.

The system analysis phase is crucial in developing an information system that works. Users must work with system personnel to identify the true nature of a problem or opportunity and develop a system to provide the information necessary for solving that problem or exploiting that opportunity. If a problem or opportunity is not correctly analyzed, the resulting information system may be useless or even detrimental.

System Analysis Phase

- Problem definition
- Requirements analysis
- Project justification

Problem Definition

The first stage in the system analysis phase is **problem definition**. System analysis is initiated by recognition of a problem or new opportunity that the current information system cannot handle. However, the appearance of a problem or opportunity does not always mean that the present system must be scrapped. It may simply mean that new features are required, or that no system currently exists to perform the needed functions.

A system analyst must quickly detect symptoms indicating that a system is becoming ineffective, and carefully gather all the facts to determine the nature, scope, and seriousness of any perceived problem. This is so because initiation of a new system or a major system modification is costly and time-consuming.

Requirements Analysis

The second stage of the analysis phase is **requirements analysis**. Here the analyst determines how the present information system performs, how the best possible system might perform, and what new system might bridge the gap between the two performance levels.

This composite portrait must, of course, be approved by key management personnel within the user group. Compromises often must be made. For example, although a "Cadillac" system might be very fast and have tight security, its cost might exceed the limits set by management. In such a case, a system analyst must identify alternative information systems to balance the needs of the users with the constraints of management (e.g., cost and time) and technology.

Project Justification

The final stage of system analysis is **project justification**. Here an analyst systematically compares alternative information systems and decides what to propose to management. It is a critical stage because it will end with management approval or rejection. Thus, the system development life cycle could be aborted here. Indeed, in a large percentage of cases, solutions are found to patch a current system, and ideas for replacement projects are not pursued. The project justification stage includes cost/benefit analysis of alternate systems, selection of the best system, preparation of a system study for submission to management, and management's final go or no-go decision.

System life Expectancy

Cost/benefit analysis is often referred to as "feasibility study." The objective is to compare costs and benefits of the alternative new information systems against the current system to determine which one to recommend. Typically, cost analysis is used to narrow the choices among alternative systems to two, or at most three. Then the analyst *qualitatively* (no numbers involved) considers the relative benefits of the two or three systems and selects the one that will best do the job. Having done so, the analyst must then sell the chosen system to management.

A **system study,** an extensive report that is sent to management, is generally accompanied by a formal oral presentation. It uses the results of the previous steps to justify the recommendation of the system analyst.

At this point, management must decide whether or not to accept the analyst's recommendations. That decision often is called the "go/no-go" decision because it determines whether to authorize the analyst to proceed with designing a replacement information system. Management may choose any one of several options at this point. It may:

1. Accept the system analyst's recommendation to proceed with design of the new information system. In this case, the remaining steps of the SDLC are activated.
2. Retain the present information system. This option may be chosen because (a) a cash-flow problem makes funds unavailable for initial investment in the new system, (b) some other department's recommendation shows more profit potential, or (c) management finds the system study to be so poorly prepared that it is not worth proceeding.
3. Repeat the system study, because one or more aspects seem to require further analysis. In this case, the analyst must reenter the system analysis phase at an earlier stage.
4. Table the study for future consideration (a variant of the second option). A new system may not be the right idea at the right time.

The project justification stage ends with the analyst's continuing the SDLC, or abandoning the project entirely, or polishing the project for another presentation to management at a future date.

SYSTEM DESIGN

The **system design** phase includes the logical design stage and the physical design stage.

Logical Design Stage

Logical design tasks must be carefully planned because the remaining stages in the system development life cycle are dependent on the logical design stage. Even the smallest error in this stage can be magnified throughout the SDLC so that it becomes a major problem when the new system is implemented. In addition, design errors identified early in this stage can be corrected much more quickly and cheaply than they can be later in the development cycle.

Logical system design shows the flow of data through an information system. It can be thought of as the information system blueprint. Much like an architect's blueprint, a system analyst's information system blueprint is a series of charts, graphs, and data layouts that describe the new information system in detail.

Physical Design Stage

The purpose of the **physical system design** stage is to convert the system blueprint into the specific detail required by programmers to develop the computer codes that transform the logical design into a working information system. An **algorithm** is the finite set of step-by-step instructions that system analysts will develop to solve the problem. **Coding** the program is the actual writing of instructions in a particular programming language to tell a computer how to operate. Programmers perform the task of coding.

A typical business information system is comprised of hundreds of thousands of lines of program code. Each line of code represents a separate operation for the computer to perform. A number of programmers are needed, and their efforts must be coordinated.

PROTOTYPING AND ITS EFFECTS ON THE SYSTEM DEVELOPMENT LIFE CYCLE

A **prototype information system** is a working information system that is built economically and quickly, with the intention of being modified. In the system analysis phase, prototyping is used to find out what uncertain users really want in an information system. In the system design phase, the analyst uses a prototype for varied reasons. To fine-tune system specifications, users are given copies of system output so they can make changes before further effort is put into programming. With a prototype, users can be trained earlier in the development process. A prototype that involves users gives them a sense of "system ownership," making them more tolerant of minor system faults after the new system is operational. Finally, a prototype can demonstrate the system to management so that key personnel can see how a long and expensive information system project is progressing.

The concept of prototyping is not new. It has been used in other fields for many years. Models of aircraft have been tested in wind tunnels since the 1920s, and architects have constructed scale models of buildings for centuries. In the information system field, however, it took the advent of microcomputers and fourth-generation languages for prototyping to become an efficient development tool. Effective use of prototyping cannot substantially change the tasks that must be accomplished to produce a new information system, but it can significantly decrease the time generally taken to develop such a system. The growing use of prototyping promises to streamline the development of information systems in general and the system analysis and system design phases in particular.

AUTOMATING SYSTEM ANALYSIS AND DESIGN

Until recently, system analysts were in a bizarre situation regarding the tools they used. They were designing large, complex computer information systems with pencils and paper. In other words, the automators were not automated! For example, the system flowchart tool might produce a final flowchart of 50 or more pages with a dozen or more symbols per page, all of which had to be drawn in pencil, using a flowchart symbol template. If a process step were omitted in the middle of page 34, much work was involved to modify the entire flowchart to insert the omitted symbol.

In recent years, automated system analysis and design programs that run on microcomputers have been marketed. These programs automate many of the system analyst's trivial but time-consuming tasks. The approach is similar to that of computer-aided design (CAD) in aiding architects and computer-aided manufacturing (CAM) in helping production designers. The software that automates system development tasks is called **computer-aided systems engineering (CASE)**. CASE products offer these automated capabilities:

- [ ] Graphics to produce and automatically change such analysis tools as **data flow diagrams (DFD),** as well as system and program flowcharts.
- [ ] Integration of other productivity tools, such as word processors and spreadsheets.
- [ ] Quality assurance functions that evaluate graphs and other CASE products for completeness, consistency, and accuracy.
- [ ] Data sharing, which allows system analysts to use several different microcomputer workstations to share graphics and data.
- [ ] Rapid prototyping, which allows quick and automatic generation of user input screens and output reports and forms.

The use of CASE products has made the design of business information systems faster, easier, and better. The investment required for CASE software purchases is typically less than $10,000, yet its increase in system analyst productivity typically exceeds 35 percent. As CASE products become more available and more comprehensive, their price is likely to decrease, and their use should dramatically increase during the next several years.

SYSTEM IMPLEMENTATION

The **system implementation** phase of the system development life cycle includes testing, installation, and training steps. During this phase, an information system is transferred to the users, and managers must ensure that systems are thoroughly tested and as error-free as possible to build confidence and acceptance in users. Frequently, managers must also budget for the type and amount of training that information system users should have.

Testing Stage

In **testing,** a new information system is checked to ensure that all of its parts are correct. Testing is one of the most important activities in the

THE BATTLE OF THE BUGS

Bugs are errors that find their way into computer software. In some cases, bugs are merely bothersome, but they can also be enormously expensive to businesses and catastrophic to military systems. Our increasing knowledge about computer construction and programming makes bugs easier to spot. However, the spread of computers into all facets of business gives bugs more places to hide.

According to one poll, computer glitches have complicated the lives of at least 91 percent of us, whether at work, at the bank, with credit card companies or airlines, or with computerized appliances at home. Bugs have delayed federal tax returns, wiped out financial records for an entire town, delayed space launches, caused gigantic overdrafts that have sent banks reeling, and raised the question of whether a life-or-death military system such as the Strategic Defense Initiative ("Star Wars") can ever be considered foolproof in its operations.

To reduce the likelihood of bugs, designers are turning to computers to design and test software, instead of leaving those tasks in the hands of human beings, who are more fallible. Large computer programs may use over 100,000 lines of code. Space and defense programs use millions of lines. Without computer aid, even a seasoned programmer might be able to write only 20 permanently usable lines of code a day.

In 1979, the General Accounting Office looked at computer use and reliability in government and learned that less than 2 percent of the $6.89 million spent for software programs could actually be used as bought. To address problems like this, companies now test programs for buyers before the programs are put into use.

Another defense against bugs—and probably the most realistic one—is to put safeguards in place to catch them. For example, the nearly 100 computers needed to fly the Boeing 767 duplicate essential operations so that another computer can compensate if a bug ruins a function.

development of an information system. Any system—whether a bridge, a piece of equipment, or an information system—can bring disaster to its users if it is not thoroughly tested and found to be satisfactory. Information system development is a huge expenditure and is important to the success of an organization. Therefore, a system must not be handed over to users without thorough testing.

Every information system performs information processing of some type. The overall purpose of testing such a system is to be sure that it processes data correctly and produces useful information. Testing should be conducted with each computer program module to ensure that its results are correct and that it has sufficient documentation. Highlight 6–1 discusses how software errors can affect information system programs.

A program must be tested to ensure that it is correct. It is difficult, if not presently impossible, to test a complex program for every condition that may cause an error. However, sufficient tests can provide reasonable surety that a program is error-free. Three types of program errors that may be encountered during the testing phase are syntax errors, run-time errors, and logic errors.

The **syntax** of a programming language is the set of rules and conventions followed when writing a program. These rules are similar to grammatical rules in any language. When the rules are violated, a **syntax error** occurs. All syntax errors must be found and corrected before a program will execute.

A second type of error that may occur is a run-time error. A **run-time error** stops the execution of a program. For example, if the program were set up to expect numerical data, and alphabetical data were entered instead, a poorly designed program would "crash," that is, stop executing. A properly written program would identify the problem, prompt the user with an error message, and permit the data to be reentered.

The third type of error, and hardest to find, is a logic error. A **logic error** will not stop program execution, but the results will not be accurate. With luck, the error will be obvious. Here's a simple example: The problem is to add 2 apples to 4 apples and determine the total number of apples. The formula should be $2 + 4 = 6$, but what if a wrong symbol, such as a multiplication sign, is typed into the computer? This would result in $2 \times 4 = 8$. The answer of 8 is correct for the formula as entered, but not for the problem intended to be solved—adding 2 apples to 4 apples. Finding the logic error in this example is easy, but finding a logic error in a complicated program can be like seeking the proverbial needle in a haystack.

The process of finding an error and correcting it is called **debugging** (Figure 6–7). After the program for an information system is debugged, it can be installed and used.

Installation Stage

After successful testing of an information system, it is installed. In **installation,** a system is made operational and put to work. This is a major component in information system development, and it may require considerable capital to support both people and equipment. In some cases, installation cost exceeds system design cost. However, the ultimate success of an information system may depend on how well the various parts of this task are carried out.

Planning is the first subtask to be completed for installation of an information system. Many information systems cause significant changes in the operating procedures of a business organization, and such changes are filled with technical and human problems. For an installation that is as trouble-free as possible, careful planning is essential.

System Implementation Phase

■ Testing
■ Installation
■ Training

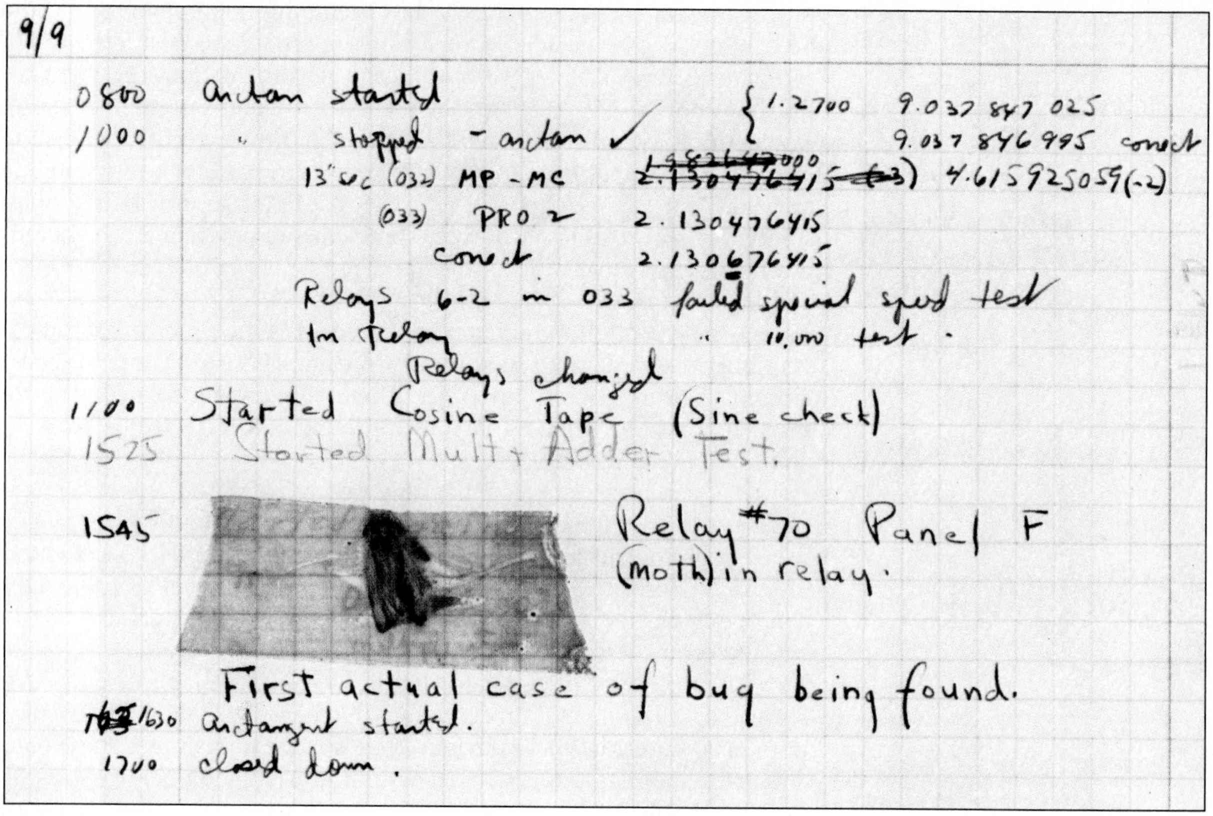

The handwritten log page reads:

```
9/9

0800   antan started
1000      "    stopped - antan ✓        { 1.2700   9.037 847 025
       13" uc (032) MP - MC                      9.037 846 995  conect
              (033)  PRO 2    2.130476415 -3)  4.615925059 (-2)
              conect          2.130676415
       Relays 6-2 in 033 failed special speed test
       in relay              "  10.000 test .
                 Relays changed
1100   Started Cosine Tape (Sine check)
1525   Started Mult + Adder Test.

1545   [photo of moth]              Relay #70  Panel F
                                    (moth) in relay.

       First actual case of bug being found.
1630   antangent started.
1700   closed down .
```

FIGURE 6-7

Pioneering computer developer Grace Hopper relates the story that in 1945, she and a team of programmers were working on the Mark II, an early large-scale digital calculator, when the computer simply quit. They couldn't determine what was wrong. Finally, they looked inside the computer and saw a small dead moth in one of the signal relays. The moth, the first computer "bug," was removed and saved for posterity in a log book now located at the U.S. Naval Museum in Dahlgren, Virginia. After that incident, whenever naval officers would check on progress when a computer was not operating, the personnel would advise that they were "debugging the program." (U.S. Navy photo)

A team of users, system developers, and managers should plan the installation. Included should be the different tasks to be completed, completion dates for each, and names of the individuals responsible for their completion.

Conversion is the replacement of an existing system with a new information system. There are four approaches to conversion: (1) direct, (2) parallel, (3) phased-in, and (4) pilot conversion (Figure 6-8).

With **direct conversion** (also called crash conversion), a new information system replaces the existing one as of a certain date, and the old system stops being used. This approach has pros and cons. Direct conversion is economical because only one system at a time is operational. How-

FIGURE 6–8
Conversion strategies for information systems.

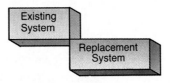

Direct Conversion
End existing system and begin replacement system immediately.

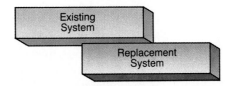

Parallel Conversion
Existing system and replacement system are both run for a specified
period of time and then the existing system is dropped.

Phase-In Conversion
Gradually phase out existing system as replacement system is gradually phased in.

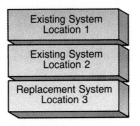

Pilot Conversion
Replacement system is installed in one location and tried out
before being installed in other locations.

ever, this approach can be risky, because there is no backup system if the new system does not work. An organization can run into operational chaos if something goes wrong with the new system. Information may not be available, reports may be delayed, management decisions may not be made, users may question the new system, and acceptance may be jeopardized.

Direct conversion may work when a new information system is not critical to the operation of an organization, or there is little resistance to the new system, or the size of the organization is small. In such instances, it is easy to recover from any loss incurred if something goes wrong. For example, a new accounts payable system for a small business would be an appropriate application for direct conversion.

With **parallel conversion,** both new and old information systems are used for a certain period of time, after which the old system is no longer used. Of all conversion approaches, parallel conversion is safest and therefore the most appropriate for critical business applications, such as customer billing and payroll. This approach provides a backup system, which is useful in case of problems with the new system. In addition, the new system can be checked against the old, permitting all of the bugs to be removed by the time it becomes the only operational system.

Nonetheless, there are disadvantages to parallel conversion. It is expensive, because two systems are used in parallel. It may create confusion. And, enough skilled personnel may not be available to operate two systems simultaneously.

With **phased-in conversion,** the new information system is installed in phases, or segments. As individual segments of the system are developed, they are installed and used. This is not a common approach, for most segments cannot be installed and used as independent units. The different segments of most information systems are interrelated and cannot work in isolation.

However, if an existing information system is being upgraded or enhanced, phased-in conversion may prove beneficial. In such a situation, the change brought about by the upgraded system is not overwhelming, and the users are exposed to the system gradually. A gradual changeover can provide lessons for users so that they are ready for the total system when it becomes operational. However, extreme caution is necessary to ensure that the installed segments really can work in isolation.

If an information system is to be used in multiple locations, **pilot conversion** may prove safe and economical. With a pilot conversion, a new system is installed in one location and tried there before installation in other locations. This approach is safe and economical because the impact of any problem is felt in only one unit of an organization and fewer users are affected.

Sometimes, pilot conversion is used in combination with other conversion approaches. For example, if an organization is installing a billing system in several subsidiary organizations, it might employ a pilot conversion approach in combination with parallel conversion. The experiences learned in that pilot location could provide valuable lessons for installing the system in other locations.

Training Stage

Training is essential to familiarize users and others with a new system so they can use it effectively. Training normally is provided for three levels of employees: (1) users, who work with the system regularly, (2) operators, who work in the computer center and run the system, and (3) managers, who must know the system's strengths, weaknesses, and impact on the organization.

User training is for employees who work regularly with a new system. It must be hands-on and may last several days or weeks. It is essential to make users thoroughly familiar with operation of the new system.

Operator training communicates operational details to those who work in the computer center of an organization and who will run the system.

User and operator training deal with operational details, but **management training** overviews a new system. The purpose is to familiarize management with major strengths and weaknesses of a system and its impact on the organization.

SYSTEM MAINTENANCE

System maintenance is the last phase in the system development life cycle of an information system. After a system has been tested, installed, and the users trained, it enters the maintenance phase. Following installation, an information system is handed over to a special group of programmers known as **maintenance programmers**. Most college graduates having their degrees in information systems or related disciplines start their careers as maintenance programmers. System maintenance may span several years, during which the changing requirements of users lead to minor modifications to the system. Most often, maintenance costs of an information system are considerably higher than the development costs. Eventually, the system reaches a point where routine maintenance is no longer sufficient, and the SDLC begins again.

FILE PROCESSING

You already know that data can be stored in files and that data in these files can be accessed and used by programs. A **file** is composed of related *records,* and each of these records is composed of *fields* that relate to the record (Figure 6–9). Files can be managed in two distinct ways: by file management systems or by database management systems.

FILE MANAGEMENT SYSTEMS

A **flat file** has no relationship or integrating structure with any other file; it cannot be cross-referenced with other files. For example, the information stored in a production file listing the parts required for a production run cannot be automatically compared to the information in an inventory file to see if the required number of parts are on hand. Each of these files must be accessed separately and the information written down and manually compared.

Software that manages flat files—their storage, access, retrieval, and use—is called a **file management system (FMS)**. Because an FMS

FIGURE 6–9
A file is composed of records and fields.

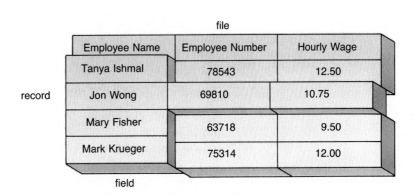

Employee Name	Employee Number	Hourly Wage
Tanya Ishmal	78543	12.50
Jon Wong	69810	10.75
Mary Fisher	63718	9.50
Mark Krueger	75314	12.00

file

record

field

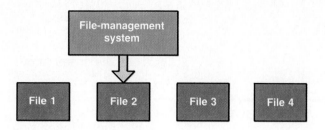

defines no relationships between files, it can access and manipulate only one file at a time (Figure 6–10). An FMS is the simplest type of program used to manage files.

Advantages

A file management system can be an easy, low-cost solution to managing flat files containing data that are rarely, if ever, cross-referenced with data in other files. Also, FMSs are appropriate for small companies having only a small number of files that must be cross-referenced. Advantages of FMSs include low purchase price, ease of operation and maintenance, and low vulnerability to data error due to hardware failures and software errors (because only one file is accessed and used at a time). FMSs often meet the needs of individuals who simply want to store lists of data, such as inventories of personal assets.

Disadvantages

File management systems and flat files do have limitations, resulting from the fact that data often are related:

- ☐ Flat files are independent and are not integrated.
- ☐ The same data are often duplicated in multiple flat files. If the data change, every occurrence of the data must be located and updated.
- ☐ Programs are dependent on the arrangement of fields in the records, called the file format. The data in a file must be stored in the exact format that the program expects.
- ☐ Programs to manage data in multiple flat files at the same time are difficult to create and maintain.

Because data used by businesses are often related, an easier and more efficient way to store and manage data was developed: databases and database management systems.

Programmable File Management Systems

Some file management systems, called **programmable file management systems,** allow users to enter programming commands that allow cross-referencing of multiple flat files. However, users are responsible for creating the code to do this, which requires users to have a great amount of programming knowledge.

To remedy some limitations of standard flat-file structures, many users rely on databases to store vital data. A **database** is a collection of related and cross-referenced data designed to minimize repetition and ease manipulation of data.

How Data Are Stored in Databases

Data are stored in a database in one of three data structures:

1. Files, which contain records and fields.
2. Tables, which contain rows and columns. The rows are called tuples (pronounced like couples), and the columns are called domains (Figure 6−11). Tables contain related tuples, just as files contain related records. In a table, each row contains the same number of columns, and data in the columns are of the same type (alphanumeric or numeric) and size.
3. Objects, which include both data and methods (procedures) that act on the data (Figure 6−12).

Advantages

Using a database instead of standard flat files has numerous advantages. First, a database reduces data redundancy. For example, a customer's address may be part of several standard flat files because each file needs the address and the files are neither related nor have any integrating structure. Thus, in a standard flat-file system, a customer's address could appear in 20

Structures in Which Data Can Be Stored in a Database

- Files
- Tables
- Objects

FIGURE 6−11
A relational database table.

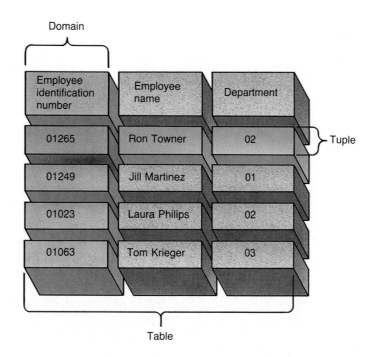

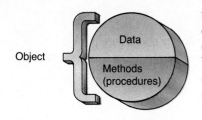

FIGURE 6–12
An object contains both data and methods (procedures) in an encapsulated form.

Advantages of a Database

- Data redundancy reduced
- Data integrity improved
- Data independence maintained
- Data security improved
- Data consistency maintained
- More powerful manipulation of data allowed
- Easier data access and use

to 30 files. If the customer's address changes, updating all those files is time consuming, expensive, and prone to error. But in a database, this redundancy disappears—the customer's address need appear in only one file, because the database management system allows files to be related. (A certain amount of redundancy in a database can be useful to support some data-manipulation tasks.)

Second, a database improves data integrity. Because a particular piece of data appears in only one or a limited number of locations, future reports are more apt to reflect any change or addition. For example, if a customer notifies a bank of an address change and the address is stored in only one location, then all other data—checking account, savings account, outstanding loans, bank-issued credit card, tax reporting, and solicitation for new services—will reflect the new address.

A third advantage is that a database maintains data independence. The database structure requires that data be independent, which means that deleting or changing selected data does not affect other data. For example, if an employee leaves, he or she will be deleted from the current-employee database, but data concerning the employee's office furniture, telephone number, travel expenditures, and other nonsalary items are not destroyed.

A fourth advantage is that a database improves data security. Because most database systems maintain their own security and all of the data are in one place, security is easier to maintain. In contrast, ensuring security is difficult for redundant data in standard multiple flat files stored on multiple disks or tapes.

Yet another plus is that a database maintains data consistency. The kind, type, and size of data are consistent for all applications. For example, the size of a specific field is the same for all applications using the database.

A database also allows more powerful data manipulation. Because data in a database can be cross-referenced and integrated, users can perform much more sophisticated data manipulations than with a file management system.

Finally, data are easier to access and use in a database. Because data are available for all applications, they do not have to be duplicated or repeated.

Disadvantages

There are also several disadvantages to using databases. First, mainframe databases are highly complex and require specialized designers and programmers to implement them. Second, mainframe databases require expensive hardware and software and highly qualified personnel to design and maintain them. Third, even though databases provide increased security, massive damage to a database can occur if an unauthorized person penetrates the system.

Also, as all data are in one location, databases are vulnerable to hardware failure or software errors. The large size of databases may make recovery from a disaster very time-consuming and costly. Making a backup copy of an entire database poses a challenge for data-processing staff,

**FBI DATABASE
EXPANSION SEEN
AS THREAT TO
CIVIL RIGHTS**

The Federal Bureau of Investigation (FBI) maintains the National Crime Information Center (NCIC) database. Housing the hardware necessary to operate the system requires a room half the size of a football field. The NCIC database consists of 12 main files and a total of about 19.4 million individual files. These files contain information on criminal arrests and convictions, missing persons, individuals with outstanding warrants, stolen vehicles, and individuals suspected of plotting against high-level government officials.

Law enforcement officials access the NCIC files more than 700,000 times a day, checking on everything from routine traffic violations to information on felony suspects. The database is a valuable resource for law enforcement, but many groups and individuals are worried that violations of civil rights may result from storing inaccurate or false information in such databases. Even the FBI, which spends $1 million a year auditing the 20-year-old system, admits "a lot of things can happen" with so many queries being made on the system each day.

Such was the case of Terry Dean Rogan of Michigan, who was arrested five times for crimes he did not commit after his wallet was stolen. He was even mistaken for a murder suspect who had used his identification. Eventually, Mr. Rogan received a settlement in the amount of $55,000 from the city of Los Angeles for failing to remove his name from its database, but the results could have been much worse.

Another worry is that the FBI cannot provide adequate security for the information stored in the NCIC. For example, the FBI's listing of drug informers could be devastating for many individuals if it fell into the wrong hands. The recent computer virus that brought the Internet computer system to a standstill is a further reminder that most computer systems have serious security vulnerabilities, especially from within. Maintaining large databases of any kind poses significant challenges for the security and privacy of the data as well as for assurance that only valid, correct data are entered into the database.

particularly if the database spans several disks, each of which contains multiple gigabytes of data.

A database system is not for everyone. There must be a real need to switch from standard flat-file to database usage. A small company or an individual with simple needs and relatively few files may not need a database system. However, other companies could not exist or function efficiently without databases.

DATABASE MANAGEMENT SYSTEMS

A **database management system (DBMS)** is software that manages the creation, storage, access, updating, deletion, and use of a database. A DBMS can access and manage multiple files, tables, or objects at the same time, linking them together if needed. Typical mainframe DBMSs are IBM's IMS (Information Management System), Cullinet's IDMS/R (Integrated Data Management System), and IBM's DB2 (DataBase II). Typical microcomputer database management systems include Paradox, dBASE, and RBASE.

A typical DBMS performs varied tasks and has numerous features that makes it attractive to businesses:

☐ Creates databases and their structures, using information provided by the database designer.
☐ Provides the vehicle for users and application programs to access, modify, and manipulate data in a database.
☐ Provides a report generator, which allows users to access the database, format data, and print or display reports.
☐ Provides security for databases, denying access to an entire database or to selected portions of a database.
☐ Provides reports to management on who accessed the database and what activity was performed.
☐ Provides reports to operators on hardware utilization, the status of current users, and other monitoring data.
☐ Provides automatic backup routines for data in the databases.

Many microcomputer-based DBMSs lack several of these features because they are not multiuser systems. The database management system needs of a single user having a microcomputer system are different from those of multiple users having a mainframe system.

DATABASE MODELS

There are four types of database models: (1) hierarchical, (2) network, (3) relational, and (4) object-oriented. Hierarchical and network models use standard files and provide structures that allow cross-referencing and integration. They have been available since the early 1970s. The relational model uses tables to store data, provides for cross-referencing and manipulating data, and provides for data integrity. The relational model became popular in the early 1980s and is used extensively. The object-oriented model, which uses objects, began making its mark in the late 1980s, and is expected to grow in popularity for applications that require complex data.

The Hierarchical Model

In a **hierarchical database,** data relationships follow hierarchies, or trees, which reflect either a one-to-one relationship or a one-to-many relationship among record types (Figure 6–13). Uppermost in a tree structure is the **root record**. From there, data are organized into groups containing parent records and child records. One parent record can have many

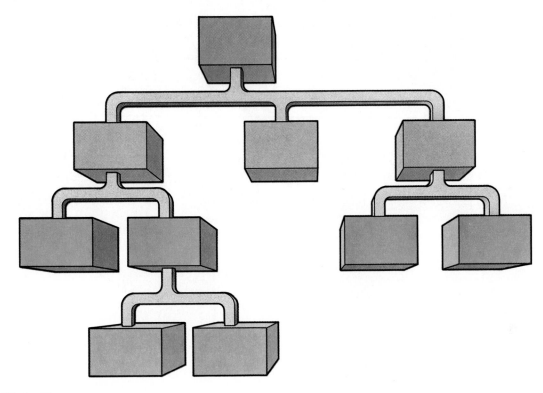

FIGURE 6–13
Hierarchical data relationships.

child records (called siblings), but each child record can have only one parent record. Parent records are higher in the data structure than child records; however, each child can become a parent and have its own child records.

Because relationships between data items follow defined paths, access to data is fast. However, any relationship between data items must be defined when the database is being created. If a user wants to retrieve or manipulate data in a manner not defined when the database was originally created, redesigning the database structure is costly and time consuming.

The Network Model

A **network database** is similar to a hierarchical database except that each record can have more than one parent, thus creating a many-to-many relationship among the records (Figure 6–14). For example, a customer might be called on by more than one salesperson in the same company, and a single salesperson might call on more than one customer. Within this structure, any record can be related to any other data element.

The main advantage of a network database is its ability to handle sophisticated relationships among various records. Therefore, more than

Database Models

- Hierarchical
- Network
- Relational
- Object-oriented

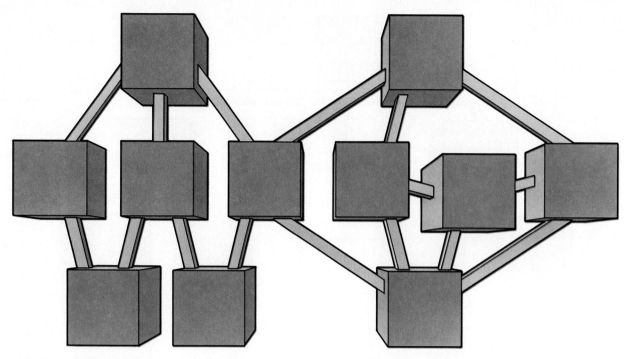

FIGURE 6–14
Network data relationships.

one path can lead to a desired data level. The network database structure is more versatile and flexible than the hierarchical structure because the route to data is not necessarily downward; it can be in any direction.

In the network structure, data access is similarly fast because relationships follow predefined paths and data relationships must be defined during the database design. However, network complexity limits the ability of users to access the database without help from the programming staff.

The Relational Model

A **relational database** is composed of many tables in which data are stored, but more is involved than just the use of tables. Tables in a relational database must have unique rows, and the cells (the intersection of a row and column—equivalent to a field) must be single-valued (that is, each cell must contain only one item of information, such as a name, address, or identification number). A database management system that allows data to be readily created, maintained, manipulated, and retrieved from a relational database is called a **relational database management system (RDBMS)**. The RDBMS, *not* the user, must ensure that all tables conform to the requirements. The RDBMS also must contain features that address the structure, integrity, and manipulation of the database.

In a relational database, data relationships do not have to be predefined. Hence, users can query a relational database and establish data

FIGURE 6–15
A database query language that
uses the query-by-example
approach.

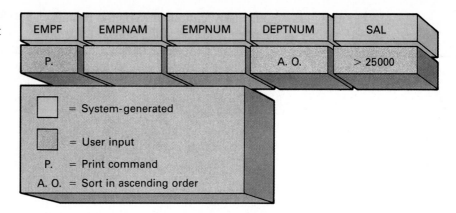

EMPF	EMPNAM	EMPNUM	DEPTNUM	SAL
P.			A. O.	> 25000

☐ = System-generated

☐ = User input

P. = Print command

A. O. = Sort in ascending order

relationships spontaneously by joining common fields. A **database query language** is a helpful interface between users and a relational database management system. Such a language helps users to easily manipulate, analyze, and create reports from data in the database. It is composed of easy-to-use statements that help nonprogrammers to use the database.

Two basic query styles are used: query by example and structured query language.

In **query by example,** the database management system displays field information and the user enters inquiry conditions in the desired fields. For example, if you want to list all employees having salaries greater than $25,000 and sort them in ascending order by department number, the screen might appear as in Figure 6–15.

Structured query language (SQL) uses commands in a structured format. For example, using structured query language, the inquiry in Figure 6–15 would appear as it does in Figure 6–16. This tells the database management system to use the fields EMPNAM, EMPNUM, DEPTNUM, and SAL from each record in the employee file (EMPF) if the employee's salary is greater than $25,000 and to sort that list by department number. Structured query language is becoming a de facto standard for relational databases.

Relational databases permit users to cross-reference data without relying on a particular structure. This places a powerful problem-solving and report-generating tool directly in the hands of those who are experts on the needs of their departments, not the programming staff. Because users can access data and generate reports without involving a programmer, relational databases can quickly increase productivity. This capability is par-

FIGURE 6–16
A database query language that
uses the structured query language approach.

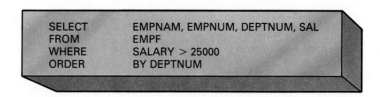

```
SELECT      EMPNAM, EMPNUM, DEPTNUM, SAL
FROM        EMPF
WHERE       SALARY > 25000
ORDER       BY DEPTNUM
```

ticularly critical in dynamic business environments, where quick cross-referencing of data is crucial to company profits.

In spite of the advantages of relational databases, the database operations of mature businesses may already be established in a hierarchical or network structure. With programming staff and users already trained in using other structures, converting to a relational database structure might have considerable cost. With thousands of programs and hundreds of databases already on-line, scrapping them and starting anew with a different database structure might not be cost-effective.

The Object-Oriented Model

Although the relational model is well suited to storing and manipulating business data, it is not well suited for handling the data needs of certain complex applications, such as computer-aided design (CAD) and computer-assisted software engineering (CASE). Business data follow a defined data structure that the relational models handle well. However, applications such as CAD and CASE deal with a variety of complex data types that cannot be easily expressed by relational models. Such programs also require massive amounts of *persistent data* (data that cannot be altered in their own private memory space), and a database for them must be able to evolve without affecting the data in memory that the application uses to operate.

An **object-oriented database** uses objects and messages to accommodate new types of data and provide for advanced data handling. A database management system that allows objects to be readily created, maintained, manipulated, and retrieved from an object-oriented database is called an **object-oriented database management system (OODBMS)**.

An object-oriented database management system must still provide features that you would expect in any other database management system, but there is no clear standard for the object-oriented model. OODBMSs are expected to evolve and be used for applications with complex data needs. They are not, however, expected to replace relational databases. Instead, the two types will work alongside each other, each being suited for different tasks (see Profile at beginning of chapter).

DATABASE DESIGN CONSIDERATIONS

Most database design is done by programming staff—usually a senior system analyst or, in larger companies, a database designer or database administrator (DBA). Design of a particular database must consider the needs of each department, the type of DBMS software already in use, staff training, and availability of system resources. Also, each department's concerns must be compatible with the company's long-range plans for DBMS usage.

A feasibility study, usually by a system analyst, identifies the needs and wants of users. The analyst must then identify what data are needed, how to capture them, and how to merge the data into existing databases. An analyst must also design methods, procedures, and standards for maintenance and sharing of data. Because a database must restrict access to sensitive data such as employee salaries or a customer's medical history, the analyst may have to consult with other departments, upper management, or company attorneys. After analyzing user needs and understanding data requirements, the analyst can begin database design.

Logical Database Design

A **logical database design** describes a database in terms of how people will use the data. During this phase, the analyst studies the data, identifying how they are grouped and how they relate to each other. The analyst must also determine which fields have multiple occurrences of data, which will be keys or indexes, and the size and type of each field.

After identifying all data to be included, the analyst enters the database information into a **data dictionary,** a data file containing a technical description of data to be stored. The dictionary includes (1) field names, (2) type (alphanumeric or numeric), size, and descriptions, and (3) logical relationships. The dictionary is a tool that a developer uses to communicate with other members of the development staff. It also provides a way of standardizing the names and lengths of data within a database structure.

Physical Database Design

An analyst, database designer, or database administrator then transforms the logical design into a **physical database design,** the actual structure of the database, in keeping with the DBMS software already in use. If multiple database management systems are available, the feasibility study should have identified which DBMS is to be used for development of the application. An analyst designs the database according to the structure of the recommended DBMS (hierarchical, network, relational, or object-oriented).

Schema and Subschema

DBMS software must know the structure of the database and the relationships among the data in it. Consequently, a database administrator creates a schema and subschema for the database. A **schema** is a complete description of database content and structure. It defines the database to the database management system, including (1) record layout, (2) names, lengths, and sizes of all fields, (3) and data relationships. A **subschema** defines each user's view, or specific parts of the database that a user can access. A subschema restricts each user to certain records and fields within the database. Every database has one and only one schema, but each user must have a subschema.

SUMMARY

A system is a set of components that interact with each other to work together toward a common goal. The four major components of a system are input, process, output, and feedback.

An information system is a set of people, data, and procedures that work together to achieve the common goal of information management. Information management gathers and processes data into reliable and accurate information in usable form and distributes the information in a timely fashion for use in decision making, problem solving, and control.

Every information system has three basic functions: (1) to accept data (input), (2) to convert data to information (process), and (3) to produce and communicate information in a timely fashion to users for decision making (output).

Managers are the key decision makers and problem solvers within an organization. Managers are responsible for using the resources available to achieve organizational goals. Each management level has specific information needs.

A transaction processing system (TPS) is an information system that records and helps manage business transactions.

A management information system (MIS) generates information for managers to use in solving structured problems. An MIS presents information through reports (scheduled, demand, and exception) and on-line retrieval. The data presented, their relationships, and their form are predetermined in an MIS. To change or add data or relationships, an MIS must be reprogrammed by the systems department.

A decision support system (DSS) is an interactive, computer-based decision system that assists management in solving structured, semistructured and unstructured problems. A DSS generates predictive reports.

An executive support system (ESS) is a specialized DSS that caters to the information needs of executives.

Development of a new information system proceeds in four phases, called the system development life cycle (SDLC): (1) analysis, (2) design, (3) implementation, and (4) maintenance. Development of a new information system is complex and requires the structured planning and scheduling skills of project management.

System analysis is composed of three stages: (1) problem definition, involving recognition of a problem or new opportunity which the current system cannot handle; (2) requirements analysis, where it is determined how the present information system performs, how the best possible system might perform, and how a new system might bridge the gap between the two performance levels; and (3) project justification, which systematically compares alternative information systems and decides which to propose to management.

The system design phase is composed of two steps: (1) the logical system design (development of a paper blueprint for a new system), and (2) the physical system design (translation of the blueprint into specific programming logic that will cause the new system to operate as planned).

Prototyping, the fast and inexpensive development of a model, can significantly reduce the development time.

Computer-aided systems engineering (CASE) software automates many of the tasks involved in system development.

The implementation phase includes three stages: testing, installation, and training. Implementation brings a new system to its productive life.

Maintenance is the last phase in the system development life cycle, during which it is updated by maintenance programmers to meet the changing requirements of users.

File processing involves the use of files to store data. A file is made up of records and fields. A file management system is software that manages storage, access to, retrieval from, and use of flat files. A file management system is low in cost, easy to operate and maintain, and low in vulnerability to data error due to hardware failures and software errors.

A database is a collection of related and cross-referenced data designed to minimize repetition and improve ease of data manipulation. Data can be stored in a database in file, table, or object form.

Database processing has these advantages: data redundancy is reduced, data integrity is improved, data independence is maintained, data security is improved, data consistency is maintained, more powerful manipulation of data is allowed, and data access and use are easier.

A database management system (DBMS) is software that manages creation, storage, access, updating, deletion, and use of a database. A typical DBMS creates databases and their structures; provides the vehicle for users and application programs to access, modify, and manipulate the data; provides a report generator for users; provides security for databases; provides management reports on who accessed the database and their activities; provides reports to operators on hardware utilization, status of current users, and other monitoring data; and provides automatic backup routines for the data in databases.

The four database models are (1) hierarchical, (2) network, (3) relational, and (4) object-oriented. Hierarchical and network models use files for storing data. Data relationships in the hierarchical databases follow hierarchies, or trees, which reflect either a one-to-one or a one-to-many relationship among the record types. Data relationships in network databases follow a many-to-many relationship among the records.

Relational databases use tables for storing data. The data relationships can be dynamically determined by the user. A relational database uses a database query language to allow users to access and manipulate data in the database; examples of query languages are query by example and structured query language. Object-oriented databases store data and procedures together in objects.

A logical design is a detailed description of a database in terms of how users will use the data. A physical design details the actual structure of a database. A schema is a complete description of database content and structure, and a subschema defines the specific parts of a database that each user can access.

Vocabulary Self-test

Can you define the following?

algorithm (p. 192)

coding (p. 192)

computer-aided systems engineering (CASE) (p. 193)

computer-based information system (p. 181)

conversion (p. 196)

cost/benefit analysis (p. 191)

database (p. 201)

database management system (DBMS) (p. 204)

database query language (p. 207)

data dictionary (p. 209)

data flow diagram (DFD) (p. 193)

debugging (p. 195)

decision support system (DSS) (p. 186)

demand report (p. 185)

direct conversion (p. 196)

documentation (p. 189)

exception report (p. 186)

executive support system (ESS) (p. 187)

file (p. 199)

file management system (FMS) (p. 199)

flat file (p. 199)

hierarchical database (p. 204)

information system (p. 180)

installation (p. 195)

interactive system (p. 186)

logical database design (p. 209)

logical system design (p. 192)

logic error (p. 195)

maintenance programmer (p. 199)

management information system (MIS) (p. 185)

management training (p. 199)

manager (p. 183)

network database (p. 205)

object-oriented database (p. 208)

object-oriented database management system (OODBMS) (p. 208)

operational (low-level) managers (p. 184)

operator training (p. 198)

parallel conversion (p. 197)

phased-in conversion (p. 198)

physical database design (p. 209)

physical system design (p. 192)

pilot conversion (p. 198)

predictive report (p. 186)

problem definition (p. 190)

programmable file management system (p. 200)

programmer (p. 188)

project justification (p. 190)

project management (p. 188)

prototype information system (p. 192)

query by example (p. 207)

relational database (p. 206)

relational database management system (RDBMS) (p. 206)

requirements analysis (p. 190)

root record (p. 204)

run-time error (p. 195)

scheduled report (p. 185)

schema (p. 209)

strategic (top-level) managers (p. 183)

structured query language (SQL) (p. 207)

subschema (p. 209)

syntax (p. 195)

syntax error (p. 195)

system (p. 179)

system analysis (p. 189)

system analyst (p. 188)

system design (p. 191)

system designer (p. 188)

Review Questions

Multiple Choice

1. Anything that enters a system is referred to as a(n) _____ .
   a. input
   b. feedback
   c. output
   d. process

2. Top-level managers are concerned with _____ .
   a. day-to-day operations
   b. short-term goals
   c. tactics for achieving goals
   d. long-term goals

3. A(n) _____ report is an MIS report that highlights activities that are out of control and need management attention.
   a. on-line
   b. exception
   c. demand
   d. schedule

4. The first phase of the system development life cycle is called _____ .
   a. implementation
   b. design
   c. analysis
   d. maintenance

5. The entire class of software that automates information system development tasks is called _____ software.
   a. project-management
   b. computer-aided system engineering (CASE)
   c. computer-aided design (CAD)
   d. computer-aided manufacturing (CAM)

6. An information system is transferred to the users and begins its useful life during the _____ phase of the SDLC.
   a. system implementation
   b. system design
   c. system maintenance
   d. system analysis

7. The _____ phase of the SDLC involves making minor adjustments to an information system that is currently in use.
   a. system maintenance
   b. system implementation
   c. system design
   d. system analysis

8. A collection of related and cross-referenced data designed to minimize repetition and ease data manipulation is called a(n) _____.
   a. flat file
   b. object
   c. master file
   d. database

9. A(n) _____ is the software that manages the creation, storage, access, updating, deletion, and use of a database.
   a. file management system
   b. database management system
   c. flat file
   d. application

10. A(n) _____ database allows users to query a database using a database query language.
    a. object-oriented
    b. network
    c. hierarchical
    d. relational

Fill-in

1. A(n) _____ is a person responsible for using available resources to achieve an organizational goal.

2. A business activity or event is referred to as a(n) _____.

3. _____ are the primary form in which an MIS presents information to users.

4. Reports generated by a DSS suggesting what might happen given certain planning decisions are called _____.

5. _____ is the structured sequence of operations required to conceive, develop, and make operational a new information system.

6. The written or graphic record of the steps carried out during the development of an information system is called _____.

7. The first stage of the system analysis phase is the _____.

8. The activity of checking a new information system to ensure that all of its parts are correct occurs during the _____ stage of the system implementation phase.

9. _____ conversion involves using both the old and new system side by side for a period of time and then removing the old system from use.

10. The _____ database model is composed of many tables in which data are stored.

Short Answer

1. What are the advantages of using a computer in an information system?

2. Describe the three basic functions of an information system.

3. Describe the information needs for each of the three levels of management.

4. Why is it important to involve users in the development of an information system?

5. What is the purpose(s) of the system analysis phase of the system development life cycle?

6. What is prototyping, and how does it affect the SDLC?

7. Describe the three structures in which data can be stored in a database.

8. Identify at least two of the advantages of database processing.

9. What is a database management system, and what is its function?

10. Describe the difference between a logical database design and a physical database design.

PART TWO

Microcomputer Application Software

Rather than radically changing social patterns they [computers] are likely to be folded into the fabric of society, altering daily life in small but cumulative ways. . . . nearly all of us will become familiar with their operation, unintimidated, and therefore easily able to appreciate and take advantage of them.

John Case, author and senior editor of
Inc. magazine.

OUTLINE

MICROCOMPUTER APPLICATION
SOFTWARE—A USER PROBLEM
SOLVING AND PRODUCTIVITY TOOL

Word Processors I Data Managers I
Electronic Spreadsheets I Graphics I
Communications

COMPONENTS OF A
MICROCOMPUTER SYSTEM USING
APPLICATION SOFTWARE

EVOLUTION OF MICROCOMPUTER
APPLICATION SOFTWARE

INTEGRATED APPLICATION
SOFTWARE

Integrated Family of Programs I
All-in-One Integrated Packages I
Integrated Operating Environment I
Background Integration

GETTING STARTED USING AN
APPLICATION PROGRAM

COMMON FEATURES OF
MICROCOMPUTER APPLICATION
SOFTWARE

Interface Features I File-Handling
Features I Other Common Application
Software Features

OBJECTIVES

☐ Describe the role of application
software.

☐ Distinguish among the five applications most in demand for
microcomputers.

☐ Identify the components of a
computer system using application software.

☐ Describe the evolution of microcomputer software.

☐ Contrast the four approaches to
integration.

☐ Recognize and describe common features of application
software.

CHAPTER SEVEN

Introduction to
Application Software
for Microcomputers

Dan Bricklin
and
Bob Frankston

Dan Bricklin, like many other students, was not fond of the tedious mathematical calculations that were required when he attended the Harvard Business School in 1978. Many of his assignments involved preparation of financial planning sheets for mock organizations. The work was repetitive and required numerous hand calculations. At times Bricklin would discover that a calculation he made in the middle of a worksheet was wrong. To correct the error, that and all dependent calculations had to be redone. This process was very time consuming and frustrating. Unlike most students, however, Dan Bricklin did not just wish for a better way; he eventually did something about it.

At about that same time, microcomputers were entering the marketplace. Initially, they were hardly more than high-tech toys for hobbyists and game players. But Bricklin saw a more practical and productive use for them. From his past computer experience, Bricklin thought that an electronic spreadsheet would be a practical idea for small computers. He teamed up with his friend, Bob Frankston, and they began to develop an electronic spreadsheet. The product, called VisiCalc, was the first spreadsheet of its kind.

The two partners literally worked around the clock to get their programming idea off the drawing board. Recalling those early days (and late nights) in *Datamation* magazine, Bricklin said, "We settled into a routine that would carry us through the end of my term at Harvard. I would go to school during the day and Bob

would sleep. We would meet in the evenings to discuss progress and problems. Then Bob would go to work on the computer for the rest of the night, when the time-sharing rates were cheaper."

In January 1979, Bricklin and Frankston incorporated as Software Arts, Inc., and soon after, in conjunction with Personal Software (later to become VisiCorp), began marketing VisiCalc. It was truly a revolutionary product, changing the microcomputer into a useful business tool. This was the beginning of the microcomputer application software industry.

VisiCalc went on to become the best-selling software of its time. In 1983, however, problems between Software Arts, Inc., and VisiCorp led to lawsuits between the two companies over the rights of VisiCalc. The lawsuits left the company in limbo in terms of the software's further development and upgrades. Bricklin and Software Arts, Inc., were eventually awarded the rights to VisiCalc, but because they had failed to react quickly to the new 16-bit technology while other companies developed new products for it, they lost their number-one position in the marketplace.

Eventually, Bricklin sold the company and the rights to Visi-Calc to Lotus, Inc., where Frankston was employed. Bricklin reentered the software business as president of a new company called Software Garden, Inc. Without his vision of the electronic spreadsheet and his commitment to make it a reality, the application software industry might not be where it is today.

Many of you won't be required to know a great deal of technical information about computers. However, most of you will be expected to understand and use *application software* to get a specific task done or solve a problem. Because microcomputers are a productivity tool in both businesses and homes, and because most people, such as yourself, are more likely to use microcomputers than large computer systems, our discussion in Part Two focuses on application software used with microcomputers.

The chapters in Part Two present several major application programs used by people and businesses to solve problems and perform the kinds of tasks that you are likely to be confronted with in your day-to-day life and work. This chapter introduces basic concepts and features of application software that are common to most microcomputer systems. Chapters 8, 9, 10, 11, and 12 describe in more detail the five most popular types of application software for microcomputers.

MICROCOMPUTER APPLICATION SOFTWARE—A USER PROBLEM SOLVING AND PRODUCTIVITY TOOL

Application software instructs the computer in how to solve a problem or perform a particular task. Application software helps you work faster, more efficiently, and thus more productively than if the job were done manually.

Dan Bricklin and Bob Frankston designed the first electronic spreadsheet for microcomputers, VisiCalc, to increase the speed and ease of calculating financial planning sheets (see Profile at beginning of chapter). Since then, microcomputers have been regarded more and more as problem solving and productivity tools for both the business and personal user. Many other tasks have also benefited from computerization. In fact, all of the tasks described in this book that are performed by computers require application software.

Five types of application software programs have emerged as the most popular and widely used with microcomputers: word processor, data manager, electronic spreadsheet, graphics, and communications.

Word Processors

At some time you probably have handwritten or typed a lengthy term paper or similar document; you know how time consuming it is to edit and rewrite—and rewrite—and rewrite—the text. A **word processor** can make the job much simpler, easier, and faster. A word processor is software that lets you create, edit, manipulate, and print text. It automates many manual tasks associated with writing in longhand or typing, such as cutting and pasting, centering, and setting margins (Figure 7–1). For example, this entire book was written and edited using word processors.

WordPerfect, Microsoft Word, and MultiMate are three of the most popular word processors. Word processors are discussed in detail in Chapter 8.

FIGURE 7–1

Two popular word processors, (a) WordPerfect and (b) Multi-Mate. Shown are the areas on the screen where you enter and edit a document. (Photos by Jo Hall/Macmillan)

Legal System
    By using computers to search through huge data banks such as LEXIS or Shepard's Citations, lawyers have shortened the time required to conduct legal precedent and case research. Subscribers to Shepard's Citations use an electronic retrieval system to: look through millions of individual cases; find whether similar or parallel cases were approved, denied, criticized, or overruled; and decide whether to use them in their arguments for the current case (Figure 1---8). Lawyers then formulate strategies based on past case decisions.
    Attorneys also use computers to keep track of their appointments, case dockets, time journals, and clients' bills. Luckily for many legal secretaries, the word processor helps them quickly prepare legal documents and briefs in time for filings, because their bosses are notorious for rewriting drafts so that just the right words and tone of voice are set.
    Many courts docket cases and trials using computers. Kurzweil's VoiceWriter may become as much an asset to the court reporter as the transcription machine. Records could be dictated directly into the voice-activated typewriter instead of first being spoken into one machine and later transcribed by a typist.

A:\FIG11   Doc 1 Pg 1 Ln 1" Pos 1"

(a)

|1 |2 |3 |4 |5 |6 |7 |
Legal System
    By using computers to search through huge data banks such as LEXIS or Shepard's Citations, lawyers have shortened the time required to conduct legal precedent and case research. Subscribers to Shepard's Citations use an electronic retrieval system to: look through millions of individual cases; find whether similar or parallel cases were approved, denied, criticized, or overruled; and decide whether to use them in their arguments for the current case (Figure 1---8). Lawyers then formulate strategies based on past case decisions.
    Attorneys also use computers to keep track of their appointments, case dockets, time journals, and clients' bills. Luckily for many legal secretaries, the word processor helps them quickly prepare legal documents and briefs in time for filings, because their bosses are notorious for rewriting drafts so that just the right words and tone of voice are set.
    Many courts docket cases and trials using computers. Kurzweil's VoiceWriter may become as much an asset to the court reporter as the transcription machine. Records could be dictated

[A:FIG11]   Insert   96%
INSERT: All characters are entered into text at the cursor position.

    <del><menu><search><print><format><change><line_del><line_ins>

(b)

DIGITIZED DISSECTION Veterinarians learn by dissecting on a computer! Yes, the answer for animal-rights activists who worry about cruelty to animals; the answer for students who might destroy valuable samples with an inept scalpel; the answer for instructors who need to recreate precisely the same laboratory experiment for all veterinary students—the answer lies in specialized application programs.

Researchers at Purdue University, among other schools, are enthusiastic about the options that digitized images offer their veterinary students. Links with the National Science Foundation's NSFnet allow image-based interactive programs to be viewed on a variety of computers at Purdue.

Video images depict the internal anatomy of animals, and students use the mouse of their computer to conduct experiments, study organ structure, or learn surgical techniques. "Real" animals thus are not required to conduct any tests.

Because dissections can be tedious, especially for new students, the ability to "delete" an erroneous action means that the student can undo a scalpel stroke—something impossible when working on a real subject. An entire lab experiment need not be scrapped because of a mistake.

Even photographs cannot compare to the clarity that students find in special veterinarian tutorial programs. Anatomical relations, and different perspectives of those relations, can be created with the digitized images. By pointing to a particular organ on the screen, students can move that part and view it from different angles. One of Purdue's goals is to create a moving image of an animal, store it on a compact disc, and then allow students to change the image to see how muscles and bones interact when the animal moves.

This kind of experimentation gives tomorrow's vets a new picture of their future patients. Students will eventually have to work with real subjects to recognize the "feel" of tissue, but fewer animals will be required for that testing.

Will the future veterinarian's black bag contain a laptop computer for use during barn calls?

Data Managers

In today's world, large volumes of data and information must be organized and accessible in different formats. The ability of people to do this job manually in a reasonable amount of time was exceeded long ago, creating a demand for machines to take over the task. Thus **data managers** were

Computers enhance the creative processes in many facets of entertainment.
For example, the music at a dance presentation you attend might be generated
at a computer keyboard, and the dancers' moves might be choreographed with
the help of a computer.

developed to store, organize, manipulate, retrieve, display, and print data
(Figure 7–2). The term data manager describes file management and database management systems. Data managers enable businesses and organizations to keep track of the vast amounts of data that they must gather
and store.

For example, a nonprofit organization conducting a fund-raising
campaign might use a data manager to store the names and addresses and

FIGURE 7-2
The data manager in PFS:First Choice can organize different types of data. For example, as shown on this input screen, data for a personal inventory system can be entered. Depending on the user's needs, the data can be manipulated into different formats. (Photo by Jo Hall/Macmillan)

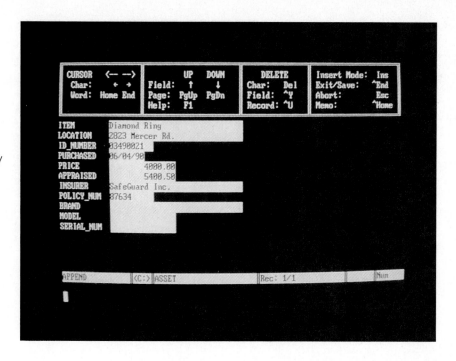

phone numbers of thousands of potential donors who must be contacted and to quickly locate pertinent information about each donor. Thus, when a fund-raiser makes a contact for a donation or receives a pledge, all pertinent data about that individual donor are available on the computer.

You might use a data manager at home to itemize valuable personal items or to list addresses, phone numbers, and birth dates of friends, relatives, or business contacts. dBASE, FoxBASE, Paradox, and RBASE are popular data managers for microcomputers. Chapter 9 will examine data managers for microcomputers in more detail.

Electronic Spreadsheets

Anyone who must keep track of and manipulate numbers can realize benefits from an **electronic spreadsheet,** the software that displays, manipulates, and prints rows and columns of data. It is similar to the paper spreadsheet document used primarily by accountants, in that both the paper version and the computer version have columns and rows in which values and labels are entered. Figure 7-3 shows a user working with both types of spreadsheet. The difference lies in the fact that data in an electronic spreadsheet can be easily edited by the user, and all other dependent figures in the spreadsheet are then recalculated automatically and the results stored.

Electronic spreadsheets can perform a wide variety of tasks, from budgeting personal income to financial planning for a corporation. Lotus 1-2-3 and Excel are two popular spreadsheets. You'll get a closer look at electronic spreadsheets in Chapter 10.

Graphics

Graphics programs display data visually in the form of graphic images. For example, even after using a spreadsheet or data manager to manipulate and organize data, it can sometimes be difficult to see relationships or to interpret that information. Presenting the information visually (graphically) is one way to make this easier.

One type of graphics program can extract and display data graphically in line, pie, or bar charts (Figure 7-4). Business managers use graphics programs to visually present statistics and other data to staff or to clients. At home, you could use graphics to create a bar graph to show if your monthly spending deviated from your budget. A popular independent, or stand-alone, graphics program is PFS:Graph. Graphics software also may be part of a larger program, such as the graphics in Lotus 1-2-3. Graphics programs are also available that enable artists to create pictures and engineers to create designs. Chapter 11 looks at graphics software in more detail.

Communications

As more individuals and organizations use computers, the need to transfer data from one computer to another has increased. Law-enforcement agencies exchange information on criminals; home users access information services such as CompuServe; and many individuals and businesses send electronic mail. To facilitate this communication among computers, **communications programs** such as the popular Crosstalk and PC-Talk are

FIGURE 7-4

The Smart Software System, by Innovative Software, Inc., allows data from a spreadsheet file to be used directly by a graphics program to generate a vivid graphic for a meeting or report. Here, a three-dimensional bar chart that shows sales of ice cream by flavor and gallons is created from data in a spreadsheet file. (Courtesy of Innovative Software, Inc.)

Employees in this office are using many different application software programs. (Courtesy of International Business Machines Corp.)

used. A closer look at communications programs and how to use them appears in Chapter 12.

COMPONENTS OF A MICROCOMPUTER SYSTEM USING APPLICATION SOFTWARE

Before application software can be used, the following computer components must be assembled:

☐ A microcomputer with sufficient RAM in main memory. The more powerful the application software, the more memory is required.

Specific memory requirements and other information are provided on the software packaging. The computer must have enough memory to accommodate the software chosen.

☐ The appropriate monitor and circuitry (in the form of a plug-in video card or built-in video circuitry) to display the application software's output. For example, if you employ application software that uses the computer's graphics mode, you will need both a monitor capable of displaying graphics and the appropriate graphics circuitry to drive that monitor.

☐ Secondary storage devices, in the form of either a hard disk drive and one floppy diskette drive, or two floppy diskette drives. The hard disk equipment provides greater storage capacities and is often required for some of today's larger programs.

☐ Any special input devices that the application requires, such as a mouse or graphics tablet.

☐ A printer or plotter if hard copy output is required.

☐ A modem and telephone for communication applications.

☐ Cables and interfaces to connect the components—for example, parallel or serial interfaces (built-in or plug-in cards).

☐ The appropriate operating system.

☐ And, of course, the appropriate application software.

☐ If the application software is to be used on a local area network (LAN), you will require the appropriate LAN version of that software and the necessary LAN hardware and operating system.

EVOLUTION OF MICROCOMPUTER APPLICATION SOFTWARE

Application software has evolved in several key areas since the earliest programs. This evolution includes improvements in:

☐ The features and power of a program.

☐ The number of programs that can reside in memory and run concurrently.

☐ The ability to share data between programs.

☐ The ease of use of a program.

☐ The number of users who can use a program simultaneously.

The proliferation of microcomputer application software brought the power of microcomputing to everyone. Before these easily understood programs were readily available, the user had to be a computing expert. It took extraordinary skills just to run the computers, much less to understand and develop the programs that made them work. However, because today's microcomputer application software is readily available and easy to learn and use, such expertise on how the computer operates is unnecessary.

The limited power of early microcomputers restricted the scope of early applications. However, as microcomputer technology evolved, there were increases in the power of microprocessors, memory capacities, and video capabilities of microcomputers. In response to these changes, users wanted their application software to do more to take advantage of the

THE CHALLENGE People who are deaf or blind, or who have muscular limitations caused at birth or by accidents, have always been challenged by their environment. They have been successful in overcoming the challenge of gaining access to public buildings, with the help of government regulations that ensure accessibility. Proposed regulations will include adding accessibility to computers for everyone.

This regulation has brought with it the challenge of adapting available computer products and equipment for this special use. Over 1600 products and devices currently on the market offer adaptations for nearly all physical challenges.

One man with cerebral palsy uses a mouth stick to manipulate his keyboard. His current job involves creating maps using computer-aided drafting equipment, and he dreams of a job working in an architect's office.

A blind NASA physicist has access to a computer that reads, writes, and can speak aloud. Using these adaptations, he is hopeful of designing equipment that will find intelligent signals from the radio noises in space.

A voice-operated computer lets a quadriplegic student answer the telephone and turn on the lights by giving voice commands. But what about those "quads" who cannot speak? Such a user can view a computer screen that shows a keyboard. A camera focused on the user's eyes senses which key the eyes are focused upon, and then types those letters to formulate a message.

Other input innovations include the ability to make keyboard selections by using a light device. The device is worn on the head, and by aiming the light at a light-sensitive keyboard, the desired key can be selected.

Yet another computerized communication tool for those who are deaf and blind is a machine that resembles a hand; it is capable of moving to form the one-hand fingerspelling alphabet. Someone who is sighted can communicate by typing on the keyboard; the hand then makes the appropriate finger motions and the deaf/blind user feels the moving hand to translate those motions into letters to receive the message.

In fact, thanks to some of the many innovations for physically challenged computer users, our authors were able to make the revisions to this text.

hardware improvements. Programmers were challenged by the demands for more. Individual applications gained more features and grew in power. The improvements meant that programs could be larger, more sophisticated, and perform better and faster.

The first microcomputers were built with the intention that only one user would access one microcomputer to run one program, or application. Only one application could be loaded into the microcomputer's main memory at one time, and that program had to finish executing before another could be loaded into main memory and executed. But advances in hardware and software technology soon allowed us to move beyond this. Improvements appeared which allowed users to more easily work with two or more applications.

One of the early improvements was a technique known as *context switching*, which took advantage of the growing memory capabilities of microcomputers. This allowed a user to load more than one application program into memory at a time. Although only one application was active at any time, context switching made it easy to switch between two or more application programs without having to quit and reload each time. The number of programs residing in memory at one time was determined by the size of the programs and the available memory.

The next challenge followed naturally: if two or more programs could be in memory, why not enable them to run simultaneously? This was called *multitasking*. Now, with multitasking capabilities and a windowing option, it appeared that two or more applications could run at the same time. In fact, only one program was running at any one time, but the microprocessor handled the switching so efficiently that it seemed that both applications were running simultaneously.

The latest advances in microprocessors, operating systems, and application software actually allow more than one program to truly execute simultaneously on a microcomputer. This is possible because the single powerful microprocessors of today's microcomputers can be divided by the software to function as multiple microprocessors of lesser power, each of which can be dedicated to the needs of a single application program.

Application software has also evolved in its ability to share data among programs. Early application software was developed with little thought of sharing and exchanging data. Each program stored data in its own format, which could not be read or used by other programs. This created many inconveniences and problems for users of different applications who wanted to share data, whether it was between two different data managers or between a spreadsheet and a word processor. This led to a proliferation of conversion programs to convert data from one format to another. Several different ways evolved for integrating programs and their data, and we will look at them in the following section on integration.

Early application software was more difficult to learn than many of today's programs. Early software was text-based and often used very cryptic codes and keystrokes to accomplish basic operations. As application-software popularity grew and more people started using it, more attention was paid to the user's needs. Commands went from keyboard based to menu based. Menus made it easier to execute needed commands, because

Evolution

- Features and power of a program
- Number of programs that can run concurrently
- Ability to share data
- Ease of use
- Number of simultaneous users

Students in this computer lab receive hands-on training in the use of different application software programs. (Courtesy of International Business Machines Corp.)

you didn't have to memorize them. Improvements in hardware allowed programs to take advantage of graphics and special input devices (such as the mouse), which improved ease of use. Development of standard user interfaces and the use of object-oriented programming are continuing this evolution.

Application software has also evolved to include multiuser versions, which allow several users to access them at the same time. They can be found on multiuser microcomputers or on LANs, enabling users to share application programs as well as the data they create.

INTEGRATED APPLICATION SOFTWARE

The data files of many early programs designed for microcomputers were not always compatible with each other. The programs were not *integrated*, i.e., data usually could not be moved electronically from one program to the other. Transferring data between programs, even when possible, was complex and tedious. Typically, the user's only recourse was to retype all the data into the receiving program, which of course defeated part of the reason for using the computer in the first place: to save time and work.

For example, if you were asked to analyze and make a graphic presentation of the sales performance of all 36 sales regions for company X, you would use a spreadsheet application for all the necessary calculations, and then use a separate graphics program to produce the graphs. The spreadsheet software allows you to do that part of the job in only five hours; the results are impressive. But remember that you still need to create bar graphs for the presentation. You spend the next hour poring over the manuals to find a way to transfer the data from the spreadsheet to the graphics program. No luck! Your only option is to spend several more hours reentering the spreadsheet data into the graphics program. This duplication could easily have been avoided if the data in the spreadsheet could have been electronically transferred to the graphics program, i.e., if the two programs were integrated.

Integrated software allows several programs to share the same data. Using the example above, a graphics application could use data directly from the spreadsheet file to create a graph. Integration also implies the use of familiar functions and a common set of commands and keystrokes among programs. However, in reality, this happens only in varying degrees. The result of integration is that the user can work faster, and more efficiently, and thus more productively than if nonintegrated programs were used (Figure 7–5).

The demand for integrated software has led to the development of four distinct approaches to integration: (1) the integrated family of programs, (2) the all-in-one integrated package, (3) the integrated operating environment, and (4) background integration. These are described below.

Integrated Family of Programs

An **integrated family of programs** is a group of independent application programs that can share data and use common commands and keystrokes. For example, if one program in the group uses the function key F10 to save (store), then all the other programs will also use F10 to save. It is faster and easier to learn each program if all have the same commands and keystrokes for the same operation.

FIGURE 7–5
Open Access II contains spreadsheet, graphics, word processor, database management, and communications programs that can share data.

Each program works independently. Because only one application program is loaded into the computer at a time, more memory is available for that application. Thus, the integrated family can be more powerful and have more features than its counterpart, the all-in-one integrated package (described below). One disadvantage is that merging data into one application or sharing data between applications can be slower and more awkward than with an all-in-one integrated package.

PFS publishes a popular integrated family of programs. It uses a common set of function keys, commands, and keystrokes.

All-in-One Integrated Packages

The **all-in-one integrated package** combines several types of applications into a single program. These packages combine some or all of the big five programs: word processor, spreadsheet, data manager, graphics, and communications. The user can conveniently switch between applications and use a common set of commands. With this kind of integrated package the user also can:

- □ Transfer data from one application to another.
- □ Combine data from several applications and transfer that collection of data to another.
- □ Set up individual fields within an application that automatically update related fields in other applications.

A limitation of the all-in-one package, however, is that it requires large amounts of the computer's primary storage capacity; many require well over 256KB because the single program contains all the applications and thus is very large. Because of this large memory requirement, some of the individual applications in an all-in-one package do not have as many features as their stand-alone equivalents. Some developers have eliminated this problem by including special functions that conserve memory and allow individual applications to retain their power.

Popular all-in-one integrated packages include Enable, Framework, and Symphony. Some programs, such as Open Access II and The Smart Software System, are designed to function either as an integrated family or combined into an all-in-one integrated package.

Integrated Operating Environment

The **integrated operating environment** uses a program called a window manager, or integrator, which permits independent applications such as word processors, spreadsheets, and data managers to work concurrently in an integrated way. With this combination, a user can retain the power and capabilities of separate programs and yet be able to share and merge data among them.

These programs use windows—separate areas or boxes on the screen—to enclose independent applications. Several applications or documents can then be displayed on the screen concurrently, and data can be

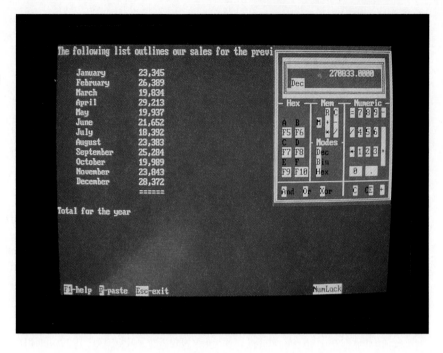

transferred among them. Presentation Manager and Windows are popular integrated operating environments.

Background Integration

Background integration places programs in memory so that they are available instantly at the touch of a key while other software is still running. These are called "terminate and stay resident" (TSR) programs. Typical programs in background integration are a calculator, calendar, appointment book, note pad, and telephone directory and dialer. These programs can be useful additions to any software. For example, the user could access a calculator while word-processing a document, or use a note pad to take notes while working in a database. SideKick is a popular example (Figure 7–6).

Types of Integrated Software

- Integrated family of programs
- All-in-one integrated package
- Integrated operating environment
- Background integration

GETTING STARTED USING AN APPLICATION PROGRAM

We'll begin by examining some concerns of users when starting an application.

When you buy an application program and bring home the box, there are a number of things you must do before you can start using the application. First, look over the documentation that comes with the program and learn how to make backup copies of the program disks. Next, read the instructions on how to install the program on your computer. Only after you've read this material completely are you ready to begin. Reading the installation instructions before starting helps you understand the entire process and may avoid mistakes.

Following the directions, make a backup copy of your application disks to protect your investment in case the original disks become damaged or erased.

Then install the program, following the instructions so that it will work properly on your particular computer. Most programs make installation relatively simple through the use of a batch file, typically called an install file. The **install file** allows you to get the application up and running quickly. It helps you to configure the program for your computer, addressing such items as:

☐ Will the program be installed on a hard disk or floppy disks?
☐ What type of monitor and video interface card does your computer have?
☐ How much memory does your computer have?
☐ Does your computer have a mouse?
☐ What type of printer and printer interface card does your computer use?

You are usually given a menu from which to choose these items, and some programs can automatically determine the type of equipment used by your computer. The install file prompts you to place the appropriate disk in drive A when needed so that its contents can be copied to the hard disk or so the appropriate setup files can be copied to the floppy diskette.

The next step is to look at the documentation to determine how to use the application. Many applications contain a text file on disk, usually called README.TXT, or something similar. The **README file** contains the latest information about the program or corrections that may not be printed in the manual. If an application contains a README file, read it before doing anything else to be sure you have the latest information. These files can be read with any text editor or word processor. Often, a README.COM file is included that can be run to read the text file.

After the program is installed, you can load and execute it. Most programs contain some set-up options that let you change the program defaults. **Defaults** are preset values that the program will use unless you specify other values. Some typical defaults that you may want to change include how data will be displayed on screen and how they will be printed. The documentation for each application program contains information on available options.

COMMON FEATURES OF MICROCOMPUTER APPLICATION SOFTWARE

In this section we'll look at a number of features which are fairly common across most application software. These features are organized in three categories: interface features, file-handling features, and other features.

Interface Features

The **user interface** is the portion of the program that the user interacts with—entering commands to direct the application software and viewing the results of those commands. Common practice in the software industry has been for each application to supply its own user interface. Unfortunately, this has resulted in a variety of different approaches to accomplishing the same tasks from one application to another.

The trend today is toward letting the operating environment supply the key elements of the user interface for each application program, instead of reinventing the wheel each time. This leads to programs having consistent interfaces, making them easier to learn and use because key operations (such as printing and file handling) are all accomplished in the same way, no matter what application program is being used. Many common features found on various application-software programs are explained below.

Command Lines. A **command line** provides a method of entering commands that requires you to type the desired command at a specific point on the display screen. Command lines are usually associated with text-based interfaces. A disadvantage of command lines is that they usually require you to memorize the exact syntax of the commands they want to use.

Menus. Many application programs also allow commands to be selected from a **menu,** which is a list of actions or options from which you can choose. Submenus often are listed under main menus because some applications have as many as *several hundred* or more commands from which to choose. Categories of commands are grouped together, and subcategories of similar commands are grouped under them. For example, a spreadsheet program may have a menu that contains a "format" command; when selected, it presents another menu that contains more explicit choices, e.g., setting dollar signs and the option of listing decimal points and zeros with number entries.

Menus can take a number of different forms. For example, Figure 7–7 shows a Lotus 1-2-3 menu. The first line is the main command line, which indicates selections available. The second line shows only those options available under the "Worksheet" command. As you scroll across the top line of the menu, the second line changes to show the suboptions available under each of the command line options.

Sometimes menus are presented in windows that overlap the display screen. These pull-down menus are increasingly popular. To use a pull-down menu, you choose from a primary menu line at the top of the screen, using either the arrow keys or a mouse to highlight and enter the selection. Doing so commands the software to pull down another menu over part of the display screen, listing the available options (Figure 7–8).

Users generally select commands from menus by one of three methods: (1) using the arrow keys or mouse to move the cursor so that it highlights the desired command, and then pressing the enter key or clicking the mouse; (2) typing the first letter (or letters) of the command; or (3) pressing the appropriate function key or key combination associated with the function.

Cursor/pointer. The **cursor** is a symbol, usually a box or line, that marks the place on the screen where the next character typed will appear or the next entry will occur. In some applications, the cursor is referred to as a **pointer**. It can also take one of several other forms: a shaded block or

Selecting from Menus
■ Arrow keys or mouse to highlight command
■ Type the first letter (or letters)
■ Press the function key or key combination

FIGURE 7–7

The second line of this Lotus Main Command Menu lists all the options available from the "Worksheet" command. (Photo by Jo Hall/Macmillan)

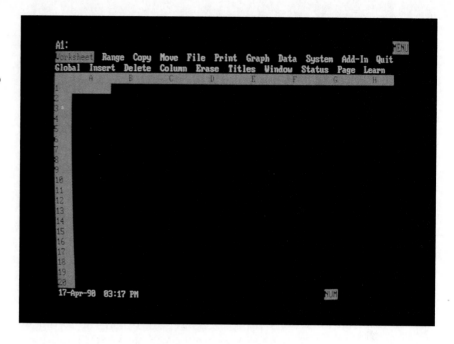

brackets; reverse video, where the background is light instead of dark; or underlined characters, among others.

Cursor movement is usually controlled by one of two means: (1) the arrow keys and associated cursor movement keys on the numerical keypad, or (2) by a mouse or other pointing device.

FIGURE 7–8

This menu from VP Planner Plus application software also shows the selections available from the "Worksheet" command. (Photo by Jo Hall/Macmillan)

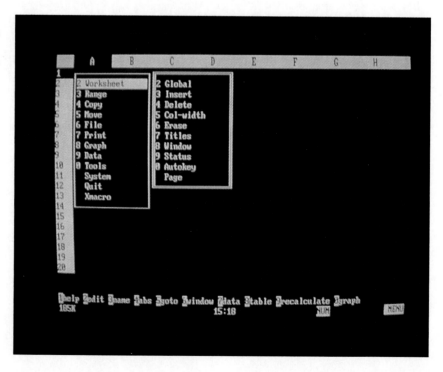

Keyboard Control. Most user interfaces, whether text-based or graphics-based, allow control of the program by making entries on a keyboard. This may involve typing commands or using various keys or key combinations to control the cursor or achieve a desired action.

Mouse Control. In a graphics-oriented interface, the mouse is often used to control a program. The mouse is used to position the cursor on the screen and for point-and-click operations such as selecting menu options or selecting icons. (Recall that an icon is a graphic image representing some action to be taken.)

Scrolling. Most computer screens display 25 lines of 80 characters each (sometimes referred to as being "80 columns wide").

If a file is too long or too wide to be created or viewed entirely on the display screen, the **scroll** feature allows you to move the edit window to create or see text that is outside the display screen. If you scroll the text vertically from top to bottom, the copy at the top of the screen will move out of sight off the top edge of the screen, leaving a blank area at the bottom for entering new data.

Scrolling can usually be accomplished in one of two ways: (1) by using various keys and key combinations, such as the Home, End, PgUp, PgDn, and arrow keys, or (2) by using scroll bars. Text-based applications use the keystroke approach. Graphics-based applications use the scroll-bar approach, but usually can use the keyboard as well. **Scroll bars** are graphic bars that contain a scroll box which you select and drag to scroll the screen (Figure 7–9).

FIGURE 7–9
This Microsoft Windows menu shows a list box, scroll bar, and buttons. (Photo by Jo Hall/Macmillan)

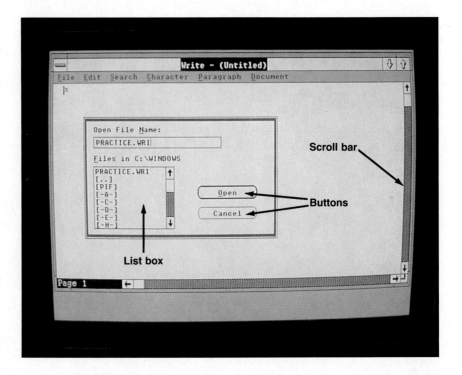

FIGURE 7–10

This WordPerfect status line gives the name of the document as well as the cursor's location by page, line, and column number. (Photo by Jo Hall/Macmillan)

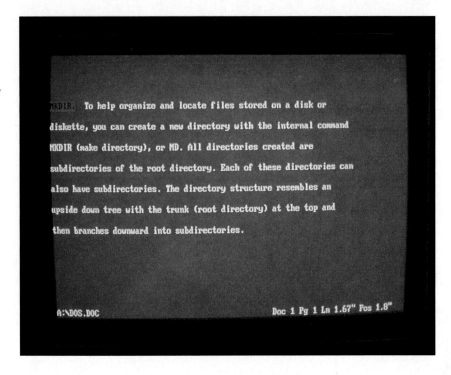

Status Lines. The **status line** at the top or bottom of a display screen provides information about the current document or file and the system (Figure 7–10). It may include the name of the document on which you are working and the cursor position (e.g., page, line, and column number); the amount of available memory and mode of operation; and the designation of disk drive being used.

Dialog Boxes. A **dialog box** usually appears in a window on the screen; it may contain a question or prompt in text form that requires a response from the user.

Message Windows. **Message windows** contain messages indicating errors or asking you to verify the next step; they prompt you to check the data entered or the command chosen.

List Boxes. When you ask for a list of files contained on the disk (for example, by selecting a directory command), this information appears on the screen in a **list box** (Figure 7–9).

Buttons. Some graphics-based interfaces present choices that appear as "buttons" to be "pushed" on the screen (Figure 7–9). These **buttons** can be selected by using a mouse.

WYSIWYG. **WYSIWYG** is the acronym for "What you see is what you get" (pronounced *wizzy wig*). The implication of this feature is that whatever you see on the display screen is exactly the way the output will look when it is printed. This feature is often found on graphics-based interfaces; however, a graphics-based interface does not necessarily mean a WYSIWYG interface.

Users of applications such as word processors find this particular feature very helpful when formatting letters, reports, and other documents that will be printed. Many programs (such as text-based applications) that don't offer this feature as a standard part of their user interfaces do offer a "preview" option that lets you view the output on screen as it will be printed. Although more convenient than waiting for the actual printing, this requires switching back and forth between the preview mode and normal program operation. The best and most convenient option is for a program to have a WYSIWYG interface.

Windows. **Windows** can be used to split the screen into two or more separate areas (Figure 7–11) so that different parts of the same file, or several different files in an application, can be displayed at the same time. Each window typically has an identification name or number found in its status line so that you can tell which file is being viewed.

File-Handling Features

Many common file-handling features can be found in application software. For example, copy, rename, delete, move, and backup commands all function similarly among programs.

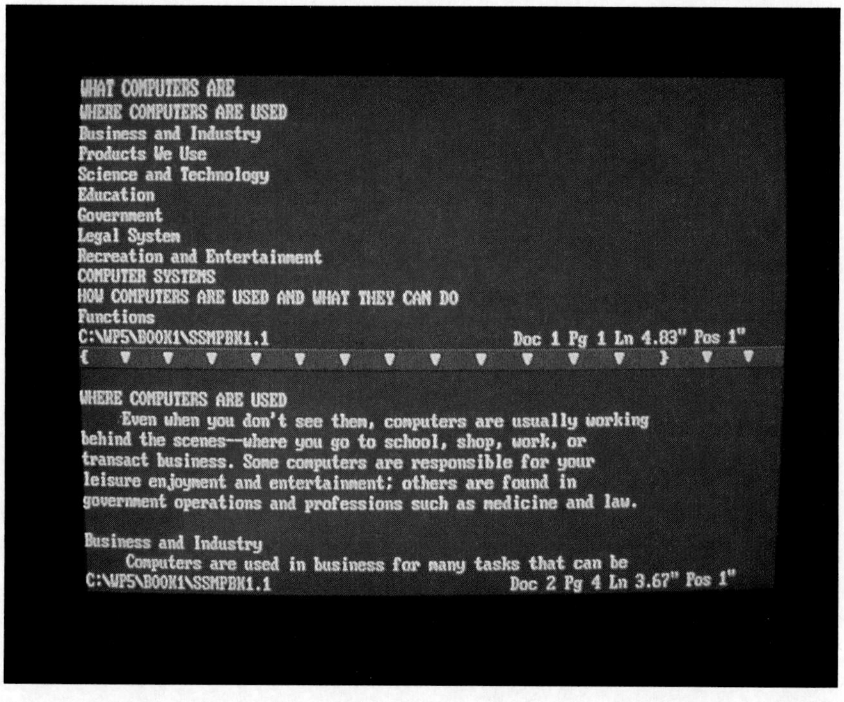

FIGURE 7–11
Two windows allow you to see different documents or files at the same time. In this example, two parts of the same document are shown on the screen, which is very handy when you need to make a comparison. (Photo by Jo Hall/Macmillan)

Copy. The copy feature duplicates an entire file. When a file is copied to the same disk, a message will indicate that the file currently on disk will be overwritten. If you choose to overwrite the existing disk file, the new file will be saved under that old file name, and the contents of the old version will be not be available. If you want to retain the contents of the original file but still save the new version to the same disk, you must select a different file name. However, if you copy a document or file to a *different* disk, it can have the exact same name, and the contents of the old file will remain intact. (This can be confusing; it can be difficult to remember which file contains the latest version.)

Rename. Sometimes it is necessary to change the name of a file or document. Using the rename feature allows assignment of a new name to an existing file or document. This feature comes in handy if a more descriptive name becomes obvious as the file or document is refined.

Delete. The delete feature allows existing files to be removed, or deleted from storage. This can be used to remove old and unneeded files and thus open up disk space for new material.

Move. The move feature allows a file to be identified and put into another location, perhaps in another directory or on another drive. This enables a user to easily manage the files that have been created with a particular application.

Backup Files. Your files represent a lot of hard work, so it is important to duplicate them as backup files on diskettes. Some application software programs include an automatic backup option in which a second copy (backup) of a file is automatically made on the same disk as the original. However, that is inadequate protection if something happens to that particular diskette. The best protection against this type of loss is to use a copy command periodically to copy each file onto a separate diskette—every few minutes, hours, or at the end of each day. How often you do so depends on how much time and energy you are willing to spend recreating the keystrokes to recapture data lost prior to backing up the file!

Other Common Application Software Features

In this section we'll examine some other features that are common among application programs.

Help. Help with questions or problems is available to users in three main ways: on-screen help, manuals, and telephone hot lines.

   □ On Screen. Most application software includes a **help window** that can be accessed from the screen by a particular function key (e.g., F1) or by the selection of a menu option. A help window lists the keys and commands available for a particular function. For example, to understand the underline function in a word-processing application, make the appropriate keystrokes or select the help menu option, and the help window that explains how to underline will be displayed. The window is usually superimposed over the display screen and offers handy reminders of the steps required to perform particular operations.

Help windows are of two types: (1) they can be generalized, in which you call for help and then select the topic desired, or (2) they can be context sensitive, so that when you request help, assistance automatically appears for the feature or part of the program in which you are involved.

☐ Manuals. Application software developers prepare written manuals and instructions for using each program. Many other books and manuals for specific software applications are available, written by people who have used them enough to become experts. These reference books are available from computer stores and bookstores.

☐ Telephone Hot Lines. Most application software developers offer help via telephone—sometimes toll free, other times at your expense—directly from troubleshooters who take calls and attempt to walk you through to a solution. Some advice is free, but oftentimes in-depth help requires that you purchase technical support, generally based on an hourly rate.

☐ One more help, which hopefully you will never need, is a data recovery service. These services use trained technicians who attempt to recover information that appears to be lost on bad disks. User groups, computer stores, and advertisements in computer magazines are sources for finding these services.

DOS Shell. Many application software programs allow you to temporarily exit from the program to return to the operating system. Although the application program is still in active memory, operating system commands such as Format, Copy, Dir, and Erase can be performed. Then you can just as quickly return to the application program, usually by typing EXIT or a similar command at the operating system prompt.

File Transfer. Some applications are integrated so that they can share data. With the capability of **transferring,** a data file created in one application (for example, a data manager) can be sent to and incorporated as part of another application (for example, a spreadsheet program). Preparing a file in a format suitable to be transferred from the current application into another application is called **exporting**.

Importing is the process of bringing an exported file into an application. For example, a file created in one data manager can be exported as an ASCII file and another data manager can import that ASCII file without the need for the entire file to be rekeyed. In a graphics-based window environment, data often easily can be "cut and pasted" from one application into an area in memory or on disk known as a "clipboard," and then moved into another application.

File Transfer

■ Exporting
■ Importing

File Conversion. Application programs sometimes use different formats for storing data on disk. When this occurs, files cannot be interpreted by another application until they are converted. **Converting** the file means to take the form in which data are stored and changing them so that they can be used by another application. This is usually done by a utility program that converts a file from its current format to the desired format. This process is often necessary when application software is issued as a new version, or release. Files created in the old version often need to be reformatted to be used by the new version.

Undo. The **undo** feature cancels any change or update just made and returns the file or document to its previous state. However, some undo features work only if no other action has been taken.

Macros. When using application software, the same sequence of keystrokes or commands may be used often. To automatically execute these repeated commands, many programs use a macro. A **macro** is a file that contains information telling the program to execute a previously recorded series of keystrokes or commands.

Two common ways of creating macros are (1) by using a macro editor to type a file that contains the keystrokes and commands to be executed, or (2) by using a macro recording function which automatically creates a macro file while you are entering the series of keystrokes and commands that are to be repeated. Both methods require that the macro file be given a separate name so that it can be accessed (or invoked) and run by selecting the macro command and supplying the macro name.

Using macros can increase the speed and efficiency of running the various types of application software.

You have been introduced to the types of application software that are available, and you've seen the many features they share. In the following five chapters you will learn some specifics of the common applications—word processors, data managers, spreadsheets, graphics, and communications.

Creating Macros
■ Use a macro editor to type a file
■ Use a macro recording function

SUMMARY

Many tasks that people perform manually can be done faster and more efficiently with a computer. Application software is a program that interacts with the system software to direct the computer to perform a task. The five most popular types of application programs for microcomputers are word processors, data managers, spreadsheets, graphics, and communications programs.

Before application software can be used, computer components must be assembled, including a microcomputer with sufficient RAM, monitor and associated circuitry, storage, input devices, printer or plotter, cables and interfaces, operating system, and possibly a modem and LAN software.

When microcomputers came on the scene, their users demanded software, and no sooner were applications developed than the hardware became more sophisticated. Both microcomputers and the application software have been in an evolutionary cycle—more power for the hardware meant that software could increase the features that were offered; more programs could reside in memory; data could be shared among and between applications; more users could access a program simultaneously; and the applications would become easier to use.

Integration of software soon followed. Integration allows several programs to share the same data, so that applications and users become faster, more efficient, and more productive. The four approaches to integrated software are the integrated family of programs, the all-in-one integrated package, the integrated operating environment, and background integration.

Application software programs have common features: interface features, file-handling features, and others.

Vocabulary Self-Test

Can you define the following?

all-in-one integrated package (p. 233)

application software (p. 221)

background integration (p. 234)

button (p. 239)

command line (p. 236)

communications program (p. 226)

converting (p. 243)

cursor (p. 236)

data manager (p. 223)

defaults (p. 235)

dialog box (p. 239)

electronic spreadsheet (p. 225)

exporting (p. 242)

graphics program (p. 226)

help window (p. 241)

importing (p. 242)

install file (p. 235)

integrated family of programs (p. 232)

integrated operating environment (p. 233)

integrated software (p. 232)

list box (p. 239)

macro (p. 243)

menu (p. 236)

message window (p. 239)

pointer (p. 236)

README file (p. 235)

scroll (p. 238)

scroll bar (p. 238)

status line (p. 239)

transferring (p. 242)

undo (p. 243)

user interface (p. 235)

window (p. 240)

word processor (p. 221)

WYSIWYG (p. 239)

Review Questions

Multiple Choice

1. _____ is the software that instructs the computer how to solve a problem or perform a particular task; it helps you work faster, more efficiently and more productively.
   a. Application
   b. An integrated program
   c. All-in-one integration
   d. Background integration

2. Software that allows several programs to share the same data is said to be _____ software.
   a. application
   b. background integration
   c. integrated
   d. transferred

3. _____ is the integrated program that combines several types of applications into one single program and allows the user to switch between applications and use a common set of commands.
   a. All-in-one integration
   b. An integrated family
   c. A communications program
   d. Background integration

4. The type of integration that places utility programs in memory and makes them available while other applications are being used is called _____ .
   a. all-in-one integration
   b. family integration
   c. utility integration
   d. background integration

5. The _____ file lists the latest information about a particular application.
   a. default
   b. list
   c. README
   d. text

6. The preset values used by the program unless the user specifies that other values should be used are known as _____ .
   a. defaults
   b. README files
   c. macros
   d. install values

7. The symbol, usually a box or line, that marks the place on the screen where the next character typed will appear or the next entry will occur is identified as the _____ .
   a. default
   b. menu
   c. command line
   d. cursor

8. Information usually found in the _____ includes information about the current document or file and the system, including the name of the

document on which you are working and the cursor position (e.g., page, line, and column number); the amount of available memory, and mode of operation; and the designation of disk drive being used.
   a. dialog box
   b. status line
   c. menu
   d. list box

9. The _____ feature allows different parts of the same file to be on the screen at the same time.
   a. dialog box
   b. menu
   c. button
   d. window

10. When a file is changed so that it can be used by another application, the process of _____ has occurred.
   a. transferring
   b. importing
   c. converting
   d. exporting

Fill-in

1. The software that instructs a computer how to solve a problem or perform a particular task is _____ software.

2. The application software that creates, edits, and manipulates text is a(n) _____ .

3. The application software that stores, organizes, manipulates, retrieves, displays, and prints data is a(n) _____ .

4. A(n) _____ is the application software that displays, manipulates, and prints rows and columns of data.

5. A(n) _____ is the application software that extracts and displays data in chart format.

6. The application software that allows a user to access an information service such as CompuServe is _____ .

7. When programs share the same data, the software is said to be _____ .

8. The text file on a disk that contains the most recent information about an application program is called the _____ file.

9. An on-screen actions/options list from which you make selections in an application program is called a _____ .

10. The place where the next character will appear is marked by a flashing symbol known as a(n) _____ .

Short Answer

1. Describe the evolution of application software. Give one example of how you might have used or will use application software in the future.

2. Explain why early microcomputers could not have used today's application software programs.

3. Identify the hardware and software needed to run an application software program.

4. What advantage(s)/disadvantage(s) do you see in an all-in-one integrated package?

5. Give an example of a program running in a background integration environment. Why is this type of program helpful?

6. What are some considerations in using the install file to start application software on your computer?

7. List and describe three common features found on application software.

8. What is WYSIWYG? Tell why it might be important.

9. Most software applications offer help to the user. Describe two forms of help.

10. What is a macro and how is one created?

OUTLINE

OBJECTIVES

- ☐ Distinguish among word processing, a word processor, and a word-processing system.

- ☐ List two advantages of a word processor over a typewriter.

- ☐ Identify several applications of a word processor.

- ☐ Describe the three basic functions of a word processor in document preparation.

- ☐ Describe the typical features of a word processor.

- ☐ Describe the concept of desktop publishing and know where it is applicable.

CHAPTER EIGHT

Word Processors

PROFILE
An Wang

One of life's great ironies is that the man who did the most to bring computerized word processing to American homes and offices could barely speak a coherent sentence of English when he came to this country. An Wang already had a degree in engineering from a Shanghai university when he ventured to the United States to continue his education. When he landed in Newport News, Virginia, however, he was far from comfortable with the English language.

Wang's government had sent him to the U.S. to continue his scientific education. However, when the civil war in China intensified, Wang decided to remain in the United States. Eventually he enrolled at Harvard, where in 1948 he completed his doctorate in applied physics.

By successfully combining his theoretical and practical work, Wang developed the magnetic-core memory for computers. He patented his invention and ultimately sold it to IBM for $500,000. Using this capital, Wang started his own electronics company in 1951. At first, his company concentrated on producing calculators, but when the market for them began to shrink, he gradually switched to manufacturing word-processing machines.

In 1972, Wang Laboratories started selling these machines, which were made from the outer shells of IBM Selectric typewriters, with memory functions handled by magnetic-tape cassettes. Within a few years, the Wang Word-Processing System had grown into an assembly of elements that included a CRT screen, multiple workstations, and programs that could be modified to process words in languages besides English. However, the system's major selling point was the fact that it could be learned and used quickly by anyone who knew how to type.

An Wang has been listed among the 10 richest men in America. Despite his riches, he lived simply until his death in 1990. One magazine reported that, although Wang had given $4 million to his alma mater, Harvard, and an additional $4 million to help rebuild Boston's performing arts center, he owned only four suits—all identical.

M any of you have been introduced to computers through their word-processing functions. Word-processing equipment is to the typewriter what the typewriter was to the pen or pencil. Since amateur inventor Christopher Sholes of Milwaukee invented the type-writer in 1873, people have been finding better ways to put words on paper—ways that are faster and more efficient than all earlier methods. The manual typewriter developed into the electric typewriter, which in turn evolved into the electronic typewriter. Now, computers and their word-processing software are the communications base for today's auto-mated office. Word processors also are essential production tools for such other users as newspapers, printers, and direct-mail companies.

Word processing is the most popular application of microcomputers, and word processing software is available for almost every computer on the market, large or small. So pervasive is the technology that almost every current document you read had its origin on a word processor.

This chapter looks at our uses of word processors, the kinds of tasks they can accomplish for us, and some of the common features we should know about.

WHAT IS WORD PROCESSING?

Word processor, word processing, word-processing system: these similar terms have different meanings. Before proceeding, let's define them.

A **word processor** is the software, or program, that manipulates the text. Word processors for microcomputers are packaged in diskette form. You may have seen them on the shelves in computer stores as 5¼″ or 3½″ disks (Figure 8–1).

Word processing is the activity of entering, viewing, storing, re-trieving, editing, rearranging, and printing text material using a computer and appropriate software.

A **word-processing system** is the combination of hardware and software used for word processing. Usually this consists of a general-purpose microcomputer, software, and printer.

However, some people use a **dedicated word-processing system,** a type of computer designed mainly for the purpose of word processing. At one time, this type of system dominated the market. But the general-purpose computer is more flexible and can be programmed for many tasks, including those described in the previous chapter—data management, electronic spreadsheet, graphics, and communications.

Most word-processing systems today are general-purpose microcom-puters into which the appropriate software is loaded. For example, when a diskette for WordPerfect (a popular word processor) is loaded into a Compaq 386 (a microcomputer), and a printer is attached, you have a word-processing system.

Most word processors perform similar tasks, and even the simplest ones allow you to type, edit, and print text quickly and efficiently. Some word processors, however, are more versatile than others. Some are diffi-cult to learn, but easy to use; others are easy to learn, but not as efficient to use. At one end of the spectrum are the very simple and inexpensive

FIGURE 8–1
A wide variety of word processors are available to suit many word-processing needs. (Photo by Larry Hamill/Macmillan)

programs for people who just want to type letters, short reports, and memos, and print them on 8½″ × 11″ paper. At the other end of the spectrum are those capable of very complex tasks, such as page layout, sorting lists, and math calculations. These features are needed for many jobs, but they may cost more and take more time to learn.

The important thing in choosing a word processor is to make sure that it has the features that *you* require. What might seem frivolous to one person may be important to another. One program may include a large dictionary to check for spelling errors, but no math functions. Another program may have the math functions, but a small dictionary (Figure 8–2).

USES AND TYPES

People who use word processors find that they have two significant advantages over a typewriter: (1) speed and efficiency in creating the documents, and (2) freedom to concentrate on the subject being written about with little concern for the mechanics of writing and typing.

The speed difference in creating documents is a result of the many editing features in word processors. It is not necessary to retype pages or "white out" words and lines. Typographical errors can be corrected and editing changes can be made on the screen before the text is actually printed. Words and paragraphs can be moved to any place in the text, and

FIGURE 8-2

This writer revises text on the screen before printing a hard copy. A typical word processing system is composed of a micro-computer, the software, and a printer.

characters can be changed, inserted, or deleted with a few keystrokes. And spelling can be automatically checked.

With the older methods of writing and typing, the words stayed where the writer put them originally. To move or delete a word or even a letter meant messy manual corrections or starting over with a clean sheet of paper. It was even more time consuming to rearrange whole sentences and paragraphs. Consequently, a writer or creator of the document often spent as much time on the typing process as on the subject being written about.

With a word processor, revisions are made electronically in the document until it is exactly right, and in a tiny fraction of the time it took on a typewriter. The final printed document is clean and neat, with no smudges where corrections have been made. With a word processor, the writer can thus concentrate on the subject and the most effective way of getting it across to the reader.

Who Uses Word Processors?

Because they are so versatile, word processors are useful to anyone who wants to type or write anything: advertising copy, outlines, reports, novels, memos, letters, term papers, scientific papers, legal briefs, or any other kind of word-based document.

In typical business offices, word processors are used to create individualized form letters and daily correspondence, as well as reports, brochures, and other published material.

Advantages of Word Processors

- Speed and efficiency in processing documents
- Freedom to concentrate on content

STROKE OF GENIUS   One of the knottiest problems in both typing and word-processing technology has been how to create a simplified input system for the complex Chinese written language. Because Chinese words are formed by an intricate and precise combination of strokes (rather than letter by letter, as in English and other Western languages), conventional Chinese typewriters have thousands of keys, one for each character. And, although Chinese computers have simpler keyboards, their word-processing functions are slow, because each character must be created artificially. One such method, called "Pinyin," requires the user to spell out spoken Mandarin Chinese with English letters, which means that the operator must know how to spell in English phonetically.

To overcome these difficulties, Canadian inventor James Monroe created a computer program that simulates the brush strokes of handwritten Chinese—by using a keyboard. With Monroe's method, an operator can form the characters by hitting a maximum of five keys on a nine-by-nine layout of 81 keys. According to China Business Machines, Inc., the first company to incorporate Monroe's system into an electronic typewriter, anyone who knows Chinese can learn the keyboard in 10 minutes and ultimately can work as fast as touch-typing in English.

Users of Word Processors

- Businesses
- Homes
- Schools
- Professionals

In schools, word processors are sometimes used in keyboarding classes to teach students to type. Teachers use them to type lesson plans and tests. School secretaries prepare school-board minutes and reports, cafeteria menus, letters to parents, and activity lists with word processors. Scholars and scientists find that using a word processor makes typing their research papers much easier.

At home, family members type personal and household correspondence, reports, and lists. Students produce neater term papers and homework assignments, and professionals, such as writers and journalists, use word processors to compose their books, articles, and newsletters.

Types of Word Processors

General-purpose word processors, like WordPerfect and WordStar, come with a variety of capabilities which attempt to meet the requirements of a variety of users. However, some packages are specifically designed to benefit a particular group of people. These specialized word processors range from easy-to-learn, easy-to-use programs for executives who must produce polished documents only occasionally, to multilanguage versions of

A Chinese phonetic keyboard. (Courtesy of International Business Machines Corp.)

word processors used by scholars who deal in translations and by businesspeople who work with international clients.

One specialized type is the executive word processor (e.g., Professional Write), which is very easy to use because of its help features and menus that quickly guide busy executives through the process. The outstanding quality of the executive word processor is its ease of use.

Other specialized word processors include Grafeas, a multilanguage word processor that can edit in 19 languages. Grafeas is not only a multilanguage word processor, but also is designed for working with complex mathematical formulas. Scientific word processors are those designed especially for mathematicians and other scientists who must communicate not only with words but with special symbols and equations. Lotus Manuscript is another word processor that simplifies the formulation and manipulation of equations.

High-powered systems for professional writers, such as Xywrite, provide complex editing features that quickly create, alter, and rearrange large blocks of text.

Types of Word Processors

- General purpose
- Executive
- Multilanguage
- Scientific
- Professional writer

HOW WORD PROCESSORS WORK

Word processors have many features and functions to help manipulate text, but the three basic functions common to all of them are (a) **text editing,** which includes entering and editing the words that make up the text; (b) **formatting,** which establishes how the document looks on the screen and when it is printed; and (c) printing the document.

Word processors handle files in different ways, but most are document-oriented, meaning that the word processor brings an entire document from the disk into the main memory so that you can work with it.

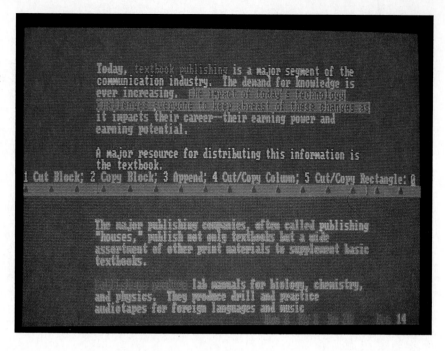

**Basic Functions of Word
Processors**

- Text editing
- Formatting
- Printing

You can create a document as large as the main memory will hold. Remember that the text stored in main memory is volatile, and changes you
make are not saved until a save command is given. If you are making
substantial changes, save the document to disk every 15 minutes so your
changes will not be lost if power to the computer is interrupted.

Many word processors allow more than two windows to be displayed. A user could, for example, view two portions of a document at the
same time, or see portions of two separate documents, or view a portion of
a document with the second window revealing any formatting codes embedded (Figure 8–3).

The two environments in which word processors operate—text-
based and graphical—differ in how users view documents and combine
graphics with text. A word processor with a graphical interface permits
WYSIWYG ("what you see is what you get"); the screen displays exactly
how the document will look when printed. A text-based interface does not
allow viewing of exactly how a document will look before it is printed
except in a "preview" mode, and text and graphics are not easily combined.

Traditionally, most word processors were text-based programs even
when used in a graphical environment. Now, however, some word processors (for example, Amí) are being designed specifically to take full advantage of the features offered by a graphical interface.

GETTING STARTED

As you assemble the components of your word-processing system, you will
want to arrange them into a work environment that offers comfort and
promotes productivity. Many organizations employ experts in the science

Design engineers work with scale models to determine an office environment that offers optimal working conditions and comfort for the user. These designs have been incorporated into this office setting. (Courtesy of TRW Inc.; inset courtesy of Hewlett-Packard Co.)

of ergonomics, or human engineering, which is concerned with the comfort and safety of workers.

Once the software is loaded into the computer, you will see the copyright notice and then be presented with either a blank screen (the work area on which to begin typing—Figure 8–4) or a menu of choices from which you will select to begin typing. The main window in a word processor is the **edit window**—the work area for entering and editing a document.

In the work area you will see the cursor, which marks the point of present activity on the screen. This location is where the first (or next) character will be entered, or where the next operation begins. The cursor

FIGURE 8–4
An edit window.

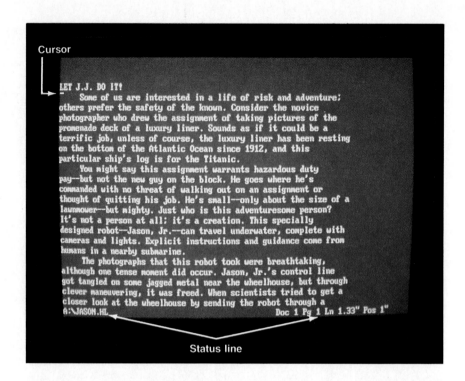

is controlled by arrow keys or a mouse, depending on your system. It can be made to jump to the first or last character on the display screen, or to the start or the end of a line. These and other cursor-movement shortcuts speed editing.

The status line at the top or bottom of the display screen (depending on which word processor you are using) provides information about the current document and the system. It may include the disk drive being used; the name of the document (also called the file name); document number; page, line, and column number (or position) on which you are working; the amount of available memory; and current mode of operation.

Word processors incorporate default settings for certain parameters like margins, line spacing, tab settings, and page length. However, you can elect not to use these and to specify different parameters or settings.

BASIC FEATURES USED TO CREATE A SIMPLE DOCUMENT

Word processors have many features and functions to help manipulate text, but within the three basic functions of word processors (text editing, formatting, and printing) are many helpful features. Although different word processors have different combinations of features, we will discuss those that are common to most of them.

Text-Editing Features

Text-editing activities include entering the words that make up the text, making deletions or insertions, and moving words, phrases, or blocks of text from one place to another. When text is entered, it is displayed on the screen and stored in the computer as a document (also called a file). Revisions can be made until the document is exactly the way the writer wants.

Modes. Text is entered in either the insert mode or the typeover mode. In the **insert mode,** when additional text is added, all text to the right of the addition automatically shifts to make room for the new material. However, in the **typeover mode,** the newly inserted characters replace or "strike over" the existing ones.

Wordwrap. The feature most unique to word processors is **wordwrap.** When this feature is activated, the user does not need to press Enter (Return) at the end of a line of text, as on a typewriter. The user just continues typing, and the program "wraps the type around" past the margin and automatically puts the words on the next line. This process continues to the end of the paragraph. At this point, pressing Enter moves the cursor down to the next line to begin a new paragraph. The wordwrap feature can be disengaged in some word processors.

If the text is not supposed to go to the end of the line—e.g., in a typed column of names—the Enter key is pressed after typing each item in the list.

A hyphenation feature offers a choice between hyphenating words at the end of a line yourself, or letting the program automatically hyphenate for you.

Inserting and Deleting. Adding a character, phrase, or block of copy to the existing text employs an insert feature. If the program is in the insert mode, the existing text automatically shifts to make room for the new text. If it is in the typeover mode, entries will strike over and replace the existing text.

The delete feature allows a character, phrase, or block of text to be removed. The remaining text automatically shifts to fill the space left by the deleted text.

Search and Replace. With the **search and replace** feature, you can make corrections throughout an entire document with only a few keystrokes. It is especially helpful when you have just finished a report and discovered, for example, that you misspelled a person's name throughout.

- ☐ In a "simple search," the program searches for a specified string of characters (the misspelled name, in this case) and highlights it and stops. You then can decide whether to change it, remove it, or move on.
- ☐ In a "conditional search," you first specify a replacement string; then the program searches for and locates all occurrences of a particular string of characters and asks you at each instance if the existing string should be replaced with the new one. If so, the program then replaces it with the change you suggested (the new name).

FIGURE 8–5

Block editing. (a) Text is marked to be moved. (b) Text is moved to end of first paragraph. (Photo by Jo Hall/Macmillan)

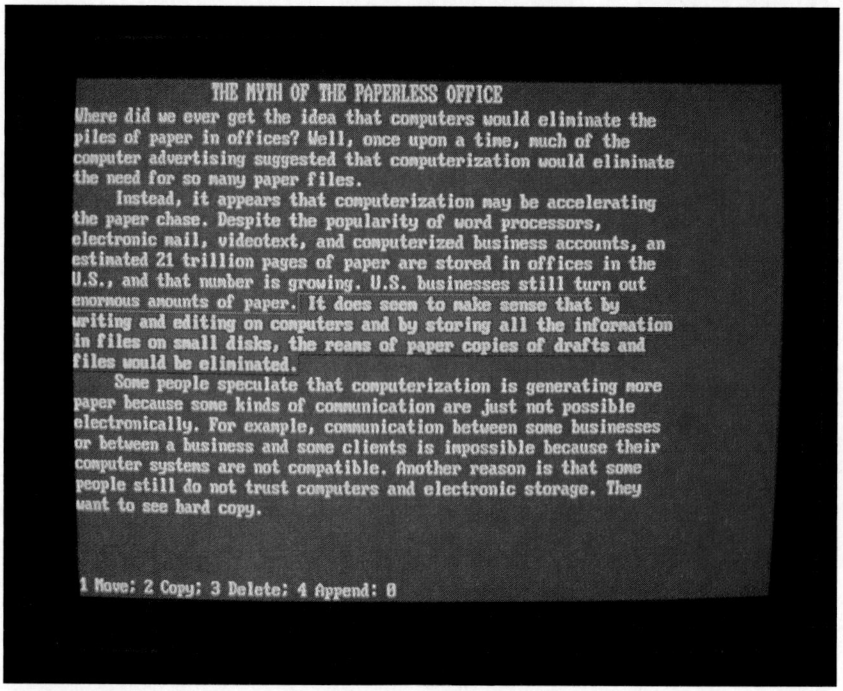

(a)

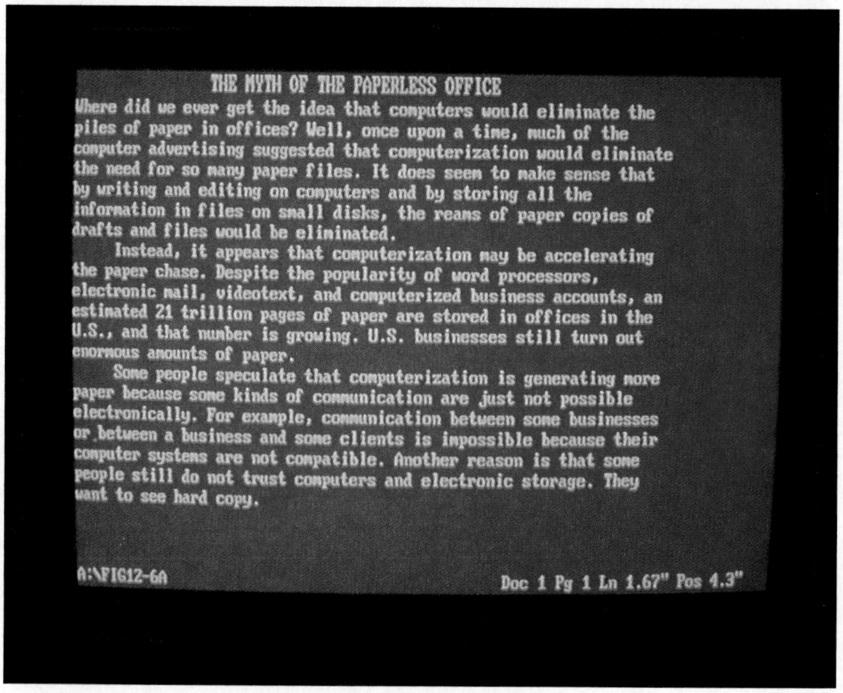

(b)

☐ In a "global" search and replace, the document is searched so that each instance of a specified string is found and automatically replaced.

Block Editing. Block actions called **block editing** permit large units of text—paragraphs, sections, or even pages—to be moved, copied, deleted, saved, or altered as a unit.

The feature requires that the user first mark both the beginning and the end of the text being changed. Then the whole block of text is manipulated according to further instructions on the screen (Figure 8–5). Block editing commands typically include delete, copy, move, append, save, boldface, underline, italics, and others.

Formatting Features

Before continuing, let's look at some typical document format features (Figure 8–6). The format of a document refers to the way it looks on the

FIGURE 8–6
Document showing format features.

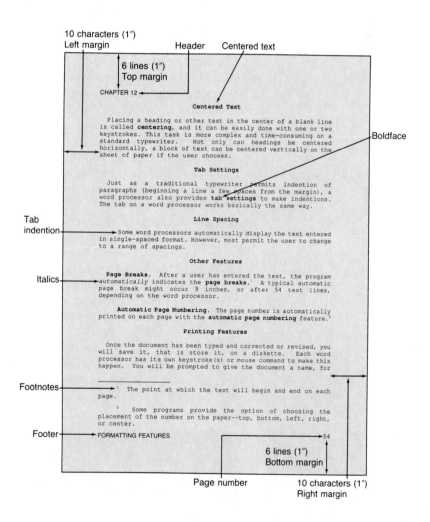

screen or after it is printed. Some features are specified before keying in the document, some during entering and editing, and others after the document is completed and right before it is printed.

The way formatting features are indicated varies, depending on whether your system uses a text interface or a graphical interface. For example, if your system uses a text interface, formatting features such as margins and tab indentions might be specified by keying-in the specification on an option menu. If your system uses a graphical interface, a specification might be entered by pointing with a mouse at positions on a ruler line across the screen or in a dialog box.

Some word processors, even though they use a text interface, measure margins, tabs, and other positions on the screen in graphic terms—in inches rather than by character position on the screen. For example, one word processor might set a left margin at 1 inch, and another system might set it at 12 character spaces.

Not all format characteristics appear the same on the screen as they will when printed. For example, some word processors display text only single spaced, but give the option of printing it double spaced.

These formatting specifications and parameters are communicated from the computer to the printer before printing starts.

Character Enhancements. Most word processors permit you to specify special enhancements to the text style when it is printed. Typical **character enhancements** are creating boldface type or italics, underlining, or a combination. Some word processors instruct you to indicate boldface by placing markers before and after the text on the screen, and that text appears boldface only when printed. Some codes are not visible on the screen unless a special command is given to reveal them. Even though a word processor may permit these enhancements, some printers are not capable of handling all of them.

Margin Settings. The specifications allocating space on the left, right, top, and bottom of a printed document are the **margin settings**. Some word processors preset the margin specifications, and they cannot be changed. Most word processors, though, allow you to specify all four margins. Margins are specified by keying in the appropriate numbers or by pointing (with a mouse) to a ruler line on the screen and "dragging" margin indicators to the desired spot on the ruler (Figure 8–7).

Justification. The feature that aligns the text flush with the margin is called **justification**. It is used to make the right margin even, the left margin even, or both (see Figure 8–8). Justification of the text may not

FIGURE 8–7
Ruler line showing margin and tab setting. (Photo by Jo Hall/ Macmillan)

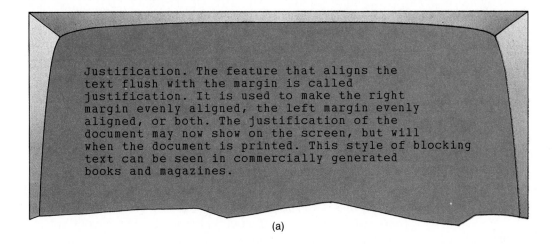

Justification. The feature that aligns the
text flush with the margin is called
justification. It is used to make the right
margin evenly aligned, the left margin evenly
aligned, or both. The justification of the
document may now show on the screen, but will
when the document is printed. This style of blocking
text can be seen in commercially generated
books and magazines.

(a)

Justification. The feature that aligns the text flush
with the margin is called justification. It is used to
make the right margin evenly aligned, the left margin
evenly aligned, or both. The justification of the
document may now show on the screen, but will when the
document is printed. This style of blocking text can be
seen in commercially generated books and magazines.

(b)

FIGURE 8–8

Justifying the text in a document changes its appearance. (a) Left justified,
ragged right. (b) Both left and right justified.

show on the screen, but it will be aligned when printed. Justification of text
can be seen in magazines and books such as the one you are reading;
notice that this paragraph is justified left and right.

Centering. Placing a heading or other text in the center of a blank line is
called **centering**. If you have ever centered a heading on a typewriter, you
know how tedious and time consuming it can be. On a word processor,
this task can easily be done with one or two keystrokes. Not only can
headings be centered horizontally, but a block of text can be centered
vertically on the sheet of paper if you choose.

Tab Settings. Just as a traditional typewriter permits indention of paragraphs (beginning a line a few spaces from the margin), a word processor

also provides **tab settings** to make indentions. The tab on a word processor works basically the same way. Most word processors have a sophisticated tab feature that simplifies typing columns of text or columns of numbers with decimal points. The feature can automatically align columns around the decimal points.

This specification is entered by keying it into your system if using a text interface, or by pointing with a mouse and "dragging" a tab indicator to the desired position on a ruler line if the system uses a graphical interface.

Line Spacing. Some word processors automatically display the text entered in single-spaced format. However, most permit you to specify a range of spacings, for example, half space, double space, or triple space. The text may still appear single spaced on the screen, but it will print as specified.

Page Breaks. After the text has been entered, the program automatically indicates the **page breaks,** that is, the point where the text will begin and end on each page when it is actually printed. You can override the automatic page break and indicate where you want the text to stop on one page and begin on another. The program usually assumes you are working with $8\frac{1}{2}'' \times 11''$ sheets of paper, so a typical automatic page break might be at 9 inches, or after 54 text lines, depending on the word processor.

Automatic Page Numbering. The page number is automatically printed on each page with the **automatic page numbering** feature. Some programs provide the option of removing the page number from only certain pages or choosing the placement of the number on the paper—top or bottom, left, right, or center.

Printing Features

Once the document has been typed and corrected or revised, you must save it—store it—on a diskette. Each word processor has its own keystrokes or mouse command to make this happen. You will be prompted to give the document a name—for example, "REPORT1"—so that you can retrieve it any time to revise or to print a hard copy.

Viewing. A graphics-based word processor enables you to continually see on the screen exactly what the document will look like when it's printed. With a text-based word processor, a special preview feature is used to see how the document will appear when it is printed. WYSIWYG and preview features are useful when a document contains footers, headers, footnotes, graphics, or other features that do not appear on the screen but will print.

Text to be Printed. When printing a document, you will probably be presented with several print options from which to make a selection. For example, you might tell the program to print only page 1, or several specific pages, or all of the pages. You can also indicate certain sections

FIGURE 8–9
Example of printing options.
(Photo by Jo Hall/Macmillan)

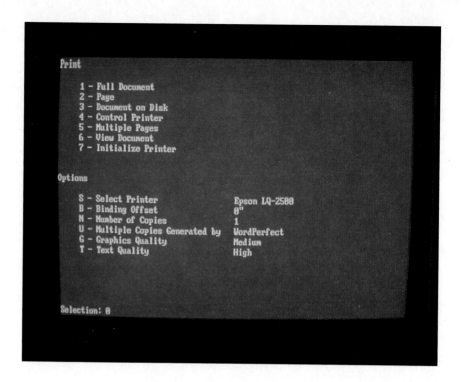

(blocks) or paragraphs to be printed. You might indicate that you want two copies of the same document printed (Figure 8–9).

Quality of Print. Other options include indicating the quality of the type when it is printed. Because many dot-matrix printers can print in several modes, such as draft or near-letter quality, you will be able to select one. With draft-quality print, the characters, which are composed of dots or lines, are formed by a single pass of the print head. Near-letter quality print results when the print head makes multiple passes over the same characters, filling in the spaces between the dots or lines.

Developments in the last few years have made near-typeset quality printing affordable for many small businesses to produce their newsletters, magazines, and brochures; the results look as good as those done by a commercial printer. Laser printers have made this possible. Some laser printers come equipped with a *page description programming language,* such as PostScript, that gives you precise control over nearly every detail of a printed page. Printers with this feature are equipped with numerous typefaces and type styles; you can specify type in any of the typefaces and styles, and in almost any size. With the trend in word processors to include more and more page-layout features, laser printers have become popular.

Page Size and Orientation. Some printers can accommodate several sizes of paper. When a printer is installed with a word processor, the standard paper size is usually 8½″ × 11″, to be printed in a **portrait**

orientation (vertical). However, you can tell the word processor and the printer to use a different size paper or a different orientation—for example, 11″ × 14″ paper (legal size), to be printed in a **landscape orientation** (horizontal) with the stationery turned on its side (depending on the printer's capabilities). Other types and sizes of forms usually accommodated are envelopes, peel-off address labels, 3 × 5 cards, and half sheets (8½″ × 5½″).

Once printing is completed and you want to stop using your word processor, you are usually asked if you want to quit or to "exit" the word processor. When you exit the word processor, the computer returns to its operating system. From here you would select another program to use, or turn off the equipment.

These basic features are common to most word processors. Developers make them as versatile as possible so that a broad spectrum of users will be able to use the same program. For example, word processors contain some features that are particularly useful to a typical business office, although a novelist who writes manuscripts at the computer might not need those features. The same word processor also might contain features that the novelist would find helpful in preparing large manuscripts, but which would be of little interest to a business. We'll describe below categories of features that appeal to particular users, but are actually found in most word processors today—manuscript preparation features, business features, and page layout features.

MANUSCRIPT-PREPARATION FEATURES

Most word processors include manuscript-preparation features for creating footnotes, endnotes, and subscript/superscript notations. In addition, they enable writers to mark segments of text to be used for other purposes—for example, to mark words and phrases in the text to automatically generate an outline, a table of contents, or an index. These are slow, tedious, and error-prone tasks when performed manually, but with a word processor having such features they are automated, faster, and easier.

Many word processors also have grammar-checking and style-checking capabilities to alert you to real or potential errors, a thesaurus to suggest words that are more varied or precise than those used originally, and a spelling checker to look for incorrectly spelled or typed words. We'll describe some of these features in more detail below.

Footnotes, Endnotes, and Comments

Both footnotes and endnotes are devices for explaining something in the main text or for listing additional sources of information. Footnotes appear at the bottom of the page and endnotes at the end of the chapter or document. Each is signaled in the body of the text by a superscript number, placed slightly above the line of type like this: [5]. With word processors, these alterations from the regular text are made with a series of keystrokes, rather than by manual manipulation of the typed page.

A **comment** feature allows you to insert notes or explanations at *any* location in a document. The comment is usually surrounded by a box so it can be easily spotted.

Headers and Footers

A **header** is a line (or lines) of text repeated at the top of each page. A **footer** is text that appears at the bottom of each page. Refer to Figure 8–6 and note where the header and the footer are placed. For example, the report's title and the author's name could be printed at the top or bottom of every page. Generally, this information is entered after the rest of the document is keyed. It is usually keyed in just one time for the entire document rather than page by page; the program automatically inserts it on every page.

Subscripts and Superscripts

Subscripts are textual additions that lie slightly below the regular line of type, such as the numbers used in chemical formulas. The formula for water, for example, would be written as H_2O. With a typewriter, you would have to roll the platen slightly to get the $_2$ in the right place.

Superscripts are textual additions that lie slightly above the regular line of type. For example, the mathematical expression "6 to the second power" is written as 6^2, and as noted above, footnotes are signaled with superscripts. Codes are inserted at the proper places for the superscript (or subscript) so that when it is printed, it appears above (or below) the line.

Macro

The macro feature helps automate some word-processing tasks. With this feature, typing a normally time-consuming phrase or other set of commands can be reduced to only a few keystrokes. The phrase or other set of keystrokes is typed and filed under a macro label or name, and then invoked each time it is needed.

For example, the name "S. J. Perelman" may be used frequently in a term paper about American humor. To avoid having to retype the full name each time (and risk misspelling it), the name is typed once, labeled with a simple abbreviation, and stored; for example, SP could be the label for S. J. Perelman. As the user keys in the document, the command (one or two keystrokes) is given to invoke that macro at each point where the name is to appear. Thus the writer types only the label SP, causing the full name to appear on the screen.

Spelling Checker and Thesaurus

A **spelling checker,** sometimes called a dictionary, locates misspelled words and typographical errors in a document. The checker compares words in a document with its dictionary of correctly spelled words, which number from 20,000 to over 100,000, depending on which word processor is used. The spelling checker highlights on the screen the words that are not in its dictionary and words that are misspelled. Options for the correct spelling are presented. The user can then decide whether or not to replace the word with the spelling-checker's recommendation.

However, a spelling checker cannot detect *misused* words that are correctly spelled. For example, in the sentence "I red the book," the spelling checker cannot know that "red" is an incorrect word; "red" *is* spelled correctly. The writer used the wrong "read," but the spelling checker cannot determine that.

Some spelling checkers allow you to add more words to the dictionary. This feature is helpful if the program's dictionary is small or if you are writing a paper using technical terms that wouldn't ordinarily appear in the dictionary. The checker will then use those added terms as part of its own dictionary. Writers who use technical terms extensively (in medical or legal papers, for example) might want to purchase a special spelling-checker program devoted to words in a particular field.

A **thesaurus** suggests synonyms for words. When you are stumped for just the right word, the computerized thesaurus can help. Usually, you access the thesaurus by highlighting the word to be replaced. With the correct command, a list of synonyms (and sometimes antonyms) is presented on the screen. Sometimes, even the synonyms have lists of synonyms (Figure 8–10).

FIGURE 8–10

Thesaurus in use. Here we highlighted the word "communication" in order to find a more appropriate word from the thesaurus. The thesaurus presented several possibilities, including "report." When we prompted the computer to seek synonyms for "report," it gave synonyms for that word, too. (Photo by Jo Hall/Macmillan)

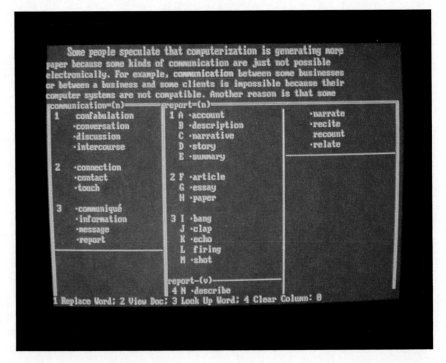

Grammar and Style Checker

A **grammar and style checker** points out possible problems with punctuation, grammar, sentence structure, and writing style. Most grammar and style checkers for microcomputers are still fairly elementary and are no replacement for good editing. Because English grammar consists of so many rules and exceptions, grammar checking demands more "comprehension" capabilities than most microcomputers can handle. But a grammar checker can examine writing in two ways:

1. It uses a few simple rules and can find some errors. For example, it can locate a period followed by two spaces and then a lowercase letter and recognize this as a capitalization error. Or it might find words used repetitiously; if you have a tendency to use "for example" quite often, the checker will point that out.
2. Another method compares words and phrases in the document with those in its file. It might locate "would of" in the document and suggest that "would have" is correct grammar.

Table of Contents, Index, Outliner

A table of contents, which is located at the beginning of a document or book, can be automatically generated by marking the headings and subheadings in the text that are to be entries in the table of contents. After marking, these items will be copied onto a page in the correct order to create a table of contents, with page numbers.

Creating an index, which appears at the end of a book, works in a similar way. The user scrolls through the text, tagging each word that is to appear in the index as an entry or subentry. Although a lot of thought still must go into planning and preparing an index, automation of the process makes it easier.

Some word processors can help you create outlines with an outliner. One type of outliner automatically inserts the outline number or letter as you type each line of the outline; a correct number or letter for each level or sublevel will turn your text into outline form, depending on how many times you indent with "tab." Another type of outliner helps organize your thoughts and text. You enter ideas as they occur; then you can easily organize and reorganize them as headings and subheadings until the outline flows as you wish.

BUSINESS FEATURES

In the business world, the word processor has several applications that go beyond the mere creation of a manuscript.

Mail Merge

A particularly useful application is the **mail merge** feature. It enables a single form letter to be addressed and personalized automatically to any

HIGHLIGHT 8–2

COMPUTERS AND CREATIVITY

Few people in science and business need to be convinced that computers are essential to their professions. But what about writers? To what degree have custom, poetic stereotypes, and fear of hardware kept them limited to pen or typewriter? Not much, it seems. *Writer's Digest,* a major trade magazine for writers, now routinely carries articles and columns about computers and the creative process. Younger writers, who learned their craft during the period when computers were first introduced into the classroom, look upon the devices as regular tools of the trade. Journalism schools and newspapers have long since assimilated computers into their instructional and operational schemes.

The unarguable merits of computerized word processing have also convinced veteran writers to take a chance with the "new" technology. Some have become almost evangelistic about it. Author/columnist William F. Buckley, Jr., for example, was instantly converted to computerized composition after seeing a primitive word processor in operation when he visited literary critic Hugh Kenner. Gene Perret, a veteran member of Bob Hope's comedy-writing team, became so impressed with computer capabilities that he carries one with him, even when he's not on a specific writing assignment. Since becoming a convert, Perret has spent a good deal of time trying to convince other team members to forsake their typewriters.

Best-selling author David Halberstam is another computer enthusiast, as is *New York Times* book reviewer Christopher Lehmann-Haupt.

What all these writers have in common is the need to produce a lot of work in a relatively short amount of time and with the least distraction possible. (Buckley reportedly dashed off a 7500-word children's book in two hours on his Epson PX–8.) For writers, computing and creativity are almost synonymous terms.

number of people. With mail merge, a form letter is created which contains specially coded characters that tell the word processor where to insert such variables as names and addresses. Then, once the process is set in motion, the computer merges the letter with the variables to produce multiple "original" copies.

With mail merge, businesses can send potential customers form letters in which the recipients' names appear in the body of the text. And, even though hundreds or thousands of these letters may have been sent out, each looks and sounds very personal. Such mass customizing would have been impossible without refinements in word processing.

Style Sheet

The **style sheet** feature also simplifies and speeds the preparation of repetitive documents. It automates text repetition and certain formatting functions by providing the user with a built-in collection of documents or the basic forms for documents. As an example of repetitive documents, a legal secretary might have a legal form that is used repeatedly with only minor changes each time it is used for a new client. A style sheet can be typed that contains the core document (the text that will be repeated for each client). Then the form is filed, to be recalled each time it is to be used, with the secretary modifying it to include the minor changes. A style sheet can also be comprised of formatting functions, such as turning on bold face, underlining, and margin changes; the style sheet then could be used anywhere it is needed throughout a document.

Law offices rely heavily on word processors. They have a particular need for standard legal documents which all include basically the same text. With a style sheet, the part that does vary can be modified for each client.

Line and Paragraph Numbering

Law offices and other businesses also produce documents that require line and paragraph numbering in the standard legal style. Many word processors offer automatic line and paragraph numbering.

Math Functions

A math function that performs simple calculations is useful to those who create documents that are mainly text, but which include some columns and rows of numbers. With this feature, calculations can be done automatically while creating, for example, a financial report or an accounting statement.

PAGE LAYOUT FEATURES

Page composition, or layout, features are included in many word processors so that businesses or personal users can type, design, and publish professional-looking newsletters, brochures, flyers, or pamphlets within the office.

Separate page-layout software is available specifically for more complex publishing efforts. This topic is discussed in more detail below under "Desktop Publishing." However, some of these features are found within many word-processing programs themselves.

Newspaper-Style Columns

One such feature creates newspaper-style columns. When the first column is full, the type flows from the bottom of the first column to the top of the next column and begins to fill that column.

WYSIWYG or Preview

After your newsletter or other publication has been designed and typed, the preview feature lets you see what the publication will look like when it is printed. It shows you, for example, what a two-page spread (left and right pages that face each other) will look like before printing, giving you the opportunity to see if the elements are arranged attractively on the page. You can then go back into the document and make adjustments if they are needed. However, if you are using a graphical interface with WYSIWYG (what you see is what you get) capability, the preview feature is not needed. The WYSIWYG feature allows you to continually see on the screen the way the publication will look when it is printed.

Type Styles

Several options of type faces, styles, and sizes are usually available with a program, assuming your printer can accommodate them. For example, you might select sans serif Roman at 12 characters to the inch, or perhaps italic Gothic at 10 characters to the inch and boldfaced.

DESKTOP PUBLISHING

Desktop publishing is a concept that combines the use of microcomputers with word processing, page-composition software, and high-quality laser printers. Anyone can use such a system to create and publish documents. Large corporate departments that want to publish in-house, managers of small businesses, and writers who like the idea of self-publishing may use desktop publishing software to produce booklets, brochures, newsletters, and annual reports. Even a 50-page magazine or a 150-page book can be designed, and its pages made up and printed using desktop publishing.

Traditional Typographic Process

To fully appreciate the benefits of desktop publishing, it is necessary to understand the traditional process of preparing professional-looking documents, using typography and a printshop. The first step is to create the basic text, using a typewriter or microcomputer. Second, decisions must be made regarding type styles and sizes, headlines, borders, and other elements that make the document more attractive or readable. The document is then sent to a professional typesetter for rekeying. The typesetter produces "galley proofs," which are returned for proofreading by the author.

After being checked for errors, the text is corrected and cut-and-pasted according to the design of the document page. In addition to "pasting up" the text in columns, space must be left to accommodate photographs and other illustrations. Finally, this "camera-ready" document (ready for the printer's camera to make printing negatives) is sent to a commercial printer who prepares a photographic plate and prints the finished document on a press. The cost for a commercially printed document runs between $50 and $250 per page.

Document Creation with Desktop Publishing

By contrast, desktop publishing allows you to create high-quality documents at significantly lower cost and in less time. The uniqueness of a desktop-publishing system lies in the page-design and composition software. It is basically a visually oriented or graphics-oriented software (as opposed to text-oriented word processing) which involves positioning and aligning text, graphics, and other elements of the document page entirely on the screen. No longer does the designer need to physically cut, arrange, add, delete, and reposition these elements, or wait for a printout to decide on changes to be made.

Besides the cost and time savings, the use of desktop publishing helps the originator control the creative process from start to finish, thus preventing errors and misunderstandings due to poor communication among originator, typesetter, and printer. It also assures consistency of appearance and quality in the case of documents such as newsletters and reports, which are produced on a regular basis and need to conform to a specific layout.

The Hardware

Sophisticated desktop publishing programs need large amounts of memory to operate properly. A typical setup requires a microcomputer with at least one floppy disk drive, 512KB or more of RAM, and a hard disk with a minimum of 10MB of memory (Figure 8–11).

Documents which are to be printed in either black and white or color can be created on a monochrome monitor. However, many newsletters, reports, graphs, etc., are printed in color for greater visual impact, so for these a color printer is necessary. A monochrome monitor can be used because color can still be represented on a monochrome monitor with varying degrees of gray shading and with patterns.

FIGURE 8–11
Desktop-publishing hardware. (Courtesy of International Business Machines Corp.)

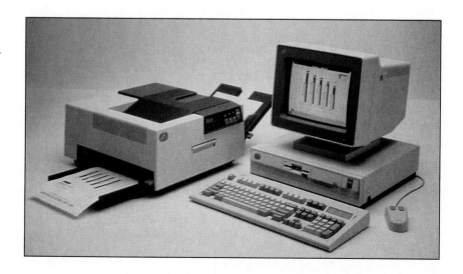

A standard color monitor is called a CGA (color graphics adaptor) monitor, with a resolution of 640 by 200 dots. For the highest-quality viewing, the serious user may want higher resolution and better color, either an EGA (enhanced graphics adaptor) monitor, with 640 by 350 dots, or a VGA monitor (video graphics array), with a resolution of 720 by 400 dots and up to 256,000 colors.

In addition to the computer's keyboard, almost all desktop publishing programs require a mouse to direct operations and to manipulate elements on the screen quickly. It is essential in free-hand graphic applications such as drawing and painting programs. Scanning devices allow desktop publishing programs to import photographs, drawings, and other visual elements into a document by electronically "reading" the picture and reproducing it on computer screen.

A modem for sending the completed document over telephone lines is also required if the document is going to be to sent to another location for final editing or printing.

Professional-quality documents using desktop publishing would not be possible without the development of laser printers, which produce high-resolution copy. Powerful printer languages, such as PostScript (which is a *page description language*) or Hewlett-Packard's LaserJet standard for printers (which is a *printer control language*), allow a wide variety of type styles, sizes, and arrangements. Internally, sophisticated and expensive laser printers are actually computers in themselves, having programs and memories that enable them to produce professional-looking documents.

The Software

Originally, most **page-composition software** for the microcomputer was developed for the Apple Macintosh—for example, Aldus PageMaker. It was Paul Brainard of Aldus Corporation who coined the term "desktop publishing." Programs have subsequently been developed for IBM and IBM-compatible microcomputers—for example, Ventura Publisher. Some software, like PageMaker, now has versions applicable to both Apple and IBM environments.

The Process

Creating Text. Though most desktop publishing programs have provisions for creating and editing text, this step is usually performed using word-processing software because of its specialized and sophisticated text creation features.

As word-processing programs have become more sophisticated, some blurring has occurred between the capabilities of word processing and desktop publishing. Software such as WordPerfect and Ashton-Tate's Byline now incorporate some desktop publishing graphics and layout features, but these programs are still primarily text oriented.

Desktop Publishing Compared to Word Processing. Most word-processing programs display the words that exist in the text and the general layout of the page, but don't give a precise picture of what the document will look like when it is printed. (A few word-processing programs do so—Amí, for example.) What dramatically separates desktop publishing from most word processing is the *immediate interaction* between text and graphics—the ability to manipulate them both on-screen simultaneously and easily. This permits spontaneous decisions and instant changes to the page being created.

The advantage of a desktop-publishing program is that it permits changing or mixing type styles (incorporating several on the same page); adding or deleting columns; increasing or decreasing the size of letters; creating headlines; adding, removing, or substituting one illustration for another; creating decorative special effects like headlines and borders; and merging all these elements quickly and with a minimum of effort. In short, the page-composition program of desktop-publishing software is used to design the "look" of the document page (Figure 8–12).

FIGURE 8–12
This publication was designed, created, and printed with a desktop-publishing system. Notice the graphics and variety in type styles. (Photo by Larry Hamill/Macmillan)

Creating Graphic Elements. An important feature of desktop publishing programs is the ability to view the document on the screen exactly as it will appear on paper. This essential WYSIWYG feature—what you see is what you get—is a major advantage over most word-processing software for producing professional-looking publications. Being able to see the entire page exactly as it will be printed allows the designer to instantly and accurately judge the balance of elements on the page and make changes to create an attractive layout.

Increasingly, serious desktop-publishing users are turning to full-page monitors (instead of the more common half-page) in order to make full use of this graphic-design characteristic. Some programs now show two pages side by side for even more creative control (Figure 8–13).

Most desktop-publishing programs permit placement of graphic elements in the document wherever desired, and then "flow" the text around the photo, chart, or illustration. Graphic elements to be included in the document are produced in one of three ways: (1) computer-generated, using drawing or painting programs and a mouse; (2) digitized, using a scanner; or (3) proprietary clip art, from a disk. All three are described below.

Drawing and Painting. Drawing or painting programs, such as MacDraw, MacPaint, PC Paintbrush, Adobe Illustrator, Crickett Draw, and others, allow you to create original artwork directly on the monitor screen using a variety of electronic drawing devices, such as a mouse or light pen. These programs may be used to create company logos or letterheads, newsletter cartoons, or other graphic illustrations which enhance the eye-appeal and readability of the document.

Scanners. One of the fastest-growing graphic aids in desktop publishing is the scanner. Remember from Chapter 2 that a scanner is a device which "reads" a photograph or other graphic representation and then converts

FIGURE 8–13
This monitor displays two pages side by side. (Courtesy of Apple Computer)

the image into a pattern of electronic digits. These digits can then be printed as a series of dots, arranged to recreate the original graphic image.

Low-end scanners, those in the $1,500 to $2,500 range, can recognize about 16 levels (shades) of gray. More expensive devices, in the $3,000 to $9,000 range, can recognize as many as 256 levels of gray. Ultimately, the quality of the printed image generated from the scanning devices is limited by the quality of the original image, the capability of the scanning device, and the resolution of the printer.

Typical laser printers today can print 300 dots per inch (dpi). By contrast, commercial typesetting machines have a resolution of over 1200 dpi. Line art, such as drawings and tables, generally reproduces well because of its high contrast. However, photographs and other visual images with more subtle changes in shading generally do not reproduce as well because the scanners are not sensitive enough to differentiate the continuous change in tones.

Clip Art. A common and cost-effective method of adding visual interest to desktop-publishing documents is the use of clip art. **Clip art** consists of pictures on floppy disk available from a variety of publishers. The user selects appropriate illustrations from these files, imports them into the desktop-publishing software, and positions them where desired on the screen. Generally, clip art files are grouped according to some theme. Illustrations are available relating to businesses or professions, holidays, hobbies, religion, travel, and sports, and there may be as many as 500 to 600 illustrations per disk (Figure 8–14).

The name clip art comes from books of artwork sold to ad agencies and printers from which they scissor or "clip out" illustrations for advertising. The generic-looking illustrations in telephone book Yellow Pages usually are clip art.

FIGURE 8–14
Clip art is available on disk for use in publications. (Photo by Larry Hamill/Macmillan)

Page Templates or Style Sheets. Another useful feature of desktop publishing is the availability of document templates, or page style sheets, now available in most desktop-publishing programs. Templates are sample forms in the software which allow you to produce newsletters, memos, invoices, reports, etc., without having to personally design the layout for each of these documents. Instead, you simply select the appropriate template and command the program to insert text and graphics in the predesigned spaces provided.

Templates are a feature in even some elementary desktop-publishing programs, allowing the creation of simple newsletters, greeting cards, banners, bumper stickers, or certificates. The most sophisticated and versatile programs offer more precise control of document elements, have more templates for a wider variety of documents, and usually include several examples to choose from. These include PageMaker (for Apple and IBM) and Ventura Publisher (for IBM and IBM-compatibles).

Printing the Publication. As mentioned earlier, the development of laser printers allowed desktop publishers to produce high-quality documents at reasonable cost. In addition to their increased resolution (density and sharpness of the printing in the finished document), laser printers differ from the less expensive and simpler ink-jet and dot-matrix printers by being more versatile.

Modern laser printers offer desktop-publishing users an almost unlimited variety of type styles, called fonts, in a wide range of sizes. A **font** includes all the letters, numbers, and symbols of one style of type, in one size. A collection of all available sizes of one font is called a *typeface*. Laser printers not only have several fonts built in (from 11 to more than 36), but cartridges are available which provide additional fonts, usually four fonts per cartridge.

Also, most printers allow the size of the type to be changed, some in fixed steps, others in infinitely scalable form within a range. Type is sized according to a vertical unit of measure called a *point*. There are 72 points to one inch. Printers with scalable type may have a range of 2 to 144 points, or approximately 1/36 of an inch to 2 inches.

An alternative to user-owned laser printers is the typesetting service. After the desktop publisher creates the document on a microcomputer, it is sent to the typesetting service on disk by mail or through a telephone modem, and is printed on a compatible system.

The cost of having a document professionally printed varies according to the quality of resolution desired in the finished product, measured in dots per inch. A minimum acceptable standard of 300 dpi may cost under $1 per page, whereas a document of over 1200 dpi could cost as much as $15 per page.

Buying Considerations

Advertising for computer products often seems to suggest that a given program will do all things for all users. Desktop-publishing software is a highly competitive field and the potential buyer/user needs to be cautious and informed before investing in a system.

How Much Desktop Publishing Will Be Done? First, a potential desktop publisher should consider realistically whether such a system is even needed. Cutting-edge technology and expensive equipment may be wasted in an office that produces only a monthly newsletter for a few employees.

Length and Type of Documents to be Created. Programs also differ in the type of document for which they are best suited. Some, such as Page-Maker, are best used for highly creative, short documents. Other software, like Ventura Publisher, is better suited for longer documents and series of similar documents that will be issued periodically.

Resolution Quality and Program Features. Not all programs are equally good examples of WYSIWYG. The quality of the visual display, the clarity of the text when different styles of type are used on the same page, and the legibility of placement tools (such as rulers and grids found in page-layout templates) make some programs more desirable for a given application than others. Also, some programs may import graphics more quickly and easily than others, but allow less precision and control of the text.

Compatibility. The compatibility of desktop-publishing software with existing computing equipment in an organization is a further consideration. In most companies, it is desirable to *network,* or interact, with the firm's existing computers. This may mean compromising some of the desired capabilities of the desktop-publishing functions if the best equipment for a particular purpose is not compatible with existing equipment.

Ease of Learning and Using. The basic commands of most desktop-publishing software can be learned in several days, but it may take several months of dedicated effort to really master the program. The ease of learning a desktop publishing system is affected by such things as the complexity of the program—how sophisticated and versatile is it? Also, the program's commands should be logical and *intuitive*—the correct way should be the natural and obvious way.

How a program addresses errors is a further consideration. A superior program will make error messages highly visible and easy to interpret, will give guidance in correcting errors, and guard against loss of data as a result of error.

Quality of Documentation and Vendor Support. Reference manuals and tutorials should be complete, should be written to anticipate questions, and should make it easy to locate topics (via cross-referencing and complete indexes.)

Another factor which affects ultimate satisfaction with a desktop-publishing system is the degree of company support available for technical help and troubleshooting. Most companies not only offer a warranty on their products, but also provide phone numbers for help when purchasers encounter difficulties. Many desktop-publishing companies also offer training in the use of their products, either directly or through third-party trainers.

Is Desktop Publishing Right for You?

New desktop publishers should realize that even the most sophisticated program is at best a very limited substitute for typographic experience and design ability. These skills come from training and practice. More than one purchaser of a desktop-publishing system has been disappointed to discover that the first document was not as attractive or professional-looking as those illustrated in the advertising for the system.

No program is a good value if it fails to do what it is supposed to, if it cannot be learned thoroughly by those expected to use it, or if more time is spent in fixing the program than in using it. Not everyone wants to devote the time and effort to become a typographic designer. What desktop publishing does is maximize the creative abilities of the people who are willing to learn and who are responsible for producing professional-looking documents at significant savings of time and money.

SUMMARY

Word processors were developed to speed the process of written communication. THey are now the foundation for today's office automation; they are essential productivity tools for offices and personal users alike.

Word processing is the activity of entering, viewing, storing, retrieving, editing, rearranging, and printing text using a computer. The software that facilitates word processing is the word processor.

Some people use a dedicated word-processing system (a special computer designed almost exclusively for the purpose of word processing), although they no longer are very popular. Most people use a general-purpose microcomputer and word-processing software. Word processors are available for most brands of computers.

There are two reasons why one might prefer a word processor over the typewriter: (1) it is faster and more efficient in making revisions and corrections, and (2) it gives the user freedom to concentrate on the subject matter rather than on the process of making revisions and corrections.

Anyone who needs to produce letters, reports, or documents of any kind can use a word processor. They are used in businesses, homes, and schools, and by professionals in all walks of life. Most general-purpose word processors contain a variety of features to appeal to a variety of users. Specialized word processors are geared to the needs of executives, multilanguage users, scientists, and professional writers.

Three basic functions common to all word processors are (a) text editing, (b) formatting, and (c) printing.

Text editing involves entering and revising the text. Formatting refers to how the document is to look, either on the screen or in its final printed form. Printing provides the necessary hard copy.

Most word processors are document oriented; that is, they bring an entire document from the disk into main memory.

The main window is the edit window, the work area where text is entered. The cursor and the status line appear in this window, providing information about the document and the system.

Word processors use default settings to specify certain parameters like margins, tabs, and line spacing. These parameters usually can be changed by the user.

Text-editing features of a typical word processor include insert and typeover modes, wordwrap, insert and delete, search and replace, and block editing.

Formatting features include character enhancements, margin settings, justification, centering, tab settings, line spacing, page breaks, and automatic page numbering.

Documents can be printed on paper in either a portrait orientation (vertically) or landscape orientation (horizontally). Laser printers with a page description programming language (PostScript, for example) give precise control over the way a page looks, with numerous typefaces, typestyles, and sizes.

Developers of word processors embed a variety of features to make a particular word processor appeal to a variety of users. They contain features for those users involved in manuscript preparation, preparation of typical business documents, and for creating brochures, pamphlets, newsletters, and other publications.

Manuscript preparation features include the capability to enter comments, footnotes, endnotes, subscripts and superscripts, headers, footers, and to create outlines, tables of contents, and indexes. A spelling checker, thesaurus, grammar/style checker, macro feature, and a math function also help users prepare manuscripts.

Businesses use the mail-merge feature to enable writing a single form letter which can be automatically addressed and personalized to any number of people. A style sheet lets the user design and store a document that will be used over and over again with minor changes; the user creates/stores a core document and retrieves it later to make changes that apply to specific situations.

The automatic page-numbering feature numbers the pages in a document, and automatic line/paragraph numbering is used by law offices to prepare legal documents.

Today's word processors include some page-layout features, which enable the user to create newspaper-style columns and to see document layout before it is printed. In systems lacking the WYSIWYG capability, layout can be checked with the preview feature. The user also has the option of several type faces and sizes in which to print.

Desktop publishing is a concept that combines a microcomputer, word processing, page composition software, and a laser printer to create brochures, newsletters, and even books. The software for desktop publishing is visually oriented (graphics-oriented) as opposed to text-oriented software used in word processing. The main difference between word processing and desktop publishing is the ability in desktop publishing to rapidly manipulate text and graphics together on-screen.

Vocabulary Self-Test

Can you define the following?

automatic page numbering (p. 264)

block editing (p. 261)

centering (p. 263)

character enhancement (p. 262)

clip art (p. 277)

comment (p. 267)

dedicated word-processing system (p. 251)

desktop publishing (p. 272)

edit window (p. 257)

font (p. 278)

footer (p. 267)

formatting (p. 255)

grammar and style checker (p. 269)

header (p. 267)

insert mode (p. 259)

justification (p. 262)

landscape orientation (p. 266)

mail merge (p. 269)

margin settings (p. 262)

page break (p. 264)

page-composition software (p. 274)

portrait orientation (p. 265)

search and replace (p. 259)

spelling checker (p. 267)

style sheet (p. 271)

subscript (p. 267)

superscript (p. 267)

tab setting (p. 264)

text editing (p. 255)

thesaurus (p. 268)

typeover mode (p. 259)

word processing (p. 251)

word-processing system (p. 251)

word processor (p. 251)

wordwrap (p. 259)

Review Questions

Multiple Choice

1. A word processor is the _____ used to create documents.
   a. combination of hardware and software
   b. software
   c. activity of entering text
   d. computer

2. The two main advantages word processors have over typewriters are _____ .
   a. price and speed
   b. speed and weight
   c. price and weight
   d. speed and efficiency

3. The three basic functions common to all word processors are _____ .
   a. graphics, editing, and complex calculations
   b. graphics, formatting, and complex calculations
   c. graphics, text editing, and printing
   d. text editing, formatting, and printing

4. The _____ appears at the top or bottom of the display screen and provides information about the current document and the system—for example, the name of the document and which disk drive is being used.
   a. command
   b. status line
   c. cursor
   d. default

5. When an additional word is added to a document in the insert mode, the existing text _____ .
   a. automatically shifts to make room for the new text
   b. is erased where the new word was added
   c. automatically scrolls vertically
   d. is automatically italicized

6. When an additional word is typed in the typeover mode, the existing text _____ .
   a. automatically shifts to make room for the new text
   b. is erased where the new word was added
   c. automatically scrolls vertically
   d. is automatically italicized

7. Actions performed on units of text are called _____ . (An example is moving an entire paragraph at one time.)
   a. justification
   b. formatting
   c. block editing
   d. character enhancement

8. The term _____ refers to how a document looks on the screen or after it is printed.
   a. block
   b. edit
   c. format
   d. enhancement

9. _____ are examples of character enhancements.
   a. Boldface and italics
   b. Line spacing and margins
   c. Justification and centering
   d. Page length and margins

10. Desktop publishing is a system that combines the use of _____ .
    a. word-processing software and a laser printer
    b. word-processing software and a dot-matrix printer
    c. word-processing software, page-composition software, and a dot-matrix printer
    d. word processing software, page-composition software, and a laser printer

Fill-in

1. Typical examples of where and by whom word processors are used are _____ , _____ , _____ , and _____ .

2. Most word-processing systems today are _____ computers into which the appropriate software is loaded.

3. The unique quality of a(n) _____ word processor is that it has the capability of dealing with complex equations, formulas, and symbols.

4. _____ -editing activities include entering the text and revising it. _____ means establishing the way the document will look after it is printed.

5. The acronym WYSIWYG means _____ .

6. The _____ is the small box or blinking line that marks the user's present location on the screen.

7. Likely to be displayed in the status line of the edit window are _____ and _____ .

8. A(n) _____ helps you find more precise or colorful alternatives for a particular word.

9. The feature that allows a single form letter to be addressed and personalized automatically to any number of people for a mass mailing is called _____ .

10. There are several page-layout features in many word processors today; _____ and _____ are two examples.

Short Answer

1. Briefly trace the evolution of word processing.

2. What is the difference between a typical word-processing system and a dedicated word-processing system?

3. Explain why creation of a document using word processing is faster than typing it on a typewriter.

4. There are several types of word processors that appeal to a specific segment of the population because of their special features. Name at least three of those population segments.

5. Compare the insert and typeover modes of entering text.

6. The feature most unique to word processors is wordwrap. Explain how wordwrap works.

7. Explain the difference between a simple search and a search and replace.

8. Describe an instance in which you think the search-and-replace feature might be used in preparing a document.

9. What is the difference between portrait orientation and landscape orientation with regard to printing a document?

10. Describe a limitation of the word processor's spelling checker.

OUTLINE

OBJECTIVES

☐ Contrast the two types of
microcomputer data
managers—file management
systems and database management systems.

☐ Identify appropriate applications
for file management systems
and database management systems.

☐ Describe common features of
data managers dealing with creating a database, maintaining a
database, manipulating a database, and generating reports.

☐ Describe ways in which data in
a database are protected.

☐ Understand what to look for
when purchasing a data manager.

☐ Define the basic components
of a hypertext data manager.

☐ Identify the basic components
of a multimedia system.

CHAPTER NINE

Data Managers

PROFILE
C. Wayne Ratliff

Most people would be surprised by the number of products in everyday use that have been developed by backyard or basement tinkerers, rather than by large corporations. Many developers of these products don't do it initially for money but for the love of the project itself. Some see a need and try to fill it, whether it be a personal need or a widespread business need.

C. Wayne Ratliff, the original author of dBASE, a microcomputer data manager, was one of those do-it-yourself individuals. As an engineer at the Jet Propulsion Laboratories in Pasadena, California, Ratliff was no stranger to writing computer programs. His credits include authoring a database management system for a NASA *Viking* space program called Lander Project. However, this project was small potatoes compared to what was to come.

In his spare time, Ratliff liked to analyze football pools. It was in the mid-1970s that the information needed to make the correct picks began to take over his living space. A better way had to be found to store all the information. In Ratliff's case, the better way was to do it yourself.

Like most entrepreneurial projects, the beginnings were humble indeed. The first formal beginnings of his program, originally called Vulcan, came about in January 1978. His first buyers were fellow computer hobbyists who acquired the program by mail order from ads he placed in a national computer magazine. The program started selling fairly well, which placed an extra burden on Ratliff. He copied the software and assembled the software manuals for each buyer by himself. Like many basement inventors, he handled the Vulcan business while working a regular job.

Ratliff wanted to concentrate more on program development itself, so he eventually left the marketing to an upcoming software marketing firm called Ashton-Tate, a firm he later joined. The Vulcan name was already being used by another company, so the name of his data manager was changed to dBASE. With Ashton-Tate marketing the program, dBASE went on to become one of the most popular programs for microcomputers.

Ratliff left Ashton-Tate in 1986 and is a founding partner in another business endeavor called Queue Associates. As for football, he was so busy that he never did get to use the program to analyze football pools!

Today's society thrives on information. To meet our ever-increasing demand for information, we require more and more data to be gathered, stored, and manipulated. In fact, many of us require so much data that it has become impossible to manage and extract the information we need in a timely fashion. To solve this problem, computers are being called upon to help manage and store the data we gather.

Computers can store a tremendous amount of data. Once stored, the data can be manipulated to produce some desired result. To facilitate a correct result, the data must be entered in a logical and orderly manner. To accomplish this, *data management software* is used.

Once the exclusive province of large system computers, data managers are equally at home on today's microcomputers. Current microcomputers, with their ever-increasing speeds and storage capabilities, have the power to handle the data storage and manipulation needs of many businesses. Microcomputer data managers allow creation of files, and use of data in those files, without having to be a programmer or mainframe specialist.

This chapter examines the types of software available for data management on a microcomputer and the major features found in these packages.

WHAT IS A DATA MANAGER?

If the data in a file are to be made available for decision-making or other applications, there must be an efficient way to organize, retrieve, and display them. Programs designed for this purpose are called **data managers**.

A library's card catalog could be thought of as a paper data manager. The card catalog (database) is organized alphabetically in a central location. By manually opening the proper drawer (file), we can search for the proper card (record). On the card will be such information as the catalog number (field) and the author's name (field). Although this works for the library, it's difficult to carry a card catalog for every database application. Electronic data managers allow us to perform the same type of operations by using a computer.

Recall in Chapter 6 that we discussed file management systems and database management systems. The following is a brief review of these data managers.

A data manager can be one of two general types of programs that manage data: (1) file management systems and (2) database management systems.

A **file management system** is a program that creates, stores, manipulates, and prints data that are stored in separate files. A file manager is often referred to as a **flat file** manager. There is no cross referencing of data between files in a file management system. Only one file can be accessed and manipulated at a time. This means the file you are working on must be "closed" before you can access records in another file. Usually these files are stored and used in their respective department locations. For example, if a person wants to use a file management system to store data for the personnel and payroll departments in a company, separate files containing data about each employee would have to be created for each department.

File managers are easy to learn and use because of their relative simplicity, compared to other types of data managers. Because a file manager can only access one file at a time, it is not as powerful or sophisticated as data managers that can access more than one file at a time, and hence the applications for which it is suited are also less sophisticated. Applications of file management systems include maintaining mailing lists; files of names, addresses, and phone numbers; inventory lists, or lists of any items; and home budgets (Figure 9–1).

Examples of file management or flat-file data managers include Q & A, Reflex, Alpha, FileMaker, and PFS:Professional File.

The other type of data manager is the database management system. **Database management systems (DBMS)** are data management programs which can access and manipulate data from more than one file at a time. Microcomputer database management systems often are relational database managers, but not always.

Because a database management system allows its user to create and access multiple files, it lends itself to more complex applications. One of the most popular applications is for accounting. Creating an accounting system involves integration of several different files, including general ledger, accounts receivable, accounts payable, and payroll. Other applications that require integration of several files—and thus are well suited to a database management system—include financial management, travel-agency management, medical-office management, and real-estate management.

Database manager systems for microcomputers include Reflex (Macintosh), Paradox, RBASE, dBASE, Powerbase, and Foxbase.

Types of Data Managers

- File management system
  - □ Flat-file
  - □ One file at a time
- Database management system
  - □ Relational
  - □ Access multiple files

FIGURE 9–1

A file management system is well suited for many uses such as managing a home budget.

In 1974, approximately 55 zoos in North America and Europe began pooling data on their animals. By the end of 1986, over 70,000 living specimens from over 200 zoos in 16 countries had been cataloged. From this database, reports covering census, breeding, age/sex distribution, and population trends are routinely generated and distributed to participating zoological facilities. Personnel at the Columbus Zoo record pertinent data about their tiger population. (Kjell B. Sandved. Insets: Macmillan Publishing/Cobalt Productions)

PICTURE THIS! Most people think of a database as storing only numeric data for applications such as accounting, or text data for applications such as mailing lists. But increasingly, video images are finding their way into database applications.

So, what would you have if you put together text, numbers, and pictures? If you were David Olszewski, you would have designed an image database of criminal suspects. This database, called Mug-Z, is a crime-fighting tool used by the San Luis Obispo County Sheriff's Department in California.

The images are combined with data such as eye and hair color, sex, age, height, weight, and race. In addition, fields can be entered for more detail, including descriptions of scars, type of offense, and aliases used. A crime victim gives as many descriptive facts as possible, which are entered as retrieval conditions into the database. From these parameters a computer lineup can be created for viewing by the victim.

In addition to retrieving images, the software allows changes to be made to the images. These changes include adding or removing mustaches, beards, and glasses, all of which may aid in making a positive identification.

FEATURES OF DATA MANAGERS

This section describes the basic features of file management systems and database management systems. These are the features that enable you to create, maintain, and manipulate information stored within files. They are common to almost all data managers, but depending on the software package, the actual commands used to execute them vary.

As noted, file managers are generally easier to learn and use because you are manipulating data in only one file. With a multiple-file data manager you can manipulate several files simultaneously, so a database manager is a more powerful system but sometimes harder to learn.

You may assume that the following features apply to both systems unless otherwise indicated.

Entering Commands

When you first access the data manager, an initial screen is brought up on the computer. From this screen you can select commands to perform various functions. Exactly how the command selections are made depends on the program you are using. Some data managers use a command line where you type in the command—Figure 9–2(a). This requires you to memorize the commands. Other data managers use a menu system—Figure 9–2(b). From the menu, which is a screen listing the

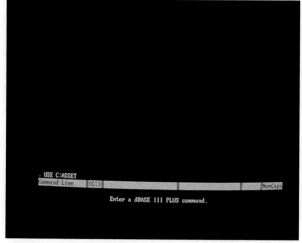

(a)

(b)

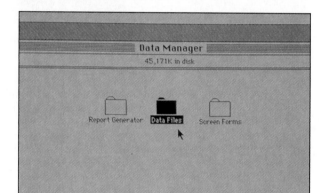

(c)

FIGURE 9-2
Entering a command using (a) command line, (b)
screen menu, (c) icons. (Photo by Jo Hall/Macmillan)

commands available, you select the proper command. This can lead to
submenus with more commands related to the one just chosen. Commands may also be accessed through icons—Figure 9-2(c). In some data
managers, you have the choice of more than one method to enter a command.

An existing file (one you have already stored) can be placed into use
by typing, selecting, or clicking (with a mouse) a load-file command. If you
are starting from the beginning, then you must create the data file.

Creating a Database

Before any data can be entered into a file, the *structure* of the data must be
defined. By defining the data structure you tell the program how to treat
the fields in each record of the file. This includes naming and setting the
length of the fields, determining the data type, and indicating which fields
are to be used as key fields. The data structures are initially defined when
the file is created.

FIGURE 9-3

Data manager data structure screen (dBASE). (Photo by Jo Hall/Macmillan)

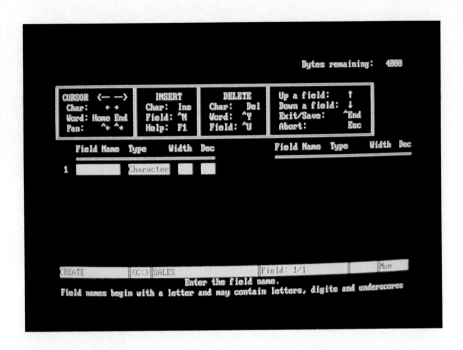

Each field is given a name, such as LASTNAME, to act as a "handle" when the data are retrieved. In many data managers, field length must be specified so the software knows how much memory space to allow for each record.

The data manager will store and manipulate data differently according to the data type, so you must specify this. Typical data types include TEXT, NUMERIC, DATE, YES/NO, TIME, and CURRENCY. Within each data type you often are able to further specify a format, such as MONTH/DAY/YEAR or DAY/MONTH/YEAR for the DATE field, or how many decimal places to use in the NUMERIC field (Figure 9-3).

Fields can also be designated as **key fields**. These are used in the sorting process. For example, a list of names may be arranged in alphabetical order by the key field LASTNAME. Most data managers allow sorting by more than one key field.

Screen Forms. A **screen form** is created to define the layout for entering data into a record. The screen form allows the fields to be positioned according to your preference (Figure 9-4). More than one screen form can be created for each record so the user can choose how the data will be displayed.

A screen form can serve more than one function. First, it provides data entry points to define records or a data dictionary where the data structures are defined. Second, it can serve as an output screen form in which field alignment is determined for printing.

Screen forms are designed from a blank screen by using the cursor to indicate the placement of the fields and their lengths, and by typing identifying labels for each field. With some data managers, this is done in response to on-screen prompts.

FIGURE 9–4
More than one screen form may
be created to display the field
names and data. The user selects which screen form will be
used.

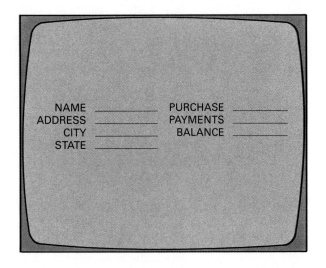

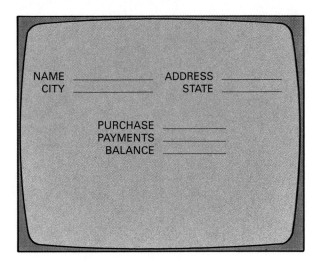

Once the screen form has been created, the data can be entered. Because most data errors can be traced back to their point of entry, the data manager provides a means of detecting errors at this point through validity checks.

Validating. Checking data for appropriateness and accuracy is called **validating**. Data-entry checks can be built into the data manager to prevent invalid data from being entered. These are often set as the data structures are being defined. Validity checks may be accomplished in the data manager by:

☐ Format checking—determining if data are in the correct format, e.g., numeric or text.
☐ Range checking—determining if the data fall within an acceptable chosen range, e.g., greater than 100 but less than 500.

□ Accuracy checking—making sure that an entry is possible, e.g., cross checking an entered product number with a list of standard product numbers in an inventory file.

Maintaining the Database

The contents of a file often need to be changed. The change may be to a field in an individual record, or it may involve an entire record within the file. In an inventory file, for example, you may need to add a new product record or delete a discontinued item. File-maintenance features include updating, adding, and deleting.

Updating. **Updating** is the process of changing the content of a record or records in a file. This updating may be adding, deleting, or changing the contents of a record—for example, it might involve entering a new address or telephone number for a person in your mailing list file. By accessing records in a file and changing the field contents, you can keep all the data current.

Adding. **Adding** to a file means to add an additional record or records to an existing file—for example, adding a new person to a customer file or a new employee in a personnel file. Some data managers put the added records at the end of the file; others place them in a spot vacated by previously deleted records; still other data managers make it possible to insert a new record at any point in the file. Adding a record may also be called "inserting" by some data managers.

Deleting. Removing records from a file is called **deleting**. A record may be deleted in direct response to a delete command prompt or may be a two-step process in which the records are first "marked" for deletion. Once marked, the records are then removed from the file. Individual fields within a record can also be deleted.

It is important to note that, after the data are deleted, those data items are no longer available. Extra care should be taken when deleting to avoid removing a field or record unintentionally. Often, a prompt such as ARE YOU SURE? (Y/N) will appear on the screen before the deletion takes place. It is wise to keep a backup copy of the file in case of accidental deletion.

Retrieving and Manipulating Data

The main purpose of the database file is to store data. To be useful, however, you must be able to access that data, either simply to see what's there, or to extract it. The data may be found by searching through an individual file, or in the case of a relational database manager, data may be pulled from multiple files using the additional features of selecting, joining, projecting, and calculating. Even when data are retrieved, it may be hard to determine what is there unless it is organized in some way, e.g., listing a column of names in alphabetical order.

Sorting. Usually, it is easier to read data if they are arranged in some predesignated order. **Sorting** records means to arrange them in order. The sort order can be numerical or alphabetical, and the data can be arranged in ascending or descending order. Sorts can be performed by both file and relational database managers.

The sort is accomplished on the previously identified key fields with the possibility of more than one key field being used. This would be done, for example, when sorting names. If the LASTNAME fields are the same, then the FIRSTNAME field might be used to further sort the data. The first key field in the sorting process is called the primary key, whereas subsequent fields are the secondary key fields. This type of sort is called a multiple sort.

Indexing. The process of **indexing** involves creating a file which contains the user's sorted-data conditions. Unlike sorting, in which the file is stored in sorted order, the index file is saved separately so that the original file remains the same. Thus, indexing allows for many different sort orderings without affecting the integrity of the original file.

Searching. **Searching** a file means to look through it and to locate data. Searching for data may also be called "finding" or "retrieving" by some systems. Only one file at a time is searched with a file management system, but a multiple file search is possible with a relational database manager.

If you are uncertain as to exactly what data you are looking for, an entire file can be searched one record at a time. Listing each record in the file allows you to visually search the file, sometimes called "browsing," until the right one is located.

More often, however, you will know what data are needed. Depending on the type of report being prepared, only selected records in a file are used. In addition, only certain fields within each record may be required.

There are different methods of selecting the required data. Among them are:

☐ Database query—accomplished by programming or through screen forms.
☐ Using a query language—programming statements or words used to specify a retrieval condition, e.g., FROM (file) SELECT (records).
☐ Query-by-example—selects given records based on conditions entered into a query screen form, e.g., BALANCE > 3.00.
☐ Using AND/OR/NOT—these commands allow compound search conditions, e.g., selecting a record where CREDIT > 2500 *AND* BALANCE = 0.
☐ Wildcard search—selects records with common character(s) in a field, e.g., specifying names starting with Ev would find Everhart, Evans, Everett, etc.
☐ Phonetic search—selects records with closely matched spellings, e.g., specifying Smith would find Smith or Smythe.

**Relational Database
Manager
Retrieval Methods**

- Selecting
- Joining
- Projecting
- Calculating

In addition to the above, which can be used with both file management and relational database management systems for an individual file, relational database managers allow complex retrieval involving more than one file.

Relational Operations. The relational database structure is used more than any other in today's powerful microcomputer databases. Because it is so popular, we'll examine four common ways in which relational databases can be manipulated.

In a relational database, data are organized into tables (files) by rows (records) and columns (fields). Relational databases can be manipulated by using selecting, joining, projecting, and calculating operations. They may incorporate one, two, three, or all four of these options. Actual command names may vary among databases, but the basic operation is the same.

Selecting. Choosing the records to be displayed from a table is called **selecting**. It is used to limit the records that are retrieved. If selecting is not used, all records from a table will be returned. For example, Figure 9–5 shows the result of a selecting operation where all records were selected in which the field named "Shift" contained the value "2nd." The selected table now lists all second-shift employees' records.

Joining. Sometimes called merging, **joining** files is combining records from two or more tables into a new table. The tables can be joined only if they contain a common key field. For example, in Figure 9–6 the customer table and the product table are joined using the common field "ItemNumber."

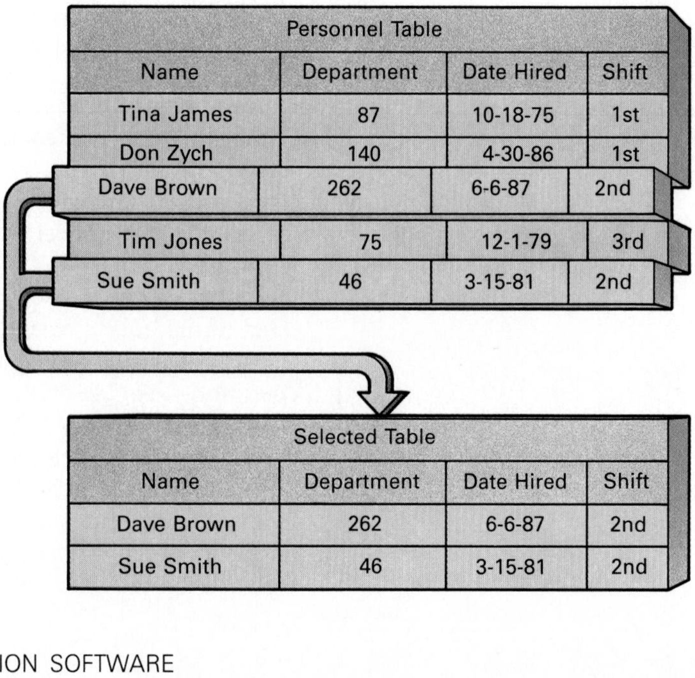

FIGURE 9–5
The selecting feature allows a new table to be created using only the rows (records) desired. Here, the records of the second-shift workers are selected and placed in a new table.

Personnel Table			
Name	Department	Date Hired	Shift
Tina James	87	10-18-75	1st
Don Zych	140	4-30-86	1st
Dave Brown	262	6-6-87	2nd
Tim Jones	75	12-1-79	3rd
Sue Smith	46	3-15-81	2nd

Selected Table			
Name	Department	Date Hired	Shift
Dave Brown	262	6-6-87	2nd
Sue Smith	46	3-15-81	2nd

Customer Table				Product Table		
Name	Current Balance	Item Number		Item Number	Description	Price/Unit
Mike Toony	60.00	100038		100038	Band saw	300.00
Jerry Layman	278.37	14066		14066	Shelving	37.95
Robert Steele	47.95	21373		21373	Hammer	9.50

Joined Table				
Name	Current Balance	Item Number	Description	Price/Unit
Mike Toony	60.00	100038	Band saw	300.00
Jerry Layman	278.37	14066	Shelving	37.95
Robert Steele	47.95	21373	Hammer	9.50

FIGURE 9–6
The joining feature allows tables to be combined through a key field. "Item-Number" is the key field above.

Projecting. Sometimes a table contains more items than are needed. The **projecting** feature can be used to create a table that is a subset of the larger table by combining only the needed rows and columns to form a new table (Figure 9–7). Here records for two specific employees are shown in a separate table.

FIGURE 9–7
By using the projecting feature, a new table can be created containing only the needed records and fields.

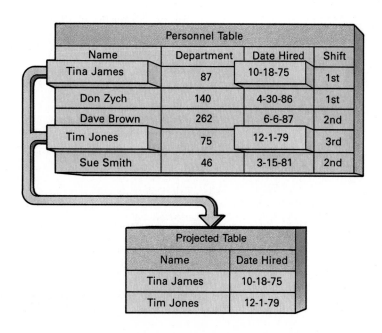

Personnel Table			
Name	Department	Date Hired	Shift
Tina James	87	10-18-75	1st
Don Zych	140	4-30-86	1st
Dave Brown	262	6-6-87	2nd
Tim Jones	75	12-1-79	3rd
Sue Smith	46	3-15-81	2nd

Projected Table	
Name	Date Hired
Tina James	10-18-75
Tim Jones	12-1-79

Calculating. The value in a retrieved field may be the result of a **calculating** process. The calculation may be the total of a QUANTITY field or the average of a BALANCE field. Often a field can be created that shows up on a generated report as a result of performing some calculation on two or more fields. After the data have been retrieved, a hard copy is often needed for others to see and use.

Printing

Sometimes it is necessary to print only the raw data rather than to arrange the output into a more formal report. The **printing** feature allows you to print the screen contents at any time. Data in a record can be sent to the printer in the same format as it appears in the user-designed screen form.

Generating a Report

All data managers allow printing of files, and many permit customizing the way that printed output will look. This customizing is possible with data managers that contain a **report generator**. With a report generator, the user defines how the report is to appear when printed. In addition to customizing the placement of fields, most report generators have these four features: headers, footers, formatting, and statistics.

Headers. The header section of a report is located at the top of the report page and contains items such as date, page number, column headings, or even a company logo.

Footers. The footer, like the header, is a separate section of the report, but it is located at the bottom of the page. The footer may contain page numbers, the user's name, or other relevant information.

Formatting. Formatting features let you control the way a report looks by setting margins, justifying text, and indicating page lengths and line spacing.

Statistics. Many report generators can perform some simple mathematical functions. Some can provide basic statistical information, such as calculating column subtotals, grand totals, averages, and counts.

Graphic Database

Traditionally, you may think of a database as storing only text data—that is, numbers or letters. Storing pictures along with text was not practical for a long time because of the large memory requirements for storing images. Increases in main and secondary storage capabilities, along with peripherals such as scanners and video cameras, have changed the way we view a database. Today, graphic or image databases are increasingly finding their way into more applications.

FIGURE 9–8
Graphic database used in the real estate business. (Courtesy of International Business Machines Corp.)

With a graphic database, a security guard can confirm a person's identification by entering their name and having a picture of the person appear on the screen along with the text data. Graphic databases are now used in the real estate business; a prospective buyer can browse through full-color pictures of homes without leaving the confines of the office (Figure 9–8).

Data Security

Data stored in a file are often sensitive or confidential. Therefore, an organization may want to restrict access to the computer and data except by authorized personnel. This restriction can be done mechanically, e.g., with a key lock on the computer. However, data managers also provide features, built into the software itself, that either prevent access or make it easy to track the intruder. Three methods used to accomplish this are data encryption, passwords, and audit trails.

Data Encryption. Data **encryption** codes data so that they appear as scrambled alphanumeric characters if retrieved by unauthorized persons. A utility program is available to *decrypt* such a file so that it can be read again.

Passwords. A **password** is a letter, number, or combination that prevents access unless the exact code is used. A data manager can be designed

Data Security

- Mechanical locks
- Encryption
- Passwords
- Audits
- File-locking

**ENVIRONMENTAL
DATABASE**

An important feature of a computerized database is that it allows all data to be stored in a central location. This allows data that otherwise might be difficult to work with to produce meaningful results.

One such database application was created by the National Oceanic and Atmospheric Administration (NOAA). The database is a compilation of many years of research on contamination along the Alaskan coastline. Over the years, information has been gathered on contaminants such as oil, radiation, pesticides, and toxic metals that are found in animals and the soil.

The database, known as the Alaska Marine Contaminants Database, saw its first big application as it was used to analyze the long-term effects of the Exxon *Valdez* oil spill in and around Prince William Sound in 1989. Because it is a database management system, scientists can retrieve data for many types of conditions. By comparing specific areas of shore, or a particular type of contamination, before and after the spill, data can be meaningfully analyzed.

Perhaps data from this application will tell scientists which method of cleaning oil from the environment will work best in future spills.

so that a password permits access to the entire data manager or only to certain files. It can also be designed so that the user needs one password to view the file and another password to change, add, or delete anything in the file.

Audit Trails. **Audit trails** show any activity in a file. For example, a typical audit trail shows what was done (deleted, changed, added), what was affected (a specific field, record, or file), when it was done (time, date), and by whom (employee identification or password).

Data security is especially critical in multiuser data manager systems. A **multiuser data manager** can be used on a multiuser computer system where more than one person has simultaneous access to data manager files. Such a system may use a minicomputer or mainframe computer to handle the database, with numerous terminals. For example, the Royal Trust Co., based in Toronto, uses a program called The Application Connection (T-A-C) to connect its microcomputers to their mainframe financial database. T-A-C allows them to use LOTUS 1-2-3 on the microcomputer as a flat-file manager to perform analysis of data stored in the mainframe. The resulting information is available much faster than if the users had to rekey data stored in the mainframe into the microcomputer.

Sometimes, however, unintended deletions, additions, or changes occur when two people work with the same file in a data manager. Errors occur because one person does not know what the other is doing; thus one person's update may be accidentally deleted by the other.

To prevent this, a data manager can restrict access or lock the file. **File-locking** permits only one user to access a file at a time. The file is not free to be manipulated by another person until it is released by the first user.

WHAT TO LOOK FOR IN A DATA MANAGER

In addition to the hardware components needed for a data manager, such as adequate memory (Chapter 7), certain software considerations are important when looking for a data manager. Equally as important is the product support available and what other users say about the product.

Before deciding on software, assess your data management requirements. Will a file manager be sufficient, or will a more powerful relational database manager be necessary? If the complexity of the database application is great, or if the amount of customizing to be done is considerable, then a database manager with a built-in programming language might be the best choice.

Program Considerations

Some program considerations to be aware of before purchasing a data manager include:

☐ Program limits—how many characters per field, fields per record, and records per file are allowed?
☐ Selecting records—what methods are used to select records?
☐ File handling—how many files can be opened at once? How many can be joined or linked?
☐ Reports—does the program include a report generator? Can you control the appearance of the report?
☐ Data file transfer—can a file be converted for use by another applications program? Also, what types of files can it be converted to and from?
☐ Speed—how fast can data be retrieved? (This is a function of both the data manager and the computer used.)

Data Manager Software

- Program considerations
  - Program limits
  - Record selection
  - File handling
  - Report generation
  - File transfer
  - Speed
- Product support
  - Help screens
  - Manuals
  - Vendor support

Product Support

Documentation and product support are very important because there will be times when you get stuck and will need assistance (Figure 9–9). When shopping for a data manager, consider the quality of assistance in the form of:

☐ Help screens—these are available while actually in the program. Are they easy to access? Are they complete and truly helpful?
☐ Manuals—are the manuals complete, clear, and well organized?
☐ Vendor support—is a phone number listed where the vendor can be reached? (Try the number: can you get through, or is it always

busy?) Is the support person able to answer your questions satisfactorily?

As a potential purchaser and user, take time to read product reviews in major computer magazines. These will indicate how users judge program reliability, how easy it is to learn and use, and how flexible the program is in meeting their individual applications.

HYPERTEXT

Hypertext is graphic-oriented software that resembles a database in that data are related; however, the data are not stored in traditional files or records. Data are stored as objects which can be arbitrarily linked together and accessed very rapidly in a multitude of ways.

Picture a stack of index cards. On each of those cards you could put one concept or idea. With hypertext, those concepts may be in the form of text, graphics, or pictures, unlike a text database. With a click of a mouse you could move from one card to another, either browsing through all the cards or moving to a specific card anywhere in the stack.

Hypertext software incorporates components of a database, text editor, and graphics editor. It uses a mouse to move through windows, click on icons, and to access pull-down menus (Figure 9–10).

Hypertext applications fall into several categories. On-line "browsers," so-called because they allow you to browse through the information, are used for manuals. These are products such as reference documents or service manuals whose contents remain essentially the same over time. Their intent is to provide the user with quick on-line information, but they usually limit the amount of customizing that can be done by the user.

FIGURE 9-10
Icon representation of features
available in HyperCard. (Photo
by Jo Hall/Macmillan)

FIGURE 9-10
Icon representation of features available in HyperCard. (Photo by Jo Hall/Macmillan)

Most microcomputer-oriented hypertext falls into the category of general purpose or user-defined products. These are products like Hyper-Card, Guide, and HyperPad, in which you can define the data and how you want them linked together.

Hypertext products can be combined with expert systems to be used as part of a problem-solving process. These types of hypertext systems are usually implemented in a workstation environment.

Cards and Stacks

Organization is the key to creating a successful hypertext application. You must be able to break down your data into small discrete units. These units of data usually fill one computer screen. In HyperCard these units are called cards, whereas HyperPad calls them pages, and Guide calls them guidelines. We will use the term *cards* in this text. Each of the cards contains text fields which may store alphanumeric data. The cards may also contain graphics or pictures.

A collection of related cards under one name is called a stack; related pages are called a pad. Notice the relationship of hypertext concepts to everyday objects: a stack of index cards; a pad of many pages.

Cards may contain the same *background*—that is, all the cards in a stack may contain the same elements, like a *screen form* in a text database. For example, if the stack were used for security identification, each card might contain an outline where a picture would go, or boxes that represent where a name and other data fields would be inserted. Each individual card would contain information only for one person.

FIGURE 9–11

HyperCard menu for creating a button. (Photo by Jo Hall/Macmillan)

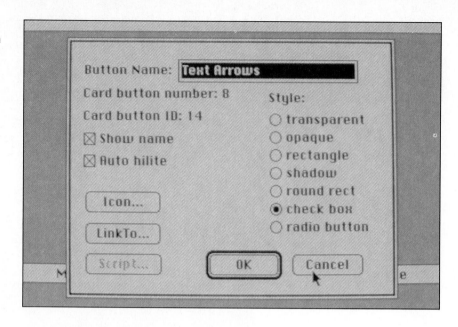

Linking Cards

To move from card to card in a stack, or page to page in a pad, the individual cards or pages must be linked together. *Linking* is the method by which you move about in a stack or pad. For the most part, the links established depend solely on you. Because you are creating the hypertext program, only you know how you see relationships in the data. Hypertext card arrangements can take many forms. They may be simple straight-line links, simple or complex hierarchal structures, or may even be a random ordering of cards.

To sort through the cards, you click on a button. A *button* can be a few descriptive words, or the words can be represented by an icon. Buttons may be user-defined icons or program-defined icons (Figure 9–11). By clicking on a button, a new card is immediately brought to the screen. Buttons can also be defined to perform functions such as activating a videodisk player or dialing a phone. For example, you might have created a stack of cards on the birds of North America. On the screen is a card of a particular bird. The card might contain a button that activates a videodisc player that would show a range map for the bird and provide audio of the bird's cries.

MULTIMEDIA

Multimedia incorporates the peripheral devices necessary to integrate text, graphic images, audio, and video (Figure 9–12). Multimedia devices allow for full-motion presentations through the use of audio and video synthesizers, CD-ROM and WORM drives for storage, and software. The software includes desktop publishing and presentation managers. The key to multimedia is that it is an interactive environment.

FIGURE 9–12
Multimedia equipment. (Courtesy of Imaging Technology Inc.)

Multimedia applications are usually implemented using high-end microcomputers call *workstations*. Workstations are desirable because of their processing speeds and available storage. For full-motion and animation applications, the computer must be able to retrieve and send a picture to the screen fast enough (sufficient frames per second) that it does not appear jittery. Potential multimedia uses are in animation, simulation, teleconferencing, education, training, engineering, and medical imaging.

Storage capabilities are increasing, making multimedia more available for microcomputers. The storage capacity of CD-ROM helps, but it is still limiting: a CD-ROM disk might store 500 megabytes of text data, but it will store only about 75 minutes of audio and about 90 seconds of video. You can see that a tremendous amount of storage is required to use multimedia with a microcomputer.

Recent enhancements in data storage techniques have paved the way for color images to be stored in a database much like a text database. The technique is called compression technology. **Compression technology** reduces the file size to only 5–10 percent of the original file size without significantly reducing the quality of the picture. For example, an E-size (34″ × 44″) color drawing might require 10 megabytes of memory. With compression technology, the file could be reduced to about 1 megabyte, which would fit nicely on one floppy diskette.

Data compression technology reduces storage demands for video images. New technologies will further reduce the storage space needed. General Electric and RCA have developed a compression technology (now owned by Intel) called ''digital video interactive'' (DVI) that reduces a file to as much as one percent of its original size. This allows one CD to hold up to one hour of full-motion video.

Multimedia can use hypertext programs, and the combination of hypertext and multimedia devices often is referred to as *hypermedia*. On a microcomputer level, many companies prefer at this time to call their systems "desktop video systems" rather than multimedia. With a desktop video system, animation software like Autodesk's Animator is used to produce motion. Individual pictures are drawn and displayed quickly, one after another, to simulate motion. Another feature of desktop video is creating overlays, which place animation and text on top of video images.

SUMMARY

Many applications once possible only on large computers are now routinely performed with microcomputers because of their expanding power and the availability of more sophisticated programs.

A microcomputer uses two main types of programs to manage data: *file management* systems and *database management* systems. These are commonly referred to as data managers. Both are programs that can create, store, manipulate, and print files. The main difference between the two is that a file management system can access only one file at a time, whereas a database management system can access multiple files simultaneously.

File management systems are suited to relatively simple applications such as mailing lists, name files, home budgets, and inventory lists. The database management concept was developed to provide more powerful data manipulation. Microcomputer database management systems are predominantly relational-type data managers. They are suited to more complex uses, such as accounting, financial management, and other multiple-file applications.

Microcomputer data managers have the following features:

- ☐ Commands for maintaining the database file, such as updating, adding, and deleting.
- ☐ Commands for retrieving and manipulating data, such as searching, selecting, joining, projecting, calculating, and sorting.
- ☐ Screen forms in which to lay out the data fields, and report generators to provide customized output.
- ☐ Methods for maintaining data security—data encryption, passwords, and audit trails.

Problems can arise with multiuser data managers if two users try to access the same file at the same time. One way to overcome this problem is to restrict file use by file-locking, which limits file access to a single user at any one time.

When purchasing a data manager, you need to consider the type—either a file manager or a relational database manager—and the level of programming language. Assess program factors, such as limits, ability to search records, how it handles and transfers files, and the speed at which data are retrieved. Other considerations are the program's reliability, ease of use, flexibility, documentation, and support.

Hypertext is graphic-oriented software that resembles a database, except data are stored as objects. These objects can be arbitrarily linked together and accessed very rapidly in a multitude of ways. Hypertext software incorporates components of a database, a text editor, and a graphics editor, and uses a mouse to move through windows, click on icons, and to access pull-down menus.

Multimedia incorporates the peripheral devices necessary to integrate text, graphic images, audio, and video. Compression technology allows large files to be stored by reducing the file size to 5–10 percent of the original file size without significantly reducing picture quality.

Vocabulary Self-Test

Can you define the following?

adding (p. 296)

audit trail (p. 302)

calculating (p. 300)

compression technology (p. 307)

database management system (DBMS) (p. 290)

data manager (p. 289)

deleting (p. 296)

encryption (p. 301)

file-locking (p. 303)

file management system (p. 289)

flat file (p. 289)

hypertext (p. 304)

indexing (p. 297)

joining (p. 298)

key field (p. 294)

multimedia (p. 306)

multiuser data manager (p. 302)

password (p. 301)

printing (p. 300)

projecting (p. 299)

report generator (p. 300)

screen form (p. 294)

searching (p. 297)

selecting (p. 298)

sorting (p. 297)

updating (p. 296)

validating (p. 295)

Review Questions

Multiple Choice

1. Which of these features can be performed by a flat-file manager? _____
   a. Selecting
   b. Sorting
   c. Projecting
   d. Calculating

2. Which of these statements is true concerning a file manager? _____
   a. Allows multiple files to be accessed
   b. Prevents data from being unnecessarily duplicated
   c. Most file managers are relational
   d. Best used for applications such as mailing lists

3. TEXT, NUMERIC, DATE, and YES/NO are _____ that the user must specify before data can be entered.
   a. screen forms
   b. validation methods
   c. data managers
   d. data types

4. Checking to see whether data fall within acceptable limits is called _____ .

   a. range checking
   b. accuracy checking
   c. file-locking
   d. format checking

5. Updating, adding, and deleting are all types of _____ features.
   a. maintenance
   b. retrieval
   c. utility
   d. security

6. Choosing records from one table is called _____ .
   a. selecting
   b. joining
   c. projecting
   d. calculating

7. Headers and footers are features used when _____ .
   a. deleting a record
   b. creating a sort
   c. calculating a field
   d. creating a report

8. A data-security method that shows activity which has taken place in a file is a(n) _____ .
   a. audit trail.
   b. password check.
   c. range check.
   d. accuracy check.

9. _____ is a procedure that permits only one user to access a file at any one time.
   a. Audit trailing
   b. File-locking
   c. Keying
   d. Data trapping

10. A device the user activates to perform a link to another card is a _____ .
   a. linker
   b. stacker
   c. button
   d. script

Fill-in

1. A file manager is also known as a(n) _____ manager.
2. Data manager commands are entered one of three ways: _____ , _____ , and _____ .
3. Fields specially designated to be used in a sort are called _____ fields.
4. A(n) _____ is created to define the layout for entering data into a record.
5. Format checking, range checking, and accuracy checking are all methods of _____ data entry.

6. Programming languages used to specify search conditions are called
   _____ .

7. A type of search that selects records which have closely matched spelling is
   a(n) _____ search.

8. Justifying text, setting page lengths, and line spacing are all types of
   _____ features in a report generator.

9. When more than one person has access through more than one computer
   (or terminal) to a data manager, it is known as a(n) _____ data
   manager.

10. Multimedia using microcomputers is often referred to as _____ .

Short Answer

1. Describe how a file management system is different from a database
   management system.

2. Why does a DBMS usually require more memory than a file management
   system?

3. Name three applications that are well suited for a file management system,
   and three that are better suited for a relational database management
   system.

4. What is the difference between sorting and indexing?

5. Describe the relational database features of joining, selecting, and
   projecting.

6. List and briefly describe four basic parts of a report generator.

7. How can an audit-trail feature help ensure data security?

8. What kind of software considerations should you take into account when
   purchasing data manager software?

9. Describe three ways in which data manager assistance can be found.

10. Briefly describe what data compression achieves for the storage of data.

OUTLINE

OBJECTIVES

- ☐ Describe the different types and uses of spreadsheets, and contrast the handwritten spreadsheet with an electronic one.

- ☐ Describe the basic procedures for loading and using a spreadsheet program.

- ☐ Explain the basic features used to create a simple worksheet.

- ☐ Describe some of the advanced spreadsheet features used for formatting and manipulating data, and list additional features that commonly are available.

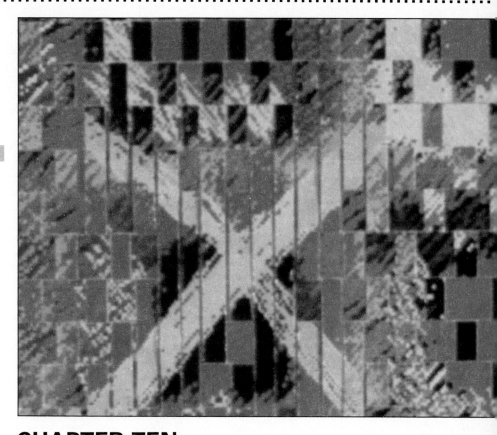

CHAPTER TEN

Spreadsheets

PROFILE
Mitchell Kapor

How does a self-described "nerd" make it big in the world of entrepreneurship and business? Mitchell Kapor did it by combining an interest in personal consciousness, antiwar activism, and interdisciplinary study of linguistics, psychology, and computer science at Yale University.

After college, Kapor entered the working world as a stand-up comic, disk jockey, and teacher of transcendental meditation. Instead of following the usual path toward corporate success by earning an MBA degree, he took his master's in psychology and became a counselor in the psychiatric unit of a small hospital.

Still, Kapor, who grew up in a Brooklyn middle-class family, was on his way to becoming a multimillionaire. Kapor first veered toward computer entrepreneurship when he came across an Apple II. While at Yale, he had found that working with mainframe computers was extremely frustrating. On campus, mainframes were often inaccessible, and they required special programming skills and punched cards for both the instructions and data. This was not so with microcomputers; they were easy to use and program. Kapor was captivated.

The microcomputer was the perfect tool for turning loose his creative instincts. He began doing freelance programming in the BASIC language for other new owners of microcomputers. His first programming job was to create a small database of patient information for a doctor.

This simple beginning led Kapor to an alliance with Jonathan Sachs, a former Data General Corporation programmer. The two devised an electronic spreadsheet that was sophisticated enough to appeal to the business world, yet could be run on a microcomputer. (A spreadsheet, as you will learn in this chapter, is a device for keeping track of and manipulating rows and columns of numbers.) The two developers called their program Lotus 1-2-3. Their spreadsheet, designed for the IBM Personal Computer and compatibles, could make projections, display results, and sort data. The documentation for Lotus was clear and concise, and the program did what it promised. Moreover, it was fast.

Lotus 1-2-3 revolutionized accounting on small computers in much the same way word processors changed writing with typewriters. Spreadsheet programs convinced the business community of the value of the relatively new microcomputer, and were the impetus that sent IBM PC sales soaring. With an alluring product, the powerful thrust of IBM's sales, and Kapor's expertise, all the elements for success were in place. First-year sales projections for Lotus were $3 million, but actual sales were $53 million. Kapor proved to be a marketing master and an advertising genius.

Kapor resigned as chief executive officer of Lotus in 1986 to spend time with his family, to continue his study of linguistics at MIT, and to consult at Lotus. Kapor's "retirement" did not last long, however, because by 1988 he was involved in another enterprise—ON Technology, developing more software for information and communications in both groupware and hypertext applications. Then in 1990, Kapor backed yet another company— GO Corp. GO's primary product is a microcomputer that recognizes handwritten input.

The earliest methods that humans used to keep track of items included tying knots in ropes, marking notches on sticks, and similar crude devices. Then came the abacus, a wooden frame with wires and beads for calculating. Gradually, as numbering systems were developed, the paper-and-pencil approach started. Each item to be counted was assigned a number, and the numbers could be added, subtracted, multiplied, and divided.

As time went on, a sophisticated means of tracking and manipulating these numbers was devised. For ease in manipulating, numbers and dollar amounts were written on paper that had been divided into rows and columns; the paper was called a *spreadsheet*.

Today, users equipped with microcomputers and spreadsheet software can manipulate numbers in rows and columns faster, more accurately, and more reliably than ever before. Spreadsheet users—including

The New York Stock Exchange is a busy place where trades must be based on the most current data available. Computers play an important part in furnishing stock brokers with the latest stock prices. This broker informs his client of late-breaking developments from data displayed on the screen in his office. (Preston Lyon/Index Stock, Inc. Inset: Macmillan Publishing/Cobalt Productions)

small-business owners, teachers, students, and especially corporate accounting giants—are asking for, and getting, still faster programs with even more capabilities, including a spreadsheet in three dimensions!

WHAT IS A SPREADSHEET?

A **spreadsheet** is simply a means of tracking and manipulating numbers—organizing them into rows and columns. The paper version of a spreadsheet is a form with horizontal and vertical lines that separate each row and column of numbers. You may have seen paper spreadsheets similar to the one in Figure 10–1. A spreadsheet can take other forms, too; each user can adapt a spreadsheet to various applications and formats.

With the development and advancement of the computer and its capabilities, the paper spreadsheet was converted to a computerized format through programs called **electronic spreadsheets**. The spreadsheet program instructs the computer to manipulate rows and columns of numbers, make calculations, and evaluate algebraic formulas. Figure 10–2 illustrates an electronic version of the paper spreadsheet shown in Figure 10–1.

Of course, merely loading a spreadsheet program into a computer cannot guarantee either the accuracy or effectiveness of any spreadsheet you create. Your spreadsheet must be organized logically so that changes in one part will not adversely affect other parts. You will see later how critical organization can be when algebraic formulas are entered to solve problems.

The first electronic spreadsheet programs operated only on large computer systems. The cost of such systems limited availability of the new technology, so most businesses and individuals still used paper spreadsheets. The development in 1979 of VisiCalc, the first electronic spreadsheet created especially for microcomputers, gave everyone easy and affordable access to this powerful tool (see the Profile of VisiCalc's developers in Chapter 7).

VisiCalc was rather crude by today's standards, because it was severely limited in the volume and size of jobs it could handle. But with the

FIGURE 10–1
A paper spreadsheet.

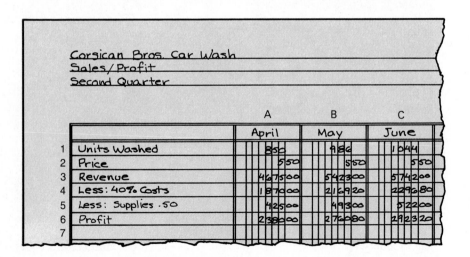

FIGURE 10–2
A screen of the paper spreadsheet as it appears when created electronically. (Photo by Jo Hall/Macmillan)

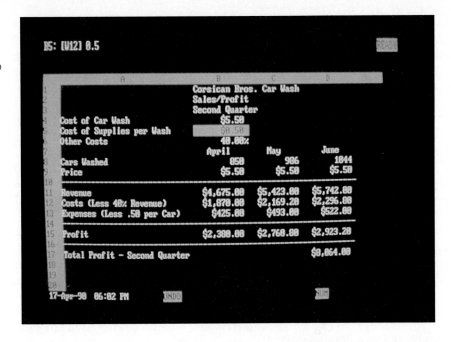

continuing development of more sophisticated hardware and software, programs improved to such an extent that most of today's computer spreadsheets allow at least 256 columns and as many as 32,766 rows, for a possible total of over 8 million spaces for entries. A paper spreadsheet of only 65 columns and 254 rows stretched out would be over 3½ feet long and more than 5 feet wide. Then, consider that some spreadsheets allow as many as 32,000 columns and 32,000 rows—over one billion cells! Can you imagine how unmanageable such a paper document would be?

Today, instead of writing and calculating each entry by hand, you can sit at a computer keyboard and use a spreadsheet program to make the necessary entries; the computer then makes all the calculations. Not only that, but the spreadsheet program can accept a correction in one item and then recalculate any of the affected numbers throughout the document. Corrections and recalculations are made by the computer. Spreadsheet programs often require repetitive keystrokes or commands, and the speed and power of the macro is especially useful.

If you wonder how an increase or decrease in one particular entry might affect the end result, the program allows you to pose "what if" questions. You can change entries on the spreadsheet, and see the outcome, but keep a copy of the original plan for comparison. For example, suppose you decided to buy a used car at a certain price: How would that choice affect other areas of your budget, such as car insurance, loan payments, automobile repair expenses, and other living expenses? What if you buy this year's model instead, and the payments are higher? A spreadsheet can analyze the effects on all these areas so that the purchase can be more closely evaluated (Figure 10–3). The spreadsheet capability of analyzing many different situations will show ramifications of each choice so that the best course of action can be taken.

The shortcuts and speed of electronic spreadsheets certainly explain their popularity. There are hundreds of spreadsheet programs available for almost any brand of computer. Spreadsheet processing is one of the most popular computer applications; it brings to accounting functions the shortcuts, speed, and accuracy that word processors bring to writing. Throughout this chapter, the term "spreadsheet" refers to an electronic spreadsheet, unless otherwise indicated.

TYPES AND USES

There are two types of spreadsheets: standard and multidimensional. The standard spreadsheet was described above. **Multidimensional spreadsheets** help you visualize spreadsheet cells as solids having three dimensions. An example is Lotus 1-2-3 Release 3, introduced in 1989. Imagine the capability of a file that can contain 256 separate layers. This three-dimensional capability helps users to divide large applications into more manageable units, to consolidate information from many separate spreadsheets, to create a centralized database, and to summarize results on multiple worksheets that have identical layouts. The speed, power, and attributes of such 3-D programs will continue to suggest new applications to their users. Figures 10–4(a) and (b) show how a 3-D application might appear.

Any application where the problem can be written in mathematical terms is a candidate for an electronic spreadsheet. There also are other considerations when using a spreadsheet to solve a problem. Consider using a spreadsheet for financial reports that are:

- ☐ Repeated regularly
- ☐ Edited
- ☐ Revised
- ☐ Made up of both variable and fixed information
- ☐ Required to be neat and legible

Editing a paper spreadsheet can be very involved. When mathematical calculations are made on calculators and entered by hand, transpositions in numbers and erroneous entries may occur. A correction that is made in one cell generally necessitates a corresponding change in the total of that particular column, and may affect other cells or totals. Therefore,

FIGURE 10–3
This woman analyzes long-range effects before making important business decisions.

FIGURE 10-4
WINGZ software, a three-dimensional spreadsheet application program for Macintosh microcomputers, lets you combine text, graphs and charts, scanned images, freehand illustration, and worksheet data in any combination, printed on any page. (Courtesy of Informix Software)

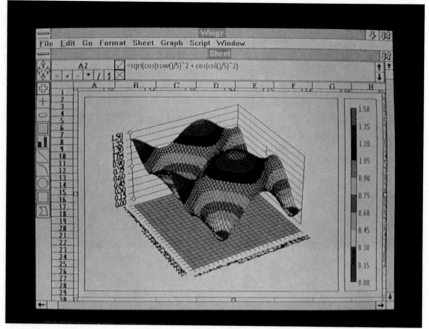

(a)

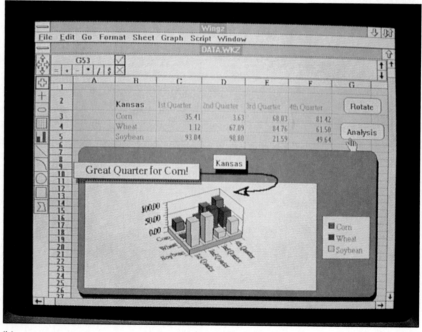

(b)

making corrections by hand involves erasures. If many mistakes are found, a paper spreadsheet could be erased to shreds before the final entries are approved.

Another drawback of the paper spreadsheet is that it sometimes must be completely rewritten. For example, if the president of a small company wants to know the effect on profit of manufacturing and selling 500 more bookcases each month, a new spreadsheet must be created. In a company that uses paper spreadsheets, the clerk would have to make the calculations, handwrite the entries, check and cross-check the totals, possibly make erasures, and then recheck the entries. Then, what if production were increased by 850? Another spreadsheet would have to be started.

However, the clerk at the company that uses electronic spreadsheets just copies the existing spreadsheet, enters the changes, and lets the computer recalculate all the figures, creating a new spreadsheet to answer each of the "what if" questions posed by the president.

Spreadsheets contain both fixed and variable information. When variable information changes in a paper spreadsheet, the erase-and-recalculate procedure begins again; in an electronic spreadsheet, the speed and power of the computer makes accurate calculations and recalculations in fractions of a second.

Finally, it is important that a spreadsheet be neat and legible for those who read it. A paper spreadsheet is only as neat and legible as the handwriting of its creator. Even extremely legible entries may lose clarity if there are many erasures. The electronic spreadsheet, on the other hand, can simply be revised and reprinted. Not only is the computer-generated spreadsheet neater, but data in the spreadsheet can also be used to create graphs and charts to represent the data visually. (Business and analytical graphics are discussed in Chapter 11.)

Accountants and businesspeople use spreadsheets to maintain important information, such as sales, expenses incurred, costs of doing business, inventory control, and projections of profits or losses. They can make sales forecasts, analyze competitors' statistics, compare discounts and markup costs, and prepare financial information, such as profit/loss statements and income statements for their banks.

Bankers use spreadsheet programs to track all day-to-day monetary transactions, create loan amortization schedules, make interest-rate computations, and evaluate potential customers' loans, among other tasks.

With spreadsheet information easily accessible, managers can make decisions about future expenditures, or can plan for expansion of products or services, or can formulate pricing strategies using the most comprehensive information available. Then, creative managers can display this spreadsheet information in graphic format.

Personal uses of spreadsheets include tracking cash flow, preparing household budgets and personal financial statements, and figuring annual income taxes, among others (Figure 10–5). People who sell from their homes items such as household products, beauty aids, and cleaning supplies can use a spreadsheet program for orders, inventory, and accounts payable and receivable. A spreadsheet could be created in table format to

FIGURE 10–5

An accounting student uses a laptop computer and a spreadsheet software program to complete his assignments at home.

help young students learn mathematical facts. Other applications depend only on your imagination!

GETTING STARTED ON A SPREADSHEET

The load feature of a spreadsheet program accesses an existing worksheet that has been saved on a disk. The usual method is to activate the load command or its equivalent from an opening menu, and enter the desired worksheet name.

Commands are generally selected from a main command menu that can be accessed by certain keystrokes. For example, Lotus invokes its Main Command Menu simply by pressing the slash (/) key. A user then chooses from the commands listed on the menu. Often, there are submenus listed under menus because some spreadsheets have as many as several hundred commands from which to choose.

Categories of commands are grouped together, and subcategories of similar commands are grouped under them. For example, a spreadsheet program may have a menu that contains a "format" command. When selected, it presents another menu that contains more explicit choices, i.e., setting dollar signs and the option of listing decimal points and zeros with number entries. Formatting choices let you change the look of the worksheet, or make the entries more readable.

The Lotus 1-2-3 Main Command Menu top line offers the selections that are available. The second line shows just those options available under the worksheet command. Scrolling across the top line of the menu changes the choices in the second line to show the options available under each category.

Modes

Spreadsheet programs have two modes of operation: a command (or menu) mode, and a ready/entry mode.

Modes

- Command mode
- Ready/Entry mode

Command Mode. When the spreadsheet is in the **command mode,** you are offered menus from which to make command selections. Usually, this is done by moving the cursor to the selection and highlighting it. Some commands may be invoked by various keys or key combinations.

Most spreadsheets offer multiple levels of command menus to accommodate the wide variety of selections. Many keys have more than one function assigned to them. For example, a key used by itself might access one function, such as making a copy. But the same key, used in conjunction with the <Shift> key, might offer a second function, perhaps creating a new window; and used with still another key, such as the <Ctrl> key, it might provide a third function, perhaps editing the spreadsheet.

Ready/Entry Mode. The **ready/entry mode** indicates that the program is ready for data entry. The program automatically shifts from the ready mode to the entry mode as soon as the first character is typed.

Typical Worksheet

Figure 10–6 shows what the spreadsheet program displays first, a relatively blank screen. This is the beginning of a **worksheet**. At this stage the

FIGURE 10–6
The typical worksheet screen.
(Photo by Jo Hall/Macmillan)

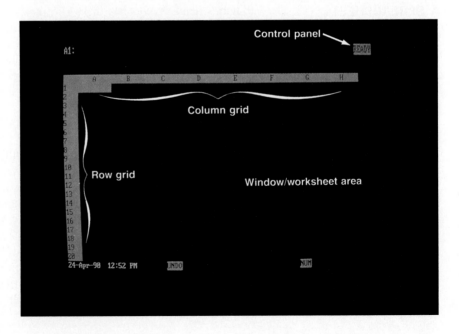

Parts of a Worksheet

- The window, area where entries are displayed
  - The numbers down the left side constitute the row grid
  - The alphabetic characters at the top are the column grid
- The control panel, area containing valuable information about activity on the worksheet.

screen is hardly impressive, but once the data are entered on the worksheet, the true power of the electronic spreadsheet can be invoked.

The worksheet has two main parts: (1) the **window,** an area on the display screen where entries are visually displayed, and (2) the **control panel,** an area that provides valuable information about activity on the worksheet.

The numbers down the left side of the screen constitute the **row** grid, and the alphabetic characters at the top of the screen are the **column** grid. Using a combination of these labels identifies specific points on a worksheet. The point where imaginary row and column grid lines intersect is the **coordinate,** or the address of that particular point. In Figure 10–7, Coordinate A1 is the point where a line down Column A intersects a line across Row 1. (Generally, the column letter is given first, followed by the row number.)

The box formed by the imaginary lines at each coordinate is a **cell.** The highlighted box in Figure 10–7 is the **cell pointer;** it indicates the **active cell,** or "current" cell. The cell pointer's size changes to reflect the width of the column it is marking. A flashing dash inside the cell pointer is the **cursor;** it indicates the position where the next character typed will appear or the next entry will occur. (We'll explain later what kinds of data are entered, and how the data get into each cell.)

Control Panel

The worksheet **control panel** is usually found at the top of the screen; it provides specific information about the worksheet. In Figure 10–6, the control panel at the top of the Lotus 1-2-3 screen contains three lines. The left-hand portion of the first line shows the coordinates where the cursor

FIGURE 10–7
The cell at Column B, Row 5 is the active cell. (Photo by Jo Hall/Macmillan)

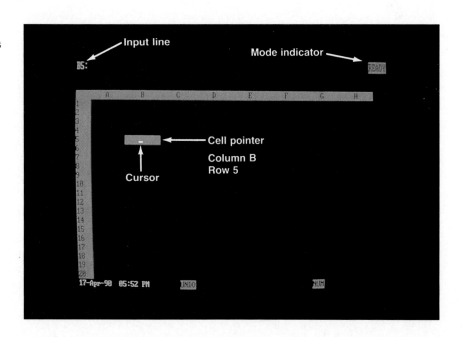

is positioned (A1). It may also indicate the cell width, show whether the cell is protected from unauthorized change, and show any contents or entry in the cell.

The right-hand portion shows the **mode indicator,** which tells whether the program is in the command (menu) mode or the ready (entry) mode. In Figure 10–6 the mode indicator READY is displayed, showing that the program is awaiting a command. The second line displays the current entry or the Lotus main command menu. The third line displays information such as the commands available under a highlighted command.

Status Line

A **status line** may include other information about the worksheet. For example, the status line in Lotus 1-2-3, at the bottom of the screen, gives the current date and time, error messages (not shown), and other status indicators such as NUM (number lock on), CAPS (all caps selected), or a prompt indicating that the worksheet should be recalculated.

Moving Around the Worksheet

Because the window lets you see only a small portion of a worksheet at any time—approximately 80 spaces across and 15 lines down—you must scroll the cell pointer "off the screen" to view the rest of the worksheet. The cell pointer can be scrolled past the right-hand margin and below the bottom of the monitor screen. For example, to reach coordinate Z100, you would scroll to the right 25 cells, and downward 99 cells. The arrow keys on the numeric keypad are used to do this.

The arrow keys move the cell pointer in the direction that the arrow points—e.g., the down arrow (↓) moves the cell pointer downward one cell at a time. By using various keys and key combinations (such as the Home, End, PgUp, PgDn), you move the cursor over larger distances quickly instead of one cell or row at a time. Another method of moving rapidly is **jumping,** where you designate which coordinates are needed, and use appropriate keystrokes to move the cursor automatically to that particular cell coordinate.

The function keys ("F" keys on the main keyboard, either at the top or down the left) are also used. For example, some programs use the F2 key to edit cell entries that contain errors or need to be changed. Many keys automatically repeat if they are held down, so it is important to maintain a light touch on the keyboard.

Templates

Recreating even relatively simple paper spreadsheets each month can take many hours to prepare the paper forms and handwrite the entries. Valuable time is wasted in rewriting the same columnar headings from month to month on blank paper forms. With an electronic spreadsheet, a **template** or blank form can be created for the required report. The template

FINDING YOUR WAY AROUND

Do you remember learning in grade-school social studies about Ferdinand Magellan, whose voyage is credited as the first circumnavigation of the world? Several computer programs are used to navigate files on computer disks, and one of them is called Magellan. These programs help locate a specific file by searching through more than one drive or directory, or application. Magellan supports most popular word processors, data managers, and spreadsheets.

This Magellan accomplishes the file/text searching through English-like queries. For example, you may need to find all references to a product or salesperson. Magellan can search 12 megabytes of files in less than 10 seconds! When Magellan finds what you are seeking, it identifies which software application was used to generate the file, and when you view the file, it appears in the same format (i.e., if viewing data from a spreadsheet, the data will be shown in that format). The application software does not need to be loaded to accomplish this feat.

Because this program is relatively sophisticated, it is necessary to follow the directions in the accompanying manual. But, the crew that follows this Magellan does not have to worry about mutiny, scurvy, sunken ships, or natives bent on murdering the captain.

contains any standard information that doesn't change; this form can be called to the screen, and data for the particular time period can be inserted.

The clerk who prepares monthly reports for the company president could create a template including headings for standard expenses such as rent, utilities, insurance, and payroll. When the report is due, the clerk simply calls up the template form and enters the name of the new month and the amounts of expenses incurred for that month. Even small companies can save time by not having to handwrite all the standard parts of these reports each time.

Defaults

Although default settings vary among spreadsheets, and can be reset by the user, some common ones are:

☐ The columns are all the same width—every column is a certain number of spaces wide.
☐ All entries that begin with a letter will be left-justified in the cell.
☐ All entries that begin with a number will be right-justified in the cell.

□ The worksheet is automatically recalculated whenever a number is changed.

□ Numbers appear without commas or beginning and ending zeros.

BASIC FEATURES USED TO CREATE A SIMPLE WORKSHEET

Different types of data can be entered into the cells. You must know what type of data are being entered, because the computer views entries based on their identifying characteristics. The two types of entries are labels (non-numeric data) and values (numeric data, which can include both constants and formulas).

Entering Labels

A **label** is text used to identify some aspect of the spreadsheet—Figure 10−8(a). A label placed at the top to identify the contents of a worksheet might appear like this:

> Bookcase Company
> Profit and Loss Statement
> for the period January to March

Other entries needing labels include the column and row headings, and any other words or text necessary to identify or clarify the spreadsheet information. Some programs automatically recognize as a label any entry that begins with an alphabetic character or certain special characters. If a label begins with numbers or other special characters that normally indicate a value—e.g., a street address or a year—specific keystrokes are required to tell the computer that the entry is a label, and not a value. Many programs include an **automatic spillover** option; if the cell label is too long to fit the column width, the text continues on, or spills over, into the next cell.

Entering Numbers

After the spreadsheet labels are entered, the **values** are inserted, both numbers and formulas—Figure 10−8(b), (c). **Formulas** are the mathematical equations for the spreadsheet program to add, subtract, multiply, and divide combinations of cells. Built-in functions, such as SUM, SIN, and MAX, can also be used in formulas; i.e., the program can automatically total, find the sine, and determine the maximum value in a list of numbers. (We'll discuss these built-in functions later in the chapter.)

Entering and Displaying Formulas

Formulas must be defined as value cells only; any cell with a label designation cannot be used for a formula. For example, the formula (D6 + D7) commands the computer to add the values found in cells D6 and D7. Some formulas may begin with a built-in function, such as the word SUM, or with a cell reference, such as D6. To identify the cell as a value and not as a label, a special character entry is usually required. The plus sign (+)

Entries

- Labels
- Numbers
  □ Values
  □ Formulas

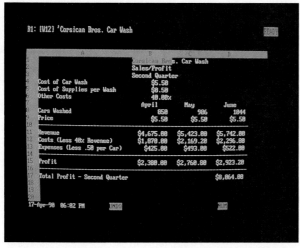

(a)

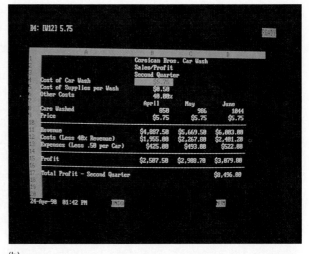

(b)

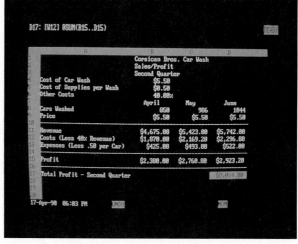

(c)

FIGURE 10–8

The cell pointer is positioned to show (a) an example of a text entry, (b) an example of a number entry, and (c) an example of a formula entry. (Photo by Jo Hall/Macmillan)

character is a common example, used to indicate that the entry following it is a value, not a label.

The basic mathematical operators used by most spreadsheets are:

* multiplication
/ division
+ addition
− subtraction

Most spreadsheet programs solve the formulas that are entered using the normal order of mathematical operations: they assume that operations enclosed in parentheses are done first, exponentiation next, then multiplication and division before addition and subtraction.

Some spreadsheets may be programmed to read and solve equations left-to-right. This procedure affects how formulas are entered. Therefore, it is important to know which method your program uses, because answers can vary drastically, depending on the method of solution. As an example, use the simple formula 10 + 10/2. If the rules of the normal order of operation were followed, the division operation would be performed first, then the addition; the answer would be 15. But, if this equation were solved from left to right, the addition operation would be performed first, then the division; the answer would be 10.

In Figure 10−8(c), the formula @SUM (B15..D15) is shown for cell D17. The computer understands that the entry in that cell is the sum total of those cells. Therefore, $8,064.00 appears in the cell, but the formula (not the total) for the cell entry is shown above the input line. The computer completes the calculation and enters the result where specified. (Remember, formulas cannot include cell references that contain labels. Also, you must indicate that the entry in cell D17 is a formula by preceding it with the appropriate keystrokes—in this case a + sign.)

Some programs let you toggle, or switch, between label and value entries just by using certain keys. This option is handy when a number, such as a date or address, needs to be entered and recognized as a label. For instance, the numbers in the year 1991, street addresses, and zip codes would ordinarily be construed as values because they begin with numbers. These entries would have to be specifically identified as labels, or the computer would recognize them as values.

Correcting Errors/Editing

Typographical errors, wrong values, or erroneous formulas can be corrected by **editing**. It is just such editing chores done on a paper spreadsheet that give accountants headaches. Errors found before they have been entered to the worksheet can be edited first on the screen, simply by making the corrections on the input/entry line. But, if the entry has already been recorded, most programs offer an "Edit" command on the menu.

Defining a Range of Cells

Designating a **range of cells** is a method of selecting specific contiguous cells. The range can consist of only one cell or of a large portion of the worksheet; that cell or cells can be copied, moved, deleted, saved, printed, or otherwise treated as a unit. This feature is a time-saving device when a large worksheet is in use.

Although spreadsheet programs vary, the usual way to identify a range of cells is to type the coordinates of the upper-left cell, followed by a delimiter—usually two periods (..) or a colon (:), followed by the coordinates of the lower-right cell. For example, if a column of numbers starting at C1 and continuing through to C200 needs to be added, entering the range of cells saves the drudgery of keying each separate row's cell label under column C. Merely keying SUM C1..C200 (or a similar formula, in most cases) tells the computer to give the total of the entries in that column. The range of cells therefore must be square or rectangular in shape (Figure 10−9).

FIGURE 10–9
A range must always be square or rectangular in shape; a single cell can be considered a range.

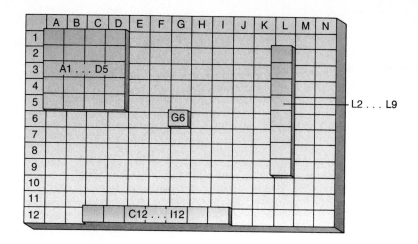

Naming a Range

A single cell, or even a range of cells, can be named for ease in identification. Going back to Figure 10–8(b), the cell containing the cost of the car wash (B4) could be named COST. Then, the formula at cell C11 for finding how much revenue was made could be stated as the number of cars washed times the cost, or +850 * COST.

Names can be added, revised, and even deleted if they are no longer useful. In large worksheets, identifying various ranges by name can speed up the process of scrolling from one portion of the worksheet to another. Specify the name of the cell or range of cells, and the program jumps directly to that area.

Recalculating/ "What If" Analyses

Some worksheets automatically recalculate the totals over the entire worksheet after a new figure is entered; others require a special menu selection (sometimes called manual recalculation) where you are given the choice of recalculating the entire worksheet or only the affected row or column. Recalculation that occurs while other operations are in process is known as the **background recalculation mode**. Some programs offer **intelligent recalculation** whereby calculation of specific rows and/or columns is controlled by the computer.

Once the spreadsheet is properly formatted and meets your approval, no doubt someone will pose some interesting, thought-provoking questions: What if we don't wash that many cars? Or, what if the price of car wax increases? Or, what if we give all the employees a bonus?

So, is it back to square 1 (or is that cell A1)? No, the spreadsheet includes the capability of *spreadsheet analysis,* a process whereby these "what if" questions can be answered simply. Copy the existing spreadsheet, revise the necessary cells, and have the computer recalculate the new version. You will than be able to review the two spreadsheets and compare results. The questions will be answered in minutes instead of days.

Recalculation

- Automatic
- Background
- Intelligent

Saving a Worksheet

The save feature stores on a disk any worksheet that you have created. You can then recall the file into computer memory at a later time and continue working or editing that particular worksheet.

The exit feature quits a worksheet without saving it. An existing worksheet can be loaded and changed to answer various "what if" questions, and then exited without overriding the original data that were stored on the worksheet. However, some programs automatically save programs as they exit. If this happens, any changes made to answer the "what if" questions are saved, and the original worksheet is permanently altered. In this case, you would create a second copy to make "what if" analyses. A number of copies could be made so that many "what if" analyses could be performed.

FORMATTING FEATURES

The **formatting** process includes various instructions and techniques that change how the contents of the cells are displayed. Format changes can be made in one of two ways: (1) globally, which affects the entire worksheet, or (2) individually, which affects an individual cell or range of cells.

Attributes

The characteristics or formatting commands available in most spreadsheets are called **attributes**. Attribute commands can:

- [ ] Change column widths.
- [ ] Set precision of numbers (the number of decimal places).
- [ ] Set justification (usually left, centered, or right).
- [ ] Determine number formats, or how the number will appear (some common number format choices are shown in Table 10–1).
- [ ] Establish character attributes (boldface, underline, italics).
- [ ] Set data types (text or value).
- [ ] Change how negative values appear—in parentheses; or preceded by DB (debit) or CR (credit); or in red.

TABLE 10–1
Common number format choices.

Integer	Whole number
Dollar	Dollar sign ($) and two decimal places
Floating point	Decimal point followed by specified number of places
Exponential	Scientific notation
Commas	Numbers displayed with commas
Leading $	Leading dollar sign ($) placed before any other format
Percent	Displayed using a percent (%) sign
Foreign currency	Displayed using foreign currency symbol, such as DM for Deutsche marks (German money)

☐ Lock cells (prevent cell entries from being changed).
☐ Hide cells (the contents of the cell are not displayed on screen).

Titles

The **titles** feature freezes rows or columns so that they stay in the window when the rest of the worksheet is scrolled. This feature is especially helpful when there are many rows and columns of numbers to scroll through and review. When the titles scroll off the window, it is difficult to remember what the numbers represent. However, the "titles" command freezes the titles and they remain on the screen so the data can be identified no matter what row or column of the worksheet you are in.

Insert Rows/Columns

There are many other formatting features. One is inserting or deleting blank rows and columns, thereby improving readability. Rows can be added to add space between headings and numbers in the spreadsheet. Underlines or other characters can be inserted by creating a blank row and using a repeating character label to insert a line or column width of a specified character—for example, an underline or a row of asterisks. New columns can be created to accommodate entries not originally planned—for example, if a company adds a new product line.

Figure 10–10 shows how a spreadsheet can look before adding some formatting instructions. Figure 10–11 shows the same spreadsheet after formatting.

FIGURE 10–10
A spreadsheet before formatting. (Photo by Jo Hall/Macmillan)

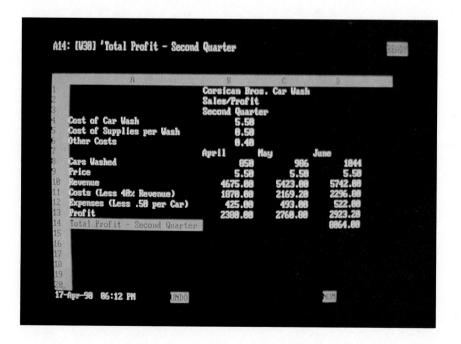

FIGURE 10–11
A spreadsheet after formatting.
(Photo by Jo Hall/Macmillan)

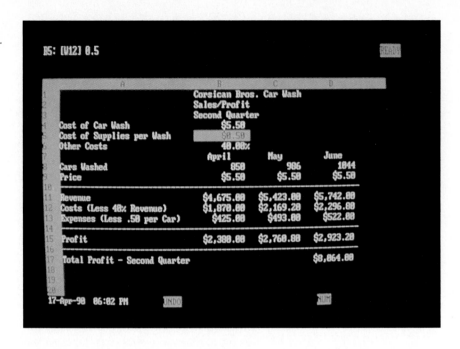

MANIPULATING FEATURES

Electronic spreadsheets have many features that make them more efficient and effective than paper spreadsheets. For example, portions of a spreadsheet can be quickly and easily moved or copied; mathematical formulas that are entered are calculated by the computer. Spreadsheet features allow you to present and manipulate values in many ways. We'll look at some common features found in spreadsheet programs.

Copying

The copy feature selects an existing cell, or range of cells, and replicates them in other cells of the worksheet. To copy labels or numbers, simply identify both the range of cells to be copied and the range of cells into which they are to be copied.

Copying formulas is a bit more involved. Sometimes you will want exactly the same formula using exactly the same cell references in both places. In this case, the computer must be instructed to copy the formula using **absolute cell reference**. For example, if the formula in cell D1—Figure 10–12(a)—is copied to cell D2 using absolute cell reference, it will appear exactly the same and will evaluate in both cases to 10 (5 + 5).

Usually, however, you will want a similar calculation but different cell references. Then you would instruct the computer to copy the formula using **relative cell references**. For example, if the formula in cell D1—Figure 10–12(b)—is copied to cell D2 using relative cell reference, it would change to B2 + C2, and evaluate to 6 (3 + 3).

FIGURE 10–12
Cell references: (a) absolute, (b) relative, and (c) mixed.

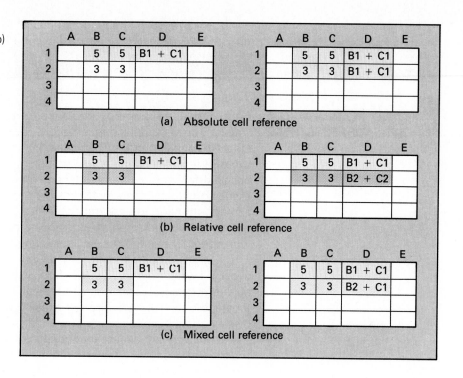

(a) Absolute cell reference

(b) Relative cell reference

(c) Mixed cell reference

Copying Formulas

- Absolute cell reference
- Relative cell reference
- Mixed cell reference

There may also be times when you will want some references in the same formula to be relative and others to be absolute. In this case, you would instruct the computer to copy the formula, using **mixed cell reference**. The absolute or relative is specified for each cell reference. For example, if the formula in cell D1 — Figure 10–12(c) — is copied to cell D2 using relative cell reference for cell B1 and absolute cell reference for cell C1, the formula in cell D2 will be B2 + C1 and evaluate to 8 (3 + 5).

Moving

The move feature allows repositioning of the contents of individual cells or ranges of cells from one location to another. With this feature, you can redesign the appearance or layout of the spreadsheet. When a range of cells is moved, any formula in the spreadsheet that will be affected by the move must be corrected. For example, if the contents of cell B2 are moved to cell B10, and the formula in cell E2 is 2 * B2, then the formula in cell E2 will have to be edited to be 2 * B10 to obtain the same results.

Sorting

Many spreadsheets can sort information by rows or columns, alphabetically or numerically. This feature usually gives many choices: allowing a search for specific numbers or labels, arranging the spreadsheet in date order, arranging in ascending or descending dollar amounts, and so on.

NO PLAIN VANILLA SPREADSHEETS HERE

Oscar Smith, president of High's Ice Cream Corp., gets the real "scoop" on his graphic presentations. Smith keeps records on all 33 stores that make up the High chain by using PlanPerfect from WordPerfect. No boring rows and columns of numbers here though, because this software allows him to create eye-catching worksheets. By using different type fonts, shades of gray, and clip-art images, he can call attention to performance in any of the individual stores. For example, he highlighted an outstanding bottom-line figure in one worksheet by using clip art of a pointing finger.

Graphs prepared from spreadsheet data from all the stores readily show if one store's productivity falls way below average for no apparent reason. This result can be highlighted by using a different typeface or choosing a different shading pattern. With this visual display, it is clear which stores are making their quotas.

An important aspect that must be factored into the data includes the weather: people consume more ice cream during a heat wave than during a blizzard. Smith compares current sales to previous sales totals from all the spreadsheet data, and then creates line graphs to visualize the data. By viewing the trends shown in the graphs, Smith can make appropriate management decisions for stores with sluggish sales.

Pie charts show that the most popular flavor of High's ice cream is still plain vanilla. Luckily, the graph that tells us that vanilla is still the all-time favorite can now be formatted with a cherry on top.

Printing

Printing the spreadsheet produces a hard copy (paper copy). To print a spreadsheet, you usually access a special print menu, and indicate the size of paper, number of copies, and margin parameters. The row-and-column grid designations can be deleted at this point to give the printed spreadsheet a more formal appearance.

A printer that can print wider than 8½" standard paper is often needed. Some programs offer a method of printing sideways, thereby offering more space to print columns and rows.

ADDITIONAL FEATURES

Spreadsheet programs vary, but some common additional features are described on the next page.

Graphing

The information entered and saved in a worksheet can be the basis for generating graphics of data in a particular worksheet—pictorial representations such as pie charts, line charts, and bar charts. The data to be graphed must be identified, the type of graph must be chosen, and titles specified and legends explained. Many spreadsheet programs require that the graph be saved as a worksheet file so that it can be recalled later with all the settings intact. (Chapter 11 contains more specific information on graphics.)

Database Functions

The worksheet data may be considered a database. Therefore, many functions can be accomplished, such as computing the average, counting cells, finding the largest and smallest numbers, computing standard deviation, finding the sum, and computing the variance. These functions are listed in Table 10–2. The name of each item listed is preceded by the letter "D" to indicate that it is a database function.

Built-in Functions

Most spreadsheets have **built-in functions** where formulas for solutions to certain standard problems have already been created and stored in the program. These functions provide shortcuts for many common tasks, typically mathematical, statistical, financial, date, string, logical, and tabular. Table 10–3 describes these built-in functions.

Most spreadsheets have dozens of built-in functions, and their names vary from program to program. The reference manual that comes with the software details the functions offered by that spreadsheet.

Electronic spreadsheet software innovations continue to make this a popular program for microcomputer users. More sophisticated applications are being developed with the multidimensional programs; these programs are a far cry from Kapor's original spreadsheet.

TABLE 10–2
Database functions.

DAVG	Computes the average
DCOUNT	Counts the nonblank cells
DMAX	Indicates the largest number
DMIN	Indicates the smallest number
DSTD	Computes the standard deviation
DSUM	Computes the total
DVAR	Computes the variance

TABLE 10–3
Built-in functions.

Mathematical function	Performs a mathematical transformation on a single value and returns a single value—for example, a SQRT(x) determines the square root of a value.
Statistical function	Accepts a list of values and provides summary statistics about those values (for example, an average function returns the average value from a list).
Financial function	Calculates the effect of interest rates on sums of money over time (for example, a payment function calculates the payment that will pay off the principal of a loan borrowed at the specified interest rate after the specified number of payments have been made).
Date function	Calculates with dates and times (for example, it can automatically enter the date and time in a report).
String function	Performs operations on text (for example, a length function indicates the number of characters in a string).
Logical function	Tests the condition of cells or performs comparisons to determine what value should be entered in a cell (for example, an IF function enters one value in the cell if the condition is true and another value in the cell if the condition is false).
Table function	Retrieves an entry from a table (for example, a "value look-up" function can search an income tax table that has been entered into the spreadsheet to find a specific number).

SUMMARY

A spreadsheet is a paper tool on which to track and manipulate rows and columns of numbers. An electronic spreadsheet uses a computer and special software to do the same manipulations faster, more accurately, and more reliably. A multidimensional spreadsheet allows cells to be visualized as solids.

A spreadsheet application is appropriate if the problem can be stated in a mathematical format; is to be repeated, edited, and revised; is made up of both variable and fixed data; and is required to be neat and legible.

A spreadsheet has two modes of operation: command mode, where the action choices are listed, and the ready/entry mode, where the program is ready for the user to move the cursor and begin making entries.

The worksheet display on a computer monitor includes the window (where entries are displayed) and the control panel (where useful information about the worksheet is typically displayed). The control panel visually reports what is happening on a given worksheet. It contains the status line, prompt line, and an input or entry line.

The numbers down the left side are the row grid and the alphabetic characters across the top are the column grid. At the intersection of an imaginary line drawn from any point on each grid lies a coordinate, or the address of a point on the worksheet. The box thus formed is called a cell. The cell pointer identifies the cell that is available for use—the active cell, or current cell. The cursor, usually a flashing dash, is inside the cell pointer.

Creating a template (blank form) that contains repetitious formats can save time.

There are two types of entries: labels are nonnumeric, or text; values are numeric data and include numbers and formulas. Spreadsheets can complete mathematical equations using the values from various value cells. Mathematical operations are performed following standard rules of operation, in this order: values in parentheses, exponentiation, multiplication and division, addition and subtraction. Recalculation of totals can be automatic, background, or intelligent.

Spreadsheets can be edited to correct typographical errors and wrong values. A range of cells can be selected to be edited or acted upon; it may be one cell or a specified portion of the spreadsheet. A cell or a range of cells can be named for ease in identification when the range is moved from one place on the spreadsheet to another, or copied, or specified for use in a calculation.

Spreadsheets contain built-in functions containing solutions to commonly encountered problems. These include mathematical, statistical, financial, date, string, logical, and tabular functions. Most spreadsheets have dozens of built-in functions that offer shortcuts; users do not have to write formulas for these built-in functions.

Formatting, or changing the look of the worksheet, can be accomplished globally or on a range of cells.

Formulas that are created can be copied to other cells, but then they must be referenced in one of three ways: absolute cell reference, relative cell reference, or mixed cell reference.

Spreadsheet data are used with graphics software to create pie, line, and bar charts for visual displays.

Vocabulary Self-Test

Can you define the following?

absolute cell reference (p. 332)

active cell (p. 323)

attributes (p. 330)

automatic spillover (p. 326)

background recalculation mode (p. 329)

built-in functions (p. 335)

cell (p. 323)

cell pointer (p. 323)

column (p. 323)

command mode (p. 322)

control panel (p. 323)

coordinate (p. 323)

cursor (p. 323)

editing (p. 328)

electronic spreadsheet (p. 316)

formatting (p. 330)

formulas (p. 326)

intelligent recalculation (p. 329)

jumping (p. 324)

label (p. 326)

mixed cell reference (p. 333)

mode indicator (p. 324)

multidimensional spreadsheet
(p. 318)

range of cells (p. 328)

ready/entry mode (p. 322)

relative cell reference (p. 332)

row (p. 323)

spreadsheet (p. 316)

status line (p. 324)

template (p. 324)

titles (p. 331)

values (p. 326)

window (p. 323)

worksheet (p. 322)

Review Questions

Multiple Choice

1. The first spreadsheet program for microcomputers was _____ .
   a. PFS:First Choice
   b. Lotus 1-2-3
   c. VisiCalc
   d. Quattro

2. The largest spreadsheet programs allow worksheets with over _____ cells.
   a. one thousand
   b. one hundred thousand
   c. one million
   d. one billion

3. The numbers at the left of a worksheet screen are the _____ .
   a. control panel
   b. row grid
   c. column grid
   d. coordinates

4. The highlighted box, also called the _____ , indicates the active cell.
   a. cell
   b. cursor
   c. coordinate
   d. cell pointer

5. A typical worksheet control panel includes all but the _____ .
   a. cell width
   b. mode indicator
   c. coordinates
   d. status line

6. A(n) _____ is the text used to identify various aspects of the worksheet.
   a. label
   b. value
   c. entry
   d. formula

7. _____ choices change the look of the worksheet or make it more understandable.
   a. Scrolling
   b. Loading
   c. Formatting
   d. Windowing

8. _____ is the feature that freezes the rows and columns and keeps them visible on the screen, even when you scroll across or down the spreadsheet.
   a. Windows
   b. Titles
   c. Hold
   d. Copying

9. One of these is not a worksheet cell reference: _____.
   a. absolute cell reference
   b. relative cell reference
   c. mixed cell reference
   d. formula cell reference

10. Selecting specific contiguous cells in a worksheet is known as _____.
    a. setting defaults
    b. entering a label
    c. defining a range
    d. designating titles

Fill-in

1. A(n) _____ is the software application that offers a means of keeping track of and manipulating numbers.

2. In a multidimensional spreadsheet, cells can be thought of as _____.

3. The alphabetic characters at the top of the worksheet screen are the _____ grid.

4. The _____ is the flashing dash that appears inside the cell pointer; it indicates the position where the next character typed will appear or the next entry will occur in a worksheet.

5. Worksheet input occurs in the _____ cell.

6. Scrolling, jumping, and using arrow keys are all methods for moving the _____ around the worksheet.

7. A worksheet form containing standard information that doesn't change and can be called to the screen to have new data entered is known as a(n) _____ .

8. SUM, SIN, and MAX are examples of _____ functions in a spreadsheet program.

9. In a worksheet, the entry C4..D10 indicates a(n) _____.

10. _____ , _____ , and _____ are the three types of entries that can be made in a worksheet.

Short Answer

1. Explain why early electronic spreadsheets did not have widespread popularity.

2. What factors indicate that a worksheet environment could be useful in solving a problem?

3. List professional and personal uses of spreadsheets.

4. Give examples of the three types of entries that can be made in spreadsheets.

5. Describe how a worksheet cell's coordinate, or address, is derived.

6. What is the standard order of mathematical operations? Explain why knowing the order of operations of a particular spreadsheet program could be critical.

7. What are three ways in which commands can be selected from worksheet menus?

8. Give two ways that errors can be corrected or editing can occur in the worksheet's cells.

9. Describe the advantages of being able to pose "what if" questions within an electronic spreadsheet.

10. Describe possible ramifications that must be considered in copying formulas in a worksheet.

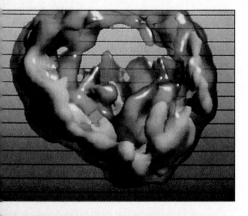

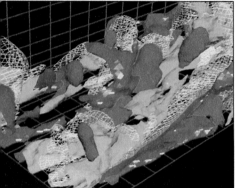

OBJECTIVES

☐ Distinguish among text graphics, bitmapped graphics, and vector graphics.

☐ Know several input and output options possible with graphics programs.

☐ Name the different types of graphics programs and briefly describe each.

☐ Describe some typical features in graphics programs.

☐ Make several suggestions for creating presentation-quality graphs.

☐ Know several areas in which computer graphics are heavily used

CHAPTER ELEVEN

Graphics for Microcomputers

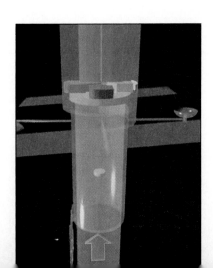

PROFILE

Stephen Wozniak and Steven P. Jobs

When Stephen Wozniak and Steven P. Jobs joined forces in the mid-1970s to form Apple Computer, Inc., it was an ideal partnership of science and salesmanship. While both men were well versed in the computer technology of the time, Wozniak was the scientific whiz kid. Jobs had a vision of creating a computer so small, powerful, and easy to use that it would have the sales appeal of a handy home appliance, and he demonstrated this vision within a remarkably short time. The first Apple computer went on sale in 1977. By 1980, when Apple stock became available to the public, the company had registered sales of $139 million—not a bad record for an enterprise that was founded on just $1,300.

Neither Wozniak nor Jobs was a college graduate when they established the company. Wozniak had attended the University of California at Berkeley before dropping out in 1972, and Jobs had spent one semester at Reed College in Oregon.

In 1974, Jobs went to work briefly for Nolan Bushnell's video game company, Atari. There, he witnessed the intellectually demanding but socially loose work style that would become a trademark at Apple.

A year after joining the Atari staff, Jobs began dropping in on meetings of the Home Brew Computer Club, a group of computer and software enthusiasts that included Wozniak. At the time, Wozniak was on the payroll of the Hewlett-Packard computer company, but Jobs (already with visions of microcomputers dancing in his head) persuaded ''Woz'' to leave his job and go into business with him. The result was Apple Computer, Inc., a firm devoted from the start to changing computers from exotic, scary, and mysterious hardware into small, attractive, friendly workhorses for the office and home.

Success eventually drove the pair of pioneers from the top of the Apple barrel. As early as 1982, Wozniak was experimenting with rock concert promotion—an interest that cost him $30 million in 2 years. He returned to college at Berkeley and graduated in 1986 with a bachelor's degree in computer science. Wozniak left Apple in 1985 and joined forces with fellow computer wizard Nolan Bushnell to produce and market a line of toy robots directed by audio signals encoded on the soundtracks of television programs or videocassettes. Jobs also left Apple in 1985. Since then, he has formed NeXT, Inc., a company that builds the powerful NeXT computers.

omputer graphics are the images and pictures jointly created by a computer program and the person using it. Although the mechanics of **computer graphics** are complex, the concept is simple. Basically, the computer can be programmed to serve two graphic functions: (1) it can create images on a screen, and (2) it can manipulate those images. The images can take many forms, depending on the imagination of the creator: graphs, drawings, paintings, portraits, architecture. It can manipulate those images to simulate such effects as depth, motion, changes in size, and shifts in perspective. These images can be line drawings or shaded solids, in black and white or in vivid color. They can range from simple bar graphs, to very complex 3-D images, to animation.

Graphics software programs allow artists and nonartists alike to use a computer for creating, editing, displaying, and printing the images and pictures.

HOW GRAPHICS SOFTWARE WORKS

Some graphics software requires a *coprocessor,* a separate processor chip inside in the computer. In many cases, you must buy this chip separately to insert in the computer. However, some computers (NeXT, for example) and workstations have a coprocessor built in. The purpose of a coprocessor is to take some of the heavy burden from the main processor (the CPU). A *math coprocessor* handles any math functions associated with creating the graphics, and a *graphics coprocessor* handles screen activities; that is, it redraws the screen quickly as changes are made to the graphic. Without a graphics coprocessor, you would wait a long time for the screen to refresh itself (redraw) when making changes to the image.

Types of Graphic Images

The software creates the images using one of three types of graphics, each produced by the computer in a different way: text graphics, bitmapped graphics, and vector graphics.

Text Graphics. **Text graphics** use any character the keyboard generates to create shapes and lines. The extended ASCII character set for the IBM and most compatibles contains a number of special characters designed just for graphics; some are shown in Table 11–1.

Bitmapped Graphics. With **bitmapped graphics,** you can create an image in much the same way as you would using traditional painting tools, like brushes and paint. In bitmapped graphics (sometimes called pixel-oriented), the individual *pic*ture-*el*ement dots, called **pixels,** make up a display screen and are turned on and off to form various shapes.

All display screens do not contain the same number of pixels. The more pixels a display has, the more detail you will see in the image—that is, the higher the resolution. **Resolution** refers to how sharp or clear an image is and the amount of detail within it.

The image you create is composed of a matrix of pixels called a **bitmap,** in which each pixel is assigned an intensity or color value. The

TABLE 11-1
Extended ASCII character set.

ASCII Value	Character	ASCII Value	Character	ASCII Value	Character	ASCII Value	Character
128	Ç	160	á	192	└	224	α
129	ü	161	í	193	┴	225	β
130	é	162	ó	194	┬	226	Γ
131	â	163	ú	195	├	227	π
132	ä	164	ñ	196	─	228	Σ
133	à	165	Ñ	197	┼	229	σ
134	å	166	ª	198	╞	230	μ
135	ç	167	º	199	╟	231	τ
136	ê	168	¿	200	╚	232	φ
137	ë	169	⌐	201	╔	233	Θ
138	è	170	¬	202	╩	234	Ω
139	ï	171	½	203	╦	235	δ
140	î	172	¼	204	╠	236	∞
141	ì	173	¡	205	═	237	∅
142	Ä	174	«	206	╬	238	∈
143	Å	175	»	207	╧	239	∩
144	É	176	░	208	╨	240	≡
145	æ	177	▒	209	╤	241	±
146	Æ	178	▓	210	╥	242	≥
147	ô	179	│	211	╙	243	≤
148	ö	180	┤	212	╘	244	⌠
149	ò	181	╡	213	╒	245	⌡
150	û	182	╢	214	╓	246	÷
151	ù	183	╖	215	╫	247	≈
152	ÿ	184	╕	216	╪	248	°
153	Ö	185	╣	217	┘	249	•
154	Ü	186	║	218	┌	250	·
155	¢	187	╗	219	█	251	√
156	£	188	╝	220	▄	252	ⁿ
157	¥	189	╜	221	▌	253	²
158	Pt	190	╛	222	▐	254	■
159	ƒ	191	┐	223	▀	255	(blank 'FF')

image is formed when the electron beam sweeps at lightning speed in thin, parallel lines across the screen, making the phosphor coating in each pixel glow to a particular intensity. Because the image resolution depends on how many dots per inch the display is capable of showing, the bitmap degrades as it is enlarged, losing some of its resolution. Also, bitmapped images have somewhat jagged edges.

Vector Graphics. **Vector graphics** (also called object-oriented graphics) mathematically define images. The images are stored as geometric descriptions. So, instead of drawing a continuous line, as you do with bitmapped graphics, you establish control points on the screen to establish the length and curve of the line. As a result, the image resolution does not depend on the display screen's number of dots per inch, as it does with a bitmapped image. Images and text print without the "jaggies" (jagged edges). Drawings do not degrade as you enlarge them; rather, they seem to "stretch," maintaining their resolution and ratio at any size. Drawings and illustrations created with vector graphics are very crisp.

Rather than scanning the entire display area, as in bitmapped graphics, here the electron beam traces the lines of the desired image. The computer tells the beam exactly to which control point it is to go and how intense the line should be. The image is then refreshed by repetition of the process.

Vector graphics use a lot of computer power and, therefore, require the computer to have a coprocessor.

Modes of Resolution

Some programs permit several degrees of resolution for bitmapped graphics. For example, you may be able to choose a 320-by-200 pixel display or a 640-by-480 pixel display. The number of choices, and the pixel number for each, depends on capabilities of both the hardware and software.

Input Options

You create graphics by sending commands, selections, and signals to the computer with an input device. A graphics program may offer several input options, including a keyboard, light pen, mouse, or graphics tablet (these devices were discussed in Chapter 2). Other input options include scanners, which digitize two-dimensional printed images, and video cameras, which digitize two- and three-dimensional images (Figure 11–1).

Output Options

Graphics programs permit you to output the images you create to one or several devices. Typical output options are:

- [ ] Save on disk—graphics can be saved on disk in several formats: (a) in a format that will use them in the graphics program again, (b) in a format that incorporates them into a document, or (c) in a format to be used by a slide show feature (discussed later).
- [ ] The computer screen—all graphics software displays the image on-screen, and most will show the effect of changes to various parameters before you save or output the image.
- [ ] A large projection screen—with special equipment, the images can be projected to a larger screen for large audiences to view.
- [ ] A dot matrix printer or pen plotter—for hard copy.
- [ ] A laser printer—for hard copy. Most laser printers will also print on acetate "cels," or transparencies, to use on overhead projectors.
- [ ] A film recorder—to produce 35 mm color slides for use with standard slide projectors. Slides are the leading form of output for business presentation.
- [ ] Transfer on disk or over phone lines to a slide service bureau—a company that converts image data into color slides or color overhead transparencies for a fee.

FIGURE 11–1
Video cameras can digitize an image and send it to a computer, where it is
stored and later manipulated or printed. (Courtesy of New Image Technology,
Inc.)

When sending the image to a printer or plotter, the program may let you
alter the size of the image and change its position on the paper. It also may
let you change the **aspect ratio**—the proportion between the width and
the height of an image. Many printers have a different aspect ratio from the
computer screen on which the graphic was created. For example, the
screen may display 20 pixels to one-half inch, but the printer may print 40
dots per one-half inch. A circle on the display screen will be printed as an
ellipse if the aspect ratio is not appropriately adapted (Figure 11–2). The
aspect ratio can be modified to correct the appearance of the graphic when
printed.

USES AND TYPES OF GRAPHICS SOFTWARE

Graphics software for microcomputers can be divided into three basic
types: paint and draw programs, design programs, and chart/graph and
"presentation graphics" programs.

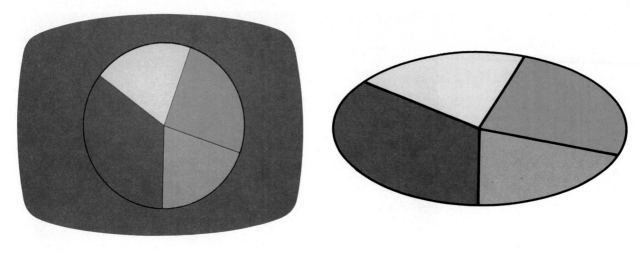

Normal circle as
drawn on screen

Distorted circle is
printed when incorrect
aspect ratio is used.

FIGURE 11–2
The effect of aspect ratio.

Paint and Draw Programs

Many programs available to consumers combine both paint and draw features (Figure 11–3), although they are also sold as separate programs. Such programs are used by artists, illustrators, advertising agencies, and businesses to create original art and illustrations, business forms, logos, and letterheads. As impressive as these programs are, however, the creativity still must come from the person using them.

Draw programs, or illustration programs, are usually vector-based (object-oriented), displaying high-quality lines and dots. This type of program helps you create freehand illustrations and line drawings. Using an input device such as a mouse, light pen, or graphics tablet, you can choose "pen" sizes to control line thickness, choose from a group of ready-drawn simple shapes like circles, squares, ovals, and textures, and then select patterns to fill those shapes. Corel Draw, Adobe Illustrator, and MacDraw II are popular drawing programs.

Paint programs are usually bitmapped (pixel-oriented) programs that let the artist work in a way similar to using a painting canvas and brush. They are best for creating solids, simulating the rich, uneven textures or colored brush strokes similar to those made with water colors and oil paint. With input devices such as a mouse, light pen, and graphics tablet, you can choose from many different pointers, or "brush" sizes, then paint an image, filling the shapes with color and texture. PC Paintbrush, Modern Artist, PixelPaint, and MacPaint are examples of paint programs. Because of the availability of high-resolution display screens and sophisticated graphics programs, computer images are now rivaling those on canvas and film in clarity and crispness.

FIGURE 11–3
Paint (a) and draw (b) programs
are used to draw illustrations or
create original art. (Photo (a) by
Jo Hall/Macmillan; photo (b)
courtesy of Time Arts)

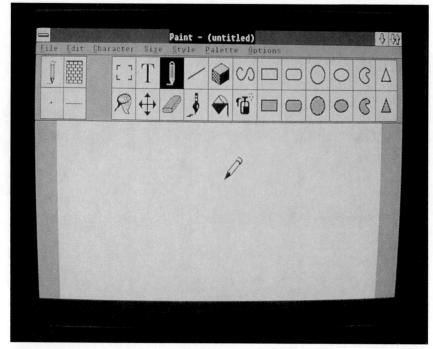

(a)

(b)

Design Programs

Design programs, most of which are vector-based, perform tasks associated with designing products or structures. These tasks can be done easier and more efficiently than by doing them manually with pen and pencil. They eliminate the need to manually erase or redraw. These programs typically use the mouse, a light pen, or a graphics tablet or digitizer for input.

They often go farther than two-dimensional drawings by creating three-dimensional objects that can be rotated and viewed from any angle. Some programs also provide **simulation** capabilities, that is, the capability of creating models of "real life" situations. For example, a skyscraper design might be mathematically tested with a program to see if it would withstand the forces of an earthquake.

In design programs, the product or structure is created in two steps. The first is to create a model (or skeleton) of the object. The second is the rendering of the model, that is, adding the surface characteristics like texture, shading, reflections, etc., to make a very realistic picture of the project.

Using the computer and design software for designing and drafting is called **computer-aided design (CAD)**. CAD programs are used primarily in the fields of engineering, industrial design, and architecture. Figures 11–4 and 11–5 show examples of what can be done using CAD.

FIGURE 11–4
CAD software is used to design and test consumer products. (Courtesy of CADKEY Inc.)

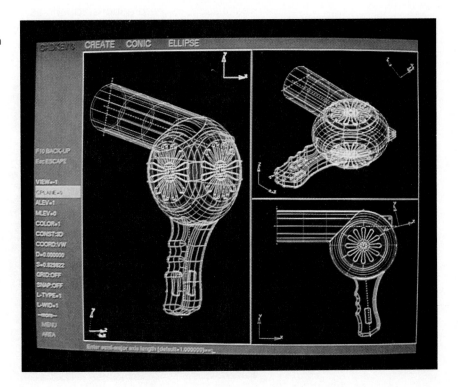

PC MEETS TV Imagine the increased learning and entertainment possibilities if your personal computer's monitor screen could also carry high-quality video images which you could manipulate. Or, what might happen if your regular television set were adapted so that you could interact with the images on the screen? Either would be a significant advancement over the flat, jerky images common in some video games and simulation training. Well, both systems are now available in the business and home markets. What the systems have in common is vivid videotaped scenes with which you can interact.

This PC/TV marriage, pioneered by Intel and N. V. Philips, has produced a great variety of games, reference works, and training and design software. Intel's Digital Video Interactive card can be inserted into a personal computer, and, with the appropriate software, allows you to inspect and analyze the workings of an actual factory, "drive" a truck along the videotaped image of a real highway, or explore detailed video pictures of Mayan ruins. With the Philips CD-Interactive player (which plugs into a regular television set), you can create a music video, take a guided tour of the human reproductive system, or consult an electronic atlas. The atlas, besides showing real moving pictures of real places, also reproduces sounds associated with those places, such as the roar of the Old Faithful geyser erupting.

FIGURE 11-5
3-D CAD enables engineers or designers to explore design alternatives and to test a product before manufacturing. (Courtesy of CADKEY Inc.)

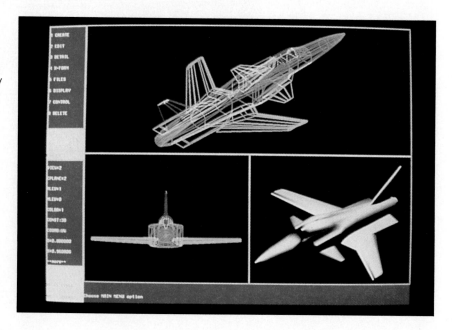

Chart/Graph Programs and Presentation Graphics Programs

A **chart/graph program,** also called a graph or an analytical program, helps the nonartist create attractive graphs and charts. The program accepts numerical data, either transferred from another program or entered directly from the keyboard, and converts those data into pictorial representations—charts or graphs—that show the relationships among the data. The use of pictorial representation of data makes it easy to compare them or to spot trends that might otherwise be difficult to see from a printed page of numbers.

Chart programs are similar to paint programs in the way the images are created by the computer—that is, they create bitmapped images. Typical business or analytical graphs produced with a chart program include bar graphs and pie charts, and line, scatter, stacked-bar, three-dimensional, and surface graphs.

Graphs and charts are not actually "drawn" by the user; rather the user points (with a mouse) or keys in the answers to specific prompts about the type of graph desired, any text or labels to appear on the graph, or other information and specifications. The computer then takes this information and draws the graph or chart.

This type of program may be a stand-alone package or incorporated as part of a spreadsheet (as in Lotus 1-2-3). A spreadsheet program that incorporates charting and graphing features was used to produce the graph in Figure 11−6(a).

A stand-alone chart program is often preferred for formal presentation—Figure 11−6(b). Chart programs incorporated in spreadsheets and other programs are adequate only for informal use; they generally are not of presentation quality. Some stand-alone programs, such as Grafix Partner and PC Storyboard, can enhance charts and graphs initially generated by charting features in other programs.

Presentation graphics programs were developed for formal business presentations. They not only help create charts and graphs, but also help organize them and provide more control while actually making the presentation. This software is considered essential by people who make formal presentations to business colleagues and clients.

Presentation software combines the typical features of a simple chart/graph program (to create the basic graphics) with features that help create, organize, and sequence a slide presentation, create audience handouts, generate speakers' notes and flip charts, and sequence and present a slide show. A slide show can be presented either on a monitor screen, with 35 mm slides and projector, or with a larger projection. (Studies show that the most-used end product for presentation software users is a 35 mm slide presentation.)

The on-screen **slide show** feature displays a series of graphics on the monitor in a predetermined order, for a predetermined time period. This produces the same effect you would get by using photographic 35 mm slides and a slide projector. A slide show of this kind is often used as a training device or for demonstrating a product or an idea. Also, equipment is available to project the image to a large screen for larger audiences,

Types of Graphics
Software

- Paint and draw programs
- Design programs
- Chart/graph programs and presentation graphics programs

FIGURE 11–6

(a) Analytical graph created with a spreadsheet package. (b) An analytical graph created with a stand-alone program. (Photo (a) by Cobalt Productions/Macmillan; photo (b) courtesy of Lasergraphics LFR)

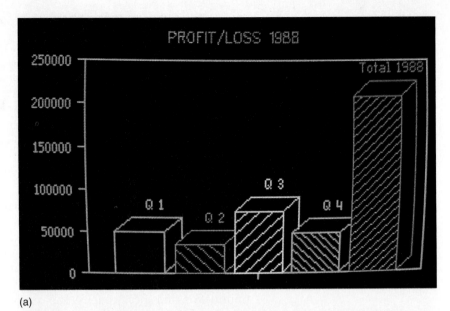

(a)

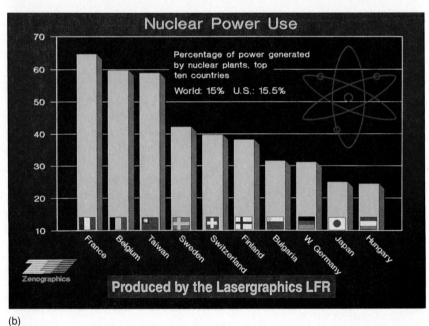

(b)

without converting the images to actual slides or overhead transparencies (Figure 11–7).

Most presentation graphics programs offer a wide selection of colors, typefaces, and drawing "tools." Harvard Graphics, Freelance Plus, Graph Plus, and Boeing Graph are popular presentation programs.

FIGURE 11-7

The graphic image can be output not only to the monitor screen but to a large-screen projector without converting the image to a slide or overhead transparency. (Courtesy of Electrohome Limited)

FEATURES OF GRAPHICS SOFTWARE

This section will familiarize you with major features and terminology associated with graphics software. Some programs are easier to use than others, and programs differ in the number and types of features offered. Some contain hundreds of features and are capable of creating every kind of graph or chart one would ever need. Some software combines elements of all three types of programs—paint and draw, design, and graphs—into one program. As hardware capabilities and software sophistication improve, the trend in designing graphics programs is to incorporate features of all three types.

Chart/Graph Types

Most chart and graph programs display at least **bar graphs,** pie charts, and line graphs. The most popular probably is the bar graph. A bar graph uses a fixed scale to compare data in simple and compound relationships. There are many variations; Figure 11–8 shows several popular types of bar graphs.

A **pie chart** shows the relationship of parts to a whole. The pie, or circle, represents the whole amount, and the segments represent proportional quantities or percentages of the whole. Some programs let you emphasize individual segments by pulling them away from the whole (exploding them), changing color, or shading them. Figure 11–9 shows a pie chart.

Line graphs show trends and emphasize movement and direction of change over a period of time. Points are plotted on the graph and then

Chart/Graph Types
■ Bar graph
■ Pie chart
■ Line graph
■ Scatter graph
■ Word chart

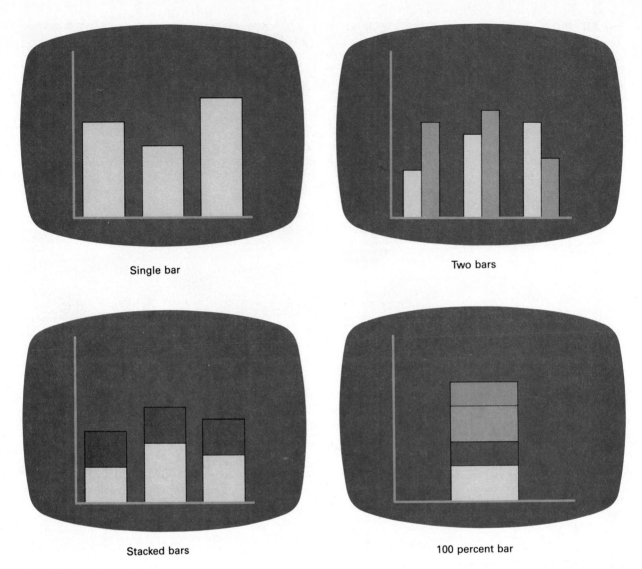

Single bar

Two bars

Stacked bars

100 percent bar

FIGURE 11–8
Several types of bar graphs.

connected by straight or curved lines (Figure 11–10). Line graphs are more appropriate than bar or pie graphs when many data points must be graphed. Line graphs that have the area between the lines or curves shaded or filled in are called **stacked-line graphs** (Figure 11–11).

A **scatter graph** shows the correlation between two sets of data. If both sets of data increase (or decrease) at the same rate, the correlation is positive—Figure 11–12(a). If one set of data increases and the other set decreases relative to the first set, the correlation is negative—Figure 11–12(b). If there is no relationship between the two sets of data, the correlation is zero—Figure 11–12(c).

FIGURE 11–9
Pie chart.

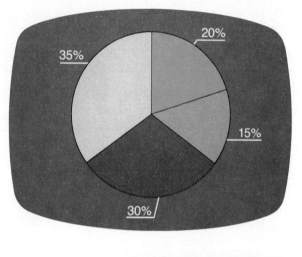

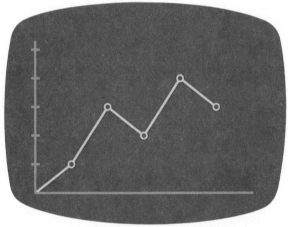

Plot points connected
by straight lines

Plot points connected
by curved lines

FIGURE 11–10
Line graphs using straight lines and curved lines.

A **word chart** (or text chart), the most popular type used in presentations, is simply a bulleted list or numbered list of text, created using different type faces and sizes, usually boldfaced or shadowed (Figure 11–13).

Slide Show

The slide show feature helps you produce a script, generate the graphs, specify slide sequence and timing, and create transitional effects (such as "fade" and "wipe"). The output can be for a "desktop presentation" (on

FIGURE 11–11
Stacked-line graph.

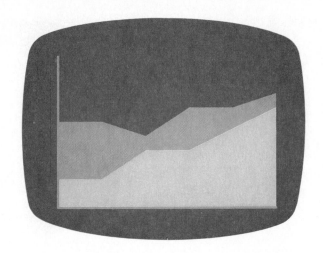

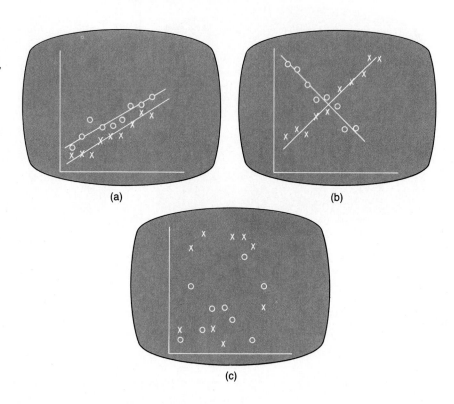

(a)

(b)

(c)

the monitor's display screen), or it can be directly projected in a larger image.

Image Manipulation

Some of the features that let you manipulate an image include the capability to (a) identify the object to be manipulated, (b) copy, (c) cut and paste, (d) drag, (e) rotate, (f) superimpose, (g) change line thickness, and

FIGURE 11–13
Word chart.

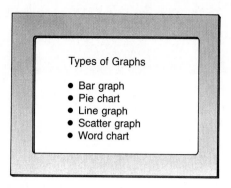

(h) change scale. These features are described below. Of course, more options give the program more flexibility.

Identify Object. This is done in one of two ways, depending on the program. The first is to **select** the object, usually using a pointer device to draw a rectangle around the object. This selected area includes both the object and the background. The second way is to **lasso** the object, also by using a pointer. However, only the object is lassoed—not the background.

Copy. The **copy** feature duplicates a selected portion of the graphic and leaves the original intact. For example, to create a repeating shape, you need only to draw it once and then use the copy feature to duplicate it as many times as needed.

Cut and Paste. The **cut and paste** feature cuts (erases) an object from the graphic and places it in a buffer so that it can be pasted (inserted) in another portion of the graphic.

Drag. The **drag** feature selects an object to be moved, or "dragged," to a new position. You then move it across the screen with a pointing device, as if you were actually dragging it.

Rotate. The **rotate** feature turns an object for viewing from other angles. Some rotate only in 90 degree increments; others rotate an object to any degree specified.

Superimpose. The **superimpose** feature moves one object over another, or over a portion of that object, without erasing either one. When separated, both images remain intact.

Line Thickness. This feature changes the line thickness of a selected drawing.

Scale. The **scale** feature changes the dimensions of an image, reducing or enlarging it, by simply telling the computer what size the image should be. Some programs are limited to certain ratios; others are more flexible, allowing you to choose specific dimensions.

GRAPHICS ON TRIAL
Faced with the need to present information to jurors in a simple, memorable manner, lawyers are resorting to computer graphics. Because so much data are involved, even in a simple trial, it is common for jurors to become bored, confused, or forgetful. To prevent such lapses, an attorney may hire a computer graphics company to create a three-dimensional animation on videotape to illustrate how a process crucial to the case happened. One company, for example, specializes in recreating airplane crashes.

In a 1989 trial concerning America's worst drunk-driving accident—which led to the deaths of 27 people—the prosecutor used computer graphics to recreate in step-by-step detail how the disaster occurred, according to police findings. Such graphics are expensive and cost from $10,000 for a 30-second exhibit to $250,000 for a 45-minute demonstration.

This method of presentation, observers say, is a mixed blessing in the cause of justice. Although it can make a complex situation easier to understand and remember, it can also distort the truth by exaggerating or oversimplifying the very thing it is supposed to illustrate. And the expense of creating the graphics puts it beyond the reach of most people involved in lawsuits.

Sometimes, though, the costs are justified. When Alpo Pet Foods sued Ralston Purina because it was advertising that its dog food could lessen the seriousness of a certain hip ailment, Alpo's attorneys commissioned a three-dimensional graphics tour of Rover's leg to show how the muscles, bones, and joints function. The show kept the jury awake—and sympathetic. It awarded Alpo more than $10 million in damages.

Template

Many programs include templates—a built-in collection of chart styles—that makes it easy for amateur artists to create graphs and charts by simply filling in the blanks and letting the computer do the rest. For example, a chart can be created by selecting a picture of the desired chart type from the program, calling up the ready-made form (chart), and typing in the raw data to be represented.

Grid

A **grid** is a pattern of horizontal and vertical lines on the display screen that helps visualize, pinpoint, and enter specific coordinates for the data. Many programs have the option of turning grid lines on or off, i.e., making them visible or invisible. When turned off, grid marks or hash marks remain on the horizontal and vertical axes to identify the scale. A scale shows the increments between the grid marks. For example, a scale may be incremented by 5, 10, or any other quantity.

Fill Pattern

A fill pattern feature produces a number of patterns, such as crosshatch or dots, with which to fill shapes so they can be easily distinguished from one another. (A fill pattern can be used in lieu of color.)

Color

Most color graphics programs offer at least 16 colors; the more sophisticated ones offer 256 true colors, from a palette of 16.7 million. The colors of the background, labels, and the graph or object can be changed in most programs. Color is an important factor in graphics presentation. It can highlight a portion of a graph to emphasize it or give it meaning, or enhance images created with paint, draw, and design programs. However, black and white is still used in graphics for newsletters and other publications. Various levels of gray shading are depicted on gray-scale monitors.

Text

The text feature lets you enter labels (text) on graphic displays. However, the flexibility of entering text varies widely among programs. Some allow entering of titles but force them into predefined positions; others permit text placement anywhere. The number of available type faces and sizes varies among programs.

Kerning

Kerning is selectively nudging letters together to improve the spacing; it gives the illusion of equal spacing between letters. For example, look at these two typeset versions of the word *Yesterday:*

Y e s t e r d a y

Yesterday

The first version has not been kerned—no special treatment of spacing between letters. In the second version, letters have been *kerned* (some space removed) for a more pleasing appearance. Note how the letters Y and e are pushed together so that the Y overhangs the e. Also note how the letters a and y are pushed together so that the tail of the y underlies the a.

Zoom

The **zoom** feature moves the window, either closer to view an enlargement of a portion of an image, or away to view the entire scene.

Pan

The **pan** feature moves the window from side to side so you can create and view a graphic that is wider than the computer screen.

Mirror

The **mirror** feature automatically draws a mirror image of the object at the same time the original is being drawn. For example, if you draw a line upward, its reflection (an identical downward line) is automatically drawn by the computer.

3-D

Some programs can show an image from various angles on a two-dimensional medium (the monitor), giving it three-dimensional perspective as though it were a tangible object.

Animation

Animation is the program's ability to simulate motion. This feature links, chains, and sequences multiple graphics to create essentially a desktop video. Engineers, for example, can see how various parts of an object will interact. Animation can also serve as a teaching tool; a graphics animation can show how the moving parts of an internal combustion engine operate. Stand-alone animation programs are available and have made possible near-broadcast quality productions on microcomputers.

Picture Library

Graphics programs include a picture library of shapes and images. The library may include simple shapes such as rectangles, circles, triangles, ellipses, and parallelograms. Many programs offer **clip art,** a selection of images—trees, animals, houses, borders, backgrounds, and business and industry icons which can be incorporated into the user's graphic creations. Separate disks of clip art with hundreds of different images are available.

CREATING BUSINESS GRAPHS AND CHARTS

A significant study done by the Wharton Business School's Applied Research Center demonstrated that graphics make the point faster and more persuasively in a presentation. It also showed that people who create and use visuals in their business presentations were perceived to be more professional and more interesting than those who did not.

Developers of graph/chart software and presentation graphics software try to create programs that reinforce the rules of good design. They make it easy for the amateur to create good graphs and charts by including suggestions on the type of graph to use, color, and other features. However, users still need to carefully plan their graphics.

Sometimes, a basic graph with no frills will suffice. But, to be most effective in a formal presentation, you should design a dynamic graph that will impress the point upon an audience. Proper design is important. A poorly designed chart or graph can be very dull—or worse, misleading.

Because many of you are headed into managerial positions, and because of the importance of graphics in the business environment, here are some basic rules for creating business graphs and charts. In general, a good presentation graph should:

☐ Be very simple.
☐ Be accurate and easy to interpret.
☐ Make a visual impact on the intended audience.

Simplicity

Keep the graph simple. Too much information makes it difficult to grasp its meaning. A graph should not show fine details or figures, but rather should *focus on general ideas* such as trends, comparisons, and movement. Keeping a graph simple increases its clarity and effectiveness; presenting complex graphs frustrates, irritates, and bores your audience.

Accuracy

The data used to create the graph must be accurate, or it may not convey the intended meaning. Also, using appropriate scales makes interpretation easier. Poorly selected scales on either the horizontal or vertical axis may cause a curve to appear more or less curved than it really is. When two graphs are to be compared, the increments between grid marks should be the same on the horizontal and vertical axes of both. Changing the distance between grid lines for a portion of a graph may cause identical data to appear different, or vice versa (Figure 11–14).

Visual Impact

Consider these factors for making a visual impact upon the audience:

☐ Balance—Maintain proper balance and spacing of elements. Make bars and columns wider than the space between them (Figure 11–15). Make sure there is enough white space around each word or idea.
☐ Emphasis—Choose design elements such as color, shape, and texture carefully. They can alter the visual effect of a graph. Emphasize the important elements. For example, a segment of a pie chart can be exploded, or a bar might be colored or shaded differently from other bars to make it stand out (Figure 11–16).
☐ Color—When using colors in slides, move from darker in the background to lighter in the foreground, because darker colors tend to recede and lighter colors tend to "jump" forward. Blues and greens are generally good background colors for graphs. In

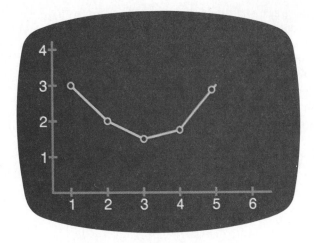

Equal distance between grid marks
on horizontal and vertical axes
gives the graph a smoother, more
realistic appearance.

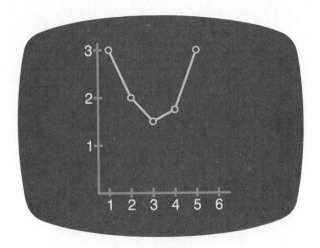

Contracted and uneven grid marks
make the curve appear to have a
severe dip.

FIGURE 11-14
Correct versus distorted scale.

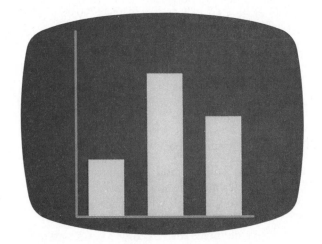

Balanced graph

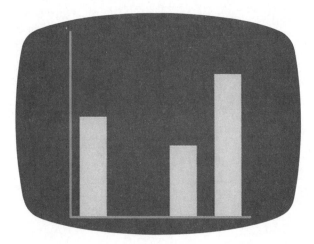

Unbalanced graph

FIGURE 11-15
Balanced versus unbalanced bar graph.

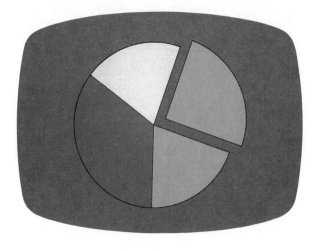

Exploded pie chart

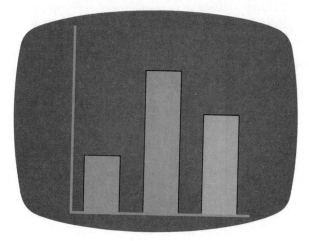

Colored bar for emphasis

FIGURE 11–16
Exploded pie chart and colored bar graph.

business situations, avoid red (it suggests failure to most business-people), unless failure is what is being conveyed. Also, if the colors red and green appear next to each other, a person with red-green color blindness may see only brown. This affliction affects approximately four percent of males in the U.S.

☐ Textures and patterns—Avoid using textures or patterns that can cause distortion. For example, solid bars stand out more than outlined bars. Vertical lines in a horizontal plane make the surface appear higher.

☐ Line Thickness—Vary the thickness or weight of plot lines (the lines that connect the data points in a graph). Or, use color shades or textures to differentiate between plot lines. Make plot lines heaviest and grid lines lightest. Don't overlay solid areas on the charts with grid lines.

☐ Text—Numbers and titles must be large enough to read. Run titles horizontally whenever possible for easier reading. This relates to the simplicity rule: if you keep graphics simple, and minimize the text, then there will be plenty of room for titles that are big enough. If you are presenting a word chart, follow the "77 rule": no more than seven lines, and no more than seven words per line.

All these factors influence where the viewer's attention will be focused and what part of the graph will be perceived as the most important. However, not all software gives you control over every aspect of creating a graph. Some allow more flexibility in graph design than others.

Roger Rabbit leaps excitedly into the room and flings his skinny cartoon arms around a real human actor. . . . On your television screen, the individual call letters of a local channel zoom in from the edge of the picture, tumble over and over toward each other, and line up in a straight, light-pulsating row. . . . A potential home buyer takes a walk through a house that's not yet been built. . . . Flying only by rows of flickering instrument gauges, a new pilot lands a crippled 747 onto a rain-slicked runway without endangering a single passenger or the multimillion-dollar aircraft. . . . In New Zealand, a marine designer tests his new yacht hull on ominously stormy seas, and stays as dry as toast throughout. . . . To get a closer look at a patient's brain tumor, a medical technician peels back the layers of skin and skull without drawing a drop of blood. . . .

None of these remarkable occurrences is magic. Rather, they're all examples of the amazing power of computer graphics. Because the "canvas" of the video screen can be altered in so many ways, an observer of computer graphics technology summarized it this way: "Anything that can be imagined can be imaged." This means that the computer can show objects and create situations that have never existed. It can take numerical data—such as the meteorological conditions that lead to the formation of a tornado—and render them into pictorial images that can be examined and understood. Computer graphics can simulate what is, what has been, and what might be in all sorts of physical conditions.

Simulation and Training

One of the most useful functions of sophisticated computer graphics is in training people to do their jobs and to do them better. Airline pilots, fighter pilots, and astronauts—to take just three examples—could not possibly learn how to operate their equipment by using actual planes and rockets. It would be too dangerous for those who are learning, and too expensive for those who pay for the equipment.

Consequently, trainees are put into realistic mockups of plane or rocket cockpits where computer graphics simulate all sorts of takeoff, flying, combat, and landing conditions. The trainees must respond through interactive controls—much like those used to play video games. If their responses are suitable, the computer-generated feedback tells the trainees so. However, if they miscalculate or are too slow in responding to "changing conditions," then they "crash," have a "near miss," are "shot down," etc. Happily, because it's all on the screen, the trainees can study their errors in safety and try it over again until they get it right. No lives are threatened, no fuel is expended, and no multimillion-dollar equipment goes up in smoke.

A commercial airline pilot might fly for dozens of years and hundreds of thousands of miles and never experience what it is like to be caught in a wind shear or face the terror of losing all engine power. Computer simulation can create these conditions and give the trainee pilot some degree of readiness, should the actual situations ever occur.

FIGURE 11–17
Commercial artists routinely use paint and draw programs to create the art for print advertisements and television commercials. (Courtesy of Lasergraphics, LFR)

Commercial Art and Illustration

The science of computer graphics strongly influenced how many kinds of commercial art and fine art are produced. Charts, logos, abstract designs, animation, and even sculpture are touched by this technology. Images for artistic purpose are first created and manipulated on a screen (Figure 11–17); then, depending on their ultimate function, the images are superimposed, printed out, or photographed for the finished project.

Newspaper artists now routinely use microcomputers to create the charts and graphs that illustrate news stories. Using printers and plotters with the graphics software, computer-assisted artists can transform on-screen images into color printouts and transparencies.

Clip art has been an essential element of newspaper advertising graphics for a long time. Until recently, these line drawings of cars, tires, turkeys, churches, pumpkins, Santa Clauses and thousands of other eye-catching objects were supplied to newspapers in book format. With such a book, a newspaper artist could illustrate an ad simply by looking through the book for a suitable illustration of proper size, clip it out, paste it down, and arrange the copy around it. Although books of clip art still are marketed, they are taking a back seat to illustrations carried on floppy or compact disks.

At one time, art departments at television stations had to use sheets of clear acetate and press-on letters to create slides. Now it's all done electronically with computers. But that is just the beginning: with computer graphics capability, artists can superimpose letters and "crawling" messages on-screen. They can "freeze" and move live images around the

FIGURE 11–18
Only the user's imagination limits the form which modern computer graphics can take. (Courtesy of Image Software)

screen, alter the colors and textures of images, and make logos pulsate and glitter—all with computer controls.

Fine Art

In the early days of computer art, one usually saw jagged science fiction-type imagery. No longer. Although computer art worked its way into mainstream visual fine art through the field of commercial art, it has graduated to the art gallery, where some computer artists now exhibit their creations (Figure 11–18). Andy Warhol, for example, created some of his last works on an Amiga microcomputer, using a mouse as his brush. Other artists, like Vibeke Sorensen (three-dimensional graphics) and Barbara Nessim (drawings), use their computers as their canvas and drawing pad.

So significant now is computer art that many art schools include a computer art program in their curriculum. Students at the School of Visual Arts in New York, for example, can earn a Master of Fine Arts degree working in a studio filled with microcomputers.

Animation was once a tedious and time-consuming matter of drawing hundreds of slightly changed images to get a few seconds of simulated motion. With computer graphics, an initial image is created, and then—through a series of data-encoding processes—the computer is able to "draw" additional images to fit a programmed pattern of motion. In 1989, the first Academy Award was presented for a totally computer-created animated film, *Tin Toy*. Although still expensive, the cost of computer animation is falling rapidly.

Graphics in Medicine

More and more, medical personnel rely on computer graphics as a diagnostic tool. Linked with a scanner, for example, a computer can render a three-dimensional image of a patient's brain and allow doctors to examine the organ in great detail and from every angle. And no exploratory surgery is involved. Black and white X-rays can be computer-enhanced and shown in color to reveal more information about the examination area.

In some universities, medical and veterinary science students can now "dissect" computer images of animals rather than actual laboratory specimens. This capability is not only less expensive for the schools, but also addresses issues raised in an age when animal-rights groups are challenging the morality of the old ways of teaching anatomy. Purdue University's School of Veterinary Medicine is just one of several institutions working toward reducing the use of animals in the test lab.

Product Design

One of the oldest and most utilitarian uses of computer graphics is in designing products. This function was followed, logically enough, by com-

FIGURE 11–19

Supercomputers analyzed millions of pieces of data before coming up with the optimum design for the hull of the *Stars and Stripes,* the 12-meter sailing yacht that won the America's Cup race held in Australia. Plausible designs were suggested and tested (by simulation) for seaworthiness and speed until the winning hull was identified. On-board computers charted the best course and suggested sail trims. (Leo Mason/Image Bank. Inset: Courtesy of Cray Research, Inc.)

puters that actually helped make the products they had helped design. This linked process has come to be called CAD/CAM, an acronym for computer-aided design/computer-aided manufacturing.

For years, engineers and architects have turned to computers for help in designing automobiles and buildings. By experimenting with various computer-aided designs for the outer shells of cars, engineers are able to create models with lower wind resistance—which leads to both greater fuel economy and road stability. Architects can "sketch" basic structures on their computers, add or subtract features, and show how the structure will look from all angles. This graphic capability enables those who will be buying or leasing the planned buildings to customize them to their needs before the first brick is laid (Figure 11-19).

Essentially, computer graphics involve the construction and manipulation of images on a screen for various artistic, business, educational, industrial, and scientific uses. The advantages of computer graphics over older forms is that they are faster and less expensive to produce, and are more versatile in their applications (Figure 11-20).

SUMMARY

Computer graphics is what we call the images created by people using computers with graphics software. Graphics software includes the programs used to create, edit, display, and print those images. The computer with graphics software can help the user (1) to create images on a screen, and (2) to manipulate those images.

Some graphics software requires coprocessors—separate chips inside the computer that take some of the load from the main processor. Computers create graphics in different ways: text graphics are created with text characters; bitmapped (pixel-oriented) graphics are comprised of bitmaps of individual pixels; and vector graphics (object-oriented graphics) are mathematically defined by establishing control points on the screen.

Some programs permit several degrees of resolution (the sharpness and clarity of the image). Pixels, or picture elements, are the individual dots that make up the display screen. The more pixels a display screen has, the higher the resolution or quality of the image.

A variety of input devices can be used, including a keyboard, mouse, light pen, graphics tablet, scanner, and video camera. Output from graphics programs can be saved on disk, viewed on a computer screen, projected on a large screen, printed, transmitted to a film recorder to make 35 mm slides, or transferred to a service bureau for conversion into color slides or overhead transparencies.

There are three basic types of graphics programs: paint and draw programs, design programs, and chart/graph and presentation graphics programs. Paint and draw features are sometimes combined into one program but are available as separate programs. Presentation graphics are those prepared for a formal presentation along with other materials for the presentation (flip charts, speeches, notes, etc.).

Graphs for presentation should be simple, accurate, and make a visual impact to get the point across.

Graphics software contains a variety of features, including different graph types, numerous image-manipulation options, color, fill patterns, grid, template, and many more.

Areas now using computer graphics include simulations and training, commercial art, fine art, medicine, and product design.

Vocabulary Self-Test

Can you define the following?

animation (p. 362)

aspect ratio (p. 348)

bar graph (p. 355)

bitmap (p. 345)

bitmapped graphics (p. 345)

chart/graph program (p. 353)

clip art (p. 362)

computer-aided design (CAD) (p. 351)

computer graphics (p. 345)

copy (p. 359)

cut and paste (p. 359)

design program (p. 351)

drag (p. 359)

draw program (p. 349)

graphics software (p. 345)

grid (p. 360)

kerning (p. 361)

lasso (p. 359)

line graph (p. 355)

mirror (p. 362)

paint program (p. 349)

pan (p. 362)

pie chart (p. 355)

pixels (p. 345)

presentation graphics (p. 353)

resolution (p. 345)

rotate (p. 359)

scale (p. 359)

scatter graph (p. 356)

select (p. 359)

simulation (p. 351)

slide show (p. 353)

stacked-line graph (p. 356)

superimpose (p. 359)

text graphics (p. 345)

vector graphics (p. 346)

word chart (p. 357)

zoom (p. 361)

Review Questions

Multiple Choice

1. Graphics are generated by a computer in one of three ways: _____.
   a. animated, simulated, designed
   b. text, bitmapped, vector
   c. modular, animated, bitmapped
   d. vector, modular, charted

2. The _____ generates 35 mm slides to be used with a standard slide projector.
   a. film stripper
   b. laser printer
   c. film recorder
   d. plotter

3. _____ are vector-based, letting the user create illustrations and line art.
   a. Draw programs
   b. Paint programs
   c. Presentation graphics programs
   d. Chart programs

4. _____ are bitmapped programs that let you create images simulating the texture of an artist's brush stroke.
   a. Draw programs
   b. Paint programs
   c. Film graphics programs
   d. CAD programs

5. Which program would you use if you were an architect using a computer to draw plans for a client's new home? _____ .
   a. draw program
   b. paint program
   c. presentation graphics
   d. design program

6. _____ programs are used by business people to make a formal presentation.
   a. Draw
   b. Paint
   c. Presentation graphics
   d. Design

7. The _____ feature in some programs allows you to use a series of graphics, displaying them on the monitor and specifying their sequence and timing.
   a. undo
   b. word chart
   c. rotate
   d. slide show

8. When one uses the _____ feature, an identical downward line will be drawn automatically when a line is drawn upward.
   a. draw and copy
   b. copy
   c. mirror
   d. pan

9. A library of ready-drawn pictures (for example, trees, houses, and business icons) is called _____ .
   a. clip art
   b. simulation
   c. draw and paint
   d. copy

10. A study at the Wharton Business School's Applied Research Center demonstrated that _____ .
    a. 35 mm slides and slide projectors are seldom used in formal business presentation
    b. graphics make the point faster and more persuasively in a formal business presentation
    c. paint and draw programs are the most popular type of graphics program
    d. design programs are the most popular type of graphics program

Fill-in

1. The _____ ratio is the relationship of the width to the height of an image.
2. _____ software lets artists and nonartists alike create pictures and images on a computer.
3. A(n) _____ chart shows the relationship of the parts to a whole.
4. A(n) _____ graph shows the correlation between two sets of data.
5. A(n) _____ chart, the most popular type of chart used in presentations, is comprised of text, sometimes in bulleted or numbered lists.
6. The sharpness or clarity of an image is referred to as its _____ .
7. A(n) _____ is a pattern of horizontal and vertical lines that guide you in entering, visualizing, and pinpointing data.
8. The _____ feature shows an image from various angles, making it look like a tangible object.
9. The ability to simulate motion is called _____ .
10. Simplicity, accuracy, and visual impact are qualities of a good _____ .

Short Answer

1. How do "text graphics" create images?
2. How do vector (object-oriented) programs differ from bitmapped (pixel-oriented) programs?
3. What do pixels have to do with resolution?
4. List several possible input devices you can use with graphics programs.
5. Name several devices to which you can output graphic images.
6. Which type of graphics software is best suited for creating solids and filling them with patterns and textures similar to those created using a brush?
7. Why is a stand-alone chart program preferred for graphs used in a formal presentation rather than using those incorporated in an electronic spreadsheet like Lotus 1-2-3?
8. What type of graph—bar, pie, or line—would best show what percentage of your budget was spent on entertainment?
9. Describe four image-manipulation features (features that let you move around the image on the screen).
10. Describe two factors to consider when trying to create a strong visual impact and assure that the viewer's focus will go to the right place on a graph.

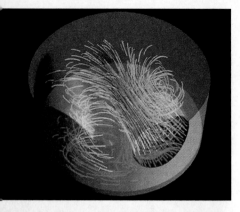

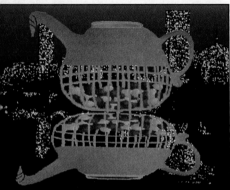

OUTLINE

COMMUNICATION BASICS

Setting Communication Parameters I
Emulating a Dumb Terminal

APPLICATION OF COMMUNICATION
SOFTWARE

MAKING THE CONNECTION

Command Mode I Data-Transfer Mode I
Automatic Dialing I Autoanswer I
Automatic Message Transfer I Pacing
Option

DATA CAPTURE

FILE TRANSFER

Transferring a File I File-Transfer
Protocols

ADDITIONAL FEATURES

Macros I File Protection I Error Handling I
Character Stripping I Break Signal I
Time On-Line Status

OBJECTIVES

☐ Define the purpose of communication software.

☐ Identify several applications for
using communication software.

☐ Describe the two general functions of a communications
package.

☐ Understand how files are transferred.

☐ List and define several common features of communication
packages.

CHAPTER TWELVE

Microcomputer
Communications

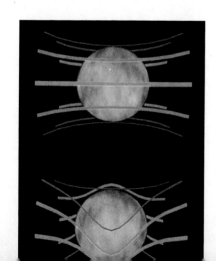

PROFILE

Grace Murray Hopper

Not many soon-to-be octogenarians make major career moves like this one, but in 1986, Grace Murray Hopper, at age 79, retired as a rear admiral in Naval Data Automation Command in the U.S. Navy to serve as senior consultant at Digital Equipment Corporation.

Admiral Hopper is widely known in the computer field for helping to develop early computers, and she is well-known among students and members of the computer industry as a lecturer and spokesperson for innovation. During her presentations, she discusses information processing and the nature and importance of information.

Hopper, a native of New York City, attended Vassar College and went on to receive her master's degree and doctorate from Yale University. Her work in computer technology has been conducted in a mixed environment that includes the academic scene, the business world, and the military.

After joining the U.S. Naval Reserve in 1944, she worked with Howard Aiken to program the Mark I, the first large-scale digital calculator. Besides teaching in colleges and universities, she was senior mathematician for Eckert-Mauchley Computer Corporation and worked for Sperry Corporation as system engineer and later staff scientist in system programming. Part of this time Hopper was on military leave. She helped develop UNIVAC I, the first large commercial computer, and she was instrumental in creating the COBOL programming language.

In 1966, she was retired at the age of 60 (the Navy thought she was too old) with the rank of commander in the U.S. Naval Reserves. Within seven months, however, Hopper was recalled to active duty. Much of her military service has been dedicated to helping run all the Navy's non-weapons computers and keeping the Navy at the leading edge of computer technology. Now, she has retired from the Naval Reserves a second time, once again moving into private industry.

Hopper has received world recognition and many honors as one of the outstanding contributors to the computer revolution. One unique honor was presented in 1969, when the Data Processing Management Association selected her as their first Computer Sciences "Man of the Year." There has been no higher award, she says, than that of the privilege and responsibility of service in the U.S. Navy.

When *Computerworld* senior editor Janet Fiderio asked her if society has become too dependent on computers, she replied, "Well, we used to be dependent on paper. What difference does it make that our information is on computer or paper?" Fiderio answered, "Computers can fail." Hopper responded, "And paper can burn."

Because of its ability to communicate and share data with other computers, the microcomputer has become an important tool for research, data gathering, and information exchange. This is evidenced by the growing number of employees who are discovering that the best place to work is at home. Their "home offices" are made possible by the sophistication of microcomputers and the ease of using communication software to link them with the "work office" or customers at remote locations.

In the past, modems and associated communications software were luxuries or extras when one purchased a microcomputer system. Today, alongside spreadsheets, databases, and word processors, communication software is becoming equally important to a complete system. This chapter examines communication software for microcomputers.

COMMUNICATION BASICS

Communication software is a program designed to control communication between two computers. Communication software:

- ☐ Establishes and maintains communication with another computer.
- ☐ Tells the computer how to send data (i.e., determines the communication parameters).
- ☐ Directs outgoing data from the keyboard or disks through the communication port and into a modem, and directs incoming data from the communication port to the screen or disk.

> **Purposes of Communication Software**
>
> - Establish and maintain communication with another computer
> - Set communication parameters
> - Direct outgoing and incoming data

There are many communication programs with a wide variety of options. But no matter how sophisticated or how basic the program, it must be able to perform two general functions: (1) set essential communication parameters, and (2) emulate a dumb terminal (defined below).

Setting Communication Parameters

Computers communicate using much the same logical sequences as people making a telephone call. First, someone initiates the call; second, at the other end the call must be received and answered. Once the connection is made, any conversation must take place in the same language, whether between two people or two computers, for the information exchange to be meaningful. If you do not understand what the other person has said, you can have them repeat it. Similarly, the computer can acknowledge an error in transmission and retransmit. Finally, when all is said and done, the communication link is broken by hanging up.

In most cases, the computer doing the calling is responsible for matching the characteristics of the computer receiving the call. To do this, four essential **communication parameters** must match:

- ☐ Baud rate of the transmission.
- ☐ Number of data bits used to create each character.
- ☐ Number of stop bits.
- ☐ Type of parity checking used for error checking during transmission.

The *baud rate* is the number of times per second that the signal being transmitted changes (modulates or demodulates). The *number of data bits* that make up a character is user-specified; in microcomputer communication, characters are made up of either seven or eight bits. Each character is surrounded by *start and stop bits,* which allow the receiving terminal to synchronize itself with the transmitting terminal on a character-by-character basis. The start bit is always a zero bit. Depending on what the receiving computer expects, there are usually one or two stop bits. The appropriate number of stop bits is also user-specified.

The *parity bit* is used to check for transmission errors. Three parity-checking options are generally used with microcomputer communication: even, odd, or none. To specify odd or even parity, the number of data bits that make up a character must be seven so that the eighth bit can be used for the parity setting. When the number of data bits is set at eight, the parity setting is always none because all the bits are used to make up the character. The "none" option can also be chosen for seven-bit characters.

The computer receiving the data adds all the "one" bits to see if they total an odd or even number. If the parity setting is odd and the bit total is odd, or the setting is even and the bit total is even, the computer assumes the data were sent correctly. If the parity setting is odd and the bit total is even, or the setting is even and the bit total is odd, the computer is alerted that an error in data transmission has occurred. Many programs allow the user to choose how a parity error is handled. For example, the user may set the program to signal that an error has occurred or to ignore the error.

Parity checking is only an elementary form of error checking. It cannot detect errors such as the loss of an entire character or larger block of data. For successful communication, both sending and receiving, computers must use the same values for each parameter. These values, along with

FIGURE 12–1
Default status screen for Crosstalk XVI communications software. (Photo by Jo Hall/Macmillan)

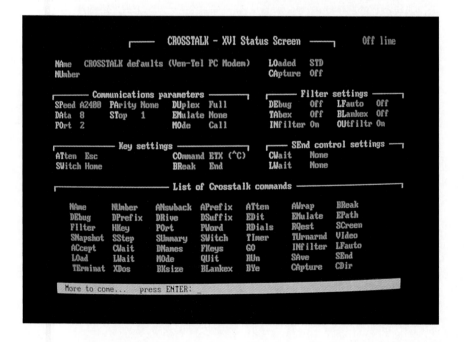

other parameters, often have default values that can be viewed and changed from a set-up menu (Figure 12–1).

Emulating a Dumb Terminal

A communication package also must cause the user's microcomputer to emulate a dumb terminal—to operate in what is called, in most programs, the terminal mode. A **dumb terminal** is a stand-alone keyboard and display screen unit that can only send data to, or receive data from, a computer to which it is connected. A dumb terminal cannot function as a stand-alone computer.

It is essential that the microcomputer emulate a dumb terminal, because most minicomputers and mainframes used in business or information services expect to see a certain type of terminal, and will only communicate with this kind of terminal. For example, if the host is a Digital Equipment Corporation (DEC) VAX system, it may expect to see a DEC VT-100 terminal. In the terminal emulation mode, your microcomputer can be configured to appear as a DEC VT-100 terminal to the host.

APPLICATION OF COMMUNICATION SOFTWARE

Much of our society is built around acquisition, manipulation, and use of information. The traditional approach to gathering information often meant long hours of research to find the appropriate sources, and then more time to pore over the vast amounts of data and to extract pertinent material. Today, however, many computerized information services have large databases that provide needed data, in usable form, in a fraction of the time needed for manual research. Databases are available for practically any topic—medicine, science, finance, weather, sports, and so on. Communication software establishes the necessary link between a microcomputer and the computers that run these databases.

In addition to providing information, services such as shopping and banking can be accomplished using communication software. You can follow your favorite stock through many of the financial services that may be reached via computer.

Communication software lets you keep in touch and exchange ideas with other professionals or with users of the same type of computer equipment through bulletin boards and electronic mail. Exchanging files from computer to computer means that information can be sent and retrieved in seconds or minutes instead of days.

Telecommuting has become an alternative workstyle for many as they use their computers at home to communicate with the computer at their office.

Popular microcomputer communication software includes Crosstalk, BLAST, PC-Talk, and Smartcom.

MAKING THE CONNECTION

Now let's examine how computers talk to each other using communication software. As noted, two computers must speak the same language to suc-

TIME TO CALL HOME
Paging devices have been around forever, it seems. You see them clipped to the belts or bulging in the purses of doctors, lawyers, account executives, and others who want to always be accessible to the world's telephones. These "beepers" emit an audible signal that alerts the wearer to call the office for a message. Some pagers display the phone number of the person calling. Usually they are hooked into a fairly small geographic paging system.

But watch out: the pager of tomorrow has arrived. And it looks like a wrist watch. Indeed, it is a wrist watch, but it's also much more. Developed as a joint venture between American Telephone and Electronics Corporation and Japan's Hattori Seiko Company, the watch/pager is built around tiny silicon chips. Its antenna is in the watch band.

Not only is the watch/pager system smaller, faster, and farther-reaching than conventional paging technology, it's also less expensive. It can display on its face the caller's phone number or short messages, such as "Call Home" or "Call Office." In fact, the device has the capacity to store and show even longer messages. Its developers hope that people who would not carry an ordinary beeper will be eager to strap on this functional piece of technological jewelry.

It's getting harder to lose ourselves!

cessfully complete a communication link. To accomplish this, both the transmitting and receiving computer must be on-line. **On-line** means the user's computer is linked to, and communicating with, another computer. **Off-line** means that no communication link is established.

To accomplish the transfer of data, both the transmitting computer and the receiving computer must have a modem. The modem converts analog signals to digital signals, and digital signals back to analog signals, so that communication can take place between the computers.

The ability to operate in both full-duplex and half-duplex modes is another feature of some programs. Communication between microcomputers, and between microcomputers and mainframes, usually takes place in full-duplex mode; however, many information services and bulletin boards operate only in half-duplex mode. (To review the full-duplex and half-duplex modes, see Chapter 5.)

Once the communication parameters are set and the computers are on-line, the link can be established. Many of the features are performed automatically.

FIGURE 12–2
Crosstalk command summary
window. (Photo by Jo Hall/
Macmillan)

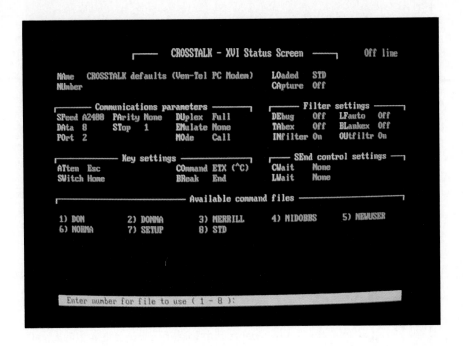

Command Mode

Most communication programs have at least two modes, a command
mode and a data transfer (or conversation) mode. In the **command
mode,** whatever is typed at the keyboard is interpreted as a command.
These commands vary among programs. A command summary window is
shown in Figure 12–2.

Data-Transfer Mode

In the **data-transfer mode,** communication actually occurs. Most programs automatically switch between the command and data-transfer
modes without disconnecting the communication link. The mode-
switching feature allows you to temporarily leave the data-transfer mode
and enter the command mode (for example, to display a disk directory,
delete a file, or activate a printer), and then to reenter the data-transfer
mode. To transfer data, however, one computer must initiate the call and
the other computer must be ready to receive it.

Call Mode. The computer that dials another computer must be placed in
the call mode. Settings are made in the call mode, such as the baud rate,
entering the phone number, and other communication parameters necessary to dial another computer.

Answer Mode. To complete a call, the computer must be on and ready to
receive it. When receiving a call, the computer must be in the answer

mode, in which it is alerted to watch for an incoming signal from the modem.

Automatic Dialing

Automatic dialing automatically dials the phone number of another computer, using information stored in a directory. A directory can contain names, telephone numbers, and communication parameters. It can also hold the **log-on sequence,** which is the series of keystrokes, account numbers, and passwords needed to access a computer or information service. With one or more keystrokes, the program automatically dials and connects to the specified computer, using the information stored in the directory (**directory storage**). To store that information, a particular communication session need be described only once; it is saved and easily accessed over and over again.

Programs differ in the amount of space available for each directory entry and for the total number of directory entries. Some, such as PC-Talk III, provide enough space for access numbers, account numbers, and passwords. In addition, they permit programming the function keys to enter a particular log-on sequence automatically. SmartCom II, among others, comes with the log-on sequences for some of the popular information services already programmed. You simply supply the account number and password to the file to make it usable.

Autoanswer

When the computer is on, the **autoanswer** feature, in conjunction with the appropriate modem, automatically answers calls from other computers. It creates a bulletin board file and receives electronic mail even when the user is not present.

Automatic Message Transfer

The **automatic message transfer** feature automatically dials a specified computer and leaves a message at a preset time.

Pacing Option

Sometimes the rate at which one computer can send data and the rate at which the other computer can receive data are not the same. Also, some receiving computers require the transmitting computer to wait for a special prompt before sending data. These situations are often found in microcomputer-to-mainframe communications. The **pacing** feature allows you to determine a specified time to wait between sending instructions. It also can instruct a program to wait for a specified character that prompts the transmitting computer to begin sending data.

DATA CAPTURE

Data capture is the process of retrieving data from a remote computer and storing it in main memory or secondary storage. A data **buffer** is an area set aside in main memory to temporarily store data. Many communication programs provide a data buffer that allows you to capture data and review, search, and edit it before saving on a disk. Or, it gives the option of discarding the contents of the buffer without saving it. A data buffer conserves disk space by allowing you to select and save only useful data.

Data received after a disk is full may be saved in a buffer or may be lost, depending on the program. Some communication programs provide a status indicator that tells how much buffer space is left. If this indicator is ignored, however, the buffer may become full and any data that overflow will be lost. With better programs, when the buffer becomes full, overflow data are automatically saved on a disk. Other programs issue a warning when the disk is full so that you can change disks or erase files from the current disk to make room. Data stored in the buffer are volatile. If the computer is turned off or data are erased before storing them on a disk, they are lost.

Another data-capturing capability in some programs is the option to send data directly to a printer as they are received. They also are usually displayed simultaneously on the screen. The printer must be able to print at the same rate that data are being sent, or data will be lost. However, use of a buffer allows communication at higher baud rates than the printer would normally handle. Print spoolers (a type of buffer) allow data to be temporarily stored and sent to the printer at the proper rate.

FILE TRANSFER

Communication programs allow transmission and reception of files between computers. This procedure is called uploading and downloading. **Uploading** occurs when data from a disk are sent to another computer, and **downloading** occurs when data are received from another computer and saved on disk. Almost all communication programs will upload and download data; otherwise, the program's usefulness would be very limited.

You can create a file on a disk before going on-line, and then upload it from that disk and send it. This procedure significantly reduces editing time spent on-line, thus lowering the cost of a communication session. Downloading lets you receive data on a disk; the data can then be read or edited off-line afterward. This process can dramatically reduce the cost of using information services such as CompuServe and The Source, where charges are based upon on-line time.

Transferring a File

In addition to capturing data, communication software allows transfer of complete files from one computer to another. Entire files are not transferred all at once, but in blocks. A **block** is a preset number of bytes that is transferred as a unit. For example, if the block size is 512 bytes, those 512 bytes sent by one computer must be received by the remote computer before the next block of data is sent. If there is an error, sending a file in blocks requires only the defective block to be resent, rather than the entire file. The block format is used both in sending or requesting a file.

Transmitting a File. When a file is sent from your computer to another, you are transmitting a file. A file may be transmitted between compatible computers—those using the same communication software—or may be transmitted between incompatible computers or systems using different communication software.

Transfer of files between dissimilar computers or computers with different software usually is much slower than between compatible computers and software. This can be caused by the systems operating at different speeds with different capabilities.

Requesting a File. In addition to transmitting a file, the caller may also request a file from the remote computer. The ability of the caller to initiate a file request eliminates the need for both computers to hang up and reestablish the contact. Built-in safeguards usually prevent the caller from roaming freely in the remote computer's files.

Whether files are sent or received, they can be checked for errors using a communication protocol.

File-Transfer Protocols

File-transfer protocols are sets of rules that ensure error-free transfer of data. They are usually supplied as built-in options that can be selected as needed. Some programs let you define a specific protocol.

Both computers in the link must use the same protocol for data transfer to take place. Because some protocols employ extensive error-checking, their use can increase data-transfer time. Some common protocols offered by communication programs include XON/XOFF, Xmodem, and Kermit.

The **XON/XOFF protocol** controls the transfer of text data. An XOFF signal tells the transmitting computer to stop sending data until it receives an XON signal to resume. In some programs, this protocol is invoked directly from the keyboard to stop data transmission temporarily. In others, it is automatic. This procedure prevents overflowing the data buffer.

The public-domain **Xmodem protocol** is widely used with microcomputers for sending and receiving nontext (binary) files between dissimilar systems. Files are sent in 128-byte blocks. If the protocol detects an error, the entire block is resent. If the block cannot be sent successfully, the Xmodem protocol terminates the transfer rather than send erroneous data. This termination warns that problems exist, either in the data or communication link. Xmodem protocol is public-domain software, or freeware, that is not copy-protected or copyrighted and is made available by its author for anyone to use.

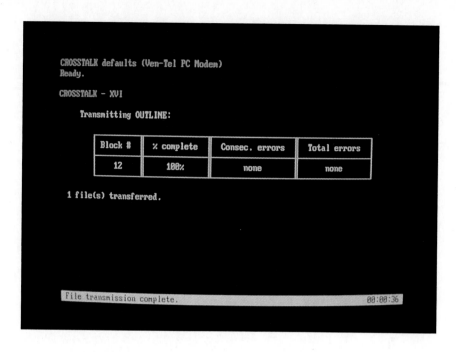

The **Kermit protocol,** developed at Columbia University, is popular on larger computers. It allows file transfer among many different types of systems.

A flexible communication program allows both text and nontext files to be sent and offers several protocols. Often, a screen will show the file transfer in progress (Figure 12–3).

ADDITIONAL FEATURES

Among other useful features often contained within a communication package is the ability to create macros, file protection, error handling, character stripping, break signals, and time on-line status.

Macros

Often you will use the communication program to call the same number. Some programs allow you to create a macro file (sometimes called a command file) that stores the log-on sequence of commands, such as the phone number and baud rate. You then have only to call up the command file, which will perform the log-on sequence automatically.

Another type of macro is the **script file,** a group of commands written in the communication package's own programming language. Script files automate the sequence of activities once the communication link is established.

File Protection

A **password** feature lets you create passwords to protect files, dialing directories, and other portions of the communication program from un-

THE NYSE AND TELECOMMUNICATION

Most brokers and specialists use preprinted slips and pencils to note the deals they make on the floor of the New York Stock Exchange (NYSE). They keep track of details such as how much stock is involved, who the parties in the deal are, and what the price per share is.

However, the paper method doesn't allow the trader the opportunity to review the details of the deal to make sure the broker wrote down and used the correct information. This paper method results in about 15 percent of the trades being questionable.

Now, there is a push for computerized trading. The person who acts as the auctioneer uses an electronic workstation while the brokers use hand-held terminals (a combination of laptop computer and telephone). The brokers enter the details of each deal on their terminals; the traders immediately see the transaction on the LCD display and lock them in or fix any mistakes. Besides eliminating the paper mess at the end of the day of trading, stockbrokers would like to see the percentage of questionable trades drop to near zero.

authorized access. This feature is valuable if sensitive data are involved, or if several people can access the communication program.

The **encryption** feature creates an unreadable version of a file before it is transmitted. A decrypt feature recreates the readable version of an encrypted file after it is received. This feature can ensure the confidentiality of a file as it is sent over communication lines.

Error Handling

There are many different ways a program can alert you to your own errors. The methods vary among programs, but a good program should indicate what the error is and, if possible, suggest steps to recover from the error.

Character Stripping

This feature lets you inspect, change, or delete any character as it leaves or enters the computer. For example, if an incoming text file contains special control characters (for formatting or printing) that are incompatible with your word processor, the program can delete those characters or change them to compatible codes.

Break Signal

The **break signal** tells the receiving computer to stop or interrupt current operation without disconnecting the communication link. (However, if the standard DOS break sequence—the Ctrl-Break sequence on IBM PCs and compatibles—were used, the risk would be extremely high of terminating the communication program, the communication link, or both.)

Time On-Line Status

Some programs monitor and display the time spent on-line during a communication session. This helps you budget the cost incurred for each communication session.

SUMMARY

Communication software is a program that controls the communication process between two computers. All communication programs must be able to set these communication parameters: baud rate, number of data bits used to create each character, number of stop bits, and type of parity checking. All programs also must be able to emulate a dumb terminal, which is a keyboard and display screen that can only send data to or receive data from another computer.

Communication programs can link computers to information services, bulletin boards, and electronic mail systems. From these services you can capture data into your computer.

Transfer of files takes place in units called blocks, which are small segments of data measured in bytes. The caller may elect to transmit a file or to request a file from a remote computer.

Two powerful features of a communication package are its abilities to upload (send data from disk to another computer) and to download (receive data from another computer and save on disk). Other features include multiple data-capturing options, switching between program modes, and multiple file-transfer protocols (the rules for the transfer of data).

Vocabulary Self-Test

Can you define the following?

autoanswer (p. 382)

automatic dialing (p. 382)

automatic message transfer (p. 382)

block (p. 383)

break signal (p. 386)

buffer (p. 383)

command mode (p. 381)

communication parameters (p. 377)

communication software (p. 377)

data capture (p. 383)

data-transfer mode (p. 381)

directory storage (p. 382)

downloading (p. 383)

dumb terminal (p. 379)

encryption (p. 386)

file-transfer protocols (p. 384)

Kermit protocol (p. 385)

log-on sequence (p. 382)

off-line (p. 380)

on-line (p. 380)

pacing (p. 382)

password (p. 385)

script files (p. 385)

uploading (p. 383)

Xmodem protocol (p. 384)

XON/XOFF protocol (p. 384)

Review Questions

Multiple Choice

1. In microcomputer communications, a character is made up of
   _____ bit(s).
   a. 8 or 9
   b. 7 or 8
   c. 0 or 1
   d. none, 0, or 1

2. The _____ feature allows you to determine a specified time to wait
   between sending instructions.
   a. pacing
   b. timing
   c. message transfer
   d. file-transfer

3. A _____ is a type of buffer that allows data to be stored and sent to a
   printer at the proper rate.
   a. print spooler
   b. register
   c. data buffer
   d. CPU

4. To ensure error-free transfer of data between two computers, the proper
   _____ must be set.
   a. voltage
   b. spooler
   c. protocol
   d. break signal

5. The public-domain _____ protocol sends and receives binary files.
   a. Kermit
   b. ASCII
   c. XON/XOFF
   d. Xmodem

6. In the _____ protocol, if a block cannot be sent without errors, it is
   not sent at all.
   a. Xmodem
   b. ASCII
   c. XON/XOFF
   d. Kermit

7. A type of macro file used to store a sequence of log-on commands is called
   a _____ file.
   a. script
   b. command
   c. program
   d. communication

8. A type of macro file used to store a sequence of program-language
   commands is called a _____ file.
   a. script
   b. command
   c. program
   d. communication

9. If you wanted to transmit private data in unreadable form so that unauthorized people could not use it, you would use the _____ feature.
   a. validation
   b. password
   c. encryption
   d. verification

10. The type of signal used to interrupt data communication without disconnecting the communication link is the _____.
    a. pause
    b. insert
    c. time
    d. break

Fill-in

1. The _____ is the number of times per second that a signal being transmitted changes (modulates or demodulates).

2. A(n) _____ is a keyboard and display screen that can only send data to and receive data from another computer.

3. The _____ is the mode in which anything typed at the keyboard is interpreted as a command.

4. The mode in which communication actually takes place is called the _____ mode.

5. A computer that is watching the modem for a signal is in the _____ mode.

6. _____ is the process of sending data from a disk to another computer via a communication link.

7. _____ occurs when data from a disk are sent to another computer.

8. Receiving data from a computer via a communication link and saving them on a disk is called _____.

9. The caller has the option of two file-transfer functions—to send or _____ a file, and to ask for, or _____ a file.

10. The sets of rules for the transfer of data are called _____.

Short Answer

1. What is the purpose of a communication package?

2. What two functions are all communication programs capable of?

3. List the four basic parameters that a communication program establishes.

4. What is the purpose of the start and stop bits that surround a character during transmission?

5. What is the function of the parity bit?

6. What are the three parity-checking options commonly available for microcomputer communication?

7. Define on-line and off-line as they relate to the communication process.

8. What is a log-on sequence?

9. Describe the autoanswer and automatic message transfer features of a communication program.

10. What is the purpose of transferring a file in blocks?

APPENDIX A

History of Computers

One view of the history of computers goes back thousands of years to the Chinese abacus as the earliest computing device. Our view will narrow that scope to advances beginning in the 1950s, the era of the first generation of commercial computers, and will concentrate on the people largely responsible for the advances.

This appendix rounds out your perspective of computers by examining how they have evolved. Computer history is filled with extraordinary advances and exciting, sometimes strange people. So remarkable has been the progress that in 1981, students used a Radio Shack TRS–80 microcomputer to outperform a 51-foot-long 1944 computer. Today's typical microcomputer would demolish the 1981 record!

VACUUM-TUBE TECHNOLOGY

In 1951 John Mauchly and J. Presper Eckert formed a company to create a commercially usable general-purpose computer, the UNIVAC I. The UNIVAC I was the first general-purpose computer designed specifically for business data-processing applications. The UNIVAC I's claim to fame was its successful 1952 presidential election prediction, with only five percent of the votes counted, that Dwight Eisenhower would defeat Adlai Stevenson. Previously, computers had been used solely for scientific or military applications. The U.S. Census Bureau immediately installed UNIVAC I and used it for over 12 years. In 1954 the General Electric Company in Louisville, Kentucky, used UNIVAC I to process the first computerized payroll. It wasn't long before other companies—including Burroughs (now called UNISYS), Honeywell, and IBM—realized the commercial value of computers to the business community and began developing their own machines.

From 1950 to 1952 the U.S. Navy and the Digital Computer Lab at MIT developed the Whirlwind computer, another early vacuum-tube, stored-program computer. One of the students involved in the Whirlwind's development was Ken Olsen, later the founder of Digital Equipment Corporation (DEC). The Whirlwind simulated high-performance trainer aircraft, contained self-diagnostics, and performed 50,000 operations per second; however, it was only about 85 percent accurate.

CHIP TECHNOLOGY

Other innovators appeared on the scene in the late 1950s. Both Jack Kilby at Texas Instruments and Robert Noyce at Fairchild Semiconductor discovered that resistors, capacitors, and transistors could be made from the same semiconductor material at the same time. Any number of transistors could be etched on silicon and thus the integrated circuit was born and refined. During this time the integrated circuit came to be called a "chip." Integrated circuits were finally mass-produced in 1962 and became instrumental in computer designs of the mid-1960s.

Miniaturization came about through various technological innovations. Combining this miniaturization with the commercial success of computers led Ken Olsen and DEC to produce the first minicomputer, the PDP–1, in 1963. Its successor, the PDP–8, was the first commercially available minicomputer. It was considerably less expensive than a mainframe, and small companies could afford to computerize their operations.

Gene Amdahl's revolutionary IBM System/360 series of mainframe computers also was introduced in the 1960s. These were the first general purpose digital computers using integrated-circuit technology. The IBM System/360 offered a "family" of computers: small but growing companies could start with a relatively small and inexpensive computer system, and as the company grew, larger and more powerful computers from the same family could be added. Because the software was compatible, programs could be shared by all the computers in the family.

By 1970 Intel had created a memory chip that could store a kilobit of information. (A kilobit translates roughly into 25 five-letter words.) Another innovation at Intel came from Ted Hoff, who further improved the integrated circuit by compressing 12 chips into 4. The arithmetic and logic functions of several chips could be contained on a single chip, called a microprocessor. This microprocessor, the Intel 4004 ("forty-oh-four"), made development of the microcomputer a possibility. However, the 4004 could handle only four bits of data at a time. Eventually, eight-bit microprocessor chips were developed.

MICROCOMPUTERS

The earliest microcomputer, the Altair 8800, was developed in 1975 by Ed Roberts. Roberts, called the "father of the microcomputer," founded a company called Micro Instrumentation Telemetry Systems (MITS). He developed the Altair to be sold in kit form to consumers (mainly hobbyists) for $395. This computer used an early Intel microprocessor and had less than 1KB of memory. Competition for the Altair appeared in 1977 in the form of Tandy's TRS−80 Model 1, sold through Radio Shack stores, and the Personal Electronic Transactor (PET) from Commodore Business Machines.

Many microcomputer companies have come and gone, but one of the great rags-to-riches stories is Apple Computer. Founded by Steven Jobs and Stephen Wozniak, the partners' first headquarters was Jobs's garage. Wozniak, the technical expert, made a microcomputer small and affordable enough for both the individual and the small businessperson. Because Jobs knew very little about circuitry or coding, he provided the marketing impetus for the small company. (See the Profile of Jobs and Wozniak in Chapter 11.)

Although the microcomputer business boomed, total accumulated sales remained below one million units until IBM entered the fray. For years IBM had manufactured and marketed office equipment and large computer systems. In 1981 they presented their IBM Personal Computer (IBM PC), using a 16-bit microprocessor. This introduction helped legitimize the microcomputer's use in business.

Also in 1981, other computer giants—Xerox and Digital Equipment Corporation—released their versions of microcomputers. The same year, Adam Osborne introduced a truly portable microcomputer, the Osborne 1, weighing only 24 pounds, with a 64 kilobyte memory, a price around $1,795, and a manufacturing time of just over an hour, using only 40 screws! Today, microcomputers are marketed by Sony, Hewlett-Packard, NEC, North Star, Zenith, and many others.

Computers have made their presence known so widely that in 1982 *Time* magazine chose the computer as its "Man of the Year," an honor awarded to someone (or in this case, some machine) who has made a difference in the world. The computer most assuredly has done so.

By 1984, the IBM PC had become the industry standard, with hundreds of companies designing software for it. IBM did not stay atop the heap for long, however. Almost every microcomputer manufacturer soon presented its version of their popular design. These "IBM PC compatibles," or "clones" are machines that run the IBM PC software and work with other IBM PC equipment. IBM PC compatibles are made by Tandy, Epson, Dell, Advanced Logic Research, Everex, and Compaq, and many others.

Another benchmark in the microcomputer revolution was the introduction by Apple of its Macintosh in the early 1980s. The Macintosh was visually oriented, and its mouse made it remarkably easy to use. It was praised for its ability to produce graphics and text of near-typeset quality, using Apple's LaserWriter laser printer.

In 1986 the Compaq DeskPro 386 computer, the first to use the powerful 32-bit Intel 80386 microprocessor, was introduced. The year 1987 saw the introduction of new microcomputers by both IBM and Apple. IBM introduced its new line, the PS/2 series, based on a new "microchannel" architecture. Apple moved into the business world by introducing its powerful Macintosh II computer. Microsoft Corporation also introduced a new operating system for microcomputers, called OS/2, that allowed application programs to take advantage of the newer computers' multitasking abilities. Steven Jobs also reentered the microcomputer market with his NeXT computer in 1988, specifically oriented toward the education market.

PROGRAMMING LANGUAGES

Concurrently, advances were being made in programming languages. High-level, English-like programming languages began to be developed in the mid-1950s. FORTRAN (FORmula TRANslator) was developed by John Backus and a group of IBM engineers as the first problem-oriented, algebraic programming language for mathematicians and scientists. Retired Rear Admiral Grace Murray Hopper (see Profile in Chapter 12) was instrumental in developing COBOL (COmmon Business-Oriented Language) as the first programming language designed for business data processing. Hopper also helped develop the UNIVAC I's compiler, a program that could translate other programs into machine language (the 1s and 0s that computers understand).

During the mid-1960s Dr. John Kemeny, a mathematics professor and president of Dartmouth, and his colleague, Dr. Thomas Kurtz, developed the computer language BASIC (Beginner's All-Purpose Symbolic Instruction Code). They later developed a version called True BASIC, which uses structured programming tools to make programs easier to read, debug, and update. Today there are numerous other high-level languages in use, including Pascal, C, and Logo. In addition, more sophisticated but easier to use fourth-generation languages began appearing in the 1980s.

SOFTWARE

The market for software had to grow as well. In 1974 Bill Gates (see Profile in Chapter 4) and Paul Allen developed Microsoft BASIC, a high-level language for microcomputers. The language was used by the MITS Altair in 1975. IBM then adopted Microsoft BASIC for its personal computers in 1981, a move that turned Microsoft into a thriving company. Most popular microcomputers—including the Apple II, Commodore 64, and Commodore PET—use Microsoft BASIC. Other successful Microsoft products include PC-DOS and MS-DOS, the operating system software that runs millions of personal computers.

The application software industry got its initial boost because Dan Bricklin, a Harvard Business School student, was not fond of the tedious mathematical calculations involved in preparing financial planning sheets, part of his assigned work. The worksheets were repetitive and required numerous hand calculations and recalculations to obtain meaningful results. Bricklin did not just wish for a better way; he teamed up with friend Bob Frankston and developed and marketed an electronic spreadsheet called VisiCalc. (See the Profile in Chapter 7.) At last businesspeople were able to justify purchasing the popular microcomputers—they now had useful software to perform business tasks. The microcomputer proved to be more than a typewriter.

VisiCalc was the first of its kind and stayed a best-selling package until 1983. At that time involvement in lawsuits prevented timely upgrades to the new 16-bit technology, and the software known as VisiCalc was not able to regain its popularity. Eventually, Bricklin sold VisiCalc and its rights to Lotus, Inc., where the popular spreadsheet Lotus 1-2-3 originated.

The late 1980s found Lotus involved in lawsuits against other spreadsheet software developers, claiming that the competition's software looked like Lotus and operated like Lotus—actions that have earned the nickname "look and feel" lawsuits.

Table A–1 lists many of the major contributors to the development of computers.

TECHNOLOGICAL EVOLUTION OF COMPUTERS

Computers have rapidly improved in speed, power, and efficiency. These changes are recognized as a progression of generations, each characterized by specific developments.

First Generation (1951–1959)

These early first-generation computers were powered by thousands of vacuum tubes. As a consequence, the UNIVAC I and others like it were physically large. The tubes themselves were large (the size of today's light bulbs), required lots of energy, and generated lots of heat.

Second Generation (1959–1965)

The device that characterized second-generation computers was the transistor. Like vacuum tubes, transistors control the flow of electricity through circuits. However, they are made of a "solid-state" semiconducting material, are smaller, less expensive, require less electricity, emit far less heat, are less fragile, and last longer. Fewer transistors were required to operate a computer.

Developed at Bell Labs in 1947 by William Shockley, John Bardeen, and W. H. Brattain, the transistor was first displayed to the public in 1948. Its inventors won the Nobel Prize in physics in 1956. This technological breakthrough allowed computers to become physically smaller, more powerful, more reliable, and even faster. Transistors were first used in computers in 1959.

TABLE A–1
Major contributors to computer development since 1950.

Date	Person	Contribution
1951	Mauchly and Eckert	Built UNIVAC I, first computer designed and sold commercially, specifically for business data-processing applications.
1950s	Hopper	Developed UNIVAC I compiler.
1957	Backus	With other IBM engineers helped develop FORTRAN.
1959	Kilby and Noyce	Developed and perfected the integrated circuit to be used in later computers.
1960s	Amdahl	Designed IBM System/360 series of mainframe computers, the first general-purpose digital computers to use integrated circuits.
1961	Hopper	Helped develop the COBOL programming language.
1963	Olsen	With DEC produced the PDP–1, the first minicomputer.
1965	Kemeny and Kurtz	Developed BASIC programming language, with True BASIC following later.
1970	Hoff	Developed the famous Intel 4004 microprocessor chip.
1975	Roberts	"Father of the microcomputer," designed the first microcomputer, the Altair 8800, in kit form.
1977	Jobs and Wozniak	Designed and built the first Apple microcomputer.
1978	Bricklin and Frankston	Designed VisiCalc, an electronic spreadsheet.
1981	IBM	Introduced IBM PC with 16-bit microprocessor.
1986	Compaq	Released the DeskPro 386 computer, first to use 80386 microprocessor.
1986	IBM	OS/2 Operating System technology.
1988	Compaq	Introduced the 80486 microcomputer
1988	Jobs	Introduced NeXT Computer
1988	Lotus	Updated the best-selling Lotus 1-2-3 spreadsheet software

Third Generation (1965–1971)

The use of integrated circuits (ICs) signified the beginning of third-generation computers. Just as the transistor miniaturized and improved the earlier vacuum-tube computers, computers with integrated circuits were smaller, more efficient, and more reliable than their transistorized predecessors. Unlike transistors and circuit boards which required manual assembly, the manufacture of ICs was automated, ultimately lowering prices. Memory technology improved and by 1969 as many as 1,000 transistors could be built on a chip of silicon.

A new computer program also came into being at this time, one that controlled the computer and its resources and used them more effectively. This new program was the operating system. It took control of the details of computer operation that human operators formerly had to exert, and thus allowed processing to proceed at computer speeds rather than human speeds.

Another phenomenon of this third generation was the introduction of *families* of computers. Previously, businesses had bought computers and programs and then found that, almost before the system was fully adapted, it was outdated or unable to grow with the firm's needs. IBM recognized this problem and created an entire product line, the IBM/360 series, which allowed for upgrading and expansion. Programs written for one computer were compatible with all other machines in the line. Businesses could upgrade or expand their data-processing operations as necessary.

In addition, Digital Equipment Corporation introduced the first minicomputer in November 1968. Its PDP–1 was substantially cheaper than a mainframe, thus making these smaller computers available to yet another business market.

Fourth Generation (1971–Present)

The significant distinction of our present fourth-generation computers is the large-scale integration (LSI) of chips containing several thousand transistors. In the mid-1970s the development of very-large-scale integration (VLSI) produced the chip called a microprocessor. Development of VLSI made the development of the microcomputer possible. This was followed by the Intel 80386 microprocessor, faster and more powerful than its predecessors.

The proliferation of application programs for microcomputers allowed home and business users to adapt their computers for word processing, spreadsheet manipulating, file handling, graphics creation, communication, games, and much more.

Fifth Generation (Future)

Although many people disagree on fifth-generation computer technology, some say that the creation and use of a computer with artificial intelligence represents that next step. The unofficial original goal was a "thinking machine" by 1990. Although expert systems are already being used for

TABLE A-2
Generations of computers and their characteristics

First Generation (1951–1959)
- Vacuum tubes
- Magnetic tape for external storage—some magnetic drums
- Punched cards for input
- Punched cards and paper for output
- Machine and assembly languages
- Human operators to set switches
- UNIVAC I, typical example

Second Generation (1959–1965)
- Transistors
- Magnetic-core storage
- Magnetic tape most common external storage, magnetic disk introduced
- Punched cards and magnetic tape for input
- Punched cards and paper for output
- High-level languages—FORTRAN, COBOL, BASIC, PL/1 and others
- Human operator to handle punched cards
- Honeywell 200, typical example

Third Generation (1965–1971)
- Integrated circuits
- Improved disk storage
- Monitors and keyboards for input and output
- More high-level languages, including RPG and Pascal
- Complete operating systems; less involvement for human operators
- Family of computers, allowing compatibility
- Minicomputers used commercially
- IBM System/360, typical example

Fourth Generation (1971–Present)
- LSI and VLSI
- Magnetic disk most common external storage
- Introduction of microcomputer
- Fourth-generation languages; application software for microcomputers
- Microcomputers used—IBM PC, typical example
- Burroughs B7700 and HP 3000 (minicomputer), typical examples

Fifth Generation (Future)
- Development of true artificial intelligence

specialized applications, true artificial intelligence—computers that can think—are still concepts of the mind.

Table A–2 lists the generations of computers and their respective characteristics. Note that programming languages, secondary storage, principal methods of input, and methods of operation also change with the generations. The future remains to be seen, of course. You may have some ideas or innovations of your own.

APPENDIX B

Issues and Trends

OUTLINE

COMPUTER CRIME
The Criminal I Difficulty of Detection and Prevention I Types of Computer Crimes
COMPUTERS AND THE RIGHT TO PRIVACY
JOB SECURITY
ELECTRONIC WORK MONITORING
HEALTH AND SAFETY
COMPUTER ETHICS
LEGISLATION
Copyright and Infringement
DIRECTIONS IN TECHNOLOGY
Artificial Intelligence I Neural Networks I Josephson Junction I Parallel Processing I
Chips I Optoelectronics
SOCIETY'S RESPONSE AND THE GLOBAL VILLAGE

Significant inventions such as the computer always crinkle our social fabric into dramatic new patterns that alter how things are produced, how we use them, and how they are protected by law. Very often, these inventions cause society to revise its ethical values, too.

Society never fully adjusts to new inventions. The automobile still haunts us, raising arguments about the need for legislation on drunk driving, seat belts, and airbags; the destruction of farmlands by interstate highways; and the legality of radar detectors. Society is now experiencing one of the first big waves of change and controversy from the introduction of computers.

Some people suggest that the computer advances of the last half century are only the beginning—that even more dramatic breakthroughs in electronics and computers loom on the horizon.

Others say the "revolution" is actually over. They say the most important discoveries have been made (computers and communication technology), and we are now in a stage of evolving or refining those technologies and adjusting to the changes in our personal lives, our economy, our work, and our world. Whatever the stage, we are clearly in the midst of the Information Age, living in an information-centered economy with all its rewards and problems.

COMPUTER CRIME

A computer crime is generally defined as one that uses computers and software for illegal purposes. This doesn't mean that all the crimes are new types of crime. On the contrary, many of these crimes, such as embezzlement of funds, alteration of records, theft, vandalism, sabotage, and terrorism, can be committed without a computer. But with a computer, these offenses can be carried out faster and with less chance of discovery and prosecution.

Computer crimes are on the rise. Just how much they cost the American public is in dispute, but estimates range from $3 billion to $5 billion or more annually.

Some reasons for the increase in computer crime are: (a) the phenomenal growth of computer availability means that more computers are in use, and thus more people are familiar with their operation; (b) more computers are tied together in satellite and other data-transmission networks; and (c) microcomputer users have easy access to huge mainframe databases.

The Criminal

Movies and newspaper stories might lead us to believe that most computer crimes are committed by teenage "hackers" who let their imaginations and technical skills get them into trouble. But a realistic look at computer crimes reveals that an offender is likely to be an employee of the firm against which the crime is committed—i.e., an "insider." And, two chances out of three, the offender will be male. The National Security Agency's logs of cases involving computer crime or computer espionage show that up to 90 percent of known security breaches are made by corporate or government insiders. Thus, organizations must protect their computer systems and data from both insiders and outsiders.

Difficulty of Detection and Prevention

Given the kind of person who commits a computer crime and the environment where it occurs, it's often difficult to identify the criminal. First, the crime may be so complex that months or years go by before it is discovered.

Second, once the crime has been revealed, it is not easy to find a clear trail of evidence leading to the guilty party. After all, there are no weapons or fingerprints as in conventional crimes.

Third, there are usually no witnesses, even though the crime may occur in a room filled with people. Who is to say whether the person at the next terminal, calmly keying in data, is doing the company's work or committing a criminal act?

Fourth, too few people in management and law enforcement know enough about computer technology to prevent the crimes. Authorities have to be familiar with the computer's capabilities within a given situation to guard against misuse. In some large cities, such as Los Angeles, police departments have set up specially trained computer crime units.

Even when an offender is caught, the investigators, attorneys, judges, or juries may find the alleged crime difficult to handle because of its complexities. However, more attorneys are specializing in computer law and studying the computer's potential for misuse.

After a computer crime has been discovered, many companies neither report it nor prosecute the person responsible. A company may not announce the crime if there was no significant loss, or from fear that the public will learn of the weaknesses of its computer system and lose confidence in its organization. Banks, credit card companies, and investment firms are especially sensitive about revealing their vulnerabilities because they rely heavily on customer trust. So, to avoid public attention, cautious companies will often settle cases of computer tampering out of court.

Types of Computer Crimes

Computer Virus/Computer Worm. A program entered into a computer with the aim of destroying or altering data and spreading that destruction to other computers is called a virus. It spreads when the infected program is shared through swapping software, logging into a network, or using a bulletin board.

A worm is a program that aims to occupy vacant computer memory and issue false and misleading commands. It spreads like a virus. Both have the effect of stopping or disrupting normal operations.

Why aren't viruses and worms detected before they cause damage? Simply because, like biological viruses and worms, people can't see them and don't know they are present—they are, after all, designed to hide themselves. They usually attack at a specific time or date set by the person who wrote and spread the program.

Data Manipulation. When a person alters data that enters or exits the computer, it is referred to as data manipulation (or sometimes, "data diddling"). Examples are changing school grades by putting false data into a school's computer system or changing credit standing by accessing credit-bureau computer files and entering or deleting information. Another type of data manipulation is "salami slicing"—skimming off a tiny bit of money from a number of accounts and diverting it into the manipulator's own account.

Time Bomb. Coding a computer program to destroy itself after it has been run a certain number of times is called a time bomb. This method of sabotage is sometimes used by disgruntled employees. It also has been used by software developers against companies that buy the software on credit. If the buyer doesn't pay for the software by the time agreed upon, then the program self-destructs. When the bill is paid, the developer tells the buyer how to "defuse" the bomb.

Trap Door. Creating a special password that gives its creator clandestine access to the system is called a trap door. The creator can thus enter a program at any time. No one else knows about it, and entries into the program will not be documented.

Data Stealing. Using a computer to steal information that has been gathered for someone else's legitimate purposes and using it for one's own purposes is called data stealing. An example is taking a client list from one company and selling it to a competitor.

Time Stealing. Time stealing is using another's computer without authorization and thus "stealing" the amount of money that would have been paid in "rent" for the time used, or "stealing" the money it takes to keep that computer in operation for its intended purpose.

Electronic Eavesdropping. Tapping without authorization into communication lines over which computer data and messages are sent is called electronic eavesdropping.

Espionage. Some people use computers to spy on military installations and private industries. In either case, the purpose is to obtain unauthorized information that will harm the victim and profit the spy. Military espionage may involve discovering battle or intelligence-gathering plans, securing weapons designs or test results, or destroying essential data. Industrial espionage covers such offenses as stealing project designs, marketing plans, financial statements, or other trade secrets from a company.

Software Piracy. As more people learn to use computers and as more uses are found for them, there is a corresponding growth in software piracy. In this case, piracy means making unauthorized copies of copyrighted computer programs for yourself or others—an illegal act. It is something like buying a popular recording, taping copies of it, and giving those copies free to family and friends. Sometimes such copying is done for resale—also illegal.

Piracy includes not only software but computer chips as well. To keep its chip technology from being pirated, the U.S. government's Lawrence Livermore National Laboratory developed a coating that protects the chip from being "taken apart" and copied. The coating resists solvents, heat, and grinding.

COMPUTERS AND THE RIGHT TO PRIVACY

Amendment IV to the U.S. Constitution, one of the Bill of Rights amendments, guarantees that "The right of the people to be secure in their persons, houses, papers, and effects, against unreasonable searches and seizures, shall not be violated. . . ."

Privacy of personal data stored in computers is not mentioned in the Bill of Rights, of course. Thus, the issue has naturally arisen as to exactly how much privacy citizens have a right to. For our purposes here, privacy means the right of control over one's personal data.

Computers alone don't invade our privacy, but they enable people to do so with greater ease and frequency than ever before. Primarily, computers assist in privacy invasion in two ways: (a) they enable organizations to stockpile and categorize a lot of information about anyone in a very small space, and (b) they allow other organizations quick access to anything and everything in the stockpile.

The federal government is the biggest stockpiler. Its numerous departments, bureaus, and offices have more than three and one-half *billion* files about American citizens. When you add the computerized files of all state agencies (health, welfare, education, law enforcement, etc.) and private institutions such as banks, hospitals, insurance companies, and credit bureaus, it is clear that none of us has a lot of privacy left if someone wants to poke about in our lives.

The Freedom of Information Act permits Americans to demand from government agencies the records that are being kept on them. But the increasing tendency of agencies to store this information in computers—as opposed to keeping it on paper—makes it more difficult for citizens to know how their lives are being affected.

Still, some organizations and institutions must know something about us if they are to work toward our own good. Doctors must have quick access to complete medical histories to cure us or save our lives. Banks need proof that our credit record is good so they can loan us money for a new car or house. Basically, the question of privacy boils down to the fair collection and use of personal data.

Here are some specific dangers that society sees in the huge personal databases that are operated by government agencies and large private organizations:

☐ *Personal data may be inaccurate.* The computer doesn't know what information is true and what is false. It simply tells what is in the file. The data may be wrong for any number of reasons: (a) a mistake by the person who gathered it originally or the one who keyed it into the computer; (b) a mismatch of the right information but the wrong name; or (c) information that was once correct, but is now out-of-date.

☐ *Personal data collected may not be secure from illegal access and use.* For example, private data sent over communication lines may be illegally intercepted. Although many organizations have established elaborate security systems, computer-related crimes and theft have increased in the last few years.

□ *One giant database containing all personal information about every member of our society could be compiled.* If all the agencies put all their data banks together, for example, it would include almost everything about us anyone could want to know.

□ *More information about people than is actually needed may be collected because of the computer's ability to store and classify vast amounts of data.* Because information about us is often very useful, and sometimes very profitable, the temptation is to amass as much of it as possible.

□ *Data collection agencies commonly combine and exchange their information.* This ominous fact compounds the danger of too much personal data being too easily accessible in one place. This enables anyone with access to get not only an individual's credit records, for example, but also health, insurance, and employment records. Even though there is legislation against *federal* agencies using the information for a purpose other than intended, there is a system called matching. In matching, one agency compares its data with another's for a specific purpose. For example, the Internal Revenue Service files are matched against welfare rolls to catch welfare cheaters.

The fact that an individual, business, or agency has these records may cause you no particular harm, *but their interpretation of the data to make decisions about you could be hazardous.* The combination of potentially inaccurate, outdated, and irrelevant information is dangerous.

JOB SECURITY

One of the most apparent social effects of the computer is the way it has altered the U.S. job market. It has changed the way work is done at every level of production—from design, to manufacture, to distribution. When computers were still in their infancy, labor union leaders predicted they would take jobs away from people. To some degree, their predictions have been correct.

Office jobs have been eliminated because a few workers using word processors are now able to turn out more letters and reports than a roomful of secretaries laboring away at "old-fashioned" typewriters. As of 1990, over 200,000 industrial robots were in use throughout the world. There are more robots and fewer people on auto assembly lines today.

Although the usefulness of robots has long been established, observers still disagree on whether their introduction will lead to extensive unemployment. For example, in 1986, a private research institute predicted that robots and other computer-assisted technology could cost American workers 200,000 jobs by 1990. But a study by a federal agency at the same time concluded that robots would cause little unemployment during the decade. The latter prediction turned out to be correct. Although there were massive layoffs in the automobile industry—a major user of robots—the job losses resulted primarily from foreign competition and overproduction.

Robots actually create some jobs, although not necessarily in the same field, industry, salary level, or education level. Someone has to design, build, sell, and maintain the robots. And some newer industries would never have been possible without them.

Thus far, the effect of these job shifts has been to weaken labor unions—not just because machines can do the work of people, but also because computers enable one worker to do a variety of related jobs as well, instead of specializing in one task. Unions were organized on the principle that a worker had a specific job and was protected in keeping it.

In response to union and societal concerns, heavily computerized companies often try to soften this reality by waiting for workers to retire or not replacing workers who resign. Some companies offer retraining and job-placement help for those who have been nudged out by computers.

ELECTRONIC WORK MONITORING

The National Institute of Occupational Safety and Health (NIOSH) estimates that more than eight million video display terminal (VDT) operators are being watched by their own computers. The term for this new way of supervising workers is *electronic work monitoring*.

How can computers monitor workers? They can count keystrokes, track data-entry errors, record the length and frequency of breaks, and measure the time it takes the operator to handle a customer-service transaction. In short, the computer can measure the quantity and, in some ways, the quality of an employee's work.

Employers claim electronic work monitoring is fair and objective. With electronic work monitoring, each employee can have a detailed, electronic record of productivity in his or her permanent file. Companies see this as a cost-effective way to measure job performance, to provide incentive pay to workers who perform beyond minimum requirements, and to make the most of the new technology to reduce cost.

Many workers see the work-monitoring issue as an invasion of their privacy and a not-very-subtle way of speeding up their work. There is room in this practice for company misuse if, for instance, company managers note only the operator's speed and give no weight to work quality. Furthermore, employees may never see data compiled about them and thus have no chance to correct any inaccuracy. Electronic work monitoring, because it is easy and automatic, could substitute machine measure for human evaluation of job performance. Finally, some employees say, this kind of measuring could allow the company to fire employees with information that only appears to be objective.

This productivity-versus-privacy argument may never be settled without laws to govern the monitoring or an agreement on the practice between the company's management and worker representatives.

HEALTH AND SAFETY

Are computers hazardous to your health? Well, the jury is still out on this question. Some worry that radiation from America's estimated 15 to 19 million VDTs may cause cataracts, cancer, miscarriages, vision problems, stress, and sterility. These charges have been researched by agencies such as the Food and Drug Administration's Bureau of Radiological Health, the Occupational Safety and Health Administration, the National Institute of Occupational Safety and Health, and the Canadian Radiation Protection Bureau. One Japanese report recommends that pregnant workers not use VDTs until more conclusive studies can be made.

The American and Canadian studies have failed to demonstrate any connection between VDT radiation and disease. The House Education and Labor Subcommittee on Health and Safety reported to Congress that it found no connection either. But it did suggest that employers and employees work together to set up satisfactory operation and work guidelines. Still, workers' fears continue, and other private and government studies are underway.

In the meantime, ergonomics, the study of adjusting the machine and the workplace to the worker, has been applied to the electronic office. Efforts are continually being made by ergonomic specialists and furniture and equipment designers to design the workplace to be safe and comfortable.

COMPUTER ETHICS

Computers pose major ethical problems for all users—government clerks, business executives, doctors, supervisors, students, and hobbyists. In addition to any laws that exist, computer ethics are needed—a standard of behavior for computer use by individuals and organizations.

A code of ethics provides a way of self-regulating conduct when the law or situation doesn't indicate a clear course of action. Here are some persistent ethical questions regarding computers:

☐ Is it an invasion of privacy to monitor an employee through his or her own computer?
☐ Is it fair for an employer to use data collected from electronic work monitoring as the only evidence for evaluating an employee?
☐ Does a company owe a worker who has been replaced by a computer any consideration other than that prescribed by labor law or contract?
☐ Should computer operators regard all data they process as completely confidential?
☐ Is it unethical to copy a program for a friend? What if he or she can't afford to buy it?
☐ Is it an invasion of privacy to snoop into other people's files, even if nothing is altered or removed? (How is it different from browsing through a filing cabinet or someone's desk, or peeking through a window?) Even if no damage is done, do computer users have a right to privacy of their files?
☐ Doesn't a company incur financial loss when it goes to the expense of tracing a computer intruder, even if nothing is changed or stolen? (Consider the salary paid to the investigator, and the lost time that could be spent on business instead.)

LEGISLATION

Because information is often randomly gathered, carelessly guarded, and easily accessible via computer technology, the assaults on personal and corporate privacy are difficult to detect and legislate against. Much of our safety under present conditions depends on the thoroughness and ethics of those who compile the data. New laws are being made; between 1985 and 1989, Congress passed 64 laws concerning information technology. Most states have also passed laws to discourage computer crime or privacy invasion.

Privacy. Laws must regard the rights of everyone who might be affected. For example: When a person or company gathers information about you, is it their property? Or do you have some right to the information, or even ownership of it? If someone acquires information you freely gave to someone else, does that constitute theft or unethical misuse? Such questions keep legislatures and courts busy.

In the 1960s and 1970s, some federal agencies and Congress realized the seriousness of the problem. Congress passed the Freedom of Information Act of 1970, which allows citizens to find out what federal agencies are keeping records on them and to secure copies to see if they are correct.

This legislation was the forerunner of a series of acts to stop unnecessary and unauthorized snooping into credit ratings (the Fair Credit Reporting Act of 1970), educational records (the Education Privacy Act of 1974), and personal finance (the Right to Financial Privacy Act of 1978). Most federal privacy legislation until the mid-1980s related to the behavior of the federal government and organizations to which it supplied funds. Now, legislation is reaching into the private sector.

To establish that the federal government has no right to keep secret records about any citizen, and to protect citizens from privacy abuses by the federal government, Congress enacted the Privacy Act of 1974.

The explosion of computer technology in the last few years led to the passage of other federal laws to protect privacy—see Table B–1.

Liability for Incorrect Information and Software Workability. Have you ever been the victim of a "computer error"? Perhaps you have been sent a check with the wrong amount printed on it, or received your class-registration form with the wrong classes listed. These errors cause more inconvenience than anything else, but some errors and losses are so great—particularly when normally reliable software malfunctions—that the courts are trying to discover just who is legally responsible for them—whether the faults are in the information, system designs, or expert systems that are used.

Incorrect Information. How much an agency or company can be held accountable for the accuracy of information it gives out remains unclear, but these organizations are becoming more vulnerable to large claims. The question of blame is quite complex, as shown by recent debates and litigations.

TABLE B-1
Key federal privacy and other computer-related legislation.

Freedom of Information Act of 1970
Allows citizens to find out which federal agencies are collecting and storing data about them and to secure copies of the records to see if they are correct.

Fair Credit Reporting Act of 1970
Provides that people have the right to inspect their credit records. If a citizen challenges data in the record, the credit agency is legally required to investigate the accuracy of that data.

Crime Control Act of 1973
Stipulates that those responsible for maintaining state criminal records that were developed with federal funds must ensure the security and privacy of the data in those records.

Privacy Act of 1974
Establishes laws to prevent federal government abuses against an individual's privacy: forbids data on individuals to be collected for one purpose and used for another without the individual's consent; gives individuals the right to find out what information the government has collected about them; allows individuals to have copies of these files and have a way to correct wrong data; requires the government agency involved to ensure that the records are up-to-date and correct and to protect them from misuse; among other provisions.

Education Privacy Act of 1974
Restricts access to computer records of grades and behavior evaluations in private and public schools. Students have the right to examine and challenge the data in their records.

Tax Reform Act of 1976
Puts limitations on the IRS in its access to personal information in bank records and its providing other agencies with that information.

Copyright Act of 1976
Protects creative and intellectual property, such as books, plays, songs, photographs, and computer programs from the moment of creation.

Right to Financial Privacy Act of 1978
Establishes restrictions on government access to customer files in financial institutions, and gives citizens the right to examine data about themselves in those files.

Privacy Protection Act of 1980
Prohibits government agents from making unwarranted searches of press offices and files.

Electronic Funds Transfer Act of 1980
Stipulates that those who offer the electronic funds transfer (EFT) check service must tell customers about third-party access to the customers' accounts.

Debt Collection Act of 1982
Sets up due-process conditions federal agencies must follow before releasing any information about bad debts to credit bureaus.

Cable Communications Policy Act of 1984
Requires cable television services to tell their subscribers if any personal information about them is being collected, used, or disclosed.

Semiconductor Chip Protection Act of 1984
Intended to prevent one company from reproducing the chip pattern of another. The act gives original developer a 10-year period of exclusive rights.

Electronic Communications Privacy Act of 1986
Makes it illegal to intercept data communication, such as electronic mail.

Computer Fraud and Abuse Act of 1986
Gives federal jurisdiction over interstate computer crimes in the private sector. Applies to computers used by the federal government and federally insured financial institutions.

Society is becoming aware of just how deeply we can be affected by wrong information. For example, incorrect data provided to air traffic controllers or drug manufacturers can have life-or-death consequences for hundreds or thousands of people.

Some providers of information and expert-system software are working within their own companies and trade organizations to prevent both potential tragedies and lawsuits. They are using two basic approaches: (a) testing and verification of data to create a more reliable product or service, and (b) limiting their liability in advance through contract provisions and disclaimer statements on their packages.

Software Workability. Who bears the cost of damages when software doesn't work? This is an ongoing battle between software manufacturers and those who buy it. Currently, software suppliers give no performance guarantee, saying they can't possibly anticipate all the software applications and ensure its usefulness. Consumers argue that software should do what it says it will.

Copyright and Infringement

Computer software is protected by federal copyright law. Many of the ethical and legal problems surrounding computer technology today are perceived to arise from copyright violations.

To discourage unauthorized copying, software developers use such methods as:

- ☐ Licensing one or more manufacturers to produce the programs and pay the developer a royalty on each program produced.
- ☐ Putting a seal on the software package and stating that when the seal is broken, the buyer is automatically agreeing that only he or she will use the software. Breaking the seal is the same as signing an agreement.
- ☐ "Copy protecting" or building "locks" into programs to prevent copying or to permit only a limited number of backup copies to be made. Unfortunately for program developers, these locks can be broken.
- ☐ Writing the software so that key instructions and codes can be found only in the documentation. Without documentation, the typical person would be unable to use the program. This forces pirates to photocopy voluminous documentation, which is far more expensive than copying a disk. A related tactic is to make the documentation difficult to photocopy.

In the United States, the Copyright Act of 1976, which went into effect January 1, 1978, specifically lists computer programs as protected from the moment of creation, instead of from the time of official registration.

The standard copyright notice includes the copyright symbol ©, year of creation, and copyright owner: © 1991 XYZ Software Co. The notice appears on the computer monitor when you turn it on and the software is installed.

The more effective that software manufacturers became in thwarting illegal copying, the more complaints they got from customers who legitimately needed extra copies of programs, some for backup and others to load on large-capacity disk drives. The result was that some customers, including the U.S. Department of Defense, quit buying copy-protected software. Manufacturers began dropping the anticopy features in their software packages. To compensate for this setback, the manufacturers stepped up prosecution of pirates and are extending their educational efforts on the consequences of unauthorized pirating.

People familiar with the variety and cleverness of computer criminals agree that more specific legislation is needed. The present laws cannot be stretched to cover all the criminal opportunities that a new technology creates.

It hardly requires a crystal ball to see more legal issues being raised and more legislation being passed as the computer continues to embed itself into the business, social, political, and personal fabrics of our lives!

DIRECTIONS IN TECHNOLOGY

The discovery and harnessing of electricity, coupled with development of vacuum tubes, brought us the first generation of computers. Then semiconductors (transistors) brought in the second generation. Integrated circuits, containing thousands of switches on a chip, were key to the third generation. Finally, microscopic circuits on a chip (LSI and VLSI) were the elements of the fourth generation. Now, scientists are looking for that technological breakthrough to propel us into the fifth generation of computers. Many argue that development of artificial intelligence will mark the beginning of a fifth generation.

Meanwhile, scientific research is being done on several fronts, all with the purpose of:

☐ Teaching computers to "think," "reason," "make decisions," and "learn from their mistakes" like humans.
☐ Increasing speed, memory, and power of computers.
☐ Making computers easier to use.
☐ Finding practical applications for the existing technology.

Artificial Intelligence

Most experts think that the next breakthrough will be artificial intelligence (AI)—the capability of machines to think and reason like humans—which, some futurists predict, will change the way we use computers. Uses for these thinking machines will be found that were never before thought possible.

Although research in AI started in the mid-1950s, it remains in the early stages of development. Specific applications for artificial intelligence being pursued in current research are expert systems, advanced robotics, natural-language processing, voice recognition, voice synthesis, and computer vision. Each is described below.

Expert Systems. Software programs that store the knowledge of a human expert and are then used as consultants in particular fields are called expert systems. For example, expert systems are used in medicine to help doctors diagnose illnesses. They are employed by service/repair technicians to analyze equipment malfunctioning. However, most of these systems do not come close to replacing human experts. They are not considered by most AI experts to be examples of true artificial intelligence.

PLC = Programmable Logic Controller

Robotics. The design, construction, and operation of robots is the field of robotics. The first industrial robot was installed in 1961. Today, they are still used mainly for simple, repetitive tasks on factory assembly lines. However, they have become sophisticated enough to be used for important and dangerous jobs, such as bomb disposal, ocean exploration, outer-space probes, coal mining, and cleanup of chemical or nuclear accidents.

MIT, Stanford University, Carnegie-Mellon University, and several other institutions and private companies are heavily involved in research to make robots even more useful. Specific research is trying to (a) make robots "intelligent," i.e., give them decision-making ability; (b) give them highly sensitive tactile capabilities; (c) provide them with a capacity to "see" in great detail; and (d) design them with dependable stabilizing systems and mobility.

To create effective walking robots, scientists at Oregon State University created their designs by watching, studying, and filming spiders and their movements over difficult terrain. The movements were digitized and computer analyzed to see how spider motions could be adapted to the much heavier robot machines.

Extreme miniaturization is a new area of robotics. Because some of these new devices are too small for the human eye to see, they are called "microbots." Their moving parts are far too tiny to be built as the elements of a regular robot would be. Instead, their design is printed on material such as polysilicon, which is then bathed in plasma or acid. These substances dissolve the material that is not a part of the printed design, leaving the microscopic parts of the robot. Scientists hope that microbots can be used to work on small, delicate machines or even can be inserted into the human bloodstream to remove cholesterol deposits or eradicate viruses.

Natural Language Processing. Finding ways to communicate with the computer, just as one person communicates with another, depends not only on the right hardware and an immense main memory, but also demands sophisticated software: a natural-language processor.

Natural language processing is the capacity of a computer to "understand" ordinary human language and translate it into instructions upon which the computer can act.

Progress already made in this area suggests that future systems using language-processing software will be able to understand language input in any form, from any speaker—English, Chinese, or whatever—and translate it into any other language.

Voice Recognition. Current systems with voice recognition capability (i.e., they allow voice input) recognize only a few thousand words at best. The computer must be "trained" to recognize the user's voice; then it accepts data or instructions through commands spoken into the computer's microphone.

There are other difficulties in voice-recognition technologies: (a) many words sound like other words; (b) different people pronounce the same word differently; (c) one word can have multiple meanings; and (d) the tone in which something is said—with sarcasm, for instance—may carry more meaning than the actual words.

Programs that improve upon these limiting factors will have to be able to interpret *all* the characteristics that make up conversation, such as inflection, sentence structure, and speed. Voice-recognition capability may ultimately become the method for giving instructions to computers or commands to robots. Responsiveness to the human voice will make computers accessible to people who can't enter data or text in traditional ways.

Voice Synthesis. Machines that "talk" to you—that have the capability of voice synthesis, or recreating the human voice—are not new. These voice-output devices respond to an inquiry with a simulated human voice. You may have heard the Coca-Cola vending machine say, "Thank you," or may have used a computerized bank teller that spoke your account balance in a humanlike voice.

A typical voice-output system speaks only a few hundred words and is limited in its ability to combine them into sentences. As sophisticated as these devices now seem, they are primitive compared to what inventors envision.

Computer Vision. Scientists hope to develop computers that will process and interpret light waves just as the human brain does. Such a system would use scanning devices to sense and interpret graphics or text-character shapes. It could then "read" text in almost every written language.

Neural Networks

Another way in which scientists seek to make machines "intelligent" like humans is neural-network computing. The concept of a neural-network computer has been around since at least 1956. A regular computer processes information in a chainlike sequence, but neural networks are organized like a grid in which information is shared and tasks are performed simultaneously—just as the brain would.

A neural network differs from an expert system in that the expert system is fed only data that will allow it to make a conclusion about a relatively narrow subject, such as diagnosing diseases. It follows the "If this is so, then what?" pattern of reasoning, and it does not increase the size of its database by its own actions. A neural network can handle broader topics and add to its database.

Josephson Junction

The Josephson Junction, developed by Brian Josephson of the University of Cambridge, is a very fast electronic switch. Its key feature is that it works at low temperatures—nearly absolute zero—where there is little resistance to the flow of electricity. This lack of resistance means that on-and-off switching operations can occur about 1000 times faster than with silicon transistors. The technology has been perfected slowly, but in 1986, Hypres, Inc. revealed the world's first commercial system using the junctions.

Parallel Processing

Another promising technique for increasing computer speed and power is already being used—parallel processing. This technology links many processors so they can handle volumes of data simultaneously instead of in sequence, as conventional computers do.

Parallel processing differs from multiprocessing. In multiprocessing, several programs can run at the same time, but each on a separate processor. Parallel processing assigns different portions of a single program to various processors. When programs run concurrently, parts of different programs share the same processor.

Although computers using this technology are being built now, they are not yet perfected or widely used. Those who do use them are spending a lot of time developing new programs and ways to use the many processors.

Chips

Some experts think that the secret to more computer power, memory, and speed lies in new chip designs. Some of the solutions being considered are:

1. Making the features (circuitry) even smaller. The amount of etched-in circuitry on a chip and how closely it is packed determines the chip's speed and power. There can be more circuitry on a chip if it is tightly packed.
2. Making larger chips or superchips. Several U.S. companies, including TRW and Motorola, are experimenting with "superchips"—larger chips with smaller features. This kind of chip will be essential where data from various sensors must be processed almost instantaneously, i.e., in real-time processing.
3. Using other substances as the semiconductor material in the chips. Although silicon is the foundation for current chip technology, scientists are considering gallium arsenide, ceramic oxides, and synthetic diamond coatings to replace silicon as the film of conducting material to use in chips. Superconductors are important because they carry electricity without the resistance that causes heat buildup in normal conductors such as copper. Thus scientists continue to look for a material that offers conductivity at the speed of light, has no resistance, and is feasible to manufacture.

4. Growing the chip circuitry organically—that is, biochips. Most of the innovations just discussed are merely improvements on current technologies. Many experts think chips with circuits can be made from living matter—biochips—and the biomolecular computer will be the technology that breaks through to a new generation of computers and artificial intelligence.

Optoelectronics

Optoelectronics, the combination of electronics and optics, may eventually become the basis of all information technology. By uniting the electron with the photon (a particle of light), greater efficiency is possible in communication and in data processing than electronics alone can achieve.

Fiber optics—the communication channel for the photon—will continue to be improved for data processing because this type of channel offers tremendous signal clarity. An engineer at AT&T Bell Laboratories has built a crude computer that uses laser beams instead of electrical signals as the on/off switching mechanism. Although it is in early development, this optical computer could lead to models that are 100 to 1000 times more powerful than today's supercomputers.

SOCIETY'S RESPONSE AND THE GLOBAL VILLAGE

Because the Information Age is still in its infancy, it is not easy to foresee all of the effects it will have on our way of life. There has been unprecedented progress in medical research and diagnosis, education, sea and space exploration, and in the relief of humans from dangerous and dull jobs. We have instant communications with the rest of the world. Computers have challenged and surpassed human beings at some intellectual games such as chess, in some technical skills such as mathematical computations, and in some assembly-line work. Most of us view this technology as a contribution and a benefit to society, not as a threat.

Here is a brief summary of observations about changes in store for our society over the next few years:

☐ More efforts will be made to find more practical uses for existing technology. The advances of the last half century are overwhelming. In fact, they still exceed our ability to adapt to them. Some technologies that have existed for several years are just now being put to use. MIT's Media Laboratory is studying and making such applications. Researchers there buy off-the-shelf equipment and program it for new uses in music, film, theater, and broadcasting. They are looking at new ways to apply the computer to the home, classroom, and office.

☐ We will continue to move from a "brawn society" to a "brain society" as the Information Age progresses. Factories will become more automated (and add to our fears of unemployment). The nature of our work life and leisure time will continue to change.

☐ Education will continue to train students in computer-assisted services, rather than teaching them physical or industrial skills. Traditional jobs will change or disappear, just as the office typing pool has. We can hope and plan for the emergence of more interesting and challenging jobs to replace the ones lost.

☐ More and more workers will telecommute to their jobs through personal computers—and not just from the suburbs to the city, but from one country to another. These changes will have significant effects on day-care centers, public transportation, office design, and parking-lot design, as well as on many other institutions. One social commentator points out that an "electronic heartland" is being opened by a new type of information worker; people are leaving cities for "quality-of-life" small towns and rural areas. With the computer, phones, fax machines, and overnight couriers, these rural areas are as technologically linked to urban centers as are other cities. People will be free to work anywhere.

☐ Shopping at home, home banking, and electronic funds transfer (EFT) in general will continue to increase and move us closer to a "cashless society."

☐ Computer crime, privacy, health and safety, and computer ethics will continue as major ethical and social concerns for at least the next few years. These issues will not be resolved quickly. No major technology is ever introduced into a society without causing waves.

☐ "Thinking" machines are a long way off, but concern about what they might do has been with us since the birth of science fiction. If indeed computers can be made that will program, repair, and reproduce themselves, there will be upheavals in law, ethics, sociology, and all the sciences that deal with social relationships. At present, fears of "computers taking over" seem groundless. However, as computers gain more autonomy of operation and become more versatile, they can become a social menace in the wrong hands.

No one can really say what the future holds, but it is fairly certain that, just as society has adapted in the past, it will continue to assimilate new technologies, trying to balance their potential good with their potential problems.

Careers in an Information Age

There was no such thing as a career in computers until the late 1940s. However, according to the U.S. Bureau of Labor Statistics, by 1961 there were about 8500 computer specialists, and today approximately 2,000,000 people work fulltime in computer jobs (operators, programmers, analysts). Another 2,000,000 or more are employed in related fields—people working in the computer industry itself, in business, and in all the other professions that rely on computers.

This means that the job market for computer professionals is strong. Even if you are not a system analyst, programmer, or other computer specialist, the likelihood is great that your job will require using computers. Computers and information handling continue to be essential parts of the work of travel agents, news reporters, law enforcers, fire fighters, editors, engineers, lawyers, teachers, scientists, many other professionals, and nearly all clerical people.

The job outlook for computer professionals is still among the best in the nation. The Bureau of Labor Statistics says that positions for computer operators, programmers, and system analysts are still among the fastest-growing fields in the United States.

This appendix describes these and other professions involving computers. Also discussed are other fields in which computers will play an important role.

SYSTEM ANALYST

System analysts are strategists and planners. They design and improve information systems. They analyze the problems of an existing information system, decide how to solve them, determine which data to collect, and develop the processing steps needed to get the proper information to each user. For this position, most companies require at least a bachelor's degree in business with knowledge or experience in software and hardware. Management background or course work is helpful.

PROGRAMMER

A programmer codes instructions that tell the computer how to solve a problem. After a system analyst designs an algorithm to solve a problem, a programmer codes that algorithm in a programming language and makes sure it all works. In a small organization, the jobs of programmer and system analyst sometimes are combined into a position called programmer/analyst. Application programmers write programs for users to solve problems; system programmers write programs that run the computer. Most programmers must have a bachelor's degree in computer science.

COMPUTER OPERATOR

A computer operator is responsible for starting and running the equipment—computer, disk drives, tape drives, printers, or other peripherals. Computer operators schedule the equipment's time for data-processing jobs, test the equipment, maintain it, load the tapes and disks onto the drives, and prepare the printers. While programs are running, they constantly monitor the equipment for mechanical failures and the environment for proper temperature and ventilation.

Formal educational requirements are not as stringent as for programmers, but because logs of activity in the computer room are usually required, operators must be able to write clear, accurate reports. Some companies require formal training, but others provide on-the-job training. Most computer operators have some college education, but it may not be required.

DATA-ENTRY OPERATOR

In the early days of computers, keypunch operators entered data into the computer by typing them onto punched cards at a keypunch machine. Today, a data-entry operator usually enters the data at a keyboard and video display terminal. Good keyboarding (typing) skills with a high degree of accuracy are required. Data-entry personnel are usually not required to have training in data processing. A high school diploma is usually sufficient.

According to the Bureau of Labor Statistics, the demand for data-entry operators will begin to decline. This reduction in personnel is due to the growing number of on-line applications in which users enter their own data and because of technology such as optical scanners where data entry is accomplished electronically.

COMPUTER SERVICE TECHNICIAN

Computers, like all machines, need maintenance and can break down. With millions of personal computers in the United States and more being purchased by businesses, there is a high demand for computer service technicians. The job of computer service technician is to install computer equipment and repair it—malfunctioning computers, damaged disk drives, tape drives, keyboards, circuit boards, etc.

In large companies, a computer service technician's job is to keep computer downtime to a minimum. Many stores that sell personal computers hire computer service technicians to install and repair the equipment they sell.

Service technicians are usually experts at using the latest testing and diagnostic devices. Training in electronics is essential, and some background in programming is an asset. The demand for computer service technicians will continue to grow for some time.

DATABASE ADMINISTRATOR

With the increasing number and size of current databases in government and businesses, there is a need for people to coordinate all the elements. Database administrators are in charge of designing, implementing, and maintaining databases. They monitor users and data security, and they direct and plan for all elements required to maintain a database. Database administrators consult with others in their organization regarding information needed and the best way to access it. They also help other managers plan data collection, storage, and organization.

This job is very technical, requiring at least a bachelor's degree in computer science or data processing. Also, excellent communication skills and some management skills are required.

INFORMATION SYSTEM MANAGER

The information system manager plans and oversees all information resources in an organization. Although this is a higher-level computer position, the actual title may vary with an organization's size and structure—Management Information System (MIS) Director, Information System Manager, or Data Processing Manager. This position requires technical knowledge about the system development process and managerial/leadership skills to oversee and motivate the programmers, system analysts, and computer operators in a data processing or MIS department. The position also requires familiarity with the organization's overall goals and information needs.

A degree in business with information-system courses is generally required. Many in this position must have a master's degree in business. Some firms, however, place less emphasis on formal business education and take their managers from the ranks of those who have worked as programmers and system analysts.

INFORMATION SERVICE CENTER CONSULTANT

Some organizations are so large that they install an information service center with a staff of information service center consultants. These people advise or train employees who need to learn a particular piece of hardware or software. The consultant might train a group of new employees or a group of experienced workers on new application software. The consultant might teach another group how to access data from a large company database.

A bachelor's degree in a related area—business or communication, for instance—is usually required. The position demands not only knowledge of the hardware or software being taught, but the ability to communicate with people and to enjoy teaching.

OTHER COMPUTER-RELATED CAREERS

Many other jobs have developed directly from the computer industry. Here are just a few:

- ☐ Sales representatives—people who sell computer equipment and software.
- ☐ Technical writers—writers with experience in a particular technical area who can explain in nontechnical terms how to install, operate, and maintain the equipment and software. They write user manuals, operation manuals, and software documentation.
- ☐ Security personnel—people who specialize in techniques to protect the computer room, hardware, programs, and the data and information stored.
- ☐ Electronic data-processing (EDP) auditors—accounting and business experts who monitor and evaluate computer operations to assure that no fraud or misuse of the system's capabilities occurs.
- ☐ Hardware developers—creators of new ideas, using the latest technology to design computer hardware and chip circuitry.
- ☐ Software engineers—people who create and write new system programs (e.g., operating systems) and new application programs for business (e.g., word processors, spreadsheets, database management software) or entertainment (e.g., video games).
- ☐ Network designers—telecommunication specialists who design and improve computer networks.

HOW COMPUTERS AFFECT OTHER JOBS

No matter what career you choose, it is likely that computers will be a major tool and that information handling will be an important function of your job. In other words, you will be a computer user. You are quite likely to be part of the entire computerized system on which the company bases its operations.

Here are some ways that computers have affected noncomputer careers:

- ☐ A graphic artist designs logos for television programs and art for music videos with computers and graphics software.
- ☐ Movie and television producers and special-effects creators produce unusual scenes with computer images and simulations.
- ☐ Journalists enter news stories directly from computer terminals or personal computers. Copy editors revise text on the computer, then electronically send it to electronic typesetting equipment and print the final story on computer-controlled presses.
- ☐ Technicians in hospital laboratories operate computerized testing equipment, store the results in a computer, and retrieve them upon request.
- ☐ Secretaries use computers for word processing and electronic mail processing. Some also implement financial applications such as budgets and expense records and use software for scheduling and travel management.
- ☐ Automobile mechanics use computer diagnostics to pinpoint engine troubles.
- ☐ Physicians prescribe diagnostic testing of their patients with computer-controlled tools. They also coordinate all phases of office management by computer.
- ☐ Teachers use computers to expedite research, design learning materials, keep student records—and teach their students how to use computers as study aids.
- ☐ Managers retrieve information from the company's databases via computers in the form of reports; they also send messages and schedule their week's appointments using computers.

Even though your chosen profession may not be that of a computer professional or specialist, you will most likely use a computer in some aspect of any career. For example, if you are a teacher, you might become the expert in computer-aided instruction (CAI) in your school; in the textile and fashion industry, you might not only be a designer, but also the expert on the company's CAD system used for designing, sizing, cutting, and manufacturing clothing. Almost every field will have specialists who combine knowledge of their field with computer skills that can enhance their positions.

A familiarity with computers will have enormous value to you in almost any job in the Information Age.

APPENDIX D

Knowledge-Based (Expert) Systems

Knowledge-based (expert) systems are used to help determine problems and assist in arriving at solutions. Increasing numbers of government and business organizations are developing expert systems to assist in more areas of operation. Edward Feigenbaum, a Stanford University professor and leading researcher in expert systems, offers this definition:

> A knowledge-based (expert) system is an intelligent computer program that uses knowledge and inference procedures to solve problems that are difficult enough to require significant human expertise for their solution. Knowledge necessary to perform at such a level, plus the inference procedures used, can be thought of as modeling the expertise of the field's best practitioners.

From this definition, it is clear that a knowledge-based system functions somewhat like an expert, solving problems that require knowledge, intelligence, and experience. Because the system depends primarily on the knowledge of human experts, it is called a knowledge-based, or an expert, system. This appendix uses these terms interchangeably.

HISTORY

Expert systems are byproducts of artificial-intelligence (AI) research conducted since World War II. Although AI research is not new, its popularity is recent, as is that of expert systems. Once exclusively a topic among AI researchers, expert systems are now seen in offices, hospitals, research laboratories, industrial plants, manufacturing shops, repair shops, oil drilling operations, and the like.

During World War II, computers were developed to perform complex numeric calculations. However, a small group of computer scientists explored the possibility of having computers process nonnumeric symbols. At about the same time, psychologists who were studying human problem solving wanted to create computer programs to mimic human intelligence. The efforts of these two groups seemed to be directed at the same objective—to create machines that would think like humans. Together, they laid the foundation of a new discipline, termed *artificial intelligence*.

In the early 1970s, a number of corporations attempted to apply AI principles to solving business problems. Several companies set up AI research groups to develop practical business applications. However, these efforts proved unsuccessful at the time. AI applications were too costly to develop, too slow in execution, not sufficiently practical, and too complex to run on existing hardware.

With the introduction of microcomputer technology came a new generation of faster, more powerful, relatively inexpensive hardware. This technology, combined with the development of programming languages suitable for artificial intelligence applications, revived research in AI. This research transformed AI applications such as knowledge-based systems into viable business applications.

CONVENTIONAL PROGRAMS VERSUS KNOWLEDGE-BASED SYSTEMS

A knowledge-based system is a set of computer programs. However, there are certain differences between conventional computer programs and knowledge-based systems:

- ☐ Conventional computer programs perform routine tasks, whereas expert systems perform specialized tasks resembling those that normally require experts.
- ☐ Conventional computer programs are developed and maintained by a computer programmer, but expert systems are developed and maintained by knowledge engineers and experts.
- ☐ Conventional computer programs rely heavily on algorithms, whereas expert systems rely on knowledge and rules of thumb (known as heuristic techniques).

□ Conventional computer algorithms operate unchanged and repetitively, whereas the knowledge incorporated into an expert system usually changes constantly and thus changes the reasoning outcome.

□ Conventional computer programs lack human reasoning, whereas expert systems mimic human reasoning.

COMPONENTS OF A KNOWLEDGE-BASED SYSTEM

A knowledge-based system has three major components and three minor ones. The major components are a user interface, a knowledge base, and an inference engine. The minor components are working (or short-term) memory, an explanation subsystem, and a knowledge-acquisition subsystem (Figure D–1).

User Interface

A user interface is a set of computer programs that links a knowledge-based system to its users. All user inputs and system-generated outputs are handled by this software. Through a keyboard, users enter commands and data. Expert system outputs are messages and output displays.

Knowledge Base

A knowledge base contains what an expert knows in a certain field. In the popular "rule-based" approach, the knowledge consists of rules and associations that simulate those used by human experts. The knowledge base is the most important component of an expert system.

Knowledge bases resemble databases, but contain knowledge instead of data. The performance of an expert system is a function of the size and quality of its knowledge base; the greater the number of rules and associations, the larger the base.

FIGURE D–1
Components of a knowledge-based system.

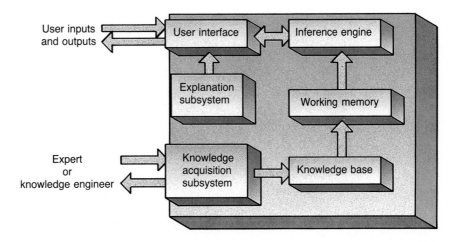

Rules and associations in a knowledge base may be constructed in the form of conditional "if-then" statements, such as:

If sales are rapidly increasing and the long-range outlook is excellent, then consider hiring more production employees.

The statement preceding the comma forms the left-hand side of the rule, and the statement following the comma forms the right-hand side of the rule. In some expert systems, rules have probabilities associated with them to indicate the degree of confidence in the conclusions. Expert knowledge also can be represented by methods other than rule-based.

Inference Engine

An *inference engine* is software that applies the rules from a knowledge base to the data provided by a user, to draw a conclusion. The inference engine is an integral part of every expert system. Two types of inference engines are used, depending upon how conclusions are drawn:

☐ In a *data-directed inference procedure*, the engine checks the left-hand side of a rule, matches it with data provided by a user, and draws a conclusion by looking at the right-hand side of the rule.

☐ In a *goal-directed inference procedure*, the engine forms a hypothesis and then tries to prove it by looking at the right-hand side of the rule and checking the left-hand side to see whether it matches the data entered by a user.

Working Memory

Working memory (also known as short-term memory or dynamic knowledge base) is the part of computer memory in which appropriate rules and data are stored for an instant during the execution of an expert system. Because the rules and data must be readily accessible to the expert system, they are copied from the knowledge base and maintained in the working memory. The contents of working memory constantly change during the execution of an expert system.

Explanation Subsystem

Most expert systems incorporate an explanation subsystem, which can respond to user requests and inquiries while the system is executing. For example, if an expert system requests additional data from a user during execution, the user might want to ask the expert system why it needs the additional data. Typically, the user would ask why by pressing a key on the keyboard or typing the word *why*. In response, the expert system would use an explanation subsystem to give the reason for requesting the additional data. This component can also be used to learn the reasoning behind the conclusion of an expert subsystem. Knowing the reasoning may help the user determine whether the conclusion is valid.

Knowledge-Acquisition Subsystem

The heart of every expert system is the knowledge transferred from an expert to the knowledge base. This transfer is accomplished by a software component known as a knowledge-acquisition subsystem. If the knowledge in a knowledge base is to be updated or retrieved, a knowledge-acquisition subsystem performs this function.

EXPERT SYSTEM SHELLS

Several commercial tools are available to help build expert systems. Such tools make it unnecessary to build expert systems from scratch. The tools are known in the industry as *expert system shells*, or shells. Most shells contain all of the components of an expert system except the knowledge base. Thus, buyers need to add only a knowledge base to create their own expert systems. Shells are available for both microcomputers and mainframes. The low-end price of microcomputer shells is approximately $50.00; some mainframe computer shells cost over $80,000.00.

KNOWLEDGE ENGINEERS

The process by which the knowledge of an expert is transformed into a knowledge base is called knowledge engineering. Special skills are required to capture the knowledge of an expert and put it into programmable form, and a new group of professionals, known as knowledge engineers, are trained to perform that role.

Knowledge engineers are important in the design and development of expert systems. The power and success of a system depend on the skills of the knowledge engineers who build it. As a result, their work requires intimate association with experts. Unfortunately, experts themselves often are unable to explain the reasoning process they employ in solving complex problems, so the task of knowledge engineers—figuring out how the experts think—is difficult. In such cases, knowledge engineers must ask the right questions to get the right information from the experts and then develop the appropriate rules for an expert system.

USES OF KNOWLEDGE SYSTEMS

Both the number of knowledge systems being developed and the number of business organizations using them are increasing, which testifies to their effectiveness. Businesses use them to detect problems faster and to assist in problem solving and decision making. Here are a few well-known systems used in diverse organizations:

DENDRAL is an expert system which examines the spectroscopic analysis of an unknown chemical compound and predicts its molecular structure. It was developed in 1965 through the joint effort of three scientists—Joshua Lederberg, Edward Feigenbaum of Stanford, and Bruce Buchanan. DENDRAL's success has led AI scientists to pursue business applications. It is available through time sharing on a Stanford University computer that can be accessed by outside chemists.

MYCIN is a landmark expert system used to diagnose infectious diseases and suggest possible therapies. The system was developed by Edward

Feigenbaum and Edward Shortliffe, both of Stanford University. MYCIN was the first expert system to use the rule-based inference procedure now used by most expert systems. It has a knowledge base of 500 rules that describe expert knowledge about diagnoses. Each rule has a probability figure associated with it to indicate its level of certainty. The performance of MYCIN is almost as good as that of physicians, an indication that this new technology has practical business applications. EMYCIN (essential MYCIN) is an expert system shell. It is MYCIN without the knowledge base, and it is marketed as a shell that can be used with other knowledge bases.

PROSPECTOR is a geological expert system used by geologists to help find valuable mineral deposits. Developed in the late 1970s by the Stanford Research Institute, it performs consultation services for investigation of sites for ore-grade deposits. PROSPECTOR can generate graphic responses in the form of maps, and can provide conclusions. With this expert system, geologists discovered a molybdenum deposit worth $100 million, a deposit that had been overlooked for many years.

INTERNIST is an expert system that helps analyze difficult clinical problems. Developed in 1974 by a computer scientist and a physician, INTERNIST models a clinician's diagnostic reasoning for a large number of diseases and their possible combinations. The procedure begins by asking a user (a physician) to describe the symptoms. The diagnostic process examines each symptom to determine what diseases could be associated with it. Each identified disease is then given a composite score—a positive score for each symptom that can be attributed to the disease and a negative score for each that cannot. The highest-scoring disease is investigated in detail first to see if the patient has all symptoms that should be present. Thus, all probable diseases are examined, and the most likely is identified.

XCON (eXpert CONfigurator) is an expert system developed at Carnegie-Mellon University for Digital Equipment Corporation (DEC). Digital uses XCON to ensure that the different components of a computer system chosen by its customers are compatible as one system. If the components are not compatible, the expert system recommends adjustments. Before this expert system was developed, only a handful of DEC experts knew enough about computer components to be sure that those chosen by a customer would work together.

DELTA (Diesel-Electric Locomotive Troubleshooting Aid) is an expert system created to help maintenance people repair diesel-electric locomotives. Developed in 1983 by General Electric, DELTA also is known as CATS–1 (Computer-Aided Troubleshooting System–1). Before this expert system was developed, GE could fix its locomotives in two ways: either fly its only repair expert, David Smith, to the locomotive, or transport the locomotive to David Smith. Both methods were expensive. DELTA was developed to transfer David Smith's expert knowledge to a computer-based system so that GE's less-expert personnel could use it. The system has a knowledge base of 1,200 rules and can print diagrams to show various parts of a locomotive. At the request of a user, it also can show a training film that displays the step-by-step procedure for fixing a problem.

GADS (Gate Assignment Display System) is an expert system used by United Airlines. It was developed by Texas Instruments to reduce travel delays and solve operating and scheduling problems at several airports. The system incorporates the knowledge of scheduling experts and has eliminated the wall-sized control boards and magnetic stick-on aircraft formerly used to schedule incoming aircraft at different terminal gates. Now, a scheduler who becomes aware of weather interference or delays can move arrivals on a computer screen and have the system automatically adjust the other aircraft to other available gates. The scheduler can examine the changes on the computer screen before setting the actual plan in motion.

LIMITATIONS OF EXPERT SYSTEMS

Expert systems do have their limitations. They can give the user only what is programmed in the system. They are expensive and work well only on problems that are specifically defined and in very specific fields.

Regardless of the advantages and limitations, expert systems are the focus of attention among people who want to extend the application and power of computers. There are those who think that the future of computers and their impact on society will depend largely upon the continued development of practical applications such as the expert system.

APPENDIX E

Buying and Caring for a Microcomputer System

Buying a microcomputer system can be fun and exciting for some people. For others, it can be difficult and unpleasant. There are hundreds of computers and thousands of ready-to-use programs from which to choose. Where do you begin? How do you narrow your choices? Without prior experience, you may feel lost amid the huge array of products.

Regardless of where you will use the computer, preparation and homework on both software and hardware will help ensure that you get what you need. It will also help ensure that, after the purchase, your computer won't sit idle because you can't do what you expected to. The average computer has about a 10-year lifespan, but a heavy user can outgrow one in less than 10 months. This kind of purchase is worth some planning!

PREPARATION

Become computer-literate. By the time you've finished this course, you will know many of the capabilities of computers and have ideas of what computers might do for you. You'll know the names of the components a typical system comprises, major applications, and how to run some software. You may even learn some programming in the BASIC or Pascal languages.

Determine what you want a computer to do for you. Why do you need one? This decision is your first and most important. You cannot evaluate various computers and software if your goals aren't clear.

You probably want a computer to help you work more efficiently. Perhaps you want it to perform two or more different tasks. Which tasks are the most important? For example, if word processing of business letters will be your computer's primary function, then a quality printer is important. If performing large spreadsheet calculations is your primary task, then large primary storage is important.

SELECTING AND EVALUATING SOFTWARE

Because software and hardware work together and because not all software runs on all computers, you must coordinate the software purchase with the computer purchase. Most people assume that you select a computer first and then software, but that actually is backwards. Investigate and select the software first, then choose the hardware that will run your software efficiently. If you are planning to program in a specific computer language, make sure that the language will work on the computer you choose.

There is an astounding array of application software from which to choose. For the IBM, its clones, and the Apple IIe and IIc, over 100,000 commercial programs are available. Here are some guidelines to help you make informed choices:

☐ *Is software available for the tasks you need to perform?* Also, is it available for your specific computer, if you already own one? Software that perfectly fits your task may not run on the computer you have in mind. Read software reviews in trade magazines, home-computing magazines, and software directories. Visit computer stores, contact people who are using the software, and ask friends who have computers to learn which packages they recommend for your job. Often, other users can tell you about helpful features and limitations of packages with which they've had experience.

☐ *What operating system controls your computer?* Examples are DOS, OS/2, Unix, and Macintosh. The software that you buy must be able to run on the operating system of your computer.

☐ *How much money do you want to spend?* The cost of the package may a factor. Some spreadsheet and database packages can cost over

$500. Also, determine if the package requires additional expenditures for more hardware or software to use it—for example, more memory or a higher resolution monitor.

☐ *Are the specific features of the package the ones you need?* If possible, ask to see it demonstrated with your own data to make sure it can do everything you wish. Keep in mind that the most expensive and feature-loaded package may not be the best for you. Most users need only a portion of the features included in most packages. You may pay for more than you need.

☐ *Will the package be easy to learn and use?* Are the commands simple to use and remember, especially the ones you'll use most often? Are the displays clear and easy to read?

☐ *Is the program menu-driven, command-driven, or a combination?* Are you comfortable with the method of controlling the program? Most novices prefer a menu-driven program, easier to learn because it presents choices in menu form on the screen. A command-driven program requires that you refer to a manual or memorize the choices and their keystrokes. (Although a command-driven program may be more difficult to learn, experienced users may prefer it. A command-driven program can be faster and less cumbersome once you have memorized the commands. Shorter, cryptic commands without menus also allow a program that is smaller, executes faster, and takes up less RAM.)

☐ *Can you understand the documentation (the written and graphic descriptions that accompany the software)?* Does it make sense to you? Does it seem accurate and complete? This can be difficult to determine at first, especially if you have never used computers and application software. Notice whether the package includes help manuals, or hints and instructions that appear on-screen when requested. These aids can help you learn and use the package. Also make sure that manuals use a D-ring or spiral binding so they will stay open easily.

☐ *How much support or assistance will you receive from the vendor or developer in troubleshooting or solving problems?* Who will provide the support—the dealer or the manufacturer? Many vendors charge fees for support because of the high cost of maintaining the personnel and facilities to answer questions. User groups in your area also are good sources of information if you have questions.

☐ *How much value will you receive for the cost?* In the past, a higher price usually meant greater capability, better documentation and support, or greater flexibility. Today, it's not so clear. A number of programs with lower price tags are as good as some higher-priced programs.

☐ *Is the program flexible and compatible?* Can the package be adapted to a wide variety of situations and hardware configurations? If you already have a computer, will the package run on it? Many programs require large amounts of RAM to operate. Generally, to operate a program most efficiently, you'll want to have more than the minimum RAM required. Some programs work with certain printers or plotters only. Make sure the package you choose is compatible with equipment you already have.

□ *Does the manufacturer revise and upgrade the program to incorporate the latest technology and advances in programming techniques?* If so, will the manufacturer provide the program upgrade to you for a reasonable fee? Will your old files be compatible with new versions of the program? If a new program is in its first version, check the credibility of the company, based on its other products (if any).

Careful evaluation and selection of application software ensures enjoyable and productive operation of your computer and effective use of the money spent. Table E–1 is a checklist of criteria to be considered when selecting new software.

TABLE E–1
Software buyer's checklist.

Tasks planned:

1. _____
2. _____
3. _____

Name of supplier:

Retail _____

Mail-order house _____

Public domain/shareware _____

Bookstore _____

Name of package _____

Operating system required _____

RAM required _____

User orientation:

Menu-driven _____

Command-driven _____

Combination _____

Additional hardware or software needed _____

Features available _____

Quality of documentation _____

Vendor support _____

Return policy _____

Warranty _____

Flexibility _____

Ability to upgrade the package _____

Price:

Package _____

Shipping, tax, etc. _____

Comparison of cost to value received _____

SELECTING A MICROCOMPUTER

You have decided what you want the computer to do, and you have selected the programs you need for your applications. Now it is time to look at hardware. Here are some guidelines, many of which are similar to the guidelines for buying software:

☐ *How much money do you want to spend?* Computer prices vary greatly. If you cannot afford an elaborate system now, perhaps you can add some components later. Be sure to ask which components are included in the price quoted. Sometimes the price tag includes only the basic computer; at other times, the monitor, printer, other peripherals, and even software are included in the price.

☐ *What equipment is available, and what do others think about it?* Table E–2 lists some manufacturers of microcomputers. Talk to friends or associates who already use or own computers. Often, they can tell you about the limitations of a particular computer, as well as its good features. Read reviews of computers and other hardware in computer magazines or newspapers.

☐ *Exactly which hardware features—monitor, printer, drives, input devices, surge protection—do you need?*

    ☐ Will you need a color monitor to run color graphics? Or will monochrome do? Do you prefer screen characters that are amber, green, or white?

    ☐ Which printer to buy depends on what you want to print, how much of it, and how fast. Business letters require letter-quality (typewriter-quality) print, or better. Rough drafts are handled nicely on a less-expensive dot-matrix printer. If you have many pages or letters to print, you will need a fast printer. If you have little to print, the most economical printer will do.

    ☐ To quickly access and save data, you will need a hard-disk drive and one floppy disk drive. Hard disks commonly come in 20-, 40-, 60-, 80-, and 100-megabyte capacities; 40 megabytes is adequate for most systems. Newer IBM, clone, and MacIntosh systems come with $3\frac{1}{2}$-inch floppy drives, but if you will be trading disks with other users who have the more common $5\frac{1}{4}$-inch drives, you may want to purchase a system having both sizes.

    ☐ A computer comes with a keyboard, but you may want other input devices: a mouse or trackball is needed for much menu-driven software; a scanner may be useful if you will be working with graphics.

    ☐ Seriously consider a surge protector to reduce the risk of electrical disturbances destroying your data or damaging equipment. (The electrical power entering your home is not as consistent as you might think. There are voltage surges and drops, power interruptions, and lightning strikes, all of which can damage equipment and data.)

TABLE E-2

Popular microcomputer manufacturers.

American Scientific	DEC	North Star
Apple	Dell	Sony
AT&T	Epson	Tandy (Radio Shack)
Atari	Hewlett-Packard	Wang
Commodore	IBM	Xerox
Compaq	NEC	

After you identify some possible systems, here are further guidelines to consider for each system:

☐ *How much main memory (RAM) does the computer have?* Does it have enough to run the software that you have selected? You might need just 640 kilobytes (for word processing), or you might need 1 megabyte or more (for graphics and spreadsheets). Software packages usually indicate the minimum amount of memory needed to use them. We recommend more than the minimum memory because larger memory capacity lets more or all of the program and your data reside in primary storage, thereby allowing the program to work faster.

☐ *Which microprocessor does the computer use, and what is the clock speed?* The amount of RAM, the microprocessor, and the clock speed all contribute to the computer's processing speed. The computer may have an 8-bit, 16-bit, or 32-bit microprocessor. Clock speed is measured from a slow 4.77 megahertz in earlier microcomputers to as fast as 33 megahertz in 32-bit computers.

☐ *Can you expand the system later?* As you use your computer, you probably will discover other applications for it and may want to add them. You might want to run larger programs later—programs that demand more RAM. Is the primary storage of the computer you've selected expandable? How many ports and expansion slots are there to accommodate more memory and peripherals? Can more disk drives be added? Can a hard-disk drive be added? Can you add graphics capabilities? If you can't anticipate future needs, at least brief yourself on how much the system can be expanded so that you won't be disappointed later.

☐ *Can you understand the documentation provided with the computer?* Read some or all of it. Reference manuals and user's manuals should be clearly written, illustrated, and easy to understand. Some vendors offer classes in the use of the hardware and software packages they sell.

☐ *In a test drive, how does the equipment perform?* You may find that you prefer one computer over another. Try the keyboards—perhaps the touch of one is more comfortable for you than another. You may even find that one type of monitor is preferable over another.

TABLE E–3
Microcomputer buyer's check-list.

Tasks planned:

  1. _____

  2. _____

  3. _____

  4. _____

Select the software _____

Microprocessor:

  No. of bits _____

  Comments _____

Amount of RAM _____

Hard-disk capacity _____

Disk drives included _____

Monitor:

  80 columns _____

  Color: Composite _____

         RBG _____

  Monochrome: White

             Amber _____

             Green _____

Printer:

  Tractor/single sheet feed _____

  Daisy-wheel/dot-matrix/laser _____

  Carriage _____

    Width: 80 columns, 132 columns _____

  Bidirectional printing _____

Quality of documentation _____

Name of vendor:

  Mail-order house _____

  General discount/department store _____

  Retail computer store _____

Vendor support _____

Maintenance _____

Service contract _____

Warranty _____

Price:

  System (includes which components) _____

  Other charges (shipping, tax, etc.) _____

□ *What level of service and maintenance does the vendor provide?* It is important to know that someone where you purchase the system is willing to answer questions if something does not work.

□ *What are the terms of the company's service contract?* Some companies offer service agreements that cover repairs after the warranty period has ended. These agreements cover a specified time period—usually one year—and include repairs on certain parts and equipment. Investigate the prices for this service. It may seem expensive to pay the lump-sum cost, but that choice may cover all repairs. You can choose to pay for any repairs yourself and hope that the total amount required ends up being less than what you would have paid for the service agreement. Table E−3 is a checklist of criteria to be considered when shopping for a microcomputer.

WARRANTIES

Become familiar with the warranty. Before you buy anything or sign any document, read the sales order and anything else you are asked to sign, front and back. A computer warranty states your rights and the degree to which the manufacturer is liable for repairs. It covers repairs during a set period of time (the warranty period) unless the damage results from improper handling, abuse, or accident. Some warranties are automatically voided if anyone other than an authorized technician repairs the equipment. Most companies guarantee hardware for 90 days. Check carefully, however; you may have as much as 18 months of protection. Software and disks are usually not covered in warranty agreements.

To protect consumers, legal experts have established for commercial transactions a set of guidelines called the Uniform Commercial Code. Article II of this code has been adopted as law throughout the United States (except Louisiana). Article II basically grants certain *implied warranties* on goods (not services) that are sold (not leased). These laws imply that computers (which are "goods sold") are "merchantable," meaning that they are at least reasonably fit and of average quality. However, printed sales agreements used by some companies try to disclaim merchantability.

If you have already signed an agreement, you may have forfeited or waived some rights; however, all is not lost. *Express warranties* may have been created during the negotiations of the sale. An express warranty is based on a salesperson's claims for the product. Document these claims by taking notes—sales personnel names, dates, and specific promises or claims. Also, check advertisements or brochures, where promises or guarantees of performance may have been made.

If problems arise in getting repairs made, negotiate with the company to the best of your ability. If that discussion brings no equitable settlement, contact an attorney to find out about other alternatives available to you.

Software warranties rarely promise that the software will work as described or do all that the advertising claims. Usually, you buy software "as is." However, there are guarantees against physical defects of a disk itself. Although many programs have been on the market long enough to establish a good track record of reliability and workability, sometimes software is rushed into the marketplace before it is fully tested. Sometimes it is released and users find problems which they report to the company; eventually a new, corrected version is issued. These facts are reason enough to read reviews and get recommendations from reliable sources.

USER GROUPS

After you've become a microcomputer owner, you may want to contact a *user group*, an informal organization of owners of microcomputers like yours. People in such organizations exchange information about hardware and software and help each other find solutions to problems they encounter. Often, members share programs they have written.

A user group is a valuable resource when you are planning to buy another piece of equipment or a new software package. More than likely, someone in the group will have used that item and can give you inside information about it. Ask your computer dealer for the name of the contact person for a local user group. Sometimes, the name and address of a national user group are included in the package with your new computer.

COMPUTER MAGAZINES

Dozens of magazines are written for microcomputer users. They review software packages, describe the latest technological advances, critique the latest hardware, and present many ideas for new ways to use your computer. Some print prewritten programs that are free for anyone to type into a computer and use. Many have columns that address users' problems and present authoritative commentary on computer concerns. Many present ideas and information from other readers on how they use their computers. Some are for users of specific computers. Their level varies from beginner to highly technical. Here are some popular magazines:

- ☐ *Byte*—monthly
- ☐ *Compute!*—monthly
- ☐ *Computerworld*—weekly
- ☐ *Home-Office Computing*—monthly
- ☐ *InfoWorld*—weekly
- ☐ *MacUser*—monthly
- ☐ *Macworld*—monthly
- ☐ *PC/Computing*—monthly
- ☐ *PC Magazine*—twice monthly
- ☐ *PC World*—monthly

WHERE TO SHOP

Software buyers can purchase through retail computer stores, mail-order houses, general discount stores, department stores, bookstores, and special discount software stores. Public domain software and shareware programs also are available at modest or no cost.

Hardware buyers can shop retail computer stores, mail-order houses, general discount stores, and department stores. There also are outlets where you can buy reliable used computers.

Retail Stores

Microcomputers and software can be purchased at general discount stores such as K Mart and at most large department stores. Radio Shack sells its own line of computers. Retail chains such as Entre and ComputerLand specialize in computers. ComputerLand, with over 800 stores, sells many name brands and models, peripheral devices, software, computer supplies, and even books and periodicals relating to computers.

There are several advantages to buying your computer at a computer store. First, they usually provide the most service and support. They are usually willing and able to answer questions or help solve problems you encounter in using your new equipment. Second, some computer stores have repair centers right in the store. If not, they will send your computer to a service center if a repair is needed. Third, you can examine what you are buying, view a demonstration, and even try the computer. A major disadvantage, however, is that you will probably pay more.

Software also can be purchased at computer stores. One advantage is that computer stores often provide the name of a contact person to answer questions and help troubleshoot. In addition, you can view a demonstration in the store. A disadvantage is that computer-store software selections are smaller, because they usually stock only the best-selling programs. Second, unless you are also buying equipment, you will receive fewer discounts.

For software purchases, a good alternative to a computer store is a specialized software discount store. For example, Egghead Discount Software has stores across the country, stocks almost every kind of software imaginable, and sells at discount prices.

Mail-Order Houses

Another option when purchasing either hardware or software is to order by mail. Advertisements in magazines offer lower-priced computers and software. Some of the products are brand names, but you may not recognize the names of others. Ordering computers and software by mail is part of a major trend in this country of buying consumer products by mail.

The advantage of buying by mail is lower price—sometimes 15–50 percent below store prices. Disadvantages include the fact that you don't get the customer service and support that you would in a computer store. In addition, you can't see what you are getting or get a demonstration. (If you don't know exactly what you want or you misunderstand the description of the equipment or software, you may be surprised when the package arrives.)

It is usually less risky to buy software, computer accessories, and supplies by mail order than it is to buy a computer. Most mail-order problems can be avoided through careful research before you purchase. Here are a few tips when ordering hardware or software by mail:

□ Check the reputation of the company selling the computer or the software. Consult a major computer magazine for articles and suggestions. Most magazines will not run an ad from a company with a bad reputation. Contact the Better Business Bureau or Chamber of Commerce in the company's city. Better Business Bureaus keep records of consumer complaints on mail-order companies. Call the company if you have questions the advertisement doesn't answer. Often, the cooperation you receive over the phone is an indication of what to expect if problems develop. If the company's representatives respond with "we just take orders" and cannot direct you to anyone who can answer your questions, beware.

☐ If it's your first time ordering from a particular mail-order house, place a small order to see if service is good.

☐ Ask how soon the order will be shipped. Usually the wait is a week or more. If orders are backlogged (for example, during certain seasons), shipment might take 4 to 6 weeks.

☐ Ask what the price of a computer system includes. Sometimes the price listed does not include the disk drive, printer, or other peripherals.

☐ Ask about return and refund policies if something does not work properly. What warranty is provided? Is it a manufacturer's warranty or does the mail-order house offer its own? Reliable companies often offer a free trial period, a money-back guarantee, and a toll-free telephone number to call in the event a problem arises. Some policies say that a product has to be defective to be returned for refund; others say that all sales are final.

☐ If your computer must be repaired, consider that you will be without it during the repair time and the time involved in shipping it back and forth—typically, one to three weeks. Also, usually you will have to pay the shipping cost if an item is returned for repair. You might want to take the machine to a local repair center instead.

Your College or University

If you are a student or employee of a larger college or university, you may be able to purchase a computer, peripherals, and software at a generous discount, often through the bookstore. "Package deals" that include a basic computer, monitor, printer, hard drive, mouse, and bundled software are common and seasonal, as at the start of the fall semester or Christmastime. Good discounts are possible because of high sales volumes and the desire of computer manufacturers to have your first computer be their brand.

Used-Computer Outlets

A viable option for those who don't really need or can't afford the hottest, latest item is the used computer. This option appeals to home users, schools, and small businesses.

Because personal computers have solid-state circuitry and few moving parts, they don't wear out like automobiles. Also, advanced new models are brought to market very rapidly each year. Because of these phenomena, a market is appearing for used PCs. A three-year-old PC may seem obsolete compared with the latest model, but most likely, it is capable of doing the job for most of us. Computer Renaissance, a chain of retail outlets for used personal computers, sells to just this type of buyer. Some new-computer stores also sell used machines that have been traded in for the latest model.

The Boston Computer Exchange, the country's largest used-computer brokerage firm and now a service available on CompuServe, helps people who want to sell and buy used computers. The Exchange keeps lists of buyers and sellers and puts them in touch with each other. When a transaction is made and the buyer is satisfied, the Exchange collects a small fee. If there is a problem, the buyer can return the item or possibly renegotiate. You can call the Exchange directly (800/262–6399). Some newspapers print their daily "BoCoEx Index" of going rates for many used computers.

Here are tips to follow when buying a used PC:

☐ Try the keyboard. Make sure that none of the keys stick and that it has the right touch.
☐ Run a piece of software that you are familiar with to try out the disk drives, the most sensitive part of a computer system.
☐ Make sure that all necessary cables are included.
☐ Try to get the computer in its original packing box (the safest way to move a computer) and have the seller include all instructions that came with the computer.
☐ Notice if the computer is very dirty, an indication that it may have not have been cared for properly.

Low-Cost Sources of Software

Literally thousands of public domain software and shareware programs are available to users. *Public domain programs,* or freeware, are programs that are neither copy-protected or copyrighted and are made available by their authors for anyone to use. The Boston Computer Society, among other user groups, is a good source of free programs, programs that cost a few dollars, or programs for which you are charged just for the cost of the disk and mailing. Some information services such as CompuServe offer their subscribers public domain programs in just about any category. Notices of public domain programs regularly appear in popular computer magazines like *Compute!*

Shareware software is available for anyone to use free, but authors request that you send a donation if you have found their particular program useful. Quicksoft in Seattle and Buttonware in Bellevue (both Washington) are shareware companies. Unlike commercial software, shareware can be copied and passed from user to user. However, the author retains the copyright to the program.

The advantages of acquiring software in these two ways are low cost and the possibility of experimenting with different types of programs. A disadvantage is that the programs are not name-brand software and thus may not be widely used, so you may have trouble finding other users who can exchange information and ideas about the product. If you have problems with the software, you may not have access to the authors to answer questions or help you troubleshoot. Also, because shareware often is acquired not from its originator but via a bulletin board or information service having wide public access, the risk of obtaining a program infected with a computer virus is greater.

CARING FOR A MICROCOMPUTER SYSTEM

Large computer systems are generally located in environmentally controlled rooms where temperature and humidity are monitored and controlled. These rooms also protect against airborne contaminants such as dust and smoke. Although microcomputers are susceptible to the same agents, they usually are located in areas that do not afford such a level of protection. Thus, microcomputer users must assume more responsibility for protective maintenance of their systems. Besides obvious don'ts, such as eating or drinking while working at a computer, some other concerns are sometimes ignored (specific precautions may be listed in the owner's manual).

Choose a place for your system that is comfortable and offers substantial support for the computer and its peripheral devices. Use a sturdy table or desktop, not subject to jostling or moving. Once the computer is set up, further movement should be minimized. When moving a computer over a considerable distance, repack it in its original box to afford maximum protection.

Protect your microcomputer from temperature and humidity extremes, magnetic fields, foreign debris, and static electricity. Table E–4 itemizes some specific factors to consider in caring for a microcomputer system.

One special rule in caring for a hard disk drive is to keep it *parked* when not in use. When the drive is parked, it locks the read/write head away from the disk. This prevents the head from bouncing into and damaging the disk if the computer is bumped or moved. Many disk drives

TABLE E–4
Microcomputer hazards.

Problem	Solution
Temperature extremes	Position computer away from sources of heat and cold. Temperature should be under 85°F.
Humidity extremes	Use humidifier or dehumidifier to allow for 50–70 percent humidity.
Magnetic fields	Place computer away from electric motors, television sets, monitors, appliances, and other magnetic fields.
Dust, smoke, food, fumes	Do not smoke, eat, drink, or leave debris near the computer.
Static electricity	Use antistatic mat, rug, or spray to reduce static electricity.

automatically park the heads; others require you to run a program to park them—see the instruction manual.

Cleaning

First, avoid the personal hazard of electrical shock:

> *Unplug the computer system* before you begin any cleaning or housekeeping chores. The system generates up to 25,000 volts of electricity, creating a shock hazard.

Second, avoid damage to the computer system itself. Do not allow liquid cleaners to get inside a monitor or computer. In general, do not use sprays or liquid cleaners around a computer, because spilling even a drop of liquid on a keyboard can cause problems, ranging from sticking keys to damaged circuit boards.

Some computers can be opened, allowing access to the internal circuitry so that it can be cleaned. Some computers do not open and cannot be cleaned inside. Clean inside a system with extreme care, because circuit boards should not be bumped or damaged. On the other hand, if dust is not removed, a buildup over time can cause heat retention, which may damage delicate parts.

You can purchase compressed air canisters to blow out dust particles without touching anything. You also can use a household vacuum cleaner externally on air vents, disk drive openings, and any other cracks or openings where dust accumulates, using a crevice tool attachment. Special computer-cleaning kits are available, complete with miniature vacuum cleaners, brushes, and other cleaning apparatus.

Vexing problems can occur if timely, preventive maintenance is not done and the equipment becomes dirty. Erratic printing can be caused by dirty contacts, bits of paper, or lint stuck inside a printer. If you provide proper preventive maintenance you can avoid a service call. Table E–5 outlines specific cleaning instructions for the hardware and software.

Other Tips

Computer systems are powered by electricity, so all general guidelines concerning electrical appliances apply to them. To repeat, *unplug electrical appliances from the source of electricity* before you do any cleaning. Do not turn on a computer before you plug it in. (This precaution avoids a surge of electricity that can damage the system.) Also, it is better for the computer to leave it on all day than to turn it on and off many times a day.

A *surge protector* is a device recommended to guard against power-line disturbances that can occur when lights flicker due to other appliances switching on and off, or when electricity is interrupted during a thunderstorm or for some other reason. If the electricity should go off, unplug the system so that when electrical power is restored, the surge of electricity will not place sensitive circuits at risk.

Computer system unit
- ☐ Extreme care should be used because of delicate circuitry inside the unit.
- ☐ Special cleaning kits are available, or have it cleaned at a computer store by a professional.
- ☐ Use air cannister to blow out dust.

Disk drives
- ☐ Experts disagree on frequency and advisability of disk drive cleaning.
- ☐ Purchase a special cleaning kit or have the drive cleaned at a computer store.

Monitors
- ☐ Use glass cleaner to keep screen clean.
- ☐ Vacuum the dust from crevices and around switches and knobs.

Keyboards
- ☐ Use moist, not dripping, cotton swab to clean keys of accumulated dirt, grease, and fingerprints.
- ☐ Vacuum particles of skin, hair, and dust from between keys.

Connections
- ☐ Use a contact cleaner to ensure proper electrical contact.
- ☐ Vacuum crevices for dust and debris.

Printers
- ☐ Use line feed and page feed selectors rather than manually advancing paper.
- ☐ Vacuum to remove dirt, lint, and paper fuzz.

Print heads (e.g., daisy-wheel thimble)
- ☐ Use a cotton swab moistened with typewriter cleaning solution or rubbing alcohol to remove ink buildup.

Protect all the components with dust covers when not in use.

If your data are particularly critical, a backup generator system or an uninterruptible power supply (UPS) may be an appropriate, if expensive, addition.

If a computer system is connected to an electrical strip on the floor, place the strip out of the way so that it does not create a dual problem: a tripping hazard for people and a shutoff hazard for the system, causing loss of data. Take special precautions if a wall switch controls power to the computer so that no one accidentally turns it off at an inopportune time, such as before work is saved or backed up.

DISKETTES

Diskettes are critical—after all, they store your valuable data—and are particularly delicate. They must never be bent, folded, twisted, subjected to temperature extremes, or paperclipped. (A paperclip not only can crease a diskette; clips kept in a magnetic paperclip container can become magnetized and can scramble data on your disk!) Handle diskettes only by touching the cardboard or plastic protective jacket. Even clean hands leave fingerprints that can obstruct a drive head when it tries to read the disk.

Unless the label has not yet been affixed to the diskette, use only felt-tipped pens to write diskette labels. To avoid denting or creasing the diskette, use only a felt-tipped pen to write on a diskette label that is already affixed to the diskette. Use paper file jackets to protect the exposed surfaces of a diskette, and store them in cardboard or plastic boxes. Diskettes that contain data should be protected from magnetic fields by not storing them on or near a computer, disk drive, or other electrical device or appliances.

The preceding advice applies particularly to the more vulnerable 5¼-inch diskettes. However, treat the more rugged 3½-inch diskettes with respect, too!

PROTECTING SOFTWARE AND DATA

As you can see, your valuable software and data are vulnerable both in the computer's internal (RAM) storage and in external diskette storage. One of the best ways to protect them is to make backup copies frequently and store at least one copy away from the computer. The safest practice is to make backup copies every 15 minutes. Although they take extra time and may be a nuisance to make, backup copies of an afternoon's work may save you half the night trying to reconstruct lost data! (Fortunately, some software, like WordPerfect, has an automatic backup feature which can be set to make a backup at whatever interval you select.)

For really valuable data, you may require additional protection in the form of safe-deposit boxes or specially built diskette vaults. Some vaults are merely tamperproof, but others are designed and insulated to withstand the high temperatures of a fire. Consider this type of storage for diskettes that contain valuable data.

EQUIPMENT, WARRANTIES, SERVICE, AND INSURANCE

Even with the best of care, a machine may require a service call. As we mentioned, most equipment is covered initially by limited warranty agreements for a specified period of time, usually from 90 days to one year. Some manufacturers offer extended warranties, on-site repair, and loaner machines. Remember that most warranties will be invalidated if you, or any other unauthorized person, try to make repairs.

A maintenance contract is a form of extended warranty. For a set fee, a maintenance contract provides authorized service on specified equipment for a period of time. Such contracts are particularly useful for equipment that contains moving parts, such as printers and disk drives.

Some people choose to take the risk of theft or loss of their computer equipment, and others elect to pay a premium and let an insurance company take that risk. Carrying insurance and paying for a service contract on a home computer are personal choices. Some homeowner's policies include coverage of computer equipment automatically, but you should consult your agent to verify your individual policy.

APPENDIX F

Structured Programming Concepts

OUTLINE

WHY YOU NEED TO KNOW ABOUT PROGRAMMING
QUALITIES OF A GOOD PROGRAM
STRUCTURED PROGRAMMING CONCEPTS
Need for Structured Programming I Control Structures I Top-Down Design and Use of Modules I Management Control I The Importance of Documentation

WHY YOU NEED TO KNOW ABOUT PROGRAMMING

You may have no intention of becoming a programmer or of programming your own software. You may be interested only in knowing how to use commercially available application programs, such as word-processing, database, or spreadsheet packages. Why, then, should you take the time to learn about programming concepts?

First, your basic knowledge of how a computer works and what it can do will increase. As your understanding increases, computers will become both less intimidating and more useful. Second, the chance that you will have to communicate with a programmer, directly or indirectly, is increasing as computers become more prevalent. Your understanding of a programmer's work and the information needed to do that work will help the two of you work together more effectively. And third, many application programs, particularly databases, incorporate fourth-generation languages (4GL) that can be easily used by nonprogrammers to take greater advantage of a program's power.

Therefore, knowledge of the basic concepts of good program design and development can be beneficial even if you don't intend to do much traditional programming.

QUALITIES OF A GOOD PROGRAM

A good program should have these characteristics:

- ☐ Correct and accurate
- ☐ Easy to understand
- ☐ Easy to maintain and update
- ☐ Efficient
- ☐ Reliable
- ☐ Flexible

A correct and accurate program will do without error what it was designed to do in accordance with the specifications laid out during program design. The program should be designed so that anyone working with it finds its logic easy to understand. It should also be designed and documented so that program maintenance and updating can be achieved with relative ease. In addition, the program should run efficiently by executing quickly and using computer resources conservatively, such as main memory.

The reliability of a program is its ability to operate under unforeseen circumstances, such as invalid data entries. For example, if a program expects a yes or no response but you type in a number, the program should recognize the error, inform you that you have made an invalid entry, and indicate the proper form of response needed by the program. Nonetheless, a flexible program operates with a wide range of legitimate input. For example, if a program requests a yes or no answer, it should accept any combination of capital and lowercase letters for the words *yes* and *no*, in addition to the single letters *Y, y, N,* and *n*.

STRUCTURED PROGRAMMING CONCEPTS

As uses for computers become more sophisticated, the software required to accomplish these tasks becomes more complicated. A method is needed to control development of programs and assure their quality. Edsger Dijkstra, a major proponent of structured programming, thinks that programming ultimately will be tested mathematically rather than by the present method of trial and error. According to Dijkstra, the presence of bugs—errors— may be merely annoying in many programming situations, such as fouled-up airline reservations; but in others, such as the launching and guidance of space flights, that presence may be a life-and-death matter. An example of such a situation occurred in 1981 when the first launching of a U.S. space shuttle was halted because software errors caused the shuttle's computers to lose synchronization.

Dijkstra and others think that traditional programming is sloppy in design. Commonly, such programming relies on specific GOTO commands, which tell the computer to go to another, sometimes distant, point in the program. The use of this command in extended programming results in enormous structural complexity and creates innumerable opportunities for errors. Structured programming is a step toward improving the design process, testing to ensure that a program is error free.

Need for Structured Programming

In the early days of computers, programming was more an art than a science, and developing a quality program was more a hit-or-miss proposition than a planned goal. Given a programming task, programmers were left on their own to create a solution in any way they could.

But three major problems arose from this free-form method: (1) long development time, (2) high maintenance cost, and (3) low-quality software. Managers found that many software projects took too long to complete; they wanted to increase the productivity of programmers. In addition, software development cost was getting out of hand. As the computer age moved forward, hardware cost began to decrease, but software development cost, especially personnel, were rising sharply. Most of the money invested in a computer system was spent on software-related cost, particularly on maintaining software. Many organizations were spending over 60 percent of their time repairing and enhancing systems that were already installed. Not only was the cost of developing, testing, and maintaining programs too high, but it was continuing to increase. To avoid these high costs, program designs had to be right the first time.

Many programs also were of low quality; they were too complex and had poor documentation. As a result, they were difficult to test and maintain, and numerous errors went undetected. Programmers in many cases lost sight of user requirements; consequently, the programs did not meet user needs.

These problems forced a search for solutions. The work of Dijkstra and others led to development of the structured programming concept. **Structured programming** stresses the systematic design and management of the program development process. Its purpose and overall goals are to:

- ☐ Decrease development time by increasing programmer productivity and reducing the time to test and debug a program
- ☐ Decrease maintenance cost by reducing errors and making program code easier to understand
- ☐ Improve the quality of delivered software by providing programs with fewer errors.

Structured programming attempts to accomplish these goals by incorporating these concepts:

- ☐ Use of limited control structures (sequence, selection, and repetition)
- ☐ Top-down design and use of modules
- ☐ Management control.

Control Structures

What is a control structure? It is a device in a programming language that determines the *order of execution* of program statements. In the late 1960s

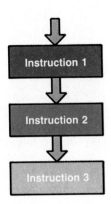

FIGURE F–1
A sequence control structure.

two mathematicians, Corrado Bohm and Guiseppe Jacopini, proved that even the most complex program logic could be expressed with three control structures: sequence, selection, and repetition (also called looping or iteration). Dijkstra put forth this same theory in his article "Notes on Structured Programming."

A **sequence control structure** executes statements one after another in a linear fashion (Figure F–1).

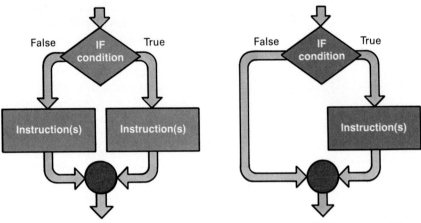

IF condition, THEN instruction(s),
ELSE instruction(s)

IF condition, THEN instruction(s)

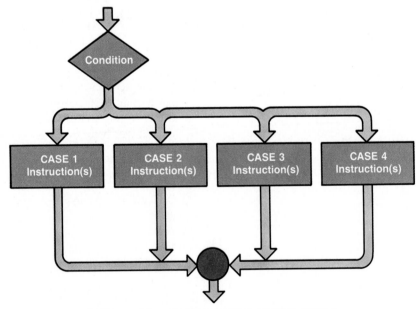

CASE condition: CASE 1, CASE 2, CASE 3, CASE 4

FIGURE F–2
Selection control structures.

FIGURE F–3
A DO WHILE control structure.

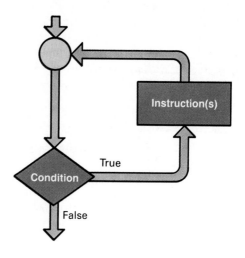

The **selection control structure** presents a number of processing options. The option chosen depends on the result of the decision criterion. Figure F–2 depicts some variations of a selection control structure.

A **repetition control structure** is used to execute an instruction(s) more than once without having it recoded. The two basic variations of this type of structure are DO WHILE and DO UNTIL. If the decision criterion (condition) is placed before the statements (instructions) to be repeated, then it is a DO WHILE loop (Figure F–3). A DO UNTIL loop places the decision criterion at the end of the statements to be repeated (Figure F–4). In this particular structure, statements are always executed at least once.

A fourth type of control structure commonly used in early programs was the unconditional branch. In many programming languages this structure took the form of a GOTO statement. It allowed program execution to jump indiscriminately to other points in the program. However, programs

FIGURE F–4
A DO UNTIL control structure.

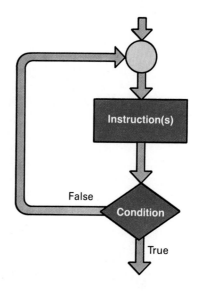

designed with several of these unconditional branches were very confusing and difficult to follow, thereby earning them the name "spaghetti code." Avoidance of unconditional branching was part of the first step toward a structured programming methodology.

Top-Down Design and Use of Modules

Structured programming also advocates a top-down approach to problem solving. **Top-down design** starts with the major functions involved in a problem and divides them into subfunctions until the problem has been divided as much as possible. Top-down design involves three major steps:

1. Defining the output, input, and major processing steps required.
2. Step-by-step refining of the major processing steps.
3. Designing the algorithms.

The first step itself involves three separate processes: first the desired outputs are defined, then the required inputs are determined, and finally the major processing tasks are specified.

In the second step, each of the major processing tasks is broken down into smaller and smaller tasks until one unit is small enough to be programmed by an individual programmer in the required time frame. This approach forces an examination of all aspects of a problem on one level before considering the next level. A programmer is left with small groups, or **modules,** of processing instructions, which are easy to understand and code. Thus, a program will consist of a main logic module that is used to control the execution of the other modules in the program. Working from the top down (from the general to the specific) rather than from the bottom up avoids partial solutions that deal with only part of a problem.

In addition, a program that uses a main logic module to control smaller modules is easier to read, test, and maintain. In structured programming, modules ensure these qualities by:

- Having only one entrance and one exit
- Performing only one program function
- Returning control to the module from which it was received.

The third step in top-down design involves designing the algorithm for each module. An **algorithm** is the finite set of step-by-step instructions that solves a problem. The main module is considered first and development then moves down by level or by path:

- In programming by *level,* each complete level of modules is coded before the next lower level is considered. In Figure F–5, programming by level would follow a numeric order.
- In programming by *path,* all modules along a path are coded in sequence before other paths are considered. In Figure F–5, programming by path would follow an alphabetic order.
- Top-down design has often resulted in a lower error rate and shorter program development time.

FIGURE F–5
Coding by level and by path.

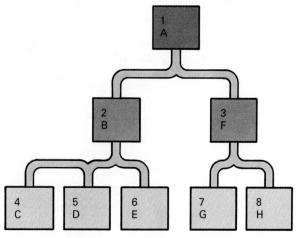

Coding by level: 1 2 3 4 5 6 7 8

Coding by path: A B C D E F G H

Management Control

Management control is an essential part of structured programming. It prevents a project from being sidetracked, keeps it on schedule, and assures that user needs are met. When many people are involved in design and development of a large program, different ideas and methods surface. To avoid conflict, a **chief programmer team** is established, consisting of specialized personnel to design and develop the program. Although the type of specialists may vary depending on the project, a typical team might consist of:

☐ Chief programmer
☐ Assistant programmer
☐ Librarian
☐ Other specialists as needed

A *chief programmer* defines portions of program development, assigns them to various team members, and takes responsibility for a project (Figure F–6). This individual reviews each member's work, coordinates integration of tasks, and conducts liaison between management and the project. The chief programmer makes sure that appropriate personnel are on the team and changes its makeup as needed.

The *assistant programmer* works directly with the chief programmer. Depending on the size of the project, there may be more than one assistant. For very large projects, separate teams of programmers are sometimes established. Each team might have a group leader who would report to an assistant programmer or directly to the chief programmer.

The *librarian's* responsibility is to maintain and make available project records, such as program listings, test results, and so on. Other specialists, such as *systems analysts* or *financial analysts,* may also be a part of

FIGURE F–6
An assistant programmer discusses a problem with the chief programmer. (Macmillan Publishing/Cobalt Productions)

a chief programmer team. The nature of each project determines their involvement. Thus, the makeup of a chief programmer team depends on the nature of the problem, in addition to management philosophy and cost factors.

One technique a chief programmer team may use before beginning to code a program is a **structured walk-through** with a systems analyst, one or more users, and possibly other system personnel. With team members present, the systems analyst discusses, or walks through, the program design. The rationale is that errors may be caught and corrected before programming begins.

The concepts of structured programming are important to remember and follow when using any programming language, whether for business or personal use. A program that adheres to these concepts will be much easier to maintain and modify than one that doesn't.

The Importance of Documentation

Documentation is the text/graphics that provides specific instructions about, or records the purpose or function of, a particular step or instruction in a program. Each step throughout the programming process should be documented. Documentation is sometimes done as an afterthought rather than as an ongoing integral part of the project, but when approached in this manner it can become an overwhelming burden of paperwork. If documentation guidelines are established and followed from the beginning of a project, the process will take less time and effort in the long run.

There are two good reasons to document a program. First, documentation leaves a clear record for someone else to understand what was done.

This record is extremely important in a business environment because it is likely that the person who later corrects an error or modifies the program will not be the same person who originally designed or coded it.

Second, documenting a program as it is developed forces reexamination of the actions taken. Thus, problems may be discovered early enough to avoid costly alterations later. Documentation is important even if you are programming for your own use.

For documentation to be of value, it must be clear, concise, and available to all who need it. Many organizations maintain a library where copies of all documentation are accessible to authorized personnel.

Most organizations keep several types of documentation during program development. Here are a few:

- [ ] Program specifications describe what the program is intended to accomplish; they help the programmer design the program.
- [ ] The program description details what the completed program actually does.
- [ ] Program design charts (flowcharts, pseudocode, etc.) outline the specific steps used in the program to produce the desired results.
- [ ] Description of testing done and errors found. Types of testing, data used, and errors found are typically recorded in separate documentation.
- [ ] Operator's manual (user's guide) provides details on how to operate the program.
- [ ] Maintenance documentation records changes made to the program, with detailed explanations.

The type of documentation kept depends on each programming department's various requirements.

Vocabulary Self-Test

Can you define the following?

algorithm (p. 452)

chief programmer team (p. 453)

documentation (p. 454)

module (p. 452)

repetition control structure (p. 451)

selection control structure (p. 451)

sequence control structure (p. 450)

structured programming (p. 449)

structured walk-through (p. 454)

top-down design (p. 452)

Review Questions

1. Why it is important to learn about programming even if you don't intend on becoming a programmer?
2. List six characteristics of a good program and explain each.
3. What were the three major problems that led to the development of structured programming concepts?
4. What is structured programming?

5. List the purpose and overall goals of structured programming and how structured programming attempts to accomplish them.

6. What is a control structure?

7. List and describe the three control structures used in structured programming.

8. What is the purpose of the unconditional branch structure and why is its use not promoted by structured programming?

9. Describe top-down design and list the three major steps involved.

10. What is a program module and what features should it have?

11. What is the purpose of management control in structured programming?

12. What is the purpose of a chief programmer team?

13. What is documentation and why is it important?

APPENDIX G

The BASIC Programming Language

OUTLINE

STARTING BASIC

Hard Disk with Microsoft GWBASIC or IBM BASIC Stored in a Directory ⏐ Hard Disk with Microsoft GWBASIC or IBM BASIC Stored on a Floppy Diskette ⏐ Microsoft GWBASIC or IBM BASIC with System Having Only Two Floppy-Diskette Drives

TYPES OF COMMANDS

MODES

Command Mode ⏐ Program Mode

BASIC PROGRAM LINES

BASIC'S CHARACTER SET AND RESERVED WORDS

BASIC'S DATA TYPES

BASIC'S DATA STRUCTURES

Constants ⏐ Variables ⏐ Arrays ⏐ Files

EXPRESSIONS AND DATA OPERATORS

Arithmetic Operators ⏐ Relational Operators

SYSTEM COMMANDS

The LIST Command ⏐ The LLIST Command ⏐ The RUN Command ⏐ Naming and Accessing Files in BASIC ⏐ The SAVE Command ⏐ The LOAD Command ⏐ The NEW Command ⏐ Editing Program Lines ⏐ The DELETE Command ⏐ The RENUM Command ⏐ The SYSTEM Command

THE PRINT STATEMENT

Printing Blank Lines ⏐ Printing Constants ⏐ Printing Variables ⏐ Formatting Output with the PRINT Statement

THE LPRINT STATEMENT

THE LET STATEMENT

THE END STATEMENT

THE REM STATEMENT

MULTISTATEMENT LINES

THE INPUT STATEMENT

BASIC stands for **B**eginner's **A**ll-Purpose **S**ymbolic **I**nstruction **C**ode. It was developed in the early 1960s at Dartmouth College by John G. Kemeny and Thomas E. Kurtz. The first version of BASIC, formally introduced in 1966, was intended as an easy-to-learn interactive language for teaching beginners how to program. Initially designed to run in a time-sharing environment, BASIC's time-sharing, interactive nature made it ideal for teaching inexperienced users because results of students' programs were available almost immediately. This provided positive feedback if the program worked or a timely chance for error correction if it did not.

BASIC gained popularity on minicomputers in the 1970s and was the first high-level language used on microcomputers. Today, almost all microcomputers have a version of BASIC available. Most of these versions use an interpreter, which converts one line at a time of BASIC code into machine language for the computer. Some BASICs use a compiler, which translates an entire program at a time into machine language. Although the compiler approach creates a smaller machine-language program that executes faster, that approach can also make it more difficult for inexperienced users to create and debug a BASIC program. An interpreted BASIC program gives users immediate feedback on whether something they have just typed has the correct syntax. Because it is easier to use, this appendix will refer to an interpreted version of BASIC.

We cannot cover the many versions of BASIC in this supplement. Our reference version is Microsoft GWBASIC 3.11. Very similar to this is IBM's version, IBM BASIC. This appendix applies equally to both. Microsoft GWBASIC is contained entirely on a disk file called BASIC. The core of IBM BASIC is contained in ROM, and extensions to the core BASIC are contained in files called BASIC and BASICA. Typing BASIC loads the core BASIC from ROM and the extensions contained in the BASIC file. Typing BASICA loads the full version of BASIC, including the core BASIC from ROM, the extensions in the BASIC file, and the extensions in the BASICA file.

It is not our purpose to teach the entire BASIC language. Instead, we cover only a subset of the language that is useful in illustrating some basic structures and concepts involved in any programming language.

STARTING BASIC

Here are three procedures for loading BASIC, depending on where the software is stored in your system.

Hard Disk with Microsoft GWBASIC or IBM BASIC Stored in a Directory

We will assume that the directory name is BASIC. If your directory name is different, substitute the appropriate name. Follow this procedure to load:

1. Be sure drive A does *not* contain a diskette.
2. Turn the computer on. DOS is loaded.
3. Make sure you are in the directory that contains BASIC. (For example, if BASIC is in a directory called BASIC, type CD\BASIC at the C> prompt to make the directory named BASIC the current directory.)
4. Type the file name BASIC and press <Enter> (IBM BASIC: type BASICA to load the full version of BASIC). (Note: On older keyboards the <Enter> key may be labeled *Return*.)

Hard Disk with Microsoft GWBASIC or IBM BASIC Stored on a Floppy Diskette

Follow this procedure to load BASIC:

1. Be sure drive A does *not* contain a diskette.
2. Turn the computer on. DOS is loaded.
3. Insert the GWBASIC diskette into drive A (IBM BASIC: Insert the diskette containing the BASIC and BASICA files into drive A).
4. Type A: at the C> prompt and press <Enter>. (Note: On older keyboards the <Enter> key may be labeled *Return*.)
5. Type BASIC and press <Enter> (IBM BASIC: type BASICA to load the full version of BASIC).

Microsoft GWBASIC or IBM BASIC with System Having Only Two Floppy-Diskette Drives

Follow this procedure to load BASIC:

1. Insert a DOS diskette into drive A.
2. Turn on the computer. DOS is loaded.
3. Remove the DOS diskette from drive A.
4. Insert the GWBASIC diskette into drive A (IBM BASIC: Insert the diskette containing the BASIC and BASICA files into drive A).

5. Type BASIC and press <Enter> (IBM BASIC: Type BASICA to load the full version of BASIC). (Note: On older keyboards the <Enter> key may be labeled *Return*.)

An Ok prompt appears on the screen after BASIC is loaded (Figure G–1); it indicates that BASIC is ready to accept commands. When you see the Ok prompt, you can begin to create, change, or run a BASIC program.

REVIEW QUESTIONS 1

1. Describe how to load BASIC on your computer.
2. What does the Ok prompt indicate after BASIC is loaded?

TYPES OF COMMANDS

BASIC includes two types of commands: system commands and programming statements.

System commands direct the operating system to perform operations on existing programs, or on programs currently being created. The BASIC system commands that we will examine are LIST, LLIST, RUN, SAVE, LOAD, NEW, DELETE, and RENUM.

Programming statements make up a program; they direct the computer to perform the desired tasks. The BASIC programming statements that we will examine are PRINT, LPRINT, LET, END, REM, INPUT, CLS, READ, DATA, RESTORE, FOR, NEXT, WHILE, WEND, IF . . . THEN, IF . . . THEN . . . ELSE, GOTO, GOSUB, ON . . . GOSUB, RETURN, DIM, OPEN, PRINT #, INPUT #, and CLOSE.

FIGURE G–1
An Ok prompt indicates that BASIC is ready to accept commands.

MODES

BASIC has two modes—the command (direct) mode and the program (indirect) mode.

Command Mode

In the command mode, programming statements and system commands are not preceded by a line number. The statements and commands are executed immediately after <Enter> is pressed:

```
Ok
PRINT 10  <Enter>        (BASIC programming statement followed by
                         pressing <Enter>)
10                       (Program statement is executed
                         immediately after pressing <Enter>)
```

BASIC system commands for handling files and displaying the contents of a program are usually executed in this mode.

Program Mode

When you precede either a programming statement or a system command with a line number, BASIC automatically goes into a program mode, or indirect mode. In this mode, programming statements and system commands that are preceded by a line number are stored in main memory before being executed:

```
Ok
100 PRINT 10  <Enter>        (BASIC programming statement preced-
                             ed by a line number and followed by
                             pressing <Enter>. The program
                             statement is stored in main memory
                             and is not executed until the
                             appropriate system command is issued)
```

To execute these stored programming statements, you must type the system command RUN and press <Enter>. After they are executed, the program instructions stay in main memory; they can be assigned a name and saved for later use.

BASIC PROGRAM LINES

A BASIC program line (also called a program instruction) always begins with a *line number,* which is used to indicate the order in which the program lines are stored in main memory. In addition, a line number is used as a reference in branching and editing (discussed later). Line numbers must be between 0 and 65529. They are typically followed by *programming statements,* although system commands can also be used in program lines. Programming statements and system commands are followed by any appropriate *expressions.* Note that maximum length of a program line in

BASIC is 255 characters or spaces. These examples illustrate typical program lines:

Line Numbers	Program Statements	Expressions
30	LET	X = 10
40	LET	Y = 100 * .06
100	PRINT	X + Y

A BASIC program file consists of a series of BASIC programming lines. We'll examine program statements and expressions shortly.

BASIC'S CHARACTER SET AND RESERVED WORDS

The characters that can be used with BASIC include alphabetic characters (uppercase A to Z and lowercase a to z), numeric characters (0 to 9), and the special characters found in Table G–1.

Reserved words are words or abbreviations that have a special meaning to BASIC. All of BASIC's commands, statements, function names, and operator names are reserved words (see list in Table G–2). Reserved words cannot be used as variable names or to start variable names; however, they can be used as part of variable names. For example, NAME is a BASIC system command and thus is a reserved word. Consequently, NAME or NAMES cannot be used as a variable name, but LASTNAME is an accept-

TABLE G–1
BASIC's special characters.

Symbol	Name
	Blank
=	Equal sign or assignment symbol
+	Plus sign
−	Minus sign
*	Asterisk or multiplication symbol
/	Slash or division symbol
^	Exponentiation symbol
(	Left parenthesis
)	Right parenthesis
%	Percent sign
#	Number (or pound) sign
$	Dollar sign
!	Exclamation point
,	Comma
.	Period or decimal point
'	Apostrophe (or single quotation mark)
;	Semicolon
:	Colon
&	Ampersand
?	Question mark
<	Less than sign
>	Greater than sign
\	Back slash or integer division symbol
"	Double quotation mark
_	Underscore

ABS	DELETE	IOCTL	OPEN	SIN
AND	DIM	IOCTL$	OPTION	SOUND
ASC	DRAW	INT	OR	SPACE$
ATN	EDIT	KEY	OUT	SPC
AUTO	ELSE	KEY$	PAINT	SQR
BEEP	END	KILL	PALETTE	STEP
BLOAD	ENVIRON	LCOPY	PEEK	STICK
BSAVE	ENVIRON$	LEFT$	PEN	STOP
CALL	EOF	LEN	PLAY	STRIG
CDBL	EQV	LET	PMAP	STR$
CHAIN	ERASE	LINE	POINT	STRING$
CHDIR	ERDEV	LIST	POKE	SWAP
CHR$	ERDEV$	LLIST	POS	SYSTEM
CINT	ERL	LOAD	PRESET	TAB
CIRCLE	ERR	LOC	PRINT	TAN
CLEAR	ERROR	LOCATE	PRINT$	THEN
CLOSE	EXP	LOF	PSET	TIME$
CLS	FIELD	LOG	PUT	TIMER
COLOR	FILES	LPOS	RANDOMIZE	TO
COM	FIX	LPRINT	READ	TROFF
COMMON	FNxxxxx	LSET	REM	TRON
CONT	FOR	MERGE	RENUM	USING
COS	FRE	MID$	RESET	USR
CSNG	GET	MKDIR	RESTORE	VAL
CSRLIN	GOSUB	MKD$	RESUME	VARPTR
CVD	GOTO	MKI$	RETURN	VARPTR$
CVI	HEX$	MKS$	RIGHT$	VIEW
CVS	IF	MOD	RMDIR	WAIT
DATA	IMP	MOTOR	RND	WEND
DATE$	INKEY$	NAME	RSET	WHILE
DEF	INP	NEW	RUN	WIDTH
DEFDBL	INPUT	NEXT	SAVE	WINDOW
DEF FN	INPUT#	NOT	SCREEN	WRITE
DEFINT	INPUT$	OCT$	SEG	WRITE#
DEFSNG	INSTR	OFF	SGN	XOR
DEFSTR	INTER$	ON	SHELL	

able variable name. Delimiters such as commas or spaces always separate
BASIC reserved words from other BASIC commands and statements.

REVIEW QUESTIONS 2

1. Describe the two general types of commands included in BASIC.
2. List and describe the two modes found in BASIC.
3. What is the function of a line number?
4. Identify the invalid line:
   a. `64101 LET X = X + 1`
   b. `98 PRINT Y`
   c. `95000 PRINT X`
5. Identify the valid characters that can be used in BASIC.
6. What is a reserved word? Give two examples.

BASIC'S DATA TYPES

BASIC allows two basic data types: numeric and alphanumeric. Numeric data can be positive or negative numbers but cannot contain commas. BASIC allows five types of numeric data: integers, fixed point, floating point, hexadecimal, and octal:

□ Integers are whole numbers between −32768 and +32768. As whole numbers, they do not have decimal points—for example, 12, −2034, 10000, 3, −2, or 346.

□ Fixed point constants are positive or negative real numbers. A real number is one that *does* contain a decimal point—for example, −1.35, 2.00, 10.5679, −3.01, 100.45, or 50.00.

□ Floating point constants are positive or negative numbers that are represented in exponential form (also called scientific form). Such a constant is made up of three parts: a mantissa, the letter E, and an exponent. The mantissa may be a positive or negative integer or a positive or negative fixed point number. The exponent may also be a positive or negative integer. Floating point constants must be in the range of 10E−38 to 10E+38—for example, 12E06 (= 12,000,000) and 3.26E−06 (= .00000326).

□ Hexadecimal numbers are those preceded with the prefix &H—e.g., &H32F and &H2B, which equal 815 and 43, respectively.

□ Octal numbers are preceded with the prefix &O and &—e.g., &O143 and &72, which equal 99 and 58, respectively.

Alphanumeric data can consist of digits, alphabetic letters, and special characters.

BASIC'S DATA STRUCTURES

BASIC can handle data using four basic data structures: constants, variables, arrays, and files.

Constants

A constant is a value that does not change throughout the execution of a program. There are two kinds of constants—string constants and numeric constants.

A *string* is a sequence of alphanumeric characters. A *string constant* is a sequence of up to 255 alphanumeric characters enclosed in double quotation marks (" "); they do not change throughout a program's execution. These are examples of string constants:

```
"HI MOM"
"$2,000,000.00"
"NET SALES"
```

Strings must be enclosed in quotation marks when keying them in.

A *numeric constant* is any numeric data that does not change throughout the execution of a program. These are examples of numeric constants:

```
-2.00
54
45E-06
435.9854
```

Precision of Numeric Constants. BASIC provides for either single- or double-precision numeric constants. A single-precision numeric constant (1) has seven or fewer digits, (2) uses the exponential form with E, or (3) has a trailing exclamation point (!). These constants are stored with seven digits of precision and are displayed with up to seven digits. These are examples of single-precision numeric constants:

```
12.4
3.21E-05
53.1!
```

For many applications, single-precision numeric constants do not supply sufficiently accurate results. For example, when there are many dependent calculations, rounding errors can significantly alter the final result. To help alleviate this problem, BASIC allows the use of double-precision numeric constants.

A double-precision numeric constant (1) has eight or more digits, (2) uses the exponential form with D (which works just like the floating point constant except that D is substituted for E, and the numbers are stored with double precision), or (3) has a trailing number sign (#). These constants are stored with 17 digits of precision and require up to 16 digits for display. These are examples of double-precision numeric constants:

```
54369813852
-4.032693D-03
6.089#
8912523.4632
```

Variables

Variables are symbolic names representing values that may change as a BASIC program is executed. A variable can be assigned a specific value, or it can be assigned a value that results from calculation. A variable name must begin with a letter, but it can contain letters, numbers, and a decimal point (e.g., AMOUNT, T5, R6.2).

Some versions of BASIC recognize no more than 40 characters in a variable name. If names are larger, only the first 40 characters will be used by BASIC. Thus, if one variable name is 40 characters long and another is 48, but the first 40 characters in each are exactly the same, BASIC sees them as the same variable. Many versions of BASIC allow for longer variable names; if the version you are using does, you will want to take advantage of this feature to create more readable programs.

As noted earlier, reserved words cannot be used as variable names, or to start a variable name, but they can be used elsewhere in a variable name.

String Variables. A *string variable* is a symbolic name representing a sequence of alphanumeric characters, or string. A string variable must always end in a dollar sign ($) to indicate that the variable represents a string. A string variable is assumed to be null (has no value) before being assigned a string value in a program. These are examples of string variables:

```
A$
CITY$
LASTNAME$
```

Numeric Variables. The last character in the name of a numeric variable can be used to indicate whether the numeral represented by the variable name has an integer, single-precision, or double-precision value:

% indicates an integer variable (e.g., QUANTITY%).
! indicates a single-precision variable (e.g., PRICE!)
# indicates a double-precision variable (e.g., PI#)

If one of these symbols is not used as the last character, then the numeric variable is defaulted to single precision (e.g., TOTAL represents a single-precision value). Before a numeric variable is assigned a value, its value is assumed to be zero (0). These are examples of numeric variables:

```
X
TOTAL
AMOUNT
T1
T2
```

Arrays

An array is a set of main memory locations that are treated as a unit. BASIC allows one and two-dimensional arrays. A one-dimensional array can be thought of as a one-column list (Figure G–2). A two-dimensional array can be thought of as a table consisting of rows and columns (Figure G–3). Arrays can hold either numeric or string data, but not both at the same time.

Files

Files extend the data-handling capabilities of BASIC. A file is composed of records and fields; records can be equated to the rows of a table, and fields

FIGURE G–2
A one-dimensional array.

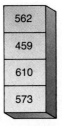

FIGURE G-3
A two-dimensional array.

24	19	23	12
31	72	45	50
27	24	18	30
46	12	21	35

to the columns of a table. However, unlike arrays, a file can contain both numeric and string data. In addition, files can be stored on secondary storage media, whereas arrays are stored only in main memory.

REVIEW QUESTIONS 3

1. Define constant. Describe the two types of constants found in BASIC.
2. Describe the difference between a single- and double-precision numeric constant. Why would you use a double-precision number?
3. What is a variable?
4. Distinguish between a string variable and a numeric variable.
5. What is an array?
6. What is a file?

EXPRESSIONS AND DATA OPERATORS

In BASIC an expression can be (1) a variable, (2) a string constant, (3) a numeric constant, or (4) a combination of constants and variables with operators to produce a single value. Operators perform mathematical or logical operations on values. BASIC divides operators into five different categories: arithmetic, relational, logical, functional, and string. In this appendix we will consider only arithmetic and relational operators.

Arithmetic Operators

BASIC maintains an *order of precedence* when evaluating expressions that use arithmetic operators. Table G-3 shows the operators in order of precedence.

Exponentiation operations, which involve raising a number to a power, are performed first. In BASIC X^Y would be represented as X^Y, and 3^2 would be 3^2.

Negation is the use of a negative sign to give a number a negative value (e.g., $-X$ or -4); negation is performed after exponentiation.

Multiplication uses the symbol * (e.g., X*Y or 3*4), and is the next operation performed.

Floating point division is performed next. It is division with real numbers and uses the slash symbol (/) (e.g., X/Y or 5.00/2.23).

Integer division is performed next. Before such division can take place, numbers must be rounded to integers. The quotient is also truncated to an integer, and the process is denoted by a backslash (\). For integer

TABLE G–3
Order of precedence of
arithmetic operators.

(handwritten notes in margin: "✓", "Read", "note", "Square Root Same priority as Exponent")

Operator	Operation	Explanation and Examples
( )	Operations in ( )	Operations always are performed inside parentheses first—5*(2/2 + 1) = 10.
^	Exponentiation *(handwritten: "also SqR")*	Raising a number to a power. (X^Y is represented as X^Y; 3^2 as 3^2) *(handwritten: ✓)*
–	Negation	Use of a negative sign to give a number a negative value. (–X; –4)
*	Multiplication	(X*Y; 3*4)
/	Floating point division	Division with real numbers. (X/Y; 5.00/2.23)
\	Integer division	Numbers must be rounded to integers and be in range of –32768 to +32767. (10\4 = 2; 25.68\6.99 = 3)
MOD	Modulo arithmetic	Gives integer remainder in integer division. (10.4 MOD 4 = 2)
+	Addition	Conventional addition. (7 + 6 = 13)
–	Subtraction	Conventional subtraction (9 – 2 = 7)

division, numbers must be in the range of -32768 to $+32767$. For example:

```
10\4 = 2
25.68\6.99 = 26\7 [rounded] = 3
```

Modulo arithmetic gives the integer value that is the remainder in integer division. The process is denoted by the operator MOD. You need to remember that numbers are rounded to integers before the division occurs. The following are two examples of modulo arithmetic:

```
10.4 MOD 4 = 2        (10\4 = 2 with a remainder of 2)
25.68 MOD 6.99 = 5    (26\7 = 3 with a remainder of 5)
```

Addition operations are next in the order of precedence, and finally subtraction operations are performed.

One factor that complicates this arrangement is that operations enclosed in parentheses override the order of precedence and are performed first. However, within the parentheses, operations follow the normal order. Consider this expression:

```
5*2/2 + 1
```

According to the order of operations, multiplication is done before division, which is done before addition. Therefore, 5*2 = 10 and 10/2 = 5 and 5 + 1 = 6. Thus, 5*2/2 + 1 = 6. Now let's change this expression to:

```
5*(2/2 + 1)
```

Operations within parentheses are done first, but within the parentheses operations follow the normal order. Thus, division is done first, followed by addition and then multiplication. Therefore, 2/2 = 1 and 1 + 1 = 2 and 5*2 = 10. Clearly, the expressions are different.

Relational Operators

Relational operators are used to compare two values. The relational operators used by BASIC are listed in Table G–4. The result of a comparison using a relational operator is either true (−1) or false (0). This result can then be used to redirect program flow. Whenever arithmetic and relational operators are combined in the same expression, *the arithmetic operators are performed first.* For example, in the expression A*B>C*D the arithmetic operations A*B and C*D are performed first. If the result of A*B is greater than C*D, the expression is true; otherwise the expression is false.

Strings can also be compared using these relational operators: =, <>, <, >, <=, and >=. When strings are compared, the ASCII code of each character is compared, starting with the first character in each string. String comparisons are used to test values and to alphabetize strings. (All strings must, of course, be enclosed in quotation marks.)

REVIEW QUESTIONS 4

1. Define a BASIC expression.
2. List the order of precedence of arithmetic operators.
3. What is the function of a relational operator?
4. Evaluate the following expressions:
   a. 8*3/2 + 10
   b. 8*3/(2 + 10)

SYSTEM COMMANDS

System commands operate on BASIC program files. The commands are usually used in the command (direct) mode, although in some cases they

TABLE G–4
Relational operators.

Operator	Relationship
=[1]	Equality
< > *same as* ≠	Inequality
<	Less than
>	Greater than
<=	Less than or equal to
>=	Greater than or equal to

[1]The equal sign has a dual role in BASIC. In addition to being a relational operator, it is also used to assign a value to a variable using the LET command.

can be used in a program mode. We will examine the most common commands used in the command mode: LIST, LLIST, RUN, SAVE, LOAD, NEW, DELETE, and RENUM.

If you type a program statement that is preceded by a line number and press <Enter>, that program line will be stored in computer memory. A BASIC program consists of a series of such program lines, just like those that make up this sample program:

```
10 REM Program Adds Two              (REM is a
   Numbers and Prints Sum            REMark or comment
                                     added for user
                                     convenience)

20 REM
30 REM Assign Values to
   Variables
40 LET X = 5
50 LET Y = 6
60 REM Calculate Sum of X and Y
70 LET N = X + Y
80 REM Display Output
90 PRINT "X", "Y", "X + Y"          (this prints
                                     headings X, Y, X+Y)

100 PRINT X,Y,N                      (this prints
                                     values for
                                     X, Y, X+Y)

999 END
```

Let's see how system commands can be used to act on this program.

The LIST Command

The LIST command displays the program currently in main memory. If the program shown above is currently in main memory, typing LIST and pressing <Enter> will display the entire program:

```
10 REM Program Adds Two Numbers and Prints Sum
20 REM
30 REM Assign Values to Variables
40 LET X = 5
50 LET Y = 6
60 REM Calculate Sum of X and Y
70 LET N = X + Y
80 REM Display Output
90 PRINT "X", "Y", "X + Y"
100 PRINT X,Y,N
999 END
```

LIST has several options that allow only specified portions of a program to be displayed. These are useful if a program listing is too long to fit on the display screen. These examples illustrate the options for viewing selected lines:

```
LIST                Lists the entire program
LIST 30 - 50        Lists lines 30 through 50
LIST -50            Lists all lines from the beginning of
                    the program through line 50
LIST 60-            Lists all lines from line 60 to the end
                    of the program
LIST 70             Lists only line 70
```

The LLIST Command

The LLIST command allows a program listing to be printed on a printer. It operates just as LIST does except that it directs the listing to a printer instead of to a display screen. The printer must be on and ready to use the LLIST command.

The RUN Command

The RUN statement is used to execute a program. With our program still in main memory, typing RUN and pressing <Enter> would produce the following output on the display screen.

```
X       Y       X + Y
 5       6        11
```

Naming and Accessing Files in BASIC

Some system commands store and retrieve files. A file is a collection of information, such as a program, stored on a floppy or a fixed disk. Each file must be given a unique file name, which is used to access the file. In addition, an optional extension may be used to help identify the file. The following list states rules for naming a file in BASIC:

- ☐ The file name can be from one to eight characters long (e.g., A or ACCOUNT1).
- ☐ An extension consists of a period (.) and one to three characters (e.g., .A, .12, .BAS).
- ☐ The file name and the extension can consist of numbers, letters, and the following special characters: $ # & @ ! % ( ) − _ { } ' ˆ (e.g., ACCOUNT1.BAS, TOTALS.$$$, MAY_ AR.BAS).
- ☐ If an extension is omitted, BASIC assumes that the file has a .BAS extension (.BAS = BASIC) and automatically appends it to the file name (e.g., if only COSTS were entered, BASIC would save as COSTS.BAS). However, the commands KILL, NAME, and OPEN do not assume an extension.
- ☐ If a file name is longer than eight characters and doesn't specify an extension, BASIC terminates the file name after the first eight characters, adds a period, and uses the next three characters as an extension (e.g., JUNEINVENTORY would be saved as JUNEIN-VE.NTO).

□ If the file name is longer than eight characters and does specify an extension, the file name is truncated to eight characters, and the specified extension is retained (e.g., JUNEINVENTORY.BAS would be saved as JUNEINVE.BAS).

□ If an extension is specified with more than three characters, BASIC truncates it to the first three (e.g., TOTALS.JUNE would be saved as TOTALS.JUN).

In a BASIC command or statement, the word *filespec* calls for this information to be supplied:

```
[d:][path]file name[.ext]
```

where [d:] represents the name of the drive where the file is or will be stored (e.g., A:, B:, or C:). If a drive is not indicated, BASIC saves or looks for the file on the default drive. [path] indicates the route, or list of sub-directories, that leads to where the file is to be saved or located. If no path is specified, BASIC saves or looks for the file in the current directory.

The SAVE Command

When a computer is turned off, everything stored in main memory is lost; therefore, a program must be reentered in order to be executed again. To avoid this, especially with longer programs, BASIC provides a way of storing programs in secondary storage with the use of the SAVE command.

The SAVE command requires that a program have a file name. In GWBASIC and IBM BASIC the file name must be enclosed in quotation marks. To save our sample program under the name SUM, type:

```
SAVE "SUM" <Enter>
```

If drive A is the current drive and you want to save the file to a diskette in drive B, type:

```
SAVE "B:SUM" <Enter>
```

There is no line number because we want the command to execute as soon as <Enter> is pressed.

The LOAD Command

When you want to put back into the computer's main memory a copy of a BASIC file that is stored on disk, BASIC uses the LOAD command. To load the SUM file back into main memory, type:

```
LOAD "SUM" <Enter>
```

If drive A is the current drive and the file SUM is stored on a diskette in drive B, we could load the program with this command:

```
LOAD "B:SUM" <Enter>
```

After <Enter> is pressed, the file SUM would be retrieved from disk and loaded back into main memory.

REVIEW QUESTIONS 5

1. What is the function of the LIST command?
2. Write the command to display the following program statements:
    a. lines 20 through 100
    b. from line 300 to the end of the program
    c. from the beginning of the program to line 120
    d. an entire program
    e. only line 85
3. Write a command to print lines 100 through 500 of a program listing directly to a printer.
4. What is the function of the RUN command?
5. Write a command that will save the file PRICE to the default drive A.
6. Assume that drive A is the current drive and the program TAX is stored on drive B. Write the command that will load the program TAX into main memory.

The NEW Command

After a program is executed it still resides in computer memory. Before you can create a new program, the existing program must be removed from main memory. Otherwise, anything you enter will be added to the existing program. To clear the computer's main memory, type:

NEW <Enter>

When <Enter> is pressed, the computer's main memory will be cleared.

Editing Program Lines

We all make mistakes; here is how to correct them. If you catch an error before pressing <Enter>, simply backspace to delete the error and retype the program line. If you have already entered the program line, the error can be corrected in several other ways. One is to retype the entire line with the desired correction; if your new program line has the same number as the existing line, the new will replace the old.

For example, if the value of Y in line 50 of our program should be 4 and the program SUM is still in main memory, simply type:

50 LET Y = 4 <Enter>

The program in main memory thus is changed. (However, the permanent copy on disk would still contain the old line 50; you must use the SAVE command to update the disk file.)

A second way to correct an error is to use the screen editing capabilities of BASIC. This approach lists just the portion of the program to be edited. For our small program you could list the entire program because it fits on one screen, but for larger programs you would list only the line(s) you wanted to edit. With the original program the command LIST 50 followed by pressing <Enter> would display only line 50: 50 LET Y = 6. You could then move the cursor to the 6 and type 4 as the correction.

At this point, the number appears correctly on the screen, but the program line in main memory would not have been updated. To update it in main memory, press <Enter> while the cursor is somewhere in the program line being edited. To confirm that changes had been made to the program in main memory, use the LIST command to view the program.

Sometimes editing a program requires adding a line. To do so, type the new program line with a line number that has not been used, and which places the new line in proper sequence. For example, if you wanted to add the heading SUMMATION OF X AND Y to the output of program SUM, you might choose the line number 85 so that it will fit into the proper place in the program, and so that other lines can be added in front of and behind it if necessary. (For this reason it is good to initially number program lines by at least 10s, to leave room for additional program lines.) The addition would be typed as follows:

```
85 PRINT "SUMMATION OF X AND Y"
```

After pressing <Enter>, type LIST and press <Enter> again to view the corrected and amended program:

```
10 REM Program Adds Two Numbers and Prints Sum
20 REM
30 REM Assign Values to Variables
40 LET X = 5
50 LET Y = 4
60 REM Calculate Sum of X and Y
70 LET N = X + Y
80 REM Display Output
85 PRINT "SUMMATION OF X AND Y"
90 PRINT "X","Y","X + Y"
100 PRINT X,Y,N
999 END
```

The DELETE Command

Sometimes you need to delete one or more program lines. There are two ways to delete a single line. Simply typing a line number and pressing <Enter> will delete that line, or the DELETE command can be used. Thus, to delete line 20 of our program, type 20 <Enter>, or type DELETE 20 <Enter>. The DELETE command can also be used to delete a range of program lines. For example:

```
DELETE 20-50     deletes lines 20 through 50
DELETE 20-       deletes all lines from line 20 to
                 the end of the program
```

```
DELETE -50        deletes all lines from the beginning
                  of the program through line 50.
```

The RENUM Command

Sometimes the increment between line numbers is too small to accommodate additions to a program. At other times you may wish to renumber program lines simply to make the increments between line numbers consistent. The RENUM command by itself renumbers an entire program, starting with 10 and incrementing each line by 10. In addition, you can specify the new line number with which to begin the renumbering, the line number from which the renumbering will start, and the increment to be used. The format for the RENUM statement is RENUM n,n,n. For example, this statement:

```
RENUM 1000, 500, 10
```

renumbers lines 500 and up so that they start with 1000 and increment by 10. Another example:

```
RENUM 100,, 20
```

This statement renumbers the entire program so that the first line number is 100 and the lines increment by 20.

You can't use the RENUM command to change the order of program lines; it can only renumber them in the same sequence. Program line numbers cannot be greater than 65529.

The SYSTEM Command

Use the SYSTEM command to exit BASIC and return to DOS: type SYSTEM and press <Enter>. When executed, the SYSTEM command erases any BASIC program that may still be in RAM, removes BASIC from RAM, and returns the system to the DOS prompt.

REVIEW QUESTIONS 6

1. What command is used to clear the computer's memory?
2. Assume the following program called SUM was loaded into main memory from disk:
   ```
   100 REM SUMMATION OF X AND Y
   110 LET X = 20
   120 LET Y = 15
   130 LET N = X + Y
   140 PRINT N
   ```
   A new line 120 was entered as follows:
   ```
   120 LET Y = 30
   ```
   If we now enter the NEW command and reload the program, what will the value of N be?
3. Describe two ways in which a program line can be deleted.

4. Write a command to:
   a. Renumber a program starting with 10 and increasing each line by 10.
   b. Renumber an entire program so that the first line number is 200 and the lines increase by 50.
   c. Renumber lines 1000 and up so that they start with 2000 and increase by 20.
5. What is the function of the SYSTEM command?

THE PRINT STATEMENT

The PRINT statement displays output on the display screen. It can be used to display blank lines, constants, variables, and the results of expressions.

Printing Blank Lines

To display a blank line, use the PRINT statement alone:

```
10 PRINT
```

Blank lines improve the visual appearance of output and make it more readable.

Printing Constants

String constants can be displayed on the screen with the PRINT Statement. When used with the PRINT statement, whatever is inside the quotation marks will be displayed on the screen when the statement is executed. (The quotation marks do not display.) For example, entering:

```
100 PRINT "GROSS PAY"
```

will display this output on the screen:

```
GROSS PAY
```

Numeric constants can also be printed using the PRINT command. However, a numeric constant is placed after the PRINT command without any quotation marks:

```
100 PRINT 30
```

When executed, this output will print on the display screen:

```
30
```

Note that positive numbers print with a leading blank space. Negative numbers print with a leading minus sign (−).

Printing Variables

A PRINT statement can print the value of a string variable. For example, suppose that the string variable A$ represents the string HELLO:

```
100 PRINT A$
```

When executed, this statement will print this output on the display screen:

```
HELLO
```

You can also print the value of a numeric variable. For example, assume the numeric variable TOTAL represents the value 365. If you write this line:

```
100 PRINT TOTAL
```

this output will appear on the display screen:

```
365
```

Printing Values of Expressions. You can print values of expressions with the PRINT statement. For example, assume the numeric variable X represents the value 10 and the numeric variable Y represents the value 20. If you write:

```
100 PRINT X + Y
```

it will print on the display screen:

```
30
```

The expressions in a PRINT statement are evaluated according to the hierarchy of operators.

Formatting Output with the PRINT Statement

BASIC divides an 80-column screen into 5 print zones of 14 columns (Figure G−4). (The number of columns in each zone may vary with different versions of BASIC.) To print values in columns, separate them with commas. For example:

```
100 PRINT "Gross Pay","Net Pay","Year to Date"
```

This will print Gross Pay in print zone 1, Net Pay in print zone 2, and Year to Date in print zone 3, as shown in Figure G−5.

If a string extends into the next print zone, then the next string to be printed must start in the first full print zone available.

A semicolon is used to print values next to each other instead of in columns defined by the print zones. For example:

```
100 PRINT "ANY";"PLACE"
```

will print on the display screen:

```
ANYPLACE
```

However:

```
100 PRINT 10;20
```

FIGURE G-4
The five print zones in BASIC.

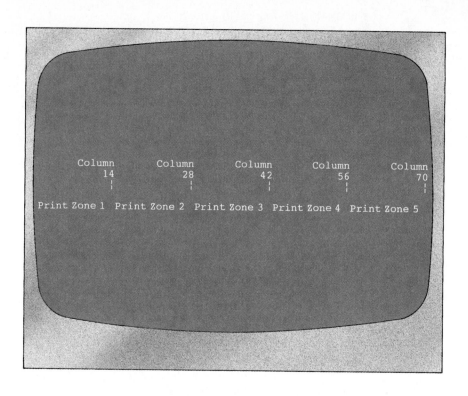

FIGURE G-5
The result of executing the program line 100 PRINT "Gross Pay", "Net Pay", "Year to Date".

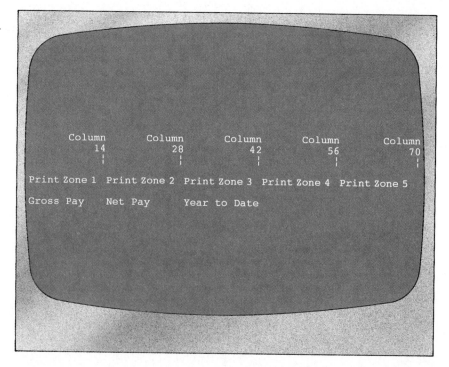

will print:

```
10 20
```

(not 1020) because positive numbers, when printed, are preceded by a blank space.

Because BASIC uses the comma as a delimiter, numeric constants cannot contain commas. If you want to print the number 10,564, this statement will *not* produce the desired result:

```
100 PRINT 10,564
```

Instead, BASIC will print 10 in the first print zone and 564 in the second print zone. The proper statement to print the numeric value 10,564 is:

```
100 PRINT 10564
```

THE LPRINT STATEMENT

Use the LPRINT statement to direct output to a printer instead of a display screen. LPRINT assumes an 80-column printer and follows the same syntax as the PRINT statement:

```
100 LPRINT "HELLO WORLD"
```

This prints the string HELLO WORLD directly to the printer. (The printer must be on and ready before the LPRINT statement is executed.)

REVIEW QUESTIONS 7

1. Write a program statement that will print a blank line. Why would you want to print blank lines in your output?

2. What output will be displayed by this statement?
   ```
   100 PRINT "TOTAL"
   ```

3. Debug (correct) any incorrect statements below.
   a. ```100 PRNT "NET SALE"```
   b. ```65000 PRINT```
   c. ```900 PRINT 'MARCH'```
   d. ```1,400 PRINT 5```

4. List the output of these statements:
   a. ```90 PRINT 40```
   b. ```100 PRINT "40"```
   How do the outputs differ?

5. What is the output of these program statements? (Assume the value of SUM is 85.)
   a. ```100 PRINT "SUM"```
   b. ```60 PRINT SUM```

6. Describe the output of these statements:
   a. ```110 PRINT 10,500```
   b. ```500 PRINT 8*2```
   c. ```300 PRINT "5 + 5"```
   d. ```1000 PRINT "SOME";"WHERE"```
   e. ```600 PRINT "NET","SALES"```

7. Write a statement that will print the string BRAVE NEW WORLD directly to the printer.

THE LET STATEMENT

The LET statement, or *assignment* statement, is used to store a value in a variable. The statement format is:

LET variable name = value that goes in that variable

Examples are:

```
100 LET X = 200
200 LET A$ = "HELLO"
```

Because the equal sign has two meanings in BASIC, it should be read *becomes* instead of *equal to* in an assignment statement to avoid confusion. For example, the statement:

```
200 LET X = X + 1
```

makes no sense if read as X *equals* X + 1 but is sensible as X *becomes* X + 1.

The word LET is optional in an assignment statement. The two examples above could also be written:

```
100 X = 200
200 A$ = "HELLO"
```

The following program uses the LET statement to assign values to variables, followed by the PRINT statement to display the results:

```
30 LET X = 5
40 LET Y = 6
50 LET N = X + Y
60 PRINT "X","Y","X + Y"
70 PRINT X,Y,N
```

When executed, the display screen will show:

```
X     Y     X+Y
 5     6     11
```

THE END STATEMENT

The END statement tells BASIC to stop execution of a program. It can appear anywhere in a program but is usually the last line. Often, it is identified with a line number made up of all 9s:

```
999 END
```

The END statement is optional. If it is not used, BASIC stops executing a program when it can find no more program lines to execute.

THE REM STATEMENT

To make programs easier to understand, debug, or change, BASIC allows REM statements (remark). For example:

```
100 REM CALCULATE GROSS PAY
200 LET GROSSPAY = HRLYRATE * TOTALHRS
```

Here the REM statement identifies the purpose of the assignment statement. The REM statement can also be used to make a program listing more readable. Segments of a program that accomplish specific tasks can be set apart from the rest of the program for easy identification by using REM statements alone or with symbols such as asterisks:

```
100 REM ***********************************
110 REM Calculate Gross Pay
120 LET GROSSPAY = HRLYRATE * TOTALHRS
130 REM ***********************************
140 REM
```

The REM statement can also be used to document the meaning of variable names:

```
10 REM CUSTADD$ = customer address
20 REM CUSTNAME = customer name
```

The REM statement is not used by the computer; it supplies information only to the person reading it. BASIC ignores all other characters in a program line after a REM statement. An apostrophe can be substituted for the REM statement. For example, the following two program lines are equivalent:

```
100 ` Calculate Gross Pay
100 REM Calculate Gross Pay
```

It is a good idea to document all written programs with REM statements, as shown here:

```
10 REM Program Adds Two Numbers and Prints Sum
20 REM
30 REM Assign Values to Variables
40 LET X = 5
50 LET Y = 6
60 REM Calculate Sum of X and Y
70 LET N = X + Y
80 REM Display Output
90 PRINT "X","Y","X + Y"
100 PRINT X,Y,N
999 END
```

MULTISTATEMENT LINES

Sometimes it is desirable to place several statements in a single program line. This is done by separating the statements with a colon (:). For example, if you wanted to print three blank lines, you could use the following statements:

```
10 PRINT
20 PRINT
30 PRINT
```

Or, you could also use one multistatement line:

```
10 PRINT:PRINT:PRINT
```

The colon is also useful for placing REM statements after other statements to document them:

```
100 LET GROSSPAY = HRLYRATE * TOTALHRS:REM
    Calculate Gross Pay
```

A program line can contain any number of statements up to 255 characters in one program line. However, because BASIC ignores all characters after a REM statement, no other statements can be added after a REM statement.

REVIEW QUESTIONS 8

1. Describe the function of the LET statement.
2. What is the function of the END statement? What happens if an END statement is not included in a program?
3. Describe what happens when the following statement is encountered by the computer:
```
400 REM CALCULATE SUM OF X + Y
```
4. Combine the following individual statement lines into a single multistatement line:
```
100 PRINT
200 PRINT
300 REM PRINT TWO BLANK LINES
```
5. What will be the output if the following lines are entered into the computer and then executed?
```
100 LET X = 5
110 LET Y = 2
120 PRINT X + Y
120 PRINT X*Y
```

THE INPUT STATEMENT

Using an assignment (LET) statement to assign values to variables is not very efficient if the values change. A more flexible way to assign values is to use the INPUT statement, which is placed where data are needed in a program. It allows a user to enter data as a program is executing. The INPUT statement can take several forms. Consider this program:

```
10 REM Calculate Sales Price
20 REM ************************
30 REM SALESP = Sales Price
```

```
40 REM DISCOUNT = Sales Discount
50 REM ITEMP = Price of an Item
60 REM ************************
70 INPUT ITEMP
80 INPUT DISCOUNT
90 LET SALESP = ITEMP - (ITEMP * DISCOUNT):REM
   Calculate Sales Price
100 PRINT "Sales Price = $";SALESP
999 END
```

When the INPUT statement in line 70 is executed, BASIC will display a ? on the screen and wait for you to input data. The value entered must match the data type of the variable, in this case a numeric variable. When that value is entered, it is assigned to the variable.

Because BASIC displays only a question mark, it can be difficult for you to know which data are being asked for by the computer. To get around this problem, the INPUT statement allows a prompt, or message, to be printed with it. The prompt is placed in quotation marks and is followed by a semicolon. For example, lines 70 and 80 in this program could be written as follows:

```
70 INPUT "What is the item price";ITEMP
80 INPUT "What is the sales discount";DISCOUNT
```

When line 70 is executed, you would be prompted:

```
What is the item price?
```

A prompt could also be added with a PRINT statement placed in the program line before the INPUT statement. However, because this operation is so common, BASIC allows the prompt to be incorporated into the INPUT statement.

A single INPUT statement can be used to enter data for more than one variable. For example, lines 70 and 80 could be combined into a single statement:

```
70 INPUT "What are the item price and sales
   discount";ITEMP,DISCOUNT
```

When this statement is executed, you are prompted:

```
What are the item price and sales discount?
```

Data must be entered in the same order in which they appear in the INPUT statement, and separated by a comma.

Let's assume the item price is $6.35 and the sales discount is 10 percent (.10). You would enter the values:

```
What are the item price and sales discount?
6.35,.1  <Enter>
```

Both string and numeric values can be entered with the INPUT statement. If incorrect values are entered (e.g., numeric data for a string variable), the computer responds with the message "Redo from start," redisplays the ? (or prompt and ?), and waits for you to enter the correct data type.

THE CLS STATEMENT

The display screen can become cluttered with prompts and difficult to read. BASIC provides the CLS, or clear screen, statement to remove the clutter. When the CLS statement is executed, all characters on the screen are erased, and the cursor is placed in the upper left corner of the screen. A sample clear screen statement is:

```
100 CLS
```

THE READ AND DATA STATEMENTS

In some programs, data remain relatively constant and do not need to be input as the program is executing. In such cases the data can be coded directly into the program. Earlier we saw that the LET statement can be used to assign data to variables. However, if data have to be changed, locating the appropriate LET statements can be difficult in a large program.

BASIC allows you to group data together with a DATA statement. DATA statements can be placed anywhere in a program as long as the data appear in the same sequence needed by the READ statement(s). Values stored in DATA statements are then assigned to the variables listed in the READ statements.

However, before any statements in a program are executed, all values stored in DATA statements must be placed in a data list; they are stored sequentially in the same order in which they appear in the program. A READ statement, when executed, takes the first datum in the data list and assigns it to a variable. For example, in this program segment:

```
100 DATA 100, 200
200 READ NUM1, NUM2, NUM3, NUM4
300 DATA 300
400 DATA 400
```

A computer will place those data in a data list:

```
100
200
300
400
```

When the READ statement is executed, it will assign 100 to the variable NUM1, 200 to NUM2, 300 to NUM3, and 400 to NUM4.

Both numeric and string data can be used in READ and DATA statements. Look at this example:

```
100 REM Example Program Using READ and DATA
    Statements
110 REM N1$, N2$ = Product Descriptions
120 REM P1, P2 = Product Prices
```

```
130 READ N1$, P1
140 READ N2$, P2
150 PRINT "PRODUCT: ";N1$,"PRICE: ";P1
160 PRINT "PRODUCT: ";N2$,"PRICE: ";P2
170 DATA "Laser Printer",4000,
    "Letter Quality Printer",1200
999 END
```

Before the program is executed, the values listed in the DATA statement are placed in a data list:

```
Laser Printer
4000
Letter Quality Printer
1200
```

When the READ statement in line 130 is executed, the string value "Laser Printer" is assigned to the string variable N1$, and the numeric value 4000 is assigned to the numeric variable P1. When the READ statement in line 140 is executed, the string value "Letter Quality Printer" is assigned to the string variable N2$, and the numeric value 1200 is assigned to the numeric variable P2.

The order of the variable types in the READ statements must match the order of the value types in the data list, or an error will occur. INPUT, READ, and DATA statements can all be combined in a single program.

THE RESTORE STATEMENT

The RESTORE statement causes the READ statement to start reading data from the top of the data list again. For example, let's insert a RESTORE statement in line 135 of our earlier example.

```
100 REM Example Program Using READ and DATA
    Statements
110 REM N1$, N2$ = Product Descriptions
120 REM P1, P2 = Product Prices
130 READ N1$, P1
135 RESTORE
140 READ N2$, P2
150 PRINT "PRODUCT: ";N1$,"PRICE: ";P1
160 PRINT "PRODUCT: ";N2$,"PRICE: ";P2
170 DATA "Laser Printer",4000,
    "Letter Quality Printer",1200
999 END
```

Now the READ statement in line 140 will take data from the top of the data list, and both N1$ and N2$ will be assigned the string value "Laser Printer," and both P1 and P2 will have the numeric value 4000.

If a READ statement is executed but there are no more data in the data list and a RESTORE statement is not executed, the computer will respond with this message:

```
Out of data in [line # where error occurred].
```

REVIEW QUESTIONS 9

1. What is the advantage of using an INPUT statement over a LET statement?

2. Write an INPUT statement that prompts you to enter a value for the variable GROSSPAY which represents an employee's gross pay.

3. Describe the function of the statement:
```
100 CLS
```

4. List the value of each variable in the following program segment.
```
100 DATA "Jim Sayer",400
110 DATA "Jan Farth",450
130 READ N1$,P1
130 RESTORE
140 DATA "Alex Wright",500
150 READ N$2,P2,N$3,P3
```

LOOPING

Often the same series of program instructions needs to be executed more than once in a program. That series could be repeated in sequence as many times as necessary, but BASIC provides a loop control structure to accomplish this task more efficiently. A loop control structure allows a program segment to be repeated as often as needed. This structure can be implemented in BASIC with FOR and NEXT statements or WHILE and WEND statements.

FOR and NEXT Statements

FOR and NEXT statements are used together to execute a series of instructions a specific number of times. The following example demonstrates these statements.

```
100 REM A FOR . . . NEXT Example
200 FOR X = 1 to 5
300     PRINT "The value of X = ";X
400 NEXT X
500 PRINT "End of Loop"
999 END
```

When the above program is executed, the output is displayed:

```
The value of X = 1
The value of X = 2
The value of X = 3
The value of X = 4
The value of X = 5
End of Loop
```

In the FOR statement in line 200, X is called the control variable, or loop index. The number 1 is the initial value, and 5 is the terminal value. Statement(s) between the FOR and NEXT statements constitute the loop body. In this example, the loop body is only one instruction, although the body can contain any number of instructions.

When line 200 is executed, the control variable (X) is set to the initial value (1). A test is performed to determine whether the value represented by the control variable is greater than the terminal value. If it is, then control is transferred to the statement following the NEXT statement, and the loop is terminated.

However, if the control variable is not greater than the terminal value, then the statements in the body of the loop are executed. Thereafter, the NEXT statement is executed. During that execution the control variable is incremented by +1. (It can also be incremented by other values, using the STEP clause, as we will see shortly.)

After the loop body has been executed, the control variable is compared to the terminal variable. If the control variable is greater, control transfers to the first statement after the NEXT statement. If the control variable is not greater, control transfers again to the first statement in the body of the loop, which is then executed once more.

The STEP clause mentioned above allows the control variable to be incremented by a positive or negative value other than +1. For example:

```
100 FOR X = 1 TO 10 STEP 2
200     PRINT X;
300 NEXT X
```

This program would result in the following output:

```
1   3   5   7   9
```

A negative STEP value causes the value of the control variable to diminish:

```
100 FOR X = 10 TO 1 STEP -2
200     PRINT X;
300 NEXT X
```

This program would result in the following output:

```
10   8   6   4   2
```

FOR and NEXT statements can also be nested or placed inside one another:

```
100 REM Outer Loop
110 FOR X = 1 TO 3
120     PRINT "Outer Loop Execution Number";X
130     TOTALOUT = TOTALOUT + 1
140     REM Inner Loop
150     FOR Y = 1 TO 2
160         PRINT "Inner Loop Execution Number";Y
170         TOTALIN = TOTALIN + 1
180     NEXT Y
190 NEXT X
```

```
200 PRINT
210 PRINT "Outer Loop Was Executed";X;" Times"
220 PRINT "Inner Loop Was Executed";Y;" Times"
9999 END
```

After you type RUN and press <Enter>, the output of this program looks like:

```
Outer Loop Execution Number 1
     Inner Loop Execution Number 1
     Inner Loop Execution Number 2
Outer Loop Execution Number 2
     Inner Loop Execution Number 1
     Inner Loop Execution Number 2
Outer Loop Execution Number 3
     Inner Loop Execution Number 1
     Inner Loop Execution Number 2

Outer Loop Was Executed 3 Times
Inner Loop Was Executed 6 Times
```

Notice that for each time the outer loop (X) executes, the inner loop (Y) executes twice.

The following program uses nested FOR and NEXT statements to print multiplication tables for 2s, 4s, 6s, and 8s:

```
100 REM This Program Prints Multiplication Tables
110 PRINT "Multiplication Tables For 2s, 4s, 6s,
    and 8s"
120 PRINT
130 FOR X = 1 TO 12
140     FOR Y = 2 TO 8 STEP 2
150         PRINT Y;" x ";X;" = ";Y * X,
160     NEXT Y
170     PRINT
180 NEXT X
999 END
```

After you type RUN and press <Enter>, the output of this program is:

```
Multiplication Tables for 2s, 4s, 6s, and 8s
2 x 1 = 2      4 x 1 = 4      6 x 1 = 6      8 x 1 = 8
2 x 2 = 4      4 x 2 = 8      6 x 2 = 12     8 x 2 = 16
2 x 3 = 6      4 x 3 = 12     6 x 3 = 18     8 x 3 = 24
2 x 4 = 8      4 x 4 = 16     6 x 4 = 24     8 x 4 = 32
2 x 5 = 10     4 x 5 = 20     6 x 5 = 30     8 x 5 = 40
2 x 6 = 12     4 x 6 = 24     6 x 6 = 36     8 x 6 = 48
2 x 7 = 14     4 x 7 = 28     6 x 7 = 42     8 x 7 = 56
2 x 8 = 16     4 x 8 = 32     6 x 8 = 48     8 x 8 = 64
2 x 9 = 18     4 x 9 = 36     6 x 9 = 54     8 x 9 = 72
2 x 10 = 20    4 x 10 = 40    6 x 10 = 60    8 x 10 = 80
2 x 11 = 22    4 x 11 = 44    6 x 11 = 66    8 x 11 = 88
2 x 12 = 24    4 x 12 = 48    6 x 12 = 72    8 x 12 = 96
```

WHILE and WEND Statements

WHILE and WEND (While END) statements are also used in BASIC to implement a loop control structure. This example illustrates a WHILE . . . WEND loop:

```
100 REM A WHILE . . . WEND Loop
110 REM ITEMP = Item Price
120 REM TOTALP = Total Price of All Items
130 REM
140 INPUT "Enter Item Price (Enter 0 to
    Quit)";ITEMP
150 WHILE ITEMP <> 0
160      LET TOTALP = TOTALP + ITEMP
170      INPUT "Enter Item Price (Enter 0 to
         Quit)";ITEMP
180 WEND
190 PRINT "Total Price of All Items = ";TOTALP
999 END
```

A WHILE statement contains a condition. In line 150 the condition is ITEMP <> 0. When the WHILE statement is executed, the condition is tested. However, the variable ITEMP must have a value assigned to it before the WHILE statement is executed, and the INPUT statement in line 140 calls for this value.

If the condition is true (i.e., if the value of ITEMP does not equal zero), the statements between WHILE and WEND are executed. When the WEND statement is executed, control is returned to the WHILE statement.

On the other hand, if the condition in the WHILE statement is false (i.e., if the value of ITEMP does equal zero), then control is passed to the first statement following the WEND statement.

REVIEW QUESTIONS 10

1. What is the function of the FOR and NEXT statements?

2. Using only the statement:
   ```
   200 PRINT X;
   ```
   in the loop body, write a FOR NEXT loop that will print the numbers 2, 4, 6, 8, and 10.

3. If the value of X is 10, will the following WHILE loop be executed?
   ```
   100 INPUT "Enter value of X";X
   200 WHILE X>10
   220 PRINT X
   230 WEND
   ```

CONTROL STRUCTURE

In the following sections we will examine several BASIC statements that alter the sequential order of execution of program lines.

The IF . . . THEN Statement

The IF . . . THEN statement provides a conditional transfer—that is, it redirects the flow of processing according to the result of a condition. *If* a condition is true, *then* the IF . . . THEN statement is used to select a specific course of action. If the condition is not true, no action is taken, and the program continues with the next line. Here's an example:

```
100 IF TOTAL >= 100 THEN TOTAL = TOTAL * .90
120 PRINT "Total Purchases = ";TOTAL
```

The IF clause in line 100 is followed by the condition that TOTAL >= 100. During execution, this condition is evaluated. If the condition is true—that is, if the TOTAL is greater than or equal to 100—the program statement(s) following the THEN clause are executed. In this case a 10 percent discount is given to those individuals purchasing 100 dollars' worth or more of merchandise. Program execution then continues with the next line. If the condition following the IF clause is false—that is, if the TOTAL is less than 100—the THEN clause is not executed. Instead, control passes immediately to the next program line.

The IF . . . THEN . . . ELSE Statement

The IF . . . THEN . . . ELSE statement allows one action to be taken if a condition is true, and another action to be taken if it is false:

```
100  IF AMOUNT > CREDIT THEN PRINT "Reject Credit
Card" ELSE PRINT "Accept Credit Card"
```

The IF clause in line 100 is followed by the condition AMOUNT > CREDIT. That condition checks to see whether the amount of purchase is greater than the credit available on a customer's credit card. If the condition is true—that is, if the amount of the purchase is greater than the customer's credit limit—the statement following the THEN clause is executed, and the message "Reject Credit Card" is printed. Control would then go to the next program line. If the condition is false—that is, if the purchase amount is less than or equal to the customer's credit limit—the statement following the ELSE clause is executed, and the message "Accept Credit Card" is printed.

To improve readability, the IF . . . THEN . . . ELSE statement can be broken across several lines.

```
100 IF AMOUNT > CREDIT
        THEN PRINT "Reject Credit Card"
        ELSE PRINT "Accept Credit Card"
```

IF . . . THEN . . . ELSE statements can also be nested:

```
100 IF BALANCE <> 0
        THEN IF AGE <30
```

```
                    THEN PRINT "Account Current"
                    ELSE PRINT "Account Overdue"
        ELSE PRINT "Account Paid in Full"
```

In this example, if a customer's balance is equal to zero, processing goes to the ELSE clause associated with the first IF statement and displays the message "Account Paid in Full." If the balance is not equal to zero, then the statements following the THEN clause are executed. In this case that step involves another IF statement, and the condition AGE <30 must be tested. If the account is less than 30 days overdue, the statement after the THEN clause is executed, and the message "Account Current" is displayed. If the account is more than 30 days past due, the condition is false, and the statement(s) after the ELSE clause are executed; in other words, the message "Account Overdue" is displayed.

REVIEW QUESTIONS 11

1. What is the function of the IF . . . THEN statement?

2. What is the value of N that will be printed in line 500?
   ```
   100 X = 12
   200 Y = 6
   300 N = X*Y
   400 If N >= 72 THEN N = N*2
   500 PRINT N
   ```

3. What is the function of the IF . . . THEN . . . ELSE statement?

4. Write an IF . . . THEN . . . ELSE statement that will print HIGH if the value of a variable NUM is greater than or equal to 100 and LOW if NUM is less than 100.

The GOTO Statement

In a BASIC program, a GOTO statement allows unconditional transfer of control to the line number specified in the statement. For example:

```
100 GOTO 420
```

transfers control from line 100 to line 420 without executing any line in between.

Indiscriminate use of the GOTO statement can create programs in which the logic is very difficult to follow, test, or modify. Many programmers recommend that GOTO statements not be used; others say that limited and controlled use is acceptable. However, a GOTO statement should never be used to transfer control into or out of a loop or subroutine. The following program illustrates how a GOTO statement can be used to implement a loop:

```
10 REM Program Using GOTO
20 REM
30 INPUT "Enter Item Price";PRICE
40 INPUT "Enter Total Number of Items
```

```
          Purchased";NUM
50 LET TOTAL = PRICE * NUM
60 INPUT "Any More Items (Enter Y or N)";A$
70 IF A$ = "N" THEN GOTO 999
80 GOTO 30
999 END
```

Line 70 tests the condition A$ = "N." If A$ is not equal to "N," the condition is false, and control passes to line 80. Line 80 then performs an unconditional transfer and sends control back to line 30. However, if the condition in line 70 is true, then control is transferred to line 999, and the program terminates. The GOTO statement in the THEN clause in line 70 is optional. The statement could also be written:

```
IF A$ = "N" THEN 999
```

The GOSUB and RETURN Statements

GOSUB and RETURN statements work together as a team. GOSUB transfers control to a specified line in a program. Execution begins at that line and continues until the RETURN statement is encountered. The RETURN statement sends control back to the line that follows the GOSUB statement. Thus, GOSUB and RETURN statements allow construction of modules, or subroutines.

Modules help structure a program, making it easier to read, modify, and debug. A common use of the GOSUB and RETURN statements is to implement a menu in a program. When a menu selection is entered, the GOSUB statement directs processing to the appropriate module. When that module is finished executing, control returns to the main program module. This example illustrates the process:

```
10 REM This Program Illustrates the use of the
   GOSUB Statement
20 REM
30 LET A$ = "Y"
40 WHILE A$ = "Y"
45       CLS
50       INPUT "Enter First Number";X
60       INPUT "Enter Second Number";Y
70       GOSUB 1000
90       IF MENU = 1 THEN GOSUB 2000
100      IF MENU = 2 THEN GOSUB 3000
110      IF MENU = 3 THEN GOSUB 4000
120      IF MENU = 4 THEN GOSUB 5000
130      PRINT:PRINT
140      INPUT "Enter Two More Numbers (Y or
         N)";A$
150      REM Allow both upper and lower case Y to
         be used
160      IF A$ = "y" THEN LET A$ = "Y"
```

```
170 WEND
180 END
1000 REM *****************************************
1010 REM Subroutine for Displaying MENU
1020 CLS
1030 PRINT "Enter 1 for Addition"
1040 PRINT "Enter 2 for Subtraction"
1050 PRINT "Enter 3 for Multiplication"
1060 PRINT "Enter 4 for Division"
1070 INPUT MENU
1080 RETURN
2000 REM *****************************************
2010 REM Subroutine to Perform Addition
2020 LET T = X + Y
2030 PRINT "The Sum of ";X;" Plus ";Y;" Is ";T
2040 RETURN
3000 REM *****************************************
3010 REM Subroutine to Perform Subtraction
3020 LET T = X - Y
3030 PRINT "The Result of ";X;" Minus ";Y;
     " Is ";T
3040 RETURN
4000 REM *****************************************
4010 REM Subroutine to Perform Multiplication
4020 LET T = X * Y
4030 PRINT "The Product of ";X;" Times ";Y;
     " Is ";T
4040 RETURN
5000 REM *****************************************
5010 REM Subroutine to perform Division
5020 LET T = X / Y
5030 PRINT "The result of ";X;" Divided by ";Y;
     " Is ";T
5040 RETURN
```

There are five subroutines in this program. The subroutine starting at line 1000 displays the menu. The subroutine starting at line 2000 performs addition; the one at line 3000, subtraction; the one at 4000, multiplication; and the one at 5000, division. The main program extends from line 10 to line 180. Lines 50 and 60 ask you to input two numbers. Line 70 branches to the menu subroutine starting at 1000. When the RETURN statement in line 1080 is executed, control is passed back to line 90.

The IF statements in lines 90 to 120 determine which subroutine should follow. If any one of the conditions in the IF statements is true, the appropriate THEN clause is executed. The GOSUB statement directs processing to the appropriate subroutine. After one of these subroutines is executed, control is returned to line 130. Also, if the value of MENU does not equal 1, 2, 3, or 4, the THEN clauses are skipped, and processing continues with line 130.

The ON . . . GOSUB and RETURN Statements

The ON . . . GOSUB statement is used to branch to any one of a number of modules, depending on the value of the variable following the ON clause. This example illustrates an ON . . . GOSUB statement:

```
90 ON MENU GOSUB 2000, 3000, 4000, 5000
```

When this statement is executed, the value of the variable MENU is evaluated. If it has a value of 1, processing branches to the first line number (2000). If it has a value of 2, processing branches to the second line number in the GOSUB list (3000), and so on.

An ON . . . GOSUB statement can be used in place of numerous IF statements and allows for more concise programs. For example, the ON . . . GOSUB statement just cited could replace the four IF statements in lines 90 through 120 in the menu program above. The program would then appear:

```
10   REM This Program Illustrates the ON . . .
     GOSUB Statement
20   REM
30   LET A$ = "Y"
40   WHILE A$ = "Y"
45        CLS
50        INPUT "Enter First Number";X
60        INPUT "Enter Second Number";Y
70        GOSUB 1000
80        ON MENU GOSUB 2000, 3000, 4000, 5000
90        PRINT:PRINT
100       INPUT "Enter Two More Numbers (Y or N)";
          A$
110       REM Allow upper and lower case Y to be
          used
120       IF A$ = "y" THEN LET A$ = "Y"
130  WEND
140  END
1000 REM ******************************************
1010 REM Subroutine for Displaying MENU
1020 CLS
1030 PRINT "Enter 1 for Addition"
1040 PRINT "Enter 2 for Subtraction"
1050 PRINT "Enter 3 for Multiplication"
1060 PRINT "Enter 4 for Division"
1070 INPUT MENU
1080 RETURN
2000 REM ******************************************
2010 REM Subroutine to Perform Addition
2020 LET T = X + Y
2030 PRINT "The Sum of ";X;" Plus ";Y;" Is ";T
```

```
2040 RETURN
3000 REM ****************************************
3010 REM Subroutine to Perform Subtraction
3020 LET T = X - Y
3030 PRINT "The result of ";X;" Minus ";Y;
     " Is ";T
3040 RETURN
4000 REM ****************************************
4010 REM Subroutine to Perform Multiplication
4020 LET T = X * Y
4030 PRINT "The result of ";X;" Times ";Y;
     " Is ";T
4040 RETURN
5000 REM ****************************************
5010 REM Subroutine to Perform Division
5020 LET T = X / Y
5030 PRINT "The result of ";X;" Divided by ";Y;
     " Is ";T
5040 RETURN
```

REVIEW QUESTIONS 12

1. What is the function of the GOTO statement?
2. Describe the function of the GOSUB and RETURN statements.
3. Describe the functions of the ON . . . GOSUB . . . RETURN statements.

ARRAYS

In the following sections we'll examine how to declare an array and work with one- and two-dimensional arrays.

Declaring Arrays with the DIM Statement

To use an array, we must first declare the existence of the array and tell BASIC its size. We do this with the dimension, or DIM, statement.

The DIM statement declares an array by defining its name and indicating its dimensions. The array name identifies the entire array and follows the same rules as a variable name. The dimension indicates the number of rows in a one-dimensional array or the number of rows and columns in a two-dimensional array, through use of a subscript. For example, a one-dimensional numeric array with 20 rows that we want to call A, can be defined as:

array name

10 DIM A(20)

subscript

A two-dimensional string array with ten rows and four columns that we want to call A$, can be defined as follows:

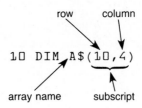

The DIM statement must come before the first occurrence of the array.

Several arrays can be defined in a single DIM statement. For example, if you needed a one-dimensional numeric array called A with 15 rows and a two-dimensional numeric array called B with 10 rows and 2 columns, this statement can be used:

```
10 DIM A(15), B(10,2)
```

Individual elements of an array are referenced by subscripts that refer to these positions. For example, in the array below the number 9 is in A(2). The subscripted variable A(2) represents the second element in the array A. The subscript enclosed in parentheses can be any valid expression, for example, A(X) or A(X + 1) are valid references to array elements. BASIC evaluates the expression to the nearest integer and uses this to access the array.

Array A Values	Subscripts
10	A(1)
9	A(2)
7	A(3)
5	A(4)

Reading Data Into a One-Dimensional Array

Data can be easily read into arrays using FOR . . . NEXT statements. This example reads data into a one-dimensional array named A:

```
100 FOR I = 1 TO 5
200     READ A(I)
300 NEXT I
400 DATA 10,20,30,40,50
```

When the FOR statement is first executed, the value of I is set to 1. When the read statement is executed, it reads the data value 10 into the first position of the array, A(1). The next time the FOR statement is executed the value of I = 2. When the READ statement is executed again, it reads the second value in the data list into the second position of the array, A(2), and so on until the array is filled.

Calculations with One-Dimensional Arrays

We can perform calculations using arrays. For example, consider this array:

Array X

3
4
7
5
6

To total the values in array X, we can use this program segment:

```
100 LET TOTAL = 0
200 FOR I = 1 TO 5
300     LET TOTAL = TOTAL + X(I)
400     PRINT I
500 NEXT I
600 PRINT TOTAL
```

Note that before the FOR statement is executed the value of the variable TOTAL is set to zero in line 100.

You can also perform calculations using several arrays and place the results in a separate array. For example, the values in array A and array B shown below can be multiplied and the result stored in an array C:

Array A	*Array B*
5	11
7	12
8	6

This program segment can be used to multiply arrays A and B and store the result in array C:

```
100 FOR I = 1 TO 3
200     LET C(I) = A(I) * B(I)
300 NEXT I
```

The values stored in array C by the above program segment would be:

```
55
84
48
```

Printing a One-Dimensional Array

Often you will want to print the contents of an array. For example, if array A contains the values 5,3,6, and 8, this program segment can be used to print the contents of array A:

```
100 FOR I = 1 TO 4
200     PRINT A(I)
300 NEXT I
```

The output from the above segment is:

```
5
3
6
8
```

Reading Data Into a Two-Dimensional Array

Data can be entered into a two-dimensional array using nested FOR. . .NEXT statements. For example, the program segment below enters data into a two-dimensional array called C with three rows and four columns:

```
100 FOR I = 1 TO 3
200     FOR J = 1 TO 4
300          READ C(I,J)
400     NEXT J
500 NEXT I
600 DATA 7,4,9,3
700 DATA 6,8,2,4
800 DATA 2,9,5,7
```

When the FOR statement in line 100 is first executed, the value of I is set to 1. This corresponds to row 1 of the array. When the FOR statement in line 200 is executed, the value of J is set to 1. This corresponds to column 1 of the array. The READ statement then reads the first value in the data list into row 1 column 1 of array C [C(1,1)]. This continues until the array is filled.

Calculations with Two-Dimensional Arrays

Consider this table:

	Product A	Product B	Product C
Q1	101	112	89
Q2	78	104	99
Q3	87	93	96
Q4	102	98	112

The table might be stored in an array called X. You might want to know the total number of all these products sold during the four quarters. You can total the two-dimensional array X using this program segment:

```
100 LET TOTAL = 0
200 FOR I = 1 TO 4
300     FOR J = 1 TO 3
400          LET TOTAL = TOTAL + X(I,J)
500     NEXT J
```

```
600 NEXT I
700 PRINT TOTAL
```

You might also want to find out the total number of products sold in Q1. You can do so with this program segment:

```
100 LET Q1TOTAL = 0
200 FOR J = 1 TO 3
300     LET Q1TOTAL = Q1TOTAL + X(1,J)
400 NEXT J
```

Note that by setting the row subscript to 1, you confine the calculation to row 1.

It's also likely that you'd want to know how many of product B were sold during the four-quarter period. The following program segment totals the second column of the array to answer this query:

```
100 LET BTOTAL = 0
200 FOR J = 1 TO 4
300     LET BTOTAL = BTOTAL + X(I,2)
400 NEXT I
```

In this case, setting the column subscript to 2 confines the calculation to column 2.

Printing a Two-Dimensional Array

An entire two-dimensional array can be output to the display screen using this program segment:

```
100 FOR I = 1 TO 4
200     FOR J = 1 TO 3
300         PRINT X(I,J);
400     NEXT J
500     PRINT
600 NEXT I
```

REVIEW QUESTIONS 13

1. What is the purpose of the DIM statement?
2. How are individual elements of an array accessed?

SEQUENTIAL FILES

BASIC allows data to be stored in sequential files. We will look at these commands: OPEN, PRINT #, INPUT #, and CLOSE.

The OPEN Command

The OPEN command has two forms:

```
line # OPEN "filename" FOR OUTPUT AS #number
line # OPEN "filename" FOR INPUT AS #number
```

The OUTPUT option specifies the sequential output mode which allows data to be written to the specified file on disk. The INPUT option specifies the sequential input mode which allows data to be read from the specified file on disk. The #number at the end of the line is used in other commands as a shorthand method of referring to the file. The word "number" is replaced with a number. (The filename used must be eight characters or less, of course.)

For example, if you wanted to create a file called EMPLOYEE and write data to it, you might type:

```
100 OPEN "EMPLOYEE" FOR OUTPUT AS #1
```

The PRINT # Command

Data is actually written to a file using the PRINT # statement, using this format:

```
line # PRINT #number,expression
```

The number must be the same one specified in the OPEN statement. The expression identifies the data being written to the file, and can be any valid BASIC expression. For example, if you wanted to write the name Rick Barnes to the EMPLOYEE file, you could use the statement:

```
100 PRINT #1, "Rick Barnes"
```

The CLOSE Command

After opening a file and writing data to it or accessing data from it, the file must be closed, using the CLOSE command in this format:

```
line # CLOSE #number
```

The number must be the same as that specified in the OPEN statement. This example creates and writes data to a sequential file:

```
100 OPEN "EMPLOYEE" FOR OUTPUT AS #1
200 PRINT #1, "Rick Barnes"
300 PRINT #1, "Terry Rice"
400 PRINT #1, "Carol Frazee"
500 PRINT #1, "Tom Ridell"
600 CLOSE #1
999 END
```

The INPUT # Command

Data can be read from a file using the INPUT # command. The format of the INPUT # command is:

```
line # INPUT #number,expression
```

The number must be the same as that specified in the OPEN statement. The expression identifies the data to be read from the file. This example reads data from a file into an array called A$:

```
100 OPEN "EMPLOYEE" FOR INPUT AS #1
200 FOR I = 1 TO 4
300 INPUT #1, A$(I)
400 NEXT I
999 END
```

REVIEW QUESTIONS 14

1. What are the two forms of the OPEN statement and what is each used for?
2. What is the purpose of the PRINT # command?
3. What command is used to close a sequential file?
4. What is the purpose of the INPUT # command?

Problem Set

1. Write a program using REM, LET, PRINT, and END statements that assigns each number below to the variable listed. Have the program calculate the average of those numbers, assigning the result to the variable AVG. The result should print to the display screen as follows:
   ```
   AVERAGE VALUE = XXX
   ```

Value	Variable
12.2	X1
9.3	X2
15.5	X3

2. Write a program using REM, LET, PRINT, and END statements that will calculate how much you will have to spend on gas for a trip of 3,452 miles. Assume the price of gasoline is $1.20/gallon and your car gets 24 miles to the gallon. Your output should appear as follows:
   ```
   Distance    Gallons    Price/Gal.    Total Cost
   XXXX        XXXX       $ XXXX        $ XXXX
   ```

3. Use the INPUT statement to write a program that asks for the name and weight in kilograms of an item and converts it to its weight in pounds. 1 kilogram = 2.2046 lbs. Your output should appear as follows:
   ```
   Item    Kilogram    Pounds
   XXXX    XXXX        XXXX
   ```

4. Use the READ/DATA statements to write a program that reads and prints these data:
   ```
   NAME              PHONE NUMBER
   Ellen Gray        (555) 444-1111
   Jay Metz          (555) 888-2222
   Warren Harris     (555) 333-1111
   ```

5. Write a program that uses a READ statement in a FOR/NEXT loop to read these data:
   ```
   Mary Appleton     222-22-2222
   Chris Young       333-33-3333
   Beth Weiss        111-11-1111
   Steve Mills       444-44-4444
   ```

Have the output printed by a PRINT statement in the FOR/NEXT loop to appear like this:

```
NAME            Social Security Number
XXXXXXXX        XXX - XX - XXXX
      .                 .
      .                 .
      .                 .
```

6. Write a program using a FOR/NEXT loop to sum the number of guests who indicated on their RSVP that they will attend your party. Use an INPUT statement to read in the data. Have the output indicate total number of guests. Use these data:

```
RSVP    # of guests
1       2
2       1
3       4
4       3
5       2
6       4
7       2
8       1
9       1
10      3
```

7. Write a program using nested FOR/NEXT loops to print out multiplication tables for 1s, 2s, and 3s in this format:

```
1 x 1 = 1        2 x 1 = 2       3 x 1 = 3
      .                .                .
      .                .                .
      .                .                .
1 x 12 = 12    2 x 12 = 24    3 x 12 = 36
```

8. Write a program using a WHILE loop and an INPUT statement to calculate a current account balance. Use these data:

```
Last period's balance            $2,406.34
Checks since last statement      $    30.72
                                 $   105.00
                                 $    79.89
                                 $     5.24
```

The WHILE loop should execute until 0 is entered to indicate that all data have been entered. Use the CLS statement to keep the display screen from becoming cluttered with prompts. The output should have this format:

```
Current Balance = $ XXXX.XX
```

9. Write a program to create a mailing list of the individuals who purchased more than $100 worth of merchandise on their store credit cards last year. Use READ/DATA statements to input data into the program. Use a WHILE loop to determine when to stop executing the program. Use an IF/THEN statement to determine if the individual should be added to the mailing list. Print names and addresses of those who purchased over $100 worth of merchandise last year. Use these data:

```
Name            Address              Credit Card
                                     Purchase
Anne Brass      121 Oak St.          $400.00
Robert Cray     25 Bay Rd.           $ 85.00
Laura Sprungl   2141 Strauss Rd.     $850.00
Tom Newton      21 River Rd.         $690.00
None            None                 $  0.00
```

10. Write a program to calculate the total cost of clamps ordered. If fewer than 1000 are purchased, the price is $1.35 each. If 1000 or more are purchased, there is a 12 percent discount. Use the IF/THEN/ELSE statements to calculate the price. Your output should read:
```
TOTAL COST = $ XXXX.XX
```

11. Write a program to convert measurements in feet to the users choice of inches, centimeters, or meters. Use a menu to choose which type of conversion is desired. Use the GOSUB and RETURN statements to place the statements for the menu and each conversion calculation in their own subroutine. Have the program use the WHILE loop to allow the user to repeat the conversion process as many times as desired. Have each subroutine output the result in this format:
```
X FEET = X (name of selected measurement)
```

12. Rewrite the program for problem 11 using the ON . . . GOSUB statement.

13. Write a program that reads these lists into one-dimensional arrays called PRICE and QUANTITY:
```
PRICE    QUANTITY
$3.45    9
$6.99    12
$8.98    6
$5.50    14
```
Have the program multiply these two arrays and store the result in an array called AMOUNT. Then have the program calculate the total amount of array AMOUNT and print the entire array as well as the total amount to the screen.

14. Read the following data into a two-dimensional array called UNITS:

	Number of Units Sold			
	Product A	Product B	Product C	Product D
Quarter 1	120	154	163	165
Quarter 2	342	154	234	321
Quarter 3	231	321	234	142
Quarter 4	132	243	254	423

Have the program calculate the total units sold for all products during the four-quarter period. Also calculate the number of units of product C sold over the four-quarter period and the total units sold during quarter 4. Print the results of each calculation on the display screen.

15. Write a program called REMINDER that creates a sequential file containing these data:
```
Savings account number 111111111
Checking account number 222222222
Credit card number 333333333
Bank card number 444444444
```

16. Write a program that reads the file REMINDER, created in exercise 15, into an array. Print the contents of the array to the display screen.

GLOSSARY

Absolute cell reference A method of copying in a worksheet where the exact formula is copied by using the same cell references.

Accounting information system An information system primarily using transaction processing systems to record transactions that affect the financial status of an organization. It maintains a historical record of transactions and is used to produce reports that give a financial picture of the organization.

Acoustic modem Also called an acoustic coupler; a type of modem with two rubber cups into which a standard telephone receiver is placed to send and receive data.

Action document A computer-produced document that becomes an input document for another information system.

Active cell The cell in a worksheet that is currently being used for data entry or data manipulation; usually indicated by the cell pointer.

Ada A programming language developed for the U.S. Department of Defense for use in military applications, Ada includes powerful control and data structures and a specialized set of commands that allow it to directly control hardware devices.

Adding Entering new records to an existing file or database.

Address bus The electrical pathway used to transmit storage locations for data or instructions.

Algorithm A finite set of step-by-step instructions for solving a problem.

All-in-one integrated package An integrated application package that combines features of several application programs into a single program.

Analog computer A computer that recognizes data as continuous *measurements* of a physical property (e.g., voltage, pressure, speed), as opposed to *counting* discrete signals, as is done in a digital computer. Compare to digital computer.

Analog data transmission Transmission of data in continuous wave form.

Analytical program See Chart/graph program.

Animation A feature of some graphics packages that rapidly displays drawings that progressively change slightly, thereby simulating motion.

Application A job or task that the user wants the computer to perform.

Application generator A fourth-generation language that allows users to enter data and specify how they are to be manipulated and output.

Application software Software that interfaces between the user and the system software, enabling the user to direct the computer to perform specific tasks.

Arithmetic and logic unit (ALU) The part of the central processing unit (CPU) that performs all mathematical and logical functions.

Artificial intelligence (AI) The ability of computers to perform humanlike thinking and reasoning.

Aspect ratio In a graphics program, the relationship between the height and width of an object. The aspect ratio may be altered to change the shape or proportions of an object.

Assembler   A language-translator program that translates assembly-language code into machine-language code.

Assembly language   A low-level language that uses mnemonic codes instead of 1s and 0s.

Asynchronous transmission   A method of data transmission in which characters are sent one at a time over a communication channel. Each character is surrounded by a start-and-stop bit that controls the transfer of that character. Compare to synchronous transmission.

Attributes   The set of characteristics used to describe a data-entry field or to describe how output will appear; often set by the user to fit a particular situation.

Audit trail   A documentation of all activity in a file. This activity includes what was done, what was affected, when it was done, and by whom.

Autoanswer   A feature of a communication package that automatically answers calls from other computers. A computer with this feature can create a bulletin board file and receive electronic mail without anyone being present at the computer.

Automated office   An office environment that combines traditional office procedures with computers and communication technology.

Automated testing   A testing process that uses software tools to mark all the paths in a program module, and then reports on which paths were executed in a test.

Automatic dialing   A feature of a communication package that allows previously stored numbers to be accessed and automatically dialed to access another computer.

Automatic message transfer   A feature in a communication package that automatically dials a computer at a preset time and leaves a message on that computer.

Automatic page numbering   An application-software feature that automatically places the consecutive page number on each page.

Automatic spillover   A worksheet option in which a cell label is allowed to continue, or "spill over," into the next cell.

Background integration   Placing of utility programs in memory to make them available while other software applications are in use.

Background recalculation mode   Mode in which recalculation of a worksheet occurs while other operations are ongoing.

Backup feature   An application program feature that makes an exact copy of an existing file. Sometimes backup copies are made in compressed form and must be expanded (using a utility program) to be useful again.

Backup file   A copy of a file to ensure that data are not lost if the original file is lost or damaged; a duplicate copy of a file.

Bandwidth   A characteristic of a communication channel that determines the rate, or speed, at which data can be transmitted over it; also called the "grade" of a channel.

Bar chart   A graph using a fixed scale to compare data in simple and compound relationships. Data may be represented as either vertical or horizontal bars.

Bar code   A series of thick and thin black bars and spaces of various widths that represent data; seen on many consumer products.

BASIC (Beginner's All-purpose Symbolic Instruction Code)   A high-level language developed at Dartmouth College as an easy-to-learn, easy-to-use language for beginning programmers.

Batch processing   A method of data processing in which data are collected and processed periodically without user intervention.

Baud rate   The number of times per second that a transmitted signal changes (modulates or demodulates).

Binary system   The base-2 numbering system; uses the digits 0 and 1 to represent computer data.

Biochip   A newer technology for designing integrated circuits by using living protein and enzymes to grow circuits; exists in theory only.

Bit   A binary digit, the smallest piece of data that can be recognized and used by a computer.

Bitmap   Dot-by-dot representation of a character or image; an image created as a matrix of dots, or pixels.

Bitmapped graphics   Graphics created with pixel-oriented images.

Block   A preset number of bytes that are transferred as a unit.

Block editing   A word-processor feature that allows editing of large portions of text as a unit.

Blocked tape   A storage technique that groups records on tape to provide more storage and faster access by reducing the number of interrecord gaps.

Blocking factor   The number of records stored between a pair of interblock gaps.

Break signal   In a communications program, a feature in which a signal is sent to stop the current operation between two communicating computers without disconnecting the communication link between them.

Broad-band channel A communication channel, such as microwave or fiber optic, that transmits data at rates as high as several megabits per second.

Buffer A temporary holding place for data; may be part of the CPU or part of an input or output device.

Built-in function A function contained within an application program to automatically perform a mathematical or logic function without manual entering of a formula.

Bulletin board system (BBS) Electronic equivalent of a conventional bulletin board. A BBS is part of a communication network where users can post messages, read those posted by other users, communicate with the system operator, and upload or download programs.

Bus An electrical path for data flow from point to point in a circuit.

Bus architecture The characteristics of a bus, such as data-transfer speed, amount of data that can be transferred, and plug-in cards that can be used.

Bus network A computer network in which each device is connected to a single communication cable by an interface. Each device can communicate directly with each other device.

Button In graphics-based interfaces, users can select items that appear on the screen as buttons to be pushed.

Byte A group of eight bits.

C A programming language that uses Englishlike statements; uses sophisticated control and data structures to make it a very concise, powerful language.

Cache memory High-speed buffer memory containing the most frequently used data or instructions.

Calculating Creating a field value through a mathematical manipulation of two or more other fields.

Calculation An information-processing task that involves performing a mathematical operation on data.

Carrier-sense multiple access (CSMA) A local-area-network access method in which a device listens to a channel to sense whether that channel is in use.

Carrier-sense multiple access/collision detection (CSMA/CD) The carrier sense multiple access (CSMA) method, with collision-detection capabilities.

Cartridge tape A form of magnetic tape similar to cassette tape but with a much greater storage density; used mainly with large computer systems.

Cassette tape A form of magnetic tape, about one-quarter inch wide; generally used for secondary storage with microcomputers.

Cathode-ray tube (CRT) A type of display that uses an electron beam to illuminate a phosphor-coated screen to form characters. A cathode-ray tube is used in most computer monitors and television sets.

Cell A data-entry point in a worksheet, defined by its row and column coordinates.

Cell pointer A highlighted box that shows the active cell.

Cellular network A network in which transmitters are placed in a checkerboard pattern throughout the system service area to enable mobile communications.

Centering An application-software feature that automatically places a word or words in the center of a defined space, such as a spreadsheet cell or document page.

Central processing unit (CPU) The processing unit of a computer. It contains the arithmetic and logic unit (ALU), control unit, and primary storage unit.

Ceramic oxide Semiconducting material made from elements such as calcium and lutetium. The material can become a superconductor at temperatures less extremely cold than is required for other materials such as gallium arsenide.

Character enhancement An application-software feature that allows altering the text style, e.g., by boldfacing or italicizing.

Chart/graph program Software used to create charts and graphs for presentation; used for pictorial representation of data. Also called analytical program.

Chief programmer team A group of specialized personnel involved in designing and developing a computer program.

Chip Another term for microchip. See integrated circuit.

Circuit switching A method of moving data through a wide-area network that opens a complete predetermined transmission route from sender to receiver before a message is transmitted.

Classification The information-processing task that arranges business transactions according to preselected criteria and groups transactions having the same criterion.

Clip art Predrawn art available on separate disks or built into a program; the user can select individual images to bring into a document or publication to enhance its appearance or to illustrate a point.

Closed architecture The inability to gain access to the internal circuitry of a microcomputer. Compare to open architecture.

COBOL (Common Business-Oriented Language) A high-level language used in business information processing, specifically designed to manipulate large data files.

Coding Writing computer program instructions in a particular programming language.

Column In a worksheet, the alphabetic labeling (A, B, C) from left to right that locates the position of a cell. Compare to row.

Command-driven program A software program that requires a command to be entered from rote memory or by consulting a manual; choices are not presented on the display screen.

Command line Method of entering commands that requires the user to type the desired command at a specific point on the display screen.

Command mode A mode of operation in which application program commands can be selected.

Comment A feature in application software that lets the user insert notes or explanations at any location in a document; usually surrounded by a box for easy spotting.

Commercial database service An online computer service in which users may access large databases of information. Like information services, these are subscriber services, but they contain information on more specialized topics.

Common carrier A company licensed and regulated by federal or state government to transmit data for customers at a regulated fee; e.g., the Federal Communications Commission regulates all telephone transmission of data.

Communication channel The medium, or pathway, through which data are transmitted between devices. This pathway may be wire cable, microwave, or fiber optic.

Communication parameters The basic parameters required for devices to communicate with each other. Four essential parameters of communication devices must match for communication to take place: (1) baud rate, (2) the number of bits used to create each character, (3) the number of stop bits; and (4) the type of parity checking used.

Communication software An application-software program that controls exchange of data between computers.

Compatibility The ability of software and hardware from one computer system to work with that of another computer system.

Compiler A language-translator program that translates a whole high-level language program at once into machine language before it is executed.

Compression technology A storage method that reduces file size to 5–10 percent of the original size.

Computer A problem-solving device that can accept data, perform certain functions on that data, present the results of those operations, and store the results.

Computer-aided design (CAD) The integration of computers and graphics to aid in the design and drafting processes.

Computer-aided manufacturing (CAM) The use of computers to control machines in the manufacturing process.

Computer-aided systems engineering (CASE) An entire class of programs (software) that automates system-analysis tasks.

Computer-assisted retrieval system (CAR) The combination of micrographics technology and computers in a system that randomly and quickly retrieves data and information stored on microforms.

Computer-based information system A set of people, data, procedures, hardware, and software that work together to achieve the common goal of information management.

Computer branch exchange A computer-based private branch exchange (PBX).

Computer crime A crime that involves the use of computers and software.

Computer ethics A set of codes or rules governing the conduct of individuals and corporations in the use of computers. The accepted standard of behavior when dealing with computers and the information they contain.

Computer graphics Images and pictures generated by a computer, software, and the person using it.

Computer-integrated manufacturing (CIM) The linking and integration of manufacturing and all other aspects of a company by computers.

Computer network Two or more computers linked by data-communication channels.

Computer numerical control (CNC) Control of milling or cutting operations by a computer.

Computer operator A person responsible for starting and running computer equipment.

Computer output microform (COM) Hard copy in the form of photographic images recorded on microfilm or microfiche.

Computer service technician A person who installs and repairs computer equipment.

Computing literacy General knowledge of what computers are, who uses them, how they are used, their functions, and their impact on society.

Concentration The process of connecting and serving more devices on a communication channel than that channel was designed to handle.

Concentrator A hardware device, often a minicomputer, that controls the process of concentration.

Concurrent access An attempt by two or more individuals or groups to use the same data simultaneously.

Contention A method for determining device access to a communication channel. Each device checks a channel to see whether it is free before sending data. Once a device begins transmission, it maintains control of that channel until transmission is complete.

Context switching A method of processing that allows several programs to reside in memory but only one to be active at a time.

Control bus The electrical pathway for all timing and controlling functions.

Control panel In an electronic spreadsheet, several lines at the top of the display screen showing information about the current worksheet (cursor position, cell width, cell protection, cell contents) and the command or activity being performed.

Control program The computer program in an operating system that manages the computer's components and resources, such as CPU time, primary storage, and input and output devices.

Control unit That part of the central processing unit that controls the sequence of events necessary to execute an instruction.

Conversion Replacement of an existing system with a new information system.

Converting Changing the data-storage format of one file so it can be used by another program having a different data-storage format.

Coordinate In a worksheet, the intersection of a row and column; defines a cell's position in a worksheet.

Copy An application-software feature that makes a duplicate of images or text selected by the user.

Copyright Act of 1976 A federal law, which actually went into effect in 1978, that specifically lists computer programs among the works protected against illegal copying, from the moment of their creation.

Cost/benefit analysis Part of the project-justification stage of the system development life cycle, often called a feasibility study; compares costs and benefits for alternative new information systems and the current system.

Cursor A special character on the computer display screen that indicates the user's present position or focuses attention on a particular point on the screen.

Cut and paste An application-software feature that "cuts" (erases) an object from a graphic or text and places it in a buffer, so that it can be "pasted" (inserted) in another area of the graphic or document—or another document.

Daisy-wheel printer A printer using a print wheel that resembles a daisy. At the end of each "petal" is a complete character (alphabet letter, number, or symbol).

Data Numbers, letters, characters, or combinations thereof that can be entered and processed by a computer. Raw facts before processing.

Database A cross-referenced collection of files designed and created to minimize repetition of data.

Database administrator (DBA) A person or a group of people who manage a database.

Database management system (DBMS) Software that allows data to be readily created, maintained, manipulated, and retrieved from a database. DBMS is the interface among programs, users, and data in a database.

Database query language A fourth-generation language used in conjunction with a relational database; acts as an interface between a user and a relational database management system to facilitate easy access to data without use of complex programming code.

Data bus An electrical pathway on which program data are transferred.

Data capture Retrieving data from a remote computer and storing it in main memory or secondary storage.

Data collection The activity of collecting transactional data for entry into a computer system.

Data communication The process of sending data electronically from one point to another.

Data dictionary A data file containing a technical description of data that are to be stored in a database; it includes the field names, types (e.g., alphanumeric, numeric), sizes, descriptions, and logical relationships.

Data-directed inference procedure Use of an inference engine to match the left-hand side of a rule with user-provided data and then draw a conclusion by looking at the right-hand side of the rule.

Data-element-to-report matrix A tabular technique that shows which file-data elements are printed out on which reports.

Data entry Entering data into a computer in a timely manner, at a reasonable cost, and with minimum error (also called input).

Data-entry operator   A person who enters data into a computer, using a keyboard and video display terminal.

Data flow diagram (DFD)   A graphic depiction of a system that concentrates on information flow rather than on treatment of the information during the flow.

Data manager   Application software that allows users to manage (manipulate, store, retrieve, display, and print) data; it may be a file management system or a database management system.

Data manipulation   Altering data that enter or exit a computer.

Data processing   The process of transforming data into useful information by a computer; sometimes called information processing.

Data stealing   A computer crime in which data gathered for a legitimate purpose are used in an unauthorized manner.

Data subsystem   The component of a decision support system (DSS) that represents the data necessary to solve a specific problem.

Data-transfer mode   In a communications package, the operational mode in which actual data transfer takes place between communicating devices.

Data transfer rate   The number of characters or bytes that can be transferred to storage media in a given amount of time.

Debugging   The process of finding and correcting a programming error.

Decimal system   The base-10 numbering system; uses digits 0 through 9.

Decision support system (DSS)   An information system designed to allow managers to interact directly with a computer for assistance with relatively unstructured decisions.

Decode   The step in the instruction cycle where an instruction is decoded and sent to the ALU along with any necessary data.

Dedicated word-processing system   A computer system designed mainly for word processing.

De facto standard   A software or hardware product that is generally accepted as a standard, even though it has not been officially declared as such.

Defaults   In application software, parameters that are automatically entered unless changed by the user.

Delete   An application-software feature that allows existing text, data, fields, records, or files to be removed.

Demand report   Management report generated only at the request of an individual.

Demodulation   The process of converting an analog signal into a digital signal.

Density   The amount of data that can be stored in a given area of a storage medium. The higher the density, the more data can be stored.

Design program   A graphics program used as a design tool to create and alter the image of an object; computerizes tasks associated with manual drafting.

Desktop microcomputer   Another name for a microcomputer, so called because it fits on a desk top.

Desktop publishing   A concept that combines the use of a microcomputer with graphics-oriented page-composition software, word-processing software, and high-quality laser printers.

Dialog box   A box that usually appears in a window on the screen; it may contain a question or prompt that requires a response from the user.

Dictionary   See spelling checker.

Digital computer   A high-speed, programmable electronic device that stores, processes, and retrieves data by *counting* discrete signals, as opposed to *measuring* a continuous signal, as is done in an analog computer. Compare to analog computer.

Digital data transmission   Transmission of data as distinct pulses, or on/off electrical states.

Digitizer   An input device that uses a pad—a graphics tablet—on which a special stylus is moved to provide data entry or indicate position.

Direct-access file processing   A method in which the records in a file are stored in random order but can be accessed directly. This method allows for faster access to data than permitted by sequential or indexed-sequential methods.

Direct conversion   A type of changeover in which an existing information system is replaced with a new information system; also called crash conversion.

Directory storage   A feature of some communication packages that allows storage of parameters required to set up communication between two computers. Users can recall this information from the directory instead of reentering it.

Disaster recovery team   A team of computer and security experts who design, monitor, and implement plans to recover data from events (fire, flood, virus attack) that destroy computer operations in an organization.

Disk operating system (DOS)   An operating system that manages the use of disk drives for storing and accessing data and programs.

Disk pack   A removable, hard-disk storage device containing multiple hard disks in a plastic case; provides increased storage capabilities for large computer systems.

Distributed database A database existing in one of these forms: (1) on-line at the host computer in a central location but also available to remote locations; (2) partially duplicated at the host computer and placed on a remote computer for processing, called segmentation; (3) entirely copied for processing at each remote location, called replication.

Distributed data processing (DDP) The concept of dispersing computers, devices, software, and data connected through communication channels into areas where they are used.

Documentation (1) The written or graphic record of the steps involved in developing or maintaining an information system. (2) Written or graphic descriptions detailing the purpose and operation of software.

DOS enhancer Operating environment that uses the DOS kernel but adds significant functions and improves the user interface. Examples include Microsoft Windows for DOS and Presentation Manager for OS/2.

DOS extender A program that adds some functionality, such as enabling direct access to more than 640K of main memory without substantially changing the way DOS operates.

DOS replacement Operating systems compatible with DOS but taking better advantage of the 80286, 80386, and 80486 chip capabilities.

DOS shell A software feature that allows the user to temporarily exit an application and return to the operating system. Commands can be performed and a command then returns the user to the application.

Dot-matrix printer An impact printer that uses a print head containing pins, usually 9 to 24, to produce characters by printing patterns of dots.

Downloading The process of receiving data from a computer and storing it on media located at the user's computer. Compare to uploading.

Draft-quality print Lowest-quality print; characters are formed using a minimum number of dots; suitable for rough drafts. Also called standard-quality print.

Drag A graphics-package feature that allows moving (dragging) an object around the drawing area.

Draw program A vector-based graphics program displaying high-quality dots and lines. Users may also draw, fill shapes, and change color while creating illustrations.

Dumb terminal A stand-alone keyboard and display screen that can send or receive data from a computer system but cannot process that data.

Dye-diffusion printer A nonimpact printer that produces images by heating a ribbon so that the dye vaporizes and diffuses onto the paper.

Dynamic knowledge base See working memory.

Edit (error) report Report generated during an updating function to supply a record of any invalid data contained in a transaction file.

Editing Correction of typographical errors, incorrect values, or erroneous formulas in an application program.

Edit window The main window in a word processor; the work area for entering and editing a document.

Electrically erasable programmable read-only memory (EEPROM) Memory that can be erased and reprogrammed electrically without removing the chip from the circuit board.

Electronic blackboard A pressure-sensitive chalkboard that digitizes and displays on a monitor whatever is written on it.

Electronic calendar An electronic scheduling system used for the same purpose as a standard paper calendar or appointment book.

Electronic data interchange (EDI) A communications protocol that allows retailers and their suppliers to conduct business transactions electronically instead of manually.

Electronic data-processing (EDP) auditor An individual who tests an information system to ensure that business transactions are processed using the desired procedures.

Electronic eavesdropping Illegal tapping into communication lines that are used by computers to send and receive data.

Electronic funds transfer (EFT) A computerized method of transferring funds from one account to another.

Electronic mail Any mail or messages transmitted electronically by computers using communication channels.

Electronic spreadsheet An application-software program that displays, manipulates, and prints data in a row-and-column format; computerized version of the paper spreadsheet used in accounting.

Electronic teleconferencing A method of communicating via computers connected through a telephone system. Each user or group of users participates in the conference by keying in their conversations.

Electronic work monitoring A process of measuring worker productivity with the use of computers.

Electrostatic printer A fast, high-resolution, non-impact printer used where complex images are needed, such as in mapping and circuit design.

Embedded microprocessor A preprogrammed microprocessor used to control the functions of a device other than a computer.

Encapsulation Combining of data and procedures into a reusable structure; a basic principle of an object-oriented programming language.

Encoding system A system in which alphanumeric characters are represented by patterns of 1s and 0s so a computer can recognize and use them. The American Standard Code for Information Interchange (ASCII) and Extended Binary Coded Decimal Interchange Code (EBCDIC) are the two most widely used encoding systems.

Encryption A data-coding scheme that codes data into unintelligible characters so they cannot be read or used by unauthorized persons.

Endnotes Notes of reference or explanation placed in a manuscript at the end of a chapter or document.

End user A noncomputer professional (such as a manager, doctor, lawyer, student, etc.) who accesses computers.

Erasable programmable read-only memory (EPROM) A type of memory that can be erased by removing it from the circuit and exposing the chip to ultraviolet light. It can then be reprogrammed.

Ergonomics The science of designing workplaces for worker comfort and efficiency.

Exception report Management report indicating activities that are out of control and thus need management action.

Execution cycle The cycle where an instruction is executed by the ALU.

Executive support system (ESS) An information system that specifically caters to an executive's special information needs in managerial planning, monitoring, and analysis.

Expert system See knowledge-based (expert) system.

Expert system shell A general-purpose inference engine and a skeleton of the knowledge base into which users can add their own special data.

Explanation subsystem The component of a knowledge-based (expert) system that can respond to user requests and inquiries as a system executes.

Exporting Preparing a file in a format suitable for transfer from the current application into another application.

Express warranty A claim, either written or verbal, about a product.

External direct-connect modem A modem that is external to a computer and connected directly to a telephone line; it reduces distortion and permits faster data transmission than the acoustic type.

Facsimile (FAX) A form of electronic mail that copies and sends text and graphics over long distances.

Fetch A step in the instruction cycle in which the instruction is located and sent to the control unit.

Fiber optic A data-communication channel in which data are transmitted and received as digital pulses of light.

Field A name given to each data item contained in a record.

Fifth-generation computer The next generation of computers, which will incorporate artificial intelligence.

Fifth-generation language One of the next generation of programming languages that will include natural languages.

File A collection of related records in which each record contains related data fields.

File locking A file-protection procedure that allows only one user to access a file at a time.

File management system (FMS) An application program that can manage (manipulate, store, retrieve, and print) data in flat files. In this system, only one file can be accessed at a time.

File-transfer protocol A set of rules for the transfer of data. Communicating devices must use the same protocol to make possible the transfer of data.

First-generation computer Computers developed and used before 1960 and which employ vacuum tube technology.

Fixed disk A hard-disk storage system of one or more nonremovable hard disks protected in a permanently sealed case.

Fixed-length record A record in which data length is set to a specific number of characters. Any unused spaces are stored as blank spaces in the records.

Flash chip A memory chip which can retain data even when its power supply is turned off.

Flat file A file having no relationship or integrating structure with any other file.

Flat-panel display A display that does not use a conventional cathode-ray tube to display characters; two types are liquid-crystal display (LCD) and gas plasma display.

Floppy diskette A flexible, mylar magnetic diskette on which data are magnetically stored, commonly used with microcomputers.

Font A collection of all the letters, numbers, and symbols of one style of type in one size.

Footer Text that appears at the bottom of a page; e.g., a page number.

Footnotes Notes of reference or explanation placed in a manuscript at the bottom of the page below the main text.

Formatting (1) Setting parameters such as margins or tabs to control the appearance of text, or setting attributes to describe how data are to be displayed. (2) Preparing a disk or diskette for use.

Formula A mathematical or logical equation from which data values are calculated.

FORTRAN (FORmula TRANslator) A high-level language designed for scientists, engineers, and mathematicians to solve complex numerical problems.

Fourth-generation computer Computers developed and in use from 1971 to the present which use large-scale integration (LSI).

Fourth-generation language A class of programming language in which users need very little programming knowledge to write computer instructions; e.g., database query languages, report generators, and application generators.

Freedom of Information Act of 1970 A 1970 federal law allowing citizens to find out which federal agencies are collecting and storing data about them and enabling them to secure copies of the records.

Front-end processor A special-purpose computer that controls the input and output functions of a main computer.

Full-duplex mode A method of transferring data over a communication channel; permits data to be transmitted and received at the same time.

Gallium arsenide A material used for making semiconductors to replace silicon because it allows faster transmission time, uses less power, is more radiation resistant, and can process both light digital data and electronic digital data on one chip.

Gas-plasma display A flat-panel monitor used in portable computers; contains an ionized gas (plasma) between two glass plates.

Gateway An interface that converts the data codes, formats, addresses, and transmission rates of one network into a form usable by another network.

Gateway service A service in which computer time is bought from many information and commercial database services at wholesale rates and sold to subscribers at a retail rate. A gateway service provides the convenience of accessing many services through one central communication line.

Generalized application software Application software that can be applied to a variety of tasks.

Generic operating system An operating system designed to be used by a wide variety of computer architectures. UNIX is an example.

Goal-directed inference procedure Use of an inference engine to form a hypothesis and then try to prove that hypothesis by looking at the right-hand side of the rule and checking to see whether the left-hand side of the rule matches user-provided data.

Grammar and style checker A feature in a word processor that points out possible problems with punctuation, grammar, and writing style.

Graphical information Information represented pictorially, e.g., pie charts and bar and line graphs; quantitative information.

Graphics Representation of data in the form of charts, graphs, or other pictorials. Also see computer graphics.

Graphics-based user interface A user interface operating in a graphics mode and using pointing devices, on-screen pull-down menus, windows, icons, and other graphical devices.

Graphics software An application program that allows users to create, edit, display, and print graphic images; may be a separate software program or integrated into another software program.

Graphics tablet A pad upon which computer users draw by moving a digitizer.

Grid A pattern of horizontal and vertical lines (sometimes just the dots representing the intersection of these lines) providing a visual aid to help enter or find data at specific coordinate positions on the screen.

Half-duplex mode A method of transferring data over a communication channel; permits data to be transmitted and received, but not at the same time.

Handheld computer A portable computer, slightly larger than a pocket calculator; it can be held in one hand.

Handshaking The process of sending prearranged signals specifying the protocol to be followed when transmitting or receiving data.

Hard copy A form of relatively stable and permanent output, such as paper or computer output microform.

Hard disk A hard metallic disk used for magnetically storing data. Its rigid construction permits higher storage densities, allowing more data to be stored; data can be accessed faster than with a floppy diskette.

Hard-disk drive The device used to transfer data to and from a hard disk.

Hardware The physical components of a computer system, such as the computer itself, input devices, and output devices.

Hashing A method used by a computer to determine where to store a record on the storage medium. The method involves performing a mathematical operation on the key field to transform it into a disk location.

Head crash When the read/write head of a hard-disk drive comes in contact with the hard disk, resulting in severe damage to the head, disk, or both.

Header Text that appears at the top of a page, often a title; sometimes repeats on every page.

Help window A feature in many application programs that can be accessed to provide information about commands or procedures.

Hexadecimal system The base-16 numbering system; uses digits 0 through 9 and letters A through F.

Hierarchical database A database structure in which data relationships follow hierarchies, or trees; there are either one-to-one or one-to-many relationships among record types.

High-level language A programming language using instructions that closely resemble human language and mathematical notation. BASIC and Pascal are examples.

History file A file created for long-term storage of data.

Hypertext Graphically oriented software in which data are stored as objects that can be arbitrarily linked and accessed. Hypertext software incorporates components of a database, text editor, and graphics editor, and uses a mouse to move through windows, to click on icons, and to pull down menus.

IBM compatible A microcomputer similar in design to an IBM, capable of using most or all of the same software.

Icon A graphic symbol used to represent an item such as a file, directory, or hardware device.

Image database Database software that allows the storage of pictures.

Impact printer A printer that produces characters by using a hammer or pins to strike an ink ribbon against paper.

Implied warranty A product warranty which implies that the goods are reasonably fit and of average quality.

Importing Bringing an exported file into an application. In a graphics-based window environment, data are "cut and pasted" from one application into an

area in memory or on disk known as a "clipboard" and then moved into another application, instead of being "imported."

Indexed sequential access file processing A method of storing and accessing data, using an index of key fields to allow records to be sequentially or directly accessed; has the advantages of both direct and sequential access.

Indexing The process of creating a file of a sorted database. The index file is saved separately, allowing the original database to be left unchanged.

Industrial espionage A computer crime in which a computer is used to steal trade secrets, such as design or marketing plans from a company.

Inference engine The component of a knowledge-based (expert) system that uses rules from the knowledge base together with data provided by a user to draw a possible conclusion.

Information Data that have been processed into an organized, usable form and are meaningful to the recipient for the task at hand.

Information filtering Removing trivial or nonessential information from the mass of information generated for a given decision. This must be a thoroughly considered and well-defined process because the decision-maker needs enough of the essential information to reach a logical decision.

Information management Process whereby information is directed to the decision maker who needs it.

Information overload Occurs when a decision maker receives trivial or nonessential information in a decision situation.

Information service An on-line computer service through which users can access large databases of general-interest information. Information services are usually offered for a fee and require a password to gain entry.

Information service center consultant A person in an organization who advises or trains employees on a particular piece of hardware or software.

Information system A set of people, data, and procedures that work together to achieve the common goal of information management. See also computer-based information system.

Information-system life cycle The life span of an information system, from its inception to its removal or redesign.

Information system manager A person who plans and oversees all information resources in an organization.

Inheritance The ability of a programming language to define how a new object (or class of objects) is like an old object (or class of objects) having a few minor differences; a basic principle of an object-oriented programming language.

Ink-jet printer A nonimpact printer that forms characters on paper by spraying ink through an electrical field that arranges the ink particles in the form of characters.

Input (1) The process of entering and translating data into machine-readable form for a computer to use. (2) Data before processing takes place.

Input device A peripheral device, such as a keyboard or a mouse, through which data are entered and transformed into machine-readable form.

Input line The place in a worksheet where data are typed before actually being entered into the program. The input line often allows editing of data before they are entered.

Input-to-file matrix A tabular technique that shows which system input documents update (or change) which system files.

Input validation The process of validating input data against possible errors.

Insert mode A mode in an application package in which adding new text results in all text to the right being moved to make room for the new text.

Installation The second task in the implementation phase of the system development life cycle, during which an information system is made operational.

Install file A batch file that helps install a program; it allows the program to be configured to the computer.

Instance An individual object that is part of a larger class of objects; it contains data and procedures necessary to perform a specific function.

Instruction cycle The fetch and decode steps in the process of executing an instruction.

Instruction set The group of instructions that define the basic operations of a computer, i.e., the arithmetic, logical, storage, and retrieval functions.

Integrated circuit (IC) A single, complete electronic semiconductor circuit contained on a piece of silicon; also called a microchip or chip.

Integrated family of programs A group of independent application programs that share the same data and use common commands and functions.

Integrated operating environment A program called a window manager, or integrator, that allows several different application-software programs to work concurrently and share data.

Integrated software Application-software programs that can share the same data.

Intelligent recalculation Recalculation controlled by the spreadsheet program.

Intelligent terminal A terminal containing a microprocessor that enables it to process data independently of the computer system.

Interactive system A system that allows a user to communicate with the computer through dialogue.

Interblock gap (IBG) The blank section of tape that separates groups of records. It provides a space for the tape to attain the proper speed for reading or writing.

Interface The connection between two or more devices, such as between the CPU and a peripheral device.

Interface subsystem The component of a decision support system (DSS) that acts as the link between a manager and the computer.

Internal direct-connect modem Similar in function to the external direct-connect modem; has all the circuitry on one circuit board, which fits into an expansion slot inside the computer.

Interpreter A language-translator program which translates a high-level language program into machine code one one line at a time. Each line is executed after it is translated.

Interprocessing A method of processing, also called dynamic linking, that allows any change made in one application to be automatically reflected in any related, linked applications.

Interrecord gap (IRG) The section of magnetic tape between individual records that allows the tape to attain proper speed for reading or writing.

Job A collection of one or more related job steps (programs).

Job control language (JCL) The portion of an operating system that allows users to specify a job's requirements in terms of computer resources and operating system services. A JCL provides a means of communicating with the operating system.

Job-cost analysis The capability of a payroll application program to allocate payroll costs to specific projects so the manager can tell how much time and money are being spent on each project.

Joining Combining records from two or more tables in a relational database management system; also called merging.

Josephson Junction An electronic switching device operated at extremely low temperatures; it is much faster than a transistor and consumes less power.

Joystick An input device that uses a lever to control cursor movement.

Jumping A cursor-movement method in a worksheet which allows direct movement to any designated cell.

Justification   An application-software feature that allows a user to move text flush to the right or left margins.

Kermit protocol   A set of rules used for sending and receiving nontext files; popular on large computers.

Kerning   In text composition or typesetting, selectively nudging letters together to improve spacing; gives the illusion of equal spacing between letters.

Keyboard   An input device, similar to a typewriter keyboard, that contains letters, numbers, special-character keys, keys that control cursor movement, and keys that can be programmed for other uses.

Key field   Within a record, a field containing data that uniquely identify that record in a file.

Keyword menu   A menu display in which the entire command or alternative action selection is listed.

Knowledge acquisition subsystem   The component of a knowledge-based (expert) system that transfers the knowledge from an expert to a knowledge base.

Knowledge base   The component of a knowledge-based (expert) system that contains a collection of facts and the rules by which those facts relate.

Knowledge-based (expert) system   Application software that specializes in one area or application to help humans make decisions or solve problems; acts as a consultant, or expert, for users.

Knowledge engineer   A person involved in gathering facts, rules, and knowledge for the knowledge base of an expert system.

Knowledge engineering   The process by which an expert's knowledge is transformed into a knowledge base.

Label   An alphanumeric designator describing the contents of an area or device; e.g., a title or heading for a report generated by an application program; the text contents of a cell in a worksheet; the contents of a diskette; etc.

Landscape orientation   "Landscape" means an image that is wider than it is high, as in a landscape painting. Such an image fits best on 8½" × 11" paper when it is turned so the 11" dimension runs left to right, or turned 90 degrees from normal reading position. "Landscape orientation" is a printing mode in which the text or image is printed in this manner. Compare to portrait orientation.

Language-translator program   A program that translates a programming language into machine code for execution by a computer.

Laptop computer   A portable computer, so-called because it is small enough to fit one's lap; usually small enough to fit in a briefcase.

Large-scale integration (LSI)   The process of putting several thousand complete circuits on a single chip.

Laser printer   A nonimpact printer that produces images on paper by directing a laser beam onto a drum, leaving a negative charge in the form of a character to which positively charged toner powder will stick. The toner powder is transferred to paper as it rolls by the drum and is bonded to the paper by hot rollers.

Lasso   Identifying a graphic element that is to be manipulated by pointing directly to that object. Only the object itself, not the background, is chosen.

Layout forms   Facsimiles of inputs, outputs, and files that indicate the data and information to be included and their format.

Letter-quality print   Print composed of fully formed characters, similar to typewriter print.

Light pen   A light-sensitive input device used to select an entry or indicate position; when touched to the display screen, it detects the presence or absence of light.

Line graph   A graph that represents data as a series of points connected by straight or curved lines; used to show trends and emphasize movement and direction of change over a period of time.

Line printer   A printer capable of printing an entire line at a time; also called line-at-a-time printer.

Liquid-crystal display (LCD)   A flat-panel display commonly used in portable computers; produces images by aligning molecular crystals when voltage is applied.

LISP   A language used to process symbol sequences (lists) rather than numbers; used frequently in artificial intelligence.

List box   Information that appears on the screen when a user requests a list of files on the disk (e.g., by selecting a directory command).

Local-area network (LAN)   A computer network in which two or more computers of the same or different sizes are directly linked within a small, well-defined area, such as a room or building.

Logical database design   A detailed description of a database, based on how a user will use the data.

Logical system design stage   The blueprint phase of designing a new information system. Descriptive tools (graphs, charts, and tables) are used to describe the appearance of inputs, outputs, and files of a new system. The products of this phase of a system development life cycle are given to application programmers, who convert a conceptual information system blueprint into an actual working system.

Logic error A computer program error caused by improperly coding either individual statements or sequences. It does not stop program execution, but will produce inaccurate results.

Logic function A function in which numbers or conditions are compared—greater than, less than, equal to, not equal to, greater than or equal to, and less than or equal to.

Logo An interactive education-oriented language designed to teach inexperienced users logic and programming techniques.

Log-on sequence A series of keystrokes, account numbers, and passwords needed to access a computer or information service.

Low-level language A programming language, such as machine language or assembler; requires the programmer to have detailed knowledge of the internal workings of the computer.

Machine language A programming language that a computer understands; based on electronic on/off states represented by the binary number system of 1s and 0s.

Macro A file in some application programs that contains a series of previously recorded keystrokes or commands that can be quickly executed with one or two keystrokes. A macro increases the speed and efficiency of making repeated entries.

Magnetic disk A mylar (floppy disk) or metallic (hard disk) platter on which electronic data can be stored; suitable for both direct-access or sequential-access storage and retrieval of data.

Magnetic-ink character recognition (MICR) A source-data input technique in which data are represented by magnetic ink characters that can be read either by humans or directly into a computer via a scanner.

Magnetic strip A thin band of magnetically encoded data used on the backs of many credit cards and automatic banking cards.

Magnetic tape An iron oxide-coated mylar strip used to magnetically store data; a sequential storage medium.

Mail merge Combining two documents into one, such as a form letter (document 1) combined with a file of names and addresses (document 2) to personalize a letter.

Mainframe computer A large-scale computer with processing capabilities greater than a minicomputer but less than those of a supercomputer.

Main memory The internal storage unit of a computer; also known as primary memory.

Maintenance programmer A special programmer responsible for the maintenance of an information system.

Management information system (MIS) A system that supplies managers with information to aid in decision making.

Management training An overview for management of a new system to familiarize them with its major strengths and weaknesses and its impact on organizational goals.

Manager A person responsible for using available resources (people, materials/equipment, land, and money) to achieve an organizational goal.

Manufacturing automation protocol (MAP) A communication link, developed by General Motors, that allows different types of computers to communicate with each other.

Margin setting A parameter that specifies the blank spaces around the left, right, top, and bottom of a document.

Master file A file that contains data of a permanent nature, such as employee salary files and inventory files.

Matching Comparing of data in one computer database with data in another computer database for a specific purpose. Used by some government agencies to detect discrepancies that might indicate fraud.

Menu In application software, a screen listing of commands, actions, or other alternatives from which users may select. The menu presents the choices from that particular point in the program. Each menu selection may perform an action or bring up another menu.

Menu-driven program A software program that presents a list (menu) of choices on the screen. These choices may be commands or directions for input.

Merging See joining.

Message In an object-oriented language, a procedure sent between objects.

Message characters The start and stop bits of asynchronous transmission and the synchronizing characters in synchronous transmission that signal when data are being sent and when a transmission is finished.

Message switching A method of moving data through a wide-area network; involves sending an entire message at once over a predetermined transmission route that is not dedicated to just one message.

Message window   Appears on the display screen as needed; often indicates errors, prompting the user to check the data entered or the command chosen.

Microchip   See integrated circuit.

Microcomputer   A small computer with processing capabilities less than those of a minicomputer; sometimes called a personal computer.

Microcomputer system   A microcomputer and its associated peripheral hardware devices and software.

Microprocessor   The CPU of a microcomputer; a single chip containing both the arithmetic and logic unit (ALU) and the control unit. It may also contain the main memory unit.

Micro-to-mainframe link   A method of connecting a microcomputer to a mainframe computer; enables a microcomputer user to share the data and computing power of a larger system.

Micro-to-micro link   A method of connecting microcomputers to one another so that they can share data; allows computers using incompatible data formats to share data.

Microwave   A data-communication channel in which data are transmitted through the air as analog signals for reception by satellites or microwave transmitting stations.

Millions of instructions per second (MIPS)   A measure of computer speed, usually used to describe large computer systems.

Minicomputer   A computer in the large-scale category that has less processing capability than a mainframe computer.

Mirror   A graphics feature that allows a mirror image of an object to appear as a user draws the original.

Mixed-cell reference   A method of copying a formula in a worksheet, in which the formula is the same and each cell reference must be specified as either absolute or relative.

Mnemonic   Alphabetic abbreviations used as memory aids.

Mode indicator   Shows whether a spreadsheet is in the command (menu) or ready (entry) mode; often found on one of the control panel lines.

Model subsystem   The component of a decision support system (DSS) that represents the mathematical formulations that define a real-life problem.

Modem   Acronym for modulator-demodulator; the device that converts signals from analog to digital form and from digital to analog form.

Modula-2   A version of Pascal with improvements in modularity, input and output, and file-handling capabilities.

Modulation   The process of converting a digital signal to an analog signal.

Module   A group of related processing instructions; part of a larger program.

Monitor   A televisionlike device used to display data.

Monitoring and control report   Report that supplies operational-level managers with information needed to control and make decisions about the operational aspects of an organization.

Motherboard   The name given to the main circuit board of a microcomputer; contains the microprocessor, memory chips, and chips that handle input, output, and storage.

Mouse   A small input device that controls the cursor position on the screen. Two types are used: (1) the electromechanical mouse, which triggers rollerball-activated switches on its underside when rolled along a flat surface, and (2) the optical mouse, which uses light beams to mark its position on a special tablet of grid lines.

Move   A software application feature that allows a file (or part of a file) to be identified and put into another location.

Multidimensional spreadsheet   An electronic spreadsheet capable of showing ranges of cells as solids (three-dimensional objects). This form allows for organization of complex worksheets.

Multimedia   The incorporation of the peripheral devices necessary to integrate text, graphic images, audio, and video.

Multiplexer   A hardware device that performs multiplexing.

Multiplexing   The process of combining transmissions from more than one device, character by character, into a single data stream that can be sent over a single communication channel.

Multipoint channel configuration   A communication channel configuration in which three or more devices are connected together and share the same communication channel.

Multiprocessing   A method of processing that uses more than one CPU and which can execute more than one set of instructions (or programs) at a time. Each processor can execute portions of each program.

Multitasking   A method of processing that allows one CPU to switch between two programs so quickly that both appear to be executing simultaneously.

Multithreading   A method of processing that can support several simultaneous functions within the same application.

Multiuser data manager A data manager that can be accessed by more than one user at a time.

Multiuser processing A method of processing that allows a computer to be accessed by more than one user at a time.

Multiuser microcomputer system A microcomputer system to which more than one person has access from separate computer terminals.

Narrow-band channel A communication channel, such as a telegraph line, that transmits data at 40 to 100 bits per second.

Natural language A computer language that can understand and translate a natural language, such as English, into commands that perform a specific operation.

Natural language processing The ability of a computer to understand and translate a natural language, such as English, into commands that perform a specific operation.

Near-letter-quality print Print made from dots rather than fully formed characters; approaches the appearance of letter-quality print.

Near-typeset-quality print Print similar in quality to that produced by commercial typesetting equipment; generally produced by laser printers.

Network database A database structure in which data use a many-to-many relationship among the records.

Network server A hardware device that provides file, print, or communication services to other network devices.

Neural network A method of making computers "think" more like humans, by organizing processing into a grid in which information is shared and tasks are performed simultaneously, just as the brain would.

Node Each computer or device in a computer network system.

Nonimpact printer A printer that produces characters without physically striking the paper.

Nonprocedural language A programming language that describes the task to be accomplished, without specifying how.

Null modem cable A cable that eliminates the need for a modem when data are transferred between two computers located near each other.

Numerical information Information represented by numbers; quantitative information.

Object A combination of data and procedures which are stored together as a reusable unit.

Object-oriented database A database model that uses objects and messages to accommodate new types of data and provides for advanced data handling.

Object-oriented database management system (OODBMS) A database management system that allows objects to be readily created, maintained, manipulated, and retrieved from an object-oriented database.

Object-oriented graphics See vector graphics.

Object-oriented programming language (OOPL) A programming language that treats a program as a series of objects and messages. Two important principles of an OOPL are encapsulation (the ability to combine data and procedures into reusable structures or objects) and inheritance (the ability of the programming language to derive a more specialized object or class of objects from a generalized object or class of objects).

Octal system The base-8 numbering system; uses digits 0 through 7.

Off-line (1) An operation or device in which data are not directly transferred to or from a computer. (2) The condition in which no communication link is established.

On-line (1) An operation or device in which data are directly transferred to or from a computer. (2) The condition in which a computer is linked to and communicating with another computer.

Open architecture Computer architecture that affords access to the internal circuitry of a computer, allowing modification through adding plug-in circuit boards. Compare to closed architecture.

Operating environment Software that can enhance an operating system's functions and improve its user interface.

Operating system (OS) The core set of programs (provided by the developer of the operating system) that controls and supervises a computer's hardware and provides services to other system software, application software, programmers, and users.

Operational (low-level) manager A manager running day-to-day operations of a business, mainly directing other personnel in implementing the tactical decisions of middle-level management.

Operator's manual Documentation containing amplified descriptions of procedures required to operate an information system, designed for personnel who actually operate and maintain the system.

Operator training Communicating the operational details of an information system to operators.

Optical-bar recognition (OBR) A data-input method that reads and interprets bar codes.

Optical card   A small card that stores data on a strip of special material, similar to a magnetic strip except that data on an optical card are encoded by a laser rather than magnetically.

Optical-character recognition (OCR)   The most sophisticated form of optical recognition; recognizes letters, numbers, and other optical-character sets by their shapes in much the same way as the human eye.

Optical laser disk   A storage medium on which data are stored and read by a laser; optical laser disks have much higher data densities than their magnetic-disk counterparts.

Optical-mark recognition (OMR)   A data-input method in which a series of pen or pencil marks on a special form are scanned and their position is translated into machine-readable code; e.g., computer-scored test answer sheets.

Optical tape   A storage medium similar in appearance to magnetic tape, but data storage is by optical-laser techniques.

Optoelectronics   The combination of electronic and optical technology for data-processing and communication applications.

Outliner   (1) A word-processor feature that automatically inserts numbers or labels on lines in an outline as they are typed. (2) A program that helps a writer organize thoughts and writing.

Output   (1) The process of translating machine-readable code into a form readable by humans or other machines. (2) The result of data processing.

Output device   A peripheral device that translates machine-readable code into a form that can be used by humans or another machine.

Pacing   In communications, a feature that allows a user to designate the amount of time between data transmissions; often used when two communicating devices send and receive data at different rates.

Packet switching   A method of moving data through a wide-area network; divides messages into packets, or blocks, and sends them over a transmission route.

Page break   An application-software parameter that controls the number of lines on a page. After this number of lines is reached, additional text is automatically placed on the next page.

Paint program   A bit-mapped graphics program that allows a user to "paint" an image by using an input device, such as a mouse, as the brush.

Pan   A graphics-package feature that moves the entire graphic content on the screen from side to side, allowing users to create and view images wider than the screen.

Parallel conversion   A conversion approach in which both new and old information systems are used for a certain period of time, after which the old system is discontinued.

Parallel interface   An interface that transmits data one byte at a time. *or more*

Parallel processing   A data-processing method in which a computer accesses several instructions from the same program at once and works on them at the same time using multiple CPUs; much faster than traditional serial-processing techniques.

Park   In a computer with a hard-disk drive, moving the read/write head away from the disk and "parking" it to prevent its bouncing on the disk and damaging the disk surface (and therefore data) if the computer is bumped or moved.

Pascal   A high-level language originally designed to teach structured-programming concepts; suited for both file processing and mathematical applications.

Password   An alphanumeric code that restricts access to those knowing the correct code.

Peripheral device   Any hardware item attached to the main unit of a computer, such as an input or output device or a secondary-storage device.

Personal computer   A microcomputer used by and under the control of one person.

Phased-in conversion   A conversion approach in which a new information system is installed in phases, or segments.

Physical database design   The actual structure of a database, based on the database management system software on the system.

Physical system design   A stage of the system development life cycle during which a logical (paper) design is transformed into an actual working system.

Picture library   A predrawn collection of shapes or objects from which a user can select.

Pie chart   A graph that uses a circle (pie) divided into segments to show the relationship of data to the whole.

Pilot conversion   A conversion approach in which a new system is installed in one location and tried before being installed in other locations.

Piracy   Illegal copying of copyrighted computer programs.

Pixel   A picture element; the smallest part of a display screen that can be individually controlled.

PL/1 (Programming Language One)   A high-level language that allows powerful computations and sophisticated data structures. It was designed to replace FORTRAN, ALGOL, and COBOL and is used largely in the oil industry.

Plotter An output device especially designed to produce hard copy of graphics.

Pointer In some applications, the cursor is often called a pointer.

Point-of-sale (POS) terminal A terminal that reads data at the source of a transaction and immediately translates them into usable information.

Point-to-point channel configuration A communication channel configuration that directly connects a computer to a single device, giving those two entities sole use of the channel.

Polling A method of determining which device needs to access a communication channel.

Port A socket on a computer to which a peripheral device can be connected.

Portable computer A microcomputer small enough to be easily carried.

Portrait orientation "Portrait" means an image that is taller than it is wide, as in a portrait painting. Such an image fits best on 8½″ × 11″ paper when it is turned so the 11″ dimension runs top to bottom, or normal reading position. "Portrait orientation" is a printing mode in which the text or image is printed in this manner. Compare to landscape orientation.

Predictive report A report generated by a decision support system.

Preliminary problem report A report created by a system analyst that includes (1) the nature and source of an information system problem, (2) the analyst's detailed analysis of the problem, and (3) the analyst's recommendation to treat the problem through normal system maintenance operations, major modification, or complete replacement of the system.

Presentation graphics Graphics suitable for a formal presentation.

Primary memory See main memory.

Printer An output device that produces hard copy, usually consisting of text but possibly containing graphics.

Printing The process of producing hard-copy output.

Privacy As related to computer data, the right of control over one's personal data.

Privacy Act of 1974 A law establishing that the federal government has no right to keep secret files about any citizen; it allows individuals to find out what data about them have been collected and how they are used.

Private branch exchange (PBX) A local-area network implemented in a star network arrangement, using an organization's existing telephone switching system.

Problem definition The first stage of the system development life cycle, which begins when a problem with the current information system is detected and is serious enough to lead to the question: Should we start planning for a new system to replace the current system?

Procedural language A programming language that specifies how a task is accomplished.

Process control Monitoring and controlling an operation.

Processing The steps a computer takes to convert data into information.

Program flowchart (PFC) A flowchart that graphically shows the processing steps of a computer program.

Program maintenance The process of correcting errors discovered in a program after it has been installed.

Programmable controller A computer-controlled unit consisting of a microprocessor, input and output modules, and a power supply; used to monitor and control machinery and processes.

Programmable file management A file-management system that allows a user to enter programming commands to cross-referenced multiple flat files.

Programmable read-only memory (PROM) A type of memory that can be programmed only once and then cannot be further altered.

Programmer A person who codes instructions in a programming language so they can be used by a computer to solve a problem.

Programmer's manual Documentation that contains step-by-step instructions for program development.

Programming language A set of written symbols that instruct a computer to perform specific tasks.

Projecting In a relational database management system, the process in which a subset of the larger table is created with only the needed rows and columns.

Project justification A stage of the system development life cycle in which information system personnel perform cost/benefit analysis of alternative systems and recommend one to management.

Project management Overall control of a one-time endeavor, or project.

Project manual Documentation detailing steps taken to develop an information system.

Prolog A language used to process symbol sequences (lists) rather than numbers; used extensively in artificial intelligence.

Prompt line In a software package, a line that asks (prompts) for a response; it may ask a question or list choices.

Proprietary operating system An operating system designed to run only on a particular computer architecture.

Protocol A set of rules and procedures for transmitting and receiving data so that different devices can communicate with each other.

Prototype information system A real, working, usable system, built economically and quickly with the intention of being modified.

Pseudocode A code that uses Englishlike phrases to describe the processing steps of a program or module.

Public domain program A software program not protected by copyright law; available for public use. Also called freeware.

Qualitative information Information that describes something without using the numerical characteristics employed in quantitative information.

Quantitative information Information that tells how much or how many; either numerical or graphical.

Query by example A query-language style in which the user inputs query conditions in the desired fields.

Random-access memory (RAM) Memory into which data and programs can be written, and from which data and programs can be read. Data stored in RAM are erased when power to the computer is shut off.

Range of cells In a worksheet, a method of selecting specific cells by identifying the upper-left cell and the lower-right cell; permits large blocks of cells to be manipulated together.

Reading Retrieving data from primary storage or from a secondary storage medium.

README file In many applications, a text file containing the latest information about the program or corrections that may not appear in the manual. These files can be read with any text editor or word processor.

Read-only memory (ROM) Memory into which data/instructions are entered during manufacturing. Contents can only be read; they are permanent and cannot be changed.

Read/write head The electromechanical component of a tape drive that performs the actual writing or reading of data onto or from magnetic tape.

Ready/entry mode A mode of operation in which a spreadsheet program indicates that it is ready to receive information. When a character is entered, the program automatically switches to the entry mode.

Real-time processing A method of processing in which results are provided fast enough to control or modify a process or provide immediate answers to queries.

Record A collection of related data items (fields). The data items are particular to that record, but fall under the general heading of the file name.

Reduced-instruction-set-computer (RISC) A computer chip designed with only the most-used instructions on it, eliminating seldom-needed instructions, to produce greater speed.

Reel-to-reel tape Magnetic tape, usually one-half inch wide, wound on reels. Typically used with large computer systems provide large amounts of secondary storage at a comparatively modest cost.

Register A temporary holding place for data or instructions that are to be worked on immediately; part of the CPU.

Relational database A database composed of many tables in which data are stored. The tables must have unique rows, and the cells must be single-valued.

Relational database management system (RD-BMS) The database management system that allows data to be readily created, maintained, manipulated, and retrieved from a relational database.

Relative cell reference A method of copying a formula in a worksheet in which the formula is the same but the cells referenced in that formula are different.

Removable cartridge A hard-disk storage system that uses a cartridge containing one or more hard disks; the cartridge can be removed from the hard-disk drive and replaced with another cartridge at any time.

Rename A software application feature that allows the user to assign a new name to an existing file or document.

Repetition control structure Also called looping; a programming control structure that allows a series of instructions to be executed more than once without being recoded.

Report file A file of information to be printed; created on auxiliary magnetic tape or disk.

Report generator A fourth-generation language that allows data to be extracted from a database and formatted into a report.

Requirements analysis A stage of the system development life cycle that involves analysis of a current system's performance to determine what the ideal system would be. The gap between the current system and the ideal system is explored to determine which system will best close the gap.

Resolution   The amount of detail that can be shown on a monitor's screen, measured by the number of pixels the screen contains.

Ring network   A computer network arrangement in which each computer or device is connected in a closed loop by a single communication channel. Communication between the source and the destination must flow through each device in turn until the message arrives at the desired device.

Robot   A reprogrammable machine that can be instructed to do a variety of tasks; often used to perform dangerous or boring tasks.

Robotics   The area of study dealing with the design, construction, and operation of robots.

Root record   The topmost record in a tree structure.

Rotate   A graphics-package feature that allows turning (rotating) an object on the screen.

Row   In a worksheet, the numeric ordering (1, 2, 3) from top to bottom that locates the position of a cell. Compare to column.

RPG (Report Program Generator)   A programming language designed for producing reports and processing files.

Run-time error   An error that causes a program to stop executing.

Salami slicing   A type of computer crime; data manipulation in which a small amount of money is skimmed from many accounts and put into one central account.

Satellite   An electronic device placed in orbit around the Earth to receive, amplify, and transmit signals; used in wide-area networks.

Scale   A feature in graphics software that lets a user change the dimensions of an image, e.g., reduce or enlarge it.

Scanner   A device that "sees" material and translates it into digital form for computer processing. Different kinds of scanners are used to "read" and digitize printed text, magnetic characters, bar codes, and images.

Scatter graph   A graph in which two sets of data points are plotted; used to show the correlation (if any) between the data sets.

Scheduled report   Management report generated regularly according to a well-established schedule.

Schema   A complete description of the content and structure of a database.

Screen form   A layout form that defines the position of data fields and provides an entry point for the data in a data manager.

Script file   A file of commands written in the communication package's own programming language.

Scroll   A feature that allows movement of an edit window to create or view text outside the display screen. Scrolling can take place horizontally or vertically.

Scroll bar   Graphic bar found at the right or bottom of some windows; the user selects and drags a scroll bar to move to the right or off the bottom of the display screen.

Search and replace   An application-software feature that enables searching for a word or phrase in a file. When found, it may be automatically replaced, or the user may be prompted to elect replacement, depending on the option selected.

Searching   Locating and retrieving data stored in a file.

Secondary storage   Computer memory external to a computer; typically used for long-term storage or large quantities of data or programs.

Second-generation computer   Computers developed and used between 1959 and 1965 that used transistors to control internal operations.

Sectors   On each magnetic-disk track, a pie-shaped division that further identifies the storage location of data.

Select   Identifying a graphic element to be manipulated by drawing a rectangle around that image. The object, background area, and any other objects in the rectangle will be selected.

Selecting   The process of retrieving only certain records in a table in a relational database management system.

Selection control structure   A programming control structure that selects a processing option based on the result of decision criteria.

Semiconductor memory   Memory in which electronic circuits are etched onto silicon wafers.

Sequence control structure   A programming control structure that executes statements in order, one after another.

Sequential-access file processing   A method of storing and accessing data in a row, or one after another. When accessing a record, all preceding records must be read first.

Serial interface   An interface that transmits data one bit at a time.

Service program   An external operating system program which provides a service to a user or application program; it must be loaded separately.

Shareware Software program available to the public; the author may request a donation if you use the program.

Short-term memory See working memory.

Simplex mode A method of transferring data over a communication channel in only one direction.

Simulation A method of creating computerized models of real-life situations; also a method of computer instruction.

Single tasking A processing method that allows only one program to execute at a time.

Single-user processing A processing method that allows only one user to access a computer at a time.

Slide show In a graphics program, a feature that allows individual graphics files to be displayed in a predetermined order for a predetermined amount of time, similar to a slide projector and slides.

Soft copy A form of volatile output, usually a screen display.

Software The instructions that direct the operations of a computer.

Sort file Any file having one or more fields in some sorted order.

Sorting Arranging data in numeric or alphabetic sequence, either in ascending or descending order.

Source-data entry The data-entry process wherein data generated at a source are entered directly into a computer in machine-readable form.

Specialized application software Application software developed for a specific use; for example, a payroll package.

Specialized common carrier A common carrier that offers a limited number of services, usually within a limited area.

Speech coding The capability of a computer to produce voice output by drawing on a large bank of actual human sounds, assembling them to form the appropriate word.

Spelling checker Also called a dictionary; a word-processor program that locates misspelled words or words not in its dictionary.

Spreadsheet A paper form divided into rows and columns for tracking and manipulating numeric data.

Stacked-line graphs Line graph in which the areas between sets of data are shaded or filled in.

Standard-quality print Lowest-quality print; characters are formed using a minimum number of dots; suitable for rough drafts. Also called draft-quality print.

Star network A computer network arrangement in which each device is connected to a centralized computer. All communications must be routed through the central host computer.

Status line One or more lines at the top or bottom of the display screen that provide information about the current file or operation in progress (typically file name, date, time, page number, error messages, etc.).

Storage Includes main memory (the internal storage unit of the computer) as well as secondary storage (external storage typically used for long-term storage of instructions or data).

Storage device Peripheral device that stores instructions or data for a computer, e.g., floppy and hard disks.

Strategic (top-level) managers Managers who make long-range, strategic decisions. Most top-level managers' time is spent in planning and organizing.

Structured programming A method of writing computer programs that emphasizes the systematic design, development, and management of the software-development process. This type of programming increases programmer productivity, improves the quality of the programs, and makes them easier to read.

Structured query language (SQL) A database query language style that uses commands in a structured format to set the query conditions.

Structured walk-through A procedure in which an analyst discusses or "walks through" the design of a computer program with members of the chief programmer team.

Style sheet A formatting feature in word processors that automates text repetition and certain formatting functions by providing a built-in collection of documents or the basic forms for documents.

Subschema A security envelope that restricts each user to certain records and fields within a database.

Subscript A distinguishing symbol, such as a letter or number, printed beside and below a character (A_1, H_2O). In a word processor, this feature signals the printer to correctly position the symbol on the paper.

Summarization The information-processing task that transforms a mass of information into a reduced, or aggregate, form.

Supercomputer The most powerful type of computer; used primarily by government agencies or organizations that process vast quantities of data.

Superimpose A graphics feature that allows a user to place one object over another without erasing either one.

Supermicrocomputer A high-performance microcomputer that contains greater processing capabilities than a standard desktop microcomputer.

Superscript A distinguishing symbol, such as a letter or number, printed beside and above a character (footnote^5, mi^2, x^3). In a word processor, this feature signals the printer to correctly position the symbol on the paper.

Supervisor program Also called monitor, executive, or kernel; the main control program in an operating system.

Surge protector Device that protects computers against power-line voltage surges caused by fluctuations in power generation or lightning strikes.

Synchronous transmission A method of data transmission in which blocks of characters are sent in timed sequences. Each block is marked by special synchronizing characters. This method is much faster than asynchronous transmission. Compare to asynchronous transmission.

Syntax The rules by which a programming language is governed.

Syntax error An error that occurs when a programming language's rules are violated in the coding of a computer program.

System A set of components that interact and work together toward a common goal.

System analysis The first three stages of the system development life cycle: (1) problem definition, (2) requirements analysis, and (3) project justification.

System analyst A specialist who works with users to determine their information needs, and then designs a system to fulfill those needs.

System clock The portion of the control unit that sends out electrical pulses used to synchronize all tasks in the CPU; instrumental in determining the speed of a processor.

System design A phase of the system development life cycle, comprised of two stages: (1) logical design, during which a paper blueprint for the new system is developed, and (2) physical design, during which that blueprint is translated into specific programming logic that will operate the new system as planned.

System designer A specialist who designs a system to fulfill the information needs of users.

System development life cycle (SDLC) A structured sequence of operations required to conceive, develop, and make operational a new information system; includes a system analysis phase, a design phase, an implementation phase, and a maintenance phase.

System flowchart A flowchart that shows the flow of information through a system and all the ways in which the information is altered as it flows.

System implementation The phase of the system development life cycle during which a completely new system or replacement system is introduced into the workplace; includes testing, installation, and training.

System maintenance The fourth phase in the system development life cycle, during which an information system is continually modified to meet the changing requirements of its users.

System manual Documentation that contains a complete technical explanation of an information system.

System operator (sysop) In an electronic network, a person in charge of operating a bulletin board system.

System software Programs that directly control and use a computer's hardware, rather than performing a specific application. An operating system is an example of system software.

System study An extensive report prepared by a system analyst at the end of the system-analysis phase; sent to management to promote a chosen information system.

Tab setting An application-software feature that sets indentions in a document and aligns columns and decimal numbers.

Tactical (middle-level) managers Managers generally concerned with short-term tactical decisions; they allocate time to staffing, planning, organizing, directing, and controlling.

Tape drive An input/output device that uses a read/write head to read and write data on magnetic tape.

Telecommunication Using communication facilities, such as the telephone system or microwave relays, to send data to and from devices. Also called teleprocessing.

Telecommuting A method of working in which a person uses a computer and a communication channel to establish a link with a remote office computer. With a personal computer (or terminal) connected to a company's computer, an off-site employee can communicate with the office.

Telemarketing (telephone marketing) A method of marketing via telephones and computer systems; often uses computerized messages to solicit orders and conduct polls.

Teleprocessing See telecommunication.

Template In an application program, a screen form that contains only entries that do not change. A template may be used as an input form as well as an output form.

Terminal A combined monitor and a keyboard, used to view output and to enter and check input; does not contain a processing unit. Also called a workstation.

Testing The stage in which a new information system is checked to ensure that it is correct.

Text A feature in a graphics package that permits adding text information (such as a title) to a drawing.

Text-based user interface A user interface that requires a user to type commands at a command line.

Text editing Changing, adding, deleting, or otherwise altering text after it has been entered into a document.

Text graphics A method of creating a graphic image, such as a shape or line, by using alphanumeric and other special characters.

Thermal-transfer printer A nonimpact printer that uses heat to transfer ink to paper to form the characters.

Thesaurus A feature in a word processor that provides alternative words (synonyms) for a given word in a document; also provides antonyms.

Third-generation computer Computers developed and used between 1965 and 1971 which first used integrated circuits (ICs).

Three-dimensional or 3-D A graphics-software feature that shows an image from various angles, giving it a three-dimensional appearance.

Time bomb A method of sabotaging a computer program so that it will destroy itself after a predetermined time or after a specific action occurs.

Time sharing A method of processing that allows more than one person access to the same computer at the same time.

Time stealing A computer crime in which time on a computer is used without proper authorization, thus stealing time.

Titles A feature in a spreadsheet package that freezes row and column titles so they remain stationary as the spreadsheet is scrolled.

Token A string of bits that is passed around a network to control message transmission.

Token passing An access method that utilizes tokens in a local-area network. To transmit a message, a device must wait for a token, hold the token while transmitting, and then release the token when finished.

Top-down design A structured-programming design concept that starts with the major functions and divides them into subfunctions until a problem has been subdivided as much as possible.

Topology The arrangement by which a computer or device is connected in a computer network.

Touch pad An input device that uses a pressure-sensitive pad to record data input where the pad is touched.

Touch screen An input device that allows entering data or showing position by "touching" the screen with a finger or other object.

Trackball An input device that uses the movement of a hand-rotated stationary sphere to control cursor movement.

Tracks On a magnetic disk, the concentric circles where data are stored. Used by a computer to identify where data are stored.

Training The third task in the implementation phase of the system development life cycle; intended to familiarize users with a system so they can operate it.

Transaction A business activity or event—for example, the receipt of an order or the sale of a product.

Transaction file A temporary file used to update master files.

Transaction log A listing of transactions that occur during a specific time period.

Transaction processing system (TPS) An information system that processes data about transactions or other events that affect the operation of a business.

Transcriptive data entry Data entry in which data generated at the source are written on a form that must be later transcribed to a computer-readable medium.

Transferring Sharing a data file created in one application program with a file in another application program without conversion.

Transistor Device made from a semiconducting material, such as silicon, to control the flow of electricity through circuits.

Trap door A special password created by the program developer; allows access to the program, but its existence is not documented.

Tree network A computer network arrangement in which devices are linked in a treelike manner through branches.

Typeover mode A mode in application software; when new text is entered, it takes the place of, or overwrites, any existing text occupying that same space.

Typeset-quality print Print quality equal to that of commercial typesetting.

Undo An application-software feature that cancels any change or update just made and returns the file or document to its previous state. Most undo features work only if no other action is taken after the change.

Updating Changing data that are stored in a file or database record on a computer.

Uploading   Reading data from a user's disk and sending it to another computer. Compare to downloading.

User   A person or group of people who use a system.

User group   A formal or informal organization of users organized to solve problems or exchange software or hardware information.

User interface   (1) The portion of a program that users interact with—entering commands to direct the application software and viewing the results of those commands. When an operating environment supplies the key elements of the user interface, programs are easier to learn and similar operations are handled the same way among applications. (2) The component in a knowledge-based (expert) system that links the system and its user.

User's manual   Documentation designed to answer common user questions about an information system; organized so that users can find answers to questions quickly and easily.

User training   Training provided to employees who work with a new system on a regular basis; intended to make them thoroughly familiar with the operation of a new information system.

Vacuum tube   Device used to control the flow of electricity through circuits in early computers.

Validating   Checking data for appropriateness and accuracy as they are entered.

Validation   A method of checking data accuracy by programming a computer to accept only a certain range or kind of data.

Value   Any number or formula used to represent data in a program.

Value-added carrier   A carrier that specializes in leasing services from common carriers and then adding extra services beyond the leased services for its customers.

Value of information   Determined by each user case-by-case; should be reevaluated periodically and viewed in terms of its incremental value and user benefit.

Variable-length record   A record in which spaces are allotted only to actual data. This eliminates storage of empty spaces.

Vector graphics   A way of depicting characters and images on a computer screen by describing them as vectors; images are mathematically defined and stored as geometric descriptions. Also called object-oriented graphics.

Verification   A method of checking data accuracy by comparing data against a known source.

Very-large-scale integration (VLSI)   Putting several hundred thousand complete circuits on a single chip.

Video display terminal (VDT)   See terminal.

Videotext   An interactive computer information service that can transmit monochrome text as well as colors and graphics. A service in which computers and phones are used for two-way communication to order goods and services.

Virtual-machine (VM) processing   A method of processing that creates the illusion of more than one physical machine, when in fact there is only one; it can run several operating systems at a time and allows each workstation or terminal to choose the operating system applicable to its particular task.

Virtual memory   A storage scheme in which data are automatically swapped in and out of main memory as needed, giving the appearance of expanded main memory storage.

Virtual storage   A method of processing that uses a secondary-storage device as an extension of primary storage.

Virus   A computer program whose purpose is to destroy or alter data and spread that destruction (infection) to other computers.

Voice-band channel   A communication channel, such as a telephone line, that transmits data at 110 to 9600 bits per second.

Voice input   See voice recognition.

Voice mail   A form of electronic mail that sends messages in the form of a computerized human voice.

Voice-messaging system   A combination telephone-and-computer system that allows messages to be sent in human voice without need for the receiver to be present to receive the message.

Voice output   The technology in which a computer uses a voice as output, either voice synthesis or speech coding.

Voice recognition   The capability of a computer to accept input in the form of the spoken word.

Voice synthesis   The capability of a computer to provide output in a simulated human voice.

Volatile   The nature of memory in RAM; when power is shut off, data are erased.

Wide-area network (WAN)   A computer network in which the computers are geographically dispersed.

Windows   (1) Separate, defined areas on a computer screen that can display data, menus, different parts of the same file, or several applications. The window typically indicates which file is being viewed.

(2) A command to split the screen horizontally or vertically so different parts of a file can be displayed simultaneously.

Wire cable   A type of data-communication channel; includes telegraph lines, telephone lines, and coaxial cables.

Word   The number of adjacent bits that can be stored and manipulated by a computer as a unit.

Word chart   The most-frequently used type of chart/graph in formal presentations; basically a list of words or phrases, sometimes preceded by numbers or bullets; often uses varied typefaces, boldface, or shadowing for effect.

Word processing   The activity of entering, viewing, storing, retrieving, editing, rearranging, and printing text material using a computer and a word processor.

Word-processing system   The combination of hardware and software used for performing computerized word processing.

Word processor   Application software (sometimes referred to as a word-processing package) that allows the user to create, edit, manipulate, and print text; generally used for creating documents such as letters and reports.

Wordwrap   A word-processor feature that automatically continues a sentence on the next line without pressing the return key at the end of that line. Any words that extend past the right margin are moved to the next line.

Working memory   That part of computer memory in a knowledge-based (expert) system in which the appropriate rules and data are stored at a given instant during the execution of the system; also known as short-term memory or dynamic knowledge base.

Worksheet   The blank spreadsheet form used for entering and organizing numeric data. It is a paper form in a noncomputerized spreadsheet and a screen form in an electronic spreadsheet.

Worm   A computer program that occupies vacant memory and issues false or misleading commands; spreads like a virus.

WORM drive (Write Once, Read Many)   A disk drive used with optical laser disks.

Writing   The process of entering data into primary storage or placing data onto a storage medium.

WYSIWYG   An acronym for "What You See Is What You Get" (pronounced "wizzy-wig"). This feature implies that what is seen on the display screen is exactly how the output will look when printed.

Xmodem protocol   A public-domain, data-transfer protocol used with microcomputers to send and receive nontext files.

XON/XOFF protocol   A protocol that enables software to control data transmission. An XOFF signal instructs the transmitting computer to stop sending data; an XON signal tells the computer to begin sending data.

Zoom   A graphics-package feature that allows enlargement of a specified area of a drawing for viewing, or pulling back and viewing the entire scene.

INDEX

Boldfaced page numbers indicate definitions.
Italicized page numbers indicate illustrations.